GRA

Anthony Rose switched careers after winning the *Observer*/Peter Dominic New Wine Writer Award in 1985. The following year he joined the *Independent* as its wine correspondent. He won the 1994 Glenfiddich Drink Writer of the Year Award and the Wine Guild of the United Kingdom's Wine Columnist of the Year Award in 1988, 1989 and 1993, as well as its trophy in 1993. He has judged wine competitions in Australia, South Africa, France, New Zealand and the United States, as well as the UK, and contributes to *Decanter, Wine, Wine & Spirit* and *L'Officiel des Grands Vins*. He has also contributed to the *Oxford Companion to Wine*, the *Harrods Book of Wine* and sundry other publications.

A former deputy editor of *Wine* and editor of *Wine & Spirit*, **Tim Atkin** is the wine correspondent of the *Observer*. He also writes for *Wine, Wine & Spirit* and *Saveur*. He won the Glenfiddich Drink Writer of the Year Award in 1988, 1990 and 1993 and the Wine Guild of the United Kingdom's Wine Columnist of the Year Award in 1991, 1992, 1994 and 1996. In 1994 he was the first recipient of the Wines of France Award. The following year he was the co-winner of The Bunch Award, described by Auberon Waugh as the 'Booker Prize of wine writing', and winner of the Waterford Crystal Wine Correspondent of the Year Award. He has contributed to a number of books on wine, as well as publishing two of his own, *Chardonnay* and *Vins de Pays d'Oc*. He is a regular member of *Wine* magazine's tasting panels and has judged wines in the UK, France and Australia.

GRAPEVINE

1997

The Definitive Wine Buyer's Guide
to over 2000 of the Best Quality,
Good Value Wines

ANTHONY ROSE
& TIM ATKIN

EBURY PRESS
London

To Mike Atkin, who sells wine at the sharp end

First published in 1996 by Ebury Press

1 3 5 7 9 10 8 6 4 2

Copyright © Tim Atkin and Anthony Rose

Ebury Press
Random House, 20 Vauxhall Bridge Road,
London SW1V 2SA

Random House Australia (Pty) Limited
20 Alfred Street, Milsons Point, Sydney,
New South Wales 2061, Australia

Random House New Zealand Limited
18 Poland Road, Glenfield
Auckland 10, New Zealand

Random House South Africa (Pty) Limited
PO Box 337, Bergvlei, South Africa
Random House UK Limited Reg. No. 954009

A CIP catalogue record for this book is available from the British Library

ISBN 0 09 185181 5

Designed and typeset by Behram Kapadia

Printed and bound by Cox & Wyman, Reading, Berks

Contents

Acknowledgements

Like its three distinguished predecessors, this completely new edition of *Grapevine* could only have been written with the help of a large number of helpful wine buyers and PRs, who organised extensive tailor-made tastings, checked the answers to our endless flow of questions and faxes, provided samples at short notice and submitted themselves to the annual *Grapevine* inquisition.

Our thanks to the following people in Britain: at Asda: Nick-Dymoke Marr, Alistair Morrell and Illy Jaffar; at Budgens: Annie Todd and Tony Finnerty; at the Co-op: Master of Wine Arabella Woodrow and Paul Bastard; at Davisons: Michael Davies; at Fuller's: Roger Higgs; at Gateway: Angela Mount; at Greenalls Cellars: Nader Haghighi, Steve Mullarkey, Kevin Wilson and David Vaughan; at Kwik Save: Master of Wine Angela Muir and Deborah Williams; at Majestic Wine Warehouses: Debbie Worton, Jeremy Palmer, Tony Mason and Emma Davis; at Marks & Spencer: Jane Kay, Viv Jawett and Chris Murphy; at Morrison's: Stuart Purdie; at Nicolas: Eric Gandon and Jill Campion; at Oddbins: Katie MacAulay, Karen Wise, Richard Macadam and Steve Daniel; at Safeway: Master of Wine Liz Robertson and Victoria Molyneux; at Sainsbury's: Mark Kermode, Gerard Barnes, Master of Wine Claire Gordon Brown and Allan Cheesman; at Spar: Liz Aked; at Tesco: Janet Lee and Nicki Walden; at Thresher, Wine Rack and Bottoms Up: Kim Tidy, Julian Twaites, Lucy Warner, David Howse and David McDonnell; at Unwins: Bill Rolfe and Gerald Duff; at Victoria Wine: Mark Davis, Geraldine Jago, Paul Stacey, Tina Hudson, Richard Lowe and Master of Wine Hugh Suter; and at Waitrose (John Lewis): Master of Wine Julian Brind and Joe Wadsack.

From the independent wine merchants: at Adnams: Simon Loftus and Rob Chase; at Avery's: Michael Peace and Master of Wine John Avery; at the Australian Wine Club: Master of Wine Phil Reedman, Craig Smith and Mark Manson; at Bibendum: Simon Farr and Rosalia Vergara; at Bordeaux Direct: Peter Greet; at Eldridge Pope: Master of Wine Robin Kinahan; at Enotria Winecellars: Master of Wine David Gleave and Monique Reedman; at Justerini & Brooks: Hew Blair; at Lay & Wheeler: Master of Wine Hugo Rose; at Lea & Sandeman, Charles Lea and Patrick Sandeman; at Peatlings: Master of Wine Robin Crameri; and at Tanners: Richard and James Tanner.

And for help with our cross-Channel chapter: at The Grape Shop: Katrina Thom; at La Maison du Vin: Master of Wine Richard Harvey; at The Wine

Society: Janet Evans and the delightful Véronique Chaumetou; at Eurotunnel: Alison Andrews and Sophie Grafton-Gratton.

At our new publishers, Ebury Press, our thanks to Margaret Little, who edited the book with cheerful efficiency, Annabel Briggs, Philippa Hayward, Caroline Buckland, Mandy Greenfield, Fiona McIntyre, and Behram and Sally Kapadia. Once again Fiona Wild read the manuscript, took out the sexist jokes and ensured political correctness. Back in the nether regions of south London, Lyn Parry pulled the book together in the last week and Helen Long helped to organise the final tastings. Mary Ensor, Rachel Foster and Samuel Rose provided coffee and tea when we needed them. And, lastly, an enormous thank you to our new agent Julian Alexander.

How to use *Grapevine*

Wines are divided into four price brackets in the UK:

Under £3
£3–5
£5–8
Over £8

and five in France:

Under 20 francs
20–30 francs,
30–50 francs
50–80 francs
Over 80 francs

Where a wine costs over £8 or 80 francs, we try to give a further indication of its price in the note. There is, after all, a big difference between something that retails at £8.49 and something that weighs in at £30.

We have made every effort to ensure that the wines we list are available, although inevitably some may be out of stock. By tasting in a concentrated two-month period, we aim to be as up-to-date as possible. Prices may also vary.

Our scores need to be looked at in the context of their accompanying tasting note. It's also important to remember that wine changes and develops in bottle – for better and for worse. Scores are not immutable or definitive. Every wine has its own intrinsic qualities and, by definition, our comments are subjective.

With two palates to consider each wine, we hope to eliminate some of our individual prejudices. Nevertheless, just because we like something, it doesn't mean that you have to, and vice-versa. If tastes were uniform, we might as well pour a few samples into a computer, give you the printout and go home.

Grapevine's scoring system and symbols

The scores and symbols used in *Grapevine* work as follows:

Quality (out of 20)

20	Nirvana
19	The suburbs of Nirvana
18	Truly outstanding
17	World-class
16	Excellent
15	Very good
14	Good everyday drinking
13	Everyday drinking
12	Drinkable (occasionally with a peg over your nose)
11	Almost drinkable
10	Almost undrinkable
9 and below	Faulty or plain disgusting

Value for money

🛍🛍🛍	Superb value
🛍🛍	Good value
🛍	Fair value
no symbol	Poor value

Unlike other guides, we score on quality as well as value for money. Hence it is perfectly possible for a wine to score 17 and 🛍, or 14 and 🛍🛍🛍. We also rate wines according to sweetness (for whites, sparkling wines and rosés) and weight (for reds and fortifieds), as well as drinkability.

Drinkability

🍾	Drink now
➡	Drink now or keep
🍾	Past it

Ratings for individual chains and merchants

Each of the chains in this guide is given a star rating out of 5. These range from one and a half stars, represented as ☆(☆), to four and a half, or ☆☆☆☆(☆). This year, no-one achieved the coveted five-star rating. We have chosen not to give star ratings to the independent wine merchants, as they are already our selection of the best specialists.

How we taste

We taste later and more thoroughly than any other guide. All the wines listed in this book were sampled between June and mid-August 1996. At each outlet we ask to look at the top-ten best-selling wines, as well as a representative range from the chain's main list. In every case, this includes wines under £5, as well as more expensive fare.

We also visit and interview every retailer in person, whether it be in France or the UK. It goes without saying that we are both independent judges. We do not write for, blend wines for, or accept advertising or funding from retailers. Above all else, we are consumers and journalists.

Another special feature of *Grapevine* is that we include wines we don't like, as well as those that we do. We believe that a critic's job is to criticise constructively, pointing out the bad as well as the good. Apart from providing a few laughs, this has a positive result: several wines that we trashed in last year's guide have not reappeared in 1997.

We try not to overdo it, though. Some of the poorest wines we taste are not listed. We see it as our role to throw out some of the truly awful bottles. Where we've left them in, they tend to be popular wines, top-ten sellers or wines with an undeservedly inflated reputation.

We aim not to go over the top in our descriptions, or to become entangled in the wayward tendrils of the vine. We try to give you enough information to make the wine sound interesting – or not, on occasions. But more than that, we have no desire to dictate what you should enjoy. Happy drinking!

The 1997 *Grapevine* Awards

Wine Merchant of the Year: Asda
For bringing a bit of much-needed pzazz to the supermarket sector, selecting an impressive, value-for-money range of wines and having the courage to challenge received retailing wisdom.

Most Improved Chain of the Year: Greenalls Wine Cellars
For taking a moribund regional wine chain and turning it into an innovative, headline-pulling national force, with a rapidly improving wine list and some of the smartest off-licences in the country.

Cross-Channel Wine Merchant of the Year: Victoria Wine
For overcoming a low-key start to establish a bustling cross-Channel presence in Calais' Cité de l'Europe, and giving customers access to the delights of the full Victoria Wine Cellars range.

By-the-Case Merchant of the Year: Bordeaux Direct
For proving that Britain's biggest mail-order operation can still deliver quality, informative literature and interest from all over the world, but especially from traditional and not-so-traditional French regions.

Independent Wine Merchant of the Year: Enotria Winecellars
For establishing the best Italian wine list in the country and complementing it with an increasing array of characterful estates from California, France and Australia.

Winemaker of the Year: Ákos Kamocsay
For adopting modern techniques at the Neszmely co-operative and using them to brilliant effect on a range of native and international grapes, raising the profile of Hungarian white wines.

Grapevine's **Wines of the Year**

This year we have again selected four cases of the year: red, white and sparkling from the high-street off-licences and supermarkets, and one from the independent merchants. These are 48 wines that we think represent a variety of characterful, value-for-money drinking. There are plenty of other outstanding wines in the pages that follow, but we picked these particular bottles for their combination of quality and availability. Stockists are listed after each wine.

Apart from the sparkling wines, most of our wines – independent wine merchants excepted – cost under £5. Most score 16 or more for quality and three stars for value for money. Where they score slightly less, it tends to be because they are inexpensive. A wine that scores 15 and 👜👜👜 and sits on the shelf at £2.99 is arguably as worthy of recognition as a £20 claret or red Burgundy.

White Wines of the Year Case

1995 Cortese del Piemonte, Contea di Castiglione
A really enjoyable Piedmontese white made by the original Aussie flying winemaker, Martin Shaw, with lime and pear fruit aromas and a surprising amount of concentration for an Italian white under £5.
Stockists: Sainsbury's; Bottoms Up (as Alasia Cortese del Piemonte); Thresher; Wine Rack

1995 Château Haut Grelot, Premières Côtes de Blaye, Joel Bonneau
Concentrated, mealy white Bordeaux with flavoursome, grapefruity Sauvignon, blending nicely with the rich textures of the Sémillon and Muscadelle grapes. Brilliant value.
Stockist: Fuller's

1995 Mâcon Vinzelles, Les Cailloux Blancs
Rich, complex, co-operative bottled Mâcon white, with masses of buttery flavour, well-judged oak and fresh acidity, made by South African Jean-Luc Sweerts. They ought to give him the keys of Mâcon for this one.
Stockist: Victoria Wine

1995 Sopron Sauvignon Blanc Private Reserve
From the outstanding Neszmely co-operative, this is a buy-and-drink-by-the-caseload Hungarian Sauvignon, with grapefruit and elderflower crispness and remarkable length of flavour for a wine at just over £3.
Stockist: Asda

1995 Welmoed Sauvignon Blanc, Stellenbosch, Welmoed Winery
Highly aromatic Cape Sauvignon Blanc, which out-Chiles Chile in the grapefruit and lemon-zip stakes. Bracingly fresh and crisp, this is the best sub-£5 South African Sauvignon we've come across.
Stockists: Booths; Co-op

1995 Clos de la Fine Muscadet sur lie, Luc and Andrée-Marie Choblet
Bracingly fresh, grower's Muscadet with remarkable intensity and a characterful *sur lie* prickle of lees-derived petillance. Amply demonstrates the quality of the 1995 vintage in the Loire.
Stockists: Bottoms Up; Thresher; Wine Rack

1995 Roussanne, Vin de Pays d'Oc

One of a stylish new range of southern French varietals at Marks & Spencer, this is a rich, honey and aniseed-like Languedoc white with exceptional weight and flavour. Good to see something other than Chardonnay emerging from the Midi.
Stockist: Marks & Spencer

1996 Errázuriz Chardonnay, La Escultura Vineyard

Tangy, ultra-fresh Chilean Chardonnay from Errázuriz's new Casablanca Valley vineyard, with 15 per cent Maule Valley material for extra weight. Vanilla oak adds sweetness and complexity here on this excellent white made by Kiwi Brian Bicknell.
Stockists: Berkeley Wines; Greenalls Wine Cellar; Oddbins; Tesco; Victoria Wine Cellars

1995 Asda Argentinian White, La Agricola

A brilliant-value blend of the aromatic native Torrontes grape, with 35 per cent Chenin Blanc for extra weight, this is an extremely fruity, yet delicately spicy, new-wave Mendoza white from the excellent La Agricola winery. Hard to beat at under £3.
Stockist: Asda

1996 Villa Maria Private Bin Gewürztraminer

Sweet, rose-petal-perfumed Kiwi Gewürz from the Auckland-based Villa Maria winery. Weighty, fresh and extremely well-made. The 1996 vintage is a vast improvement on 1995 in New Zealand.
Stockist: Oddbins

1995 Nottage Hill Riesling, South Eastern Australia

The best of Hardy's Nottage Hill range by far, this is an intensely aromatic, lime and citrus fruity South Eastern Australian Riesling, with excellent weight, body and soul. They even have the courage to package it in a flute bottle.
Stockist: Victoria Wine

1995 Müller-Thurgau, Messmer, Pfalz

Floral, sweet-pea-scented Müller-Thurgau, with lightweight 9.5 per cent alcohol, good concentration and elegant, grapey freshness. Müller-Thurgau doesn't come any better than this.
Stockist: Oddbins

Red Wines of the Year Case

1994 Montepulciano d'Abruzzo, La Luna Nuova, Casalbordino, Madonna dei Miracoli

A brilliantly packaged, ultra-modern, oak-influenced Montepulciano made by Meerlust's winemaker, Giorgio dalla Cia. This smooth, chocolatey red takes the normally rustic Montepulciano d'Abruzzo into a new dimension.
Stockist: Fuller's

1994 Mas des Bressades, Costières de Nîmes, Roger Mares

A splendidly aromatic, come-hither Provençal Syrah with blackberry and black-olive fruit flavours and exuberantly crunchy acidity and concentration. A very serious red at a laughable price.
Stockist: Majestic

1990 Château Noblet, Côtes de Bourg, Union des Producteurs de Pugnac

Vigorously fruity, characterful *petit château* claret from the Pugnac co-operative from the fine 1990 vintage, whose tannins and fruit have mellowed beautifully in harmony.
Stockist: Booths

1994 Bright Brothers Old Vines Estremadura Red

This is a vibrantly fruity, succulent Portuguese blend with masses of peppery spice and well-judged oak character from talented oenologist Peter Bright. The garish red label is almost as loud as the winemaker.
Stockist: Asda

1994 Saint Martin des Tocques, Corbières

Hugely fruity, intense angostura bitters-perfumed Languedoc red with Syrah-derived freshness and personality. A stunner for under £5, which shows that southern appellations can be just as good as modern vins de pays.
Stockists: Berkeley Wines; Greenalls Wine Cellar

1994 Marqués de Griñon Rioja

Made entirely with Tempranillo grapes from the Rioja Alavesa, this is an elegant, well-judged marriage of oak and soft, strawberry fruitiness at a very good price, from aristocrat Carlos Falcó.
Stockists: Berkeley Wines; Greenalls Wine Cellar; Fuller's; Majestic; Oddbins; Tesco; Waitrose; Bottoms Up; Wine Rack; Thresher;

1994 Santa Carolina Malbec

Intense, peppery Chilean red made by Pilar Gonzalez at the Santiago-based Santa Carolina winery. A tarry, sagey Malbec with masses of sweet fruit and flavour. Maybe Argentina isn't the best place to find South American Malbec after all.

Stockists: Bottoms Up; Waitrose; Wine Rack; Thresher

1994 Maipo Cabernet Sauvignon Reserve, Carmen

Serious, concentrated Maipo Valley Cabernet Sauvignon with beautifully balanced oak, cassis fruit and acidity. Winemaker Alvaro Espinoza has excelled himself with this stylish, age-worthy Chilean red. Beats every red Bordeaux we can think of at under £6.

Stockist: Marks & Spencer

1995 Orobio Tempranillo, Rioja

Stylish, super-value, deeply coloured Rioja with sweet, succulent fruit, good structure and well-judged oak. Lovely stuff. Modern Rioja at its vibrant best.

Stockist: Oddbins

1994 Argiolas Costera, Cannonau di Sardegna

Tarry, massively oaked, powerfully structured Sardinian red made from the local Cannonau grape, otherwise known as Grenache. Leafy, complex stuff, which demonstrates the sort of quality emerging from southern Italy at the moment.

Stockist: Victoria Wine

1995 Beyerskloof Pinotage

Chunky, vibrantly coloured, oak and raspberry fruity Pinotage from Kanonkop winemaker, Beyers Truter. Plenty of character, as you'd expect, from South Africa's most distinctive red grape variety.

Stockists: Bottoms Up; Oddbins; Victoria Wine; Wine Rack

1993 Barossa Valley Merlot

Full-flavoured, coffee-bean oaky, sumptuously textured Barossa Valley Merlot, which manages to combine ripe mulberry fruit flavours with a silky, green-pepper undertone. One of a number of excellent own-label Australians at Tesco.

Stockist: Tesco

Sparkling Wines of the Year Case

Sonoma Pacific Brut NV
From Piper Heidsieck's California outpost, this is a fresh, youthful, Pinot Noir/Chardonnay-based fizz with an attractive mousse, which has established itself as one of the best West Coast sparklers.
Stockist: Fuller's

Henri Macquart Champagne Brut
Creamy, flavoursome, sub-£12 house-Champagne showing good ripeness and some bottle-aged character. One of the best high-street fizzes on the market at this price.
Stockists: Greenalls Wine Cellar; Berkeley Wines; Cellar 5

'R' de Ruinart Champagne Brut
Rich, honeyed, old-style, non-vintage Champagne from an under-rated quality-conscious Grande Marque house. Lots of rich, toasty Champagne flavours at under £20, with commendable maturity and complexity.
Stockists: Greenalls Wine Cellar; Berkeley Wines; Cellar 5

Sainsbury's Cava
Indicative of the improved quality we've seen this year from Spain's sparkling wines, this is a surprisingly complex, nicely mature Cava, with malty fruitiness and lively acidity.
Stockist: Sainsbury's

Pongracz Cap Classique NV
Successful Champagne-style blend of Pinot Noir and Chardonnay with an extremely fine mousse and mature, bottle-developed flavours. One of the New World's best-value sparklers at just under £11.
Stockist: Majestic

Waitrose Blanc de Blancs NV
Rich, bready, all-Chardonnay Champagne with a mouth-filling mousse and lots of buttery flavours. One of a number of impressive own-label Champagnes at Waitrose.
Stockist: Waitrose

Cuvée Trésor, Bouvet-Ladubay NV
Stylish Saumur sparkler with plenty of appley aromas and honeyed richness, fresh tangy acidity and considerable length of flavour. About as good as Loire sparkling wine gets.
Stockist: Victoria Wine

1993 Green Point, Domaine Chandon
The red fruits character of the Pinot Noir grape is abundantly apparent in this Victorian-based blend of Pinot Noir and Chardonnay from the thinking woman's winemaker, Dr Tony Jordan. As you might expect from a Moët et Chandon-owned subsidiary, this is a good Champagne substitute.
Stockists: Widely available

Drappier Carte d'Or Brut Champagne NV
You can almost taste whole strawberries in this deliciously full-flavoured, Pinot-dominated négociant Champagne. We'd be happy to drink a lot of this any time, anywhere.
Stockists: Bottoms Up; Thresher; Wine Rack

Chevalier de Melline Champagne, Blancs de Blancs Brut NV, Union Champagne
Lemony, elegant, Chardonnay-derived Champagne, from the Union Champagne co-operative, with yeasty, brioche characters and a soft mousse.
Stockist: Marks & Spencer

Tesco Champagne Premier Cru Brut
Rich, honeyed, commendably mature own-label Champagne with soft, strawberry fruity Pinot Noir characters and a delightful cushion of bubbles.
Stockist: Tesco

1989 Waitrose Brut Vintage, Marne et Champagne
A wine that is just getting into its stride, this is an intense, tightly structured vintage Champagne showing promising complexity for a comparatively young fizz.
Stockist: Waitrose

Independent Wine Merchants'
Case of the Year

Adnams
1995 Abadia da Cova, Ribera Sacra, Albarinho
From a vineyard situated on the slopes above the River Miño, this is a peach and ripe pear-like, unoaked Galician white with superb concentration and fresh acidity. A good-value introduction to one of Spain's most sought-after wine styles.

Australian Wine Club
1995 Tim Adams The Fergus
Made predominantly from Grenache with small amounts of Cabernet Franc, Shiraz and Malbec, this is a ginger and pepper-spicy Clare Valley blend with masses of powerful alcohol and raspberry, plum and damson fruit. The best red wine we've had yet from Tim Adams.

Avery's
1992 Clos du Val Cabernet Sauvignon, Napa Valley
Frenchman Bernard Portet, whose family hails from Bordeaux, is at his confident best working with Cabernet Sauvignon. This silky, but structured, age-worthy California red has superb cassis and cedary oak characters, and will benefit from another five to ten years in bottle.

Bibendum
1994 De Trafford Merlot, Stellenbosch
Substantially oaked, concentrated, well-structured Stellenbosch Merlot with masses of colour, black-cherry and cassis fruit and ripe, silky tannins. The sweet vanilla oak complements the fruit beautifully in this classy Cape red. One of the best reds we've ever had from South Africa.

Bordeaux Direct
1995 Domaine Emmanuel Dampt, Vieilles Vignes, Chablis
Super-ripe, honeyed, deliciously aromatic Chablis with sumptuous old-vine concentration and a steely backbone of acidity. Super stuff, which shows you just how good Chablis can be.

Eldridge Pope
1995 Genetin, Pouilly-Fumé, Vieilles Vignes, Domaine François Tinel
Intense, minerally, super-crisp Sauvignon Blanc with genuine old-vine richness and concentration, and a nettley undertone. Grower's Pouilly-Fumé at its complex best.

Enotria Winecellars
1995 Condrieu, La Côte, Cuilleron
A wine whose fabulous aromas of honeysuckle and ripe apricot make you want to plunge your nose into your glass and hold it there all day. From young grower, Yves Cuilleron, this is stunningly concentrated, essence of Viognier at its sensual best. Even at £23 a bottle, this is good value for money.

Justerini & Brooks
1994 Saint Romain, Sous Le Château, Coste Caumartin
From the hillside village of Saint Romain, behind the better-known communes of Meursault and Puligny-Montrachet, this is a tightly focused, extremely well-made Chardonnay with finely crafted oak influence and piercingly austere, citrus fruit characters. Should age well for at least five years.

Lay & Wheeler
1993 Henschke Keyneton Estate Shiraz/Cabernet Sauvignon/ Malbec, Barossa Valley
Deeply coloured, sweetly oaked, aromatically complex Barossa blend of mainly Shiraz and Cabernet Sauvignon with mulberry and cassis fruit, well-judged vanilla oakiness and smooth tannins. Well up to the usual high standards of Australia's top red wine estate.

Lea & Sandeman
1992 Querciabella, Chianti Classico
From an ultra-modern winery in the town of Greve, this is an extremely impressive, characterful Chianti, especially for a 1992, with sagey, savoury notes and a sweet middle palate of plum and black-cherry fruit.

Thomas Peatling
Peatlings Manzanilla
Savoury, super-fresh, olive and almond-friendly Manzanilla from the Sanlúcar house of Barbadillo, with a dry, flor-yeasty tang. Brilliant value at just over £4. Pass us those tapas, please.

Tanners
1995 Erdener Treppchen Riesling Auslese, Weingut Meulenhof
Peachy, intense, beautifully defined Mosel Riesling from a top vineyard site in the Mosel Valley, showing sumptuously juicy primary fruit flavours, super concentration and fine balancing acidity.

Introduction

Diversity rules, OK

Which country stocks a greater variety of wine styles than any other? Where can you find bottles from China, Uruguay and Mexico brushing neck-labels with wines from Spain, France, Italy and Australia? The answer is Britain, a country that imports an enormous range of wines and whose consumers, believe it or not, are considered the most discriminating in the world.

Did we say discriminating? A glance at the shelves of your average corner shop might convince you otherwise. Bottle upon dusty bottle of Liebfraumilch, Muscadet, Beaujolais, Bordeaux Rouge and Lambrusco are hardly evidence of good taste. But such places conceal what is really going on in Britain. We are living through a wine consumers' revolution – a seismic change in the quality, and origin, of what we drink.

Everywhere we've tasted this year, the message has been the same. The wines that have dominated the thinking of British retailers for the last 20 years are on the skids. Of course there are still people who enjoy sugary, over-sulphured Hock, who continue to spend good money on mean, tartly tannic clarets. But they're in a shrinking minority.

In the past, our celebration of diversity has rung hollow to a degree. There was never a shortage of interesting stuff on supermarket, high-street or independent wine merchants' shelves, but the big sellers, the wines that people drank in their millions, always came down to the same uninspiring line-up. Not any more. Now Britain's celebrated range of wine styles is being enjoyed by everyone.

Auf wiedersehen* Liebfraumilch? *Au revoir appellation contrôlée?

Which wines are no longer relevant? Step forward, Germany's soupy mass-market blends. We all know that the Mosel, Rheingau and Pfalz can produce some of the greatest wines in the world, but none of them is called Liebfraumilch, Hock or Niersteiner Gutes Domtal. We're light years away from the time when German wines were regarded with the same respect as top Bordeaux or Champagne. As the latest 12 per cent slump in German wines makes clear, the British public is voting with its feet and collective palate.

The traditional regions of France are struggling, too. And once again, they've had it coming. In a market where Côtes du Rhône sits beside Barossa Valley Grenache, where Mâcon Blanc shares shelf-space with Chilean Chardonnay, where claret is increasingly contrasted with Argentine Cabernet Sauvignon, under-performing French regions have nowhere to hide.

Sure enough, France and its *appellation contrôlée* wines continue to lose sales to the New World. The unfavourable exchange rate hasn't helped. But one statistic is hugely significant. Five years ago, two in five bottles of wine sold in Britain were French. Today, we're talking one in four – and struggling.

Italy's familiar names haven't fared much better. Lambrusco, the frothy, not-so-adult answer to lemonade, is declining, along with vapid Valpolicella, watery Soave and limp-flavoured Chianti. To replace them, we're turning to richer, fruitier wines from Sicily, Sardinia, Puglia and the Abruzzi and new-wave styles from Tuscany, Piedmont, Trentino and the Veneto.

Much of the inspiration for this wine-drinking revolution has come from the New World, especially Australia. Traditionalists who said that the New World wouldn't establish a bridgehead in Britain have been proved wrong. Dramatically wrong. With the installation of temperature-controlled fermentation in places as geographically distant as Australia's Riverland and South Africa's Olifants River, enabling winemakers in warm climates to preserve the fruit in their wines (and still produce them at competitive prices), the New World is challenging the supremacy of the Old.

Hang on a tick, you're thinking to yourself. What about my bottles of Vosne-Romanée? That case of Cos d'Estournel I've been keeping for years? Well, our advice is to cherish them and, if you can afford it, to go on buying the great wines of Europe. But we're talking chalk and cheddar here. Our quarrel is not with genuinely fine wines, by which we mean those that demonstrate a real spirit of place and the capacity to age. The wines we – and you – are fed up with come from lazy, cynical, time-serving producers who sold us rubbish for years and assumed we wouldn't notice. Well, we did. And now we're doing something about it.

France fights back

The news from France isn't all bleak, however. The Languedoc-Roussillon, that huge chunk of land between the Rhône and the Pyrenees, has responded to the challenge of the New World with vigour. Varietal wines, or *vins de cépage* as they're known locally, are a match for honest, flavoursome Chardonnay, Sauvignon Blanc, Cabernet Sauvignon and Merlot from anywhere.

The region also produces increasing numbers of characterful, indigenous styles, many of them from under-valued *appellations contrôlées* such as Saint Chinian, Coteaux du Languedoc, Costières de Nîmes and Corbières. At the same time, it has started to use more characterful white grapes like Marsanne, Roussanne and Viognier to good effect.

If France has started, somewhat belatedly, to take the New World seriously, then its fightback has been helped by the quality of the 1995 vintage – the best and most consistent since 1990 – as well as by wine shortages, and price increases, in neighbouring Spain and Italy.

Introduction

There are signs that some of the more traditional regions are changing for the better, too. We've seen some really good Mâcon whites this year, especially in the £5–10 range. And the Loire Valley generally, and Muscadet *sur lie* in particular, produced a range of excellent wines in 1995. Basic Muscadet is still losing ground to the New World and the south of France. But the best *sur lie* wines are increasingly crisp, concentrated and well-made.

Bordeaux also had a good to very good vintage in 1995. The trouble with France's most famous wine region is its size. The best stuff from the *crus classés* such as Châteaux Margaux and Palmer can be wonderful, yet basic Bordeaux Rouge is frequently dire. Still, hype apart, 1995 Bordeaux *en primeur* offers from independent wine merchants were more voluminous than they've been since the great 1990 vintage. The 1995 whites are generally good, too.

Eastern Europe's first winemaking star

Eastern Europe has also moved up a gear in 1996. The white wines from Hungary are particularly noteworthy, but Bulgaria and the Czech Republic, of all places, have impressed us this year, too, with new-style wines from David Wollan and Nick Butler.

Why has Hungary suddenly come good? The answer is a combination of outside investment, the strongest economy in Eastern Europe and winemaking talent. Flying winemakers – those peripatetic oenologists derided by traditionalists – can pat themselves on the back here. Without the likes of Kym Milne, Nick Butler and Hugh Ryman, Hungary's wines would not be where they are today.

Flying winemakers have passed on their knowledge to local oenologists, such as Ákos Kamocsay, *Grapevine 1997's* winemaker of the year, who have combined their understanding of vineyards and indigenous grapes with new vinification techniques to produce the best wines that Eastern Europe has come up with in years.

Hungary's whites are finally showing genuine varietal character, especially its Sauvignon Blanc, Pinot Gris and wonderfully aromatic Irsai Oliver. The austere, bone-dry Furmints from the Tokay region may be a little harder to appreciate, but the quality is excellent. Tokay will have something really exciting to shout about when the release of sweet wines from the excellent 1993 vintage unveils the first modern styles made by French and Spanish companies such as AXA and Vega Sicilia.

The hand of God

Argentina is another of this year's success stories. In the past, poor winemaking – not to mention the Falklands War and the infamous 'hand of God' incident, when Diego Maradona scored with his fist in a World Cup football match with

England – have conspired against Argentine wines. The quantity was there all along (Argentina is the world's fifth-largest wine producer), but the quality was all but absent.

This time last year, Chile was doing all the South American running, but Argentina is catching up fast. Excellent wines from Norton and Catena have already drifted across the Atlantic, while for value for money it's almost impossible to beat the whites and reds emerging from the ultra-modern La Agricola winery, from Balbi and from Peter Bright's consultancy at Peñaflor. We think Argentina has the potential to make a real impression in Britain, especially with grapes such as Tempranillo, Bonarda, Torrontes, Cabernet Sauvignon, Syrah and Malbec.

Having said that, Chile's better-equipped wine industry will retain the edge over Argentina for some time to come, with brilliant Merlot, Chardonnay and Sauvignon Blanc at under £5. But, in the longer term, the two Andean neighbours could complement one another rather well. Argentina's warmer climate can make the full-flavoured reds, while Chile can take care of the aromatic whites and more delicate reds.

South Africa makes its move
South America isn't the only chunk of the New World to have impressed us in 1996. There have been encouraging improvements from South Africa, too, particularly with good-value Sauvignon Blanc and a number of classy Chardonnays in the £5–8 bracket. Basic South African reds are still struggling a little, although the potential is there, as Wine Rack's excellent Winelands range demonstrated in the high street. Despite the variable quality, the Mandela effect means that everyone wants to drink Cape wines at the moment. The result is a shortage of premium wine, particularly native Pinotage red, and rapidly rising prices.

The Spain just waiting to be tasted
Back in the Old World, Spain has benefited from the investment and soul-searching of recent years. We've had impressive, really characterful wines in 1996 from such diverse sources as Cava, Rioja, Somontano, Navarra, Galicia and Jerez, indicating that Spain is once more a force in world winemaking. Rioja deserves special praise. We've selected two of our red wines of the year from the region and have enjoyed many more. New ideas and better, more modern winemaking have transformed the face of Spain's foremost red wine region.

And what about England?
There have even been signs that England, with a fine vintage in 1995, can produce wines capable of competing for quality and value with the Loire Valley.

Introduction

We've tasted a number of enjoyable wines from Denbies, Britain's largest producer, and Notting Hill-based Aussie John Worontschak this year, which have changed our minds about English wines. Well, almost. Fingers crossed for a few more hot summers and autumns.

Must improve

Those are this year's star turns. But who disappointed us in 1996? Who, not to put too fine a point on it, are we going to dump on? First up in the stocks, surprisingly perhaps, is **Australia**. As a result of two small harvests in a row, Australia has struggled with quality and supply under £5. Cheap Aussie wine is frequently a disgrace, far less enjoyable than similarly priced wines from Chile, South Africa and southern France.

Not all sub-£5 wines from Down Under are poor, and most of the big companies have reacted sensibly to shortages. Key brands such as Lindeman's Bin 65 and Penfolds' Koonunga Hill have held their prices in anticipation of the effects of the 1996 harvest, the biggest on record for Australia. Early sightings suggest that the quality of the vintage should put Australia back on track.

The same is true of **New Zealand**. The 1996 vintage was a vast improvement on its predecessor, but with the legacy of the difficult 1995 vintage still on our shelves, this has not been New Zealand's year. There's plenty of goodwill towards the country that has transformed our attitude towards Sauvignon Blanc, but with so much refreshing Sauvignon from Chile and, increasingly, South Africa, New Zealand is in danger of pricing itself out of the market.

In France, the traditional under-performers continued to under-perform. As we said in our first few paragraphs, too many basic appellation wines are a disappointment, with **Bourgogne Rouge, Beaujolais, Muscadet, Rosé d'Anjou, Côtes du Rhône and Bordeaux Rouge** the worst offenders. Well-made wines under £5 are rare from such sources.

So much so, that they are increasingly irrelevant to British wine drinkers. Beaujolais is the obvious case in point. Quality Beaujolais exists, but is mainly made in the ten *crus*, Fleurie and Morgon among them, by individual growers. At the sub-£5 entry level, high yields and the addition of sugar to boost alcohol levels make Beaujolais look fruitless next to its modern counterparts in the New World and southern France. And with the southern hemisphere releasing new wines in our spring, Beaujolais Nouveau – once a cause for cheerfully celebrating the new vintage – has become embarrassing.

Germany is also in danger of suffering vinous meltdown. A handful of fine estate wines cannot begin to reverse the appalling image that Germany has created for itself by taking the lowest possible road. What's to be done? The new panacea is to call in the flying doctor, in the shape of a handful of Australian winemakers, to produce fruitier but drier wines, which are less reliant on sackfuls of sulphur. Wines with names such as Almond Grove, Northern Star and Devil's Rock may not set the world ablaze, but in the depths of the Schwarzwald, something is finally stirring. Let's hope it's not too late.

Further to the east, one wine-producing country continues to lag behind its competitors in the former Eastern Bloc – **Romania**. Most of the old-fashioned Romanian reds and whites we've come across from the land of Count Dracula deserve to have a stake driven firmly into the bottle. We've started to see slight improvements, but Romania has a very long way to go before it can produce wines that are palatably clean and fruity on a consistent basis.

California doesn't have a problem making palatable wine. Indeed, some of the best Chardonnay, Zinfandel, Merlot, Pinot Noir and sparkling wines of all come from the West Coast. But California's wines are increasingly polarised: many of its basic, sub-£5 wines are sweet, confected and not terribly distinguished, while its top wines are frequently over-priced. It's worth paying £12 or more to buy wines from the likes of Acacia, Ridge, Saintsbury and Au Bon Climat, but too many wineries are providing poor value for money.

Wine dinosaurs

The wine world is evolving so fast, with thrilling new wines emerging by the vintage, that some traditional names look increasingly old-fashioned these days. Maybe our palates have changed, but wines that we used to enjoy now seem rather dull. Wineries that badly need a transfusion of new ideas include Torres in Spain, Château Musar in the Lebanon, Quinta de Bacalhôa in Portugal, and Marqués de Murrieta in Spain. Come on, guys, if Gallo can reinvent itself as a producer of premium wines, anything is possible.

Flying winemakers do it on the ground

Perhaps they should enlist the services of a top flying winemaker. There is certainly no sign of the airborne division's influence waning in the high street. Quite the opposite, in fact. The technical rule-book has been used to good effect to improve basic wines from Eastern Europe, South Africa, Chile, Portugal and even parts of France and Italy. There may be an element of conformity to the wines, but the benefits of cleanliness and professionalism are more than adequate compensation. The flying doctors of winemaking have brought freshness and flavour to everyday wines, unearthed interesting local varieties and injected new life and hope into creaking wine industries around the globe. More power to their pipettes.

The end of the £1.99 bottle

Flying winemakers have done a lot to build the image of countries like Hungary, Bulgaria and Portugal. In the process, they've helped them to climb out of the

Introduction

bargain basement, where workers are poorly paid, there's no money to invest in the future and producers are tempted to cut corners.

Everyone, from retailers to grape pickers, seems to have realised that really cheap wines are a dead-end. We're happy to see the back of the £1.99 wine, not because we're against inexpensive wines *per se*, but because the effect of last year's £1.99 price war was to drag the market into the gutter and delude the public into thinking that wine is cheaper, or should be cheaper, than it actually is. £1.99 wine is almost inevitably rot-gut rubbish, which makes no contribution to anyone's enjoyment or appreciation of wine.

This year, the battleground has shifted from the £1.99 bottle to the £2.99 wine. Even at this level, finding something drinkable has become a game of Russian roulette. A combination of variable vintages and unfavourable exchange rates has conspired to take the price of most drinkable wines over £3 a bottle. Argentina still limbos under the £3 bar, as do Hungary, Bulgaria, Italy and the south of France. But when you bear in mind that more than £1 per bottle goes on excise duty, VAT and production costs, we feel that true value for money is to be found in the £3.50–£5 price range.

Segmentation and propositions

The big high-street news story of the year turned out to be – after a huge balloonful of hot air – a non-story. Oddbins was rumoured to be up for sale. The Wimbledon-based chain may no longer be the only innovator in the high street, but in a decade it has done a huge amount to champion quality and innovation. Tesco, Thresher and Greenalls Wine Cellars were all linked, as they say, to a possible purchase, but since parent company Seagram's supply deal terms were allegedly too onerous, no-one was prepared to take Oddbins on, hook, line and contra-deal sinker.

We're glad Oddbins is still around, but the high street as a whole remains volatile. Segmentation, not a pretty word, has been uppermost in the minds of the strategic thinkers behind the big companies. Thresher started it by tailoring Wine Rack, Bottoms Up and Thresher Wine Shops to the need of the locality. But the arrival of the dynamic Nader Haghighi at Greenalls Wine Cellars has added panache (and further segmentation) to a sector in danger of being squeezed out by the supermarkets.

If people go to supermarkets for one-stop shopping, reasons Haghighi, why not make the high-street off-licence more convenient? To this end Haghighi, once the boy-wonder of street-trading in Iran, has persuaded his bosses at Greenalls to ease the purse strings to allow him to indulge his passion for concepts and what he calls 'propositions'. The result is the first series of off-licence cafés, to be followed by more off-licence-cum-convenience-stores, off-licence-cum-newsagents and off-licence-cum-video-stores.

Can the high street cope with all this diversity? Whether there's room, between the mighty empires of Victoria Wine and Thresher, for a third force remains to be seen. Victoria Wine and Thresher themselves are both seriously looking at the 'Booze Barn' idea – huge wine warehouses in big shopping malls, where customers can browse and buy in bulk. Watch out Majestic?

Cork

Thresher has also made a success of its wine buyer's guarantee, which allows customers to bring back any bottle they don't like and replace it with something else. It's only a thought, but how many of them return to their local branch with a corked wine?

Our informal research indicates that the problem of tainted wine is still substantial.

When a cork's good, there's nothing to beat the satisfying ritual of pulling it, plop, from the bottle. Unfortunately, far too many wines are corked – affected by the foul-smelling TCA mould. Facing a rate of around one in every 20 bottles, the wine trade is taking cork taints seriously and looking at alternatives.

Marks & Spencer and Safeway were among the first to experiment with plastic corks. Sainsbury's, too, has tried plastic corks on a number of its wines, with a view to getting rid of corks altogether. Tesco is planning to try out screwtop bottles in the autumn of 1996, with a view to gauging consumer reaction. Château Pétrus in a screwcap? Maybe not, but screwcaps may well prove superior to cork, even for wines that need to be cellared for five years or more. We feel that corks should be scrapped for all everyday wines in favour of plastic corks or, better still, well-designed screwcaps.

Chips with everything

Because of the affinity between wine and oak, small barrels are often the favoured medium for the fermentation and maturation of full-bodied reds and non-aromatic whites. Oak adds something like 60 pence to the cost of a bottle of wine. All very well on expensive white Burgundy or California Chardonnay, but for everyday wines, the cost of French oak barrels can be prohibitive. The result is the increasing use of oak chips.

Like hickory chips on a barbecue, these are added to the grape juice in the winemaker's pillowcase, sock or some similar garment, to try to replicate the character that oak lends to fine wines. When the winemaker knows what he or she is doing, the result is a wine where the oak chips add extra complexity. Unfortunately, far too many wines suffer from an overdose of oak chips. The result is wines with coarse, bitter flavours that dry your mouth out.

You may notice, when you read our descriptions in *Grapevine*, how often we refer to oak, or if not to oak itself, then to wines that are 'chippy', 'sawdusty',

Introduction

'splintery' or 'charry'. All these terms – and many more – describe the effect of oak or oak chips (the latter jokingly referred to by Australian winemakers as microcasks), which have become part and parcel of winemaking. So much so that the winemaking wheel has turned full circle and bottles now declare their contents 'Lightly Oaked' or even 'Unoaked'. The backlash has begun.

Back labels

Ideally, back labels ought to tell you everything you need to know about a wine – its grape variety (or varieties), its style and, where appropriate, its brush with oak. Supermarkets often pay lip-service to providing such information, but all too often on back labels – an area where they can provide practical help – they fall flat on their faces. We've come across back labels in incomprehensible foreign languages, back labels with irrelevant guff, and back labels that are hopelessly uninformative. What, for instance, does 'a wine made from a blend of local grapes...' tell you, us or anyone else?

At least we've been amused by some of the more extravagant, travel-speak back labels. We liked Sainsbury's Chilean red '...from vineyards situated amongst the fertile foothills of the snow-capped Andes Mountains', and giggled at a humble English white, the 1995 Northbrook Springs White, Bishops Waltham produced from the 'free-draining southern slopes of the Hampshire Downs'. Welcome to claptrap country...

Picnic at Vampire's Leap

Talking of which, something else we've noticed this year is the tendency among European producers to adopt Australian-sounding names: Two Rivers, Downs Edge, Bear Ridge, Deer Leap and Block IV Chardonnay. At least Vampire's Leap is a conscious attempt at a spoof. Nevertheless, huge numbers of European wines are turning towards Devil's Creek and Donkey's Ridge. Whatever next. Rhino's Horn?

See you next year.

Asda ☆☆☆☆

Address: Asda House, Southbank, Great Wilson Street, Leeds LS11 5AD

Telephone/fax: 0113 2435435; 0113 2418146

Number of branches: 207

Opening hours: 9.00am to 8.00pm Monday to Saturday; 11.00am to 5.00pm Sunday; some stores open until 10.00pm

Credit cards accepted: Access, Visa, Switch

Discounts: £1 off any six bottles of still wine, providing the retail price is over £1.95. Buy any five bottles of the same sparkling wine or Champagne over £3.99 and receive a sixth free

Facilities and services: Glass loan; nationwide in-store tastings

Special offers: Regular promotions (buy any two and save around £1) and special buys/wine of the month

Top ten best-selling wines: 1995 Frascati Superiore; Muscadet de Sèvre et Maine, Celliers du Bellay; Cape Medium White, Simonsvlei; Lambrusco 8 per cent; Hock, Augustus Weinkellerei; 1995 Chianti, Piccini; Claret, Yvon Mau; 1992 Luvico Suhindol Cabernet Sauvignon; Sicilian Rosso; Cape Red, Simonsvlei

Range:

GOOD: Southern France, Italy, Portugal, Eastern Europe, Chile, Argentina, South Africa

AVERAGE: Spain, Loire, white Burgundy, Bordeaux, Beaujolais, Rhône, England, Germany, Australia, New Zealand, Port and Sherry, Champagne and sparkling wines

POOR: United States

UNDER-REPRESENTED: Red Burgundy, Alsace

There's a buzz about Asda at the moment, a sense of purpose visible in everyone, from the lowliest shelf-packer to Archie Norman, the media-hungry chairman. There's also evidence of a bit of fun. How many British supermarket groups would decorate their reception with giant papier mâché toffees and Licorice Allsorts?

The same two commodities are visible in the wine department, currently one of the most interesting in the country. So enthusiastic is *Loaded*-reading category manager, Nick Dymoke-Marr, that at times you want to attach a few guy-ropes and sandbags to his legs, lest he take off through the roof. 'We've made massive progress in the last 12 months,' says Dymoke-Marr, a man who has never lacked self-confidence. 'We're the fastest-growing wine retailer in the country at the moment, showing 29 per cent growth, which is 15 per cent ahead of the market.'

He makes no secret of his admiration for the unstuffiness of the 'Oddbins culture'. Supermarkets, he feels, are often 'dreary places to buy wine. There's no theatre, no passion.' His aim is to create the same sort of atmosphere within a supermarket wine department. 'No one else is trying to do that in this country,' he adds.

How is he going to achieve it? The first step has been to install a 'beer, wines and spirits supervisor' in every one of Asda's 207 booze departments. This is an example of what Dymoke-Marr calls 'the power of the person'. For him it's a way of selling the range to customers. 'We don't want wine buffs, who'll scare the hell out of people. We want polite, well-presented sales people who are enthusiastic about what they do.'

A series of countrywide in-store tastings, conducted by Jayne Bridges, the former Thresher PR person, is another part of Asda's strategy for getting its message across. Between 50 and 150 people pay £3 a time to come and hear about wine, with discounts on selected bottles after the tasting. 'Twenty thousand customers have attended our tastings this year,' says Dymoke-Marr. 'The whole thing is self-funding and self-propagating.'

Again with the consumer in mind, Asda restructured its wine department just over a year ago to group wines by style, rather than by country. Dymoke-Marrr says this makes it easier for shoppers to try new things and understand the range, although we have found it poorly signposted in at least one store.

All this activity looks impressive enough, but is it justified by the quality of the wine range? After this year's *Grapevine* tasting, our impression is broadly positive. Interesting new wines have arrived from Portugal, Italy, Germany, Eastern Europe and Argentina, and the chain has consolidated its strengths in Chile and the south of France.

Asda doesn't have the biggest range in the high street, but it does have one of the best-selected. 'We're not interested in stocking 900 wines,' says Dymoke-Marr. 'I want a regularly changing range of 350 lines, where there are always new things in store. I don't see the point of stocking eight different Chiantis.'

The last 12 months have witnessed a spot of self-criticism in the wine department. 'We've addressed our range,' admits Dymoke-Marr. 'The general level was up and down before, and we wanted to sort that out.' As a result, nearly half of the list has changed. As well as off-the-peg wines, there have been new projects with winemaking consultants, such as Aussies Nick Butler, Ben Riggs and Peter Bright and Chilean Andres Ilabaca. But a lot of 'turkeys' have been sacrificed. 'We haven't got time to deal with people who don't perform,' he explains.

The wine department has expanded from three to four this year, with the appointment of marketing manager Penny Thair from Greenalls Cellars. Otherwise, it's the familiar line-up of lobster-loving Dymoke-Marr, buying manager Alistair Morrell and trainee buyer and fashion consultant Illy Jaffar.

The team has focused on creating what Dymoke-Marr terms 'a bit of theatre in the wine department', with regular wines-of-the-month promotions on wines at £5 and above. These are part of a wines-for-special-occasions 'bookcase' of around two dozen finer wines. Other props for selling pricier wines include barrels, bins and lively point-of-sale material.

This hasn't stopped Asda focusing on the cheaper, volume end of the market. In fact, its selection of sub-£3 wines is arguably the best in the country. The chain's average bottle price has moved over £3 to £3.04, and Liebfraumilch has dropped out of the top-ten best-sellers for the first time. But a lot of Asda customers are still after bargain-basement wines.

Sadly, at least as far as we're concerned, this includes a pair of wines at £1.99. 'We don't shout about it, but we do sell a red and a white at £1.99,' says Dymoke-Marr, who concedes that they are effectively loss-leaders. 'Wine is something everyone should enjoy at every price point, and these are wholesome and clean-tasting.'

A more significant fact is that Asda's fastest-growing price sector is between £4 and £6, admittedly from a lower base. It can also shift smaller quantities of expensive wine, such as 30 cases a week of Penfolds Bin 389 at nearly £10.

Whatever the price point, Asda customers seem to like what they find in the department. They spent a record £150m on wine last year, and more and more of them include wine as part of their weekly shop. 'Five years ago, only 5 per cent of our customers bought wine from us,' says Dymoke-Marr. 'We've doubled that, but there's still a lot of work to do.'

White

Under £3

ARGENTINA

1995 Asda Argentinian White, La Agricola   15/20
Dry 💰💰💰 ▐
A brilliant-value blend of the aromatic native Torrontes grape with 35 per cent Chenin Blanc for extra weight, this is extremely fruity and delicately spicy. Hard to beat under £3.

CHILE

Alto Plano Chilean White, Concha y Toro   13/20
Dry 💰💰 ▐
A soft Chilean Bordeaux-style blend of the Semillon and Sauvignon grapes, whose fragrant, lime-like character reminds us of a palatable New World Riesling.

FRANCE

1995 Muscadet de Sèvre et Maine, Vinival   14/20
Dry 💰💰💰 ▐
A change of supplier has improved Asda's basic Muscadet beyond all recognition. A fresh, appley, crisply turned-out Nantes country white.

1995 Spring Vale, Vin de Pays de l'Aude   13/20
Off-dry 💰💰 ▐
Clean, pleasantly palatable southern French white from the Foncalieu winery. Finishes a little bitter.

GERMANY

Hock Medium White, Augustus Weinkellerei   12/20
Medium sweet 💰 ▐
Very basic German white blend with grapefruit-segment characters and a depressing lack of freshness.

Northern Star German White

Off-dry 🍷🍷🍷 🍾

14/20

Made by Aussie flying winemaker Nick Butler in a consciously mould-breaking style, this is a successful modern German white with ripe banana and peach-like fruit allied to refreshing crispness and spritz, Fritz.

HUNGARY

1995 Badger Hill Hungarian White, Irsai Oliver

Dry 🍷🍷🍷 🍾

14/20

With the floral fragrance of clove pinks and full, spicy fruitiness, this crisp, zesty aromatic white made by Ákos Kamocsay at the Neszmely co-operative is the perfect solution for Alsace Gewürz-lovers on a budget.

1995 Asda Hungarian Chardonnay

Off-dry 🍾

11/20

Flat, musty, sweetish Eastern European Chardonnay, which does few favours for the world's trendiest grape variety.

1995 Asda Hungarian Muscat

Off-dry 🍷🍷 🍾

13/20

Easy-drinking, grapey Muscat with soft, simple fruitiness and fresh acidity.

ITALY

Lambrusco Bianco, Coltiva, 8 per cent

Sweet 🍷 🍾

12/20

Water-white, sweetly grapey, lemonadey alternative to Hoopers Hooch.

1995 Frascati Superiore, Cantina del Bacco

Off-dry 🍷🍷 🍾

13/20

Plumpish, unoaked, faintly spicy Roman white, which lacks a bit of acidity and zip.

1995 Coltiva Il Bianco, Vino da Tavola

Dry 🍷🍷🍷 🍾

14/20

A nutty, fresh, extremely commercial blend of Italian grapes from the regions of Tuscany and Emilia-Romagna, made by Chilean star, Andres Ilabaca, of the Canepa winery.

1995 Riva Trebbiano di Romagna   12/20
Dry
The Chilean connection is maintained here by the presence of Casablanca-based winemaker Gaetane Carron. We preferred last year's effort to this rather ordinary, high-acid *bianco*.

PORTUGAL

1995 Bela Fonte, Vinho da Mesa Branco   13/20
Dry
Soft, baked-apple-style Portuguese white made by leading Iberian oenologist José Neiva.

SOUTH AFRICA

Cape White Medium, Simonsvlei   12/20
Medium dry
Fine if you like the rather sickly combination of banana and boiled sweets. Otherwise, best avoided.

SPAIN

1995 Remonte Navarra Blanco, Co-operativa Vinicola Murchantina   13/20
Dry
A fresh, basic northern Spanish co-operative quaffer apparently made from the neutral Viura grape, whose tart acidity is the wine's most distinctive feature.

UNITED STATES

Asda Californian White   10/20
Medium dry
A confected West Coast blend of Colombard and Chenin Blanc with a touch of Muscat, from California wheeler-dealer Jason Korman. Soupy stuff.

£3–5

AUSTRALIA

1995 Kingston Estate Chenin/Verdelho   14/20
Off-dry 👜👜 🍾

Sweetish, tropical fruity, warm-climate blend of Chenin Blanc and Verdelho from the irrigated Murray Valley in South Australia's Riverland. One of the better sub-£4 Australian whites on the market.

Asda South-East Australia Semillon/Chardonnay, Yaldara   13/20
Off-dry 👜 🍾

Sweetish, straightforward Aussie white with a few splinters lending a toffeeish note to the blend.

1994 Cranswick Oak-Aged Marsanne   16/20
Dry 👜👜👜 🍾

Toasty, intensely rich, honeysuckle-scented Marsanne from the people who also make the rather less exciting Barramundi wines. A characterful, oaky, enticingly spicy Aussie triumph.

1995 Koonunga Hill Chardonnay, Penfolds   16/20
Dry 👜👜👜 🍾

Classy, complex, barrel-fermented Aussie Chardonnay with butter and toffee-fudge richness balanced by beautifully judged, refreshing acidity.

1994 Peter Lehmann Barossa Valley Semillon   15/20
Dry 👜👜 🍾

A wine with the typical herby aromas and lemony flavours of the Semillon grape in the Barossa Valley, made by characterful raconteur, Peter Lehmann.

CHILE

1995 Rowan Brook Sauvignon Blanc Reserve, Canepa   15/20
Dry 👜👜👜 🍾

Zesty, ultra-crisp Curicó Sauvignon Blanc made by the youthful Andres Ilabaca, who can take credit for helping to pioneer excellent-value, new-wave whites in Chile.

1995 Rowan Brook Chardonnay Reserve, Canepa, Mataquito Valley   14/20
Dry 🍷 ▮

Sweetly oaked, honeyed Chardonnay made by Andres Ilabaca from grapes grown in one of Chile's innumerable river valleys, in this case the Mataquito Valley.

ENGLAND

1995 Carden Vale English White   15/20
Off-dry 🍷🍷🍷 ▮

A really impressive, zesty English white from the Three Choirs Vineyard, which shows that some of the fuss made about the 1995 vintage was worthwhile. England's answer to Touraine Sauvignon.

FRANCE

1995 Southern Cross Chardonnay/Viognier, Vin de Pays d'Oc 14/20
Off-dry 🍷🍷 ▮

From the Val d'Orbieu winery, this is a ripe, well-made Midi blend of the two trendiest white grapes around. It's hard to discern the presence of 45 per cent Viognier, but the wine is still attractively drinkable.

1995 Southern Cross Grenache/Chardonnay, Vin de Pays d'Oc
13/20
Off-dry 🍷 ▮

A southern French combination (or Cross, geddit?) of international Chardonnay and the ubiquitous Midi grape, Grenache Blanc. Ripe, mealy, but a shade plonky.

1995 Domaine Saint François Sauvignon Blanc, Vin de Pays d'Oc
15/20
Dry 🍷🍷🍷 ▮

Zingy, grapefruity, brilliant-value Sauvignon made by Jean-Luc Lafarge at the Foncalieu winery. Nettley in the Loire style, but with ripe, southern weight.

1995 Entre Deux Mers Cuvée Frimont, Yvon Mau   13/20
Dry 🍷 ▮

The fruit concentration apears to have done a runner on this Bordeaux blend of mainly Sauvignon, with some Semillon and Muscadelle. Time to call Hercule Poirot.

1994 Muscadet de Sèvre et Maine sur lie, Domaine Gautron 15/20
Dry 💰💰 ▯

White-peppery, concentrated, characterful Muscadet with ripe pear flavours and a fresh prickle of lees-derived gas.

1995 Cuckoo Hill Viognier, Château de Raissac, Vin de Pays d'Oc
16/20

Off-dry 💰💰💰 ▯

Nick Butler has had a huge impact on the quality of the wines made at the Languedoc's Château de Raissac since leaving Hungary. This ripe honeysuckle and peach-like example of southern France's most sought-after grape is a flavoursome, beautifully balanced stunner.

1995 Montagne Noire Chardonnay, Vin de Pays d'Oc 15/20
Dry 💰💰💰 ▯

Cleverly made, toasty-oaky southern French Chardonnay, which is far subtler than last year's more overtly chipped style. A fresh, clean, well-crafted white from the Foncalieu winery. Very good value at under £4.

1995 James Herrick Chardonnay, Vin de Pays d'Oc 15/20
Dry 💰💰 ▯

Elegant, minerally Chardonnay from Englishman James Herrick's southern French vineyards near Narbonne, showing restrained, spicy oak and melony fruitiness.

GERMANY

1995 Wild Boar Vineyards Riesling 14/20
Off-dry 💰💰 ▯

The result of Nick Butler's first foray into Black Forest gâteau territory, this is a fresh, appealingly commercial, modern expression of the Riesling grape, tinged with blackcurrant leaf and lime.

HUNGARY

1995 Sopron Sauvignon Blanc Private Reserve 15/20
Dry 💰💰💰 ▯

From the outstanding Neszmely co-operative, this is a buy-and-drink-by-the-caseload Hungarian Sauvignon, with grapefruit and elderflower crispness and remarkable length of flavour for a wine at just over £3.

1995 Mecsekalji Chardonnay Private Reserve 14/20
Dry 🍾🍾 |

For an extra 50 pence, this is considerably more interesting than the basic Asda Hungarian Chardonnay. Again from Neszmely, it's a crisp, fruit-steered style with a refreshing citrus-like tang.

ITALY

1995 Soave Classico Superiore, Boscaini 15/20
Dry 🍾🍾🍾 |

A weighty, full-flavoured Soave, which has just managed to limbo under the £4 pole. Fresh, nutty pear and apple fruitiness and zesty acidity.

1995 Frascati Superiore, Colli di Catone 15/20
Dry 🍾🍾🍾 |

Bracingly fresh, ginger-scented, characterful Roman white made from a blend of Malvasia del Lazio and Malvasia di Candia by the quality-conscious producer, Antonio Pulcini.

1993 Recioto di Soave, Castelcerino 13/20
Sweet 🍾 |

Sugary, orange-peel and brandy-snap-like Italian sticky, blended from Garganega and 5 per cent Trebbiano di Soave. Recioto di Soave, made from dried Soave grapes, can be wonderfully intense, but this is a rather flat-footed effort.

PORTUGAL

1995 Bright Brothers Sercial/Arinto, Vinho Regional Extremadura 15/20
Dry 🍾🍾🍾 |

With so much Chardonnay and Sauvignon Blanc on the market, it's a delight to come across an innovative white wine made from indigenous grape varieties, such as Portugal's Sercial and Arinto. Spicy, lemony, pungently aromatic, tangily fresh combination from Lisbon-based Aussie Peter Bright.

1995 Fiuza Barrel-Fermented Chardonnay, Vinho Regional Ribatejo 15/20
Dry 🍾🍾 |

Ripe New World-inspired southern Portuguese Chardonnay with pineapple fruitiness and rich toffee-fudge and toasty notes. A wine for Banoffee pie lovers.

SOUTH AFRICA

1995 Kumala Chenin/Chardonnay 13/20
Off-dry 🍷 🍾
A quaffable Cape blend of Chenin and Chardonnay from the Sonop Wine Farm, which should have moved on to the next vintage by the time you read this – we hope so.

SPAIN

1995 Terra Alta Garnacha Blanca 13/20
Dry 🍷 🍾
A basic expression of a basic white Spanish variety, given the oak character treatment by Nick Butler and Mark Nairn in a moderately successful attempt to inject a bit of interest.

£5–8

AUSTRALIA

1995 Château Reynella Chardonnay 16/20
Dry 🍷🍷🍷 🍾
With its powerful flavours and toffee and caramel richness, this is a ripe, but still youthful, Australian Chardonnay made at BRL-Hardy's home base south of Adelaide. Lots of concentration and complexity for just under £7.

FRANCE

1995 Sancerre La Vigne des Rocs, Henri Bourgeois 16/20
Dry 🍷🍷🍷 🍾
Steely, dry, honeyed Sancerre showing the quality of the 1995 vintage in the Loire Valley. Modern and intense, with typical grassy Sauvignon Blanc undertones and good structure.

1995 Château du Trignon, Côtes du Rhône Blanc 15/20
Dry 🍷🍷 🍾
An equal blend of Grenache Blanc, Clairette, Bourboulenc and Roussanne made at a winery in Gigondas, this mealy, almondy-fresh white presents the modern face of white Rhône.

1995 Saint Véran, Domaine des Deux Roches   16/20
Dry 🍾🍾🍾 ▬

Minerally, youthful, grapefruity Mâconnais Chardonnay showing an astonishing degree of buttery complexity for an unoaked white.

GERMANY

1995 Wiltinger Braunfels Riesling Kabinett, Jordan & Jordan
15/20

Medium dry 🍾🍾 |

Fresh, piercingly aromatic, green apple-like Mosel Riesling with crisp, sweet-and-sour acidity. Good value at just over a fiver.

NEW ZEALAND

1995 Saint Clair New Zealand Sauvignon Blanc   14/20
Dry 🍾 |

A trans-island blend of Kiwi Sauvignon Blanc made by Coopers Creek winemaker, Kim Crawford. Given the lean, dilute vintage, this is a creditable, green-bean-like Sauvignon Blanc at a slightly inflated price.

1995 Saint Clair New Zealand Chardonnay   16/20
Dry 🍾🍾🍾 |

More successful than the Sauvignon Blanc, this Chardonnay from the same winemaker is a smokily oaked, citrus-fruity white, which is almost Chablis-like in its cool-climate elegance.

SPAIN

1995 Raimat Chardonnay, Costers del Segre   14/20
Dry 🍾 |

Unoaked Catalan Chardonnay from a modern, New World-influenced winery near Lerida, showing sweetish, banana-like fruit and tart acidity.

Red

Under £3

ARGENTINA

1995 Asda Argentinian Red, La Agricola   15/20
Medium-bodied 🛍🛍🛍 🍾
With its attractive sun-emblem label, this brilliantly commercial Argentine blend of Bonarda, Malbec and Cabernet Sauvignon is the sort of wine that should break down any lingering post-Falklands, post-Maradona prejudices. A meaty, spicy, robustly fruity red.

BULGARIA

1992 Lovico Suhindol Cabernet Sauvignon, Domaine Boyar   12/20
Medium-bodied 🍾
A raisiny, old-fashioned, oak-chippy Bulgarian Cabernet Sauvignon moving in a counter-revolutionary direction.

CHILE

1995 Alto Plano Red, Concha y Toro   14/20
Medium-bodied 🛍🛍🛍 🍾
Unoaked, blackcurrant-pastille-scented Chilean *tinto*, constructed around the Cabernet Sauvignon grape. A good-value, claret-busting blend.

FRANCE

1995 Spring Vale Rouge, Vin de Pays de l'Aude   14/20
Medium-bodied 🛍🛍🛍 🍾
An encouragingly modern, southern French red made in a Beaujolais style and showing lush, if simple, blackberry fruitiness. Great value.

Asda Merlot, Vin de Pays d'Oc, Skalli   14/20
Medium-bodied 🛍🛍🛍 🍾
A smooth, spicy, lightly tannic Midi Merlot blended for Asda by Fortant de France in Sète. Another top-value rouge.

HUNGARY

1995 Asda Hungarian Kekfrankos   12/20
Light-bodied 👜 ▮
A light, peppery quaffer made from Eastern Europe's characterful Kekfrankos grape blended with a dash of Kekoporto.

1995 Asda Hungarian Merlot   13/20
Medium-bodied 👜👜 ▮
Not massively true to type, but this Hungarian Merlot has a bit more weight, mid-palate sweetness and tannin than the Kekfrankos.

ITALY

1995 Coltiva Il Rosso, Vino da Tavola   13/20
Light-bodied 👜👜 ▮
The red counterpart to Chilean Andres Ilabaca's *bianco*, this light, cherried sub-Valpol blend is approachable, if one-dimensional

1995 Riva, Sangiovese di Romagna   14/20
Light-bodied 👜👜👜 ▮
Making up for a slightly dull, dry white, Gaetane Carron has produced a soft, spicy, lightly peppery, central Italian *rosso* with sweet, easy-drinking tannins.

1995 Montepulciano d'Abruzzo, Cantina Tollo   14/20
Medium-bodied 👜👜👜 ▮
In a similar vein, this is an aromatic, thirst-quenching red, with crisp loganberry fruitiness and juicy acidity.

Sicilian Rosso, Vino da Tavola di Sicilia   13/20
Light-bodied 👜👜 ▮
A sweetish, morello-cherry-like Sicilian blend of the local Nero d'Avola with Sangiovese and Barbera.

PORTUGAL

1995 Bela Fonte Tinto, Vinho da Mesa   11/20
Medium-bodied ▮
Raisiny, confected, oak-chipped plonk with a dose of commercial sweetness to help it on its way down – the sink?

SPAIN

1995 Remonte Navarra Tinto   14/20
Full-bodied 🍾🍾🍾 ▯
An appealing, Garnacha-based northern Spanish alternative to Beaujolais, with softly fruity, raspberryish flavours and a nip of dry tannins on the aftertaste.

UNITED STATES

Asda Californian Red   12/20
Medium-bodied ▯
A confected, raspberry-jelly-like wine pieced together from out-takes that should have stayed on the cutting-room floor. Sweet, soupy and hollow. This was a silver-medal winner at the 1996 International Wine Challenge, so maybe you should avoid the bronzes.

£3–5

AUSTRALIA

1995 Asda South Eastern Australia Shiraz/Cabernet, Yaldara 11/20
Light-bodied ▯
A wine that tastes considerably older than something from the 1995 vintage. Dilute and prematurely ageing, with a confected oak character.

1995 Rosemount Cabernet/Shiraz   13/20
Light-bodied ▯
Soft, mawkish, tutti-frutti red using the carbonic-maceration vinification technique to not particularly good effect.

CHILE

1995 Rowan Brook Cabernet/Malbec, Mataquito Valley   14/20
Medium-bodied 🍾🍾 ▯
Light, well-made Chilean claret substitute, blending Cabernet Sauvignon with the comparatively rare (for Chile) Malbec in a fruity, no-nonsense style.

1995 Rowan Brook Zinfandel
Medium-bodied 🎒🎒🎒 ❘

15/20

One of the very few examples of Zinfandel grown outside California, Andres Ilabaca's tobacco-ish, raspberry fruity red is an unoaked delight with a characteristically spicy finish.

1995 Terra Noble Merlot
Medium-bodied 🎒🎒 ▪▪—

15/20

This is a considerable step up from the first vintage of the new Chilean venture advised by Loire specialist, Henry Marionnet. Grassy, carbonic-maceration-style, unoaked Merlot, with attractive depth and juiciness and faintly rustic tannins.

1994 Rowan Brook Cabernet Sauvignon, Winemaker's Reserve, Mataquito Valley
Medium-bodied 🎒🎒 ▪▪—

15/20

Overtly oaked, cedary Chilean Cabernet Sauvignon from the Canepa winery, with mint and blackcurrant-pastille fruit characters to the fore, and a chewy aftertaste that may soften with a few more months in the bottle.

FRANCE

Asda Claret, Yvon Mau
Medium-bodied 🎒 ❘

13/20

Basic, chewy red Bordeaux, which struggles to compete with similar-priced wines from Chile and Argentina.

1995 Montagne Noire Syrah/Merlot
Medium-bodied 🎒🎒🎒 ❘

15/20

Richly coloured, perfumed Languedoc blend made at the impressive Foncalieu winery. The blackberry fruitiness of the Syrah grape comes through strongly on the palate and is complemented by well-judged oak character.

Asda Fitou
Full-bodied 🎒🎒 ❘

14/20

The reliable Mont Tauch co-operative, which seems to supply Fitou to half of Britain, has produced a typically well-made, unoaked blend of Carignan and Grenache with garrigue and rosemary notes.

1995 Mas Segala, Côtes du Roussillon Villages 14/20
Full-bodied 🍷🍷 ➡

A more substantial Midi rouge, in which the addition of some Syrah to the basic Grenache and Carignan has given the wine extra backbone and a drier aftertaste.

1994 Domaine de Grangeneuve, Coteaux du Tricastin 14/20
Medium-bodied 🍷 🍶

Soft, peppery, unoaked carbonic-maceration-style blend of Grenache, Cinsault and Syrah from the southern Rhône. Starts well, but comes over all plonky on the palate.

1995 James Herrick, Cuvée Simone, Vin de Pays d'Oc 16/20
Full-bodied 🍷🍷🍷 ➡

Named after his charming Californian wife, Simone, James Herrick's first Languedoc venture into red wine is a triumph, showing tarry, aromatic Syrah character and fleshy, sweet fruit and southern spiciness. Still chunky, but should soon soften into a memorable sub-£5 red.

ITALY

1995 Chianti Piccini 13/20
Light-bodied 🍷 🍶

Light, approachable, cherried Chianti with a shaving of oak character.

1994 Barbera d'Asti, Cascine Garona 13/20
Medium-bodied 🍷 🍶

A soft, approachable, oak-chippy Barbera from an area better known for its fizzy, sweet whites.

1993 Rosso del Salento, Santa Barbara, Vino da Tavola 15/20
Medium-bodied 🍷🍷🍷 🍶

A modern take on a traditional Puglian style of red, with the sun-dried, sweetly raisined Mediterranean character of fruit elegantly lifted by refreshing acidity. A real mouthful of southern Italy.

1993 Squinzano Rosso, Santa Barbara 12/20
Full-bodied 🍶

The best thing about this pruney, vinegary, rustic red is its name – make that the only thing.

1994 Chianti Colli Salvanza, Colli Senesi   15/20
Medium-bodied 👛👛👛 ●—

A wine that looks and tastes a lot more expensive than its sub-£4 price tag would suggest, this is a rich, chocolatey, spicy Sangiovese-based Chianti with well-judged oak and refreshing acidity.

1994 Rozzano, Villa Pigna   15/20
Full-bodied 👛👛 ●—

Wannabe super-Tuscan red from the Marches region of central Italy, this is a hefty wine in a hefty bottle with masses of oak and spicy, sage-like stuffing, only slightly let down by a touch of astringency.

PORTUGAL

1994 Bright Brothers Old Vine Red, Vinho Regional Estremadura
15/20
Medium-bodied 👛👛👛 ▮

Vibrantly fruity, succulent Portuguese blend, with masses of peppery spice and well-judged oak character, from talented oenologist Peter Bright. The garish red label is almost as loud as the winemaker.

1994 Fiuza Oak-Aged Cabernet Sauvignon   16/20
Medium-bodied 👛👛👛 ▮

Elegant, almost New Zealand-like Cabernet Sauvignon, which is remarkable given that the wine was made in the warm Portuguese south. Fine tannins, smoky oak and green-pepper fruitiness make this restrained red a brilliant alternative to claret.

SOUTH AFRICA

1995 Kumala Cabernet/Shiraz   14/20
Full-bodied 👛👛 ●—

A spicy, plummy Cape blend of Cabernet and Shiraz grapes, which tastes and smells more like a Pinotage. No bad thing on a well-made wine such as this.

1995 Stellenzicht Block Series Zinfandel   15/20
Full-bodied 👛👛 ●—

A meaty, rustic, sweetly oaked, warm-climate Zinfandel with powerfully structured, blockbuster fruit intensity and firm tannins.

1994 Kanonkop Bouwland Red   14/20
Full-bodied 🛍 ●━
A rather chunky South African attempt at a Bordeaux-style blend of Merlot, Cabernet Sauvignon and Cabernet Franc. Lots of colour, lots of fruit, but far too much tannin.

SPAIN

1995 Terra Alta Cabernet/Garnacha, Rovira   13/20
Medium-bodied 🛍 ▮
There's lots of sweetish, Garnacha fruit here, strengthened by the addition of Cabernet Sauvignon, but the wine pulls up short and dry.

1995 Terra Alta Bush Vine Garnacha   14/20
Medium-bodied 🛍🛍 ▮
From the same team of Nick Butler and Mark Nairn, this Catalan Garnacha has borrowed the Aussie old-vine concept to produce a highly drinkable, strawberry fruity red, which doesn't hide its quality under a bushel.

1992 Asda Rioja Crianza   11/20
Light-bodied ▮
A talcum-powder and desiccated coconut-like confection which does a disservice to Spain's leading red-wine region. If you like Don Darias, you might enjoy this one. We didn't.

El Mesón Rioja, CVC   15/20
Medium-bodied 🛍🛍 ▮
It's hard to believe that this sweetish, mature, attractively oaked, non-vintage Rioja only costs 70 pence more than the Asda own-label. A silky, elegant, Pinot Noir-like Rioja with vanilla and raspberry fruitiness.

UNITED STATES

1995 Sebastiani Zinfandel   12/20
Medium-bodied ▮
Sweet, confected, boiled-sweets and lollipop-like Californian Zinfandel made, we assume, with the cola-drinker in mind.

£5–8

AUSTRALIA

1993 Château Reynella Cabernet/Merlot, McLaren Vale   16/20
Full-bodied 🍷🍷 ▪—

A firm, structured, age-worthy, McLaren Vale blend of the Bordeaux grapes, Cabernet Sauvignon and Merlot, infused with sweet American oak and cinnamon-tinged spice.

CHILE

1995 Cono Sur Pinot Noir Reserve   16/20
Medium-bodied 🍷🍷🍷 ▪—

It's a shame that rangy Ed Flaherty has moved to the Errázuriz winery, because this is his best-ever Pinot Noir Reserve, made like a modern Côte de Beaune red Burgundy with attractively spicy oak, wild strawberry fruitiness and medium-weight tannins. Pity Asda could only secure 500 cases of the wine.

FRANCE

1993 Domaine de la Baume, Vin de Pays d'Oc   15/20
Full-bodied 🍷🍷 ▪—

A markedly Australian-style, Cabernet Sauvignon-based southern French blend with lashings of sweet, smoky oak and tightly structured tannins. Could do with a year in the bottle to soften the abrasive edges.

1993 Château de Parenchère, Bordeaux Supérieur   15/20
Medium-bodied 🍷🍷 ▮

An old Asda favourite, showing supple Merlot-like fruit characters and attractive, mint and cassis vivacity. The lean streak of the 1993 vintage pokes through on the finish.

1993 Château Peybonhomme-Les-Tours, Côtes de Blaye, Cru Bourgeois   16/20
Medium-bodied 🍷🍷🍷 ▮

A controversial red Bordeaux, which is the only *cru bourgeois* outside the Médoc and is currently engaged in legal wrangles to remain so. Soft, forward, well-balanced claret made in a mellow, mini-Saint Emilion mould. The discreet charm of the bourgeoisie.

ITALY

1990 Barolo, Angelo Veglio   15/20
Full-bodied 👜👜 🍷
Well-priced for a Barolo from one of the best post-war vintages in Piemonte, this all-Nebbiolo-grape red is typically tarry, dry and tannic. Make sure you drink it with suitably robust food.

SPAIN

1991 Barón de Ley Rioja   16/20
Medium-bodied 👜👜👜 ▮
Oaky, Cabernet Sauvignon-influenced Rioja Reserva, which is just getting into its stride. An attractively fruity, well-oaked red.

Over £8

FRANCE

1993 Moulin-à-Vent, Les Hospices   11/20
Medium-bodied ▮
A hollow, fruitless Beaujolais *cru* with fungal undertones and little Gamay fruitiness. Everything but the flashy label belongs in a hospice for the moribund.

1993 Penfolds Bin 389 Cabernet/Shiraz   17/20
Full-bodied 👜👜👜 🍷
Gorgeous rich, blackberry succulence and sweet cedary oak are the hallmarks of this deeply hued Penfolds classic red, which is already showing delightful richness of fruit and length of flavour. Will go on and on, ad infinitum.

Sparkling

£3–5

SPAIN

Asda Cava Brut   15/20
Dry 👛👛 ▮
From Spanish sparkling-wine giant Codorniu, this blend of Xarel-lo, Parellada and (crucially) Chardonnay is one of the better Cavas on the market, with creamy, tangy fruitiness and good lift.

£5–8

AUSTRALIA

Cranswick Pinot/Chardonnay, Riverina   15/20
Off-dry 👛👛 ▮
A yeasty, big-bubbled Aussie fizz for lovers of lemon-sherbet sweets and Vegemite sandwiches.

Over £8

FRANCE

Asda Champagne Brut   14/20
Dry 👛 ▮
Cheap for Champagne at under £12, this is a fresh, youthful fizz, which lacks an added dimension of depth and finesse.

Asda Champagne Rosé Brut   15/20
Dry 👛👛 ▮
From the same supplier, Nicolas Feuillatte, and at the same price as the Asda own-label, this salmon-pink, strawberry fruity Champagne is soft, mouth-filling stuff with fresh acidity and fine bubbles.

Nicolas Feuillatte Blanc de Blancs Brut   15/20
Dry 🍾🍾 ▯

Still on the young side, but this all-Chardonnay co-operative Champagne should fill out nicely over the next year, allowing the promising raw material to strut its stuff.

UNITED STATES

Scharffenberger Mendocino Brut   16/20
Dry 🍾🍾🍾 ▯

A *Grapevine* wine of the year in 1996, this Anderson Valley California sparkler is a fine-moussed, creamy fizz with a vanilla ice-cream richness. One of the New World's finest.

Fortified

£3–5

SPAIN

Asda Fino Sherry, Barbadillo   14/20
Off-dry 🍾🍾🍾 ▯

Fresh, tangy, aromatic Fino at an unbelievable price. A little bit of sweetness makes the wine more commercial.

Asda Amontillado, Barbadillo   13/20
Medium sweet 🍾 ▯

Confected crème caramel-like medium Sherry with rather light, almondy flavours. True Amontillado should be drier and more interesting than this.

£5–8

PORTUGAL

Asda Vintage Character Port, Smith Woodhouse   15/20
Full-bodied 👜👜 |
Raisiny sweet and slightly nutty, swilling Port from the Symington stable. We find the fortification a little heavy-handed.

Asda 1988 Late Bottled Vintage, Smith Woodhouse   15/20
Full-bodied 👜👜 ━
Deeper in colour and richer in flavour, this is a chocolatey Port with peppery spice, rich fruit and a fiery finish.

Asda Tawny Port   15/20
Full-bodied 👜👜 |
The sweetest of Asda's own-label Ports, this is a softly mature, aromatic Tawny, with attractive raisin and nut fruitiness.

Booths ☆☆☆☆

Address: 4, 5 & 6 Fishergate, Preston PR1 3LJ

Telephone/fax: 01772 251701; 01772 250066

Number of branches: 23

Opening hours: Vary from store to store, but the majority are open 8.30am to 6.00pm Monday and Tuesday; 8.30am to 7.00pm Wednesday and Thursday; 8.30am to 8.00pm Friday; 8.30am to 6.00pm Saturday; 10.00am to 4.00pm Sunday (16 stores only)

Credit cards accepted: Access, Visa, Switch, Delta

Discounts: 10 per cent off a mixed case

Facilities and services: In-store tastings at weekends; sale or return on party purchases; free glass loan

Special offers: Promotions and bin-end offers

Top ten best-selling wines: Alta Mesa Portuguese Red; Nicole French Vin de Table White; Bulgarian Cabernet/Merlot; Nicole French Vin de Table Red; Peter Mertes Hock; Gabbia d'Oro Rosso; Santa Carolina White; Bellefontaine Merlot Vin de Pays d'Oc; Château Laval, Costières de Nîmes; Gyöngyös Hungarian Chardonnay

Range:

GOOD: Red Bordeaux, red and white Burgundy, regional France, Australia, New Zealand, Spain, Chile

AVERAGE: White Bordeaux, Loire, Beaujolais, Rhône, Alsace, Germany, Italy, Eastern Europe, South Africa, United States, Champagne and sparkling wines

POOR: None

UNDER-REPRESENTED: Portugal

In 1925 *Country Illustrated* described E.H. Booth as the Fortnum & Mason of Preston. 'In the large wine and spirit department of their business, customers are offered a large selection, while Messrs Booth and Co.'s bottled wines and blended spirits have attained well-deserved popularity.' *Plus ça change*, we thought after this year's tasting, although 'the Waitrose of the North' is perhaps a more appropriate moniker for a company that today has 23 branches.

Strategically located in the wealthier market towns of Cheshire, Lancashire and the Lake District, the stores of this family-owned, Preston-based chain of supermarkets tend to be small, by supermarket standards. Six or seven stores have the full range of 550 wines, while 13 are considerably smaller. The top ten stores account for 80 per cent of the wines and spirits turnover.

Last year, Booths headhunted Chris Dee as their wine buyer, when he divested himself of the last of his three wine shops, Vins Extraordinaire. Oddbins had already bought one, and the council put a double-yellow line outside another, so he decided that if he couldn't beat the supermarkets, he might as well join one.

Only 27, Dee already has 13 years of wine experience behind him. After picking up Michael Broadbent's pocket guide to wine in a bookshop, the Adrian Mole of wine started boning up at the age of 14 3/4. 'By the age of 16, I could recite all the Port vintages and the whole of the 1855 classification of Bordeaux,' he says.

After Terry Herbert opened an innovative wine shop in York, Dee's home town, Chris helped pour the wine at customer tastings and developed a taste for it himself. He worked with Addison Vintners in London before returning 'oop North, where working for a venture-capital business gave him the nous to start his own wine business in Bradford in 1991.

From the off, Dee has clearly relished the challenge of moving from a range of 100 to 700 wines, especially as Edwin Booth, one of the company's family directors, has allowed him to create his own list. His first act was to chop the unwieldy range back to a more manageable 550. He admits that it's taken him a year to understand why some things sell and others don't. But in that time he's laid the foundations of one of the most individual supermarket ranges in the country. The list also runs to 200 beers and 300 spirits.

Dee is keen on southern Italy, non-mainstream Spain and interesting grape varieties, such as Garnacha. He also believes that the south of France has huge untapped potential. Chile will be a developing area at Booths, and he predicts a great future for Argentina and regional Australia.

Half of Booths' customers are 'very price-orientated', according to Dee. For this group, which buys wines on promotion and gondola-end offers, a bottle of wine is just an add-on to the groceries.

'But a large part of the range is aimed at the next 40 per cent of customers, anxious for information, innovation and new and interesting things,' he adds. It is for this group, for instance, that Booths has expanded its in-store wine-tasting programme this year, with at least four wines available at weekends. 'Selling wine's a bit like the fashion business,' says Dee. 'Supermarkets have even started to hold regular spring and summer sales.'

In creating a buzz around the wine shelves, Dee acknowledges the tremendous help he gets from Booths' staff, who are fabled for their friendliness and helpfulness with customers. That's where Booths can get away with selling rare birds, such as the Coriole Sangiovese or the Pazo de Barrantes Albariño, that wouldn't normally stroll off a supermarket shelf.

For its fine-wine customers, Booths has an extensive range, some bought *en primeur* and all sold at good to remarkable prices. Where else would you find a 1988 La Tâche at £185 a bottle, or a well-priced selection of 1982 clarets, a £30 Oppenheimer Herrenberg Eiswein rubbing shoulders with a Blue Nun? 'I want people to think they've got a bargain. It's what selling fine wine in a supermarket's about.'

Booths has come a long way since 'China House' was founded by Edwin Booth in Blackpool in 1847. With the Adrian Mole of wine rapidly developing one of the most interesting, high-quality ranges in the country, the company's 150th anniversary should provide plenty of excuses to pop a few Booths' Champagne corks.

White

Under £3

CHILE

1995 Santa Carolina White, Maule Valley, Santa Carolina   15/20
Dry 🍾🍾🍾 🍷
Tangy, grapefruity Sauvignon-like white made by Pilar Gonzalez. Refreshing and flavoursome. Stunning value.

FRANCE

Nicole Vin de Table   13/20
Dry 🍾🍾 🍷
Clean, appley basic white *vin de table* with more freshness than most at this price.

1993 Muscat à Petits Grains, Vin de Pays des Collines de la Moure, Hugh Ryman   16/20
Sweet 🍾🍾 |
Sweet, marmaladey Midi sticky, with scented, eau de Cologne-like aromas and reasonable balance. A poor person's Monbazillac.

GERMANY

Peter Mertes Hock Tafelwein, Peter Mertes   13/20
Medium dry 🍾🍾 |
On the dry side for basic German Hock, this is crisp, aromatic and pleasantly grapey.

ITALY

Trebbiano delle Marche, Vino da Tavola, Collezione Bodio   14/20
Bone dry 🍾🍾🍾 |
Tea-leaf and ginger aromas and cherry-stone fruit make this zesty dry white an intriguing buy at under £3.

£3–5

AUSTRALIA

Kingston Chenin/Verdelho, Murray Valley, Kingston Estate   15/20
Dry 🍾🍾🍾 |
An unusual combination of grape varieties has produced a highly drinkable, comparatively restrained Aussie white with pear and melon-fruit ripeness.

1995 Booths Chardonnay, South Eastern Australia, Miranda   14/20
Off-dry 🍾🍾 |
Classic Aussie Chardonnay from irrigated vineyards in Griffith, New South Wales, with smoky oak character and ripe melon and barley-sugar fruitiness.

CHILE

1995 Andes Peak Chardonnay Casablanca, Santa Emiliana   14/20
Off-dry 🍾🍾 |
Opal-fruits-style Chardonnay with some confected sweetness and a bitter twist.

FRANCE

1995 Fortant Viognier, Vin de Pays d'Oc, Fortant de France 14/20
Dry 👛👛 ▮
A teeny bit dilute perhaps, but this is a fresh, well-priced, faintly apricotty, southern French interpretation of the Rhône Valley's fashionable white grape.

1994 Touraine Sauvignon, La Chapelle de Cray   15/20
Bone dry 👛👛👛 ▮
Nettley, minerally mini-Sancerre at an attractive price.

White Burgundy, Bourgogne Blanc, Cave de Lugny   14/20
Dry 👛👛 ▮
Fruity, well-made, unoaked Chardonnay from the reliable Lugny co-operative. The sort of thing the Mâconnais should be producing more often at under £5.

HUNGARY

1995 Gyöngyös Estate Chardonnay, Matraalja, Hugh Ryman 14/20
Dry 👛👛 ▮
Fresh, zingy, lightly oaked, greengage-style Hungarian Chardonnay from Hugh Ryman. A vast improvement on recent disappointing vintages.

ITALY

1995 Frascati San Antonio, Colli di Catone   15/20
Bone dry 👛👛👛 ▮
For his top Frascati, Antonio Pulcini uses a high proportion of the premium Malvasia di Lazio and Malvasia di Candia grapes. The result is a zesty, refreshing, nutty Roman white that would happily complement a plate of white fish.

SOUTH AFRICA

Welmoed Sauvignon Blanc, Stellenbosch, Welmoed Winery 16/20
Dry 👛👛👛 ▮
Highly aromatic Cape Sauvignon Blanc, which out-Chiles Chile in the grapefruit and lemon-zip stakes. Bracingly fresh and crisp, this is the best sub-£5 South African Sauvignon we've come across.

£5–8

AUSTRALIA

1994 Ninth Island Chardonnay, Tasmania, Tasmania Wine Company   15/20
Dry 🍶 |
From Australia's coolest wine region, this is an understated, unoaked Chardonnay made by the formidably intelligent Dr Andrew Pirie. Honeyed but crisp.

FRANCE

1994 Riesling Muhlforst d'Alsace, J. Luc Mader   15/20
Dry 🍶🍶 |
Modern, fruity, almost New World-like Alsace Riesling with notes of fresh lime and ripe pear.

NEW ZEALAND

1995 Esk Valley Sauvignon, Hawkes Bay, Esk Valley Estates   16/20
Dry 🍶🍶🍶 |
Fresh, deliciously crisp, restrained Kiwi Sauvignon Blanc, which proves once again that the North Island made better, more concentrated whites than the South Island in this vintage. A wine that's the equal of a good Sancerre – only cheaper.

Over £8

SPAIN

1994 Albariño de Pazo de Barrantes, D.O. Rias Baixas, Bodegas Pazo de Barrantes   17/20
Bone dry 🍶🍶🍶 |
Complex, expensive-looking Galician interpretation of the local Albariño grape. Richly concentrated, unusually flavoured and refreshingly austere, with undertones of lime zest and toast. Superb stuff.

Red

Under £3

FRANCE

Nicole Rouge, Vin de Table, GVG 13/20
Medium-bodied 🍶🍶 ▪
Softly juicy, cheap French red that still manages to deliver flavour and freshness.

ITALY

Gabbia d'Oro Rosso, Vino da Tavola, Cantina Gadoro 12/20
Light-bodied ▪
Light, sugary, sub Piat d'Or *rosso*.

Sangiovese delle Marche, Vino da Tavola, Collezione Bodio 14/20
Medium-bodied 🍶🍶🍶 ▪
A bracing, lightly fruity central Italian red made from Tuscany's Sangiovese grape and better-priced than many a Chianti.

PORTUGAL

Alta Mesa Red, Vinho Regional Estremadura, Co-op de São Mamede da Ventosa 13/20
Medium-bodied 🍶🍶 ▪
Clove-spicy, robustly fruity, sweetened southern Portuguese red made by the softly spoken José Neiva. Middle, rather than high, table fare.

£3–5

ARGENTINA

1995 Parral Malbec Sangiovese, Trapiche 13/20
Light-bodied 🍶 ▪
Cooked, jammy Argentine blend of Malbec and Sangiovese produced, by the taste of it, from high-yielding vineyards.

CHILE

1994 Palmeras Cabernet Sauvignon, Nancagua, Santa Emiliana
14/20

Medium-bodied 🛍🛍 ⚬

An oak and blackcurrant-pastille-style Chilean Cabernet Sauvignon with minty aromas, but a hard, high acid finish.

FRANCE

1995 Château Laval, Costières de Nîmes, Louis Mousset   13/20
Medium-bodied 🛍 ⚬

Light, Beaujolais-style quaffer from southern Rhône négociant Louis Mousset. Not terribly distinguished for a wine bearing the new Costières de Nîmes appellation.

1995 Bellefontaine Merlot, Vin de Pays d'Oc, Paul Boutinot   14/20
Medium-bodied 🛍🛍 ⚬

Claret-like southern French Merlot blended by Franco-Mancunian merchant Paul Boutinot. Lots of cherry and damson fruit, tannin, colour and a warm-climate, dry finish.

1994 Côtes du Ventoux, La Falaise, Paul Boutinot   13/20
Medium-bodied 🛍 ⚬

Light, slightly souped-up Provençal red, again 'blended' by Paul Boutinot. Slowly rolling downhill – the wine, that is.

1995 Fortant Pinot Noir, Vin de Pays d'Oc, Fortant de France
13/20

Medium-bodied 🛍 ⚬

The cherry and raspberry characters of the Pinot Noir grape are suppressed by dry tannins on this Languedoc red, but at under £4 this well-packaged *vin de pays* is a drinkable alternative to red Burgundy.

GREECE

1995 Vin de Crète Red, Kourtaki   14/20
Medium-bodied 🛍🛍 ⚬

A spicy, angostura-bitters-style Greek red, which reminds us of something from the Languedoc. A well-made modern blend with a rasp of tannin.

ITALY

1992 Copertino, Cantine Monaci   13/20
Full-bodied

Leathery, rum'n'raisin-like red from Italy's southern heel. An old-fashioned style that needs food.

1994 Merlot Lavis, Trentino, Cantina La Vis   15/20
Medium-bodied

Light, grassy, elegant north Italian Merlot with lively acidity. A stylish alternative to claret at under £5.

SOUTH AFRICA

1995 Kumala Cinsault/Pinotage, Western Cape   15/20
Full-bodied

A well-made, warm-climate blend of Cinsault and the indigenous South African Pinotage. Sweetly ripe, red fruit flavours with a characterful slice or three of baked banana.

SPAIN

1995 Guelbenzu Jardin, Navarra   15/20
Full-bodied

Super-rich, peppery Navarra red made from old Garnacha vines, which is still a little raw. The borders may be on the green side, but there's plenty of fruit in this particular garden.

UNITED STATES

Apple Hill Barbera Cabernet Franc, California   13/20
Medium-bodied

Less confected than many a cheap Californian red, this is a pale-coloured, soft, slightly rustic blend of Barbera and Cabernet Franc.

£5–8

AUSTRALIA

1993 Leasingham Domaine Shiraz, Clare Valley   14/20
Full-bodied 🍷 |
Coconut essence and sweet American oak-like characters filled out with soft, spicy, blackberry fruit. Rather one-dimensional.

FRANCE

1994 Côtes du Rhône Les Arbousiers, Domaine Réméjeanne 15/20
Medium-bodied 🍷🍷 |
Pure, fruity, Grenache-dominated Côtes du Rhône, with sumptuous strawberry-sweet fruit and fine tannins. A beautifully balanced red.

1990 Booths Oak Aged Claret, Bordeaux, Patrice Calvet   15/20
Medium-bodied 🍷🍷 |
Gracefully maturing, lightly oaked, supple own-label claret from the excellent 1990 vintage. It's good to see a supermarket avoiding the lowest common denominator.

1990 Château Noblet, Côtes de Bourg, Union des Producteurs de Pugnac   16/20
Medium-bodied 🍷🍷🍷 |
Vigorously fruity, characterful *petit château* claret from the Pugnac co-operative, also from the fine 1990 vintage, whose tannins and fruit have mellowed beautifully in harmony.

1994 Domaine de L'Hortus Classique, Coteaux de Languedoc, Pic St-Loup, Jean Orliac   16/20
Full-bodied 🍷🍷🍷 |
Refreshing, thirst-quenching, Syrah-influenced Languedoc estate red from one of the Midi's best young growers. Lovely spice and blackberry fruit.

1994 Mas Champart, Saint Chinian   15/20
Full-bodied 🍷🍷 |
From Isabelle and Matthieu Champart, this is a concentrated, herb-infused red from the hills of Saint Chinian. A wine to chew on.

1980 Château de Canterrane, Côtes du Roussillon, Maurice Conte 13/20
Full-bodied

An idiosyncratic red from an extensive wine estate in the Roussillon, which deliberately releases its bottled wines with at least ten years of age. Some might enjoy these leathery old flavours, but we think the wine's past its sell-by date.

Over £8

AUSTRALIA

1993 Coriole Sangiovese, McLaren Vale, Coriole Vineyards 16/20
Medium-bodied

One of the very few Sangioveses from Down Under. Stephen Hill has made an intriguing red with more (southern) Italian than Australian character. This is a concentrated, oak-aged Sangiovese with elegantly balanced acidity and tannins.

SPAIN

1989 Marqués de Murrieta, Reserva Especial Ygay, Rioja 13/20
Medium-bodied

The label may have been given a new lease of life, but the wine hasn't changed much. Baked, rather rustic Rioja with a vinegary edge.

Rosé

Under £3

FRANCE

Louis Chatel Rosé, Vin de Pays d'Oc, Domaines Listel 12/20
Off dry

Alcoholic, copper-coloured dry rosé with dull, neutral fruit flavours. A style that doesn't appear to travel very well.

£5–8

SPAIN

1994 Rioja Rosado, Rioja Alavesa, Bodegas Artadi 14/20
Off dry 🍶🍶 ▮
Raspberryish, smoky, abundantly fruity Garnacha that is two-thirds of the way to being a red. A refreshing, weighty, food-friendly rosé.

Sparkling

£5–8

SPAIN

Palau Brut, Cava, Mont Marçal 14/20
Dry 🍶🍶 ▮
Lemon-fresh, clean Champagne-method Spanish fizz made in the fruity, modern style. A good-looking Cava.

Over £8

FRANCE

Booths Champagne NV, Jacquart 15/20
Dry 🍶🍶🍶 ▮
A well-priced, own-label co-op Champagne with a tingling freshness and the delicate strawberry fruitiness of the Pinot grapes, Noir and Meunier.

Fortified

£5–8

SPAIN

Booths Manzanilla, Emilio Hidalgo   16/20
Bone dry 🍾🍾🍾 ❙
Super-fresh, delicate, savoury, dry Sherry from the outstanding Hidalgo winery.
An incredible bargain at this price. Bring on the almonds and olives.

Over £8

PORTUGAL

Churchills White Port   16/20
Dry 🍾🍾 ❙
A wood-aged white Port with crème brûlée smokiness and a dry, almost
Amontillado-like maturity.

Booths Finest Reserve Port, Quinta de la Rosa   13/20
Full-bodied ❙
Spirity, rather cooked, own-label Port with rustic tannins and prematurely aged
fruit characters.

Budgens ☆(☆)

Address: 9 Stonefield Way, Ruislip, Middlesex HA4 0JR

Telephone/fax: 0181 422 9511; 0181 423 2263

Number of branches: 104, of which 8 are Fresh Save stores

Opening hours: 8.30am to 8.00pm Monday to Friday; 8.00am to 8.00pm Saturday; 9.00am to 6.00pm Sunday

Credit cards accepted: Access, Visa, Switch

Discounts: 5 per cent on case sales

Facilities and services: By-the-case sales; in-store tastings

Top ten best-selling wines: Budgens Vin de Table Red; Bordeaux Blanc; Budgens Claret; Château Bassanel, Minervois; Blanc de Blancs Special Cuvée; Budgens Liebfraumilch; Merlot del Veneto; Frascati Superiore; Vin de Pays d'Oc Chardonnay; Tocai del Veneto

Range:

GOOD: None

AVERAGE: White Burgundy, Bordeaux, Loire, regional France, Alsace, Germany, Eastern Europe, England, Italy, Spain, South Africa, Australia, California, Chile, Champagne and sparkling wines, Sherry

POOR: Red Burgundy, New Zealand

UNDER-REPRESENTED: Argentina

'We're getting there,' says Tony Finnerty with something approaching resignation, 'they've offered to buy me a second horse this year.' British retailing's answer to the Lone Ranger continues to ride a Tonto-less trail. While Somerfield and Morrison's have expanded their wine-buying teams in the last 12 months, Budgens still expects Finnerty to organise, run and star in the whole show.

So dependent is the operation on his expertise that when a new store in Oxford found (perfectly normal) tartrate crystals on the corks of two bottles of fine wine recently, Finnerty had to drive down on a Sunday to explain what it was. For Budgens' sake, we hope he doesn't fall under a bus. If he did, the wine department would collapse overnight.

The days in solitary are clearly getting to Finnerty. Pacing the confines of his office in Ruislip, he longs for the wide open prairies of the New World. 'It's very frustrating not being able to visit these places,' he says. 'I've been promised an assistant; but I'm not holding my breath.'

So, for the time being, Finnerty works on alone. His main priority over the past 12 months has been to 'realign' the range to make sure 'the right wines are targeted to the right stores'. 'We used to tailor ranges according to the style of the store,' he adds, 'rather than to what local customers wanted.' In the past, Budgens' Ascot shoppers were treated to a wall of Hock and Lambrusco, when Pimms or Champagne might have been more appropriate.

The realignment seems to be working. Hock and Lambrusco have slipped out of Budgens' top ten, but volume sales are up by 4 per cent across the range. 'We've achieved greater sales with our higher-priced wines,' says Finnerty, 'especially with our New World wines.' Other winners this year have been the Languedoc-Roussillon and southern Italy.

In numerical terms, the range has remained constant at around 320 wines, but Finnerty has increased his listings from Australia, South Africa, Chile and southern France, while cutting back on Germany and Italy. Most of these wines are bought off the peg. Budgens' own lines are restricted to a core range of Soave, Valpolicella, Lambrusco, Hock, Liebfraumilch, claret, Muscadet, et al. 'Other than that, I try to go for exclusive wines,' says Finnerty, 'because we don't have the volume to justify a huge range of Budgens' own labels.'

Despite the restricted range, Finnerty has not been afraid to list off-the-wall wines, be it Trebbiano from Australia, Dornfelder from Germany or Cabernet Franc from California. 'We tend to do quite well with weird and wonderfuls,' he says. 'We can't compete with Tesco and Sainsbury's on buying power, but we can offer something original and unusual in the high street.'

How does Finnerty tempt Budgens' more conservative customers to try new things? 'We've introduced floor stacks, bins and proper wine stands,' he says, 'and we've started to put wine next to other things, like pasta, bread and the in-store deli.'

The other method is cut-price specials, a regular fortnightly offering of up to five discounted wines. Finnerty reduces prices from £3.99 to £2.99 and from £4.99 to £3.99, rather than offering £1.99 wines. 'We might sell 60,000 cases at £1.99, but in the end all you do is drag your profit margin down.' Cut-price wines encourage customers to experiment. 'We bring the wines down to people,' according to Finnerty, 'and they follow them back up when they revert to their normal price.'

The Budgens' estate continues to grow, with 110 stores the target for 1997.

New sites take a variety of forms. Budgens bought Carters of Faringdon near Oxford in 1996, inheriting a range of fine wines (complete with tartrate crystals), as well as opening stores of its own. These took the form of regular Budgens stores, as well as Fresh Saves (Budgens' answer to Kwik Save) and a new series of garage forecourt convenience stores launched in partnership with Q8 and Mobil.

Guess who buys the range for all these different formats? You guessed it, Tony Finnerty. And a decent job he does too, although we found little to inspire us at Budgens. If the range is to develop and lose some of its rougher edges, the buying department must be strengthened. Go on, give the guy a break.

White

Under £3

BULGARIA

1995 Domaine Boyar, Preslav Chardonnay/Sauvignon Blanc 14/20
Dry 👅👅👅 🍾
Ultra-fresh, lightly oaked Bulgarian blend of the two premium varieties, Chardonnay and Sauvignon Blanc. On this evidence, Bulgaria is beginning to give Hungarian whites a run for their forints.

FRANCE

Vin de Pays de l'Aude, Les Celliers de Montroyal   11/20
Off-dry 🍾
Basic, sweetened-up, baked-apple white plonk de plonk.

Blanc de Blancs, Cuvée Spéciale, Montreuil-Bellay, Vin de Table Français   11/20
Off-dry 🍾
Ageing Loire-based white with dull, gluey flavours, residual sweetness and a rasp of acidity.

1995 Bordeaux Blanc Sec
13/20
Dry 🍷🍷 🍶
Well-priced white Bordeaux with a modicum of fresh fruit character.

Domaine de Pascaly, Vin de Pays de l'Aude, Les Celliers de Champsbilloux
12/20
Dry 🍶
Southern French blend of Mauzac and Chenin Blanc grapes, made in a baked, rather old-fashioned style.

1995 Chardonnay Dulac, Vin de Pays de l'Ile de Beauté
12/20
Dry 🍶
With its aroma of wild Corsican mushrooms, this cool-fermented, unoaked Chardonnay is not exactly a 'fun-guy'.

GERMANY

1995 Budgens Liebfraumilch
11/20
Medium sweet 🍶
Very dilute, slightly grapey German white. Still, depressingly, among Budgens' top-ten best-sellers.

MACEDONIA

Macedonian Country Wine
13/20
Dry 🍷🍷 🍶
Lime-zest and celery-like Macedonian white, which is clean, well-made and surprisingly drinkable. Alexander the Great loved it too, apparently.

£3–5

AUSTRIA

1994 Grüner Veltliner Kremstal, Johann Müllner
13/20
Bone dry 🍷 🍶
Faintly resinous, softly fruity, commercial example of Austria's most widely planted grape variety.

CHILE

1995 Viña Casablanca Sauvignon Blanc, Curicó   15/20
Dry 👜👜 ▮
Fresh melon and passion fruity Chilean Sauvignon Blanc from 1996 *Grapevine* winemaker of the year, Ignacio Recabarren.

1995 Viña Tarapacá Chardonnay, Maipo   13/20
Dry ▮
Alcoholic, lumpen Chilean Chardonnay from a showpiece winery near Santiago. With so much money, the white wines should be a bit better.

ENGLAND

1994 High Ridge Fumé   13/20
Dry ▮
Tart, rather charmless attempt at a Loire Sauvignon Blanc, using the Germanic crossing, Bacchus, with a hint of oak character.

FRANCE

1995 Mâcon-Igé, Les Vignerons d'Igé   15/20
Dry 👜👜 ▮
Still one of the better-value white Burgundies on the market, the most recent vintage of this flavoursome Mâconnais Chardonnay is crisp, unoaked and pleasantly dry.

1995 Bourgogne Blanc, Chardonnay, Charles Viénot   15/20
Dry 👜👜 ▮
Smooth, comparatively rich white Burgundy showing peachy fruit and decent weight for a sub-£5 wine.

GERMANY

1995 Rüdesheimer Rosengarten, Gustav Adolf Schmitt   13/20
Medium sweet 👜 ▮
A step up from Liebfraumilch, this is a spicy, floral-fruity Müller-Thurgau-based blend from the Nahe region, in a distinctive blue bottle.

1993 Flonheimer Adelberg, Auslese   14/20
Sweet 💰💰 🍶
Still inexpensive for an Auslese at under £4, this is a peachy, scented Müller-Thurgau white with a hint of grapefruity, Scheurebe-like fruitiness.

ITALY

Budgens Soave, Pietro Sartori   13/20
Dry 💰 🍶
Neutral, inoffensive, vaguely nutty Italian dry white.

Tocai del Veneto, Pergole del Vento, Zonin   14/20
Dry 💰💰 🍶
A fresher, more interesting Veneto white, with buttery fruit flavours unencumbered by oak.

1995 Frascati Superiore, Casale del Grillo   15/20
Dry 💰💰 🍶
Clean, zesty, modern Roman white with mouth-filling fruit, balancing ripeness and flavour and a crisp acidity.

NEW ZEALAND

Waimanu Dry White, Corbans   10/20
Off-dry 🍶
Distinctly musty Kiwi white with marked acidity and tart, sweetish, lemon-meringue flavours. New Zealand struggles to make palatable wine for under £4.

SOUTH AFRICA

Clear Mountain Chenin Blanc   13/20
Off-dry 💰 🍶
Sweetish, dilute Cape quaffer made from the ubiquitous Chenin Blanc grape.

£5–8

AUSTRALIA

1995 Rosemount Semillon/Chardonnay 15/20
Dry 🍬🍬 |
Fresh, attractively oaked, cream soda-like Aussie blend of Semillon and
Chardonnay. It's good to see Rosemount restraining the oak on its whites and
optimising fruit flavours.

Red

Under £3

BULGARIA

1994 Stara Zagora, Merlot/Cabernet Sauvignon 14/20
Medium-bodied 🍬🍬🍬 |
On the sweet side, but this lightly oaked Bulgarian blend, by appointment to
King Simeon II, no less, is soft and palatably juicy.

FRANCE

1994 Vin de Pays de l'Agenais, Les Vignerons de Beaupuy 11/20
Medium-bodied |
Made from the south-west French Bouchales grape, this is a rough, rasping,
high-acid co-operative plonk, which shouldn't be let out after dark.

**Domaine Saint Roch, Vin de Pays de l'Aude, Les Celliers de
Champbilloux** 13/20
Medium-bodied 🍬🍬 |
Fresh, fruity, paysan blend of Terret and Carignan grapes with sweet, spicy fruit
and a rustic aftertaste.

SPAIN

1991 Diego de Almagro, Valdepeñas, Crianza   13/20
Medium-bodied 💰💰 🍾
A prize to the reader who tells us who the bearded conquistador on the label
is. A very oaky, commercial Rioja taste-alike with sweet strawberry fruit and no
shortage of splinters.

£3–5

CHILE

1991 Viña Casablanca, Cabernet Sauvignon   14/20
Medium-bodied 💰 🍾
Essence of blackcurrant aromas and rather lean Cabernet fruit from Chile's San
Fernando Valley.

1994 Viña Tarapacá, Cabernet Sauvignon   15/20
Medium-bodied 💰💰 🍾
Super-ripe, old-fashioned Chilean Cabernet Sauvignon from the Maule Valley,
showing rich, toffee and cassis notes and good concentration.

FRANCE

Budgens Vin de Table, Joseph Verdier, 1 litre   10/20
Medium-bodied 🍾
Sweetened, chewy rot-gut rouge. Good for extinguishing the barbecue.

Budgens Claret, Dulong   14/20
Medium-bodied 💰💰 🍾
Smooth, well-made, Merlot-based claret with youthful tannins and lively acidity.

1994 Costières de Nîmes, Fontanilles   13/20
Full-bodied 💰 🍾
Soupy, faintly bitter, splintery Provençal red in which tannins have overwhelmed
the fruit.

1995 Château Bassanel, Minervois, Paul Jeanjean   15/20
Medium-bodied 🍷🍷🍷 ▯

Modern, deep-hued, cherry and raspberry fruity Minervois blend with approachable tannins and plenty of spicy flavour for a sub-£4 red.

1995 Château Saint Louis, Corbières   14/20
Medium-bodied 🍷🍷🍷 ▯

Super value at just over £3.50, this garrigue-scented Languedoc red from grower Philippe Pasquier-Meunier, is a well-made, succulent blend with a slightly dry finish.

1994 Château Malijay, Côtes du Rhône, Fontanilles   14/20
Medium-bodied 🍷🍷 ▯

A blend of Grenache, Syrah and Cinsault, which outperforms its lowly status. A smooth, alcoholic, southern Rhône quaffer.

GERMANY

1994 Rheinhessen Dornfelder, Gustav Adolf Schmitt   13/20
Light-bodied 🍷 ▯

Light, cherryish, damson-skin German red with soft tannins. Just about worth buying as a curiosity.

GREECE

Vin de Pays de Crète, Kourtaki   14/20
Medium-bodied 🍷🍷 ▯

Spicy, angostura-bitters-style Greek red, which reminds us of something from the Languedoc. A well-made, modern blend with a rasp of tannin.

ITALY

Merlot del Veneto, Pergole del Vento, Zonin   14/20
Light-bodied 🍷🍷 ▯

Soft, commercial, unoaked Veneto Merlot with a faint grassiness and easy-drinking tannins.

NEW ZEALAND

Waimanu Red 13/20
Medium-bodied 💰 🍾

A 'Bordeaux meets Burgundy in New Zealand' blend of Cabernet Sauvignon and Pinot Noir from the Corbans winery. Combines raspberry sweetness with a rather tart acidity.

SOUTH AFRICA

Clear Mountain Pinotage 13/20
Medium-bodied 💰 🍾

Beginning to dry out, but this mature Cape red has still got enough leafy, sweetened Pinotage character to be drinkable at under £4.

SPAIN

1989 Viña Albali Reserva, Valdepeñas 15/20
Medium-bodied 💰💰 🍾

Mellow, baked-banana and oak-style red from the edge of Spain's central plain. A mature, fruity, well-structured *tinto* at a good price.

1991 Lagunilla Rioja Reserva 16/20
Medium-bodied 💰💰💰 🍾

A very well-knit, vanilla and sweet summer-pudding-like Rioja with excellent balance of freshness, fruit and backbone. And all for under £5.

UNITED STATES

1994 Pepperwood Grove Zinfandel 15/20
Medium-bodied 💰💰💰 🍾

Not quite up to the high standards of the 1993, but even so, at under £4.50, this is a light but authentic expression of Californian Zinfandel with juicy, tobacco-ish fruit framed by American oak and robust tannins.

£5–8

FRANCE

La Croix de Teyssier, Saint Emilion 15/20
Medium-bodied 🛍🛍 ▮
Softly textured second wine of Château Teyssier, made in a ready-to-drink, Merlot-based style with some sweet vanilla oak.

Sparkling

Under £3

SPAIN

Espuma Prima Golden Sparkling Wine, Muscat 13/20
Sweet 🛍🛍 ▮
Lemonadey, frothy Spanish cross between Asti Spumante and Lambrusco. Mmm...

£3–5

AUSTRALIA

Flinders Creek Sparkling Rosé 13/20
Off-dry 🛍 ▮
Sweet, raspberry and rhubarb confection from New South Wales. Still fair value at under a fiver.

Over £8

FRANCE

Germain Champagne Brut   15/20
Dry 🍾🍾 ▮
Young, tangy, fruity Champagne, halfway to a superior New World fizz in style, with attractive Pinot Noir strawberryishness.

Brossault Rosé Champagne   14/20
Dry 🍾🍾 ▮
Copper-coloured, cut-price rosé Champagne with bland, strawberry-cup fruitiness and fresh acidity.

Co-op ☆☆(☆)

Address: National Buying, Marketing and Distribution Group, PO Box 53, New Century House, Manchester M60 4ES

Telephone/fax: 0161 834 1212; 0161 827 5117

Number of branches: 2,500 licensed branches

Opening hours: Varies from store to store

Credit cards accepted: All major credit cards

Discounts: Occasionally on large orders

Facilities and services: Glass loan and in-store tastings in selected superstores; home delivery arranged at local level

Special offers: To Co-op members; monthly promotions

Top ten best-selling wines: Co-op Lambrusco Bianco; Co-op Liebfraumilch; Bulgarian Russe Cabernet Sauvignon/Cinsault; Co-op Hock; Co-op Laski Rizling; Co-op Corbières Rouge; Co-op Claret; Co-op Bulgarian Cabernet Sauvignon; Co-op Vin de Pays des Côtes de Gascogne; Co-op Valencia Red

Range:

GOOD: Spain, Australia, Chile

AVERAGE: Bordeaux, Beaujolais, Burgundy, regional France, Eastern Europe, Portugal, Italy, Germany, England, South Africa, Argentina, New Zealand, Champagne and sparkling wines

POOR: United States

UNDER-REPRESENTED: None

We haven't visited all the Co-op's 2,500 licensed branches yet, but we did manage one northern foray this year to the Allandale Co-op. Here, in Postman Pat country, we were pleasantly surprised to find the sumptuously juicy, Rioja-like 1992 Enate Tempranillo/Cabernet, one of our favourite wines in last year's edition of *Grapevine*. Unfortunately, the locals must have discovered it at the same time, because when we went back for more there was none left.

We were not too complimentary last year about the lack in its smaller stores of the more exciting side of the Co-op wine range. As the Co-op is an 'all things to all men' organisation, with stores ranging in size from the Hexham and Aberdeen superstores to survival outfits in the remotest corners of the back of the beyond, it was clearly a problem for the central buyers in Manchester – Master of Wine Arabella Woodrow and Paul Bastard – to penetrate, as it were, the smaller stores.

This has a lot to do with the old-fashioned structure of the Co-op itself, which is more like a sprawling nationwide collection of municipalities than a business. Yet even at the Co-op, whose different member societies jealously guard their independence from the Kremlin, aka Co-op HQ in Manchester, business efficiency has begun to make itself felt.

Compared with a decade ago, when the Co-op had no control over its own stores and depots could stock what they liked, things have changed for the better. And with centralised ordering getting into its stride, we are assured by the Co-op's buyers that more of the better wines are getting into a greater number of stores.

Every year we have the structure of the convoluted organisation known as the Co-op explained to us, and every year we come away a little bit wiser – until we sit down and try to put it on paper. However, we think we've finally cracked it, so, at the risk of repeating ourselves, it may be worth briefly unravelling for you the labyrinthine complexities of the Co-op.

Basically, the Co-op is the umbrella body for 51 different co-operative societies. The biggest is the Co-operative Wholesale Society Retail (CWS Retail). Arabella Woodrow and Paul Bastard buy the wines for CWS Retail and an extended group called Co-operative Retail Trading Group (CRTG), but not necessarily for other parts of the co-operative movement. Co-operative Retail Services (CRS) is a rival organisation, with members including Co-op Leo's, Lo-cost and Pioneer.

There was a possibility last year that CWS Retail and CRS would merge, but the much-vaunted union did not materialise. The CRS has in fact recently taken itself off to Rochdale, where it's planning to adopt a different logo from the Co-op and to trade under the Pioneer name. So Arabella Woodrow and Paul Bastard still buy for only 1,232 out of the total of 2,500 Co-op stores nationwide.

The other 1,268 may take the Co-op's core own-label range, but beyond that they buy wines through their own particular organisation. So with only 30 per cent of the respective wine ranges overlapping, you're less likely to find the Woodrow/Bastard selection in Welsh, south-western England and central Manchester stores, where the Co-op HQ has less control over the range stocked.

Co-op

Three years ago the Co-op bottled more than half the wine range itself. But since it ditched its bottling plant in exchange for a supply agreement, only 50 or so wines of the 550-strong range are bottled at Irlham. There's a slight tax advantage – about 2.5 pence a bottle – but, looking at a number of wines in the dreary own-label range, we feel that the advantages of bottling in the country of origin outweigh the price advantage of own-bottling in the UK.

As we commented last year, many of the wines in the basic own-label range are pretty uninspiring. They nevertheless constitute the bulk of sales, and Arabella Woodrow and Paul Bastard have capitalised on a sales growth of more than 20 per cent to source wines that wouldn't previously have been given shelf-room at the Co-op, such as Carmen and the Long Slim white and red from Chile, and a Mexican Petite Sirah.

The Co-op's wine buyers admit that the chain has lagged behind in the New World, but they are busy putting that right – Australia goes from strength to strength, and now that the once-iffy regimes of emerging wine countries such as Argentina, Chile and South Africa no longer pose a problem for its politically right-on customers, the Co-op is moving full steam ahead and taking its customers with it.

It was for its politically correct stance over apartheid that the Co-op lost out on sales of South African wine. Now South African wines are doing particularly well and the Co-op is supporting the first black merchant – Cape Afrika – in South Africa. The Co-op is proud of the lead it takes on ethical issues, too, symbolised by its arrangement with the World Wildlife Fund, which receives 5 pence on every bottle of Koala Creek.

Brazil is 'not just a gimmick' in the wine range, according to Paul Bastard, although the wines, which leave something to be desired, 'will be better in the future', he promises. There are two new own-label New Zealand wines this year and four new Argentine wines, including the Lost Pampas red and white, whose name may or may not be connected with the wine department taking maternity leave *en masse*.

Customers obviously thrive on the wacky names dreamt up by the punsters in the wine department. Bad Tempered Cyril, the Tempranillo-Syrah blend from the south of France, has done well for the Co-op. Hungaroo, an Australian-Hungarian joint venture, has also been a success. The latest addition to the department of fun labels is Fair Martina, a southern French white made from the Vermentino grape (geddit?), featuring a saucy postcard beach-front belle. Any resemblance to a well-known Czech tennis player is purely coincidental.

In Europe, the Co-op has added eight new wines to the Beaujolais and Burgundy section over the year and a new oak-aged claret. The new Rioja supplier, Berberana, is a change for the better. There's a new-wave Chardonnay in Castillo de Monjardín, as well as new wines from the up-and-coming Viñas del Vero in Somontano. Sales of Spanish wines have nevertheless dropped off and Germany, in line with the national trend, is way down.

Hungarian wines are popular and Bulgaria still makes the top ten with two reds. Thanks to a huge residue of conservative-minded customers at the Co-op, French wines also continue to do well. The Co-op Claret and Corbières feature in the Co-op's top-ten best-selling wines, but there is evidence of a move from *appellation contrôlée* wines to better-value *vins de pays*.

This year Arabella Woodrow and Paul Bastard have continued to move the Co-op range into interesting new areas. No doubt a CWS Retail/CRS merger would have helped the much-needed process of assimilation of the better wines into the stores. Even so, some of the good news at least finally appears to be filtering through from Co-op HQ to smaller stores and their members.

White

Under £3

ARGENTINA

1995 Mission Peak White 14/20
Dry 👜👜 ▮
An aromatic, full-flavoured white blend of Chenin Blanc, Ugni Blanc and the local Torrontes grape, with attractive floral fruitiness.

AUSTRALIA

Koala Creek Dry White Wine 13/20
Off-dry 👜👜👜 ▮
Fresh, grapey Aussie white at an extraordinary price. Tangy and not overly sweet, this is the ideal party quaffer.

CHILE

Tierra del Rey Chilean White
Dry 🍷 ❘
Made from the local Sauvignon Vert grape, this is a basic, faintly gluey white, which lacks the zing you'd normally expect from the grape variety.

12/20

CROATIA

Co-op Laski Rizling
Medium sweet ❘
Resin and furniture-polish aromas make this cheap Croatian white taste like a cross between a Retsina and a Lieb. Mmmm...

11/20

FRANCE

Co-op Vin de Pays des Côtes de Gascogne
Dry 🍷🍷 ❘
Appley, austere Gascon white, with sharp acidity, from Yves Grassa. A little dilute and short on flavour.

13/20

GERMANY

Co-op Liebfraumilch, Rheinhessen
Medium sweet 🍷 ❘
Fresh, grapey, bog-standard Lieb, with rose-petal undertones and decent acidity.

12/20

Co-op Hock
Medium sweet 🍷 ❘
Sweet-and-sour, floral, Müller-Thurgau-based Hock with pleasingly quaffable fruitiness.

12/20

ITALY

Co-op Lambrusco Bianco, 4 per cent
Sweet 🍷🍷 ❘
Lemonadey, fruit-cocktail white with sherbety fizz and sweetness. Fine, but is it a wine?

12/20

£3–5

ARGENTINA

1996 Lost Pampas Oak-Aged Chardonnay   14/20
Dry 👛👛 🍾

Well-made, fresh, heavily oaked Argentine Chardonnay made by Aussie Peter Bright at the Peñaflor winery. Good value at under £4.

BRAZIL

Amazon Chardonnay, Rio Grande do Sul   12/20
Off-dry 🍾

Sweet and simple, rice-pudding-flavoured Brazilian Chardonnay. We wouldn't cross the Amazon to secure a bottle of this.

CHINA

1993 Dragon Seal Chardonnay   14/20
Dry 👛 🍾

A barrel-fermented Chardonnay from the slopes of the Yan Mountain near Beijing, this is a buttery, well-made, softly fruity white with subtle oak integration. Curiously, it also comes wrapped in a Chinese hairnet.

FRANCE

1995 Winter Hill White, Vin de Pays de l'Aude   13/20
Off-dry 👛👛 🍾

Last year we felt that the label description 'French wine made by Australians' was laughably silly. But the 1995 Winter Hill is considerably fresher than the 1994, with crisp apple acidity and residual sweetness.

Fair Martina Vermentino, Vin de Pays d'Oc   14/20
Dry 👛👛 🍾

Made by Aussie Nick Butler at Château de Raissac, this is a spicy Mediterranean white with the typically sharp acidity of the Vermentino grape. We also like the saucy, pier-end label.

GERMANY

Co-op Morio Muskat, Pfalz, Saint Ursula 14/20
Off-dry 🍾🍾🍾 |
With its curious aromas of overripe melons and exotic guava fruitiness, this is an appealing, fresh and distinctive German white with restrained sweetness.

Co-op Müller Thurgau, Rheinhessen, Saint Ursula 14/20
Off-dry 🍾🍾🍾 |
Ultra-fresh, thirst-quenching grapefruit and honey-style quaffer, which leaves most Lieb and Hock in the starting blocks.

HUNGARY

1995 Hungaroo Pinot Gris, Neszmely 15/20
Dry 🍾🍾🍾 |
Aussie Nick Butler (the 'roo' in the Hungaroo) may have moved on, but the techniques he brought to Hungary have inspired this fresh, richly spicy, well-balanced Pinot Gris from the refurbished Neszmely winery.

ITALY

1995 Monferrato Bianco, Araldica 13/20
Dry 🍾 |
Basic, north-west Italian white from the Araldica co-operative, with lively green-apple fruitiness and rather sour acidity.

1995 Co-op Frascati, Cantina Produttore Frascati 15/20
Dry 🍾🍾🍾 |
Fresh, rich, nutty Roman blend with thirst-quenching acidity for balance and excellent length of flavour for a sub-£4 white.

NEW ZEALAND

1995 Co-op New Zealand Semillon/Sauvignon, Montana 15/20
Dry 🍾🍾 |
From the difficult 1995 vintage, this is a successful blend of Semillon and Sauvignon Blanc, with soft, well-rounded herbal fruitiness and green-bean notes.

PORTUGAL

1995 Fiuza Sauvignon Blanc, Vinho Regional Ribatejo 15/20
Dry 👜👜👜 🍶
Nettley, ripe, well-made Sauvignon Blanc from the well-travelled Australian winemaker, Peter Bright. This is just one of several good wines available under the Fiuza label.

1995 Campo dos Frades Chardonnay, Vinho Regional Ribatejo 15/20

Dry 👜👜👜 🍶
Stylish, lightly oaked, modern Chardonnay made by Australian Peter Bright in his adopted Portuguese home. Delicate citrus-fruit flavours and excellent weight and balance.

SOUTH AFRICA

1995 Welmoed Sauvignon Blanc 16/20
Dry 👜👜👜 🍶
Highly aromatic Cape Sauvignon Blanc, which out-Chiles Chile in the grapefruit and lemon-zip stakes. Bracingly fresh and crisp, this is the best sub-£5 South African Sauvignon we've come across.

1995 Kumala Chenin/Chardonnay 13/20
Off-dry 👜 🍶
A quaffable Cape blend of Chenin and Chardonnay from the Sonop Wine Farm, which should have moved on to the next vintage by the time you read this – we hope so.

SPAIN

1995 Co-op Spanish Pyrenean Chardonnay/Riesling, Covisa, Somontano 14/20
Dry 👜👜 🍶
From the northern Spanish region of Somontano, which specialises in elegant, cool-climate wines, this is an unusual but successful blend of Chardonnay and Riesling, with fresh pear fruitiness and a crisp, grapey tang.

1994 Castillo de Monjardín Unoaked Chardonnay 15/20
Dry 👜👜 🍶
Rich, tropically fruity, but refreshingly unoaked Chardonnay from Spain's Navarra region, with considerable complexity for a sub-£5 Chardonnay.

£5–8

CHILE

1995 Caliterra Casablanca Chardonnay 16/20
Dry 🍾🍾🍾 ▮

One of Chile's leading Chardonnays, this Casablanca-sourced white from Brian Bicknell has a crisp, grapefruity, subtly oaked style with a Pacific-influenced, cool-climate tang.

NEW ZEALAND

1995 Millton Vineyard Semillon/Chardonnay, Gisborne 15/20
Dry 🍾🍾 ▮

Characteristically off-the-wall white from biodynamic specialist James Millton's ugly-bug ball in North Island's Gisborne. A weird combination of flavours, including ginger, celery, green malt and some honeyed fruitiness.

Red

Under £3

BULGARIA

Bulgarian Russe Cabernet/Cinsault 13/20
Medium-bodied 🍾🍾 ▮

Soft, damsony Bulgarian blend of Cabernet Sauvignon and Cinsault with a peppery twist.

Co-op Bulgarian Cabernet Sauvignon, Liubimetz 13/20
Medium-bodied 🍾🍾 ▮

A chocolatey, winter-warming, non-vintage Cabernet Sauvignon with vanilla oak-chip characters and smooth tannins.

CHILE

Tierra del Rey Chilean Red, Viña Tocornal   13/20
Medium-bodied 👜👜 🍾
Blackcurrant-pastille, faintly chewy claret substitute from Chilean giant, Concha y Toro.

FRANCE

Co-op Corbières   11/20
Medium-bodied 🍾
Prematurely aged, pruney Languedoc plonk with farmyardy overtones.

SPAIN

Co-op Valencia Red   12/20
Light-bodied 👜 🍾
Chewy, fruity summer red, with lightweight tannins and a rather rustic edge.

£3–5

ARGENTINA

1995 Co-op Argentina Malbec/Sangiovese, Trapiche   14/20
Medium-bodied 👜👜 🍾
Soft, strawberry fruity, attractively drinkable Argentine blend of Malbec and Sangiovese, with a firm backbone of tannin and some spicy notes.

AUSTRALIA

1995 Kingston Estate Shiraz/Mataro   14/20
Medium-bodied 👜👜 🍾
Mint-humbug and spicy oak-style Aussie blend of Shiraz and Mataro (aka Mourvèdre), with some raspberry-lollipop fruitiness and a soft finish.

BRAZIL

Amazon Cabernet Sauvignon   11/20
Medium-bodied

Baked, warm-climate Cabernet Sauvignon with dry tannins and a mercifully short finish.

CHINA

1993 Dragon Seal Cabernet Sauvignon   14/20
Medium-bodied

Well-made, herbaceous Cabernet Sauvignon from China's Huailai County, with light blackcurrant fruit and smooth tannins.

FRANCE

Co-op Claret   12/20
Medium-bodied

Soupy, drying claret with awkward tannins and little charm.

1994 Domaine Serjac Grenache, Vin de Pays des Côtes de Thongue   13/20
Medium-bodied

A modern, raspberry fruity, southern French Grenache, which is let down by a rather hot finish.

Co-op Merlot/Cabernet, Vin de Pays d'Oc   13/20
Full-bodied

A youthful, vibrantly fruity Bordeaux-style blend, with a few raw edges and hardish tannins.

Co-op Oak-Aged Claret, Calvet   14/20
Medium-bodied

A well-crafted, pleasantly oaked young claret from the Bordeaux house of Calvet, with plenty of cassis fruit and a firm, mildly astringent backbone.

Co-op Côtes du Rhône   13/20
Medium-bodied

Old-style Grenache-based Côtes du Rhône, with smooth if simple strawberry fruit flavours and a leathery undertone.

HUNGARY

1994 Hungaroo Merlot   12/20
Light-bodied
Pale, light, oak-chipped and rather confected Merlot, which demonstrates that Hungary makes better whites than reds.

ITALY

Monferrato Rosso   14/20
Medium-bodied
Piedmontese blend of Dolcetto and Barbera grapes, with fresh plummy fruit and thirst-quenching acidity. A good everyday red.

Villa Mantinera Montepulciano, Vino da Tavola di Molise   13/20
Full-bodied
Sweetly raisined Mediterranean *rosso* with robust tannins and acidity. Needs suitably rustic peasant food.

MOLDOVA

1994 Kirkwood Moldova Cabernet Sauvignon   13/20
Full-bodied
A vibrantly coloured, beetrooty Moldovan blend of Cabernet Sauvignon and Merlot, with a sackful of oak chips lending a dry finish.

NEW ZEALAND

1994 Co-op New Zealand Cabernet/Merlot, Montana   14/20
Medium-bodied
Cool-climate, red Bordeaux-style blend from New Zealand's biggest winery, with green-pepper fruitiness and light, supple tannins.

SOUTH AFRICA

1993 Long Mountain Shiraz   14/20
Full-bodied
Sweet, licoricey, mature Cape Shiraz, with an alcoholic rum-punch finish, from Orlando's Robin Day of Jacob's Creek fame.

1994 Robertson Cabernet Sauvignon   15/20
Medium-bodied 👝👝 ▯
Australian-style Cape Cabernet Sauvignon with sweet vanilla-oak characters and juicy mint and blackcurrant fruitiness.

1995 Kumala Cabernet/Shiraz   14/20
Full-bodied 👝👝 ▬▬
A spicy, plummy Cape blend of Cabernet and Shiraz grapes, which tastes and smells more like a Pinotage. No bad thing on a well-made wine such as this.

SPAIN

1995 Co-op Spanish Pyrenean Tempranillo/Cabernet   15/20
Medium-bodied 👝👝👝 ▯
Modern, juicy, unoaked Spanish blend of Tempranillo and Cabernet Sauvignon, with succulent raspberry fruit flavours, from the Viñas del Vero winery in Somontano.

Co-op Rioja, Berberana   14/20
Medium-bodied 👝👝 ▯
A lightly oaked, attractively fruity young Rioja with elegant strawberryish fruitiness.

1992 Marqués de Monistrol Merlot   15/20
Medium-bodied 👝👝👝 ▯
Charry American oak, ripe blackcurrant fruit and good acidity make this modern Iberian red a characterful buy in a classy package, at under £4.

£5–8

FRANCE

1995 Fleurie, Mommessin   15/20
Medium-bodied 👝 ▯
Vibrant young Gamay from the Beaujolais *cru* of Fleurie, with ripe cherry and banana fruitiness and refreshing acidity.

1994 Vacqueyras, Cuvée du Marquis de Fonseguille   16/20
Full-bodied 🛍️🛍️🛍️ ▬

Hefty, abundantly fruity, spicy southern Rhône blend – Grenache and Syrah with smaller quantities of Mourvèdre and Cinsault – with throat-warming alcohol and a solid backbone of tannins. Good mini-Châteauneuf-du-Pape.

SPAIN

1992 Palacio de la Vega Cabernet Sauvignon   15/20
Full-bodied 🛍️ 🍾

A boldly modern, oak-aged Cabernet Sauvignon from one of the best producers in Navarra, with structured cassis fruitiness and dry vanilla oak. Drink up.

Over £8

ARGENTINA

1991 Weinert Malbec   15/20
Full-bodied 🛍️ 🍾

Old-fashioned, tarry, tea-leaf and raisin-style Malbec from one of Argentina's most traditional wineries, made from concentrated, low-yielding vines. A wine for *Spectator* readers.

Rosé

£3–5

SPAIN

1995 Gandia Grenache Rosé   13/20
Medium dry 🛍️ 🍾

Sweetish, Day-Glo-pink rosé from the California-sounding Hoya Valley, made in a commercial blush style by Spain's Vicente Gandia. A bit mawkish.

Sparkling

£3–5

SPAIN

Co-op Cava NV Brut   14/20
Dry 👛👛 ⏐
Toasty, mature Spanish fizz with a soft, sweetish mousse and good length of flavour for a sub-£5 Cava.

Davisons ☆☆☆

Address: 7 Aberdeen Road, Croydon, Surrey CR0 1EQ

Telephone/fax: 0181 681 3222; 0181 760 0390

Number of branches: 77

Opening hours: 10.00am to 2.00pm and 5.00pm to 10.00pm Monday to Saturday; 12.00pm to 2.00pm and 7.00pm to 9.00pm Sunday

Credit cards accepted: Access, Visa

Discounts: 8½ per cent on mixed or unmixed cases

Facilities and services: Free glass loan; home delivery in local area; occasional in-store tastings; by-the-case sales

Special offers: Occasional promotions focusing on specific countries; 1995 Bordeaux *en primeur*

Top ten best-selling wines: 1995 Hardy's Stamp Series Semillon/Chardonnay; 1995 Vin de Pays des Côtes de Gascogne, Cépage Colombard; 1995 Le Chardonnay de Gibalaux, Vin de Pays d'Oc; 1995 Jacob's Creek Semillon/Chardonnay; 1994 Liebfraumilch, Eduard Wolf; 1991 Romanian Classic Pinot Noir; Don Gulias Tinto; 1994 Domaine de La Serre Merlot, Vin de Pays d'Oc; 1994 Jacob's Creek Shiraz/Cabernet; 1995 Conde de Castilla Tinto, Navarra

Range:

GOOD: Bordeaux, Burgundy, Rhône, Beaujolais, regional France, New Zealand, Port

AVERAGE: Loire, Alsace, Germany, Spain, Australia, Chile, Argentina, Champagne and sparkling wines

POOR: United States, South Africa, Eastern Europe

UNDER-REPRESENTED: Portugal, Italy

With its Gothic lettering and mock-Tudor exteriors, Davisons' chain of Home Counties stores looks terribly old-fashioned. From the outside nothing appears to have changed at the family-owned company in the last year – or, cruel observers might add, since it was founded back in 1875 by the great-grandfather of the current managing director, Michael Davies.

But appearances can deceive. The majority of the shops may look as if they could do with a re-fit, or at the very least a rendezvous with a paintbrush, but Davisons has been busy over the last 12 months, following its takeover of City wholesaler Mayor Sworder.

Davies and former Mayor Sworder boss and Master of Wine Martin Everett spent a good deal of time combining their two lists in 1996. The two companies possessed complementary strengths, according to Davies. Davisons could provide a certain amount of knowledge of the New World, as well as an array of older vintages in Bordeaux, Burgundy and Port. Mayor Sworder was strong in Spain, Germany, Beaujolais, the Loire, the Rhône, Burgundy and the Languedoc-Roussillon, especially at the individual domaine level.

How has it all panned out? So far, fine and dandy. 'I feel Mayor Sworder has given us another dimension,' comments Davies. 'If you take two lists and select the best from each of them, you're bound to come out on top.' To cement their commercial relationship, Davies and Everett went on a three-part tour of France this year, visiting suppliers in every part of the country except Alsace and the Loire.

The concentration on France was more than an excuse to eat good food and indulge a love of travelling, however. France still accounts for around 44 per cent of Davisons' sales, with the next biggest country, Australia, a long way behind at 15 per cent. The new list, complete with tasting notes and useful information on suppliers, is even more biased towards France - over half of the wines are from across the Channel. At this rate, it won't be too long before someone puts Mr Davies up for the Légion d'honneur.

Having predicted a couple of years ago that Australia would be outselling France in his stores by the turn of the century, Davies has now changed his mind. He believes that the Languedoc-Roussillon, with its varietal *vins de pays* and more traditional appellation wines, is giving the Aussies a run for their marketing dollars.

New World listings have continued to arrive this year (from Chile, Argentina and California, as well as New Zealand, the subject of a 20-wine promotion), but the main focus has been on France. In particular, Davies has improved his selection of characterful wines from difficult areas, such as Alsace, the Rhône and Beaujolais.

The French theme was also present in the 1995 *en primeur* offer of red Bordeaux. 'It's part of our rôle as an independent wine merchant,' says Davies. Davisons has always bought fair quantities of claret *en primeur* to offer to its customers once it has matured in bottle. But this was the first time it has offered what Americans call 'futures' through the shops.

Davies says his selection of older clarets, Burgundies and Ports is 'nigh on unique' in the high street. 'Where else can you walk into an off-licence and find a bottle of nicely mature 1990 Clos du Marquis sitting there on the shelf? A lot of people come to us because of that.' This may be true – customers can choose from 100 clarets and 17 different vintages – but we still feel the list could do with a clear-out in places.

So who shops at Davisons? The answer is a steady, rather than brimming, flow of fairly traditional wine drinkers reluctant to trawl the bottom of their wallets. 'We haven't increased sales by volume or value,' says Davies with his usual candour. 'I'd love to say that we're selling masses of wine over £5, but it's not true.'

The thing about Davisons, rather like Unwins, is that it isn't trendy or street-wise. 'Not everyone feels at home walking into an Oddbins or a Bottoms Up,' says Davies. 'Our stores are cosy and friendly. When you go in there, we want you to feel it's your local wine merchant.'

This, in part, is why Davies is reluctant to give the shops a much-needed face-lift. One or two shops have been upgraded (and considerably better they look, too), but we sense that sales will have to improve before Davies gets on the phone to Dulux.

Martin Everett argues that 'The most important thing is to get what's inside the stores right first.' And he has a point – why spend millions on design consultants if your list isn't worth the coloured paper it's printed on?

The takeover has certainly provided a lot of good new wines from Mayor Sworder, as well as an excuse to junk a few horrors from the old Davisons list. But Davisons still seems to be putting more effort into its wholesale division and pubs than into its stores at the moment. Davies admits that pubs are easier to run, especially in the current retail climate. 'If you're investing in a new site, it's much easier to gauge the profitability of a pub than a shop.'

Tasting at Davisons, you are aware of the weight of the past. Paintings and photographs of Michael Davies' ancestors eye you from every wall. Davies himself is acutely aware of his responsibilities. 'Everything here is geared up for generation after generation. I genuinely believe we'll be here in another 100 years.'

To a certain extent, such independent-mindedness is a good thing. But it has a down side, too. Despite the improvements over the last year, there is still a certain reluctance at Davisons to take risks. If the shops, as opposed to the pubs, are to remain competitive in the high street, their exteriors will have to match the quality of the best wines on the shelves inside.

White

Under £3

GERMANY

1994 Liebfraumilch, Eduard Wolf, Pfalz 13/20
Medium sweet 🍶🍶 |
Decently floral, Müller-Thurgau-based German quaffer with enough acidity to prevent it from cloying.

£3–5

ARGENTINA

1995 Norton Estate Torrontes 15/20
Dry 🍶🍶 |
Extremely fragrant, Muscat-like Argentine white made from the indigenous Torrontes grape by one of Mendoza's leading estates. The finish is on the alcoholic side.

AUSTRALIA

1995 Hardy's Stamp Series Semillon/Chardonnay 14/20
Off-dry 🍶🍶 |
Sweetish, big-company Aussie white blend with sweet-and-sour fruit characters and crisp acidity. Refreshingly unoaked.

1995 Jacob's Creek Semillon/Chardonnay 14/20
Dry 🍶 |
Ever-reliable, fruity super-blend of Australia's biggest-selling branded wine. Lemon-crisp, fresh and lightly oak-chipped.

CHILE

1995 Caliterra Chardonnay, Curicó · 14/20
Dry 👜 🍾

Sweet, tropical fruity Chilean Chardonnay with a soft texture and ripe peach and banana flavours.

1995 Caliterra Sauvignon Blanc, Curicó · 14/20
Dry 👜 🍾

Ripe, forward Sauvignon Blanc from the Curicó region of Chile's fertile central valley. Caliterra wines are made in a deliberately approachable style by the Errázuriz winery.

FRANCE

1995 Vin de Pays des Côtes de Gascogne, Cépage Colombard, Plaimont · 14/20
Dry 👜👜 🍾

Tangy, grapefruity, medium-bodied Gascon white made from the superior (anything is superior to Ugni Blanc) Colombard grape.

1995 Le Chardonnay de Gibalaux, Vin de Pays d'Oc · 14/20
Dry 👜 🍾

Buttery, unoaked southern French Chardonnay, which starts out well enough but falls by the wayside for lack of fruit and concentration.

1995 Domaine de Lacquy, Vin de Pays des Terroirs Landais · 14/20
Bone dry 👜 🍾

Citrus-crisp south-west French blend of Colombard, Ugni Blanc and Gros Manseng, made for summer sipping by the Atlantic. Good with oysters.

1995 James Herrick Chardonnay, Vin de Pays d'Oc · 15/20
Dry 👜👜 🍾

Elegant, minerally Chardonnay from Englishman James Herrick's southern French vineyards near Narbonne, showing restrained, spicy oak and melon fruitiness.

NEW ZEALAND

1995 Nobilo White Cloud 14/20
Off-dry 🍶🍶 ▮
A Kiwi white that never lets you down, this zesty, off-dry blend of Müller-Thurgau with a dollop of Sauvignon Blanc for aromatic freshness is a good introduction to New Zealand.

UNITED STATES

Shelby Vineyards Semillon/Chardonnay 14/20
Dry 🍶🍶 ▮
Fresh, apple and pear-like California white in a good-looking package, from super-blender Jason Korman.

£5–8

AUSTRALIA

1995 Ironstone Semillon/Chardonnay 15/20
Dry 🍶🍶 ▮
Ripe, melon and grapefruit-like Western Australian blend, which tastes more like Sauvignon Blanc than either of the two grapes in the blend.

FRANCE

1995 Sauvignon de Touraine, Domaine des Sablons 14/20
Bone dry 🍶 ▮
Ageing, dry Loire Sauvignon Blanc with muted aromas and crunchy acidity.

1995 Château de La Jannière, Muscadet de Sèvre et Maine Sur Lie 16/20
Bone dry 🍶🍶🍶 ▮
Reflecting the excellent quality of the 1995 vintage, this is a crisp, concentrated, weighty Muscadet with notes of aniseed and ripe apple and a refreshing *sur lie* petillance.

1994 Pinot Blanc d'Alsace, J Becker 15/20
Dry 🍶🍶 ▮
Fresh and extremely characterful for (the often rather neutral) Pinot Blanc, this is an Alsace white with ripe pear fruitiness, good weight and zip.

1994 Mâcon Uchizy, Domaine Talmard
Dry 👜👜👜 🍾   16/20

Super-ripe, ginger-spicy, estate-bottled Mâcon Villages white, with complex, honeyed Chardonnay fruit unobstructed by oak.

NEW ZEALAND

1995 Oyster Bay Chardonnay, Marlborough
Dry 👜👜👜 🍾   16/20

Chablis-like South Island Chardonnay from the brother-and-sister team of Jim and Rosemary Delegat, with citrusy acidity balanced by buttery, barrel-fermented richness.

Over £8

AUSTRALIA

1995 Chateau Xanadu Chardonnay
Dry 👜👜 ➥   16/20

Restrained, barrel-fermented Western Australian Chardonnay, which is still tight and youthful at the moment but should evolve into a top-notch white over the next two to five years. One for Coleridge fans.

FRANCE

1995 Saint Véran, Domaine de l'Ermite, Gérard Martin
Dry 👜👜 ➥   16/20

Rich but old-fashioned southern Mâconnais grower's Chardonnay with minerally, idiosyncratic complexity. A wine that grows on you.

1994 Sancerre, Domaine Millet-Roger
Bone dry 👜 🍾   15/20

From the under-rated 1994 vintage in the Loire, this is a grassy, tangily austere Sancerre, which lacks a teeny bit of mid-palate fruitiness and weight.

1992 Mâcon Clessé, Domaine Emilian Gillet, Jean Thévenet
Off-dry 👜👜👜 🍾   17/20

Made by one of Burgundy's most individual producers, this is an extraordinarily ripe, almost tropical fruity Chardonnay with masses of concentration, some residual sweetness, but lovely balancing freshness and acidity.

NEW ZEALAND

1995 Nautilus Sauvignon Blanc   14/20
Dry

An austere Marlborough Sauvignon Blanc from the difficult 1995 vintage. The aromas reminded us of lemon-scented bath soap. There was certainly no New Zealand water shortage in 1995.

Red

£3–5

ARGENTINA

1993 Norton Estate Cabernet Sauvignon   15/20
Full-bodied

Blackcurrant-leaf aromas, sweet black-cherry fruitiness and fine-grained tannins make this one of the best sub-£5 Argentine reds on the market.

AUSTRALIA

1994 Jacobs Creek Shiraz/Cabernet   13/20
Medium-bodied

Minty, ripe, faintly medicinal, best-selling Aussie blend of Shiraz and Cabernet Sauvignon, let down by a rasp of added acidity.

1995 Peter Lehmann Grenache   15/20
Full-bodied

Supple, juicy, easy-drinking Grenache from the Baron of the Barossa, Peter Lehmann, showing strawberry fruitiness and plenty of warm alcohol.

FRANCE

1994 Domaine de La Serre Merlot, Vin de Pays des Côtes de Thongue　　14/20
Medium-bodied 🍯 ▮

Pleasantly rustic Languedoc red made from Bordeaux's Merlot grape with plenty of colour and plum-like fruit.

1995 Château de Valcombe, Costières de Nîmes　　10/20
Full-bodied ▮

Pongy, over-sulphured aromas, dullish flavours and dry tannins create a fatal imbalance here.

1993 Prieuré Donnadieu, Saint Chinian　　14/20
Full-bodied 🍯 ▮

Peppery, intense, traditional Midi blend with cedary tannins and a rather drying, rustic finish.

1994 Domaine Saint Martin, Vin de Pays des Côtes de Thongue
15/20
Full-bodied 🍯🍯 ▮

Robustly chewy, Cabernet-like Languedoc red made at Domaine de l'Arjolle and showing plum-skin fruit and a hint of vanilla oak.

1995 James Herrick, Cuvée Simone, Vin de Pays d'Oc　　16/20
Full-bodied 🍯🍯🍯 ▬

Named after his charming Californian wife, Simone, James Herrick's first Languedoc venture into red wine is a triumph, showing tarry, aromatic Syrah characters, fleshy, sweet fruit and southern spiciness. Still chunky, but should soon soften into a memorable sub-£5 red.

ROMANIA

1991 Romanian Classic Pinot Noir　　12/20
Medium-bodied ▮

Beetrooty, basic, sweetened-up Pinot Noir from the land of Count Dracula. Not a threat to red Burgundy – even at £3.30 a bottle.

SPAIN

Don Gulias Tinto, Vino de Mesa   11/20
Medium-bodied
Coarsely oaked, very basic Spanish plonko. One banderillo short of a bullfight.

1995 Conde de Castilla Tinto, Navarra   10/20
Full-bodied
Cooked, raisiny, extracted old-fashioned Spanish tinto with hefty dry tannins and insufficient fruit for our taste.

UNITED STATES

Shelby Vineyards Barbera/Cabernet   15/20
Medium-bodied
Clove and ginger-scented, pleasantly oaked blend of Barbera and Cabernet (Sauvignon, we presume) from wheeler-dealer Jason Korman, with lively, fresh cherry fruit characters and thirst-quenching acidity.

£5–8

AUSTRALIA

1994 Church Block Red, Cabernet/Shiraz/Merlot, Wirra Wirra
     16/20

Full-bodied
Sweet, massively fruity, but finely tuned Aussie classic from Ben Riggs at McLaren Vale's Wirra Wirra winery, showing lots of alcohol and minty, blackcurrant fruitiness with a polished veneer of spicy oak.

FRANCE

1992 Château de Mendoce, Côtes de Bourg   13/20
Medium-bodied
Leafy, soft, but rather insubstantial Right Bank claret from the worst vintage of the last decade. Rain stopped play here.

1993 Vacqueyras, Château des Roques, Edouard Dussor   16/20
Full-bodied 💰💰💰 ▬
Powerfully fruity, intense expression of southern French Grenache with rich, peppery, brown-sugar-like fruit flavours and heady alcohol. Two somersaults to the glass.

1992 Lirac, Domaine Duseigneur   16/20
Full-bodied 💰💰💰
Very youthful and concentrated for a 1992, this is a chunky, blackberry fruity, Syrah-like southern Rhône red from grower Jean Duseigneur.

1994 Côte de Brouilly, Domaine de la Voûte des Crozes   16/20
Medium-bodied 💰💰 ▬
Good, concentrated Gamay from grower Nicole Chanrion, with plenty of sweet morello-cherry fruit flavours and excellent structure for ageing.

1994 Juliénas, Le Chapon, Domaine Jean Buiron   15/20
Full-bodied 💰 ▬
A less charming expression of the Gamay grape with more traditional, heftily extracted tannins and flavours.

SOUTH AFRICA

1995 Mulderbosch Faithful Hound Merlot/Cabernet   15/20
Medium-bodied 💰
Rather lean Cape Bordeaux blend from an estate that is better known for its Sauvignon Blancs. Pleasantly grassy and oaky with an unmistakably South African bite.

SPAIN

1991 Valserrano Crianza, Rioja Alavesa   16/20
Medium-bodied 💰💰💰
A Rioja Alavesa blend of Tempranillo, Mazuelo and Graciano grapes, showing well-judged oak, succulent tannins and notes of vanilla and sweet red fruits.

Over £8

ARGENTINA

1991 Navarro Correas, Colleción Privada   14/20
Full-bodied
Dusty, old-fashioned Argentine blend of Cabernet Sauvignon, Cabernet Franc and Merlot in a naff, frosted bottle complete with Mouton-Rothschild look-alike label.

FRANCE

1990 Château de Cardaillan, Graves   14/20
Medium-bodied
Prematurely aged, browning-red Bordeaux, which is beginning to dry out. Should be a bit better than this, given the much-touted vintage.

1994 Fleurie, Domaine de la Grand Cour, Dutraive   16/20
Medium-bodied
Flavoursome, domaine-bottled Beaujolais with lively red fruit flavours, good concentration and thirst-quenching acidity. About as exciting as Fleurie gets. Shame about the £9.15 price tag.

1993 Saint Joseph, Les Grisières, André Perret   17/20
Medium-bodied
André Perret is one of the best growers in the white wine appellation of Condrieu. It might be auto-suggestion, but this stylish, elegant 1993 northern Rhône Syrah, with its sweet blackberry fruit and stylish oak, smells a little like Viognier. Intriguing...

1990 Château Les Ormes de Pez, Cru Bourgeois, Saint Estèphe
17/20

Medium-bodied
From the best Bordeaux vintage of the last decade, this is a stylish, opulently fruity, judiciously oaked *cru bourgeois* claret with plenty of ageing potential and substance, from one of Bordeaux's leading figures, Jean-Michel Cazes.

1988 Les Brulières de Beychevelle, Haut-Médoc   16/20
Medium-bodied
Nicely mature, coffee-bean oaky Second Label claret from Saint Julien's Château Beychevelle, with good structure, softening tannins and a core of sweet, gamey fruitiness.

Rosé

£5–8

FRANCE

1995 Château de Sours Rosé, Bordeaux 15/20
Dry 👜👜 ❘
Deeply coloured, modern Bordeaux rosé verging on a *clairet* (sic) in style, this
raspberry and rhubarb-fruity pink is drinkably fresh but will age nicely, too.

Sparkling

£5–8

AUSTRALIA

Killawarra Brut, Southcorp 14/20
Off-dry 👜👜 ❘
Fresh, sherbety, sweetish Aussie fizz with simple, tropical fruit flavours.

Killawarra Rosé, Southcorp 15/20
Off-dry 👜👜👜 ❘
Bronze-pink, strawberry fruity, sweetish party fizz, also from the Southcorp
Group.

Fuller's ☆☆☆☆

Address: Griffin Brewery, Chiswick Lane South, London W4 2QB

Telephone/fax: 0181 996 2000; 0181 996 2087

Number of branches: 72

Opening hours: 10.00am to 10.00pm Monday to Saturday; 11.00am to 10.00pm Sunday

Credit cards accepted: Access, Visa, Switch

Discounts: One free bottle with every unmixed case; 10 per cent on a case at the Brewery Store

Facilities and services: Glass loan with 50 pence deposit per glass; free home delivery locally; in-store Saturday tastings

Top ten best-selling wines: Winter Hill White; Moët et Chandon NV; Winter Hill Red; Jacob's Creek White; Tocornal Chardonnay; Jacob's Creek Red; Brossault Brut; Berticot Sauvignon; Chablis Vauroux; Nottage Hill Chardonnay

Range:

GOOD: Red Bordeaux, Rhône, Burgundy, regional France, Spain, New Zealand, Australia, Chile, Champagne and sparkling wines

AVERAGE: White Bordeaux, Loire, Italy, Eastern Europe, United States, Argentina, South Africa

POOR: Portugal

UNDER-REPRESENTED: Alsace, Germany

When Roger Higgs, Fuller's wine buyer, is in the dock with a QC problem, it's usually quality control that's on his mind. But this time the QC in question was being paid a fat fee by Unwins to oppose Fuller's application for a licence to open a new store in Surrey's commuter belt. Dorking, according to Unwins, didn't need any more Riojas. The licensing justices disagreed, however, and while Unwins and its co-sponsors Thresher found themselves on the wrong end of an expensive fee, Fuller's had its new store and Dorking got more Riojas.

Dorking was one of a number of new sites opened in 1996 by Fuller's, whose small but thoroughly well turned-out estate has increased in size from

65 to 72 stores. Almost all the new Fuller's are in busy London areas: Putney High Street, Fulham Road, South Kensington, Old Brompton Road and Parson's Green.

Fuller's is best-known, of course, for its prize-winning London Pride, its Chiswick Bitter and ESB beers, all brewed at the Griffin Brewery in Chiswick. And with around 200 pubs in London and the Home Counties, Fuller's off-licences account for only 10 per cent of its total business. But the policy of taking on city centres is deliberate.

With its new range of 600-plus wines and more competitive prices, Fuller's is confident that it can take on Victoria Wine and Thresher. It plans to open an average of six or seven stores a year, mainly in central London, aiming to reach 100 by the millennium. Forty-six of the stores, called Gold stores by Fuller's, take the full range. Most of the rest are Silver stores, which stock the majority of the range. Three Bronze stores hold out as the old-style high-street 'offie'.

With 600 wines, the list may not be as big as Oddbins', nor does Fuller's have quite the geographic spread of the high-street chain for which Roger 'Higgsy' Higgs used to work. In fact, while Oddbins may be the model, from the point of view of image and enthusiastic staff, Higgs doesn't want Fuller's to be seen as a second-rate Oddbins. By stamping his own personality on the range, Higgs has already put Fuller's streets ahead of its independent high-street-chain rivals, Unwins and Davisons.

France still dominates the Fuller's agenda, with one-third of all its wine sales. But Fuller's sells more Australian, Chilean and South African wine than German or Italian, which come second and third respectively in the national league table. The New World is the focus of Roger Higgs' introduction to Fuller's sober new grey and burgundy wine list. Written by Higgsy, the list highlights his personal tips, with endearing *Grauniad*-style typos such as 'Les Qunits Sauternes 1994, a lovely stucky in an ideally sized bottle'.

Higgs admits that, even after two years in the job, 'there's still plenty of work to be done': 1997 will see a clutch of new Argentine wines from Catena and Peter Bright; Chile is still growing; and Australia, with 18 per cent of Fuller's wine turnover, remains its most important New World country. South Africa though, which started well in 1996, 'bit itself in the bum with its pricing', says Higgs, especially with Pinotage, which he refuses to sell.

The south of France is a developing area at Fuller's and there are some exciting things happening in Spain, says Higgs, citing new Navarra wines from Nekeas and Marqués de Griñon in Rioja. Although he pledged to revamp the Italian range this year, Higgs was forced to boot it out of play as a result of the small 1995 crop and rising prices. Californian wines too have yet to strike a chord with Fuller's customers.

Staff training and incentives are a feature at Fuller's, where throughout the year Peter Lehmann, Peter Dawson of BRL-Hardy, Tony Jordan from Moët et

Chandón's Green Point, Wingara and Montana all put on tastings for staff at the company's smart new wine warehouse, the Brewery Store, next to the Griffin Brewery. Nine groups of taster training managers carry out tastings with staff, who are offered incentives, such as trips to wineries, based on percentage sales of table wine.

Since Higgs joined Fuller's from Oddbins two years ago, Fuller's has upped its wine profile as customers have got to know the shops and Higgsy's range of wines better. The Christmas Champagne deal helped to bring in a lot of new customers and sales have been up 12 per cent over the year, with the average spend on wine – including fizz – now up to £4.50.

Fuller's customers like seeing new things in the range, as well as a good selection of ongoing bin ends. Some of the bigger shops, such as Richmond and Putney, sell considerably more wine than beer, spirits or any of the other convenience items normally sold in an off-licence. It may be a while before Fuller's becomes better known for its wine than its London Pride, but you can be sure that Higgsy's working on it.

White

Under £3

ARGENTINA

1995 Bright Brothers Argentine White   14/20
Dry 👜👜👜 ▮

A spicy, fragrant, richly fruity Argentine blend of Chenin Blanc and the Muscat-like Torrontes, from travelling Aussie winemaker Peter Bright.

FRANCE

1995 Winter Hill White, Vin de Pays de l'Aude   13/20
Off-dry 👜👜 ▮

Last year we felt that the label description 'French wine made by Australians' was laughably silly. But the 1995 Winter Hill is considerably fresher than the 1994, with crisp apple acidity and residual sweetness.

£3–5

ARGENTINA

1995 Torrontes Mendoza, Bodegas Jacques et François Lurton
15/20

Dry 🍾🍾🍾 ▮

Made at the Escorihuela winery in downtown Mendoza, this is a beautifully perfumed, lime-juicy Argentine white with plenty of flavour and zip.

AUSTRALIA

1995 Lonsdale Ridge Victoria Colombard
15/20
Dry 🍾🍾🍾 ▮

Extremely characterful for a cheap Aussie white, this is a tangy, aromatic, citrus and passion fruity Colombard from the quality-conscious, Mildura-based Wingara operation.

1995 Rawson's Retreat Bin 21 Semillon/Chardonnay/Colombard
15/20

Dry 🍾🍾🍾 ▮

Lime-fresh, ice cream soda-like blend of Semillon, Chardonnay and Colombard from Australia's biggest winery, Penfolds, proving that big-volume wines can show character in the right hands.

1995 Oakland Colombard/Semillon/Sauvignon Grant Burge
14/20
Dry 🍾 ▮

Sweetish, faintly confected blend of Colombard, Semillon and Sauvignon Blanc from Barossa Valley winemaker, Grant Burge. Decent enough, but £1 overpriced at £5.

CHILE

1996 Tocornal Chardonnay
12/20
Dry ▮

Bitter, coarsely oaked sub-£4 Chardonnay, which is one of the few white wine disappointments we've had from Chile this year.

1996 Santa Ines Sauvignon Blanc   15/20
Dry 👝👝👝 ▯

Classically Chilean, zesty Sauvignon Blanc, with fresh melon and Florida grapefruit characters, from the De Martino family.

1995 Caliterra Chardonnay, Curicó   15/20
Dry 👝👝 ▯

Flavoursome, ripely fruity Chilean Chardonnay with a touch of smoky oak and good weight.

1995 Louis Felipe Edwards Chardonnay   13/20
Off-dry ▯

Clumsy, rather unbalanced Colchagua Chardonnay with sweetish banana fruit flavours and a bitter, extracted aftertaste. Another disappointment.

1995 Santa Ines Barrel-Fermented Chardonnay   15/20
Dry 👝👝 ▯

Oaky, toffee-fudge-like Chilean Chardonnay with Burgundian aspirations. Pretty good stuff for under a fiver, this is cheese to Louis Felipe Edwards' chalk.

FRANCE

1995 Terret Sauvignon, Vin de Pays d'Oc, Domaine des Martin, Jacques Lurton   14/20
Dry 👝👝 ▯

A blend of the Vermouth grape Terret with Sauvignon Blanc, this is a fresh, grapefruity Languedoc white with a sharp twist of acidity.

1995 Château Haut Grelot, Premières Côtes de Blaye, Joel Bonneau   16/20
Dry 👝👝👝 ▯

Concentrated, mealy white Bordeaux with flavoursome, grapefruity Sauvignon blending nicely with the rich textures of the Semillon and Muscadelle grapes. Brilliant value.

1995 Berticot Sauvignon, Côtes de Duras   14/20
Dry 👝👝 ▯

Rather muted in the aroma department, but this zippy, faintly gooseberry fruity Gironde white is a decent buy at under £4.

GERMANY

1994 Kirchheimer Schwarzerde Beerenauslese, Pfalz, half-bottle
16/20

Very sweet 👛👛👛 ●━

Golden-hued, luscious, honey and marmalade-like German sweetie, with enough tangy acidity to cut through the syrup.

ITALY

1995 Pinot Grigio Pecile, Grave del Friuli, Bidoli   15/20
Dry 👛👛👛 🍾

It's almost impossible to find well-priced quality wines from Italy's best white wine region, Friuli, so this smartly packaged, concentrated, peachy Pinot Grigio is something of a bargain.

SOUTH AFRICA

1996 First Cape Chenin Blanc   13/20
Dry 👛 🍾

A juicy, early-released Cape white with boiled-sweet flavours and rather tart acidity.

1995 Springfield Estate Sauvignon Blanc   15/20
Bone dry 👛👛 🍾

With aromas of elderflower and freshly mown lawns, this is a grassy, crisply dry Cape white, which could only be made from Sauvignon Blanc.

SPAIN

1995 Castillo de Montblanc, Conca de Barbera   14/20
Dry 👛👛👛 🍾

Attractively oaked, ripe pear-flavoured, mini-Graves-style Spanish blend of the native Macabeu and Parellada grapes at an attractive price.

1995 Castillo de Montblanc Chardonnay, Conca de Barbera   14/20
Off-dry 👛👛 🍾

Well-priced, modern Spanish Chardonnay from Hugh Ryman, with perceptible sweetness and oak character. Commercial stuff.

1995 Durius Blanco Marqués de Griñon   15/20
Dry 👜👜 ▮

Nettley, ultra-fresh northern Spanish blend based on the Sauvignon Blanc grape, showing aromatic lift and lemony fruit.

1995 Nekeas Barrel-Fermented Chardonnay, Navarra   14/20
Dry 👜 ▮

An ambitious Navarra Chardonnay from the Nekeas winery, which should have been taken out of new oak barrels a bit earlier to avoid the splintery effect. A shame, because the basic fruit quality is first-class.

£5–8

ARGENTINA

1994 Catena Agrelo Vineyard Chardonnay   15/20
Off-dry 👜 ▮

From the most dynamic winery in Argentina, this is a sweetish, oatmealy, Californian-style Chardonnay made by American Paul Hobbs, with good weight and peachy flavours. We found the finish a little cloying.

AUSTRALIA

1994 Penfolds Barrel-Fermented Chardonnay   14/20
Dry 👜 ▮

Old-fashioned, nutty, rather ponderous white with a copse of smoky oak to the fore. We prefer the more delicate new style evident in Penfolds' 1995 white wines.

1994 Mitchelton III Goulburn Valley White   16/20
Dry 👜👜 ▮

A southern Rhône-style blending Marsanne, Viognier and Roussanne and made in Victoria's Goulburn Valley, this is a dry, complex, if slightly austere white, which is built to age. A wine that improves in the glass.

1995 Basedow Barossa Valley Chardonnay   16/20
Dry 👜👜 ▮

Deeply coloured, intensely oaky, Barossa Valley Chardonnay. Short on subtlety, but long on sweet vanilla, cinnamon spice and burnt-butter character.

1995 Madfish Bay Oak-Fermented Chardonnay, Western Australia   17/20
Dry 🍷🍷🍷 ▬

Made by John Wade, one of Western Australia's star winemakers, this is a classy, richly flavoured Chardonnay, which combines textured fruit and buttered popcorn characters with elegant acidity.

1995 Katnook Coonawarra Sauvignon Blanc   17/20
Dry 🍷🍷🍷 ▬

Ripe gooseberry and passion fruity Sauvignon Blanc from a South Australian region better known for its red wines. Intensely concentrated, moreish stuff, which should age well too.

CHILE

1995 Caliterra Casablanca Chardonnay   16/20
Dry 🍷🍷🍷 ▮

One of Chile's leading Chardonnays, this Casablanca-sourced white from Brian Bicknell is a crisp, grapefruity, subtly oaked style with a Pacific-influenced, cool-climate tang.

FRANCE

1995 Mâcon Igé Vieilles Vignes, Caves d'Igé, Oak-Aged   13/20
Dry ▮

Vegetal, clumsily oaked white Burgundy from a Mâcon co-operative whose white wines we've enjoyed a lot more in previous vintages.

1995 Fat Bastard Chardonnay, Vin de Pays d'Oc   15/20
Dry 🍷🍷 ▮

A ripe, attractively oaked, New World-influenced southern French Chardonnay with throat-warming alcohol and peachy fruitiness, from winemakers Thierry Boudinaud and Guy Anderson. Not to be confused with Bâtard-Montrachet.

1995 Saint Véran, Domaine des Deux Roches   16/20
Dry 🍷🍷🍷 ▬

Minerally, youthful, grapefruity Mâconnais Chardonnay showing an astonishing degree of buttery complexity for an unoaked white.

GERMANY

1992 Serrig Herrenberg Riesling Kabinett, Bert Simon, Mosel Saar Rüwer   15/20
Medium dry 👛👛 🍾
Fresh, intensely aromatic, featherweight Mosel Riesling with mineral and petrol aromas and crisp apple fruitiness.

SOUTH AFRICA

1995 Neil Ellis Sauvignon   16/20
Dry 👛👛👛 🍾
Like a cross between a top-notch New Zealand Sauvignon Blanc and a Sancerre, this is a richly grapefruity, beautifully crafted white from Elgin, one of the Cape's most exciting cool-climate areas

1995 Hoopenburg Chardonnay   15/20
Dry 👛👛 🍾
Intense, butterscotchy Cape Chardonnay with considerable elegance and finesse. Shame the packaging looks so cheap.

1995 Jordan Chardonnay, Stellenbosch   16/20
Dry 👛👛👛 ➖
With a whacking 14 per cent alcohol, this is a rich, nutty/oaky Burgundian-style Cape Chardonnay, with fermentation lees-derived lemony freshness and good weight. Another tacky package, though.

Over £8

AUSTRALIA

1993 Miranda Golden Botrytis Semillon/Riesling, half-bottle   16/20
Very sweet 👛👛 🍾
Very sticky, very sweet essence of botrytis blend of Semillon and Riesling, with liquid barley-sugar and mandarin-orange flavours. Less old-fashioned than it looks.

FRANCE

1995 Chablis, Domaine le Verger, Cuvée Vieilles Vignes, Alain Geoffroy   16/20
Dry 🛍🛍 ▥⊸
Rich, structured, old-vine Chablis from an excellent vintage, with minerally complexity and thirst-quenching acidity. One for the cellar.

1993 Pouilly Fuissé, Dr B. Leger Plumet, Clos du Chalet   16/20
Dry 🛍 ▥⊸
From one of the best domaines in Pouilly Fuissé, this is a concentrated, honeyed white showing the austere acidity of the vintage.

1995 Coteaux du Layon, Chaume, Domaine des Forges   17/20
Very sweet 🛍🛍🛍 ▥⊸
Intense, hugely concentrated Loire sweetie from the excellent 1995 vintage. When Chenin Blanc tastes as good as this honey and apple-like stunner, it's well worth paying £9 a bottle.

1995 Sancerre Cuvée Flores, Vincent Pinard   17/20
Dry 🛍🛍🛍 ▥⊸
Made by the winningly named Vincent Pinard (*pinard* is French for plonk), this is an elegant, finely crafted Sancerre with minerally intensity of flavour. This is about as good as Sauvignon Blanc gets. *Pinard* it certainly isn't.

SPAIN

1994 Augustus Chardonnay, Penedès   15/20
Dry 🛍 ▮
Deeply coloured, beery, toffee-fudge-style Catalan Chardonnay, which is not for the faint of heart or palate. Very rich, if a little over-the-top.

Red

Under £3

ARGENTINA

1996 Bright Brothers Argentine Red   14/20
Medium-bodied 🍷🍷🍷 ▮
Argentina's rather well-priced answer to Beaujolais, this is a banana and strawberry fruit quaffer, which almost bounces out of the glass at you.

FRANCE

1995 Winter Hill Vin de Pays de l'Aude   13/20
Medium-bodied 🍷🍷 ▮
Softly fruity, deeply coloured Languedoc blend of Merlot and Carignan made at the Foncalieu winery. Pleasant blackberry and plum-skin red, which won't rot your gut.

£3–5

ARGENTINA

1996 Bright Brothers Tempranillo   15/20
Medium-bodied 🍷🍷🍷 ▮
Abundantly fruity, deeply coloured Argentine Tempranillo, which outclasses anything from Spain at the price. It's youthful, but accessible, and oozing blackberry fruitiness and silky tannins.

1995 Malbec/Tempranilla, Jacques Lurton, Mendoza   14/20
Medium-bodied 🍷🍷 ▮
Another highly promising Argentine red, this time from Frenchman Jacques Lurton, with chocolate and ripe plum-fruit flavours and a hint of drying oak.

AUSTRALIA

1995 Hardy's Stamp Series Shiraz/Cabernet   14/20
Medium-bodied 🍷 ▮

Sweetish, ginger-spicy, Aussie blend of Shiraz and Cabernet Sauvignon with simple, mint-humbug flavours.

1995 Peter Lehmann Barossa Grenache   15/20
Full-bodied 🍷🍷 ▮

Supple, juicy, easy-drinking Grenache from the Baron of the Barossa Valley, Peter Lehmann, showing strawberry fruitiness and plenty of warming alcohol.

CHILE

1995 Concha y Toro Merlot   15/20
Medium-bodied 🍷🍷🍷 ▮

Soft, succulent, quintessence of blackcurrant-style Merlot, with masses of youthful, juicy fruitiness, from Chilean giant Concha y Toro.

1995 Santa Ines Cabernet/Merlot   15/20
Medium-bodied 🍷🍷🍷 ▮

An excellent sub-£4 claret substitute, with lots of sweet, minty fruitiness, good structure and tannic backbone.

1995 Terra Noble Merlot   15/20
Medium-bodied 🍷🍷 ▬

This is a considerable step up from the first vintage of the new Chilean venture with Loire specialist, Henry Marionnet, as consultant. Grassy, carbonic maceration-style unoaked Merlot, with attractive depth and juiciness and faintly rustic tannins.

FRANCE

Montagne Noire Syrah, Vin de Pays d'Oc   14/20
Medium-bodied 🍷🍷 ▮

From the Foncalieu winery, this is a juicy, exuberantly fruity Syrah with well-crafted, medium-weight tannins.

1995 Carignan Vieilles Vignes, Vin de Pays d'Oc, Jacques Lurton
14/20

Full-bodied 👜👜 ▮

Robust, meaty, full-bodied Mediterranean red with a dusting of garrigue spice. Good to see a flying winemaker working with an unloved grape like Carignan.

1995 Domaine de Sérame Syrah, Vin de Pays d'Oc   14/20
Full-bodied 👜 ▮

Peppery, inky, but approachable southern French Syrah from Bordeaux-based Jacques Lurton, with ripe, black-cherry fruitiness and a rough aftertaste.

1995 M. le Merlot Vin de Pays d'Oc   15/20
Full-bodied 👜👜 ▬▬

We're not sure about the back label – *'Christophe Barbier, un homme, un vin'* – which almost reads like a passage from Baudelaire's *Les Fleurs du Mal*, but this structured, oak-infused Midi Merlot is a very demanding drop at under £5. The package is either swanky or wanky, depending on your point of view.

1995 James Herrick, Cuvée Simone, Vin de Pays d'Oc   16/20
Full-bodied 👜👜👜 ▬▬

Named after his charming Californian wife, Simone, James Herrick's first Languedoc venture into red wine is a triumph, showing tarry, aromatic Syrah character and fleshy, sweet fruit and southern spiciness. Still chunky, but should soon soften into a memorable sub-£5 red.

ITALY

1994 Teroldego Rotaliano, Ca Donini   14/20
Medium-bodied 👜👜 ▮

Black cherry-scented, northern Italian thirst-quencher with juicy sweet tannins and a refreshing twist of acidity.

1994 Montepulciano d'Abruzzo Barrique, La Luna Nuova, Casalbordino, Madonna dei Miracoli   15/20
Medium-bodied 👜👜👜 ▮

A brilliantly packaged, ultra-modern, oak-influenced Montepulciano made by Meerlust's winemaker, Giorgio dalla Cia. This smooth, chocolatey red takes the normally rustic Montepulciano d'Abruzzo into a new dimension.

PORTUGAL

1994 Bright Brothers Baga 15/20
Full-bodied 💰💰💰 🍷
Cracked pepper-scented, intensely spicy Portuguese red with robust tannins, made from the highly acidic Baga grape of Bairrada. Impressive for a sub-£4 red.

SOUTH AFRICA

1994 Bellingham Shiraz 12/20
Full-bodied 🍷
Beetrooty, hard, alcoholic Cape Shiraz with too much oak for its own good. Hard to see the Shiraz for the trees.

SPAIN

Marino Tinto Vino de Mesa, Bodegas Berberana 13/20
Full-bodied 💰 🍷
Sawdusty, but decently made, Spanish plonk with sweetish, raisiny fruit flavours and a whack of alcohol. It's under £3 at Kwik Save.

1995 Castillo de Montblanc, Conca de Barbera 12/20
Medium-bodied 🍷
Dryish, oak-chippy blend of Tempranillo, Cabernet Sauvignon and Merlot from Hugh Ryman, showing astringent tannins and high acidity.

1994 Castilla de Manzanares Cabernet Sauvignon, La Mancha
12/20
Medium-bodied 🍷
An oak-chippy, dry Spanish Cabernet Sauvignon from Don Quixote country. A bit basic. One for Sancho Panza's donkey.

1995 Tierra Secca Tempranillo/Cabernet, La Mancha 14/20
Full-bodied 💰💰 🍷
A more impressive La Mancha red blend of Tempranillo and Cabernet Sauvignon, made by Californian Ed Flaherty and showing chunky blackcurrant fruitiness and some oak character. One for Don Quixote's horse, Rosinante.

1994 Marqués de Griñón Rioja 15/20
Medium-bodied 💰💰 🍷
Made entirely with Tempranillo grapes from the Rioja Alavesa, this is an elegant, well-judged marriage of oak and soft, strawberry fruitiness at a pretty good price.

1994 Nekeas Crianza Tempranillo/Cabernet Sauvignon, Navarra
15/20

Medium-bodied 🍷🍷 ▮
Well-made, sweetly oaked Navarra blend of Tempranillo and Cabernet Sauvignon with notes of vanilla, blackberry and green pepper.

UNITED STATES

Thornhill Barbera   13/20
Medium-bodied ▮
A hot, jammy Californian red, which tastes more like a warm-climate Pinot Noir than Piemonte's Barbera.

£5–8

AUSTRALIA

1995 Oakland Cabernet/Mourvèdre/Grenache
14/20
Medium-bodied 🍷 ▮
Sweetish, simple, hole-in-the-middle Aussie blend of Cabernet Sauvignon, Mourvèdre and Grenache, unrealistically priced at around £5.50.

1992 Rouge Homme Coonawarra Shiraz/Cabernet
16/20
Medium-bodied 🍷🍷🍷 ▮
For the same money, you could buy a bottle of this sweetly oaked, elegant Coonawarra blend of Shiraz and Cabernet Sauvignon made by Lindemans winemaker Paul Gordon. Lovely stuff at an excellent price.

1993 Hardy's Bankside Shiraz, South Eastern Australia
16/20
Full-bodied 🍷🍷🍷 ▭▬
Dense, richly textured, cinnamon-tinged cross-regional Shiraz from Australia's number two, BRL-Hardy. Attractively spicy, with a firm backbone of tannin.

1994 Moculta Shiraz
16/20
Full-bodied 🍷🍷🍷 ▭▬
Ripe, chocolatey, sweetly oaked Barossa Valley Shiraz with vibrant licorice and blackberry fruit. No other region makes heart-stopping Shiraz like this.

1993 Mitchelton III Goulburn Valley Red
Full-bodied 16/20

Sagey, minty Victorian blend of Rhône grapes from Mitchelton winemaker, Don Lewis, showing coffee-bean oak and full-flavoured, but elegant, blackberry fruit with good acidity.

1994 Best's Great Western Dolcetto, Victoria
Medium-bodied 15/20

An unusual, cherry-fruity Aussie interpretation of north-west Italy's Dolcetto grape, this is a refreshing, pasta-bashing red at a rather inflated price.

1994 Grant Burge Barossa Cabernet
Medium-bodied 16/20

Minty, substantially oaked Barossa Valley Cabernet Sauvignon with sweet, chocolate and licorice notes and elegant cassis fruitiness.

CHILE

1994 Valdivieso Reserve Cabernet Franc
Medium-bodied 16/20

From a winery that makes some of the best reds in Chile, this is a sumptuous, chocolatey, well-oaked Lontue Cabernet, with minty intensity and structured tannins.

FRANCE

1995 Château Gazeau, Bordeaux Supérieur
Medium-bodied 14/20

From a château that sounds as though it was invented by Perrier, this is a smooth, attractively balanced, green-pepper-style claret with the lean finish you'd expect for a 1993.

1993 Bourgogne Pinot Noir, Martin
Medium-bodied 14/20

Light, but authentic red Burgundy from Côte de Beaune-based grower, Maurice Martin. Decent raspberryish Pinot Noir with a dry aftertaste.

1993 Valréas Domaine de la Grande Bellane, Côtes du Rhône Villages   15/20
Full-bodied 👜👜 🍷

An organic blend of 75 per cent Syrah and 25 per cent Grenache, this is a peppery, clove-spicy, Côtes du Rhône Villages with excellent ripe raspberry fruit and robust tannins.

1994 Château Sainte Agnès, Vieilli en Fût, Coteaux du Languedoc, Pic Saint Loup   17/20
Full-bodied 👜👜👜 🍷

One of the best reds we've tasted from the south of France, this densely textured, hugely concentrated, oak-aged blend of 75 per cent Syrah and 25 per cent Grenache is a stunning expression of blackberry-fruity Syrah with spicy, perfectly judged oak.

SOUTH AFRICA

1994 Woodlands Pinot Noir   14/20
Medium-bodied 👜 🍸

Sweetly brambly, liquid raspberry-like Cape Pinot Noir with a jammy, dry, warm-climate twist.

1994 Hoopenberg Merlot   16/20
Medium-bodied 👜👜 🍷

Maybe a bit pricey at nearly £7, especially given the cheap packaging, but this is a ripe, mouth-filling, coffee-bean oaky red with the structure to age.

Over £8

ARGENTINA

1994 Catena Malbec, Mendoza   17/20
Full-bodied 👜👜👜 🍷

Concentrated, mulberry fruity Mendoza Malbec from Nicolas Catena's Esmeralda winery, showing fine-grained, elegant tannins and savoury, herbal flavours with the weight and acidity to age.

AUSTRALIA

1993 Robertson's Well Coonawarra Cabernet   16/20
Full-bodied 👜👜 ➡–
Intense, finely textured Cabernet Sauvignon with masses of sweet blackcurrant fruit, well-judged vanilla oak and refreshing acidity. Should age well.

1994 Grant Burge Old Vine Shiraz   17/20
Full-bodied 👜👜👜 ➡–
Massively concentrated, smoky oak Barossa Valley red made from old Shiraz vines with abundant aromas of spicy blackberry fruit and real complexity. Super stuff.

FRANCE

1992 Château Haut Bages Monpelou, Pauillac   16/20
Medium-bodied 👜👜 ▮
From the generally ropey 1992 vintage, this is a forward, cedary, softly fruity, sub-£9 red Bordeaux – a good price for a good *cru bourgeois*.

1992 Château Haut Faugères, Grand Cru, Saint Emilion Grand Cru   16/20
Medium-bodied 👜👜 ▮
Sexy, modern, Merlot-based Right Bank claret with sweet vanilla oak and fleshy, softly textured fruitiness, which finishes a litttle on the dry side.

1992 Morey Saint Denis, Domaine Arlaud   16/20
Medium-bodied 👜👜 ▮
Modern, mulberry fruity, spicily oaked red Burgundy from négociant Denis Philibert. Highly drinkable Pinot Noir.

Rosé

£3–5

FRANCE

1995 Domaine de Raissac Cabernet Rosé   14/20
Dry 🍾🍾 ▮

Delicate Languedoc rosé in which the grassy character of the Cabernet Sauvignon grape is attractively apparent, along with some dry, redcurrant fruit flavours.

Sparkling

£5–8

AUSTRALIA

1992 Seaview Pinot Noir/Chardonnay   15/20
Dry 🍾🍾 ▮

From the Penfolds stable, this is a beer-yeasty, Champagne-method blend of Pinot Noir and Chardonnay, with mature, old-style fruitiness and a nutty aftertaste.

Over £8

FRANCE

Brossault Champagne Brut NV   14/20
Off-dry 🍾 ▮

Coarse, basic Champagne, which is rather sweet and overpressed.

Joseph Perrier Champagne NV   16/20
Dry 🍾🍾🍾 ▮
Complex, malty, strawberryish non-vintage Champagne from the underrated Grande Marque house of Joseph Perrier. One of *Grapevine's* fizzes of the year last year, and still bang on form.

UNITED STATES

Sonoma Pacific Brut NV   16/20
Dry 🍾🍾🍾 ▮
From Piper Heidsieck's California outpost, this is a fresh, youthful, Pinot Noir/Chardonnay-based fizz with an attractive mousse, which has established itself as one of the New World's best sparkling wines.

Fortified

£3–5

FRANCE

1994 Domaine de Brial Muscat de Rivesaltes, half-bottle   15/20
Very sweet 🍾🍾 ▮
Boudoir-scented, exotically grapey, Roussillon fortified white, with sweet lemon-meringue flavours and a knee-capping whack of alcohol.

Greenalls Wine Cellars

Including:

Wine Cellar ☆☆☆(☆)
Berkeley Wines ☆☆☆
Cellar 5 ☆☆

Address: PO Box 476, Loushers Lane, Warrington, Cheshire WA4 6RR

Telephone/fax: 01925 444555; 01925 415474

Number of branches: 26 Wine Cellar, 72 Berkeley Wines, 283 Cellar 5, 70 Greenalls Food Stores, 14 Night Vision

Opening hours: 10.00am to 10.00pm Monday to Sunday

Credit cards accepted: Access, Visa, Switch, Delta, Amex

Discounts: Party planning, sale-or-return offers and quantity discounts up to 15 per cent on wine

Facilities and services: Glass loan; home delivery by Wine Cellar and by arrangement with Berkeley Wines; in-store tastings on Saturdays at Wine Cellar

Special offers: Promotions, including 20 per cent off a case at Wine Cellar

Top ten best-selling wines:

Wine Cellar

Vino de Chile Red; Sliven Merlot/Pinot Noir; 1994 Philippe de Baudin Chardonnay; Bucklow Hill Dry White; Bucklow Hill Dry Red; Hardy's Stamps of Australia Shiraz/Cabernet; Lindemans Bin 65 Chardonnay; Penfolds Koonunga Hill Chardonnay; Bucklow Hill Semillon Chardonnay; Penfolds Bin 202 Riesling

Berkeley Wines

Jacob's Creek Dry Red; Jacob's Creek Semillon/Chardonnay; Liebfraumilch; Hardy's Stamps of Australia Shiraz/Cabernet; Moët et Chandon Brut; Bucklow Hill Dry White; Seppelts Great Western Brut; Lindemans Cawarra/Chardonnay; Lambrusco Bianco; Vino de Chile Red

Cellar 5

Liebfraumilch; Lambrusco Bianco; Muskat/Ugni Blanc Rousse; Sliven Cabernet
Sauvignon; Sliven Merlot/Pinot Noir; Bucklow Hill Dry White; Vino de Chile
Red; Bucklow Hill Dry Red; Valpolicella, Villa Mura, Sartori; Hardy's Stamps of
Australia Shiraz/Cabernet

Range:

GOOD: Australia, Chile, United States, Champagne and sparkling wines

AVERAGE: Bordeaux, Burgundy, regional France, Rhône, Loire, Italy, Spain,
Portugal, England, Eastern Europe, South Africa, Argentina

POOR: Germany

UNDER-REPRESENTED: None

Only Wine Cellar stocks the full range. For Berkeley Wines and Cellar 5 see
our introduction below.

As we sipped cappuccinos in the sunshine, Wine Cellar's Parisian-style cafeteria
was pulling in the Walton-on-Thames high-street crowd: pensioners, women
with children taking a break from shopping, and, at one table, spies in suits from
a competitor. An old couple straight out of central casting bought a decanter
and a bottle of Port, which were extravagantly gift-wrapped in front of our eyes
and those of Greenalls' exuberant managing director, Nader Haghighi.

'No fine-wine buyers, Nader?' we enquired. 'At ten o'clock in the morning,
you don't expect fine-wine buyers to be out of bed,' he commented. The new,
lavishly appointed store's recently acquired on-licence was not yet in force, so
waiters in French-style uniforms served nothing more intoxicating than coffee
and croissants against a collage of French pastoral scenes.

The long-term plan for Greenalls' new Wine Cellars, though, is to encourage
customers to read the wine list instead of their *Daily Mail*, and to open and try
a bottle of wine at the table. 'We want Wine Cellar to have the continental feel
of a Soho or Parisian café,' said Haghighi, pinching a baguette between thumb
and forefinger. The croissants and baguettes, to the evident surprise of one of
the waitresses, are expensively transported, three times a week, part-baked, by
lorry from Paris.

Meanwhile at the back of the store, where fine wines rub shoulders with
Hooper's Hooch and Twinings Iced Earl Grey, there's something of the feel of
a mini-Harrods food hall, with high-class coffees and other de luxe products
such as hand-made Belgian chocolates, the Fauchon range of luxury foods,
crystal glasses and decanters. Bottles stand temptingly, or lie on the limed-oak

shelves with handwritten tags dangling neatly from their necks, like Pierre Cardin ties.

Whichever way you look at it, Wine Cellar is unique. Combining a first-rate off-licence with a Parisian-style café inevitably adds a touch of the surreal to the British urban scene. What's the aim? According to Haghighi, it's to create a place with a relaxed enough ambience to encourage browsing. 'The biggest problem with the off-licence is attracting customers and attracting women in particular,' he says. 'We've found the solution.'

With a bottle of wine available to drink at shelf-price plus £2, and a machine that chills down a white in five minutes, the cafeteria 'makes the ambience for the customer more enjoyable, especially for the wine consumer', according to Haghighi. The hours are 8.30am to 10.30pm, with the drink licence running from 10.00am to 10.00pm.

As part of Haghighi's plan to turn Greenalls Cellars into a national force, Wine Cellar focuses on the south of England. As our summer deadline approached, there were five Wine Cellars in the south – Epsom, Walton-on-Thames, Welwyn Garden City, Chiswick and Banbury – and 17 in the north and Midlands, with Horseferry Road in Saint James's, Baker Street and Sevenoaks in the pipeline. Haghighi's aim is to be running between 35 and 40 Wine Cellars by the beginning of 1997.

Looking at the Greenalls group as a whole, you could be forgiven for regarding Wine Cellar as a cunning ploy to dress the mutton of its sprawling, regional chain as lamb. In fact, the ambitious Haghighi has nothing less than a complete shake-up of Greenalls in view. Thwarted in his attempt to buy Oddbins in the summer of 1996, he has turned his attention to revamping the more dowdy elements of the Greenalls off-licence empire.

Apart from the investment in Wine Cellars, Haghighi has increased the number of Greenalls Food Stores to 70 and upped the number of Night Visions to 14. Night Vision is a specialist video brand, like Blockbuster, but with an off-licence attached. Greenalls Food Stores are local, community-based convenience operations, which in turn have a different range and give varying shelf-space to wine, depending on the location.

Cellar 5, the traditional corner-shop off-licences, which form the bulk of the Greenalls estate, are not about to up sticks and go, but Haghighi, as you may have guessed, has plans for them, too. Greenalls, in Haghighi-speak, is 'repositioning' Cellar 5. As we went to press Haghighi was testing a new 'booze and news' concept to be called Hugglers. If it works, 100 or so Cellar 5s will be converted to Hugglers, a sort of off-licence-cum-newsagent that will be open long hours.

Haghighi's strategy for turning Greenalls into a major high-street force is dictated, at least in part, by external pressures. 'The supermarkets have squeezed the traditional off-licence and cross-Channel shopping has put even more pressure on them in the last three to four years.' But he also has his own vision of the off-licence of the future. 'If the proposition was limited to just selling drinks, we'd have to think twice about the future. But we're always looking for other reasons to bring customers into shops.'

Last year we pointed out that Haghighi, once operations director at Thresher, seemed to be creating an amalgam of the best of Oddbins and Thresher. But Haghighi denies that his approach to the off-licence is just a collage of his two competitors. 'Our job is to bring in extra traffic, to see what's missing, to create a flexible brand tailor-made to the needs of the local community. Our proposition has got so much legs [sic] and is so unique that we're able to compete.'

Concepts, not to mention propositions, are all fine and dandy of course, but a reputation for quality, value and choice of wines is what brings thirsty customers back for more. Here wine buyers Kevin Wilson and David Vaughan have increased the total range to 650-odd wines. The wines are all mouthwateringly set out in Wine Cellar's glossy new list, whose recipes, photos and chatty introductions to countries give it a more original look than last year's Oddbins-clone effort.

Reports on the ground suggest that not all the wines in the well-stocked Wine Cellar list are available, however. And the trickle-down effect means fewer wines in stores where convenience products have greater priority. Berkeley Wines has a range of some 450–500 wines, depending on the size of store, Greenalls Food Stores up to 300, with Night Vision around 250. Cellar 5s take only a small core range of 100 wines.

After a certain amount of early gerrymandering, however, the range is beginning to take on an identity of its own. Among others, there is a handful of distinctive, well-chosen wines from Argentina, the United States and even England. Prices too, which we previously criticised for being too high, are now more in line with the competition. And there are some good promotions, including 20 per cent off all cases for a limited period.

In the past year, because of price rises, the Australian range has been chopped back a bit – from 110 wines down to 90 – to accommodate the three new key value-for-money areas: South America, southern France and South Africa. A Chilean red is the number-one best-seller at Wine Cellar, and South America has increased its share of the listings cake, or possibly gâteau, at Greenalls from 29 wines to 45.

There are now some 35 South African wines, and the Languedoc-Roussillon, with 14 new wines, is up to 50. Elsewhere in France, the Loire is in slow decline, but the fall in Muscadet has in part been compensated for by some better Muscadet *sur lie* from individual properties.

1996 was not without its frustrations for Greenalls and Haghighi. The acquisition of Oddbins would have given them the nationwide presence they so badly seek. But it's still been a lively year, with performance starting to match some of the extravagant claims. 'We're bucking the trend through dedication, working with suppliers, improving buying priorities, enhancing the range and improving training,' says Haghighi.

So keep your eyes wide open, because Nader Haghighi is not finished with you or the high street yet. In fact, if you wander out to your local off-licence for a bottle of wine, and end up stopping off for a cappuccino and croissant, then emerge with an armful of magazines, luxury goods and videos, either you're in imminent danger of arrest or you've been Naderised.

White

£3–5

ARGENTINA

1996 Balbi Vineyards, Dry White　　　　　　　　　14/20
Dry 👛👛 |
Full, pear-droppy Mendoza white with spicy richness. Could do with a little more acidity for balance.

AUSTRALIA

1994 Penfolds Bin 202, Riesling　　　　　　　　　14/20
Off-dry 👛👛 |
Commercial, well-made, lemon meringue pie-like Riesling created with the Liebfraumilch connoisseur in mind.

1996 Bucklow Hill Dry White, Southcorp　　　　　　　　　15/20
Dry 👛👛👛 |
Same price, same grape, but we preferred the zesty freshness and concentration evident in this aromatic, lime and lemon-scented dry white.

1996 Bucklow Hill, Semillon/Chardonnay, Southcorp   15/20
Dry 👜👜👜 ▮

Fruit-dominated Aussie blend from the voluminous 1996 vintage, with nicely textured, ripe peach characters and pleasantly juicy softness.

1995 Lindemans Bin 65 Chardonnay   15/20
Off-dry 👜👜 ▮

Toffee and pineapple-fruity Aussie super-blend from winemaker Philip John. In a short vintage, he's maintained the Bin 65 hallmark of ripeness and approachability.

1995 Penfolds Koonunga Hill Chardonnay   16/20
Dry 👜👜👜 ▮

Classy, complex, barrel-fermented Aussie Chardonnay with butter and toffee-fudge richness balanced by beautifully judged, refreshing acidity.

CHILE

1995 Cordillera Estate Chardonnay   15/20
Dry 👜👜 ▮

Ripe, oaky, grapefruit-segment-scented dry white with a buttery texture and refreshing acidity.

1995 Santa Carolina, Chardonnay/Semillon   14/20
Off-dry 👜👜 ▮

Golden-hued, smoky, partially barrel-fermented blend of Chardonnay and Semillon, with sweet barley-sugar characters and lively acidity.

FRANCE

1994 Philippe de Baudin Chardonnay, Vin de Pays d'Oc   14/20
Dry 👜👜 ▮

A faintly bitter, assertively oaked southern French Chardonnay from Australians BRL-Hardy, with ripe, tropical fruit flavours.

Calvet, Two Rivers, Sauvignon/Semillon   15/20
Dry 👜👜 ▮

Daringly packaged Bordeaux blend of Sauvignon Blanc and Semillon, with a clean, grapefruity tang in a perceptibly New World-influenced style.

HUNGARY

1995 Château Megyer, Tokay, Furmint　　　　16/20
Bone dry 👜👜👜 ♪
Spicy, assertively dry Hungarian white made from the indigenous Furmint grape of the classic Tokay region, and showing sweet pipe-tobacco aromas and concentrated fruit flavours.

ITALY

1995 Soave, Villa Mura, Sartori　　　　　　13/20
Dry 👜 ♪
Ultra-clean, ultra-safe Soave, with fresh acidity but rather thin flavours.

1995 Principato, Pinot Grigio, Ca'vit, Vino da Tavola delle Venezie　　　　14/20
Dry 👜👜 ♪
Soft, melony, pleasantly fruity Veneto Pinot Grigio with a crisp orange-peel tang.

ROMANIA

1995 Block IV Chardonnay　　　　　　　　14/20
Off-dry 👜 ♪
At last, a drinkable white wine from Romania, made by the team of Stephen Donnelly and Christophe Baron. A light, banana-fruity New World-style Chardonnay, which, by Romanian standards, is Le Montrachet.

SOUTH AFRICA

1995 Welmoed, Chardonnay　　　　　　　13/20
Dry ♪
Over-oaked, one-dimensional Cape Chardonnay, with boiled sweets character and a charry aftertaste.

UNITED STATES

1995 Glen Ellen Proprietor's Reserve Chardonnay　　14/20
Off-dry 👜 ♪
Sweetish, oak-chipped, but highly commercial California Chardonnay with toffee and ripe apple fruit flavours.

£5–8

CHILE

1995 Casablanca Sauvignon Blanc, Santa Isabel Estate, Casablanca Valley 16/20
Dry 👜👜👜 ▮

A candidate for the title of Chile's best Sauvignon Blanc, this rich but dry, gooseberry and lemon-zest-like white shows that, with fruit from the Casablanca Valley, South America can compete with the best of New Zealand and South Africa.

ENGLAND

1994 Downs Edge Vineyards Fumé 15/20
Dry 👜👜 ▮

Elegantly oaked, well-crafted, dry English white with crisp, nettley fruit flavours, made from unspecified grapes.

1994 Chapel Down Vineyards Bacchus 15/20
Dry 👜👜 ▮

Nutmeg and grapefruit-like English white made from the Geisenheim-developed Bacchus, a Sylvaner-Riesling crossing with the workhorse Müller-Thurgau grape, aptly described by Chapel Down as England's answer to Loire Valley Sauvignon Blanc.

FRANCE

1995 Domaine de Raissac, Viognier 16/20
Dry 👜👜👜 ▮

Rich, ripe, apricot jam-like Languedoc white made from the ultra-trendy Viognier grape by Aussie Nick Butler. Nicely balanced and a bargain for Viognier.

1995 White Burgundy, Cave de Viré 13/20
Dry ▮

Clumsy, old-fashioned white Burgundy from the Mâconnais Viré co-operative, with bitter tannins and a hot fermentation character.

UNITED STATES

1994 Château Sainte Michelle Chardonnay, Washington State
15/20

Dry 🝔 ▮
Cinnamon and buttered toast-like Chardonnay from one of Washington State's largest producers. Well made, if a little shy on the finish.

Red

£3–5

AUSTRALIA

Bucklow Hill Dry Red, Australia, Southcorp
13/20
Full-bodied 🝔 ▮
Simple, minty, blackcurranty red from Down Under with some added oak character.

Nanya Estate Grenache/Pinot Noir
14/20
Medium-bodied 🝔🝔 ▮
The Ganja label may have gone, but this ripe, raspberry jam-like, warm-climate blend of Grenache and barely perceptible Pinot Noir is still reasonable value at under £4.

1995 Peter Lehmann Grenache
15/20
Full-bodied 🝔🝔🝔 ▮
Minty, pure, sweetly aromatic Grenache with pure, raspberry-like fruit flavours, throat-warming alcohol and soft tannins.

1995 Hardy's Stamps of Australia, Shiraz/Cabernet
13/20
Medium-bodied ▮
Slightly confected, mint-humbug character and dry oak made this BRL-Hardy bottom-of-the-range red expensive at over £4.

BULGARIA

Sliven Merlot/Pinot Noir   13/20
Medium-bodied 💰 🍷
Dry, rather rooty blend of Merlot and Pinot Noir from the Sliven region of Bulgaria.

CHILE

Vino de Chile Talca Red   13/20
Medium-bodied 💰 🍷
Simple, rather rustic claret alternative from the southern end of Chile's Central Valley.

1995 La Palma Cabernet/Merlot, Rapel Valley, La Rosa   14/20
Medium-bodied 💰💰 🍷
A little dry on the finish, but this sub-£4, sweetly blackcurranty Chilean blend is a good, ripe alternative to claret.

1994 Palmeras Estate Cabernet Sauvignon, Santa Emiliana   14/20
Medium-bodied 💰 🍷
Vanilla oaky, dry Chilean Cabernet Sauvignon, where you can just about see the fruit for the trees.

1995 Domaine Apalta Cabernet Sauvignon, Santa Cruz, Villa Montes   15/20
Full-bodied 💰💰 🍷
Made by Aurelio Montes at his Apalta vineyard in Colchagua, this is a characterful, peppery, raspberry fruity Cabernet Sauvignon, which reminded us of a California Zinfandel.

1995 La Palma Estate, Reserve Cabernet Savignon, Rapel Valley, La Rosa   15/20
Medium-bodied 💰💰 🍷
Savoury oaky, well-crafted Chilean Cabernet Sauvignon from the reliable Santa Rosa winery, with attractively sweet, cassis and plum fruit flavours.

FRANCE

1994 Claret, Calvet   13/20
Medium-bodied 💰 🍷
Drinkable, if basic, four-square claret from the négociant house of Calvet.

1994 La Croix Belle, Le Champ du Coq, Vin de Pays des Côtes de Thongue   14/20
Full-bodied 🍷 ➡-

Excellent, pure blackberry fruit quality and inky purple colour slightly let down by a dryish finish. The wine may soften with another six months in bottle.

1994 Château de Paraza, Cuvée Spéciale, Minervois   15/20
Full-bodied 🍷🍷 ▮

Traditional, well-structured Languedoc blend with masses of herby aromatics and impressive concentration.

1994 Saint Martin des Tocques, Corbières   16/20
Full-bodied 🍷🍷🍷 ➡-

Intense, hugely fruity, angostura bitters-perfumed Languedoc red with Syrah-derived freshness and personality. A stunner for under £5.

HUNGARY

1994 River Route Merlot, Hungary   12/20
Medium-bodied ▮

Ageing, tomato juice-like Hungarian Merlot, made with a shot of Vladivar vodka in mind, we assume.

ITALY

1995 Valpolicella, Villa Mura, Sartori   14/20
Light-bodied 🍷🍷 ▮

Good-value, trattoria-friendly Valpol, with soft, easy-drinking cherry fruit flavours.

PORTUGAL

Alta Mesa, Red   13/20
Medium-bodied 🍷🍷 ▮

Sweetish, deep ruby-coloured Portuguese quaffer, with raspberry and raisin fruitiness and a touch of oak character to soften the wine's rustic edges.

SOUTH AFRICA

1995 Landscape Merlot/Cabernet   15/20
Full-bodied 👜👜 ▬

Super-ripe, if slightly raw, oak and blackberry fruity Cape blend, which tasted like a Pinotage to the *Grapevine* team. But then rather a lot of South African reds do.

1995 Ruitersvlei Estate Cinsault, Paarl   13/20
Full-bodied 🍾

Jammy, rooty, old-fashioned Cape red with simple flavours.

SPAIN

1992 Palacio de Leon   13/20
Full-bodied 🍾

Massively oak-chippy, coconut macaroon-style red with a drying finish. Bounty Bars are cheaper.

1994 Marques de Griñon Rioja   15/20
Medium-bodied 👜👜 🍾

Made entirely with Tempranillo grapes from the Rioja Alavesa, this is an elegant, well-judged marriage of oak and soft, strawberry fruitiness at a pretty good price.

UNITED STATES

1994 Saddle Mountain Grenache, Columbia Valley, Washington State   14/20
Full-bodied 👜👜 🍾

Ripe, sweetish, Washington State Grenache with bramble fruit flavours and head-banging alcohol. Good value at under £4.

£5–8

AUSTRALIA

1995 Tyrrells Pinot Noir, South Eastern Australia   15/20
Medium-bodied 👜👜 🍾

Full, eucalyptus and vanilla oak-perfumed Pinot Noir with ripe, strawberry jam-like, warm-climate flavours.

CHILE

1994 Casablanca Cabernet Sauvignon, Casablanca Valley, Santa Isabel Estate   16/20
Medium-bodied 🍷🍷🍷 ▬

Classy, barrel-aged Chilean Cabernet Sauvignon from master winemaker Ignacio Recabarren, showing restrained vanilla pod and sweet cassis-like fruit flavours. An elegant Casablanca red. Here's looking at you, Ig.

FRANCE

1995 Mâcon Rouge Supérieur, Cave de Buxy   15/20
Medium-bodied 🍷🍷 🍾

Structured, plummy southern Burgundy Gamay from the Buxy co-operative, halfway between Burgundy and Beaujolais, both stylistically and geographically.

1995 Two Rivers Merlot/Cabernet, Bordeaux   13/20
Full-bodied 🍾

A botched attempt at a New World-style of red Bordeaux, this is too extracted and dry for its own safety.

GERMANY

1992 Dornfelder, Grosskarlbacher Osterberg Trocken, Rainer Lingenfelder   16/20
Medium-bodied 🍷🍷🍷 🍾

Deeply coloured German curiosity from the quality-minded Rainer Lingenfelder's Rheinpfalz estate, with concentrated black cherry and plum fruitiness and refreshing Italianate acidity.

ITALY

1995 Remole Chianti, Marchesi de' Frescobaldi   15/20
Medium-bodied 🍷🍷 🍾

From the Rufina house of Frescobaldi, this is a herby Sangiovese-based red with plenty of freshness and lively cherry fruitiness.

SOUTH AFRICA

1993 Welmoed Cabernet Sauvignon   12/20
Full-bodied

Marmitey, cooked, dry Cape Cabernet Sauvignon with a bitter finish.

SPAIN

1994 Cosme Palacio, Rioja   16/20
Medium-bodied

Modern, structured Tempranillo Rioja with well-handled spicy oak and the blackberry fruit intensity to age for a year or two in bottle. Rich, succulent stuff.

UNITED STATES

1993 Reds from Laurel Glen   15/20
Full-bodied

A West Coast blend of everything that winemaker Patrick Campbell could get his hands on, this is a robust Californian quaffer with good concentration and backbone.

1993 Columbia Crest Merlot, Columbia Valley, Washington   15/20
Medium-bodied

Silky, soft, coffee-bean-scented Washington State Merlot, with dry tannins that are beginning to dominate the sweet fruit.

1992 Columbia Crest Cabernet Sauvignon, Columbia Valley, Washington   16/20
Medium-bodied

Cheaper by £1 and better balanced than the Merlot, this is a more vibrantly fruity, elegantly oaked Washington State Cabernet Sauvignon with commendable length of flavour.

1992 Villa Mount Eden, Cabernet Sauvignon   14/20
Full-bodied

A cross-regional California Cabernet Sauvignon from the Napa Valley-based Villa Mount Eden winery, this is an alcoholic, very oaky and rather charmless concoction.

1994 Villa Mount Eden, Zinfandel   14/20
Full-bodied
Plonky, alcoholic and somewhat short of fruit intensity. California makes better Zins than this formulaic red.

1993 Firesteed, Pinot Noir, Oregon   15/20
Medium-bodied
Mature, gamey, New World-style Pinot Noir from Oregon, with sweet oak, ripe juicy fruit and a warm aftertaste..

1995 Clos de Gilroy, American Grenache, Cuvée Saint Marcel, California   16/20
Full-bodied
From the literary-pastiche king of the Santa Cruz Mountains, Randall Grahm, this is an intensely fruity, Marcel Proust-inspired Remembrance of Things Past in the southern Rhône. Described by Grahm himself as having 'the peppery, strawberry rhubarbarity of Grenache'. Judge for yourself.

Over £8

AUSTRALIA

1993 Rosemount Estate, Show Reserve Cabernet   16/20
Full-bodied
Nicely maturing, coffee-bean oaky Coonawarra Cabernet Sauvignon with sweet, succulent fruit and smooth tannins.

1994 Mount Langhi Ghiran, Shiraz   16/20
Full-bodied
Intense, minty and freshly milled pepper-like Victorian Shiraz with a tightly bound core of spicy blackberry fruit. Success in recent vintages has encouraged the owners to push the price over the £10 mark.

FRANCE

1990 Châteauneuf du Pape, Domaine Chante Cigale   16/20
Full-bodied
From the excellent 1990 vintage, this is a heady, enticing, alcoholic, spicy Grenache-based blend, which is at its peak now.

1989 Côte Rôtie, Les Ravines, Delas Frères   15/20
Full-bodied 💰 🍾

Gamey, drying northern Rhône Syrah, which is a little hollow in the middle, from the Tournon-based négociant house of Delas Frères.

SPAIN

1994 Pago de Carraovejas, Ribera del Duero   15/20
Medium-bodied 💰 🍾

From a region whose wines are often on the pricey side, this is an idiosyncratic blend of 75 per cent Tempranillo and 25 per cent Cabernet Sauvignon, with leafy, cassis fruit concentration and fine-grained tannins.

Rosé

£3–5

ARGENTINA

Balbi Vineyards, Syrah, Argentina   15/20
Off-dry 💰💰💰 🍾

Exuberant, cherry and strawberry fruit thirst-quencher from Argentina with a crisp dry finish. Chill for optimum enjoyment.

ITALY

1995 Le Trulle, Puglian Rosé   13/20
Dry 💰 🍾

A lightish, simple cherry-stone rosé made from southern Italy's Negroamaro grape. Kym Milne can do better than this dilute example.

£5–8

FRANCE

1995 Château de Sours Rosé, Bordeaux   15/20
Dry 👜👜 ▮
Deeply coloured, modern Bordeaux rosé verging on a *clairet* in style, this raspberry and rhubarb-fruity pink is drinkably fresh but will age nicely, too.

Sparkling

£5–8

FRANCE

1992 Cray, Crémant de Loire   15/20
Dry 👜👜👜 ▮
Elegant, attractively poised Loire fizz with tangy citrus-fruit crispness and Chardonnay finesse.

Over £8

FRANCE

Henri Macquart Champagne Brut   16/20
Dry 👜👜👜 ▮
Creamy, flavoursome sub-£12 house Champagne showing good ripeness and some bottle-aged character.

'R' de Ruinart Champagne Brut   17/20
Dry 👜👜👜 ▮
Rich, honeyed, old-style non-vintage Champagne from a quality-conscious Grande Marque house. Lots of rich, toasty Champagne flavours at under £20.

Kwik Save ☆(☆)

Address: Warren Drive, Prestatyn, Clwyd LL19 7HU

Telephone/fax: 01745 887111; 01745 882504

Number of branches: Approximately 1,000

Opening hours: 9.00am to 5.00pm Monday to Wednesday and Saturday; 9.00am to 8.00pm Thursday and Friday; 10.00am to 4.00pm Sunday

Credit cards accepted: Not generally accepted, although Switch and Delta in some stores

Discounts: None, but whole range 'competitively priced'

Facilities and services: In-store tastings in top branches

Special offers: Occasional special parcels ; regular monthly promotion

Top ten best-selling wines: Liebfraumilch; Hock; Lambrusco Bianco 4 per cent; Rouge de France; Lambrusco Rosé 4 per cent; Lovico Suhindol Cabernet Sauvignon/Merlot; Flamenco Red; Flamenco Medium White; Les Forges, Vin de Pays de l'Aude; Les Oliviers, Vin de Table Rouge

Range:

GOOD: Regional France, Hungary

AVERAGE: Bordeaux, Spain, Portugal, Italy, Bulgaria, Romania, Australia, Argentina, Champagne and sparkling wines

POOR: Germany

UNDER-REPRESENTED: United States, Burgundy, South Africa, Chile and just about anything over £3.50

For frozen burgers, sliced white bread and other staples of the delightful British diet, Kwik Save has established itself as one of the cheapest stores in the country. Margins are small, prices are low and frills are kept to a puritanical minimum. You won't find extra-virgin olive oil and caviar at Kwik Save, but if it's the basics you're after, this is the place to save some money.

The same could be said of the Kwik Save wine range, which numbers a greater percentage of sub-£3 bottles than any we've come across. You will search in vain for *cru classé* claret, New World estates or super-Tuscan reds, but most of the leading wine styles are covered – and covered well, as a rule. As Richard Graves, the Prestatyn-based chain's buying controller puts it with a smile, 'We can sell wines at £4.99, you know, but we have to offer people a £2 off voucher first.'

The company did not have a brilliant year in 1996, appointing a management consultant to look at its business after disappointing half-year figures. But, as wine consultant and Master of Wine Angela Muir points out, 'Wine is not in the same boat as the rest of the company.' Sales of the 100-strong wine range have increased threefold since Muir was appointed nearly four years ago.

Despite a commitment to provide some of the cheapest wines in the high street, Kwik Save has had to put up its prices this year. 'Even with our lightweight margins policy,' explains Muir, 'an increasing number of our wines have had to be offered at over £3 because of exchange rate problems.' This applies to France and Australia in particular.

The dreaded £3 hurdle was not as difficult to clear as Muir had anticipated, however. 'Some things respond by dying on us, but in one or two cases we were relieved that sales went up with the prices. We don't intend to relax our margins, but we do feel that we can be a bit more adventurous about some of the wines we choose as a result.'

So, thanks to the currency markets, a mould-breaking 35 per cent of the wines on Kwik Save's shelves have crept over £3. Just as well, really. It's 'almost impossible' to find good wines under £3 these days, according to Muir, although she says that 'We can do it on some wines, because £2.99 at Kwik Save is £3.49 in anyone else's language.'

This is true enough, but in its search for low-priced wines, Kwik Save is facing a rapidly drying source of supply – Spain, southern France, Argentina, Germany, Italy, Eastern Europe and (amazingly, given the costs involved) Australia. Other parts of the vinous world are more or less off-limits.

Kwik Save strengthened its wine department this year, with the addition of Justin Addison as wine and spirits buyer, working alongside Richard Graves and Angela Muir. The set-up works as follows: Muir sources a selection of wines and Addison and Graves talk money and make the final cull. 'They decide what to buy and how much of it to take,' says Muir, 'but I have an absolute veto over everything, except the stuff we sell at £1.99. And even then I do my best to make sure that it's drinkable.'

Muir admits that 'We're not doing a frightfully esoteric job.' Instead, what she and the Kwik Save team seek to offer is 'good value, everyday drinking'. Her way of introducing a frisson of interest into the range in future will be to reduce the number of core lines and 'bring in more special parcels, while stocks last'.

Given her background and obvious love of finer wines, Muir would clearly like to include better things. 'It's not a question of dreaming about what I want to see,' she says, 'but sometimes it would be nice to move off the valley floor.' Nevertheless, Muir recognises that she has to take the Kwik Save customer with her (not always an enticing prospect). 'I can't risk the whole range on the assumption that people are going to trade up. We have to have some turnover lines, too.'

The stubbornness (not to mention the low incomes) of many of its shoppers is a problem for Kwik Save. When the chain tried to phase out £1.99 plonk this year, it found that winos and drink-anything slurpers went elsewhere for their cheap vino. Stuff them, would be our reaction. No-one, not even Kwik Save, can make money on £1.99 wines.

The reluctance of customers to reach deeper into their pockets restricts the range to the very cheap and cheerful. Muir has worked miracles in Australia, travelling to the southern hemisphere to blend some really good basic whites and a red, and some of her French and Eastern European wines are more than respectable, but the woman is only human. No-one can find drinkable £2.99 wines from South Africa, New Zealand and Bordeaux.

How can Kwik Save introduce new flavours to its customers and persuade them to spend more on wine? One solution has been a series of in-store tastings, launched this year in some of the better stores. Let's hope they get punters excited about something other than Lambrusco and Flamenco Red. Because if Kwik Save can get its shoppers to trade up, the buying team is well placed to introduce more interesting wines. For the time being, however, the range is stuck in the bargain basement.

White

Under £3

AUSTRALIA

Pelican Bay Medium Dry White, McWilliams   14/20
Medium dry 🍾🍾🍾 ▮
Very impressive for a sub-£3 Aussie white, this blend of Fruity Gordo and Colombard is an aromatic, grapey, citrus fruity quaffer from the Griffith-based McWilliams winery.

Pelican Bay Dry White, McWilliams   14/20
Dry ♠♠♠ ▮
An ultra-fresh, lightly oaked blend of Colombard and Semillon, which gives an early indication of the improved quality of the 1996 vintage. Amazing at under £3.

BULGARIA

1995 Preslav Chardonnay/Sauvignon, Vintage Blend   13/20
Dry ♠♠ ▮
Modern, smoky, citrus fruity Bulgarian blend of the two premium varieties, Chardonnay and Sauvignon Blanc, made in a refreshing, New World-influenced style.

FRANCE

Vin de Pays de l'Hérault Blanc, Domaines Virginie   13/20
Dry ♠♠ ▮
Crisp, zesty Vin de Pays des Côtes de Gascogne-like dry white from the giant Domaines Virginie operation, with attractively tangy freshness.

1995 Grenache Blanc/Colombard, Vin de Pays d'Oc, Val d'Orbieu
                                                    12/20
Dry ▮
Tart, unbalanced Languedoc-Roussillon blend of flabby Grenache Blanc and appley Colombard.

1995 Bordeaux Sauvignon, Cuvée VE   14/20
Dry ♠♠♠ ▮
VE stands for Vite Epargne (Franglais for Kwik Save, ho ho!). This is a reliably fresh, nettley Sauvignon Blanc from Bordeaux négociant, Calvet.

Skylark Hill Very Special White, Vin de Pays d'Oc, Viennet   13/20
Dry ♠♠ ▮
'Very special' might be pushing it a bit, but this southern French blend from the Viennet family domaine is a spicy, full-bodied white with a green-apple bite of acidity.

GERMANY

1995 Valley Home Riesling, Saint Ursula   13/20
Medium sweet 🍷 ▮
Grapey, sweet, one-dimensional attempt at a modern-style German white. The attempt to throw you off the German scent extends to a Bordeaux bottle and the somewhat inappropriate name.

HUNGARY

1995 Hungarian Country Wine, Pinot Gris/Riesling   13/20
Off-dry 🍷🍷 ▮
Lightly spicy, fragrant, well-made Hungarian blend of Pinot Gris and Riesling. A poor person's Alsace.

1995 Hungarian Chardonnay, Mor Region   11/20
Off-dry ▮
Lean, unbalanced Hungarian white dignified only by the word Chardonnay on the label.

1995 Hungarian Pinot Gris, Neszmely   14/20
Dry 🍷🍷🍷 ▮
Weighty, flavoursome, new-wave Hungarian Pinot Gris from the remodelled Neszmely winery. Fresh and pleasantly peppery.

ITALY

Soave, Venier, GIV   14/20
Dry 🍷🍷🍷 ▮
Blended by Kwik Save's own Master of Wine, Angela Muir, this is a soft, ultra-fresh apple-and-pear fruity Veneto white with good weight for a sub-£3 Soave.

SPAIN

Marino, Vino de Mesa Blanco, Berberana   13/20
Dry 🍷🍷 ▮
With a label that looks like a cross between a fried egg and a nuclear explosion, this is a clean, soft seafood white from Rioja giant, Berberana.

Jun Carillo, Fruity Spanish White, Navarra   13/20
Dry 🍾🍾 ▮
Crisp, lime-fresh, northern Spanish white made from the zesty Viura grape.
Pleasant, if rather light.

£3–5

AUSTRALIA

1996 Pelican Bay Chardonnay, Southcorp   14/20
Dry 🍾🍾 ▮
Very fresh, tropical fruity Aussie Chardonnay, with elegantly balanced acidity
rounded out by a hint of smoky oak.

BULGARIA

1995 Barrel-Fermented Chardonnay, Preslav   14/20
Dry 🍾🍾 ▮
We're not entirely convinced that this Chardonnay ever saw the inside of a
barrel. Micro-casks, perhaps. Nevertheless, it's a crisp, well-made new-wave
Bulgarian white with peachy fruitiness and smoky oak.

FRANCE

Skylark Hill Chardonnay, Vin de Pays d'Oc   12/20
Dry ▮
Coarsely flavoured, baked-apple Languedoc-Roussillon Chardonnay, which is
beginning to tire a bit.

SPAIN

1994 Hoya Valley Chardonnay, Gandia   14/20
Dry 🍾🍾 ▮
Ripe, peachy, cleverly packaged Iberian stab at a California Chardonnay, with
oak chip in the ascendant.

Red

Under £3

AUSTRALIA

Pelican Bay Red, McWilliams   14/20
Medium-bodied 👜👜👜 ▮
Juicy, easy-drinking, raspberry fruity Aussie blend from the Riverina-based McWilliams operation.

BULGARIA

1992 Reserve Merlot, Domaine Sakar   14/20
Medium-bodied 👜👜👜 ▮
Smoothly mature, substantially oaked, vanilla-like red. For Rioja lovers on a tight budget.

1992 Reserve Gamza, Lovico Suhindol   14/20
Medium-bodied 👜👜👜 ▮
Savoury, vibrantly fruity, mature red made from one of Bulgaria's most interesting indigenous varieties, with thirst-quenching dry acidity and pure, peppery flavours.

1994 Merlot/Cabernet Sauvignon, Liubimetz   13/20
Full-bodied 👜👜 ▮
Sweet fruit, coconutty oak and a rasp of dry tannins make this Bulgarian blend of Merlot and Cabernet Sauvignon a reasonable buy at around £2.50.

1993 Domaine Boyar Cabernet Sauvignon, Straldja   14/20
Medium-bodied 👜👜👜 ▮
The best balanced of Kwik Save's half-submerged raft of Bulgarian reds, this is a nicely weighted, cassis and cherry fruity Cabernet Sauvignon with attractively smooth flavours.

FRANCE

Vin de Pays de l'Hérault Rouge, Domaines Virginie   13/20
Full-bodied 💰💰 🍷
Reasonably well-balanced, bargain-basement *rouge* with lots of colour and firm blackberry fruitiness.

Les Garrigues, Vin de Pays des Cevennes   13/20
Full-bodied 💰💰 🍷
Faintly peppery, flavoursome blend of Grenache, Syrah and Merlot, with plump, spicy fruitiness and hardish tannins.

Minervois, Val d'Orbieu   14/20
Full-bodied 💰💰💰 🍷
Massively spicy, thyme and angostura bitters-scented Languedoc red, with firm, hot-climate tannins and a good dose of sweet blackberry fruit.

1995 Cabernet Sauvignon, Vin de Pays d'Oc   13/20
Full-bodied 💰 🍷
Attractively grassy Cabernet Sauvignon aromas give way to somewhat dry, over-extracted tannins.

Skylark Hill Very Special Red, Vin de Pays d'Oc, Viennet   12/20
Full-bodied 🍷
An unusual blend of Tempranillo and Syrah, this is a beetrooty, oak-chipped red, which finishes with a rasp of dry tannin. Very Ordinary.

Skylark Hill Merlot, Vin de Pays d'Oc, Gabriel Meffre   14/20
Medium-bodied 💰💰💰 🍷
A vast improvement on the 'Very Special' red, this rich, concentrated Midi Merlot is a well-judged, blackcurrant fruity red at an attractive price.

ITALY

Valpolicella, Venier, GIV   13/20
Light-bodied 💰 🍷
Light, almost rosé-like Italian quaffer with soft raspberry-cordial fruit characters.

1995 Montepulciano d'Abruzzo, Venier, GIV   12/20
Medium-bodied 🍷
Basic, plonky Abruzzo red showing coarse plum-skin fruit characters and hard, dry tannins.

PORTUGAL

1994 Alta Mesa, Vinho Regional Estremadura 13/20
Full-bodied 👜👜 🍾
Cherry fruity, sweetened-up southern Portuguese red blend with an almondy, rustic bite.

José Neiva, Vinho Regional Estremadura 13/20
Full-bodied 👜 🍾
Plummy, sweetly fruity, coffee-bean oak-like Portuguese red with a rustic dry edge.

ROMANIA

1995 Young Vatted Pinot Noir, Dealul Mare 13/20
Medium-bodied 👜 🍾
Oaky, modern-style Pinot Noir, which is a welcome change of direction from the old, tomato-skin-style we know and dislike.

1995 Young Merlot, Danube Meadow 13/20
Medium-bodied 👜 🍾
We like the basic material here, but the raw tannins could do with a polish.

SPAIN

Marino, Vino de Mesa Tinto, Berberana 13/20
Full-bodied 👜👜 🍾
Sawdusty Spanish quaffer with sweetish, raisiny fruit flavours and a whack of alcohol.

Jun Carillo, Navarra 12/20
Full-bodied 🍾
Chewy, confected, oak-chippy Navarra Garnacha with excessively robust tannins.

Promesa Tinto Joven, Vino de Mesa, Cosecheros y Criadores
12/20

Full-bodied 🍾
Jammy, chunky Spanish table wine, which promises a lot more than it delivers.

£3–5

ARGENTINA

1996 Balbi Malbec/Syrah   14/20
Medium-bodied 👜👜 ▯
Youthful, exuberantly fruity Argentine red from the San Rafael-based Balbi winery, showing notes of chocolate and ripe plums.

AUSTRALIA

Pelican Bay Shiraz/Cabernet Sauvignon, McWilliams   14/20
Medium-bodied 👜👜 ▯
Minty, pleasantly smooth, Aussie barbecue red with sweet, juicy fruit and soft tannins.

BULGARIA

1992 Domaine Boyar Cabernet Sauvignon Reserve, Elhovo   11/20
Medium-bodied ▯
Stewed, pruney, old-fashioned Bulgarian red with confected black-pastille characters. Said to be a favourite of His Majesty King Simeon II.

FRANCE

1995 Côtes du Rhône, François Dubessy   13/20
Light-bodied 👜 ▯
Light but quaffable southern Rhône plonk from an appellation that has recently been re-admitted to the Kwik Save list.

Skylark Hill Cabernet Sauvignon/Shiraz, Vin de Pays d'Oc, Calvet
                                                        14/20
Medium-bodied 👜👜 ▯
Pleasantly smooth, chocolatey blend of Cabernet Sauvignon and Shiraz, as the French now appear to call it, made by Bordeaux négociant, Calvet.

1995 Claret, Cuvée VE, Calvet   13/20
Medium-bodied 👜 ▯
Youthful, lightly grassy red counterpart to the Cuvée VE white. Finishes a little thin.

1995 Berloup Royale, Saint Chinian, Val d'Orbieu   15/20
Medium-bodied 🍷🍷🍷 🍾

Characterful, intensely fruity Saint Chinian blend, with ripe cherry and rosemary notes and accessible, sweet tannins.

1995 Domaine Trianon, Saint Chinian, Domaines Virginie   13/20
Full-bodied 🍷 🍾

Oak-chippy, dry and plummy. We prefer the more vibrant Berloup Royale from the same appellation.

1994 Côtes de Malepère, VDQS, Domaine des Bruyères   14/20
Medium-bodied 🍷🍷 🍾

Made from a blend of Merlot, Cabernet Sauvignon, Grenache and Cinsault, this elegant Carcassonne *rouge* is a good claret substitute at around £3.50.

SPAIN

1994 Tempranillo, Berberana   15/20
Medium-bodied 🍷🍷🍷 🍾

Modern, attractively oaked, all-Tempranillo Rioja with intense strawberry fruit flavours and soft tannins.

Sparkling

£3–5

SPAIN

Cava Brunet Brut Reserve   14/20
Off-dry 🍷🍷 🍾

Well-packaged, softly fruity Cava, with sweetness for added commercial appeal.

Over £8

FRANCE

Louis Raymond Champagne, F. Bonnet   13/20
Dry 🛍 ▯
Coarse, cut-price fizz with undistinguished flavours, big bubbles and insufficient bottle age.

Bonnet Brut Heritage Champagne, F. Bonnet   15/20
Dry 🛍🛍 ▯
From the same house, this is a more interesting, toasty, sweetish non-vintage Champagne with an attractively soft mousse.

Fortified

Under £3

SPAIN

Moscatel de Valencia, Gandia   13/20
Very sweet 🛍 ▯
Honey and candied orange-peel-like Spanish sticky, with well-judged fortification and a confected aftertaste. More of a kitchen accessory than a wine.

Majestic ☆☆☆☆

Address: Odhams Trading Estate, Saint Albans Road, Watford WD2 5RE

Telephone/fax: 01923 816999; 01923 819105

Number of branches: 58

Opening hours: Generally 10.00am to 8.00pm Monday to Saturday; 10.00am to 6.00pm Sunday. A few stores have slightly different hours

Credit cards accepted: Access, Visa, Switch, American Express, Diners

Discounts: 'Substantial' discounts on Champagne and sparkling wines over £5.99; 10 per cent off six unmixed bottles; 15 per cent off an unmixed case; and 20 per cent off five cases. Discounts on multi-buys

Facilities and services: In-store tastings, and 13 themed tasting weekends per year; delivery within a 30-mile radius; glass loan

Special offers: Special offers and 'deals' always available

Top ten best-selling wines (by volume): Domaine Le Puts; Fortant Grenache; Mâcon Villages, Louis Page; Pinot Grigio del Veneto, Pasqua; Blanc de Blancs, Henri Lambert; Montagny Premier Cru, Louis Page; Vin de Pays de l'Hérault Rouge; Lindemans Cawarra Semillon Chardonnay; Penfolds Bin 35 Cabernet Sauvignon/Shiraz; Côtes du Rhône Lys d'Or

Range:

GOOD: Bordeaux, Burgundy, Beaujolais, Loire, Rhône, regional France, Germany, Spain, Australia, New Zealand, Champagne and sparkling wines

AVERAGE: Alsace, Italy, Portugal, United States, Chile, South Africa

POOR: Eastern Europe

UNDER-REPRESENTED: Hungary, New World estates

Like a Monopoly-board whizz-kid, John 'Midas' Apthorp, Majestic's chairman, has opened eight new branches during the past year, bringing his tally to 58 stores. The high street may be struggling, but not Majestic. Enjoying a virtual monopoly of its own in the wine warehouse business, Majestic has found

159

Majestic

a formula that works. For the first time since he took over the company, ex-Bejam tycoon Apthorp's Majestic posted a healthy million-pound-plus profit last year.

Majestic's deals-obsessed buyer Tony Mason has been playing the monopoly game himself this year. His insatiable appetite for a coup was aroused following a tip-off that the Swedish monopoly was about to dump huge stocks of wines. Deemed uncompetitive and inefficient, the monopoly was disbanded after privatisation, but was prohibited from dumping its stocks in Sweden.

Enter Mason, on an SAS flight to Stockholm. He tasted a range of mature stocks, which had been kept in excellent condition in cellars tunnelled into the hillsides. As usual, he didn't mess about. Within a day, he was back from Stockholm with 37 lorries in tow containing 40,000 cases of wines, all of which were sold to customers at knockdown prices over the summer.

The average price of a bottle at Majestic has gone up to £4.60 (from £4.04 last year). 'We're getting better at wine that's worth its price tag, whether it's cheap or expensive,' says Debbie Worton, Majestic's marketing manager. With a range of 800 wines from 17 countries (plus 75 sparkling wines and 76 beers and lagers) to choose from, customers are increasingly prepared to buy higher-priced wines. 'Rumour has it,' adds Mason drily, 'that we still sell Liebfraumilch in Croydon, but at 2,000 cases a year, that's just over half a bottle per day per store.'

Customers are continuing to desert France, for South America in particular and the New World in general. Burgundy and the south of France are just about holding their own, but the other so-called classic regions – Bordeaux, Rhône and the Loire – are not doing so well. 'I've got a feeling that wine drinkers between 18 and 30 are not drinking French wine,' says Mason, who is such a staunch Francophile that he blends in with the French growers like a baguette in a boulangerie. Mason is optimistic, though, that the plentiful and largely high-quality 1995 vintage will reverse this trend.

After taking on fine-wine buyer, Chris Hardy, last year, Majestic offered the 1995 vintage of Bordeaux en primeur – a first for the wine warehouse company. 20 red Bordeaux were offered, around 1,000 cases in all, plus 100 cases of California's 1995 Ridge Montebello. 'It was a bit of a revelation, we sold out very quickly,' says Mason. Hardly surprising, given that First Growth Château Mouton-Rothschild, for instance, was offered at £520 a case, when everyone else was selling it at over £600.

Majestic still has a lot of traditionally-minded customers crying out for a good claret. As the successful 1995 Bordeaux en primeur sales indicated, it's not basic claret they're after, but good crus bourgeois in the £8–10 range. It's the same story with Spain, where Majestic do well with Reserva Riojas and wines such as the Guelbenzu from Navarra at over £5 a bottle.

The New World door has well and truly opened and customers are rushing through it. Chile, represented by Santa Rita, Undurraga, Montenuevo (Canepa) and Carta Vieja, the star performer, has been Majestic's fastest-growing country this year. Not difficult, mind you, considering its previously threadbare range of Chileans. And on the back of a Mason foray to the United States, California sales doubled. The list includes the likes of Calera, Joseph Phelps, Ridge, Jade Mountain, Clos du Bois and Clos du Val, but Beringer and Mondavi provide the bulk. Last year, Majestic sold 6,000 cases of Beringer in the £6–£21 price range.

Majestic's response to a patchy South African list was to go to the monolithic Bergkelder. 'They have a big range and we found some really nice wines', says assistant buyer, Jeremy Palmer. Majestic believes there's massive latent demand for South African wines, but its use of the scatter-gun approach to see what will sell and what won't is questionable. Even if the sprawling Bergkelder does comprise a number of individual estates, it still peddles some rather old-fashioned stuff.

The Great Barrier Reef is about the nearest Majestic's wine buyers have come to interesting growers' wines from Australia. 'We've tried to do other things with Australia, but it hasn't worked,' says Mason. Tried and tested Penfolds and Lindemans are what customers want, apparently. This is surprising to us. With Chile and South Africa performing well, perhaps someone at Majestic should invest in a Qantas ticket to the Aussie vineyards.

Majestic customers are still mainly middle-class males with well-lined pockets, who think Majestic *vaut le détour*. But backed up by its enthusiastic, knowledgeable staff, Majestic is also widening its focus, supplying businesses, restaurants, wine bars, directors' dining rooms and the like. 'Five years ago, we were an esoteric minority company,' says Worton. 'Today, we're expanding our customers and broadening the age band. Now everyone's heard of Majestic.'

The new properties this year are in Winchester, the City, Chelmsford, Gidea Park, Reigate, Richmond, Brighton and Peterborough. To turn itself into a truly nationwide company, Majestic now has Leeds, the North and Scotland in its sights. The only problem is finding suitably large locations for converting into wine warehouses.

With expansion in mind, Majestic was anticipating a flotation at the time of going to press. Raising more money would enable the company to buy derelict sites and build more Majestics, while creating a market value for the shares. John Apthorp would then be on the road towards the opening of Majestic's 100th store in the year 2000, with 30 more to follow in the new millennium. Let's hope he's not assessed for street repairs.

White

Under £3

FRANCE

Blanc de Blancs, Henri Lambert   13/20
Dry 👛👛 ▮
Crisp, green apple fruit with a faintly coarse aftertaste, made by Yonne-based merchant Henri Lambert from indeterminate white grape varieties unlikely to include Chardonnay.

1994 Domaine le Puts, Vin de Pays des Côtes de Gascogne, Hugh Ryman   14/20
Dry 👛👛 ▮
Cox's apple and boiled-sweets-style Gascon white, retaining a surprising degree of freshness for a '94.

£3–5

AUSTRALIA

1995 Kalinga Creek Semillon/Chardonnay   13/20
Off-dry 👛 ▮
Fresh, sweetish, confectionery-shop Semillon/Chardonnay, presumably from somewhere in Australia's irrigated Riverland.

1995 Lindemans Cawarra Semillon/Chardonnay   14/20
Dry 👛👛 ▮
Herby, vanilla-fudge-like blend, also made by Southcorp, with a medicinal aftertaste (which is surprisingly appealing). An extra 30 pence goes a long way Down Under.

CHILE

1995 Santa Rita Reserva Sauvignon Blanc   15/20
Dry 👛👛 ▮
Typical of a style that Chile has made its own, this is a tangy grapefruit and tropical fruit Sauvignon Blanc from one of the country's biggest wineries.

ENGLAND

1995 Northbrook Springs White, Bishops Waltham   14/20
Off-dry 💰 ▮
Floral, sweet-pea-like English white made by self-confident Aussie John Worontschak from grapes that just about managed to ripen on the Hampshire Downs.

FRANCE

1995 Fortant de France Sauvignon Blanc, Vin de Pays d'Oc   14/20
Dry 💰💰 ▮
A flavoursome, lime-cordial-like Languedoc white from the Skalli winery in Sète. A good-value quaffer, with an understated Sauvignon Blanc character.

1995 Muscadet de Sèvre et Maine Sur Lie, Château la Touche
15/20
Bone dry 💰💰💰 ▮
A fragrant, richly fruity, organic Muscadet with good weight and characteristic petillance from vinification on its yeast lees.

1995 Chardonnay Vin de Pays d'Oc, Bessière   14/20
Dry 💰💰 ▮
A modern, banana-fruity, southern French Chardonnay, unoaked for maximum flavour impact. The sort of wine the Mâcon region ought to be making at this price.

1995 Bourgogne Chardonnay, Emile Trapet   13/20
Dry 💰 ▮
Faintly bitter Burgundian Chardonnay claiming to be a selection from the best vineyards. Pretty basic stuff.

1993 Château Haut Mazières, Bordeaux   16/20
Dry 💰💰💰 ▮
Stylishly packaged Bordeaux white showing richness, crisp acidity and subtle sweet oakiness. A Semillon-based stunner at under £5.

1994 Chardonnay, Vin de Pays d'Oc, Hugh Ryman   14/20
Dry 💰💰 ▮
A well-made southern French Chardonnay from Hugh 'Grant' Ryman, who has employed a bagful of cellar techniques to add complexity to this peach and melon-fruity, lightly oaked white.

1993 Andante Muscat Gewürztraminer, Ribeauvillé   13/20
Off-dry
Light, sweetened-up, somewhat pointless blend of Alsace's two main aromatic varieties. Both appear to have suffered from the partnership. Time for a divorce.

GERMANY

1993 Cuvée Constantin Rivaner Trocken, Max Ferdinand Richter
15/20
Bone dry
A startlingly dry, lime-crisp Rivaner white from Germany's Mosel Valley. Worth a try at under a fiver.

1994 Jacob Zimmermann Kabinett 1995, Herxheimer Herrlich, Pfalz   12/20
Medium sweet
A gluey, sweet confection, which isn't much better than Liebfraumilch. Not even the Bordeaux bottle can rescue it.

ITALY

1995 Pinot Grigio del Veneto, Vino da Tavola, Pasqua   13/20
Dry
Flat, ripe pear-like north Italian white, with alcohol compensating for lack of flavour.

1994 Chardonnay Atesino   14/20
Dry
Refreshing, unoaked Trentino Chardonnay made by Kiwi Rebecca Salmond, with attractive melon fruit flavours and crisp acidity.

NEW ZEALAND

Waimanu Premium Dry White   10/20
Off-dry
Faintly musty Kiwi white with marked acidity and tart, sweetish, lemon-meringue flavours. New Zealand struggles to make palatable wine under £4.

1995 Stoneleigh Riesling
Off-dry 👜👜 🍾 15/20

A distinctive Kiwi Riesling, with citrus and blackcurrant flavours rounded out by a touch of sweetness and zesty acidity.

SOUTH AFRICA

1995 Drostdy-Hof Chardonnay
Dry 👜 🍾 14/20

Lemon-fresh, boiled-sweets-style Cape Chardonnay, which would have benefited from lower yields in the vineyard.

UNITED STATES

1994 Bel Arbor Sauvignon, Vintners Selection, Mendocino
Dry 👜 🍾 14/20

Smooth, soft, American-style Sauvignon Blanc from Mendocino County, with herby, licoricey notes but negligible varietal character.

£5–8

AUSTRALIA

1994 Ironstone Semillon/Chardonnay, Margaret River
Dry 👜👜👜 🍾 16/20

From the Margaret River-based Cape Mentelle winery, this is a pithy, herby, grapefruity blend of Semillon/Chardonnay, with intensity of flavour and a zing of carbon dioxide gas.

1994 Preece Chardonnay 1994, Mitchelton
Dry 👜👜 🍾 15/20

Lightly oaked, elegant, green olive-like Victorian Chardonnay with a fresh, cool-climate acidity and good length of flavour.

CHILE

1995 Santa Rita Medalla Real Chardonnay, Casablanca
Dry 👜👜👜 🍾 16/20

A crisp Chilean Chardonnay with grapefruity, citrus-like flavours and polished French oak handling.

FRANCE

1995 Reuilly, Beurdin   16/20
Bone dry 🍾🍾🍾 |

Delicate, nettley Loire Sauvignon Blanc. Close your eyes and it could almost be Sancerre, give or take the £6 price tag.

1995 Sancerre Les Mouchottes, Jean Dumont   16/20
Bone dry 🍾🍾🍾 ▬

Ultra-fresh, delicate Sancerre with subtle minerally flavours, rich fruit and structure and a tangy acidity.

1995 Beaujolais Blanc, Duboeuf   14/20
Dry 🍾 |

From the comparatively rare appellation of Beaujolais Blanc, this is a decent, yeasty Chardonnay, which finishes on the lean side.

1994 Ardèche Chardonnay, Vin de Pays de l'Ardèche, Louis Latour   12/20
Dry |

Pongy, farmyardy Rhône white made by Burgundian merchant Louis Latour. On this evidence, he'd be better off staying in Beaune.

1993 Bourgogne Hautes Côtes de Nuits Blanc, Vaucher   12/20
Dry |

Lean, coarsely made hillside white Burgundy from the Nuits Saint Georges-based négociant, Labouré-Roi. The sort of thing that gives white Burgundy a bad name.

1994 Grand Ardèche Chardonnay, Vin de Pays de l'Ardèche, Louis Latour   14/20
Dry 🍾 |

Louis Latour is certainly bold in charging £7 for a *vin de pays* white. This is a buttery-oaky Chardonnay with lots of alcohol sweetness and reasonable fruit concentration. But 'Grand' Ardèche is almost a contradiction in terms.

1993 Vouvray, Marc Brédif   16/20
Off-dry 🍾🍾🍾 ▬

Concentrated, off-dry, estate Vouvray, which has managed to squeeze the best from the Chenin Blanc grape in an average vintage. Honeyed but refreshing.

GERMANY

1994 Scharzhof Riesling, Weingut Egon Müller-Scharzhof   16/20
Medium dry 👜👜 ➡

A classic Mosel Riesling from one of the best estates in Germany. With light-fingered, crisp apple fruitiness and a hint of the garage forecourt, this is a wine with plenty of staying power.

ITALY

1995 Chardonnay del Salento Barrique, Vigneti di Caramia   15/20
Dry 👜👜 🍾

A ripe, pungently oaky, New World-style Chardonnay made in the boot-heel of Italy by Aussie, Kym Milne. Rich, spicy and mouth-filling Puglian white, which finishes a tad dry.

NEW ZEALAND

1995 Twin Islands Sauvignon Blanc   15/20
Dry 👜👜 🍾

With its pungent gooseberry and cat-litter-tray aromas, this Hawkes Bay/Marlborough blend from the Australian Yalumba winery is a well-made introduction to the Kiwi style.

1995 Twin Islands Chardonnay   16/20
Dry 👜👜👜 🍾

Chablis-like blend of Kiwi North and South Island Chardonnays made by the Australian Yalumba winery. Lightly oaked for complexity, this is a deliciously flavoursome white.

1995 Oyster Bay Sauvignon Blanc, Marlborough   16/20
Dry 👜👜👜 🍾

Surprisingly soft and full of stuffing for the cool 1995 vintage, this broad Sauvignon Blanc with its rich, green-bean flavours is one of New Zealand's best.

1995 Oyster Bay Chardonnay, Marlborough   16/20
Dry 👜👜👜 🍾

Chablis-like South Island Chardonnay from the brother-and-sister team of Jim and Rosemary Delegat, with citrusy acidity balanced by buttery, barrel-fermented richness.

SOUTH AFRICA

Fleur du Cap Chardonnay 1995   14/20
Dry 🌡 🍾
Old-fashioned, toffee-fudge-like Cape Chardonnay, which starts off well enough, but then abruptly falls over the edge of Table Mountain.

SPAIN

1994 Marqués de Riscal Rueda Blanco   14/20
Dry 🌡 🍾
A characterful north-west Spanish blend made in Rueda by one of Rioja's most famous bodegas from the local grapes, Viura and Verdejo. A crisp tapas-bar white.

1990 Marqués de Murrieta Rioja Blanco Reserva   15/20
Dry 🌡🌡 ⬤—
Tea-leafy, substantially oaked, traditional white Rioja with searing acidity and a Sherry-like aftertaste. A highly idiosyncratic white made in a near-extinct style.

UNITED STATES

1994 Beringer Fumé Blanc, Napa Valley   13/20
Dry 🍾
A barrel-fermented, top-heavy Napa Valley Sauvignon, which is trying to be a Chardonnay, but ends up falling between two staves.

1993 Coastal Ridge Chardonnay   13/20
Off-dry 🍾
A sweet, buttered popcorn and toffee-oaky California Chardonnay. Strictly for Coca-Cola drinkers.

Over £8

ENGLAND

1992 Thames Valley Vineyards Fumé   16/20
Dry 🛍 ▮

Aussie John Worontschak's best white is one of England's leading wines, although we think £9 a bottle is pushing it a bit. Barrel-fermented lychee and elderflower-scented blend that may change your mind about our national vineyards.

FRANCE

1994 Chablis Saint Martin, Domaine Laroche   15/20
Dry 🛍 ▮

Oak-dominated négociant Chablis at a rather optimistic price. Good life and zip, but finishes a bit tart for the weight of oak.

1993 Gewürztraminer Grand Cru Vieilles Vignes Sonnenglanz, Bott-Geyl   17/20
Medium dry 🛍🛍🛍 ▬▬

Pot-pourri-scented, sweetish Alsace Gewürz from a celebrated *grand cru* site. Rich, powerful, spicy stuff, with enough acidity to keep it on its feet when you've fallen under the table.

GERMANY

1989 Oberemmeler Rosenberg Riesling Auslese, Von Kesselstatt
16/20
Sweet 🛍🛍 ▬▬

Highly concentrated, flavoursome Mosel Valley Riesling from one of our favourite estates, showing grapey, juicy fruitiness and a licoricey aftertaste. All this at under 10 per cent alcohol.

UNITED STATES

1993 Mondavi Napa Chardonnay, Napa Valley   12/20
Off-dry ▮

Stale, cheesy, rancid-butter California Chardonnay padded out with sweetness. Mondavi can do better than this.

Red

Under £3

FRANCE

Vin de Pays de l'Hérault, Chais Beaucairois   13/20
Medium-bodied 👛👛 ▮
It's hard to find anything drinkable at under £2.50, so this cherryish, deeply coloured Midi red is a rare bird.

ITALY

Sangiovese, Daunia   12/20
Light-bodied 👛 ▮
A light, raspberry-lollipop and damson-skin plonk from Puglia.

Il Paesano Merlot del Veneto   12/20
Light-bodied 👛 ▮
Soft, sweetened, faintly grassy Veneto Rosso made from the Merlot grape.

£3–5

AUSTRALIA

1994 Kalinga Creek Shiraz/Cabernet   14/20
Medium-bodied 👛 ▮
Minty, blackcurrant-cordial-style Aussie blend with some added oak character. A decent introductory red.

CHILE

1994 Santa Rita Reserva Merlot, Maule Valley   15/20
Medium-bodied 👛👛👛 ▮
Coffee-bean oak and grassy, lead-pencil fruitiness make this Chilean Merlot a very drinkable, structured, food-friendly, sub-£5 red.

FRANCE

1995 Fortant de France Grenache, Vin de Pays d'Oc   13/20
Medium-bodied 🍷 🍾

A juicy, drinkable, if one-dimensional Midi red, made from southern France's most widely planted grape variety by contemporary arts and wine specialists, Fortant de France.

1995 Côtes du Rhône, Les Chevaliers aux Lys d'Or   14/20
Medium-bodied 🍷🍷 🍾

A more substantial southern French rouge, again made using the Grenache grape as a base. Peppery and medium-bodied, with tannins adding an extra dimension.

1995 Cot, Oisly et Thésée   14/20
Medium-bodied 🍷 🍾

Cot is Loire jargon for south-west France's Malbec grape. This softly fruity, Beaujolais taste-alike from the Oisly et Thésée co-operative dries a bit on the finish.

1995 Domaine des Murettes, Minervois, Viviane et Jean-Louis Bellido   15/20
Full-bodied 🍷🍷 ➖

Concentrated, structured, fragrant red from the hills of the Minervois, at a good price for a domaine red.

1993 Tricastin, Domaine Vergobbi   13/20
Full-bodied 🍷 🍾

A raisiny, old-fashioned southern Rhône rouge with a rustic dry finish.

1994 Crozes-Hermitage, Louis Page   14/20
Medium-bodied 🍷 🍾

Made by Burgundy merchant Labouré-Roi, this is a deeply coloured, faintly spicy, but rather hollow, northern Rhône Syrah.

1993 Château la Perrière, Bordeaux   13/20
Medium-bodied 🍾

Light in colour and aroma, with insufficient fruit to counter the dry tannins and a green, grassy edge – or should that be border?

ITALY

1993 Montepulciano d'Abruzzo, Barone Cornacchia   15/20
Full-bodied 💰💰 ▮
Rich, raisin-sweet Abruzzo red with savoury dry tannins. A mouthful of fruit and good value at just over £4.

1988 Notarpanaro, Taurino, Rosso del Salento   15/20
Full-bodied 💰💰💰 ▮
Old-fashioned, but still youthful, southern Italian *rosso*, with complex flavours of red fruits and raisins and the leathery undertones of maturity.

NEW ZEALAND

Waimanu Premium Dry Red   13/20
Light-bodied 💰 ▮
A Bordeaux-meets-Burgundy admixture of Pinot Noir and Cabernet Sauvignon from Corbans winery, combining raspberry sweetness with rather tart, green-edged acidity.

SPAIN

1992 Puerta Vieja Crianza, Rioja   14/20
Medium-bodied 💰💰 ▮
Smooth, well-priced, coconut and vanilla-sweet Rioja, now at its peak.

1995 Guelbenzu Jardin   15/20
Full-bodied 💰💰 ▭
Super-rich, peppery Navarra red made from old Garnacha vines, which is still a little raw. The borders may be on the green side, but there's plenty of fruit in this particular garden.

1994 Marqués de Griñon, Rioja   15/20
Medium-bodied 💰💰 ▮
A more modern interpretation of Rioja's Tempranillo grape, with vibrant strawberry fruitiness and lightly charred oak.

UNITED STATES

1993 Bel Arbor Merlot   13/20
Medium-bodied 💰 ▮
A chewy, basic, coarse, oaked California red with a jammy-sweet aftertaste.

£5–8

AUSTRALIA

1993 Ironstone Cabernet Shiraz, Margaret River & Swan Valley
15/20

Medium-bodied 🛍🛍 🍾
Green-bean-style blend from Western Australia made by David Hohnen and his Mentelle team. Supple, fine-grained tannins, pure cassis fruit and thirst-quenching acidity.

1993 Preece Cabernet Sauvignon, Mitchelton
14/20
Medium-bodied 🛍 🍾
Light, minty Victorian Cabernet Sauvignon with rather obvious sweet fruit flavours. At this price, we'd expect more concentration and finesse.

CHILE

1992 Santa Rita Medalla Real Cabernet, Maipo
15/20
Medium-bodied 🛍🛍 🍾
Combining ripe blackcurrant fruit and rather softish dry tannins, this is typical of mid-priced Chilean Cabernet Sauvignon, with a veneer of vanilla oak for good measure.

FRANCE

1993 La Cuvée Mythique, Val d'Orbieu, Languedoc
16/20
Full-bodied 🛍🛍🛍 ⬤▬
Broad, herby, flavoursome Languedoc blend with thyme and rosemary aromas. Val d'Orbieu's top red is a richly endowed, plummy modern classic.

1995 Régnié, Duboeuf
14/20
Light-bodied 🛍 🍾
A fresh, pleasantly cherryish expression of the Gamay grape from the 'King of Beaujolais' Georges Duboeuf. More like a Beaujolais-Villages than a full-throttle *cru* Beaujolais.

1995 Chénas, Domaine des Pierres, Georges Trichard   16/20
Medium-bodied 💰💰 ▮

A more exciting manifestation of the Gamay grape, if the word exciting and Gamay aren't a contradiction in terms. This grower's Chénas has the structure and raspberry fruit we expect of a wine selling at £7.50.

1995 Moulin à Vent, Clos des Maréchaux, Duboeuf   14/20
Medium-bodied ▮

Moulin-à-Vent is often the most concentrated and long-lived Beaujolais *cru*. This oak-aged example is a little too dry for its own good.

1995 Bourgueil, Les Cent Boisselées, Pierre-Jacques Druet   15/20
Medium-bodied 💰 ▬

Deeply coloured, pungently grassy Cabernet Franc from one of the Loire Valley's best growers. An elegant, well-defined red with crisply refreshing acidity.

1992 Saint Emilion, Cave Co-op   14/20
Medium-bodied 💰 ▮

Leafy, light, drink-now Right Bank Merlot, which is decently priced and surprisingly drinkable for a 1992.

1993 Château Duplessis, Moulis, Cru Bourgeois, Lucien Lurton
14/20

Medium-bodied 💰 ▬

A youthful, structured, coffee-bean oaky claret from the Moulis appellation. A tad sawdusty and lean.

1993 Bourgogne Hautes Côtes de Beaune, Tasteviné   15/20
Medium-bodied 💰💰 ▮

Well-made hillside red Burgundy showing attractive Pinot Noir perfume, a touch of new oak and solid backbone. One of the better cheap Bourgogne Rouges on the market.

1994 Domaine de la Janasse, Vin de Pays de la Principauté d'Orange
15/20
Full-bodied 💰💰 ▬

Richly hued, southern Rhône *vin de pays* from a domaine based at Châteauneuf-du-Pape. Solid, violet-scented, rustic red with plenty of character.

1994 Mas des Bressades, Costières de Nîmes, Roger Mares   17/20
Full-bodied 👜👜👜 ➡

A splendidly aromatic, come-hither Provençal Syrah with blackberry and black-olive fruit flavours and exuberantly crunchy acidity and concentration. A very serious red at a laughable price.

1994 Lirac, Château d'Aqueria   15/20
Full-bodied 👜👜 ➡

A contrast in style, based on the Grenache grape and showing a thick, roughish texture and a kernel of fruit sweetness.

ITALY

1992 San Crispino Sangiovese di Romagna, Ronco   15/20
Medium-bodied 👜👜 🍾

A mature, well-structured oak-aged Sangiovese, which would probably cost £2 more if it came from Chianti. Plenty of cherryish flavour and character for the price.

1994 Montepulciano d'Abruzzo Vigna le Coste, Barone Cornacchia   15/20
Full-bodied 👜👜 ➡

Rustic, chocolate and damson-skin Montepulciano d'Abruzzo with masses of colour and youthful tannins. A big, beefy red.

SOUTH AFRICA

1994 Drostdy-Hof Merlot   15/20
Medium-bodied 👜👜 🍾

Refreshingly juicy, attractively oaked Cape Merlot made in an elegant, cool-climate style. An excellent alternative to red Bordeaux.

1992 Simonsig Shiraz, Stellenbosch   14/20
Full-bodied 👜 ➡

A very rustic Cape Shiraz, which, in common with many South African reds, ends up tasting a bit like a Pinotage. Drinkable, but make sure you bring a knife and wear a hair-shirt.

1993 Uitkyk Cabernet Shiraz   15/20
Medium-bodied 👜👜 ➡

A more modern Cape red, still showing baked, earthy flavours, but with sufficient mint and spicy oak character to keep the palate entertained.

1989 Fleur du Cap Cabernet Sauvignon 12/20
Full-bodied
Shagged-out Cape Cabernet, which probably tasted better three years ago – or possibly not.

SPAIN

1994 Guelbenzu, Navarra 15/20
Medium-bodied
The modern face of Spanish winemaking is apparent in this elegant, well-crafted Cabernet Sauvignon-like Navarra red. Our only minor criticism is that the oak dries the palate a little.

UNITED STATES

1992 Coastal Ridge Cabernet Sauvignon 13/20
Medium-bodied
Sweet, jammy, confected fruit-pastille red – 'obviously' from California.

1992 Jardin du Soleil Zinfandel 13/20
Medium-bodied
Baked banana and tinned raspberry-flavoured Zinfandel. A rather coarse, jammy number, which would send you sprinting, starkers, from the Garden of Eden.

1993 Kautz-Ironstone Cabernet Franc 16/20
Medium-bodied
Made in the foothills of the Sierra Nevada, this bears little resemblance to Cabernet Franc as we know it. Nevertheless, it's a sweetly oaked, well-priced red that could be a strawberryish Pinot Noir.

Over £8

AUSTRALIA

1991 Wynns Coonawarra Cabernet Sauvignon 15/20
Full-bodied
A smoky, cleverly oaked, vanilla and blackcurrant-pastille Cabernet Sauvignon from Australia's leading red wine region. We prefer the 1992 vintage.

1991 Lindemans Limestone Ridge Shiraz/Cabernet, Coonawarra
17/20

Full-bodied 👜👜👜 ▬–

The quality of the grapes shines through in this elegantly made, age-worthy Coonawarra blend of Shiraz and Cabernet Sauvignon. Coffee-spicy oak and ripe, pure mint and cassis fruit flavours make this a deliciously succulent Aussie red.

FRANCE

1995 St Amour Domaine des Pierres, Georges Trichard   16/20
Medium-bodied 👜👜👜 ▬–

Textbook *cru* Beaujolais with soft, juicy, sweetly textured raspberry fruitiness. Beautifully balanced, intense expression of Gamay at its best.

1995 Saumur Champigny, Cuvée Terres Chaudes, Domaine des Roches Neuves   16/20
Medium-bodied 👜👜 ▬–

Thierry Germain makes some of the most succulent Cabernet Franc reds in the Loire Valley. This lively Saumur Champigny combines cherry fruit, soft tannins and crisp acidity in a refreshing whole. Not quite as good as the landmark 1990.

1991 Cornas, Jean-Luc Colombo   14/20
Medium-bodied 🍾

Cinnamon-spicy, souped-up northern Rhône Syrah from media darling Jean-Luc Colombo. The Cornas from his own vineyards is considerably more interesting.

1992 Château Meyney, St-Estèphe, Cru Bourgeois   16/20
Medium-bodied 👜👜👜 🍾

Even in mediocre vintages such as this, the enjoyable Cordier style emerges. This is a light, well-made Médoc claret with new oak sweetness and surprisingly concentrated, supple fruit.

1993 Château l'Evéché, Pomerol   13/20
Light-bodied 🍾

Light on fruit, heavy on your pocket.

1990 Château Cantemerle, Médoc   15/20
Medium-bodied 👜 🍾

Strongly oaked, and a teeny bit short of stuffing for a *cru classé*, especially one from the much-touted 1990 vintage.

1987 Aloxe Corton, Domaine Latour, Louis Latour   16/20
Medium-bodied 👜👜 ▮

Drying, slightly vegetal Pinot Noir from one of the 1980s' lesser vintages. For all that, it has some mature, gamey fruit flavours and reasonable length on the palate.

1992 Savigny-Vergelesses, La Bataillère, Albert Morot   17/20
Medium-bodied 👜👜👜 ▭

Rich, unfiltered, modern-style Côte de Beaune red Burgundy, with wild strawberry fruitiness, subtle new oak and well-managed tannins. When red Burgundy is as good as this vibrant Pinot Noir, you can see why Pinotphiles make so much fuss about it.

1990 Savigny-Vergelesses, La Bataillère, Albert Morot   16/20
Medium-bodied 👜👜 ▭

Not as open or exuberant as the playful 1992, but this is still a substantial, concentrated red Burgundy, which has something in reserve.

1989 Corton Grand Cru, Domaine Latour, Louis Latour   15/20
Medium-bodied 👜 ▮

Advanced *grand cru* from the négociant house of Louis Latour. We'd expect a 1989 to taste fresher than this rapidly maturing red.

1989 Corton Grancey Grand Cru, Louis Latour   16/20
Medium-bodied 👜👜 ▮

Another Corton, another *grand cru*, but this is considerably more interesting than the straight Corton. It has good depth and sweetness of fruit flavour and shows the plumpness of the vintage.

SPAIN

1991 Marqués de Murrieta Rioja Tinto Reserva   15/20
Medium-bodied 👜 ▭

Old-fashioned Rioja from one of the most traditional bodegas. Oaky, faintly Sherry-like red with rasping acidity and just about enough fruit for balance.

1993 Guelbenzu Evo   17/20
Medium-bodied 👜👜👜 ▭

Iberian stab at a New World style, which has been given the full oak-barrel treatment. This ripe, chocolatey blend of mainly Cabernet Sauvignon with a splash of Merlot reminds us of a top Coonawarra red.

UNITED STATES

1993 Mondavi Napa Pinot Noir, Napa Valley   14/20
Full-bodied 🍷 |
An alcoholic, heavy Californian Pinot Noir with pleasantly oaked, red fruit character. The Mondavi Reserve is a better buy.

1993 Clos du Bois Merlot   14/20
Medium-bodied 🍷 |
Light, chewy, oaky, overpriced Sonoma blend of Merlot and Cabernet Sauvignon. Better value abounds in Australia and Chile.

1991 Clos du Val Pinot Noir, Napa Valley   14/20
Medium-bodied 🍷 |
Plump, ginger-scented Carneros Pinot Noir made by Frenchman Bernard Portet, which is rapidly approaching the end of its life. Pinot Noir is not really Portet's forte.

Sparkling

£5–8

AUSTRALIA

Yaldara Reserve Brut NV   14/20
Off-dry 🍷🍷 |
Basic, Marmitey Aussie fizz, with lemony acidity and some sweetness for balance.

Yaldara Rosé NV   14/20
Off-dry 🍷🍷 |
Pale salmon-pink, attractive raspberryish fruit and commendable freshness and zip.

FRANCE

Bouvet Ladubay Saumur NV   15/20
Dry 🍾🍾 ▮
Appley, structured Loire fizz based on the Chenin Blanc grape. A well-made, mouth-filling sparkler.

Over £8

FRANCE

De Telmont Grande Réserve Brut NV   14/20
Dry 🍾 ▮
A Majestic stalwart, this youthful, well-priced Champagne needs another year in the bottle to soften up.

Oeil de Perdrix NV, Léonce d'Albe   16/20
Dry 🍾🍾🍾 ▮
Delicate onion-skin rosé Champagne, showing elegant strawberry fruitiness and a refreshing, tapering aftertaste.

NEW ZEALAND

Nautilus Cuvée Marlborough NV   15/20
Dry 🍾🍾 ▮
A Pinot Noir-dominated fizz made by Australian winery Yalumba, this is a tangy, lemon sherbet and pineapple-style refresher with good weight.

SOUTH AFRICA

Pongracz Cap Classique NV   16/20
Dry 🍾🍾🍾 ▮
Successful Champagne-style blend of Pinot Noir and Chardonnay with an extremely fine mousse and mature, bottle-developed flavours. One of the New World's best-value sparklers at just under £11.

Marks & Spencer ☆☆☆

Address: 57 Baker Street, London W1A 1DN

Telephone/fax: 0171 935 4422; 0171 487 2679

Number of branches: 293

Opening hours: Variable

Credit cards accepted: Switch, Delta and Marks & Spencer's own card

Discounts: 12 bottles for the price of 11, whether the case is mixed or unmixed

Facilities and services: By-the-case sales; home delivery through Marks & Spencer Wine Cellar (fee per delivery, irrespective of size, is £3.99); in-store tastings

Special offers: Wines of the month

Top ten best-selling wines: White Lambrusco; Oudinot Champagne; Vin de Pays du Gers; Chablis; Cava; Domaine Saint Pierre; Italian white; Italian red; Mandeville Chardonnay; Bucks Fizz

Range:

GOOD: White Burgundy, Chile, Australia, Champagne and sparkling wines

AVERAGE: Loire, Bordeaux, red Burgundy, regional France, Argentina, New Zealand, Italy, Spain, Portugal, Germany, California, Sherry, Port

POOR: Eastern Europe, United States

UNDER-REPRESENTED: Rhône, South Africa

Company tasting rooms tell you a lot about a supermarket's corporate culture. Some are festooned with posters, some are strewn with cardboard boxes, and others are so clean you could eat your lunch off the floor. The inner sanctum of the Marks & Spencer wine department falls squarely into the third category: all scrubbed white surfaces and gleaming taps. Outside the door, food technologists pad down identical corridors dressed in identical uniforms.

The comparison may sound a little unfair, but the twin objectives of cleanliness and conformity still characterise large swathes of the 200-strong M&S wine range. It is no coincidence, in our view, that the company is so popular in Singapore, a country where jaywalkers are flogged and it's illegal to chew gum. M&S is the Singapore of the supermarket sector – cautious, middle-class and highly profitable.

The search for safety and reassurance has resulted in a series of close relationships with suppliers worldwide – Domaines Virginie and Domaine Mandeville in the south of France, La Chablisienne in Burgundy, Rosemount in Australia, Trapiche in Argentina, AGE in Spain, Celliers des Samsons in Beaujolais and the Loire, Montana in New Zealand, Klosterhof in Germany, the KWV in South Africa, Geyser Peak in California and Girelli in Italy.

The result is a rather mixed bag of wines. Sometimes you feel Marks & Spencer's choice is spot-on; at other times, you wonder what they're trying to achieve. Not that the wine range stands still: 40 per cent of the list is new this year, according to wine buyer and Leeds United fan Chris Murphy. 'The rest is our core range, which will be there for evermore,' he says.

The range may be developing, but the suppliers remain pretty much the same. Is this always in the customer's interest? One example will suffice. Murphy went out to New Zealand on what he calls 'the best visit I've ever had' to quadruple the M&S range of Kiwi wines from two to eight. Selecting a decent range mainly from the pretty ropy 1995 vintage in New Zealand was never going to be an easy job. You'd expect to have to shop around a bit to find a few good parcels, but Murphy bought all eight wines from Montana. There's nothing wrong with New Zealand's largest wine producer, but whatever happened to diversity?

Murphy and fellow buyer Jane Kay try to visit all their suppliers at least twice a year – once during the vintage and once when the wines are bottled. This shows admirable dedication to the cause, but is it really necessary? 'If you get out at harvest time,' explains Kay, the only supermarket buyer in Britain with a degree in oenology, 'you can see the quality and quantity of the grapes coming in. That way, you have a greater palette of wines when you go back to make up blends.'

Some might accuse M&S of interfering too much, but Murphy sees the relationship with suppliers as a two-way process. He also rejects the charge of complacency. 'We do do comparative tastings. But if your current supplier can produce exciting new wines that stand out in tastings, what's the point of trying something new? We wouldn't change just for the point of changing.' Fair enough, but our feeling is that the ties with Girelli, Trapiche, Geyser Peak, the KWV and Domaines Virginie could be loosened a little.

Apart from New Zealand, the main areas of development have been South America, where Jane Kay has sourced some excellent Chilean wines from Carmen and La Rosa, and Australia, where the partnership with Rosemount has produced some genuinely exciting new wines from Orange and McLaren Vale.

After some initial reluctance on the part of M&S's rather conservative customers to buy New World wines, that sector now accounts for 25 per cent of sales. 'People are increasingly open to new things,' says Jane Kay. Inevitably, this means that classic areas are suffering a little, with the exception of white Burgundy, where La Chablisienne continues to turn out super-value wines.

M&S is not perhaps the best place to find weird and wacky wines, but a varietal Counoise and two new southern French whites made from Roussanne and Vermentino are promising signs of a willingness to try new things.

The same is true of the lead that Jane Kay has taken in introducing plastic corks at M&S. (The hard work nearly paid off in more than one respect when the subject came up in her Master of Wine exams this year.) There are now 15 wines in the range bottled with plastic corks and, encouragingly, there have been no subsequent shifts in sales patterns.

'It's possible we'll move over entirely to plastic corks,' says Kay, 'except for wines that we expect to develop in the bottle over a period of time. Plastic corks are great, but they're less forgiving than natural ones. And because of possible problems with leakage and oxidation, they demand a higher level of discipline when it comes to quality control.' More work for M&S's team of white-coated technologists.

The other area where M&S deserves praise is for its bright and informative labelling. Waffle is kept to a minimum and the packaging invariably makes you want to take individual bottles off the shelf and place them in your basket. Only Asda has a wine range that looks as good.

M&S's growing band of customers, from Hong Kong to Paris, Singapore to Marble Arch, would seem to agree with us. Value and volume increases in wine are both running at 'over 10 per cent' (as precise as the press office is prepared to be) and new shops are opening at a steady rate. Bordeaux is the latest.

'We've never offered better value for money,' says Murphy, 'and that's reflected in the sales.' Providing this has required a more adaptable approach to profit margins – still some of the highest in the high street overall. M&S offers half a dozen wines under £3 and, to find something drinkable, has had to be a little more flexible. It now offers a promoted red and white every month, and a 12-for-11 deal on mixed and unmixed cases. It has also begun to promote certain wine and food combinations.

More than any other supermarket, M&S finds it easy to sell higher-priced wines, as demonstrated by the presence of a Chablis and a Champagne in its top-ten best-sellers. There is also a rotating range of a dozen finer 'dinner-party wines' in the top 20 stores, which includes good clarets and red Burgundies and even the odd Aussie red. Shouldn't that be TV dinners?

The biggest challenge over the next 12 months for M&S's two buyers is at the other end of the wine market – Germany. 'As a buyer, you've got two choices,' says Jane Kay. 'Either you accept that Germany makes a few very good wines and a majority of not very good wines, or you do something about it.' Working with Klosterhof and Kiwi winemaker Jamie Marfell, M&S is doing its best to make more modern, attractively packaged wines under £5. 'We believe we can turn Germany around,' says Chris Murphy. While they're at it, the buying team could look at California, Argentina, South Africa and parts of Italy, too.

White

Under £3

1995 Vin de Pays du Gers, Plaimont   14/20
Dry 👜👜👜 ▮
A zesty, south-west French blend of mainly Ugni Blanc, with a dollop of Colombard for added zing. A top-ten seller at M&S.

£3–5

AUSTRALIA

Australian Medium Dry, South Eastern Australia, Lindemans
14/20
Off-dry 👜👜 ▮
It's an indication of the low esteem suffered by Riesling that the name of the grape doesn't even appear on the label of this fragrant, lime- and melon-like Aussie white. Come on, mates, there's nothing to be ashamed of.

1995 Bin 501 Semillon/Chardonnay, Southcorp   15/20
Dry 👜👜 ▮
Fresh, lightly oaked blend of Semillon and Chardonnay, made by Philip 'Bin 65' John at Lindemans and showing good, ripe pear-like richness and weight.

1995 Honey Tree Semillon/Chardonnay, Rosemount   16/20
Dry 🍷🍷🍷 ▮

A richer, oakier, more characterful blend of the same two grape varieties. Weighty, complex stuff, in which the herbal freshness of the Semillon and the butter-fudge fruitiness of the Chardonnay are extremely well married.

CHILE

1995 Casa Leona Chardonnay, La Rosa   16/20
Dry 🍷🍷🍷 ▮

From the La Rosa winery in Rapel, this is an excitingly concentrated, unoaked, butterscotch and citrus fruit-style Chardonnay with superb length. M&S may have moved on to the 1996 by the time you read this.

1994 Lontue Chardonnay, Viña San Pedro   14/20
Dry 🍷 ▮

Developed, tropical fruity, unoaked Chilean Chardonnay, made by Frenchman Jacques Lurton. Time for a new vintage.

FRANCE

1995 Vin de Pays des Côtes de Gascogne, Plaimont   15/20
Dry 🍷🍷🍷 ▮

A sizeable proportion of Colombard gives this grapefruity Gascon white added flavour and richness. A very good-value quaffing white.

1995 Gold Label Chardonnay, Vin de Pays d'Oc   13/20
Dry ▮

Lightly splintery Languedoc Chardonnay from Domaines Virginie. Decently made, but marred by a bitter aftertaste.

1995 Domaine Mandeville Chardonnay, Vin de Pays d'Oc   15/20
Dry 🍷🍷🍷 ▮

A much more interesting Languedoc Chardonnay from a model vineyard in the Aude. Peachy, rich and unoaked, this is still bang on form.

1995 Domaine Mandeville Viognier, Vin de Pays d'Oc   14/20
Dry 🍷 ▮

Not quite as good as the 1994, this is a delicately apricotty Viognier, which appears to have suffered from higher vineyard yields.

1995 Roussanne, Vin de Pays d'Oc, Domaines Virginie   15/20
Dry 🍾🍾🍾 ▮

One of a new range of southern French varietals at M&S, this is a rich, honey-
and aniseed-like Languedoc white with exceptional weight and flavour.

1995 Vermentino, Vin de Pays d'Oc, Domaines Virginie   14/20
Bone dry 🍾🍾 ▮

Another interesting Mediterranean varietal, with herby, lemony fruitiness and a
note of pine resin.

1995 Chardonnay, Vin de Pays du Jardin de la France, Celliers des Samsons   13/20
Dry 🍾 ▮

Sharp, northern French Chardonnay from the Haut-Poitou co-operative. Lacks
fruit and charm.

1995 Vouvray, Domaine de la Pouvraie   14/20
Medium 🍾 ▮

Honeysuckle-scented, appley Chenin Blanc with enough sweetness to mask the
grape's rasping acidity.

GERMANY

1995 Johannisberg Riesling, Klosterhof   14/20
Off-dry 🍾 ▮

Simple, zingy, fruity, modern Rheingau Riesling from the Klosterhof co-operative
in Erbach, with a clean, elegant finish.

1995 Zell Castle Riesling Spätlese, Klosterhof   15/20
Medium 🍾🍾 ▮

Subtler German Riesling, this time from the Mosel. A light, delicate wine with
the lime and green-apple flavours typical of the region.

ITALY

1995 Bianco di Puglia, Girelli   13/20
Dry ▮

Neutral, rather over-priced blend of Bombino Bianco (not one we'd heard of,
either) and Trebbiano, which lacks southern Italian weight and character.

1995 Bellaura Bianco di Sicilia, Casa Vinicola Calatrasi   14/20
Dry 👜👜 ▮
A crisp, if innocuous, ripe pear-flavoured white, which is less interesting than its mix of grape varieties (Catarratto, Trebbiano and Viognier) would suggest.

1995 Pinot Grigio della Toscana, Le Rime   14/20
Dry 👜 ▮
Lightly peachy, unoaked, stainless-steel-fermented Tuscan blend of Pinot Grigio and a smidgeon of Sylvaner from the Banfi operation. A bit dilute.

Chardonnay delle Tre Venezie, Girelli   13/20
Dry 👜 ▮
Very light, unoaked, northern Italian Chardonnay, which could just as easily have been made from the flavourless Trebbiano.

1995 Malvasia del Salento   15/20
Dry 👜👜👜 ▮
Stem-ginger and butter-like southern Italian white, with plenty of character and weight and a prickle of carbon dioxide gas.

1995 Frascati Superiore, Pallavicini   14/20
Dry 👜 ▮
Clean, if rather dull, Roman blend of Malvasia del Lazio, Malvasia di Candia and Trebbiano Toscano. We'd like to see a bit more concentration from an estate-bottled Frascati.

NEW ZEALAND

1995 Kaituna Hills Sauvignon Blanc, Marlborough, Montana   14/20
Bone dry 👜 ▮
So green it's almost still on the vine, this cool-climate, cool-vintage Sauvignon Blanc has rather tart flavours of artichoke and runner bean. Fine, if you like that kind of thing.

1995 Kaituna Hills Chardonnay/Semillon, Gisborne, Montana
   14/20
Dry 👜 ▮
Another Kiwi white that appears to have suffered from the adverse weather conditions during the 1995 vintage. Lean, green and lightly oaked.

1995 Kaituna Hills Chardonnay, Gisborne, Montana   15/20
Dry 💰💰 🍾
Richer and fruitier than the other two Kaituna Hills whites, this is a pleasantly spicy, light-bodied Chardonnay with crisp, refreshing acidity.

URUGUAY

1995 Uruguayan Chardonnay, Juanicó   14/20
Off-dry 💰💰 🍾
Uruguay is not Latin America's best-known wine-producing country, but this sweetish, unoaked, stainless-steel-fermented Chardonnay with its fresh green apple notes shows that things are moving in the right direction.

£5–8

AUSTRALIA

1995 Rosemount Chardonnay, Hunter Valley   15/20
Dry 💰💰 🍾
Rosemount has lightened its Chardonnays in recent vintages, we're pleased to say. This peachy fruity, full-flavoured, but lightly oaked Hunter Valley white is a case in point.

FRANCE

1995 Sancerre, Les Ruettes, Cave de Sancerre   15/20
Dry 💰💰 🍾
From the much-improved Sancerre co-operative, this is good-value Sancerre at under £7, with light, nettley fruit and carbon dioxide freshness.

1994 Jeunes Vignes, La Chablisienne   16/20
Dry 💰💰💰 🍾
A hardy annual at M&S, this young vine declassified Chablis from the excellent La Chablisienne co-operative never lets your tastebuds down. No oak, but plenty of buttery fruit.

1995 Petit Chablis, La Chablisienne   15/20
Dry 💰 🍾
In a leaner style, this is a crisp, lemony, unoaked Chablis with delicately flavoured Chardonnay fruit.

1994 Chablis, La Chablisienne   16/20
Dry 💰💰💰 |

For an extra pound, you get a lot more concentration for your money, from this classic, unoaked Chablis. Minerally and attractively honeyed, with a thrust of crisp acidity. You can see why this is in M&S's top-ten best-seller list.

1993 Montagny Premier Cru, Cave de Buxy   14/20
Dry 💰 |

A nutty, smoky oaky, maturing Côte Chalonnaise Chardonnay from the reliable Buxy co-operative. Let down by a coarse, bitter finish.

NEW ZEALAND

1995 Saints Gisborne Chardonnay, Montana   16/20
Dry 💰💰💰 |

Barrel-fermented, coconutty Kiwi Chardonnay from the North Island's Gisborne region, with rich vanilla flavours balanced by citrusy acidity. We want to be in that number...

UNITED STATES

1995 Canyon Road Sauvignon Blanc, Geyser Peak   14/20
Dry 💰 |

Spearminty, rather odd Californian white with ripe grapefruit and gooseberry characters. A decent attempt at a more characterful West Coast-style of Sauvignon Blanc than the norm.

1995 Canyon Road Chardonnay, Geyser Peak   15/20
Dry 💰💰 |

Sweetish, lightly oaked, tropically fruity blend of Chardonnay, Chenin Blanc, Colombard and Semillon, made by Australian Daryl Groom at the Geyser Peak winery. The southern hemisphere does this sort of thing £1 cheaper.

Over £8

AUSTRALIA

1994 Orange Vineyard Chardonnay, Rosemount Estate   17/20
Dry 🍾🍾🍾 ▮

The most elegant of Rosemount's extensive range of Chardonnays, sourced from winemaker Philip Shaw's own cool-climate vineyard in Orange, New South Wales. Beautifully balanced, with cashew nut, popcorn and citrus fruit flavours.

1993 Capel Vale Chardonnay, Special Reserve   15/20
Dry 🍾 ▮

Hefty, barley-sugared, richly worked Western Australian Chardonnay with masses of alcohol and buttered Brazil-nut fruit. A bit pricey at nearly £11. Perhaps half the money went on the faded silver label.

FRANCE

1990 Chablis Premier Cru, Grande Cuvée, La Chablisienne   13/20
Dry ▮

An ageing Chablis, which has seen a number of better days. Starting to come over all leesy and yeasty.

Red

Under £3

FRANCE

1995 Domaine Saint Pierre, Vin de Pays de l'Hérault, Domaines Virginie   12/20
Medium-bodied ▮

Beetrooty blend of Merlot, Syrah and Alicante, with soft tannins and slightly sweetened damson fruit.

£3–5

ARGENTINA

1995 Trapiche Cabernet Sauvignon/Merlot   14/20
Full-bodied 🍷🍷 ▮
Ripe, slightly raisiny Argentine red made from the classic Mendoza combination of Cabernet Sauvignon and Malbec. South America's answer to the Mediterranean south of Italy.

1992 Trapiche Malbec Oak Cask Reserve   14/20
Full-bodied 🍷 ▮
Still youthful, aggressively oaked Argentine Malbec with plum-skin and vanilla characters.

AUSTRALIA

1993 South Eastern Australia Shiraz, Southcorp   15/20
Full-bodied 🍷🍷 ▮
Licoricey, appealingly funky, oak-matured Shiraz blend from every corner of South Australia.

1994 Bin 505 Shiraz/Cabernet, Southcorp   14/20
Medium-bodied 🍷 ▮
Less vibrant than the straight Shiraz, this is a dry, oak-chipped Aussie blend with smooth fruit and an unbalanced aftertaste.

1995 Honey Tree Shiraz/Cabernet, Rosemount   14/20
Medium-bodied 🍷 ▮
Light, quaffable, fruit-juicy Aussie red with simple cherry and blackcurrant flavours.

BULGARIA

1991 Svischtov Cabernet Sauvignon   11/20
Medium-bodied ▮
Rooty, tomato-skin Bulgarian Cabernet Sauvignon with coarse oak character and drying fruit. Switched-off rather than Svischtov.

CHILE

1994 Casa Leona Cabernet/Merlot   15/20
Medium-bodied 👝👝👝 ▪
Leafy, pine-flavoured Chilean Cabernet Sauvignon with a splash of Merlot.
Chile's equivalent of a luncheon claret.

1994 Central Chile Cabernet Sauvignon, Carmen   15/20
Medium-bodied 👝👝 ▪
Distinctively Chilean, essence of blackcurrant-style blend of mainly Cabernet
Sauvignon and Merlot, which has benefited from the soft touch of winemaker
Alvaro Espinoza.

FRANCE

1995 Domaine Mandeville Merlot, Vin de Pays d'Oc   14/20
Medium-bodied 👝👝 ▪
Soft, deeply coloured, grassy Languedoc Merlot with juicy blackcurrant fruit,
supple tannins and a nip of acidity.

1994 Fitou, Mont Tauch   14/20
Full-bodied 👝👝 ▪
Typically characterful Fitou blend of Carignan and Grenache from the excellent
local co-operative in the hills of the Languedoc. A chunky, thyme- and spice-
scented barbecue red.

1994 Domaine Saint Germain, Minervois   13/20
Full-bodied 👝 ▪
Baked, faintly plonky, carbonic-maceration Minervois blend of Syrah, Grenache
and Carignan.

1995 Domaine Mandeville Syrah, Vin de Pays d'Oc   13/20
Full-bodied 👝 ▪
Purple-hued, rather extracted, declassified Minervois from the Mandeville
winery. May soften with a few more months in the bottle. It certainly needs to.

1995 Portan, Vin de Pays d'Oc, Domaines Virginie   13/20
Full-bodied 👝 ▪
Made from the unusual Portan grape crossing, this is a chunky, raspberry and
bubble-gum-like red with soft tannins.

1995 Merlot, Vin de Pays d'Oc, Domaines Virginie   11/20
Medium-bodied 🍾

Green tannic, pongy Languedoc Merlot from Domaines Virginie. Best avoided, unless you've got a peg over your nose.

1994 Gold Label Cabernet Sauvignon, Vin de Pays d'Oc, Domaines Virginie   14/20
Medium-bodied 💰💰🍾

Green-pepper and capsicum aromas, lightish blackcurrant fruit and soft tannins make this a drinkable alternative to red Bordeaux.

1994 Gold Label Pinot Noir, Vin de Pays d'Oc, Domaines Virginie
11/20

Full-bodied 🍾

Extracted, raw, dry Languedoc red proving that good Pinot Noir is a rare and temperamental beast in the Midi. A bit like the Himalayan yeti.

ITALY

Merlot del Veneto, Girelli   13/20
Medium-bodied 💰 🍾

Light and dilute, sweetened-up Venetian confection, apparently made from the Merlot grape.

1994 Rosso di Puglia, Girelli   13/20
Medium-bodied 💰 🍾

A faintly spicy Puglian blend of Primitivo and Negroamaro, which would have benefited from more fruit concentration, less filtration and lower yields.

1995 Cardillo Rosso di Sicilia, Casa Vinicola Calatrasi   15/20
Medium-bodied 💰💰💰 🍾

A much more characterful and true-to-type combination of Sangiovese and herby Nero d'Avola, with soft tannins and plain chocolate and black-cherry notes.

NEW ZEALAND

1994 Kaituna Hills Cabernet/Merlot, Marlborough, Montana 13/20
Medium-bodied 💰 🍾

Weedy, under-ripe, would-be Bordeaux blend from New Zealand's South Island. Too light to support the weight of oak.

SOUTH AFRICA

1995 South African Merlot, Vinfruco   14/20
Medium-bodied 🍷🍷 |

Grassy, softly fruity Cape Merlot with sweetened blackcurrant and vanilla characters and an earthy, rustic aftertaste.

SPAIN

Peñascal, Vino de Mesa Tinto, Antonio Barcelo   13/20
Medium-bodied 🍷 |

Oak-chippy, table-wine blend of Tempranillo and Garnacha, with flavours of overripe banana and desiccated coconut.

Rioja, AGE   13/20
Medium-bodied |

Young, light, sweetish, unoaked Côtes du Rhône-style red, which bears little resemblance to Rioja as we know and love it.

1993 Roseral Rioja Crianza, AGE   14/20
Medium-bodied 🍷 |

More mature, lightly oak-aged Rioja blend of Tempranillo and the rare Mazuelo, showing delicate, if dilute, wild-strawberry fruitiness and a sheen of new oak character.

URUGUAY

1995 Uruguayan Merlot/Tannat   13/20
Medium-bodied 🍷 |

Robust Uruguayan blend of Merlot and Tannat, with decent black-cherry fruitiness and high acidity.

£5–8

AUSTRALIA

1994 Langhorne Creek Cabernet Sauvignon   14/20
Full-bodied 🍷 |

Coarse, mint-humbug fruity, American-oak-influenced Langhorne Creek Cabernet Sauvignon, which tastes more like a Shiraz or a Grenache.

1994 Rosemount Estate Shiraz   17/20
Medium-bodied 💰💰💰 ▐
Spicy, succulent, really attractive Shiraz blended from vineyards in McLaren Vale and Langhorne Creek, showing perfectly judged American oak and excellent definition.

CHILE

1994 Maipo Cabernet Sauvignon Reserve, Carmen   17/20
Medium-bodied 💰💰💰 ▐
Serious, concentrated Maipo Valley Cabernet Sauvignon with beautifully balanced cassis fruit, oak and acidity. Alvaro Espinoza has excelled himself with this stylish, ageworthy Chilean red. Beats every red Bordeaux we can think of under £6.

FRANCE

1995 Fleurie, Celliers des Samsons   15/20
Medium-bodied 💰 ▐
Text-book expression of the Gamay grape at its most abundantly fruity. Concentrated, juicy, exuberantly fresh, red fruit-like Beaujolais *cru*.

1993 Bordeaux Matured in Oak, Dourthe Frères   13/20
Full-bodied ▐
Saturated with coarse dry oak, this is an extracted, rather hefty claret of little finesse.

ITALY

1994 Villa Cafaggio, Chianti Classico   15/20
Medium-bodied 💰💰 ▐
Almond and cherry fruity, refreshingly dry Chianti Classico with plenty of Sangiovese character, good spicy concentration and an attractive aftertaste. Characterful stuff.

NEW ZEALAND

1994 Saints Hawkes Bay Cabernet/Merlot, Montana   16/20
Medium-bodied 🍾🍾🍾 ▮

A New Zealand response to Bordeaux's Saint Julien, this is an elegant, supple-textured Cabernet/Merlot blend with refreshing acidity and lightness of oak. A grassy, delicately crafted red.

SPAIN

1992 Gran Calesa, Costers del Segre   15/20
Medium-bodied 🍾🍾 ▮

Mature, coffee-bean oaky blend of the Franco-Spanish grape varieties, Cabernet Sauvignon, Tempranillo and Merlot, from a pioneering winery just outside Lerida. A softly sweet red, halfway between Rioja and Bordeaux in style.

1988 Marqués del Romeral, Gran Reserva Rioja, AGE   16/20
Medium-bodied 🍾🍾🍾 ▮

Very good value for an eight-year-old Gran Reserva Rioja, this is a delicate, mature, sweetly oaked, vanilla and wild strawberry-like red made from a blend of Tempranillo, Mazuelo and Graciano grapes.

UNITED STATES

1994 Canyon Road Cabernet Sauvignon, Geyser Peak   13/20
Medium-bodied ▮

Basic, oaky, pretentiously packaged Californian blend of Cabernet Sauvignon and Ruby Cabernet from the Geyser Peak winery.

1994 Canyon Road Merlot, Geyser Peak   13/20
Medium-bodied ▮

Soft, quaffable California blend of mainly Merlot with a bit of Ruby Cabernet and Cabernet Sauvignon. Would be good at half the price – provided it had twice the fruit.

Over £8

AUSTRALIA

1993 Rose Label McLaren Vale Shiraz, Rosemount   18/20
Full-bodied 🍷🍷🍷 ➻
Made from low-yielding, old-vine McLaren Vale Shiraz, this is a classic in the
making, with subtle, spicy oak and pure blackberry fruitiness allied to some
remarkably complex flavours. Hats off to winemaker Philip Shaw.

1992 Capel Vale Shiraz   16/20
Full-bodied 🍷🍷🍷 ▮
Peppery, smooth, northern Rhône-style Shiraz, showing Côte Rôtie-like acidity
and elegance. Drier than many Aussie reds.

1992 James Halliday Coonawarra Cabernet Sauvignon   15/20
Medium-bodied 🍷 ▮
Blended by Australia's best-known wine writer, this is a decent, if rather
unexciting, Coonawarra Cabernet Sauvignon, with good-quality blackcurrant
fruit but two, rather than three, dimensions.

FRANCE

1992 Beaune, Clos des Couchereaux, Louis Jadot   16/20
Medium-bodied 🍷🍷 ▮
From one of the best merchants in Beaune, this is a highly drinkable red
Burgundy with spicy new oak and attractive red fruit flavours. Our only
reservation is that the alcohol is on the high side.

1990 Moulin de Duhart, Pauillac, Domaines Rothschild   15/20
Medium-bodied 🍷 ▮
The second wine of Château Duhart-Milon tarted up with lots of new oak.
We'd expect a bit more finesse from the Rothschilds in a great vintage such as
1990.

1989 Les Plantes du Mayne, Saint Emilion Grand Cru   16/20
Medium-bodied 🍷🍷 ▮
Rich, concentrated Merlot, which is approaching its peak, showing evolved
flavours of chocolate, coffee-bean oak and a solid backbone of tannin.

ITALY

1990 Amarone della Valpolicella, Speri   15/20
Full-bodied 👛👛 ➡
Made by Carlo Speri and marketed by Girelli, this is a concentrated, damson fruity, powerfully alcoholic blend of the Valpolicella grapes Corvina, Rondinella and Molinara. Still lively and rich.

1990 Brunello di Montalcino, Val di Suga   16/20
Full-bodied 👛👛 ➡
Vigorous, well-structured Brunello with leafy, almost leathery characters, classy new oak and food-welcoming tannins. A modern Italian classic.

Rosé

£3–5

FRANCE

1995 Rosé de Syrah, Domaines Virginie   14/20
Off-dry 👛 🍾
Soft, sweetish, redcurrant and strawberry summer-pudding rosé.

Sparkling

£3–5

ITALY

Malvasia/Prosecco, Zonin   14/20
Off-dry 🍾🍾 🍷
Sweetish, easy-drinking blend of Malvasia and Prosecco grapes, best drunk within sight of the Bridge of Sighs.

Rosato Spumante, Zonin   13/20
Off-dry 🍾 🍷
Taking its colour from a dash of Merlot , this pink-tinged rosé is a light, sweet, strawberry-cup confection.

SPAIN

Cava, Segura Viudas   13/20
Off-dry 🍾 🍷
Young, fruity, crunchy Cava made from the traditional trio of Macabeo, Xarel-lo and Parellada. Refreshing but simple.

£5–8

AUSTRALIA

1993 Australian Chardonnay, Blanc de Blancs, Southcorp   14/20
Off-dry 🍾 🍷
An all-Chardonnay Aussie fizz made at Seppelts Great Western winery. A sweetish, big-bubbled sparkler that lacks finesse.

NEW ZEALAND

Bluff Hill Sparkling Wine, Montana   15/20
Dry 🍾🍾🍾 🍷
Fresh, transfer-method Kiwi sparkler with tangy acidity and creamy-textured fruit. An elegantly balanced fizz.

Over £8

FRANCE

Veuve de Medts, Premier Cru Brut, Union Champagne   15/20
Dry 🍾🍾 |
Improved from last year's blend with added reserve wine, this is a fruity, easy-drinking Champagne from the Union Champagne co-operative.

Chevalier de Melline Champagne, Blancs de Blancs Brut, Union Champagne   17/20
Dry 🍾🍾🍾 |
Lemony, elegant, Chardonnay-derived Champagne, also from the Union Champagne co-operative, with yeasty, brioche characters and a soft cushion of mousse.

1989 Oudinot Grand Cru, Champagne Oudinot   16/20
Dry 🍾🍾 |
The Pinot Noir character is particularly strong in this strawberry fruity vintage Champagne backed up by refreshing acidity and a delicate spume.

1990 Champagne de Saint Gall, Premier Cru, Brut   17/20
Dry 🍾🍾🍾 |
Rich *premier cru* Champagne from a great vintage, with excellent weight and concentration. A lovely, malty mouthful.

1985 Champagne Orpale, Union Champagne   14/20
Dry |
Surprisingly tart and coarse for a 12-year-old Champagne, with green malt fruit characters and a bitter aftertaste.

Fortified

£3–5

SPAIN

Fino Sherry, Williams & Humbert   15/20
Dry 🍷🍷🍷 🍾
Fresh, nutty, Marmitey Fino, with a tang of zesty acidity. Great value.

Medium Amontillado Sherry   13/20
Medium 🍷 🍾
Sweetened, aged blend of Amontillado and Oloroso, which leaves the wine between two soleras.

Over £8

PORTUGAL

10 Year Old Port, Morgan Brothers   14/20
Full-bodied 🍷 🍾
Pale, tawny-style Port with spirity, fiery fruit and a raisiny-sweet middle.

20 Year Old Port, Morgan Brothers   15/20
Full-bodied 🍷 🍾
A richer, toffee and almond-sweet Port, showing attractively mature characters and a spirity aftertaste.

Morrison's ☆☆

Address: Junction 41 Industrial Estate, Carr Gate, Wakefield, West Yorkshire WF2 OXF

Telephone/fax: 01924 870000; 01924 875120

Number of branches: 81

Opening hours: Majority 8.30am to 8.00pm weekdays; 8.00am to 6.00pm Saturday; 10.00am to 4.00pm Sunday

Credit cards accepted: Access, Visa, Switch, Delta

Discounts: Up to 10 per cent on six bottles of specific wines

Facilities and services: Occasional in-store tastings; free glass loan.

Special offers: Regular bin-ends and other themed promotions

Top ten best-selling wines: Morrison's Hock; Morrison's Liebfraumilch; Morrison's Lambrusco Bianco; Morrison's Portuguese Rosé; 1995 Marquis de l'Estouval, Vin de Pays de l'Aude; Gabbia d'Oro Rosso; 1995 Merlot del Veneto, Vigneti del Sole; Romanian Country Red; Morrison's Rioja Tinto; 1995 Escoudou, Vin de Pays de l'Hérault Blanc

Range:

GOOD: Regional France, Germany, Champagne and sparkling wines

AVERAGE: Australia, United States, Spain, Loire, Bordeaux, Bulgaria, Chile, New Zealand, South Africa, Portugal

POOR: Romania, Italy, Hungary, Greece

UNDER-REPRESENTED: England, Argentina, Burgundy

'How many wines do you stock?' a well-meaning wine journalist once asked the dynamic Yorkshire entrepreneur Ken Morrison. 'Sell, laddie, not stock,' replied the sixty-something chairman and managing director of the eponymous supermarket chain.

Mr Morrison's stack-it-high approach is taken seriously in the wine department. Wander along the aisles of a Morrison's store and you're in danger of tripping over the point-of-sale material and special offers. 'The store-within-

202

a-store approach gives people time to browse,' says wine buyer Stuart Purdie. 'And the longer they're in here, the more they buy.'

Morrison's north and Midlands-based stores are pleasant places to shop. The 'street concept', whereby supermarkets are designed to look like high streets (the irony of this won't be wasted on hundreds of bankrupt bakers, butchers and greengrocers up and down the country), encourages a relaxed feel, true to the company's market-trader origins. As Purdie puts it: 'You're not being rammed up the backside by Mrs Smith trying to get to the cornflakes.' You should be so lucky.

Competitive prices are the focus of attention here, with the emphasis on what a Turkish bazaar trader once termed 'big cheapness'. Some of the deals are outrageously good for the consumer, if not necessarily for the supplier. Hearing that the Swedish drinks monopoly was flogging off some surplus stock this year, Stuart Purdie leapt aboard a plane to Stockholm and came back with 38,000 cases of bargains – including a delicious 1992 Ürziger Würzgarten Riesling Spätlese from Robert Eymael at £3.15 a bottle, £3 below the normal retail price (now sadly sold out).

Indeed, you can often find the best prices on given wines at Morrison's, although Asda and occasionally Somerfield run it pretty close. The other strong point in Morrison's favour is that all of its 81 stores carry the entire 380-strong wine range. Many of the chain's competitors list window-dressing wines in only a handful of top stores.

Morrison's best stores also carry a supplementary fine wine range (anything from Mouton-Cadet to the second wines of top Bordeaux châteaux depending on the store), although Purdie dislikes the term. 'I would much rather call them "wine-rack wines",' he says.

The wine range doesn't change enormously from year to year at Morrison's. Purdie has expanded his North American range, listing new wines from California, Oregon and Washington State. South Africa and Chile have also benefited from fresh additions. (The New World as a whole now accounts for just over 9 per cent of Morrison's wine sales.) But continuity is the watchword at Morrison's.

There has been evidence of trading up by wine drinkers over the last 12 months, according to Purdie, with Hock, Liebfraumilch and Lambrusco, the Muzak of winemaking, in decline. Nevertheless, he admits that: '£2.99 is still a crucial price point. In some cases we've had to squeeze our margins to hit it. We're a supermarket above all, not just a wine merchant, and we have to recognise that most of our customers are frightened of spending more than £4 on a bottle of wine.'

Purdie has been with Morrison's for five years now. In the first two or three years, he changed the range substantially, introducing wines that might once have seemed revolutionary in Bradford and Wakefield. 'Someone said I'd been smoking wacky baccy when I bought our first Australian sparkling wine four years ago,' he remembers.

Perhaps he ought to take a few more puffs on the joint, as we've begun to feel that his range needs fresh inspiration. Morrison's has updated its packaging this year, dispensing with the yellow and black 'M' on its 60-strong own-label range, but other parts of the list would benefit from a spring-clean, too.

Purdie's workload is a heavy one. So the imminent arrival of a new number two (still to be appointed when we went to press) may enable him to make more forays into the vineyard and cellar. This would bring in a few more original wines. It would also, pace Ken Morrison, boost sales even further.

White

Under £3

BULGARIA

1995 Bear Ridge Chardonnay, Lyaskovets, Kym Milne   12/20
Dry
Sawdusty, resinous aromas and tart, Granny Smith apple flavours don't quite add up to a balanced whole.

FRANCE

1995 Escoudou, Vin de Pays de l'Hérault Blanc, Caves de Saint Arnould   11/20
Off-dry
A very basic, baked southern French cheapie, with a touch of sweetness and a coarse, bitter aftertaste.

1995 Winter Hill, Vin de Pays de l'Aude   13/20
Off-dry
Last year we felt that the label description 'French wine made by Australians' was laughably silly. But the 1995 Winter Hill is considerably fresher than the 1994, with crisp apple acidity and a hint of residual sweetness.

GERMANY

Morrison's Hock, Zimmermann-Graeff   13/20
Medium sweet 👜👜 🍾
Sweet, but not cloyingly so, this is a well-made, basic Hock with floral, grapey fruitiness and a refreshing acidity.

Morrison's Liebfraumilch, Zimmermann-Graeff   13/20
Medium sweet 👜👜 🍾
Pretty similar in style, with a shade more acidity and Germanic bite.

ITALY

Morrison's Lambrusco Bianco, 8.5 per cent   11/20
Medium sweet 🍾
Coarse, fruitless, rather dull Lambrusco, in which the sparkle is the only redeeming factor.

PORTUGAL

Val Longa White, Borges   14/20
Dry 👜👜👜 🍾
A light, gingery, northern Portuguese blend of local varieties, with dry, super-crisp acidity and a distinctive, nutty character. Interesting stuff.

£3–5

AUSTRALIA

1995 Coldridge Estate Chenin/Chardonnay/Colombard   13/20
Off-dry 👜 🍾
Straining to limbo under the £3.50 barrier has done this normally reliable Aussie white few favours. It's drinkable enough, but lacks real excitement and depth.

Wyndham Estate TR2 Riesling   13/20
Medium 👜 🍾
A very sweet, lemon-and-lime confection, which falls into the one-glass wonder category. Make sure there are six of you around the table when you open the bottle.

CHILE

1995 Gato Blanco Sauvignon Blanc, San Pedro   15/20
Dry 👝👝👝 ⌷

Typical of the 1995 vintage in Chile, this soft, full, grapefruity Sauvignon Blanc has plenty of aroma and fresh flavour for the price.

1995 Castillo de Molina Reserve Chardonnay, San Pedro   15/20
Dry 👝👝👝 ⌷

Another Chilean white made by Frenchman Jacques Lurton at the super-modern San Pedro winery. The toasty, coconutty oak may attract the odd termite, but the freshness and pineapple fruitiness add a sheen of class to the wine.

ENGLAND

1993 Three Choirs Estate Premium, Medium Dry   14/20
Medium 👝👝 ⌷

With its pungent elderflower and gooseberry aromas, this hedgerow-style West Country white is a refreshing, off-dry summer picnic quaffer.

FRANCE

1995 Château de Laurée, Bordeaux Blanc Sec   14/20
Dry 👝👝 ⌷

The aromas on this Bordeaux blend of Sauvignon Blanc, Semillon and Muscadelle are a little underwhelming, but the wine is fresh, delicately grassy and clean on the palate. A little more fruit concentration wouldn't go amiss.

1994 Château Saint Galier, Graves Blanc   13/20
Dry ⌷

The 1994 vintage of this oak-aged Graves blend is beginning to flag, so look out for the 1995, as the underlying wine is well made.

1993 Mâcon Villages, Jean-Pierre Teissèdre   13/20
Dry ⌷

Another wine that needs a change of vintage. It's full and honeyed, but a little flabby around the jowls.

1994 Muscadet de Sèvre et Maine sur lie, Domaine des Charmilles   14/20
Dry 🍾 ▮

A step up from basic Muscadet, with rounded pear and apple fruitiness. Still, it lacks the zip of fresh *sur lie* Muscadet.

1994 Pinot Blanc, Vin d'Alsace, Tradition, Preiss Zimmer   15/20
Dry 🍾🍾 ▮

Ripe, peachy white from the under-appreciated Pinot Blanc grape, which cloys far less than many Alsace wines. Attractive, refreshing stuff.

1995 James Herrick Chardonnay, Vin de Pays d'Oc   15/20
Dry 🍾🍾 ▮

Elegant, minerally Chardonnay from Englishman James Herrick's southern French vineyards near Narbonne, showing restrained, spicy oak and melony fruitiness.

GERMANY

1995 Zeltinger Himmelreich Riesling Kabinett, Ewald Pfeiffer
15/20

Medium 🍾🍾🍾 ▮

With its sweet pea, floral fragrance, light-bodied, grapey fruitiness and characteristically crisp Germanic acidity, this is a very good introduction to the potential delights of Mosel Valley Riesling.

1993 Franz Reh Spätlese, QmP   14/20
Medium sweet 🍾🍾 ▮

In its distinctive blue bottle, this blend of German grape varieties is a step up from the Liebfraumilch and Hock brigade – or should that be Gruppe. Grapey, floral and slightly oily.

ITALY

1994 Orvieto Classico, Uggiano   13/20
Dry 🍾 ▮

A basic, rather diluted Umbrian quaffer with apple-purée fruitiness and medium weight.

NEW ZEALAND

1995 Sacred Hill Sauvignon Blanc, Hawkes Bay 15/20
Dry 🍯 ▮
From the comparatively decried 1995 Kiwi vintage, this is a restrained Hawkes
Bay Sauvignon Blanc with herbal, Semillon-like fruitiness. But, at nearly £7, it's
no steal.

ROMANIA

1994 Romanian Chardonnay, Murfatlar 12/20
Off-dry ▮
Flat, resinous, sweetened-up Romanian Chardonnay made by resident Aussie
Graham Dixon. Hungary and Bulgaria make far better whites than this.

SOUTH AFRICA

1995 Bottelary Sauvignon Blanc, Stellenbosch 14/20
Dry 🍯 ▮
There's some grassy, genuine Sauvignon Blanc character in this attractively
packaged Cape white, but it doesn't stick around for long.

UNITED STATES

1994 Sutter Home Chardonnay 15/20
Off-dry 🍯🍯 ▮
A well-made and well-priced California Chardonnay from a company that
specialises in sticky Blush wines. Ripe, sweet and buttery, with toffee-fudge and
spicy oak undertones.

£5–8

UNITED STATES

1992 Willamette Valley Vineyard Chardonnay 12/20
Dry ▮
A rancid-butter, Burgundian-style Chardonnay that has seen better days. Lots of
them.

Red

Under £3

FRANCE

Minervois Cellier La Chouf   14/20
Medium-bodied 🍶🍶🍶 |
Soft, approachable Languedoc red with the emphasis on cherry fruitiness and
a whiff of Mediterranean herbs.

1995 Marquis de l'Estouval, Vin de Pays de l'Aude   11/20
Medium-bodied |
Hard, beetrooty, traditional rot-gut *rouge*. The kind of wine that Brussels gives
people money to distil.

1995 Winter Hill, Vin de Pays de l'Aude   14/20
Medium-bodied 🍶🍶🍶 |
Deeply coloured, chocolatey red with grassy, Merlot-style fruit filled out by a
dose of Carignan. Succulently drinkable.

ITALY

Gabbia d'Oro Rosso   12/20
Light-bodied |
Light, sugary, sub-Piat d'Or *rosso*.

1995 Merlot del Veneto, Vigneti del Sole, Pasqua   14/20
Light-bodied 🍶🍶🍶 |
A fresh, softly fruity Venetian red with green-pepper and damson-skin fruitiness
and a thirst-quenching acidity. A good summery quaffer.

PORTUGAL

Val Longa Red, Vinho de Mesa, Borges   14/20
Medium-bodied 🍶🍶🍶 |
A deep-hued Portuguese red at a come-hither price, showing peppery, almost
Côtes du Rhône-like aromas and a nip of dry tannin.

ROMANIA

Romanian Country Red Cabernet Sauvignon/Merlot   11/20
Medium-bodied
From the vineyards of Oltina on the Black Sea, this is far less lyrical than its origins would suggest. Bitter, raisiny and overcooked.

SOUTH AFRICA

Noble Cape Red, Paarl   12/20
Medium-bodied
Old-fashioned, sweetly soupy, hot-region Cape red made from a pot-pourri of grape varieties.

£3–5

AUSTRALIA

1995 Coldridge Estate Shiraz/Cabernet Sauvignon   13/20
Medium-bodied
Simple, tutti-frutti Aussie red with a raspberry-lollipop sweetness and tart acidity.

CHILE

1994 Castillo de Molina, Cabernet Sauvignon, San Pedro   14/20
Medium-bodied
A modern Chilean Cabernet Sauvignon made by former *Grapevine* winemaker of the year, Jacques Lurton, at the San Pedro winery. The oak character blends well with the fresh, finely textured blackcurrant fruitiness.

FRANCE

1995 Côtes du Rhône Villages, Florence Vinaton   14/20
Medium-bodied
Youthful, assertively fruity southern Rhône red with plenty of colour and Beaujolais-style suppleness.

Coteaux du Languedoc, Tradition — 14/20
Full-bodied 👜👜👜 🍾

With a label that looks like a naff duvet cover, this Grenache-based Midi red packs a lot of flavour and tannin for a £3.20 wine. A robust, chunky, autumnal rouge.

1995 Château Jougrand, Saint Chinian — 14/20
Full-bodied 👜👜 🍾

A vivid, purple-hued Languedoc red that underlines the value for money of which the south of France is capable. A savoury, black-cherry fruity blend with attractively herby undertones and tannin.

1994 Domaine du Crouzel, Corbières — 14/20
Full-bodied 👜👜 🍾

The spicy, rosemary-scented character of this Syrah, Carignan and Grenache blend has been mellowed by oak ageing. The result is a subtle, satisfying dry red with faintly rustic tannins.

1994 Chais Cuxac, Cabernet Sauvignon, Vin de Pays d'Oc — 13/20
Full-bodied 🍾

Serge Dubois, the normally reliable winemaker at the Cuxac co-operative seems to have got carried away with the oak staves on this rather astringent, southern French Cabernet Sauvignon.

HUNGARY

1994 Chapel Hill Cabernet Sauvignon, Balatonboglar — 12/20
Medium-bodied 🍾

Unbalanced, tomato-skin-style Cabernet Sauvignon with drying tannins. Kym Milne's Hungarian whites are vastly superior to this.

ITALY

1994 Chianti Classico, Uggiano — 13/20
Medium-bodied 👜 🍾

Cocktail-cherry flavours and dry, oaky tannins make this Chianti somewhat atypical.

MOROCCO

Moroccan Cabernet/Syrah, Berkane   13/20
Full-bodied 🍷 ▮
Pruney, minty Moroccan plonk, which just about passes the magic carpet test. The label is a lot of fun.

ROMANIA

1994 Romanian Pinot Noir Special Reserve   12/20
Medium-bodied ▮
You can just about discern the long-suffering Pinot Noir character on this ageing, beetrooty Romanian plonk. Drink with bortsch.

SPAIN

Morrison's Rioja Tinto, Bodegas Navajas   12/20
Medium-bodied ▮
Aromas of sawdust and green malt dominate this confected Rioja blend.

1992 Remonte Cabernet Sauvignon Crianza, Navarra   15/20
Medium-bodied 🍷🍷 ▮
Mature, oak-aged Navarra Cabernet Sauvignon, whose vanilla-rich fruitiness is reminiscent of a good Rioja rather than a red Bordeaux.

UNITED STATES

1993 Sutter Home California Cabernet Sauvignon   14/20
Medium-bodied 🍷🍷 ▮
Pleasantly ripe, commercial, green-pepper-style California Cabernet Sauvignon with palate-pleasing tannins.

£5–8

FRANCE

1992 Château Caronne Sainte Gemme, Haut Médoc, Cru Bourgeois   14/20
Medium-bodied 🗑 ▮
This cedary-red Bordeaux has developed a few premature wrinkles, as you might expect for a 1992, but it's light and drinkable, if a shade dry on the finish.

UNITED STATES

1993 Willamette Valley Vineyards Pinot Noir   14/20
Medium-bodied 🗑 ▮
Considerably better than the 1991 vintage that we've also come across this year, this oaky, structured Oregonian Pinot Noir has some attractive red fruit characters. Shame about the dry, over-alcoholic finish.

Over £8

FRANCE

1993 Château Teyssier, Saint Emilion Grand Cru   14/20
Medium-bodied 🗑 ▮
Firm, still youthful Right Bank Bordeaux with Merlot-derived sweetness undermined by a green streak of flavour and acidity.

Rosé

Under £3

FRANCE

1995 Rosé d'Anjou, Vincent de Valloire   11/20
Medium |
Sickly sweet, gluey, tart Loire rosé. Strictly for masochists or, if you happen to be having a dinner party, sadists.

PORTUGAL

Morrison's Portuguese Rosé, Borges   12/20
Medium 🍷 |
Lightly fizzy, Mateus rosé clone with a small measure of raspberry fruitiness and thirst-quenching acidity.

SPAIN

Marino Rosé, Berberana   13/20
Off-dry 🍷🍷 |
Spain's answer to Tavel rosé, with soft, slightly sweetened-up fruitiness and plenty of alcohol. Needs fresher acidity.

Sparkling

£3–5

AUSTRALIA

Barramundi Brut, Cranswick Smith   13/20
Off-dry 🍷 ▮
Brashly Australian, tropical and citrus-fruit fizz with mouth-filling flavours and all the finesse of an Aussie Rules wing-back.

ITALY

Gianni Asti, 7.5 per cent   14/20
Sweet 🍷🍷 ▮
A fresh, grapey, sherbety fizz with soft, palate-soothing sweetness. A refreshing drop at the end of a meal.

SPAIN

Cristalino Brut, Cava   14/20
Dry 🍷🍷 ▮
Typical of the improvements we've noted in Cava over the last year, this is a fresh, comparatively elegant, lemony fizz with a crisp, dry finish.

Over £8

FRANCE

Nicole d'Aurigny Brut Champagne   13/20
Dry 🍷 ▮
Tart, youthful, first-base fizz with none of the yeastiness that makes Champagne distinctive. Don't bother reading the French back label.

Paul Hérard, Blanc de Noirs, Demi-Sec   15/20
Off-dry 🍾🍾 ▮
On the dry side for a demi-sec, but this Morrison's stalwart is as good as ever, with its soft, malty mousse, strawberry fruitiness and refreshing, balanced acidity.

Fortified

£3–5

GREECE

Mavrodaphne of Patras, Koutakis   12/20
Full-bodied ▮
Sweet, tawny-hued, earthy Peloponnese plonk. Not even Nana Mouskouri could persuade us to down this.

Nicolas ☆☆☆(☆)

Address: 157 Great Portland Street, London WIN 5FB

Telephone/fax: 0171 436 9338; 0171 637 1691

Number of branches: 9

Opening hours: Varies from store to store

Credit cards accepted: Access, Visa, Switch, American Express

Discounts: 10–20 per cent off selected wines and Champagnes (can be by the bottle). Twice a year, three-for-the-price-of-two offer on selected Bordeaux, and 15 per cent discount on 40-odd brands of Champagne

Facilities and services: Glass loan; home delivery free in central London; 48-hour countrywide delivery service; in-store tastings; free gift wrapping; 'butler' service

Special offers: See under discounts

Top ten best-selling wines: Petites Récoltes Vin de Pays des Côtes de Thau white; Petites Récoltes Vin de Pays du Comté Tolosan white; 1991 Réserve Nicolas Bordeaux; 1993 Crozes Hermitage Rouge; 1995 Saint Véran; 1994 Château Lacaussade Saint Martin Côtes de Blaye; 1994 Château La Grave Bechade; 1995 Côtes de Provence Rosé; Champagne Chaudron et Fils; 1987 Château Pichon Longueville Baron, Pauillac

Range:

GOOD: Bordeaux, Burgundy, Loire, Rhône, Beaujolais, Alsace, Savoie, south-west France, Champagne and sparkling wines

AVERAGE: Provence, Languedoc-Roussillon, Jura, Italy

POOR: Spain

UNDER-REPRESENTED: Germany, Australia, United States

Nicolas

Old hands who remember Nicolas for nothing more than its infamous litre bottle of *vin de table* should take another peek. When Nicolas sold the tarnished family silver to Rémy Martin in 1984, Rémy began the process of improving the chain's downmarket image. In 1988 Pierre Castel, one of France's biggest wines and spirits distributors, bought Nicolas and set about converting it into a high-class, international wine merchant with the accent firmly on French wines.

Nearly 1,300 products adorn the wine list with around 800 in the shops at any one time. The main difference between France and the UK is that the London shops stock an assortment – albeit little more than token – of New World wines. While in France only 20 of the 1,300-strong range are non-French, there are 200 non-French wines in the UK. France is always the focus, though. 'We do better in French wine than in New World,' says UK manager Eric Gandon. 'We are able to sell French wine more easily.'

This is what Nicolas is all about. The staff are French, they are trained in how to sell French wine, and customers come mainly to buy French wines. 'It's not that we want to be seen as invaders,' says Gandon discreetly, 'but we're trying to convey the ambience of a French shop. People like to come in and speak French.'

Nicolas's claim that its wines are typical of their appellations is borne out by a cornucopia of unusual wines, such as Jurançon Sec, Vouvray Moelleux, Savoie and Grain Sauvage from Jura. Lesser-known wines like these offer a different taste from Chardonnay and the more limited French selections available in the high street. And although not always the cheapest, Nicolas's line-up of traditional clarets and Burgundies definitely *vaut le détour*.

The staff are highly knowledgeable and, just as important, keen to impart their knowledge of the wines they're selling, advising on a wine to suit a particular dish or vice-versa, like sommeliers but without the starchy superciliousness. Members of staff undergo La Maîtrise Caviste Nicolas, a four-year course with an exam each quarter. Attention to detail is an important part of the job, right down to tissue-wrapping individual bottles.

True to his Gallic form, Alain Favereau, who buys 30 million bottles a year for Nicolas, styles himself as 'architect, selector and builder' of the range. He never knows what a wine costs before tasting it and never meets a producer unless he's tasted the wine first. He also makes a virtue of his refusal to squeeze suppliers so hard that they have to compromise on quality.

The Nicolas range is still developing. Over the past year the wines from the Ardèche have grown in number and the Paris-centred chain has at last begun to discover the delights of the Languedoc-Roussillon and the value to be had there. A handful of new, small red Burgundy producers has been added to the list, too.

Nicolas

Nicolas doesn't want to be seen as cheap, which is just as well really. 'We are a bit more expensive than the high-street chains, who are working on small profit margins,' says Gandon, 'and our strategy is not necessarily to buy the cheapest.' The problem is that Nicolas's mark-ups are sometimes too high. Why, for instance, buy the red Burgundy, Domaine Maillard, for £14.50, when you can get it at Waitrose for £9.50? Or what about the 1990 Les Ormes de Pez, £22.50 at Davisons and £5 more expensive at Nicolas?

Nicolas was affected more than most by the selective consumer boycott of French goods in protest at French nuclear testing in the autumn of 1995; but, since the beginning of 1996, the market has picked up, with turnover growing by 20 per cent at Nicolas's first eight shops. A ninth shop opened in December 1995 in Covent Garden, and there are plans to open up to 20, all in the London area.

This healthy rate of growth compares with 8 per cent growth in France. But Nicolas' French shops have done well, compared with a general growth rate in France of between 1 and 2 per cent, and their performance has been boosted by cross-Channel shopping. With 250 shops in Paris, and strength in Lyons, Nicolas also extends as far north as Lille, Boulogne, Caen and Le Havre.

The shops look and feel good, more like the well-appointed treasure chest of an independent wine merchant than an off-licence, with bins for everyday wines, wooden racks filled with fine wines standing upright and lying down, separate spaces for handy half-bottles of fine wines, malt whiskies and Champagnes, and newly installed cigar cabinets.

Promotions have become an important part of Nicolas's business: Champagne deals, a third bottle free on a selection of wines and a monthly special offer. In fact, Champagne accounts for 25 per cent of turnover. There are regional French promotions and Nicolas pays a lot of attention to its window and shop displays.

After seven years, Nicolas has finally started to get its message across. Spreading the word has something to do with its affordable Petites Récoltes range of 16 *vins de pays* at £3.95. Improved service and a nod in the direction of more competitive prices are further welcome developments. Nicolas has the finest, the most varied and in some instances the wackiest range of French wines of any UK chain. If only it could bring prices more into line with the rest of the British market.

White

£3–5

FRANCE

1995 Petites Récoltes Nicolas, Vin de Pays du Comté Tolosan
13/20

Dry 🍷 ⅃

Soft, dry, southern French summer white, made from an interesting blend of five grape varieties (Len de l'el, Muscadelle, Dauzac, Semillon and Sauvignon) and showing fresh, pear-like fruit.

Vin de Pays du Jardin de la France, Cépage Chenin, Leon d'Aubert
13/20

Bone dry 🍷🍷 ⅃

Fresh, tangy introduction to the Loire's Chenin Blanc grape, with a typical crisp, lightly honeyed, pear-and-apple fruitiness.

1994 Bordeaux Blanc, Réserve Nicolas
14/20

Dry 🍷 ⅃

Buttery, rounded, lightly toasty Bordeaux Blanc, in which the weight and flavour of the Semillon grape is attractively prominent.

£5–8

FRANCE

1995 Muscadet sur lie Comte de Malestroit, Château de la Noé
15/20

Bone dry 🍷🍷 ⅃

Classic bone-dry, honeyed Muscadet with the richness and concentration of the 1995 vintage and plenty of *sur lie* zip.

1995 Chasselas Vieilles Vignes Réserve, Pierre Sparr et Fils, Alsace
16/20

Dry 🍷🍷 ⅃

Spicy, broad Pinot Gris-like Alsace white with excellent concentration and balancing acidity, made from a rarely seen grape variety.

1995 Muscat Senner, Réserve Particulière, Jean Geiler, Cave Vinicole d'Ingersheim   16/20
Dry 🍾🍾 ▮

A blend of one-third Muscat Ottonel and two-thirds Muscat d'Alsace, this is another aromatic, well-made Alsace white, which finishes with a crisp, dry flourish.

1994 Jurançon Grain Sauvage, Cave des Producteurs de Jurançon
                                                   16/20
Dry 🍾🍾🍾 ▮

An idiosyncratic white made from a highly idiosyncratic grape, the Pyrenean Gros Manseng, showing assertive passion fruit flavours and a distinctive, honeyed twist.

1995 Quincy, Pierre Druet   17/20
Bone dry 🍾🍾🍾 ▮

Minerally, dry, well-structured Loire Sauvignon Blanc with lots of the flintiness you normally associate with top-notch Pouilly-Fumé and very elegant, citrus fruit flavours.

1995 Chardonnay, Vin de Pays des Coteaux de l'Ardèche   16/20
Dry 🍾🍾🍾 ▮

A pure, unoaked, well-balanced southern French Chardonnay from a co-operative that has mastered the art of warm-climate winemaking. Delicately buttery, concentrated stuff.

1995 Saint Véran Les Ombrelles, Terroirs Mâconnais   15/20
Bone dry 🍾 ▮

Fresh, floral, slightly dilute southern Mâconnais white made in a crisp, dry, stainless-steel-fermented style.

Over £8

1995 Menetou-Salon, Domaine Chatenoy, B.Clement et Fils 16/20
Bone dry 🍾🍾 ▮

Broader and more gooseberry-fruity in style than the Quincy, this is another characterful Loire Sauvignon Blanc, with notes of blackcurrant leaf and fermentation, lees-derived complexity and richness.

1993 Montagny Premier Cru, Cave des Vignerons de Buxy   17/20
Dry 🍷🍷🍷 ➡-

One of the best co-operative white Burgundies we've tasted, this is a stylishly oaked Côte Chalonnaise Chardonnay from the Buxy co-op, showing the class you'd expect from a Puligny Montrachet, rather than a more humble Montagny.

1992 Chablis Grand Cru Vaudésir, Les Vaux Sereins   17/20
Dry 🍷🍷 ➡-

Hazelnutty, barrel-fermented *grand cru* Chablis from the landmark 1992 vintage, showing masses of richness and toasty intensity of flavour and the structure to age for a good five years plus. A bit pricey at nearly £30.

1993 Condrieu, Marcel Guigal   18/20
Dry 🍷🍷🍷 ➡-

Powerful, brilliantly made peach and honeysuckle-scented Condrieu from one of the northern Rhône's leading producers. The oak is perfectly handled, allowing the Viognier grape's distinctive character to shine through. There are times when it's worth paying nearly £27 for a wine as good as this.

1990 Brut de Lafaurie, Bordeaux, Domaine Cordier   16/20
Dry 🍷🍷 |

We always wondered what Sauternes did with the grapes that didn't nobly rot on the vine. Now we know. This is a rich, dry, honeyed, nutty blend of Semillon, Sauvignon and Muscadelle from Cordier's top Sauternes property, Château Lafaurie-Peyraguey.

1992 Gewürztraminer, Jean Geiger, Cuvée Sainte Marguerite, Cave Vinicole d'Ingersheim   17/20
Off-dry 🍷🍷🍷 ➡-

Elegant, richly textured, late-harvest-style Gewürz from the excellent Ingersheim co-operative, with exotic lychee flavours, good weight and fresh balancing acidity.

1988 Château Bethanie, Fruitière Vinicole d'Arbois, Arbois Blanc, Savagnin   18/20
Bone dry 🍷🍷🍷 ➡-

Delicious, rich, but dry Jura curiosity, which tastes like a compote of dried fruits marinated in Fino Sherry. Made from the rare Savagnin grape (not to be confused with Sauvignon), this is a stunningly complex one-off wonder.

1990 Vouvray Le Peu de la Moriette Moelleux, Vieilles Vignes, Jean-Claude Pichot   18/20
Sweet 🍷🍷🍷 ●–

From one of the great post-war Loire vintages, this is a stunningly good, concentrated Loire sticky, which shows the Chenin Blanc at its best. Wonderfully honeyed and rich, yet superbly balanced by fresh acidity.

1992 Vouvray La Grande Dame Moelleux, Jean-Claude Pichot
                                               16/20
Sweet 🍷🍷 ●–

The lesser vintage shows through here in this faintly fungal, botrytised Chenin Blanc. Still, it's got good appley, honeyed Vouvray character.

Red

£3–5

FRANCE

1995 Vin de Pays du Comté Tolosan Rouge, Petites Récoltes 14/20
Light-bodied 🍷🍷 ▮

Soft, light summer quaffer made from a bewildering combination of Duras, Fer Servadou, Syrah, Gamay, Merlot, Tannat and Cabernet grapes, with thirst-quenching cherry fruit and barely perceptible tannins.

1994 Vin de Pays de la Principauté d'Orange, Petites Récoltes
                                               13/20
Light-bodied 🍷 ▮

Basic, carbonic-maceration red blend of Grenache, Syrah, Carignan, Cabernet and Merlot, which could be cheaper, given the lack of substance and fruit.

1995 Domaine des Bois du Garn, Côtes du Vivarais, Vignerons Ardéchois   14/20
Medium-bodied 🍷 ▮

Pungent aromas of bitters and spice, and soft blackberry fruit, make this Grenache/Syrah blend a pleasant, if lightweight, Rhône glugger.

1994 Latour de France, Côtes du Roussillon Villages   14/20
Full-bodied 👜 🍾

Latour de France used to be the leading *cru* in the Roussillon until its fall from grace. This chunky, full-flavoured co-op red partly redresses the balance.

1991 Réserve Nicolas Bordeaux Rouge   15/20
Medium-bodied 👜👜 🍾

Fresh, grassy, sub-£5 claret with an attractive bottle-aged complexity and silky tannins. It's well worth paying an extra £1 or so for drinkable house-red Bordeaux like this.

£5–8

FRANCE

1993 Saumur Rouge, Réserve Nicolas, Cave des Vignerons de Saumur   14/20
Medium-bodied 👜👜 🍾

A stalky, green-pepper-scented Loire Cabernet Franc with the light fruit of the 1993 vintage and drying, austere tannins.

1993 Crozes Hermitage, Cave de Tain l'Hermitage   14/20
Medium-bodied 👜 🍾

As you'd expect from the watery 1993 vintage, this is a light, simple Syrah from the co-operative that dominates the appellation. Time to move on to the 1994.

1994 Château La Grave Bechade, Côtes de Duras   15/20
Medium-bodied 👜👜 🍾

Grassy Merlot and Cabernet Franc-style Duras red, with soft, forward, ripe fruitiness. An interesting alternative to Right Bank *petit château* Bordeaux.

1993 Cahors, Clos de la Coutale, V. Bernede et Fils   16/20
Full-bodied 👜👜 🠒

Good tarry, robust Malbec with a smattering of Tannat and Merlot for backbone and suppleness respectively. A herby, sage-like red, which is developing well in bottle.

1994 Château Lacaussade Saint-Martin, Premières Côtes de Blaye
16/20
Medium-bodied 🍷🍷🍷 ▪

Fresh, fruity, modern-style red Bordeaux from the Blaye hills, with succulent red fruit characters and oak-aged suppleness. We'd like to see a few more clarets like this in the high street.

1991 Château Guerry, Côtes de Bourg
14/20
Medium-bodied 🍷 ▪

Drying, Merlot-dominated Right Bank claret, which shows the fallibility of the 1991 vintage. There's more skeleton than flesh here.

Over £8

FRANCE

1994 Saint Joseph Rouge, Cave de Tain l'Hermitage
15/20
Medium-bodied 🍷 ▪

Thick, roasted, faintly agricultural Syrah from the Tain co-op, showing the cherried elegance of Saint Joseph, but needing an extra dimension.

1994 Lirac, Domaine de la Mordorée, Delorme
16/20
Full-bodied 🍷🍷 ▬

Punchy, structured, deeply coloured Grenache/Syrah blend, full of concentrated blackberry fruit and black-olive notes. A wine with plenty of poke.

1993 Mercurey Premier Cru, Les Champs Martins, Domaine F & L Saier
14/20
Medium-bodied 🍷 ▪

A wine whose ripe, gamey aromas are let down by a very dry finish. At around £15, we'd expect more weight from the fabled 1993 vintage.

1992 Maranges Premier Cru, La Fussière, Domaine B. Bachelet Père et Fils
16/20
Medium-bodied 🍷🍷🍷 ▪

From one of the lesser-known appellations of the Côte de Beaune, this is pure, textured, wild strawberry-like Pinot Noir with lots of village character from a top grower in a good vintage.

1993 Chorey-Lès-Beaune, Domaine Maillard   16/20
Medium-bodied 👝👝👝 ▮

Stylish, modern, spicily oaked village red Burgundy from a consistently reliable estate. With the structure of the excellent 1993 vintage, it needs another year or two to reach its peak. But don't be afraid to drink it now.

1992 Beaune Premier Cru, Les Boucherottes, Louis Jadot   16/20
Medium-bodied 👝👝 ▬

A ripe, gamey, raspberryish Côte de Beaune Pinot Noir from one of Burgundy's leading négociants, showing excellent concentration and structure, tapering to a dry finish. Needs food.

1986 Volnay Fremiets, Clos de la Rougeotte, Bouchard Père et Fils
         15/20
Medium-bodied 👝 ▮

Ageing, garnet-hued premier cru red Burgundy from négociant Bouchard Père et Fils. Genuine old-style Pinot Noir, which will soon be eligible for a free bus pass.

1991 Château Tour du Haut Moulin, Haut-Médoc, Cru Grand Bourgeois, Lionel Poitou
         16/20
Medium-bodied 👝👝 ▬

From the curate's egg 1991 vintage, this is a stylish, concentrated, beautifully oaked Médoc claret from a château whose reputation is on the rise. Complex, luscious stuff.

1993 Château de Clairefont, Margaux   14/20
Medium-bodied ▮

The second wine of Château Prieuré-Lichine in a second-rate vintage. Dry, over-oaked and rather charmless.

1991 Château Tour des Termes, Saint Estèphe, Cru Bourgeois
         16/20
Medium-bodied 👝👝👝 ▮

This silky, mature, cru bourgeois red Bordeaux, with sweet, roasted coffee-bean aromas and velvet-textured fruit, is the perfect Christmas claret.

1990 Château Les Ormes de Pez, Cru Bourgeois, Saint Estèphe
17/20

Medium-bodied 👛👛 ▬
From the best Bordeaux vintage of the last decade, this is a stylish, opulently fruity, judiciously oaked *cru bourgeois* claret with plenty of ageing potential and substance, from one of Bordeaux's leading figures, Jean-Michel Cazes.

1981 Château Cap de Mourlin, Saint Emilion, Grand Cru Classé
16/20

Medium-bodied 👛👛 🍶
Surprisingly sprightly for a 16-year-old, this Merlot-dominated claret is a sweet, gamey, mature, Right Bank red with a leathery, dry finish. Great if you're 50-something.

Rosé

£3–5

FRANCE

1995 Vin de Pays des Coteaux de Peyriac Rosé, Petites Récoltes
15/20

Dry 👛👛👛 🍶
Pale, fresh, redcurranty, dry rosé made from a hotchpotch of Grenache, Cinsault, Syrah and Cabernet Sauvignon grapes. A refreshing summer rosé.

£5–8

FRANCE

1995 Les Clos de Paulilles, Collioure Rosé
16/20
Dry 👛👛 🍶
Fresh, deeply coloured, modern-style Roussillon rosé made by the owners of the arts-promoting Château de Jau winery. A full, structured, raspberryish rosé designed to accompany food.

1995 Château de Fonscolombe, Coteaux d'Aix, Cuvée Spéciale

16/20

Dry 🍷🍷 |

Very pale, subtle, elegant Provençal rosé with dry, cherried fruitiness and a long, tapering aftertaste. A southern French rosé that travels well.

Sparkling

£5–8

FRANCE

Monmousseau Touraine Blanc de Blancs, Cuvée J.M. Brut   15/20
Dry 🍷🍷 |

Rich, honeyed Chenin Blanc with a greenish, earthy undertone. A flavoursome, well-made alternative to Champagne.

Over £8

FRANCE

1989 Champagne Jeanmaire Grand Cru Chardonnay Brut   16/20
Dry 🍷🍷🍷 |

A very well-priced, all-Chardonnay *blanc de blancs* vintage Champagne, with toasty freshness and elegantly balancing acidity, particularly for the comparatively warm 1989 vintage.

Fortified

Over £8

FRANCE

1991 Mas Amiel, Maury, Charles Dupuy   16/20
Full-bodied 🎒🎒 ➡

Appealingly rustic, fortified *vin doux naturel* from the wild hills of Maury in the Roussillon, with a mixture of prune and raspberry-jam fruitiness and a tobacco-ish aftertaste. At 16 per cent alcohol, this is an interesting after-dinner drink.

1995 Château de Calce, Muscat de Rivesaltes   16/20
Sweet 🎒🎒🎒 ➡

A rich, top-quality Rivesaltes Muscat, brilliantly made to bring out the exotic, aromatic grapeyness of the Muscat à Petits Grains and Muscat d'Alexandrie varieties. Oak fermentation adds richness, complexity and weight to this fresh, fortified white.

Oddbins ☆☆☆☆(☆)

Address: 31–3 Weir Road, London SW19 8UG

Telephone/fax: 0181 944 4400; 0181 944 4411

Number of branches: 216 (plus 6 Oddbins Fine Wine Stores)

Opening hours: Generally 10.00am to 9.00pm Monday to Saturday; Sunday opening times vary – please ask your local branch for details

Credit cards accepted: Access, Visa, Switch, American Express

Discounts: 10 per cent on mixed cases during weekly tastings; 5 per cent on mixed cases at any time; seven bottles for the price of six on Champagne and sparkling wines at £5.99 and above

Facilities and services: Regular in-store tastings; home delivery free within locality of the shop (minimum one case); glass loan (with deposit)

Special offers: Regular promotions on Champagne and sparkling wines, malt whisky and beer

Top ten best-selling wines: Heidsieck Dry Monopole; Cuvée Napa Brut; 1995 Lindemans Cawarra Colombard/Chardonnay; Glenloth Dry White; Penfolds Rawson's Retreat Bin 21; 1995 Oddbins White, Domaine de Jöy; 1995 Oddbins Red; Perrier Jouët Champagne; Lindemans Bin 65; 1995 Montana Sauvignon Blanc

Range:

GOOD: Burgundy, Bordeaux, Rhône, Alsace, regional France, Spain, Germany, Chile, California, Australia, South Africa, Champagne and sparkling wines

AVERAGE: England, Italy, Eastern Europe, Argentina, New Zealand

POOR: None

UNDER-REPRESENTED: Portugal

You can tell it's spring in the wine trade when a familiar whisper starts to circulate at tastings. With first cuckoo-like seasonality, Oddbins is said to be up for sale. Rumours of the brash, Wimbledon-based chain's impending demise seem to coincide with the appearance of the first daffodils – and to disappear just as quickly.

But in 1996 things were different. This time, Canadian parent company Seagram appeared ready to part with its unruly charge, providing someone would pay the £50 million-plus asking price. Prospectuses were prepared and likely buyers were canvassed (unofficially, of course. Officially, as the speak-your-weight Seagram PR person will tell you with a straight face, Oddbins has never been up for sale).

Various competitors were said to be on the verge of concluding a deal. First Greenalls Cellars, then Tesco, and finally Thresher in the guise of Whitbread were linked to the sale. In the case of Whitbread – the last and apparently the most serious of the suitors – negotiations seem to have failed at the eleventh hour because of a disagreement over product contra-deals. Seagram, like Whitbread, regards its off-licence chain as a handy place to sell its own booze – which helps to explain the presence of Mumm Cuvée Napa and Perrier-Jouët in Oddbins top-ten best-sellers.

Whatever may have happened behind closed boardroom doors, Oddbins survived – to the relief of staff, customers, journalists and anyone who values what's left of diversity in the British high street. For what it's worth, Seagram has committed itself to the future of the wacky off-licence chain. But with its new-found interest in Hollywood, Seagram must regard Oddbins as an increasingly minor part of its business. As one high-street competitor put it: 'For Seagram, Oddbins is a minnow in a very large and potentially dangerous fish tank.'

The spring and early summer brouhaha coincided with movement at the top of the company. Derek Morrison, who ran Oddbins for 11 years, retired to be replaced by Richard Macadam, formerly marketing, buying and logistics director. John Ratcliffe, who was being groomed for the managing director's office, chose to stay at Seagram UK as commercial director instead. Perhaps he knows something we don't. Morrison's departure was one of several senior management changes, which also saw senior buyer Steve 'The Nose' Daniel promoted to marketing and buying executive.

But enough of corporate details. Whatever its place in Seagram's future plans, Oddbins continues to do what it does best – buying and selling exciting, flavoursome and innovative wines from all over the world. To go on doing so during what the staff newsletter described as the 'least comfortable six months in the company's 32-year history' is a tribute to the buying team of Steve Daniel, Nick Blacknell, Adrian Atkinson and Katie MacAulay, as well as to the people who work in Oddbins' 216 branches.

Oddbins

Richard Macadam is confident that, after a 'tough time', Oddbins is back on track. 'Seagram has promised to invest in growing the estate at a rate of 15 new stores per year for the next three years,' he says. The upper limit is 300 shops. More importantly, Seagram has agreed to provide the cash to install Epos in every store (at an estimated total cost of around £1m – one-third of Oddbins' annual profit). 'Epos will give us much more flexibility,' adds Macadam. 'We'll have sales information coming back daily, as opposed to monthly.'

The 'tough time' does not appear to have affected Oddbins' consumers. Since October 1995, according to Steve Daniel, the chain has seen a 'massive upturn', with sales up 10 per cent by value for the first six months of 1996.

The Oddbins formula remains fairly consistent – good service, an irreverent list packed with goodies and Ralph Steadman drawings, and an off-the-wall approach to the subject of wine in general. 'We've tweaked a few areas this year,' says Daniel, 'by adding a few Chilean wines at the top end and increasing our range of South African wines. But otherwise, we've continued to do what we're good at.'

The Cape has been the main focus of activity this year. After a stand-offish, some might say snooty, attitude to South African wines in the past, Oddbins jumped into the deep end in 1996, listing new things from Haute Provence, Fauré, Villiera, Veenwouden, Sentinel, Clos du Ciel and Thelema.

'The South Africans have improved a lot over the last two years,' says Daniel. 'But the reds are going to take a little longer to sort out. The other problem with South Africa is that the boutique producers are tiny and the parcels only last you a month.' Our feeling is that, having lost ground to its high-street competitors in the Cape, Oddbins has now caught up with everyone but Thresher and Waitrose.

Another deliberate area of neglect, English wines, was also remedied in 1996, with the listing of two really good whites from Denbies and Australian John Worontschak. Norton from Argentina is also new to the list this year. And Oddbins has continued to increase its range from the Languedoc-Roussillon, too. 'It's getting better and better every year,' says Daniel. 'And, like the rest of France, the Languedoc-Roussillon had a good vintage in 1995. The only problem is the exchange rate against the franc.'

Australia is not quite as dominant as it once was – earning Oddbins the sobriquet 'Ozbins' in some quarters – but wines from Down Under still account for 30 per cent of sales. Other areas of the New World are catching up, with Chile leading the pursuing pack with 10 per cent of sales, ahead of California and South Africa.

All this adds up to a 1,200-strong wine range, with 250 new lines each year. Isn't the list a little unwieldy? 'We turn the stocks; that's the difference between us and our competitors,' says Daniel. Epos should make it easier to get the right wines into the right branches at the right time.

The policy, as ever, is to buy small parcels on an ad hoc basis, with the tiniest lots sourced for Oddbins' six Fine Wine Stores. These seem to specialise in providing a home for all manner of quirky, and sometimes over-priced, Californian oddities. In general, however, the minimum purchase is 200 cases, which may or may not last the year. 'Our remit is not to offer a constant range,' says Daniel. 'A wine doesn't have to be available for 12 months.'

The key to selling such a broad, complex and constantly changing selection of wines is the enthusiasm of the average Oddbins' manager, still among the best-informed in the business. This is part of the reason why, at £4.97, Oddbins' average bottle sale is impressively high. For California wines it is even higher, at £6 – although this may reflect some over-optimistic West Coast price tags.

Personal store-manager recommendation counts for a lot here, as does the opportunity to brush shoulder pads with the stars. Oddbins' eager-to-learn customers get the chance to 'meet the winemakers' at two well-attended annual fairs in London and Edinburgh, now into their sixth year.

There were still only half a dozen shop-within-a-shop Fine Wine Stores at the time of writing, but two more are on the cards. 'It's very important to find the right place and the right size of shop,' says fine-wine buyer, Katie MacAulay. 'We'd like to open something in the north of England.'

Not that Fine Wine Stores are the only place to buy fine wines. Oddbins will once more be offering 1995 Bordeaux on the shelf, as opposed to *en primeur*, when the wines are released in late 1997. It has bought 35 wines and 'invested a lot of money', according to Steve Daniel. So if you thought you'd missed out on the 1995 jamboree, Oddbins will be worth a visit later in the year.

'Our consumers will have the benefit of looking at the quality of the 1996 vintage before they buy the 1995s,' adds Daniel. 'They don't have to take the risk that others do.' Oddbins has also bought 1994 Ports from 10 houses, and in the late summer of 1996 was about to set off for Burgundy to look at the 1995s.

Oddbins is justifiably proud of its on-shelf initiative with the 1995 clarets – a repeat of what it did in 1990. 'We'll make everyone else look daft, as ever,' says Richard Macadam. This is a little disingenuous. The days when Oddbins ran rings round its competitors may be past, now that Bottoms Up, Wine Rack, Greenalls Wine Cellar and Victoria Wine Cellars have pulled up their socks and garters, but the creative, appealingly quirky chain remains a national British treasure. Whether Seagram, with its eyes fixed on Los Angeles, continues to regard it as such is another matter. Let's hope so.

Wines marked OFW only are available only at Oddbins Fine Wine Stores.

White

Under £3

SOUTH AFRICA

1996 Namaqua Chenin Blanc, Olifants River   13/20
Off-dry 🍷🍷 |
Fresh, cool-fermented, pear-droppy Cape Chenin Blanc from the irrigated
Olifants River region. Good party quaffer.

SPAIN

Marino, Vino de Mesa Blanco, Berberana   13/20
Dry 🍷🍷 |
With a label that looks like a cross between a fried egg and a nuclear explosion,
this is a clean, soft seafood white from Rioja giant, Berberana.

£3–5

AUSTRALIA

1995 Woodford Hill Dry White   14/20
Off-dry 🍷🍷 |
'Dry' might be an overstatement, but this opulent, Riesling-based Aussie white
from Southcorp is an extremely commercial, opal fruity aperitif white.

1995 Lindemans Bin 65 Chardonnay   15/20
Off-dry 🍷🍷 |
Toffee and pineapple-fruity Aussie super-blend from winemaker Phillip John. In
a short vintage, he's maintained the Bin 65 hallmark of ripeness and
approachability.

1995 Penfolds Koonunga Hill   16/20
Dry 🍷🍷🍷 |
Classy, complex, barrel-fermented Aussie Chardonnay with butter and toffee-
fudge richness balanced by beautifully judged, refreshing acidity.

1995 Penfolds Rawson's Retreat Bin 21 Semillon/Chardonnay/Colombard   15/20
Dry 💰💰💰 ▯

Lime-fresh, ice cream soda-like blend of Semillon, Chardonnay and Colombard from Australia's biggest winery, Penfolds, proving that big-volume wines can show character in the right hands. Super stuff.

Glenloth Dry White, South Eastern Australia, Southcorp   13/20
Off-dry 💰 ▯

Sweetish, lemon meringue pie-like white with soft, one-dimensional tropical fruit flavours.

1995 Lindemans Cawarra Colombard/Chardonnay   14/20
Off-dry 💰💰 ▯

Good basic, quaffing Aussie blend of Colombard and Chardonnay, with a hint of toffee and ripe melon fruitiness.

CHILE

1996 Errázuriz Sauvignon Blanc, La Escultura Estate   15/20
Dry 💰💰💰 ▯

Intensely grassy, grapefruity Chilean Sauvignon Blanc from the cool-climate region of Casablanca, showing the weight and concentration of low-yielding vines.

1996 Errázuriz Chardonnay, La Escultura Estate   16/20
Dry 💰💰💰 ▯

Tangy, ultra-fresh Chilean Chardonnay from the same Casablanca Valley vineyard, with 15 per cent Maule Valley material for extra weight. Vanilla oak adds sweetness and complexity here.

1996 Casa Porta Chardonnay   15/20
Dry 💰💰 ▯

From a Catalan-owned vineyard in the Cachapoal Valley, this is a toasty, leesy, partially barrel-fermented Chilean Chardonay, with fresh, lemony fruit and a note of toffee fudge.

ENGLAND

1995 Yellow Hammer, Harvest Wine Group 16/20
Dry 🍾🍾🍾 ▮
Honeysuckle-scented, almost Viognier-like English white from the excellent 1995 vintage, with surprising weight and balance and crisply assertive acidity. Exciting stuff from Aussie John Worontschak.

1995 Denbies Pinot Blanc 15/20
Dry 🍾🍾 ▮
Fresh, nettley English Pinot Blanc from the country's largest wine producer, Denbies, with ripe pear notes and a refreshing spritz. A distinct improvement on previous releases.

FRANCE

1995 Cuvée de Grignon Blanc, Vin de Pays de L'Aude, Foncalieu
14/20
Dry 🍾🍾 ▮
Characterful, aniseedy Languedoc white from the Foncalieu winery, with ripe apple flavours and a blade of crisp acidity.

1995 Philippe de Baudin Sauvignon Blanc, Vin de Pays d'Oc 15/20
Dry 🍾🍾 ▮
Gooseberry and passion-fruit flavours abound in this soft, southern French Sauvignon from BRL-Hardy's winery near Béziers.

1995 Philippe de Baudin Chardonnay, Vin de Pays d'Oc 15/20
Dry 🍾🍾 ▮
Richly commercial, southern French Chardonnay with a noticeable Australian stamp from BRL-Hardy. Textured, full-bodied, lightly oaked stuff.

1995 Domaine Saint Hilaire Chardonnay, Vin de Pays d'Oc, André Hardy 16/20
Dry 🍾🍾🍾 ▮
From a domaine that pioneered new-wave varietal wines in the south of France (André Hardy is nothing to do with BRL-Hardy, by the way), this is a weighty, unoaked Chardonnay with buttery, lightly spicy fruit and a zesty tang of acidity.

1995 Oddbins White, Domaine de Jöy, Vin de Pays des Côtes de Gascogne 14/20
Dry 👜👜 🍾

Fresh, softly fruity New World-influenced Gascon white with a zesty twist. A bit pricey.

GERMANY

1995 Müller-Thurgau, Messmer, Pfalz 16/20
Medium 👜👜👜 🍾

Floral, sweet pea-scented Müller-Thurgau, with lightweight 9.5 per cent alcohol, good concentration and elegant, grapey freshness. Müller-Thurgau doesn't come any better than this.

HUNGARY

1995 Nagyrede Pinot Gris Reserve 14/20
Dry 👜👜 🍾

Smoky, white peach-like Pinot Gris made by Aussie flying winemaker, Kym Milne, at the Nagyrede winery, with attractively honeyed weight and balancing acidity.

ITALY

1995 Segesta Bianco, Vino da Tavola di Sicilia 13/20
Bone dry 👜 🍾

Resinous, sharply acidic Sicilian white made from the local Catarratto and Inzolia grape varieties.

1995 Colli Amerini Bianco, Terre Arnolfe 15/20
Dry 👜👜👜 🍾

Surprisingly successful kitchen sink of Italian varieties (Trebbiano, Verdelho, Grechetto, Garganega and Malvasia Toscana), with full, white-pepper and ripe pear fruitiness and a tonic-water-like zip.

1995 Greco di Puglia 15/20
Dry 👜👜 🍾

Refreshing, well-made Mediterranean white made by Aussie Kym Milne in the boot-heel of Italy, showing plenty of indigenous character and a spicy, orange-peel tang.

1995 Sauvignon, Grave del Friuli, Bidoli   15/20
Bone dry 👜👜 🍾

Elegant, nettley, almost Loire-style Sauvignon Blanc from Italy's best white wine region, with zippy, thirst-quenching acidity. Stylishly packaged.

NEW ZEALAND

1996 Villa Maria Private Bin Gewürztraminer   16/20
Medium dry 👜👜👜 🍾

Sweet, rose-petal-perfumed New Zealand Gewürz from the Auckland-based Villa Maria winery. Weighty, fresh and extremely well made.

1995 Montana Sauvignon Blanc   14/20
Dry 👜 🍾

Light, pleasantly grassy, large-volume Marlborough Sauvignon Blanc, which should have moved on to the superior 1996 vintage by the New Year. A good effort in a difficult vintage.

SOUTH AFRICA

1996 Van Loveren Colombard/Sauvignon Blanc   13/20
Dry 👜 🍾

Decently made, if dilute, warm-climate Cape blend with a smidgeon of grassy Sauvignon Blanc character.

1996 Van Loveren Colombard/Chardonnay   14/20
Dry 👜👜 🍾

From the same Robertson winery, this is a grapefruity, modern, almost Chilean-style blend of Colombard and Chardonnay, with clean, citrusy acidity.

SPAIN

1995 La Cata Blanca, Penedès   13/20
Dry 👜 🍾

Made by Californian Ed Flaherty, this is a soft, faintly soupy blend of Catalonia's Xarel-lo and Parellada grapes. Drink up.

1995 Marqués de Griñon Durius, Vino de Mesa   15/20
Dry 👜👜 🍾

Nettley, ultra-fresh, northern Spanish blend based on the Sauvignon Blanc grape and showing good aromatic lift and crisp, lemony fruit.

UNITED STATES

1994 Mariquita 12/20
Medium dry 🍾
Gooey, coconut and toffee-fudge-like Californian white with a note of eucalyptus. Too mawkish for our liking.

£5–8

AUSTRALIA

1995 d'Arenberg The Olive Grove Chardonnay, McLaren Vale
16/20
Dry 🍾🍾🍾 🍾
Fresh, sweetly oaked, citrus and passion fruity McLaren Vale Chardonnay, with nice richness, good length of flavour and elegant acidity. Almost lives up to the back-label guff.

CHILE

1995 Errázuriz Reserva Chardonnay, La Escultura Estate 17/20
Dry 🍾🍾🍾 ➡
Near perfectly judged, barrel-fermented Casablanca and Maipo Valley Chardonnay made by Kiwi Brian Bicknell. Creamy, intensely fruity white, which demonstrates the full range of the winemaker's art.

1995 Errázuriz Wild Ferment Chardonnay 15/20
Dry 🍾 🍾
Fermented with wild, as opposed to dry, yeasts, this is a honeyed, buttery, barrel-fermented Chardonnay that lacks the verve and intensity of the Reserva. Maybe it just needs a little more time to settle.

FRANCE

1995 Coteaux du Giennois, Balland-Chapuis 15/20
Bone dry 🍾🍾 🍾
Characterful, if rather austere, Loire white with minerally, flinty undertones and nettley fruit. Poor person's Pouilly-Fumé.

1995 Pinot Blanc/Auxerrois, Mann
16/20
Dry 💰💰💰 |

Ripe, perfumed, lightly spicy Alsace blend of Pinot Blanc and Auxerrois, with a surprising amount of depth, weight and character. A richly concentrated white, clearly made from low-yielding vines.

1993 Bourgogne-Hautes-Côtes de Nuits, Jaffelin
16/20
Dry 💰💰💰 |

Showing the lean, lemony acidity of the vintage and plenty of sweet vanilla oak, this is a modern, well-made Hautes Côtes Chardonnay at a pretty good price, from the improving house of Jaffelin.

1995 Menetou-Salon Morogues, Cuvée Eric, Domaine Henry Pellé
17/20
Bone dry 💰💰💰 ▪—

Flavoursome, aniseed and elderflower-like Sauvignon Blanc, labelled in homage to the late Eric Pellé, showing masses of rich, concentrated fruit.

GERMANY

1995 Westhofener Aulerde Bacchus Kabinett, Wittman
15/20
Medium dry 💰💰 |

Floral, delicately aromatic Rheinhessen white made from the Bacchus crossing. Fresh and zippy, but finishes a little green.

1994 Riesling Kabinett Halbtrocken, Messmer
16/20
Off-dry 💰💰 ▪—

Structured, stylish Pfalz Riesling with notes of honey and blackcurrant leaf and a tight core of acidity.

1994 Ockfener Bockstein Riesling Kabinett, Von Kesselstatt
16/20
Medium dry 💰💰 ▪—

Classically petrolly Mosel Riesling, with intense, sweet-and-sour flavours and a crisp green-apple bite. Refreshing stuff from a very classy producer.

ITALY

1995 Villa Gioiosa Grechetto dell'Umbria, Vino da Tavola
14/20
Dry 💰 |

French oak-fermented, Umbrian Grechetto with yeasty, lees-derived flavours and a splintery finish. A rather botched attempt at an international style.

NEW ZEALAND

1996 Villa Maria Private Bin Sauvignon Blanc 16/20
Dry 💰💰💰 ▮
Super-value Kiwi Sauvignon Blanc with passion fruit and gooseberry flavours and a lot more richness than the 1995.

1996 Villa Maria Private Bin Chardonnay 16/20
Dry 💰💰💰 ▮
Rich, complex, appealingly oaked New Zealand Chardonnay with tropical fruit notes, good length of flavour and assertively tangy acidity.

SOUTH AFRICA

1996 Haute Provence Vineyards Sauvignon Blanc 15/20
Bone dry 💰💰 ▮
Nettley, refreshing, cool-climate Cape Sauvignon Blanc with a crisp, elderflower tang and good length of flavour. South Africa's answer to Menetou-Salon.

1996 Haute Provence Vineyards Semillon 16/20
Dry 💰💰💰 ▮
From the same Franschhoek winery, this is a really flavoursome, elegantly concentrated, tea-leafy Semillon with excellent length and character.

1996 Sentinel Chardonnay, Stellenbosch 16/20
Dry 💰💰💰 ▮
Youthful, barrel-fermented Stellenbosch Chardonnay with toast and butterscotch flavours and citrus-fruit acidity. Complex for a £6 Chardonnay.

SPAIN

1994 Viñas del Vero Barrel-Fermented Chardonnay, Somontano
16/20
Dry 💰💰💰 ▮
Typical of the value-for-money Chardonnays emerging from the cool-climate, northern Spanish region of Somontano, this is an intense, buttery-textured Chardonnay with fresh, lemony acidity and well-judged oak.

1994 Viñas de Gain Blanco, Rioja Alavesa 16/20
Dry 💰💰💰 ▮
Barrel-fermented, modern-style blend of Viura and Malvasia, with spicy oak and lemon-peel fruitiness underpinned by considerable richness and a fine backbone of acidity. The best white Rioja we've tasted in ages.

UNITED STATES

1994 Sterling Vineyards Chardonnay   14/20
Off-dry 💰 ▮
Sweetish, nutty, full-blown Napa Valley Chardonnay from the Seagram-owned
Sterling winery. Finishes a little hot and alcoholic.

1995 Fetzer Viognier, Napa County   15/20
Dry 💰 ▮
Confected, apricot jam-like Viognier – currently the hot white grape in
California. Ripe and flavoursome, if a little over-priced at nearly £7.

Over £8

AUSTRALIA

1995 Green Point Chardonnay   16/20
Dry 💰💰 ▬
Classy, cool-climate Chardonnay from a Yarra Valley winery best-known for its
elegant fizz. This is a crafted, full-flavoured, toast and lemon butter-style white
with the acidity to age.

1994 Petaluma Chardonnay   17/20
Dry 💰💰💰 ▬
From the hills of South Australia's Piccadilly Valley, Brian Croser's richly
complex, well-structured Chardonnay combines cool-climate citrus and stone-
fruit flavours with Burgundian barrel-fermentation techniques. Restrained for an
Aussie Chardonnay.

1993 De Bortoli Noble One, Botrytis Semillon, half-bottle (OFW
only)   15/20
Very sweet ▮
Old-fashioned, brandy-snap and mandarin orange-like Semillon sticky, which is
gooey with botrytis, but lacks balancing acidity.

CHILE

1995 Casablanca Santa Isabel Barrel-Fermented Chardonnay
16/20

Dry 👛👛 ❘
Nutty, mealy, intensely flavoured Casablanca Valley Chardonnay from the master of Chilean white wines, Ignacio Recabarren. A spicy, lemony white with toasted oak overtones.

1995 Santa Carolina Reserva de Familia Chardonnay   16/20
Dry 👛👛 ❘
Pineapple-chunk aromas and toasty, citrus fruit flavours make this a good, if still youthful, Chilean Chardonnay, with excellent underlying finesse.

FRANCE

1995 Sancerre La Croix au Garde, Domaine Henry Pellé   17/20
Bone dry 👛👛👛 ➡
Refreshing, flinty, tightly bound Sauvignon Blanc with nettley intensity and impressive length of flavour. Super Sancerre.

1993 Puligny-Montrachet, Louis Carillon   17/20
Dry 👛👛👛 ➡
From one of the best and oldest family-owned domaines in the village of Puligny-Montrachet, this is an intense, minerally, lightly honeyed Chardonnay with beautifully integrated oak and a sturdy backbone of acidity.

1993 Chassagne-Montrachet, Fontaine Gagnard   16/20
Bone dry 👛👛 ➡
Just up the road in neighbouring Chassagne-Montrachet, Richard Fontaine-Gagnard has produced a contrasting style of white Burgundy, with tight, spicy fruitiness and an austere knife-blade of acidity.

1995 Sancerre Cuvée Pierre, Joseph Balland-Chapuis (OFW only)   17/20
Dry 👛👛 ➡
Very pricey, even for a Sancerre, at nearly £20, but this super-ripe, late-picked dry Sauvignon Blanc takes the style to the limits of complexity, with rich, honeyed, botrytis-like notes and delicious length of flavour.

GERMANY

1995 Hochheimer Herrnberg Riesling Kabinett, Franz Künstler
16/20

Medium 🍯🍯 🍷
Aromatic, grapefruity Rheingau Riesling, which is almost reminiscent of the Scheurebe grape, with modern, tangy sweetness and exotic citrus fruit flavours.

1995 Hochheimer Hölle Riesling Spätlese, Franz Künstler　17/20
Medium sweet 🍯🍯🍯 🍷
A step up in concentration, grapey ripeness and intensity, this is a wonderfully fresh Riesling with a lemony intensity that explodes on the palate.

ITALY

1993 Torcolato, Maculan, Vino Dolce Naturale
16/20
Very sweet 🍯🍯 🍷
Made from dried grapes for extra concentration and complexity, this is a tangy, sweet, lemon-peel fresh Italian sticky from the quality-conscious Maculan winery.

1992 Acininobili, Maculan, half-bottle
18/20
Very sweet 🍯🍯🍯 🍷
An even more concentrated version of the same winery's Torcolato, this is a small oak-fermented, intensely sweet stunner to rival the finest Sauternes. Yours for only £24 a half-bottle.

SOUTH AFRICA

1995 Hamilton Russell Chardonnay (OFW only)
16/20
Dry 🍯🍯 🍷
Consistently among South Africa's best Chardonnays, this cool-climate, barrel-fermented white is an elegant, butterscotchy, cinnamon-spicy number with perfectly poised acidity and the concentration to age.

UNITED STATES

1994 Estancia Reserve Chardonnay
14/20
Dry 🍷
Sweet, vulgar, toffee-fudge-like California Chardonnay with charry oak and wild yeast-derived flavours. On the heavy side, and optimistically priced at nearly £12.

1994 Landmark Overlook Chardonnay   16/20
Dry 🛍🛍 ▬

Youthful, cinnamon oaky, ultra-fresh Sonoma Chardonnay, with buttery richness underpinned by refreshing acidity and considerable complexity.

Red

£3–5

ARGENTINA

1995 Norton Sangiovese, Mendoza   14/20
Medium-bodied 🛍🛍 ▮

Soft, raspberry fruity, well-made Argentine interpretation of Tuscany's Sangiovese grape. More New World than Chianti – as you'd expect from Mendoza's warm climate.

1995 Norton Malbec, Mendoza   15/20
Medium-bodied 🛍🛍 ▮

Inky-hued, richly concentrated, aromatic Malbec with impressive structure and blackberry fruit for a £4.99 red.

1996 Norton Cabernet Sauvignon, Mendoza   16/20
Medium-bodied 🛍🛍🛍 ▬

Equally inky, vibrantly perfumed, cassis and black-cherry fruity Cabernet Sauvignon from one of Argentina's leading wineries, with considerable power and tannic backbone.

1995 Norton Merlot, Mendoza   14/20
Full-bodied 🛍 ▬

Licoricey, damson-skin and black-cherry-like Merlot with hardish tannins on the back palate. Perhaps this should have been blended with the Cabernet Sauvignon.

1995 Balbi Malbec   14/20
Full-bodied 👜👜 🍾
Another good-value Argentine red, with more oak, sweet chocolate and bramble fruitiness and a rough-edged finish. A pound cheaper than the Norton reds.

CHILE

1995 Errázuriz Merlot, Curicó   15/20
Medium-bodied 👜👜 🍾
Luscious, ultra-juicy Chilean Merlot, made by Kiwi Brian Bicknell before his return to New Zealand. Finishes with a pleasantly grassy tang.

1995 Villa Montes Malbec   14/20
Full-bodied 👜 ▬
Smoky, black-cherry and plum-fruity red from the airborne Aurelio Montes, with dry, extracted tannins and a mouth-puckering aftertaste.

1995 Errázuriz Cabernet Sauvignon, El Descanso Estate, Curicó
16/20
Medium-bodied 👜👜👜 ▬
Profoundly minty, cassis fruity, refreshing Chilean Cabernet Sauvignon with impressive concentration and intensity at this price. A stunner from Brian Bicknell.

FRANCE

1996 Oddbins Red, Château de Jau, Vin de Pays Catalan   13/20
Medium-bodied 👜 🍾
Basic, rustic Roussillon plonk from the art-loving Château de Jau winery. This has been a lot better in previous vintages.

1995 Cuvée de Grignon, Vin de Pays de l'Aude, Foncalieu   14/20
Medium-bodied 👜👜 🍾
Decent Languedoc rouge, with pleasant rusticity and gluggable blackberry fruit. Much better value than the Oddbins Red.

1995 Métairie du Bois Syrah, Vin de Pays d'Oc, Foncalieu   15/20
Full-bodied 👜👜👜 ▬
Hugely coloured, freshly aromatic, peppery southern French Syrah, with vibrant blackberry fruitiness and chewy, but still sweet, tannins.

1995 Philippe de Baudin Merlot, Vin de Pays d'Oc   14/20
Medium-bodied 👜 🍾
Succulent, chocolatey, Midi Merlot, with dry, splintery tannins, from the BRL-Hardy operation.

1995 Philippe de Baudin Cabernet Sauvignon, Vin de Pays d'Oc
14/20
Medium-bodied 👜 🍾
Dry, coffee-bean oaky, Languedoc Cabernet, which has been softer and fruitier in previous vintages.

1994 Château de Lascaux, Coteaux de Languedoc   15/20
Full-bodied 👜👜 ▭▬
Sandalwood-spicy, thyme-scented Languedoc blend with lots of blackberry fruit and a hottish, tannic aftertaste.

ITALY

1994 Castel del Monte Rosso, Torrevento   13/20
Full-bodied 🍾
Baked, southern Italian plum and damson-skin-like red, with marked acidity and rather coarse, extracted tannins.

1993 Cent'are Rosso, Duca di Castelmonte   14/20
Full-bodied 👜 🍾
Lightly coloured, cedary oaky Sicilian red, which is beginning to dry a little on the palate.

SOUTH AFRICA

1995 Genus Shiraz   14/20
Medium-bodied 👜 🍾
From the Simonsvlei co-operative, this is an oak-dominated, cherry fruity Shiraz, which would taste better with fewer splinters.

1995 John Fauré Cabernet/Shiraz, Paarl   15/20
Full-bodied 👜👜 🍾
Sweetly fruity, attractively oaked Cabernet/Shiraz blend with juicy blackcurrant characters and refreshing acidity. It'll be a while before this one's ready for a Requiem.

SPAIN

1995 Vega Sindoa Tempranillo, Navarra

14/20

Full-bodied 👜👜 |

Solid, well-made, modern, strawberry fruity Navarra Tempranillo with a firm, chewy finish.

1995 Orobio Tempranillo, Rioja

15/20

Medium-bodied 👜👜👜 ━

Stylish, super-value, deeply coloured Rioja, with sweet, succulent fruit, good structure and well-judged oak. Lovely stuff.

1995 Artadi Tinto, Rioja

16/20

Medium-bodied 👜👜👜 ━

A succulent, vibrantly fruity blend of Tempranillo, with a touch of white Viura for added acidity, made in the modern style with the emphasis squarely on fruit flavours rather than oak.

UNITED STATES

1994 Sterling Redwood Trail Pinot Noir

15/20

Medium-bodied 👜👜 |

Jammy, warm-climate, loganberry fruity Californian Pinot Noir, with recognisable varietal character – more than you can say for most red Burgundies at the price.

1994 Sterling Redwood Trail Cabernet Sauvignon

14/20

Medium-bodied 👜 |

Easy-drinking, soft-centred California Cabernet Sauvignon, with pleasant black-pastille characters but little in the way of complexity.

£5–8

ARGENTINA

1994 Norton Privada

16/20

Medium-bodied 👜👜👜 ━

The top cuvée from Mendoza's Norton winery, this is a ripe, softly textured but intensely concentrated Cabernet-based blend with stylishly integrated vanilla oak. One of Argentina's top reds, made in an encouragingly modern style.

AUSTRALIA

1995 Yaldara Reserve Shiraz   15/20
Full-bodied 👜👜 ▬
Pungently sweet, South Eastern Australian Shiraz, with masses of oak and mint-humbug fruitiness and a whack of alcohol. Assertive, head-banging stuff.

1994 d'Arenberg The Old Vine Shiraz, McLaren Vale   15/20
Full-bodied 👜👜 ▬
Big, if one-dimensional, McLaren Vale Shiraz with sweet, ripe blackberry fruit and a sheen of new oak. Heart on sleeve time.

1995 Wirra Wirra Original Blend Grenache/Shiraz   16/20
Full-bodied 👜👜👜 ▬
From one of McLaren Vale's leading wineries, this is a rich but finely textured southern Rhône-style blend made from low-yielding vines. A warmingly alcoholic, sumptuously fruity red.

CHILE

1994 Cono Sur Selection Reserve Cabernet Sauvignon   15/20
Medium-bodied 👜👜 |
Cassis fruity, assertively oaked Chilean Cabernet Sauvignon made by American Ed Flaherty. Dries a little too much on the finish to be worthy of the Reserve tag.

1995 Viña Porta Merlot, Valle del Cachapoal   16/20
Full-bodied 👜👜 |
With its coffee-bean oak and green-pepper aromas, this is a concentrated, structured, blackberry fruity Chilean Merlot from the Catalan-owned Viña Porta winery.

1995 Errázuriz Merlot Reserva   17/20
Medium-bodied 👜👜👜 ▬
From the vineyard that surrounds Errázuriz's Aconcagua Valley winery, this is a very classy, finely textured, blackcurrant and black-cherry-like Merlot, with well-judged new oak and the concentration to age for five years or more.

FRANCE

1995 Vacqueyras, Domaine de Cabassole 16/20
Full-bodied 👝👝 ●–
Youthful, heady, Grenache-based grower's red from the southern Rhône, with chunky, licorice and pepper notes and sweet, plummy fruitiness.

1994 Mas Cal Demoura, Coteaux du Languedoc 16/20
Full-bodied 👝👝 ●–
Modern, concentrated Languedoc red in which the Syrah grape is aromatically apparent. The wine is just beginning to soften into something really interesting.

1994 Côtes du Rhône, Cépage Syrah, Lionnet 16/20
Full-bodied 👝👝 ●–
From Cornas-based producer Jean Lionnet, this is a Côtes du Rhône with a difference. Apart from the £8 price tag, it's made entirely from Syrah, and it shows in the wine's tightly wound tannins and peppery spice.

ITALY

1995 Torre del Falco, Torrevento, Murgia Rosso, Vino da Tavola
15/20
Medium-bodied 👝 |
Forward, aromatic, southern Italian *rosso* with pleasant strawberry fruitiness, rounded out by cedary oak.

SOUTH AFRICA

1996 Sentinel Shiraz, Stellenbosch 16/20
Full-bodied 👝👝👝 ●–
Impressively coloured, sweetly oaked Cape Shiraz with a chocolatey, almost treacley texture, and masses of sweet blackberry fruit and complexity. Proves that Australia doesn't have a monopoly on fine Shiraz.

1995 Landskroon Unfiltered Shiraz 13/20
Full-bodied |
Leathery, old-fashioned Cape Shiraz with rustic tannins and a vinegary aftertaste.

1995 Beyerskloof Pinotage   16/20
Full-bodied 🎒🎒🎒 ▬

Chunky, vibrantly coloured, oak and raspberry fruity Pinotage from Kanonkop winemaker, Beyers Truter. Plenty of character, as you'd expect, from South Africa's most distinctive red grape variety.

UNITED STATES

1994 McDowell Syrah, Mendocino   13/20
Full-bodied ▮

Rather extracted, one-dimensional Mendocino County Syrah, with swingeing alcohol and dry tannins.

Havenscourt Roti   15/20
Full-bodied 🎒🎒 ▮

A southern Rhône-inspired Californian blend from Jason Korman, with peppery spice and sweet red fruits and vanilla flavours rounded out by heady alcohol and brown-sugar notes.

Over £8

AUSTRALIA

1994 d'Arenberg Dead Arm Shiraz   15/20
Full-bodied 🎒 ▬

Named after a fungal vineyard disease, possibly on the wrong side of a six-pack of Cooper's Sparkling Ale, this is a strappingly alcoholic, American oaky Shiraz with muscle-bound tannins and fruit flavours. Not for quiche eaters.

1993 Tim Knappstein Cabernet Sauvignon (OFW only)   16/20
Medium-bodied 🎒🎒 ▬

From amateur pilot Tim Knappstein, this is an elegant, blackcurrant and coffee-bean oaky South Australian Cabernet Sauvignon, which is drinking nicely now but should age well for another five years.

CHILE

1994 Concha y Toro Reserve Cabernet Sauvignon   15/20
Full-bodied 🎒 ▬

Sagey, aromatic, ambitiously priced Chilean Cabernet in which excellent raw material is obscured by rather dry tannins. Too late for an egg-white fining to remove some tannin?

UNITED STATES

1994 Franciscan Oakville Estate Zinfandel   15/20
Medium-bodied 🍷 |
Decent, if unexciting, Napa Valley Zinfandel, with ripe, wild strawberry fruitiness and supple tannins. Should be a pound or two cheaper.

1993 Franciscan Oakville Cabernet Sauvignon   15/20
Full-bodied 🍷 |
Simple fruit and oak. Drinkable enough, but we expect a bit more from a Napa Valley Cabernet Sauvignon at nearly £9 a bottle.

1994 Ravenswood Napa Valley Zinfandel   16/20
Full-bodied 🍷🍷 ▬
From one of California's top Zinfandel producers, this is a densely-textured, peppery, powerfully fruity red, which is so assertive that it all but smacks you in the face. Needs time.

Sean Thackrey Pleiades V Old Vines   17/20
Full-bodied 🍷🍷🍷 ▬
From part-time book-binder and Rhône freak Sean Thackrey, this is a rich, six-way blend of Syrah, Grenache, Zinfandel, Carignan, Nebbiolo and Mourvèdre, with elegantly oaked, cherry-fruit concentration and good ageing potential.

1993 Rutz Pinot Noir, Russian River Valley (OFW only)   15/20
Medium-bodied |
Excessively oaky, drying Russian River Pinot Noir, which was probably more enjoyable a year ago.

1993 Rocking Horse 'Old Paint' Zinfandel (OFW only)   14/20
Full-bodied |
Deeply coloured, massively alcoholic Napa Valley Zinfandel, with extracted, leathery tannins and cowering fruit flavours.

1993 Les Côtes Sauvages, Edmunds Saint John (OFW only)   16/20
Full-bodied 🍷🍷 |
Another southern Rhône-inspired California blend of Grenache and Mourvèdre, with a little Syrah and Carignan for good measure, this is a spicy, Mediterranean-like red with good concentration and richness and a warmish, tannic finish.

Rosé

£5–8

UNITED STATES

1995 McDowell Grenache Rosé   14/20
Off-dry 🍷 🍾
Sweetish, full-flavoured, strawberryish California rosé, which ought to be at least £1 cheaper.

Sparkling

Over £8

AUSTRALIA

1991 Green Point Blanc de Blancs (OFW only)   16/20
Dry 🍷🍷🍷 🍾
A limited release, all-Chardonnay Yarra Valley sparkling wine from Moët et Chandon's Green Point winery. Rich, mature, attractively toasty fizz, which is better than most Champagne at the price.

FRANCE

Heidsieck Dry Monopole NV   15/20
Dry 🍷🍷 🍾
An improvement on recent releases, this is a malty, Pinot-influenced non-vintage blend, which finishes rather coarsely.

Perrier Jouët NV   14/20
Off-dry 🍾
Young, tangy, green-flavoured Champagne with added sweetness to compensate for the absence of bottle age. Poor value at over £17.

UNITED STATES

Mumm Cuvée Napa Brut NV   15/20
Dry 👜 🍾
Frothy, big-bubbled, hugely popular Napa Valley fizz, with youthful, tangy fruit
but no great complexity. The Mumm Cuvée Napa Rosé is a better bet.

Fortified

£5–8

AUSTRALIA

Seppelt DP 63 Rutherglen Show Muscat, half-bottle (OFW only)
                                                         17/20
Very sweet 👜👜👜 ▬
Viscous, rose-petal and raisin-like Rutherglen sticky, with mature, almond
fruitcake flavours and age-derived complexity in a stylish Italianate bottle. A
wine that grabs you by the nose and pulls you into the glass.

Safeway ☆☆☆(☆)

Address: Safeway House, 6 Millington Road, Hayes, Middlesex UB3 4AY

Telephone/fax: 0181 848 8744; 0181 573 1865

Number of branches: 371

Opening hours: 8.00am to 8.00pm Monday to Saturday, or 10.00pm in selected stores; 10.00am to 4.00pm Sunday

Credit cards accepted: Access, Visa, Switch, Delta

Discounts: May wine fair; selection of price promotions every week, including Multisaves and Linksaves; 5 per cent off a case of any six wines over £2.99 per bottle

Facilities and services: Occasional in-store tastings; free glass loan in selected stores

Top ten best-selling wines: 1995 Safeway Soave; Safeway Cava Brut; Safeway Lambrusco Bianco 7.5 per cent; 1995 Hock; 1995 Liebfraumilch; 1995 Safeway Bulgarian Country Red Merlot/Pinot; 1995 Safeway Sicilian Red; 1995 Safeway Côtes du Rhône Red; 1994 Safeway Minervois; 1993 Safeway Romanian Pinot Noir, Special Reserve

Range:

GOOD: Regional France, Eastern Europe, England, Chile, Australia, organic wines

AVERAGE: Burgundy, Bordeaux, Loire, Alsace, Rhône, Portugal, Spain, Italy New Zealand, South Africa, Champagne and sparkling wines

POOR: Germany, United States

UNDER-REPRESENTED: None

'The Revolution is Coming', proclaimed a Safeway press release earlier this year. Barricades were erected, the emergency services were primed and journalists sat fidgeting at their typewriters. Would Bolshevik flags flutter from the company rooftop? Would Jack Hanford, the cute kid who features in the supermarket's television ads, be forced to abdicate?

Safeway

In fact, the revolution in question was a major re-think of the wine department. The first sign that things were about to undergo a few changes came with the wholesale clear-out of a large number of own-label wines in a summer bin-end sale. But this was only a prelude to what Safeway termed a wholesale 're-designing' of the range in the autumn of 1996.

Late summer deadlines meant that we didn't have the chance to see the new ideas in action. But the gist is that Safeway wants to help shoppers make more informed choices about the wines they place in their supermarket trolleys. It may not bear comparison with the storming of the Winter Palace, but Safeway is convinced that its customers want to know more.

How does it all work? Well, there are two main concepts behind the new, consumer-helpful layout. First, the Safeway Style Guide, which explains wine styles to busy shoppers with words, rather than symbols, and helps identify the wines on the shelves. Wines will be divided into 'Dry and Crisp', 'Dry and Smooth', 'Dry and Full', 'Medium' and 'Sweet/Dessert' for white; and 'Light and Soft', 'Smooth and Mellow', 'Dry and Firm' and 'Rich and Mature' for reds.

Second, there is the Safeway Quality Guide, which groups wines by quality and complexity – awarding them Bronze, Silver or Gold status. Bronze wines will be everyday drinking wines, while Golds will be reserved for 'special occasion' bottles. Just think, you could pick up more medals than the British Olympic team in a single sweep through the wine department!

This is all part of the Safeway 2000 project, launched in 1994 to cut costs, increase productivity and attract more family shoppers, in a successful move to boost sales per square foot. More specifically, it's about 'helping people to negotiate the Great Wall of wine in-store,' according to Liz Robertson, Safeway's perky quality and selection controller.

There's been plenty of movement in the wine department over the last year. 'We shook the bag and everyone had a go at buying something different,' says Robertson. With the arrival of the talented Julie Marshall from Sainsbury's, the department is back to full strength, with four buyers (Marshall, Russell Burgess, Piarina Hennessey, and buying controller Clive McLaughlin) and Liz Robertson charging around the world in search of new wines.

Most of these are presented to the Safeway shopper for the first time during the May and October wine fairs. The former tends to highlight the new vintage from the northern hemisphere; the latter does the same for Australia, Chile, South Africa and New Zealand. Many of these wines are 'bought almost out of the fermenting vat', according to Robertson, who subscribes to the DIY (Drink It Young) school of wine consumption.

In terms of new wines, the focus this year has been on Italy, Australia, South Africa, South America and the Languedoc-Roussillon. This has meant a reduction in the number of what Robertson calls 'quirky wines', namely the English and organic ranges. 'We're careful not to make as much noise about them as we used to,' she adds. 'You won't see 15 English wines in a Safeway supermarket.'

The fact that the Safeway Organic Wine Challenge was not held this year is coincidental, however. The event was cancelled because of EU bureaucracy requiring organic competitions to be registered with the Commission. More ammunition for John Redwood? No, thank goodness. Robertson promises that the Challenge will be back in 1997 and insists that Safeway is still 'interested and involved' in organics.

Robertson's latest crusade is to 'get a vintage on every wine we sell, apart from claret and Champagne'. Does it matter to the consumer that his or her bottle of Lambrusco is labelled with its year of production? Robertson thinks it does. 'It means control from our end to the customer's end. It's the clearest handle you can get on a wine and its quality, and it helps us to exert extra control over the supplier.'

In common with the rest of the supermarket sector, Safeway has had to be very competitive in its pricing over the last 12 months, running regular promotions as well as its two wine fairs. It has abandoned the £1.99 bottle, but will drop down to £2.29 on occasion. The focus on core lines has seen 'some of the more eclectic lines vanish off the top', says Robertson. 'But we've ended up with a more broadly based range with a much stronger structure.'

Most of the 11 per cent sales growth has come from southern hemisphere and Eastern European wines, both of which are Safeway strengths. France is holding its own, but Germany is 'slowly shuddering to a standstill'. Robertson says that, 'If we took out Liebfraumilch and Lambrusco we'd be selling as much wine from the southern hemisphere as the north in two years' time.'

Safeway has been at its most innovative in Eastern Europe in recent vintages, especially with its move to Young Vatted, as opposed to old, shagged-out reds.

In Hungary, Bulgaria and the Czech Republic it has tended to work with flying winemakers, a breed that Liz Robertson is extremely enthusiastic about. 'A third of what we sell overall is made by flying winemakers,' she says, 'but it's far too exciting to stop.' Nevertheless, Safeway has encouraged local winemakers, such as Benjamin Bardos and the brilliant ÁKos Kamocsay, to produce some very promising new wines.

So what does it all add up to? The 400-strong range is not the biggest among the multiple grocers – that particular gong belongs to Tesco – nor would it win awards for label design (we're talking about pre-revolutionary times here), but the overall quality is good, and sometimes outstanding. Some of the quirkier wines may have been sacrificed to the Great God Profit, but this is still the place to find organic Chiantis, Aussie Marsannes, Hungarian Pinot Gris and weird Kiwi whites. If it all goes to plan, the revolution should make such wines even easier to find on the shelves.

White

Under £3

FRANCE

1995 Chenin Blanc, Vin de Pays du Jardin de la France, Domaine Baud   13/20
Dry 🜂🜂 ▮
Clean, modern apple and pear-like Loire white showing the distinctive, crisp acidity of the Chenin Blanc grape.

GERMANY

1995 Hock   11/20
Sweet ▮
Basic, soupy, floral Hock with a note of Müller-Thurgau fragrance.

1995 Liebfraumilch, Rheinhessen   12/20
Sweet 🜂 ▮
Slightly drier than the Hock, crisper on the palate, and drinkable to boot.

ITALY

Safeway Lambrusco   11/20
Sweet ▮
Flat, banana-scented sweetie, with a faint prickle of gas just about keeping it ticking over.

1995 Le Monferrine Moscato d'Asti, 5.5 per cent   14/20
Sweet 🜂🜂🜂 ▮
For the same money, you'd be better off buying this grapey, sherbety, low-alcohol summer quaffer made from the aromatic Muscat grape in Italy's north-east.

1995 Safeway Sicilian Dry White   14/20
Dry 🜂🜂🜂 ▮
A zesty, crisp Sicilian blend of the local Catarratto and Inzolia grapes made by ubiquitous Aussie winemaker, Kym Milne. Finishes with a twist of bitter lemon.

£3–5

AUSTRALIA

1995 Safeway Semillon/Chardonnay, S.E. Australia 13/20
Off-dry � ▮
Tropical fruity, rather simple, warm-climate Aussie blend from Penfolds. Less interesting than its experimental yellow plastic cork.

1995 Rawson's Retreat Bin 21 Semillon/Chardonnay/Colombard
15/20
Dry 555 ▮
Lime-fresh, ice cream soda-like blend of Semillon, Chardonnay and Colombard from Australia's biggest winery, Penfolds, proving that big-volume wines can show character in the right hands.

1995 Breakaway Sauvignon Blanc/Semillon, South Australia 14/20
Dry 5 ▮
Light, faintly oaky Sauvignon Blanc-dominated white blend from the hairier-than-life Australian, Geoff Merrill.

1993 Longleat Marsanne, Goulburn Valley 15/20
Dry 5 ▮
One of Australia's rare examples of the northern Rhône's Marsanne grape, this Victorian classic is rich in aromas of honeysuckle and eucalyptus. Wine's answer to a good Islay malt whisky.

BULGARIA

1995 Chardonnay, Rousse region 14/20
Dry 5 ▮
One of the new-wave Bulgarian whites made as part of a special project by Australian David Wollan at the Russe (sic) winery, this is a fresh, lemon-zippy white with restrained oak character.

1993 Bulgarian Chardonnay Reserve, Rousse region 15/20
Dry 555 ▮
From the same team, this coconut and vanilla-flavoured Chardonnay, fermented in new American oak, points the way forward for Bulgarian whites.

CHILE

1994 Casillero del Diablo Barrel-Fermented Chardonnay, Casablanca   16/20
Dry 🍾🍾🍾 ▮

Despite the diabolical guff on the back label, this fresh, grapefruity, oak-influenced Chardonnay from Concha y Toro has the sort of weight and buttery richness you'd expect from a wine at almost twice the price.

FRANCE

1995 La Coume de Peyre, Vin de Pays des Côtes de Gascogne
13/20
Dry 🍾 ▮

Basic, tangy Gascon white from the Plaimont co-operative, with pleasant apple fruitiness.

1995 Safeway Chardonnay, Vin de Pays d'Oc   14/20
Dry 🍾🍾 ▮

Made by John Weeks, the Australian consultant at Domaines Virginie, this is a well-made, melony southern French Chardonnay with a shaving or two of oak character.

1995 Domaine du Rey, Vin de Pays des Côtes de Gascogne   15/20
Dry 🍾🍾🍾 ▮

A rare vegetarian white from a country where non-meat-eaters are regarded with the same suspicion as Greenpeace protesters. In this context, vegetarian means that no animal products have been used in the processing. It may not make any perceptible difference to the flavours, but this nettley, grapefruity blend of Colombard and Ugni Blanc is a lot more than just a gimmick.

1995 Safeway Bordeaux Blanc Sec, Aged in Oak, Prodiffu   14/20
Dry 🍾🍾 ▮

A mini-Graves-like white Bordeaux blend with well-handled oak and pleasantly herby aromas.

1995 Vieux Manoir de Maransan, Côtes du Rhône   15/20
Dry 🍾🍾 ▮

A rich, mealy, unoaked southern Rhône blend made by Australian consultant, Nick Butler, in a modern, ultra-fruity style.

1995 Philippe de Baudin Sauvignon, Vin de Pays d'Oc   15/20
Off-dry 🍷🍷 ❘
A full, come-hither, southern French Sauvignon Blanc from Aussie giant, BRL-Hardy. It's ripe and rich, with flavours of passion fruit and grapefruit, and a tangy acidity for balance.

1994 Château Haut Bonfils, Bordeaux Semillon, Barrel-Fermented   13/20
Dry 🍷 ❘
From Hugh 'Grant' Ryman, this soft, flat-footed Gironde white is starting to show its age.

GERMANY

1993 Ruppertsberger Nussbein Riesling Kabinett, Pfalz   14/20
Medium dry 🍷🍷 ❘
Soft, juicy, almost tropical fruity Riesling with the grapefruity tang more commonly associated with the Scheurebe grape.

1994 Auslese, Pfalz, Saint Ursula   14/20
Sweet 🍷🍷 ❘
Rich, honeyed, well-priced Auslese from the giant Saint Ursula winery, with a blackcurrant-leaf tang suggesting the presence of Bacchus or Scheurebe grapes.

HUNGARY

1995 Pinot Grigio, Nagyrede   16/20
Dry 🍷🍷🍷 ❘
An incredible find from Hungary, especially at under £3.50, this is a rich, honeyed, Alsace-like Pinot Grigio made by Benjamin Bardos at the Nagyrede co-operative.

1995 Matra Mountain Oaked Chardonnay, Nagyrede   14/20
Dry 🍷🍷 ❘
Made by Kym Milne at the Nagyrede winery near Budapest, this is a lime-crisp, vanilla-oaky Chardonnay with plenty of flavour for relatively few dinars.

1995 River Duna Sauvignon Blanc, Special Cuvée, Bataszek 15/20
Dry 🍷🍷🍷 ❘
A delicate, Loire Valley taste-alike from the progressive Neszmely winery, showing crisply refreshing, varietal characters. Better than any Sauvignon de Touraine we've come across at this price.

1995 Neszmely Estate Barrique Sauvignon Blanc, Neszmely 16/20
Dry 🍷🍷🍷 ▬

An experimental, limited-edition Sauvignon Blanc from the same source, oak-fermented in the Bordelais style for extra complexity. This subtle, lightly spicy, intensely gooseberryish white is outlandishly good value at under £5. Let's hope for greater quantities and the same quality next year.

1994 Chapel Hill Barrique-Fermented Chardonnay, Balaton 15/20
Dry 🍷🍷 ▮

An extra year in bottle has seen this oak-fermented Hungarian Chardonnay develop in an interesting direction, allowing it to gain in honeyed complexity.

ITALY

1995 Zagara Grillo, Vino da Tavola di Sicilia, Kym Milne 15/20
Bone dry 🍷🍷🍷 ▮

The winningly named Marsala grape, Grillo, is responsible for this zesty, juniper-like, tangy dry white with its refreshing bite of crisp acidity. Who says flying winemakers only make wines from Chardonnay and Sauvignon?

1995 Safeway Soave 15/20
Dry 🍷🍷🍷 ▮

With its distinctive cherub label, this rich, broadly buttery, own-label Soave is one of the best cheap Italian whites on the market. It's almost enough to give Soave a good name.

MOLDOVA

1995 Kirkwood Chardonnay, Moldova 13/20
Off-dry 🍷 ▮

The touch is a little bit lighter than last year on this oak-chipped, lemon and toffee-like Chardonnay from Hugh Ryman's Moldovan outlet, but it's still on the confected side.

PORTUGAL

1995 Bright Brothers Fernão Pires/Chardonnay, Ribatejo 15/20
Dry 🍷🍷🍷 ▮

Full-bodied, fragrant, modern-style Portuguese white made by resident Australian Peter Bright, combining the indigenous Fernão Pires with the ubiquitous Chardonnay. A rich, spicy, lightly oaked blend. Good, but not quite as exciting as last year's *Grapevine* wine of the year.

SPAIN

1995 Viña Malea Oaked Viura, Vino de la Tierra Manchuela   13/20
Dry 🍷 🍶
It says lightly oak-aged on the label, but this central Spanish white made from the Viura grape is surrounded by a palisade of oak. There's a wine in there somewhere, but perhaps someone should send out for a buzz-saw.

1995 Somontano Chardonnay, Covisa   15/20
Dry 🍷🍷🍷 🍶
From a tiny Aragonese appellation, which is rapidly establishing itself as Spain's most interesting new area for Burgundy-style reds and whites, this is an inexpensive, cool-climate Chardonnay with rich, spicy weight and a hint of smoky oak.

UNITED STATES

1995 Stony Brook Chardonnay, California   14/20
Dry 🍷 🍶
Made by organic lifestyle proponents Fetzer, this is a commercial, oaky West Coast Chardonnay with attractive melon fruitiness and sustainability.

£5–8

AUSTRALIA

1994 Penfolds Organic Chardonnay/Sauvignon, Clare Valley   15/20
Dry 🍷🍷 🍶
A comparatively unusual Clare Valley combination of rich Chardonnay and crisp Sauvignon Blanc, rounded out with sweet vanilla fudge-like oak. Made in an elegant style with pithy, refreshing acidity.

1995 Rosemount Semillon/Chardonnay, S.E. Australia   13/20
Off-dry 🍶
One of the few dull wines we've tasted this year from the much-improved Rosemount winery. There's nothing actually wrong with this cross-regional Semillon/Chardonnay blend. We just found it a bit commercial and over-oaky.

1995 Hunter Valley Chardonnay, Rosemount 15/20
Off-dry 🍾🍾 |
Opulent, honeyed, tropical fruity Aussie Chardonnay with sweet oak and toffee-fudge richness from Rosemount Estates. It's the kind of thing that would appeal to Australian wine neophytes.

FRANCE

1994 Gewürztraminer, Alsace 15/20
Off-dry 🍾🍾 |
Perfumed, boudoir-scented Alsace Gewürz, with classic aromas of rose petal and lychee, plenty of sumptuous fruit characters and a waterbed of rich alcohol.

1994 Safeway Chablis, Cuvée Domaine Yvon Pautre 16/20
Bone dry 🍾🍾🍾 |
Superb, minerally, own-label Chablis sourced from the praiseworthy La Chablisienne co-operative, with a touch of oak for extra flavour, roundness and complexity.

NEW ZEALAND

1995 Villa Maria Private Bin Sauvignon Blanc, Marlborough 15/20
Dry 🍾🍾 |
Tart, catty Kiwi Sauvignon from the Marlborough region. One of the better-value, commercial whites produced in New Zealand in 1995.

1995 Millton Semillon/Chardonnay, Gisborne 15/20
Dry 🍾🍾 |
Characteristically off-the-wall white from biodynamic specialist James Millton's ugly-bug ball in Gisborne. A weird combination of flavours, including ginger, green malt and honey.

SPAIN

1993 Cune Monopole, Barrel-Fermented Rioja 14/20
Dry 🍾 |
Traditional, abundantly oaky white Rioja blend of Viura and Malvasia, which has seen better days. Time for a new vintage, perhaps.

Red

Under £3

BULGARIA

1995 Safeway Bulgarian Country Wine Merlot/Pinot, Sliven   13/20
Light-bodied 👜👜 🍾
Modern, strawberry fruity blend of Bordeaux with Burgundy in Bulgaria, with a veneer of chippy oak.

1995 Safeway Young Vatted Cabernet Sauvignon, Haskovo   13/20
Full-bodied 👜 🍾
A densely coloured, hugely tannic Cabernet Sauvignon, which has changed supplier this year. We applaud the modern thinking behind this all tank-fermented red. It's just the execution that lets it down.

ITALY

1995 Safeway Sicilian Red, Calatrasi   14/20
Medium-bodied 👜👜👜 🍾
A raisiny, plum and damson-skin-style Mediterranean red made from Sicily's Nero d'Avola grape, with robust tannins and good grip.

MOROCCO

Domaine Sapt Inour, Appellation Zenata Contrôlée   10/20
Full-bodied 🍾
Aaaaah...the smell of week-old camel dung.

£3–5

AUSTRALIA

1995 H.G. Brown Bin 60 Shiraz/Ruby Cabernet, S.E. Australia
14/20

Full-bodied 👜👜 ⌡
Youthful, cross-regional Aussie red blend, which tastes considerably more advanced than the vintage would suggest. Spicy, chocolatey stuff with coarse oak flavours. Still, pretty good for under £4.

1994 Breakaway Grenache/Shiraz , South Australia   13/20
Medium-bodied ⌡
Soft, sweet, simple, minty Australian attempt at a southern Rhône blend from Geoff Merrill, who usually makes more interesting wines than this.

BULGARIA

1995 Bulgarian Aged-in-Oak Merlot, Rousse   12/20
Medium-bodied 👜 ⌡
Dry, rubbery oak smothers the Merlot fruit on this Australian-made Bulgarian red.

1991 Due Mogili Vineyard Cabernet Sauvignon, Rousse   12/20
Medium-bodied 👜 ⌡
Due Mogili is apparently Bulgarian for Twin Peaks. We were hard pushed to find even one, on this drying vulgar Bulgar. No Bafta Awards here.

CHILE

1994 Tocornal Cabernet/Malbec, Rapel Valley   14/20
Full-bodied 👜👜 ⌡
Sweetly oaky, chocolate and ginger spicy Chilean Merlot made by American Ed Flaherty at the massive Concha y Toro winery.

1995 Safeway Chilean Cabernet Sauvignon, Molina-Lontue   15/20
Medium-bodied 👜👜👜 ⌡
From Frenchman Jacques Lurton, working at the recently modernised San Pedro winery, this is a cassis and green-pepper-style Cabernet with the emphasis on chewy fruit richness.

266

FRANCE

1995 Safeway Beaujolais, Deschamps/Mommessin 14/20
Light-bodied 👜👜 🍾
Refreshingly juicy, strawberry and banana-fruity Gamay with attractive, thirst-quenching acidity.

1995 Safeway Côtes du Lubéron 14/20
Medium-bodied 👜👜 🍾
A cross between a Beaujolais and a Côtes du Rhône, this Grenache/Syrah blend has been given a grind of the metaphorical pepper mill by Hugh Ryman.

1995 Safeway Côtes du Rhône 13/20
Medium-bodied 👜 🍾
A fresh, lightly peppery, but somewhat under-fruited, basic Côtes du Rhône from the Valréas co-operative.

1994 Safeway Minervois 12/20
Full-bodied 🍾
Dry, hard and astringent. The Languedoc – and Safeway – can do much better than this.

1994 Château Montner 1994, Côtes du Roussillon Villages 13/20
Medium-bodied 👜 🍾
A four-square blend of Syrah, Grenache and Carignan with charmless, dry tannins and raisiny fruit.

1994 Château La Tour de Béraud , Costières de Nîmes 13/20
Full-bodied 👜 🍾
Rustic, dry Provençal red, whose spicy aromas are more attractive than its rather coarse, astringent character. Not as good as last year's vintage.

1995 Domaine de Picheral Merlot, Vin de Pays d'Oc 15/20
Full-bodied 👜👜👜 ▬
Well-structured, organic Midi Merlot, with plenty of pure blackcurrant fruitiness imbued with Mediterranean spices, and finely honed tannins.

1994 La Baume, Cuvée Australe Syrah/Grenache, Vin de Pays d'Oc 13/20
Full-bodied 👜 🍾
Over-oaky, astringent, Australian-influenced blend from BRL-Hardy's southern French winery near Béziers.

1995 Vieux Manoir de Maransan, Cuvée Spéciale, Côtes du Rhône 15/20
Medium-bodied 👜👜 ❘

Super-soft, enticing southern Rhône red made in a spicy, fruit-oriented style by consultant Nick Butler.

1993 Bourgueil, Cuvée Les Chevaliers, La Cave des Grand Vins de Bourgueil 15/20
Medium-bodied 👜👜 ❘

Classic Loire Valley Cabernet Franc at a give-it-a-try price, this is a soft, ripe, grassy red with herby undertones and refreshing length of flavour.

Safeway Claret, Aged in Oak, Bordeaux, Calvet 15/20
Medium-bodied 👜👜 ❘

In the annual struggle to find a drinkable sub-£5 claret, Safeway has done well to come up with this firm, almost stylish red Bordeaux, showing ripe, decent-quality fruit and well-judged oak.

ITALY

1995 Zagara Nero d'Avola, Vino da Tavola di Sicilia 14/20
Medium-bodied 👜👜 ❘

Made by Spanish flying winemaker, Susana Fernández, this is a light, damsony refresher from Sicily with attractive indigenous character.

1995 Safeway Chianti 13/20
Light-bodied 👜 ❘

Light, easy-drinking beginner's Chianti with a smidgeon of Sangiovese character, from Tuscan giant, Rocca delle Macie.

1994 Safeway Casa di Giovanni, Vino di Tavola di Sicilia 14/20
Full-bodied 👜👜 ❘

Raisin and chocolate-style *rosso* from Sicily, with rustic, peasant charm. Will Giovanni please report to *Grapevine* HQ for identification.

1993 Salice Salentino Riserva, Puglia 15/20
Full-bodied 👜👜 ❘

Savoury, mature red from the boot-heel of Italy, with masses of pruney fruit and concentrated, powerfully alcoholic spiciness.

HUNGARY

1994 Chapel Hill Barrique-Aged Cabernet Sauvignon, Balaton
12/20

Medium-bodied
Flatter than the surface of Lake Balaton, this oak-aged Cabernet Sauvignon is fast losing whatever fruit it had. Even in the hands of an Australian winemaker such as Kym Milne, Hungarian reds struggle with the elements.

MOLDOVA

1995 Kirkwood Cabernet/Merlot, Hugh Ryman   12/20
Full-bodied
Cooked, beetrooty, undistinguished red from the footballing Republic of Moldova. Perhaps we should serve this to their players after the match at Wembley.

PORTUGAL

1994 Fiuza Merlot, Ribatejo   15/20
Medium-bodied
Extremely elegant for a Portuguese red, this smooth, green-pepper-scented Merlot with its stylish oak and smart package is another of Peter Bright's many successes this year.

ROMANIA

1993 Safeway Romanian Pinot Noir Special Reserve, Dealul Mare
10/20

Medium-bodied
Stewed, dry, oak-aged Pinot Noir with a musty Eastern European twang, this is apparently a VSOC (very stale old crap), a quality-approved wine under the Romanian wine regulations.

1987 Safeway Romanian Cabernet Sauvignon Special Reserve, Dealul Mare   11/20
Medium-bodied
Old-fashioned, shagged-out Cabernet Sauvignon with the tomato-skin character typical of pre-revolutionary Romanian reds. Fine if you like Black Sea sun-dried tomatoes.

SOUTH AFRICA

1995 Landskroon Cinsault/Shiraz, Paarl   14/20
Full-bodied 🍾🍾 ▬
Extremely youthful, juicy, super-oaky Cape blend with flavours of bubble gum and blackberry. Powerful stuff.

1994 Simonsvlei Pinotage Reserve, Paarl   15/20
Full-bodied 🍾🍾 🍾
A sweetish, blackberry-and-apple-pie-like example of South Africa's most distinctive red-wine style, showing smooth, dry tannins and a stave or two of oak.

1994 Simonsvlei Shiraz Reserve, Paarl   14/20
Full-bodied 🍾 ▬
Ripe, raunchy, abundantly oaked Cape Shiraz with sweet, tobacco-ish fruitiness made by Philip Louw at the Simonsvlei co-operative.

SPAIN

1995 Viña Albali Tempranillo, Valdepeñas   13/20
Medium-bodied 🍾 🍾
Farmyardy aromas and sweet, aromatic, Tempranillo fruitiness make this youthful Spanish quaffer a bit of a mixed bag.

1989 Safeway Aged in Oak Valdepeñas Reserva   13/20
Medium-bodied 🍾 🍾
Mature, softly fruity Rioja taste-alike, with coconutty oak and a drying finish.

1992 Agramont Tempranillo/Cabernet, Navarra Crianza 15/20
Medium-bodied 🍾🍾 🍾
Assertively, but not aggressively, oaked Navarra blend with sumptuous fruitiness and plenty of warm-climate spice.

UNITED STATES

1994 Stony Brook Cabernet Sauvignon, California   15/20
Medium-bodied 🍾🍾 🍾
Silky, commercial, sweetly oaked West Coast Cabernet Sauvignon from the Fetzer winery, with luscious blackcurrant fruit characters. As smooth as a Baywatch hunk's pectorals.

£5–8

AUSTRALIA

1995 Rosemount Shiraz/Cabernet Sauvignon, S.E. Australia   13/20
Medium-bodied
Mawkish, rather simple, tutti-frutti Aussie blend with soft tannins and vanilla oak. A little too tame for an over-£5 red.

1995 Hardy's Barossa Valley Cabernet Sauvignon/Merlot   15/20
Medium-bodied
Sweetly mature, almost Rioja-like blend from South Australia's Barossa Valley, with opulent, sweet vanilla oakiness balanced by soft, cassis fruitiness.

1993 Hardy's Bankside Shiraz, S.E. Australia   16/20
Full-bodied
Dense, richly textured, cinnamon-tinged cross-regional Shiraz from Australia's number two, BRL-Hardy. Attractively spicy, with a firm backbone of tannin.

1993 Hardy's Coonawarra Cabernet Sauvignon   15/20
Full-bodied
Firm, minty, faintly medicinal Coonawarra Cabernet Sauvignon with lots of smoky oak and a green edge of hard tannins.

1994 Penfolds Clare Valley Shiraz/Cabernet Sauvignon   16/20
Full-bodied
From Penfolds' organic vineyards in South Australia's Clare Valley, this is a massively inky, silky-textured blend, with beautifully judged sweet oak and toffee and blackberry fruit characters. At under £7, this is the best-value organic red we've encountered.

CHILE

1992 Villard Cabernet Sauvignon, Rancagua   15/20
Medium-bodied
Mature, spearminty Chilean Cabernet Sauvignon from the widely travelled, multilingual Frenchman, Thierry Villard. An elegant, leafy red, which is just beginning to dry. Drink now.

FRANCE

1993 La Cuvée Mythique, Vin de Pays d'Oc 16/20
Full-bodied 👝👝👝 ➡

Made by France's largest winery, Val d'Orbieu, this is a pioneering southern French blend, which uses Cabernet Sauvignon to enhance the Mediterranean character of the region's indigenous grapes. A rich, spicy, thyme and angostura bitters-style number, with chocolatey sweet tannins and well-judged Allier oak.

ITALY

1994 Tenuta San Vito, Chianti Putto 16/20
Medium-bodied 👝👝👝 ▯

Proving that organic wines are more than just a gimmick at Safeway, this is a juicy, cigar-box-scented, beautifully poised Chianti showing the Sangiovese grape at its most alluring.

SOUTH AFRICA

1993 Kanonkop Kadette, Stellenbosch 14/20
Full-bodied 👝 ➡

A blend of two-thirds Cabernet Sauvignon to one-third Pinotage from the Cape Pinotage Crusader, Beyers Truter, there's a core of sweet blackberry fruit here, but it's overshadowed by rustic dryness.

SPAIN

1991 Faustino V Rioja Reserva 16/20
Medium-bodied 👝👝 ▯

The man on the label of this frosted bottle may look like a cross between George III and old man Steptoe, but this is a nicely mature, licoricey Reserva Rioja, with attractive wild strawberry fruit flavours and restrained oak.

UNITED STATES

1993 Fetzer Zinfandel, California 15/20
Full-bodied 👝👝 ▯

An easy-drinking California Zin, with a veneer of smoky oak and succulent raspberry fruitiness, from organic gardeners, Fetzer.

Over £8

FRANCE

1993 Saint Julien, Barton & Guestier   15/20
Medium-bodied 🍷🍷 ▮
Good for a 1993 claret, this village blend from négociant Barton & Guestier has
a touch of spicy oak and mellow, coffee-bean and blackcurrant characters.

1992 Sarget du Château Gruaud-Larose   16/20
Medium-bodied 🍷🍷 ▮
The second wine of Saint Julien-classified property, Château Gruaud-Larose,
this is a supple, forward, but attractively complex red Bordeaux with a
surprising amount of fruit concentration for such a watery vintage.

1993 Gevrey Chambertin, Domaine Rossignol-Trapet   16/20
Medium-bodied 🍷🍷 ▬
From the excellent 1993 harvest in Burgundy, this is a modern, spicily oaked,
intensely fruity Pinot Noir, which has the guts and staying power of the vintage.

Rosé

£3–5

AUSTRALIA

1995 Breakaway Grenache, South Australia   14/20
Off-dry 🍷 ▮
Like an Australian Tavel with added sweetness, this is a ripe, alcoholic rhubarb
and raspberry fruity rosé from the characterful Geoff Merrill.

Sparkling

£3–5

AUSTRALIA

Safeway Australian Sparkling   14/20
Off-dry 🍾🍾 ❘
From Seppelt's Great Western winery, this is a typically soft, commercial, sherbety fizz, which is ideal for Christmas parties.

SPAIN

Safeway Cava Brut   14/20
Dry 🍾🍾 ❘
From Spanish Cava giant Freixenet, the company that brought you Cordon Negro, this is a lemony, tangily crisp fizz with an earthy bite.

£5–8

AUSTRALIA

Carrington Extra Brut   15/20
Dry 🍾🍾 ❘
One for the Bloomsbury set, this is a ripe, tropically fruity sparkler from Orlando, showing a mouth-filling mousse and fresh acidity. Mrs Dalloway probably served this one.

ITALY

Safeway Asti Spumante   13/20
Medium dry 🍾 ❘
With its confected lemon bath-soap scent, this rather sickly Asti Spumante will only be of interest to Lambrusco lovers and the sweet of tooth.

Over £8

FRANCE

Safeway Albert Etienne Champagne Brut   15/20
Dry 👛👛 🍾
From the Grande Marque house of Massé, this is a creamy, well-made, own-label Champagne with a good dose of reserve wine to soften the youthful tang.

1990 Safeway Albert Etienne Champagne Vintage   16/20
Dry 👛👛👛 🍾
Toasty, intense, richly textured vintage Champagne from the house of Marne et Champagne, this high-quality fizz is a real bargain at around £15.

Fortified

£3–5

FRANCE

1995 Domaine de Brial, Muscat de Rivesaltes, half-bottle   12/20
Sweet 🍾
Clumsy fortification has made this Roussillon sticky rather spirity and short of fruit. Send for the Cathars.

Sainsbury's ☆☆☆☆

Address: Stamford House, Stamford Street, London SE1 9LL

Telephone/fax: 0171 921 6000/ 0171 921 7160. Or freephone: 0800 636262

Number of branches: 365

Opening hours: Branch-specific. Regular late-night opening

Credit cards accepted: Access, Visa, Switch, American Express

Discounts: 5 per cent off six bottles of wine (which can be mixed) plus multi-buy offers, special offers and special purchases

Facilities and services: Home delivery through Sainsbury's *The Magazine* and Wine Direct; free glass loan; in-store tastings on an *ad hoc* basis

Special offers: See discounts

Top ten best-selling wines: Sainsbury's Bianco di Verona; Sainsbury's Soave; Sainsbury's Liebfraumilch; Sainsbury's Hock; Sainsbury's Lambrusco Bianco; Sainsbury's Vin Rouge de France (1.5 litre); Sainsbury's Romanian Pinot Noir; Sainsbury's Bulgarian Cabernet Sauvignon; Sainsbury's Navarra; Sainsbury's Bordeaux Rouge

Range:

GOOD: Bordeaux, Loire, Languedoc-Roussillon, Australia, New Zealand, Chile, Bulgaria, South Africa, Italy, Champagne and sparkling wines

AVERAGE: Beaujolais, Burgundy, Rhône, Alsace, Germany, Portugal, Spain, Argentina, Hungary, England

POOR: California

UNDER-REPRESENTED: None

The chatty Allan Cheesman newsletter is back, along with the man himself. Early sightings of the Big Cheese in a Pringle sweater raised fears that some of his old sharpness had been blunted by a sojourn in fresh fruit and flowers. But any such anxieties were soon allayed by the reappearance of the pinstripe suit and its well-toned occupant. The return of Cheesman, already a legend in his own dinnertime, has been like watching a Madame Tussaud's waxwork come to life.

Cheesman has certainly had a busy year as a wine judge. By sitting in on a panel (but not, he stresses, voting) that awarded the Supermarket of the Year gong to, er, Sainsbury's, Cheesman raised the eyebrows and hackles of his competitors. Then along came the Glenfiddich awards, and the never knowingly self-effacing Cheesman protested his innocence when only two writers were shortlisted, both of whom have worked for, er, Sainsbury's. Sainsbury's 0; Own Goals 2.

Why was Cheesman brought back? Well, Sainsbury's performance has lagged behind its competitors, whose introduction of loyalty-card schemes and accelerating sales figures left Sainsbury's looking distinctly flat-footed. 'When Allan Cheesman went,' says senior buyer Mark Kermode, 'it was possible to make a lot of noise quite quickly. Now you have to work that much harder to make an impact.'

It's been a tough year, but the wine department appears to be coping with the hurricane conditions. It claims to have outperformed the company generally, even if the perception of Sainsbury's as a plodder has put some shoppers off. Wine sales continue to grow, albeit at a slower rate. After the introduction of a 5 per cent discount on six bottles and a free cardboard carry-case offer in autumn 1995, sales growth hit double figures. Neck-and-neck with Tesco, and perhaps just a nose behind now, Sainsbury's currently has around 15 per cent of the take-home market, the sector that itself accounts for 75 per cent of the total wine market.

Last year, a few weeks after his return to the expanded drinks department at Sainsbury's, Cheesman pledged in particular to do something about reviving France, to look closely at staff training and to rid Sainsbury's, if he could, of the £1.99 bottle. How has the man measured up? Rising prices throughout Europe have effectively killed the £1.99 bottle, even if the likes of Somerfield and Asda still use it as a one-off promotion price. The result is that 'the price-point battlefield' has jumped from £1.99 to £2.99, where Sainsbury's have around 80 wines in the range.

The focus has returned to France too, but despite Cheesman's self-confessed Francophilia, the Cantona effect has more to do with factors beyond even Cheesman's control. 'France has seen the impact of the New World and come out of denial. And the French franc has finally weakened against the pound,' says Kermode. 'There are natural forces such as vintage at work as well.' This is true. The 1995 vintage in France compared favourably with that in much of Europe.

France now accounts for 32 per cent of Sainsbury's sales, more or less in line with the national average. At the basic level, Sainsbury's claret, red Bordeaux, red and white Cuvée Prestige wines from Château Carsin and red Burgundy (more so than the white) are classic, good-value blends. Sainsbury's project with wine consultant Jacques Lurton in the Loire has paid dividends, too, with a new-wave, fruitier Chenin Blanc, although the Sauvignon is less inspiring.

Dramatic strides in the Midi are reflected in an expanded and improved southern French range. Moving into fine wine territory, Sainsbury's has used the resources of Bill Blatch, a Bordeaux broker, to source some useful 1989 and 1990 vintage châteaux. We were underwhelmed, on the other hand, by Sainsbury's new Classic Selection, a group of on the whole safe, rather than adventurous, wines, mostly from négociants.

Italy accounts for about 21 per cent of Sainsbury's sales. 'The exciting thing is the switch from Lambrusco, which is in swift decline, to proper wine,' says Kermode. This is the fourth vintage in which Sainsbury's has collaborated with the rambunctious Australian Geoff Merrill and Italian giant, Gruppo Italiano Vini. From 2,000 cases four years ago, shelves are now buckling under the weight of nearly half a million cases, and the quality, especially of the Grechetto and Pinot Grigio, is excellent.

Spanish reds have made strides and another rumbustious, well-travelled Australian, Peter Bright, has continued to mix blends with some panache, putting his experience of working with native Portuguese grapes to good effect in Italy, Argentina and Portugal itself. We wondered last year if the somewhat unlikely duo of Merrill and Bright could keep up with the demands of so much travel, while continuing to maintain varietal character and regional identity. So far so good.

In the light of Sainsbury's claim to outsell competitors by three to one in Eastern Europe, it is miffed to see Safeway hogging the Eastern European limelight. 'People see Bulgarian reds as a good alternative to French reds,' says Kermode. 'We've had to invest quite a bit of time in Bulgaria and Romania. Prices are firming up and the competition is increasing, with Germany and Holland buying Eastern European wines, too.' He accepts, however, that the balance of the range is a bit out of kilter, with whites less interesting than the reds.

Sainsbury's made two visits in 1996 to Australia and New Zealand, the results of which will filter through during 1997. New World sales account for 16 per cent of business, of which 7.5 per cent is Australia. We were impressed by the basic ranges from both Chile and South Africa. South America overtook South Africa this year, but Kermode's view is that South Africa will come back and Chile go into short supply, because of worldwide demand.

Whether from a Malvinas or Maradona hangover, customers are still resistant to Argentine wines. Pity, really, because at the £2.99 level, Argentina's reds and whites are among the best-value wines on the market. Sainsbury's accept that they haven't cracked good California wine under £5. 'We admit it's a weakness in the range, but California just can't compete on value at those prices.'

Sainsbury's has paid more than lip-service to staff training over the past year. A tailor-made, in-house training programme for staff has been set up, with videos on how to display the wines and food and on wine matching. 'The biggest focus is on how we serve the customer,' says Kermode. 'A quantum leap has to be made to improve the level of knowledge of our people in the stores, making staff more wine literate to bridge the gap between them and the customer.'

The size of the range is similar to last year at around 500 wines from 21 countries. 'Proliferation is sometimes desperation,' says Mark Kermode, with a side-swipe at the acknowledged enemy, Tesco. 'Is size of range so important?' He points to the fact that even though the high-street specialists have the advantages of a bigger range and more knowledgeable staff, they're struggling.

Kermode acknowledges that Sainsbury's needs to do more on the marketing front, whether it's more information on food and wine matching or on style of wine, but he's wary of gimmicks: 'Viognier is a fashionable grape, but it's a brave grower who plants it. Our philosophy is a return to core values and getting the best possible wines. It's hard enough for our customers to grapple with traditional wines.'

It has tried to break up the supermarket 'sea of wine' using sections featuring monthly 'hot spots', such as Italy, South America, Montilla, and rosés for summer drinking. But Sainsbury's recognises that it could do more research to find out what customers want. 'In terms of public perception,' says Kermode, 'the booze section is fairly sterile and needs to be livened up.'

No fireworks then in the wine department. Pyrotechnics are neither Sainsbury's nor Allan Cheesman's style. Under Cheesman, Sainsbury's has quietly plugged away to produce one of the best basic supermarket ranges in the all-important £3–£5 price bracket. Cheesman's espousal of the three Vs – value, variety and versatility – may not be headline-grabbing virtues, but they are still three compelling V-signs to poke at his rivals.

NB: Wines marked with an asterisk (*) are also available at Sainsbury's Calais (see page 586).

White

Under £3

ARGENTINA

*Sainsbury's Mendoza Country White, Trapiche   14/20
Dry 👜👜👜 ▮
Fresh, tropical fruity Argentine blend of Criolla and Chenin Blanc made at the Peñaflor winery by boisterous Australian winemaker, Peter Bright. An affordable, lime-flavoured white.

BULGARIA

*Sainsbury's Lyaskovets Chardonnay   12/20
Off-dry 👜 ▮
Blowsy, oak-chipped Bulgarian Chardonnay from airborne Aussie winemaker, Kym Milne.

FRANCE

*1995 Sainsbury's Vin de Pays du Gers, Les Chais de la Forge
                                                         13/20
Dry 👜👜 ▮
Fruity, modern, early-picked Gascon white with light, grapefruity freshness.

GERMANY

*Sainsbury's Liebfraumilch, Zeller Barl Kellerei   11/20
Medium sweet ▮
Cardboardy, uninspired German quaffer, which does nobody any favours, least of all the wine consumer.

*Sainsbury's Hock, Zeller Barl Kellerei   12/20
Medium sweet 👜 ▮
Cheap, unbalanced, sweet-and-sour Müller-Thurgau-based blend with a featherweight 9 per cent alcohol.

HUNGARY

*Sainsbury's Hungarian Irsai Oliver 14/20
Dry 🍯🍯🍯 ▮

Fragrant, spicy, Alsace-like dry white from Kym Milne, making the most of an interesting indigenous grape at the Balatonboglar co-operative on the shores of Lake Balaton.

ITALY

*Sainsbury's Bianco di Verona, Vino da Tavola della Provincia di Verona, Fratelli Fabiano 13/20
Dry 🍯🍯 ▮

Light, banana-fruity north Italian *bianco* with a refreshingly bitter twist. A rather grandiose-sounding name for a relatively humble dry white.

*Sainsbury's Lambrusco Bianco, Donelli Vini 12/20
Sweet 🍯 ▮

Banana- and lemonade-flavoured alternative to Two Dogs. Why do you ask?

£3–5

ARGENTINA

1995 Trapiche Oak-Cask Chardonnay, Tupungato Valley, Mendoza 13/20
Dry ▮

Splintery, toffee-fudge-like Chardonnay with a hole in the middle.

AUSTRALIA

*Sainsbury's Australian Chardonnay, Southcorp 12/20
Dry ▮

Coarse, gluey, oak-chippy Australian white, which should be at least £1 cheaper.

Sainsbury's Australian Semillon/Sauvignon, Rothbury 13/20
Dry ▮

Over-oaked, over-acid Aussie Bordeaux-style blend that lacks balance.

CHILE

*Sainsbury's Chilean White Wine   14/20
Dry 🍾🍾🍾 ❙

A refreshing lemon-and-lime-style white based on Chile's Sauvignon Vert grape. Excellent value at under £3.50.

*Sainsbury's Chilean Sauvignon Blanc, Maule Valley, Santa Rita
                                                        14/20

Dry 🍾🍾 ❙

Somewhat muted in the aroma department, but this Maule Valley Sauvignon from one of Chile's largest producers is a bit more interesting on the palate, with some appealing grapefruity zing and crispness.

FRANCE

1995 Sauvignon Blanc, Vin de Pays du Jardin de la France   13/20
Dry 🍾 ❙

Commercial Loire Valley white made by French wine consultant Jacques Lurton. Rather short of aroma and Sauvignon zip.

*1995 La Goelette Muscadet de Sèvre et Maine sur lie   16/20
Bone dry 🍾🍾🍾 ❙

Rich, complex, weighty Muscadet from an excellent vintage, showing characteristic, lees-derived verve and bone-dry acidity. Believe it or not, this is an exciting Muscadet.

*1995 Sainsbury's Gaillac   15/20
Dry 🍾🍾🍾 ❙

Ripe pear and white-pepper-scented Gaillac dry white, with plenty of richness and off-the-wall flavours. A welcome break from Chardonnay and Sauvignon Blanc.

*1995 Domaine Saint Marc Sauvignon Blanc, Vin de Pays d'Oc, M. Servage   14/20
Dry 🍾 ❙

Made at the Foncalieu winery by Western Australian winemaker, Michael Goundrey, this is a grapefruity, refreshing Sauvignon Blanc with good weight and warm-climate ripeness.

1995 Château Les Bouhets, Bordeaux Blanc   15/20
Dry 🎒🎒 ⬗

Christophe Ollivier has produced a crisp, aromatic, almost Kiwi-style Sauvignon Blanc with notes of elderflower and capsicum fruitiness.

*1994 Château Carsin, Bordeaux Blanc   15/20
Dry 🎒🎒 ⬗

Australian Mandy Jones makes some of the best sub-£5 Bordeaux whites, here using oak-ageing and New World techniques on a traditional blend of 85 per cent Semillon and 15 per cent Sauvignon Blanc. The result is an elegant, vanilla-oaky, Graves-like white with crisp acidity.

*1995 Sainsbury's La Baume Sauvignon Blanc, Vin de Pays d'Oc
                                                              15/20
Off-dry 🎒🎒 ⬗

A full, come-hither, southern French Sauvignon Blanc from Aussie giant, BRL-Hardy. It's ripe and rich, with flavours of passion fruit and grapefruit and a tangy acidity for balance.

*1995 Sainsbury's La Baume Chardonnay, Vin de Pays d'Oc   13/20
Off-dry ⬗

Basic, smoky-oaky, Aussie-influenced Languedoc Chardonnay, in which technology triumphs over local character. Fine if you like smoked bananas.

1995 Chardonnay, Vin de Pays d'Oc, Cave de la Cessane   15/20
Dry 🎒🎒🎒 ⬗

For around 50 pence less, you can treat yourself to a bottle of this fresher, more characterful Chardonnay, in which oak character and lemony fruit are pleasantly harmonious.

*1995 James Herrick Chardonnay, Vin de Pays d'Oc   15/20
Dry 🎒🎒 ⬗

Elegant Chardonnay from Englishman James Herrick's southern French vineyards near Narbonne, showing restrained oak and melony fruitiness.

*1994 Vouvray, La Couronne des Plantagenets, Demi-Sec   14/20
Medium 🎒🎒 ⬗

A good example of Chenin Blanc's distinctive combination of appley fruitiness and searing acidity, produced in a medium style to file down its tougher edges.

ITALY

*Sainsbury's Soave, Pietro Sartori   12/20
Dry 🍷
Lean, basic, neutral Soave with a whiff of the chemistry lab. Presumably in Sainsbury's top ten because of the Soave name, rather than the quality of the wine.

*Sainsbury's Garganega, Vino da Tavola del Veneto, Geoff Merrill
14/20
Dry 💰💰 🍷
Crisp, almost bracing Venetian white using the leading Soave grape to good effect.

Sainsbury's Sicilian Inzolia/Chardonnay   13/20
Dry 💰 🍷
The character of the local Inzolia grape doesn't really come through in this basic, clean, fruity white.

*1995 Bianco di Custoza, Geoff Merrill   14/20
Dry 💰💰 🍷
The result of a tripartite collaboration between the giant Italian group GIV (Gruppo Italiano Vini), Sainsbury's and cricket-mad Aussie Geoff Merrill, this is a light, scented, Veneto white with refreshing acidity and pear-like fruitiness.

*Sainsbury's Grechetto dell'Umbria, Vino da Tavola dell'Umbria, Geoff Merrill   16/20
Dry 💰💰💰 🍷
An unusual Umbrian white, with good honeyed weight and richness of fruit, pepped up by distinctive crispness and acidity. One of the best sub-£5 whites on the market.

*Sainsbury's Pinot Grigio, Atesino   15/20
Dry 💰💰💰 🍷
Rich, spicy dry white, with attractive weight, peach-like fruitiness and length of flavour.

1995 Cortese del Piemonte, Contea di Castiglione   16/20
Dry 💰💰💰 🍷
A really enjoyable Piedmontese white made by the original Aussie flying wine-maker, Martin Shaw, with lime and pear fruit aromas and a surprising amount of concentration for an Italian white under £5.

*Sainsbury's Chardonnay delle Tre Venezie 14/20
Dry 🍷 ▌
A wine that has been better in previous incarnations. Clean, fresh, but a little tart and short of fruit.

NEW ZEALAND

*1995 Nobilo White Cloud 14/20
Off-dry 🍷🍷 ▌
A Kiwi white that never lets you down. This zesty, off-dry blend of Müller-Thurgau with a dollop of Sauvignon Blanc for aromatic freshness is a good introduction to New Zealand wine.

PORTUGAL

*Sainsbury's Ribatejo Sauvignon Blanc, Fiuza 15/20
Dry 🍷🍷🍷 ▌
Nettley, ripe, well-made Sauvignon Blanc from well-travelled Peter Bright. One of several good wines available under the Fiuza label.

SOUTH AFRICA

*Sainsbury's South African Cape Dry 13/20
Dry 🍷 ▌
Pear-droppy, dilute, cool-fermented dry white from the hot Worcester region of the Cape. One horn short of an impala.

*Sainsbury's South African Reserve Selection Chardonnay 15/20
Dry 🍷🍷 ▌
A well-made Cape Chardonnay with spicy, barrel-fermented oak and good middle-palate richness and a fresh, lemony fruitiness. Precisely the direction in which Cape Chardonnay should be moving.

SPAIN

1993 Marqués de Cáceres White Rioja Crianza 15/20
Dry 🍷🍷 ▌
Fresh, dry, characterful Viura-based white Rioja made in a modern style but with enough French oak and vanilla flavour to retain its interest as a distinctive style.

UNITED STATES

* Sainsbury's California White Wine, Canandaigua   11/20
Dry
Stewed, bitter, hollow California cheapie. At under £3.50, the West, *pace* Jim Morrison, is not the best.

*Southbay California Chardonnay   13/20
Dry
Rather dilute, wet-wool-like, resinous California Chardonnay, which is at least drier than last year's confection, but still lacks fruit quality.

£5–8

CHILE

*1995 Santa Rita Chardonnay Estate Reserve, Maipo Valley 16/20
Dry
Grapefruity, crisply turned-out Chilean Chardonnay with stylish, toasty, well-handled French oak, refreshing acidity and length of flavour.

FRANCE

*1994 Domaine de Grandchamp, Sauvignon Blanc, Bergerac Sec
                                                              13/20
Dry
A flat, rather overpriced Dordogne white which has lost some zip and fruit complexity. Curiously subdued. Better in previous vintages.

*1995 Sainsbury's Classic Selection Sancerre, Fouassier   15/20
Bone dry
Decent, rather than enthralling, Sancerre with an alcoholic punch masking the Sauvignon Blanc fruitiness.

*Sainsbury's White Burgundy, Rodet   14/20
Dry
Decent, commercial white Burgundy with a touch of vanilla sweetness.

*1994 Sainsbury's Classic Selection Chablis, Domaine Sainte Céline, Paul Brocard   14/20
Bone dry

Lean, austere Chablis from a normally reliable grower, Paul Brocard. Don't drink this before or after a visit to the dentist.

1994 Sainsbury's Classic Selection Pouilly Fuissé   14/20
Dry

Classic is not the first word that leaps to mind to describe this lumpen, rather ordinary, Mâcon Chardonnay.

1990 Clos St Georges, Graves Supérieures   14/20
Very sweet

Honeyed, slightly bitter sub-Sauternes from négociant Peter Sichel, with burnt-toffee notes.

ITALY

1994 Chardonnay Atesino, Barrique-Aged, Vino da Tavola   15/20
Dry

Fresh, yeasty, almost beery, oaked Italian Chardonnay from Aussie Geoff Merrill, showing the sort of length of flavour and complexity that also characterise his Australian wines.

NEW ZEALAND

1995 Stoneleigh Sauvignon Blanc, Marlborough   16/20
Dry

Classically aromatic Marlborough Sauvignon Blanc from a lean vintage, cleverly transformed into a well-priced, green-bean-like alternative to Sancerre.

*1995 Grove Mill Sauvignon Blanc, Marlborough   14/20
Off-dry

Not as good as the Stoneleigh Sauvignon Blanc, despite its more expensive price tag. A lightish, sweetened-up Sauvignon Blanc, which demonstrates the austerity of the vintage.

---

*1995 Matua Valley Eastern Bays Chardonnay   16/20
Dry 🍾🍾🍾 ▮

The amusing Spence brothers are among the most consistent Chardonnay producers in New Zealand. This blend of Poverty Bay and Hawkes Bay Chardonnays could almost be a well-made white Burgundy, such are its elegance and richly oaky complexity.

1995 Oyster Bay Chardonnay, Marlborough   16/20
Dry 🍾🍾🍾 ▮

Chablis-like South Island Chardonnay from the brother-and-sister team of Jim and Rosemary Delegat, with citrusy acidity balanced by a buttery, barrel-fermented richness.

SOUTH AFRICA

1995 Danie de Wet Grey Label Chardonnay   16/20
Dry 🍾🍾🍾 ▮

Danie de Wet, the acknowledged master of Robertson Chardonnay, has done it again. This is a beautifully balanced, minerally Chardonnay, with subtle oak integration and elegant, citrus-fruit flavours.

Red

Under £3

ARGENTINA

*Sainsbury's Mendoza Country Red Wine, Trapiche   14/20
Medium-bodied 🍾🍾🍾 ▮

A good example of the quality of basic red wines emerging from Argentina. This is a fruity, spicy blend enhanced by subtle oak character.

BULGARIA

*Sainsbury's Bulgarian Cabernet Sauvignon, Rousse   13/20
Medium-bodied 💰💰 ▯

Modern, blackcurrant-pastille fruity Bulgarian red from Rousse. Better than almost all red Bordeaux at the price, but still on the rooty side.

*Sainsbury's Bulgarian Merlot   14/20
Medium-bodied 💰💰💰 ▯

A smooth, modern, fruit-steered Bulgarian Merlot from the go-ahead Rousse winery. Extremely good value at under £3.

ROMANIA

*Sainsbury's Romanian Pinot Noir, Calugaresca Winery, Dealul Mare   14/20
Medium-bodied 💰💰💰 ▯

Inexpensive, oak-aged Pinot Noir, which has more sweet, brambly fruit than the clapped-out reds we're used to from Romania.

£3–5

ARGENTINA

Sainsbury's Mendoza Cabernet Sauvignon/Malbec   13/20
Full-bodied 💰 ▯

Tarry, warm-climate Andean blend made by Peter Bright at the Peñaflor winery. On the basic side.

1993 Trapiche Oak Cask Cabernet Sauvignon   13/20
Medium-bodied ▯

Splintery, old-fashioned, dry, over-oaked Cabernet Sauvignon made by the enormous Trapiche winery.

AUSTRALIA

*Sainsbury's Tarrawingee Shiraz/Cabernet, Kingston Estate 11/20
Medium-bodied ▯

Dull, basic Aussie blend with tart, unbalanced acidity and chippy oak. Pointless.

Sainsbury's Tarrawingee Grenache   13/20
Full-bodied 🍾 ▮
Minty, oaky, alcoholic Grenache with enough spice to provide interest. Still shown up by South Africa and Chile.

Sainsbury's Tarrawingee Shiraz/Mourvèdre   14/20
Full-bodied 🍾🍾 ▮
The best of Sainsbury's Tarrawingee range (aboriginal for 'pass the oak chips, mate'), this is a blackberry-sweet, oaky blend of southern Rhône grapes with refreshing acidity.

CHILE

*Sainsbury's Chilean Red Wine, Canepa   14/20
Medium-bodied 🍾🍾🍾 ▮
A well-made, mint and blackcurrant-style Chilean blend of Cabernet Sauvignon, Merlot and local Pais grapes, with attractively sagey weight and exuberance.

*Sainsbury's Chilean Merlot, Canepa, San Fernando Valley   15/20
Medium-bodied 🍾🍾🍾 ▮
A ludicrously well-priced, juicy, deep-hued Chilean Merlot with succulent, green-pepper fruitiness unencumbered by oak.

Sainsbury's Chilean Cabernet Sauvignon/Merlot, Maule Valley, Curicó Co-operative   13/20
Medium-bodied 🍾🍾 ▮
This Bordeaux-style blend lacks the vibrancy of the varietal Merlot. Vanilla oak and dry tannins make it rather austere and chewy.

*Sainsbury's Chilean Cabernet Sauvignon, Canepa, Curicó   13/20
Medium-bodied 🍾 ▮
Well-made, capsicum-scented Cabernet Sauvignon from the southern end of Chile's Central Valley. Finishes a bit lean and green.

FRANCE

*Sainsbury's Bordeaux Rouge, Ginestet   14/20
Medium-bodied 🍾🍾 ▮
Commendably drinkable, youthful red Bordeaux, unoaked for maximum fruit impact.

---

*Sainsbury's Cahors   14/20
Medium-bodied 🍷🍷 ▮

Herby, tarry, Malbec-based dry red from south-west France, with fairly robust tannins.

*Sainsbury's Claret, Jean-Paul Jauffret   14/20
Medium-bodied 🍷🍷🍷 ▮

Youthful, juicy red Bordeaux – sorry, claret – with grassy fruit and a sweet, cassis-like middle.

*Sainsbury's Cuvée Prestige Claret   15/20
Medium-bodied 🍷🍷🍷 ▭

Made by the talented Aussie, Mandy Jones of Château Carsin, this deep-hued red Bordeaux has plenty of structure, and damson and cassis fruit enhanced by new oak ageing. A wine that lives up to the audacious claim on the label.

*1994 Domaine Saint Marc Syrah, Vin de Pays d'Oc   13/20
Full-bodied 🍷 ▭

From the New World-inflenced Foncalieu winery in the Languedoc, this dark ruby Syrah is rather dominated by oak and extracted dry tannins.

*1993 Saint Chinian, Les Mourgues, Val d'Orbieu   14/20
Medium-bodied 🍷🍷 ▮

A garrigue-scented, essence of Languedoc blend, with angostura bitters and rosemary notes and a rustic edge.

*1994 Château Borie-Azeau, Corbières, Val d'Orbieu   15/20
Full-bodied 🍷🍷🍷 ▮

Marginally cheaper than the Saint Chinian, but smoother, richer and more concentrated with a chocolatey, plum-like fruitiness and a spicy aftertaste.

*1995 Sainsbury's La Baume Merlot, Vin de Pays d'Oc   14/20
Full-bodied 🍷 ▮

Structured, Aussie-made Languedoc Merlot with sweet oak tannins and a core of supple, black cherry fruit. Only the drying finish lets it down.

*1994 Sainsbury's La Baume Cabernet Sauvignon, Vin de Pays d'Oc   13/20
Full-bodied ▮

Someone should have siphoned this out of the barrel a few months earlier, as the oak creates a hard, sawdusty impression on the palate. A pity, because this could have been a rather good red.

ITALY

Sainsbury's Sicilian Nero d'Avola/Merlot, Settesoli   14/20
Medium-bodied 👜👜 ▮

A soft, raisiny southern Italian red combining the local Nero d'Avola grape with the more international Merlot. The result is pleasant, if a little uninspiring.

Biferno Rosso, Campo Marino   15/20
Full-bodied 👜👜👜 ▮

Intensely herby, aromatic Italian *rosso* made from the Negroamaro grape, with smooth, ripe, raisiny notes and a kernel of sweetly robust tannins.

*1994 Sainsbury's Cabernet Sauvignon, Barrique-Aged, Atesino
14/20

Medium-bodied 👜 ▮

A New World-influenced combination of toasty, coffee-bean oak and green-pepper Cabernet characters. The wine could do with a bit more middle.

SOUTH AFRICA

Sainsbury's South African Cinsault/Pinotage, Vinfruco   14/20
Medium-bodied 👜👜👜 ▮

Stem ginger and sandalwood aromas lead into a well-made, juicy, modern blend of traditional Cape varieties. A very decent wine at a decent price.

*Sainsbury's South African Cabernet Sauvignon, Vinfruco   15/20
Medium-bodied 👜👜👜 ▮

Another stunner from South Africa, showing ripe, supple fruit, sweet oak, minty complexity and super length of flavour.

SPAIN

*Sainsbury's Navarra, Agronavarra   14/20
Medium-bodied 👜👜 ▮

Modern, juicy blend of Tempranillo and Cabernet Sauvignon grapes produced in a Beaujolais style to emphasise the plum and blackcurrant suppleness. Finishes a bit dry.

---

*Sainsbury's Rioja, Olarra   15/20
Medium-bodied 👜👜 ▮

A classic Rioja blend of Tempranillo and Garnacha grapes enhanced by American oak sweetness. Deliciously refreshing, with an attractively mature, strawberry fruitiness.

UNITED STATES

*Sainsbury's California Red Wine, Canandaigua   11/20
Medium-bodied ▮

Heavy, confected California plonk. Few countries manage to produce wines as unpleasant as this, at £3.50 a bottle.

*Southbay California Pinot Noir   15/20
Medium-bodied 👜👜 ▮

Tawny-coloured California Pinot Noir, which is still hanging in there, with attractively mature raspberry and strawberry fruitiness and a touch of sweet oak.

£5–8

CHILE

1991 Santa Carolina Cabernet Sauvignon Reserve   15/20
Medium-bodied 👜👜 ▮

Made by Pilar Gonzalez from grapes grown at Santa Rosa Vineyard in Chile's Maipo Valley, this is sweet essence of blackcurrant, with refreshing acidity and length on the aftertaste.

1993 Santa Carolina Merlot Reserve   15/20
Medium-bodied 👜👜 ▮

Younger, oakier Santa Carolina red from the San Fernando Valley. A wine for ageing Abba fans.

FRANCE

*Sainsbury's Red Burgundy, Rodet   15/20
Medium-bodied 👜👜 ▮

Solid, characterful Pinot Noir from the Mercurey-based house of Antonin Rodet, rounded out by a spell in oak barrels. Well-priced Bourgogne *rouge*.

1995 Juliénas, Château des Capitans, Robert Sarrau   15/20
Medium-bodied 💰💰 🍷

From négociant Robert Sarrau's own vineyards, this is a lively, cherry Beaujolais *cru* with elegant Gamay fruitiness and thirst-quenching acidity.

1993 Cave de la Cessane Grenache/Syrah, Saint Chinian
16/20
Full-bodied 💰💰💰 🍷

Licoricey, intensely fruity, well-structured Languedoc red matured in French oak. The fragrant Syrah component gives the wine added life and interest.

1990 Château de Crouseilles, Madiran   15/20
Full-bodied 💰💰 🍷

A mature, vanilla-oaky Tannat showing the grape's characteristic bite, rusticity and capacity to age. An ambitious and successful co-operative red.

1991 Château La Voulte Gasparets, Corbières   16/20
Full-bodied 💰💰💰 🍷

Intensely rosemary-scented developed Corbières from one of the best estates in the Languedoc. The gamey, meaty tannins cry out for a good chunk of beef (French beef, *ça va sans le dire*).

1993 Sainsbury's Classic Selection, Saint Emilion   15/20
Medium-bodied 💰💰 🍾

A youthful, oak-imprinted Bordeaux red, which manages to avoid the excessive green streak that mars many a 1993. Firm, classic (as the label implies) Right Bank claret.

PORTUGAL

*1993 Quinta da Bacalhôa Cabernet Sauvignon   13/20
Medium-bodied 🍷

Soupy, cooked, old-fashioned Portuguese Cabernet, which is living on its past reputation. Has a useful back label – as long as you're fluent in Portuguese.

SOUTH AFRICA

*1995 Sainsbury's South African Pinotage Reserve Selection   16/20
Full-bodied 💰💰💰 🍾

Beyers Truter, the king of Cape Pinotage, has produced a French-oak-aged corker. Inky purple in colour, packed with concentrated, spicy Pinotage fruit, and promising much for the future.

1994 Fairview Cabernet Sauvignon   15/20
Medium-bodied 🝪🝪 ▬
A more extracted style of Cape Cabernet from wine- and cheesemaker Charles Back, with savoury French oak characters and sweet cassis fruit to the fore.

SPAIN

1990 Orobio Reserva Rioja, Cosecheros Alavesas   15/20
Medium-bodied 🝪🝪 ▮
Coconutty oak and cherry-raspberry fruitiness make this mature, barrel-aged Rioja an enjoyable introduction to Spain's best red-wine region.

Over £8

AUSTRALIA

1991 Wynns Coonawarra Cabernet Sauvignon   16/20
Full-bodied 🝪🝪🝪 ▬
Elegant, sweetly oaked, coffee-bean and cassis-flavoured Cabernet Sauvignon from Australia's leading cool-climate region, showing concentrated fruit and fine-grained tannins.

FRANCE

*1993 Gevrey Chambertin, Maurice Chenu   15/20
Medium-bodied 🝪 ▮
Oak-rich, faintly soupy village Burgundy from one of the best recent vintages. Well-made, chocolatey Pinot Noir.

1990 Château Vieux Chevrol, Lalande de Pomerol   14/20
Medium-bodied 🝪 ▮
Dullish, ageing Merlot from Pomerol satellite appellation, Lalande de Pomerol. Might appeal to ultra-traditionalists, but we found its rusticity overdone.

1990 Château Coutelin Merville, Cru Bourgeois, Saint Estèphe

16/20

Medium-bodied 🍾🍾🍾 ▄▄
Savoury-oaky, meaty, mature Left Bank claret with intense fruitiness, strappingly firm backbone and the ability to age for a few years yet.

Rosé

£3–5

FRANCE

*Bordeaux Clairet, Pierre Coste   14/20
Dry 🍾🍾 ▌
Juicy, deeply coloured, green-pepper-scented Bordeaux rosé with considerable weight, good depth of flavour and a sophisticated dry finish.

1995 Sainsbury's Domaine de la Tuilerie Merlot Rosé, Vin de Pays d'Oc   15/20
Dry 🍾🍾🍾 ▌
Made entirely from the Merlot grape, this bronze-pink rosé is a delicately balanced, raspberry fruit number with a pleasingly moreish quality.

Sparkling

£3–5

AUSTRALIA

*Sainsbury's Australian Sparkling Wine, Seppelt   13/20
Off-dry 👜 ▮
Fresh, lemon-sherbet confection from Seppelts Great Western winery, made in a light, innocuous style.

£5–8

AUSTRALIA

1992 Seaview Sparkling   15/20
Dry 👜👜 ▮
From the Penfolds stable, this is a beer-yeasty, Champagne-method blend of Pinot Noir and Chardonnay, with mature, old-style fruitiness and a nutty aftertaste.

NEW ZEALAND

Montana Lindauer Brut   15/20
Dry 👜👜👜 ▮
Fresh, transfer-method Kiwi fizz with tangy acidity and creamy-textured fruit. Elegantly balanced.

SOUTH AFRICA

*Madeba Brut   15/20
Dry 👜👜👜 ▮
A Robertson blend of the Champagne grapes Pinot Noir and Chardonnay, this has more going for it on the palate than the nose. Still, it's a creamy, pleasantly fruity Champagne alternative at a good price.

SPAIN

*Sainsbury's Cava   15/20
Dry 🍾🍾🍾 |

For the same price, you can buy a bottle of this complex, nicely mature Cava with malty fruitiness and a lively acidity.

Over £8

FRANCE

*Sainsbury's Blanc de Noirs Champagne   16/20
Dry 🍾🍾🍾 |

Still on the youthful side, this rich, strawberry fruity Champagne, made entirely from Pinot Noir grapes at the Champagne Palmer co-operative, is extremely good value at around £12.

*Sainsbury's Extra Dry Champagne, Duval-Leroy   15/20
Dry 🍾🍾 |

Crisp, fruity, elegant own-label Champagne from the house of Duval-Leroy, with an attractive degree of bottle-aged maturity.

*1990 Sainsbury's Vintage Champagne, Blanc de Blancs   17/20
Dry 🍾🍾🍾 |

From the Gruet co-operative at Bethon in the Côte Sézannaise, this is a finely balanced, all-Chardonnay Champagne with a delicate, creamy mousse and very good length of flavour. A class act.

Fortified

£3–5

PORTUGAL

Sainsbury's Madeira   15/20
Full-bodied 🍾🍾 ▬
Baked, toffee-sweet Madeira with flavours of coffee and caramelised sugar and a tangy, palate-cleansing aftertaste.

SPAIN

*Sainsbury's Pale Dry Fino Sherry, Morgan Bros   14/20
Off-dry 🍾🍾 ▮
Salty, tangy, well-made basic Fino with a teaspoonful of sweetness to round it out.

Sainsbury's Aged Amontillado Sherry, 37.5 cl., Del Ducado 15/20
Dry 🍾🍾🍾 ▮
Almondy, savoury dry Amontillado Sherry with the freshness and nuttiness you would expect from a well-made, mature Sherry.

Sainsbury's Oloroso Sherry, 37.5 cl., Morgan Bros   16/20
Dry 🍾🍾🍾 ▮
Fresh, dry, old-style Oloroso which, despite what Orson Welles used to imply, is best when it's dry. Classy, oak-matured *crème brûlée* style.

Over £8

PORTUGAL

Sainsbury's 10 Year Old Tawny Port, Noval   16/20
Full-bodied 🍾🍾🍾 ▬
Traditional, youthful tawny, which has still got plenty of sweet, chocolatey fruit, good weight and a spicy intensity. Very Portuguese in style.

Somerfield
(including **Gateway**) ☆☆(☆)

Address: Somerfield House, Whitchurch Lane, Bristol BS14 OTJ

Telephone/fax: 0117 9359359; 0117 9780629

Number of branches: 610 (including 28 Food Giant)

Opening hours: Varies from store to store, but generally 8.00am to 8.00pm Monday to Saturday and 10.00am to 4.00pm Sunday

Credit cards accepted: All

Discounts: 12 bottles for the price of 11, excluding Price Check wines, on any unmixed case

Facilities and services: Occasional in-store tastings

Special offers: Regular 'Price Check' promotions

Top ten best-selling wines: Somerfield Lambrusco Bianco; Somerfield Liebfraumilch; Somerfield Hock; Somerfield Muscadet; Somerfield Claret; Somerfield Vin de Pays des Coteaux de l'Ardèche Rouge; Somerfield Bulgarian Cabernet Sauvignon; Somerfield Valencia Dry White; Somerfield Bulgarian Country White; Somerfield Vin de Pays des Coteaux de l'Ardèche Blanc

Range:

GOOD: Italian red, French country wines

AVERAGE: Australia, Germany, Chile, Bordeaux, Burgundy, Rhône, Italian white, Portugal, New Zealand, United States, Champagne

POOR: Spain, Eastern Europe

UNDER-REPRESENTED: New World sparkling wines

Angela Mount is a remarkably busy wine buyer. She selects all the wines in Somerfield's list, deals with journalists, suppliers and designers, writes a column in the company's in-store magazine, travels to vineyard areas, dictates press releases and answers the telephone. Where some of her competitors have half a dozen wine buyers to help run the department, Ms Mount is reluctant to delegate. You get the impression that, if she had to, she'd find time to make and bottle the wines, too.

As you would expect, she's made quite an impact since she moved to Bristol from Safeway in 1990. At the time, Somerfield itself, or Gateway as it was known, was struggling. But right from the start, Mount's energy and enthusiasm ensured a higher profile for the wine department. She is clearly someone who believes that all publicity is welcome, whatever form it takes. Last year she even seemed to welcome one rival buyer's description of her as 'the scum of the earth'.

Nevertheless, a person can only do so much on her lonesome. 'Think back three years,' she says, 'and we were losing market share. Things weren't easy. Now we're in a position to announce a stock-market flotation'.

The arrival of David Simons as chief executive in February 1993 was a tremendous boon for the embattled chain. He renegotiated the company's debts, pumped a lot of money and new ideas into the stores, and changed their name from Gateway to Somerfield, a moniker that suggests holiday camps for wayward children.

Like a Soviet Communist regime combing the archives for incriminating photographs, it's taken time to air-brush the Gateway brand from the retail scene. Mount assures us that the last Gateway will have disappeared by the spring of 1997 and is delighted at the news. 'It carries a lot of baggage with it,' she says.

In the brave new Somerfield world, the focus is on 'fresh food and high-street retailing'. Not surprisingly, given the urban locations of many stores, they vary considerably in size. This affects the extent of the wine range. One hundred stores have the full 350-wine list, a further 300 have 80 per cent of it and the remaining 200-odd take about 60 per cent or less. This, according to Mount, keeps her on her tootsies. 'I have to get the core range right. I can't hide the basics behind the innovation.'

We're not so sure. In our view, the Somerfield range has a split personality. In the blue corner, there are interesting wines from Italy, the United States, Australia, Germany, Chile, Portugal and France; in the red, a worryingly dull set of basic wines, many of which feature among Somerfield's top-ten best-sellers. Just when we were starting to feel more positive about the chain's range, we tasted a rubbery 1995 South African Pinotage and a horrendous Valencia Dry White from Gandia, both of which carry the Somerfield brand. In short, the 130 own-label wines are not the calling card they might be.

Mount herself admits that parts of the range are still weak, namely Iberia, Eastern Europe and (for the bargain-basement lines) Germany. Perhaps that's why she's recently appointed a new assistant buyer, Mark Jerman, to help with the shoulder-straining workload. Some of these areas will be addressed in the short term, with revamped selections. Others, as Captain Oates might have put it, may take some time.

Somerfield's customers are becoming more adventurous, with 'lots of interest' in Chile, South Africa, the south of France and, of course, Australia (accounting for 8 per cent of sales on its own). Mount believes that her Price Check promotions, launched in May 1993 as a way of offering very good deals on specific wines for a two-week period, have 'encouraged people to experiment by reducing the financial risk'.

Some of Mount's competitors are unhappy about Price Check, claiming that regular £2.19 offerings merely lower the tone of the market. Mount denies this: 'I'm promoting our range by introducing it to the consumer,' she says. 'We make it very clear what the normal prices are, and a lot of people continue to buy the wines once the two-week blast has ended.'

The *Grapevine* team is equivocal about the concept. If it enables Somerfield wine drinkers to taste Chilean Cabernet Sauvignon at a good price, then fair enough. But many of the promoted lines don't taste terribly wonderful – even before the discount – and are sometimes sold at a loss. Very cheap prices screw the producer, as well as, in the final analysis, the customer.

Still, you can't fault Somerfield for creating interest in its wine range. It has produced informative leaflets (written by guess who?) on Chardonnay, Cabernet Sauvignon, Australia and summer drinking, complete with no-frills food and wine suggestions: 'Fish and chips, rather than lobster thermidor,' as Mount puts it.

One casualty this year, as in most multiple grocers, has been the fine-wine racks. These have been replaced by a series of two bottle mini-units incorporated into the main body of the wine range at strategic spots. This reflects the fact that only 15 per cent of Somerfield's wine sales retail above £5 and that the wine-rack wines were accumulating dust.

Even with Price Check promotions, Mount admits that it's getting harder and harder to keep prices under £3. Italy, Spain and South Africa have less wine to sell to the UK, so prices (as the theory of supply and demand says they must) have increased. Not even Angela Mount can change that.

White

Under £3

BULGARIA

Somerfield Bulgarian Country White, Welschriesling and Misket 13/20

Medium dry 💰💰 🍾

Spicy, encouragingly modern Bulgarian blend of the central European Welschriesling and Misket grapes rounded out with a touch of sweetness.

FRANCE

1995 Somerfield Vin de Pays des Côtes de Gascogne 13/20
Dry 💰💰 🍾

A fresh, crisp, apple and pear-like blend of Ugni Blanc and Colombard from Musketeer and Condom country. All for one? Or a packet of three?

GERMANY

Somerfield Hock, Rudolf Müller 13/20
Off-dry 💰💰 🍾

Fight your way past the sulphur dioxide and there's a tangy, grapefruity, Müller-Thurgau-based white struggling to get out.

Somerfield Liebfraumilch, Rheinberg Kellerei 12/20
Medium sweet 💰 🍾

Clean, floral, pleasantly fruity and fresh. One of the less offensive supermarket Liebs.

ITALY

Isola del Sole, Dolianova 12/20
Off-dry 🍾

A lead-pencil-scented, Nuragus-based Sardinian white with rather flat, baked apple fruit.

Somerfield Lambrusco Bianco, Casa Vinicola Donelli 12/20
Medium sweet 💰 🍾
A blend of no fewer than five different varieties. That's an awful lot of grapes for a simple, lemonadey concoction. It's frothy, man.

PORTUGAL

Estorila, Ribatejo, Vinho de Mesa 13/20
Dry 💰💰 🍾
A blend of the indigenous Fernão Pires and Mouriscas grapes, showing soft, lemony fruitiness and a distinctively earthy, Portuguese tang.

SOUTH AFRICA

Somerfield South African Dry White, Simonsvlei 13/20
Off-dry 💰💰 🍾
Soft, simple, sweetish, pear-droppy Cape Chenin Blanc made by the Simonsvlei co-operative. Fine if you liked boiled sweets.

SPAIN

Somerfield Valencia Dry White, Gandia 11/20
Dry 🍾
Made from the local Merseguera grape at the enormous Gandia winery, this is a dull, old-fashioned Spanish white. Sour and dilute.

£3–5

AUSTRALIA

Berri Estates Unwooded Chardonnay 14/20
Off-dry 💰 🍾
Soft, alcoholic, unoaked, warm-climate Chardonnay from the irrigated Australian Riverland. One-dimensional – but it's a pretty big dimension.

1995 Rawson's Retreat Bin 21 Semillon/Chardonnay/Colombard, Penfolds 15/20
Dry 🝆🝆🝆 ▮
A lime-fresh, ice cream soda-like blend of Semillon and Chardonnay from Australia's biggest winery, proving that large-volume wines can show character in the right hands.

1995 Jacob's Creek Chardonnay, Orlando 14/20
Off-dry 🝆 ▮
One of the biggest-selling wines in Britain. You can see why this commercial, sweetish, toasty oaky Chardonnay is so popular.

1995 Koonunga Hill Chardonnay, Penfolds 16/20
Dry 🝆🝆🝆 ▮
Classy, complex, barrel-fermented Aussie Chardonnay, with butter and toffee-fudge richness balanced by a beautifully judged, refreshing acidity.

CHILE

1996 Somerfield Chilean Sauvignon Blanc, Canepa 15/20
Dry 🝆🝆🝆 ▮
Zesty, ultra-fresh Chilean Sauvignon Blanc made by the lugubrious Andres llabaca and showing lemon and gooseberry fruitiness.

1995 Caliterra Chardonnay, Curicó 15/20
Dry 🝆 ▮
Sweet, tropical fruity Chilean Chardonnay with a soft texture and ripe peach and banana flavours.

1995 Caliterra Sauvignon Blanc, Curicó 15/20
Dry 🝆 ▮
Ripe, forward Sauvignon Blanc from the Curicó region of Chile's fertile central valley. Caliterra wines are made in a deliberately approachable style by the Errázuriz winery.

FRANCE

Somerfield Vin de Pays des Coteaux de l'Ardèche, UVICA 13/20
Dry 🝆🝆 ▮
A full, fruity, well-made southern French blend with clean appley acidity and good weight.

1995 Domaine Bordeneuve, Vin de Pays des Côtes de Gascogne Blanc, Grassa   14/20
Dry 🍷🍷🍷 ▮

Highly aromatic, modern Gascon white from the bearded Yves Grassa. The addition of a small percentage of the south-west French Gros Manseng grape lends the wine an extra dimension of grapefruity zest.

Chais Cuxac Viognier, Val d'Orbieu   15/20
Dry 🍷🍷 ▮

A well-priced introduction to the Midi's most fashionable white variety, demonstrating the grape's floral, apricotty aromas and characteristic plumpness.

Somerfield Entre Deux Mers, Yvon Mau   13/20
Off-dry 🍷 ▮

Basic, bog-standard Bordeaux white blend of Sauvignon Blanc and Semillon with a dose of sweetness.

1995 Chardonnay Vin de Pays du Jardin de la France   13/20
Off-dry 🍷🍷 ▮

Floral, sweetish, decently made Loire Chardonnay from one of France's largest *vin de pays* regions.

1994 Somerfield Chardonnay, Vin de Pays d'Oc   13/20
Dry 🍷 ▮

Made for Somerfield by Languedoc-based Englishman James Herrick, this is a medium-weight, toffee-apple-like, lightly oaked Chardonnay that has lost some of its freshness.

1995 Domaine de la Tuilerie Chardonnay, Hugh Ryman
15/20
Dry 🍷🍷🍷 ▮

Ripe, plump, juicy Languedoc Chardonnay from flying winemaker Hugh Ryman, with a light touch of oak character adding extra complexity. A bargain at under £4.

1994 Bordeaux Blanc Oak-Aged, Louis Eschenauer   15/20
Dry 🍷🍷 ▮

Delicately oaked, Graves-style Bordeaux blend, with texture and weight derived from the Semillon grape.

GERMANY

1994 Somerfield Rheinhessen Spätlese, Rheinberg Kellerei   14/20
Medium sweet 👜👜 🍾
Fresh, melon-scented, Müller-Thurgau-based white with attractive, grapey fruitiness and honeyed sweetness.

1994 Somerfield Rheinhessen Auslese, Rheinberg Kellerei   15/20
Medium 👜👜👜 🍾
Honeyed, rich, affordable Auslese, with grapefruity flavours adding freshness and zip to the sweetness.

1995 Somerfield Niersteiner Spiegelberg Kabinett, Rudolf Müller
14/20

Off-dry 👜👜 🍾
A light, floral, zippy, Müller-Thurgau-based medium white with crunchy, grapefruity acidity.

HUNGARY

1995 Gyöngyös Chardonnay, Hugh Ryman   14/20
Dry 👜👜 🍾
Fresh, zippy, lightly oaked, greengage-style Hungarian Chardonnay from Hugh Ryman. A vast improvement on recent, disappointing vintages.

1995 Gyöngyös Sauvignon Blanc, Hugh Ryman   14/20
Dry 👜👜 🍾
A good vintage for Hungarian whites has helped to boost the aromatic intensity of the Sauvignon Blanc grape in this lemon-zesty, crisp, dry white.

ITALY

1995 Somerfield Frascati, Pallavicini   14/20
Dry 👜 🍾
A nutty Roman blend of Trebbiano Toscano and Malvasia di Candia, with surprising depth of flavour and refreshing acidity.

1994 Chardonnay del Salento, Le Trulle, Kym Milne   15/20
Dry 👜👜 🍾
Aussie Kym Milne has made a full-flavoured, oak-influenced Chardonnay in the heel of Italy. Fresh, but weighty.

NEW ZEALAND

1995 Timara Dry White, Montana   14/20
Off-dry 🝑 🍾
Notes of tinned asparagus and gooseberry fruit make this a well-priced starter bottle for New Zealand wine neophytes.

PORTUGAL

1995 Bairrada Branco, Caves Aliança   13/20
Dry 🝑 🍾
Baked, almost resinous, northern Portuguese blend of Bical, Maria Gomes, Sercial and Rabo, showing good acidity and a bitter aftertaste.

SOUTH AFRICA

Huguenot Hills South African Chardonnay   11/20
Dry 🍾
Fruitless (in both senses of the word), dilute Cape white. Spot the Chardonnay, if you can.

1995 Bellingham Sauvignon Blanc, Paarl   15/20
Dry 🝑🝑🝑 🍾
Nettley, grassy Cape Sauvignon Blanc, which has succeeded in capturing the grape's distinctive character – no mean achievement for a warm-climate area. A lively, zippy dry white.

SPAIN

1994 Gandia Chardonnay, Hoya Valley   14/20
Dry 🝑🝑🝑 🍾
Cleverly packaged to resemble a New World Chardonnay, this comes from Spain's eastern seaboard. For an oaked Chardonnay at just over £3 it's an attractively fruity, commercial white that would look good on any dinner table.

UNITED STATES

1994 Redwood Trail, California Chardonnay   15/20
Dry 🝑🝑 🍾
An interesting, well-priced (for California) Chardonnay, with considerable, oak-aged complexity for a sub-£5 wine. An elegant, spicy, buttery-textured white.

£5–8

AUSTRALIA

1995 Rosemount Semillon, Hunter Valley   16/20
Dry 🍷🍷🍷 ▬
Modern, lightly oaked, mealy Hunter Valley Semillon from Rosemount winemaker Philip Shaw, showing herby undertones and attractively textured fruitiness. Intensely refreshing.

1994 Penfolds Barrel-Fermented Chardonnay   14/20
Dry 🍷 |
Old-fashioned, nutty, rather ponderous white, with a copse of smoky oak to the fore. We prefer the more delicate new style evident in Penfolds' 1995 white wines.

FRANCE

1995 Somerfield White Burgundy, Cottin   15/20
Dry 🍷🍷 |
Spicy, lightly oaked, fruity white Burgundy from the reliable Labouré-Roi stable, made in an approachable, New World-influenced style.

1995 Somerfield Gewürztraminer d'Alsace, Cave de Turckheim
    15/20
Dry 🍷🍷 |
Classic rose-petal and lychee aromas and a rich, weighty concentration of fruit lifted by fresh acidity.

1995 Sancerre, Fouassier   16/20
Bone dry 🍷🍷🍷 ▬
Youthful, estate-grown, minerally, super-fresh Sancerre at an excellent price.

NEW ZEALAND

1995 Coopers Creek Chardonnay, Gisborne   16/20
Dry 🍷🍷🍷 |
Butterscotchy, well-oaked Kiwi Chardonnay made in a Burgundian style by the exuberant Kim Crawford. An elegant, spicy, cool-climate white from the Chardonnay capital of New Zealand's North Island.

Red

Under £3

ARGENTINA

Somerfield Argentine Red, San Juan, Peñaflor   13/20
Medium-bodied 👜👜 ▮
An Italianate blend of Barbera and Sangiovese, made by Peter Bright at the Peñaflor winery, showing sweet, strawberry fruit and dry tannins.

BULGARIA

Somerfield Bulgarian Country Red, Merlot and Pinot Noir, Sliven Region   11/20
Medium-bodied ▮
Plonky, boot-polish aromas and simple, old-fashioned, pre-revolutionary flavours. Let us know if you find any Pinot Noir character here. It escaped our attention.

1989 Somerfield Bulgarian Cabernet Sauvignon, Melnik   10/20
Medium-bodied ▮
Leathery, dry, unreconstructed red. Best left under the bed in a chamber pot.

FRANCE

Vin de Pays des Bouches du Rhône Rouge, Lucien de Noblens
                    12/20
Light-bodied 👜 ▮
Light, peppery, carbonic-maceration southern French red with soft tannins and a plonky aftertaste.

PORTUGAL

Leziria Tinto, Vinho de Mesa Tinto   13/20
Medium-bodied 👜👜 ▮
A spicy, sweetly fruity, raisiny blend of the native Portuguese varieties, Bobal and Monastrell. A good party red.

£3–5

AUSTRALIA

1994 Rawson's Retreat Bin 35, Cabernet/Shiraz   14/20
Full-bodied 🍷 🍷
A minty, sagey Aussie blend of Cabernet Sauvignon and Shiraz, in which dry oakiness dominates the sweet blackcurrant fruit. Not as good as the Rawsons white.

CHILE

Somerfield Chilean Cabernet Sauvignon, Montes   14/20
Medium-bodied 🍷🍷 🍷
Slightly rustic-nosed Chilean Cabernet Sauvignon with juicy, underlying blackcurrant fruit and fine-grained tannins.

FRANCE

Somerfield Vin de Pays des Coteaux de l'Ardèche Rouge, UVICA   13/20
Medium-bodied 🍷🍷 🍷
Fresh, peppery, softly fruity southern French Grenache-based blend with a rustic bite of dry tannin.

1994 Château Le Clairiot, Bordeaux   14/20
Medium-bodied 🍷 🍷
Forward, drinkable, supple-textured blend of Merlot, Cabernet Sauvignon and Cabernet Franc, showing ripe Merlot characters and medium-weight tannins.

1994 Domaine La Tuque Bel Air, Côtes de Castillon   15/20
Medium-bodied 🍷🍷 🍷
Deeply coloured, youthful, firmly structured claret from the Castillon hills. On the chewy side, but showing some sweet chocolatey fruit, too.

1994 Somerfield Oak Aged Claret, Peter Sichel   14/20
Medium-bodied 🍷 🍷
A blend of (mainly) Cabernet Sauvignon, with some Merlot and Cabernet Franc, aged in oak for eight months. The result is a mellow, well-made claret, which dries a little on the aftertaste.

1995 Somerfield Côtes du Rhône, Le Cellier de Roussillac   13/20
Medium-bodied 🍷 ▮

Basic, decently crafted, modern-style Côtes du Rhône with a soft raspberry fruitiness. Pulls up rather short.

1993 Crozes-Hermitage, Cellier de Noblens   15/20
Medium-bodied 🍷🍷🍷 ▮

Unoaked, abundantly aromatic northern Rhône Syrah with spicy, blackberry fruit and medium weight. A characterful example of Crozes-Hermitage under £5.

Claret, Louis Eschenauer   13/20
Medium-bodied 🍷 ▮

Muted aromas and drying flavours suggest that this own-label Bordeaux red is getting on a bit. But it's a decent claret at the price.

1994 Somerfield Mâcon Rouge, Labouré-Roi   15/20
Medium-bodied 🍷🍷 ▮

The back label claims that this is 100 per cent Pinot Noir, 'the only grape permitted in red Burgundy', but we suspect there may be more than a touch of (perfectly legal) Gamay in this youthful, cherryish blend.

1993 Château de Caraguilhes, Corbières   13/20
Full-bodied ▮

An organic blend of Carignan, Grenache, Syrah and a little Mourvèdre, in which the fruit is on the hard shoulder and the rustic tannins are doing 100mph in the fast lane.

1993 Château Valoussière, Coteaux du Languedoc   15/20
Full-bodied 🍷🍷 ▮

Aromatic, oak-aged Languedoc blend from Midi merchants Jeanjean, with vigorous, chocolatey fruit sweetness and dry, splintery tannins. Nearly very good indeed.

Fitou, Cuvée Rocher d'Embrée, Mont Tauch   14/20
Full-bodied 🍷🍷 ▮

Typically well-crafted example of the Languedoc's best-known wine from the Mont Tauch co-operative, showing thyme-like herbiness and sun-baked, sweetly ripe fruit. Pass the Factor 15.

1994 Vacqueyras Vieux Clocher, Arnoux   14/20
Full-bodied 👜
Rich, Grenache-anchored southern Rhône red with plenty of peppery bite, alcohol and rough-edged tannin.

ITALY

1994 Somerfield Lazio Rosso, Casale del Giglio   14/20
Light-bodied 👜👜
A blend of Merlot and Sangiovese from a region once graced by idiot-savant, P. Gascoigne Esq. A grassy, lightly fruity, refreshing red with quaffable juiciness.

I Grilli di Villa Thalia, Rosso di Sicilia   15/20
Medium-bodied 👜👜👜
Raspberry and loganberry aromas and smooth, raisiny southern Italian fruit. A wine in which the grassy Cabernet Sauvignon character lends freshness and structure to the Nero d'Avola, Sangiovese and Syrah grapes. Brilliant value at around £3.60.

1994 Montepulciano d'Abruzzo, Umani Ronchi   14/20
Medium-bodied 👜👜
Cherryish Adriatic *rosso* made from the refreshing Montepulciano grape. A good wine-bar red.

1993 Chianti Classico, Montecchio   13/20
Medium-bodied 👜
Smooth, commercial but slightly soulless Chianti, with obtrusive dry tannins poking through the Sangiovese fruit.

1992 Copertino   14/20
Full-bodied 👜👜
A Salento blend of Negroamaro, Malvasia Nera and Montepulciano grapes, with mature, leathery, raisiny fruit characters and coffee notes. A wine for traditionalists.

PORTUGAL

1995 Quinta da Pancas, Sociedad Agricola Purio   15/20
Full-bodied 👜👜 ▬
Riper in style than the 1994, this chunky, deeply coloured, youthful Portuguese blend of Cabernet Sauvignon and Periquita is a real find. Packed with cassis and black-cherry fruitiness and blessed with the structure to age.

SOUTH AFRICA

1995 Somerfield South African Pinotage   11/20
Full-bodied ▪
Dry, chewy, vinegary Cape red. One to sprinkle over your fish and chips.

1995 Kumala Cinsault/Pinotage, Sonop   15/20
Full-bodied 🍷🍷🍷 ▪
A well-made, warm-climate blend of Cinsault and the indigenous South African
Pinotage. Sweetly ripe, red fruit flavours with a characterful slice or three of
baked banana.

Landema Falls South African Cabernet Sauvignon   15/20
Medium-bodied 🍷🍷🍷 ▪
Juicy, ripe, green-pepper Cape Cabernet Sauvignon with a minty undertone
and gripping tannins.

Huguenot Hills Cape Red   12/20
Medium-bodied ▪
Basic, sweetened-up, Beaujolais-style Cape plonk with baked, raspberry
fruitiness. Guaranteed to drive the Huguenots back whence they came.

UNITED STATES

Somerfield Californian Dry Red, Sebastiani   14/20
Full-bodied 🍷🍷 ▪
A west-coast blend of Cabernet Sauvignon and Petite Sirah, with sweet,
exuberant fruit flavours of plum and strawberry. One of the few drinkable
Californian wines under £4.

1994 Redwood Trail Pinot Noir, Sterling Vineyards   15/20
Medium-bodied 🍷🍷 ▪
Recognisably New World Pinot Noir at an affordable price. Wild strawberry
fruitiness, soft tannins, lollipop-sweet alcohol and a veneer of vanilla oakiness.

£5–8

AUSTRALIA

1992 Hardy's Bankside Shiraz   15/20
Full-bodied 👜👜 ▮

Cinnamon, clove and nutmeg aromas and sweet, spicy, chocolatey fruit smoothed over with vanilla oak. Good-value Aussie Shiraz.

1992 Penfolds Bin 407 Cabernet Sauvignon   14/20
Full-bodied 👜 ▬▬

It's still youthful, but this South Australian Cabernet Sauvignon is over-oaked for the weight of fruit in the glass. Not one of Penfolds' greatest hits.

FRANCE

1992 Château Latour Ségur, Lussac Saint Emilion   15/20
Medium-bodied 👜👜 ▮

From one of the galaxy of Saint Emilion satellites, this is a light, elegant red, which reminded us more of the Côte d'Or than of Bordeaux. Maybe no bad thing in 1992.

1993 Château Saint Robert, Graves   15/20
Medium-bodied 👜👜 ▬▬

Youthful, coffee-bean and vanilla oaky red, made in a modern style and showing considerable structure and cassis fruitiness for the vintage.

1993 Château Baron Ségur, Montagne Saint Emilion   13/20
Medium-bodied ▮

Dullish, rather dilute Right Bank claret, which appears to have suffered from the wet weather that bedevilled the 1993 vintage.

ITALY

1995 Somerfield Chianti Classico, Conti Serristori, Villa Primavera   13/20
Medium-bodied ▮

Commercial, if pricey, soupy Chianti Classico, which tastes as if it comes from further south. Allegedly, of course.

1990 Salice Salentino, Azienda Agricola Taurino   15/20
Full-bodied 👜👜 🍾

A blend of 80 per cent Negroamaro and 20 per cent Malvasia Nera, with traditional southern Italian flavours of prune and raisin backed up by dryish tannins.

LEBANON

1989 Château Musar, Bekaa Valley   12/20
Full-bodied 🍾

Raisiny, old-fashioned, over-alcoholic, vinegary Lebanese red, which barely survived the ravages of war. A curiosity that has had its day, but is still popular with fogeys, young and old.

Over £8

FRANCE

Domaine de la Solitude, Châteauneuf-du-Pape   16/20
Full-bodied 👜👜👜 ➖

Modern, peppery, Grenache-based Châteauneuf-du-Pape, with a spicy, brown-sugar fruitiness, substantial weight and richness, and a firm backbone of tannin. Will age for another three to five years.

Rosé

£3–5

FRANCE

1995 Domaine de la Bouletière, Vin de Pays des Coteaux de Cabrerisse   14/20
Dry 👜👜 🍾

Pale pink, organically grown Languedoc rosé made in a delicate, thirst-quenching style for those posing pouch moments.

1995 Rosé de Syrah, Vin de Pays d'Oc, Val d'Orbieu　　　14/20
Dry ⚶ 🍾
Middle-of-the-road, strawberry-cup-style rosé from France's largest winery, Val d'Orbieu with refreshing acidity and zing.

Sparkling

£3–5

SPAIN

Somerfield Cava, Blanc de Blancs　　　　　　　　　　14/20
Dry ⚶⚶ 🍾
Blanc de Blancs is a rather silly description for a wine that can only be made from white grapes. Be that as it may, this is a fresh, drinkable fizz with youthful, lemony fruit.

£5–8

FRANCE

1991 Crémant de Bourgogne, Caves de Bailly　　　　　14/20
Off-dry ⚶ 🍾
Lemony, yeasty, aged Burgundian sparkler, with a light mousse but rather hefty sweetness and alcohol.

SPAIN

Codorniu Brut Chardonnay, Première Cuvée　　　　　16/20
Dry ⚶⚶⚶ 🍾
Unusually for a Cava, this is made entirely from the distinctly un-Spanish Chardonnay grape. Just as well, because this has a lot more finesse, flavour and richness than most Iberian fizz.

Over £8

FRANCE

Prince William Non-Vintage Champagne, Palmer   14/20
Dry 🛇 ▮
A well-priced, Pinot-dominated own-label Chardonnay for supporters of the
Windsor family and Orange people. A fruity, decent, if unspectacular, fizz.

Prince William Blanc de Blancs, Michel Gonet   13/20
Off-dry ▮
Big-bubbled, distinctly coarse Champagne with confected Chardonnay fruit
flavours. Not a great advertisement for Champagne or the royals. Off with its
head!

Prince William Rosé, Henri Mandois   15/20
Dry 🛇🛇 ▮
Considerably more interesting than the Blanc de Blancs, showing the fragrant
strawberry fruitiness of the Pinot Noir grape and bronze-hued finesse.

Fortified

£5–8

FRANCE

Muscat de Frontignan, Vin de Liqueur   12/20
Very sweet ▮
A dried fig and stale honey-style sticky from the south of France. Coarse and
unshaven.

Spar ☆☆

Address: 32–40 Headstone Drive, Harrow, Middlesex HA5 5QT

Telephone/fax: 0181 863 5511; 0181 863 0603

Number of branches: 2,450, of which 1,967 are licensed

Opening hours: Varies, but an average of 96 hours a week per store

Credit cards accepted: At individual retailer's discretion

Discounts: At individual retailer's discretion

Facilities and services: Glass loan and in-store tastings in some branches; 450 retailers belong to the Spar Wine Club

Special offers: Promotions of two bottles for £5

Top ten best-selling wines: Spar Lambrusco; Spar Liebfraumilch; Spar Valencia; Spar Bulgarian Country Wine; Spar Hock Tafelwein; Spar French Country Wine; Spar Soave; Jacob's Creek Red/White; Spar Valpolicella; Spar Claret

Range:

GOOD: South Africa

AVERAGE: Bordeaux, regional France, Germany, Italy, Spain, Hungary, Bulgaria, Australia, Chile

POOR: Sparkling wines

UNDER-REPRESENTED: Portugal, Burgundy, Alsace

Spar is a curious set-up. More numerous than either Thresher or Victoria Wine, its 1,967 licensed stores make Spar the second-biggest off-licence group in the country. Yet its endearingly loose structure, consisting of mostly independent convenience shops, deprives it of any headline-grabbing focus.

In essence, Spar sees itself as the do-gooding corner-shop ally of the little person in the community, in the struggle against the all-powerful supermarket groups. Spar (the name comes from the Dutch for thrift) is basically a top-up store away from the high street, providing a local service for anyone who wants a bottle of wine any time of the day or night to go with their daily loaf or *Daily Mail*.

Spar

Thirty-seven stores, mainly in city centres, are now open 24 hours a day, compared with just ten a year ago. This may be accounted for by the fact that a surprising number of Spar shoppers are young people. Wine at Spar accounts for 15 per cent of turnover, but sales continue to rise. Last year sales were up by 25 per cent.

In line with the general off-licence trend towards – excuse the marketing speak – segmentation, Spar stores are being split into three types, each 'selected for its relevance to local needs', as the marketeers would have it. Spar Neighbourhood is the archetypal convenience store and the main resource for the local community. Spar Express, in busy urban areas, is smaller, open longer hours and puts more emphasis on fresh produce. Spar supermarkets are the biggest stores, with the widest range of services and at least 4,000 different lines.

Technically Spar is a symbol group, in which members pay a levy for the symbol. Like Russian dolls, each individual retailer is part of a local guild, which in turn reports to a higher national guild and eventually to a European guild. Next stop the world?

In all, there are 22,000 Spars in 26 countries. The bigger Spars (the biggest is 15,000 square feet) are owned by the Spar Landmark organisation itself, an umbrella body for Spar's retail and wholesale divisions and for Landmark cash and carry. In all, about 350 Spars are organisation-owned.

Since Spar's wine buyer Liz Aked took over the reins of power from Philippa Carr at the end of 1994, she has increasingly stamped the range with her own ideas and personality. While Carr made sure that Spar had the traditional areas of Europe covered, Aked's mission has been, in her own words, 'to take the New World by the scruff of the neck'. Concentrating on good-value New World wines, the emphasis has been on Chile, Australia and South Africa. In Europe, southern Italy has also got more of a look-in.

The new wines from South Africa and Chile in particular have given the Spar range a glossier, more streamlined look. Aked also intends to add a Sauvignon Blanc from the 1996 vintage to the own-label Chilean Chardonnay, Cabernet and Merlot and to make California her new mission. Australia presents more of a problem, now that it's virtually abandoned the sub-£4 field to its competitors, but boosted by the ever-reliable Jacob's Creek, Oz is clinging on to New World pole-position at Spar.

Already, the increased bias towards the New World can be measured by the drop in sales of French, Italian and German wines from 70 to 55 per cent; 15 per cent of sales still come from Spain, with 10 per cent each from Australia and Eastern Europe, and the rest from Chile, South Africa and California. According to Aked, 'South Africa has been the star-turn of the first part of 1996. It's really motoring.'

The average price of a bottle of wine at Spar is around £3.35, with an average lowest price of £2.75, which descends to a Scrooge-seducing £2.45 in the Spar Christmas promotion. Aked won't tear her hair out if she's 20 pence less competitive than some on a Montepulciano d'Abruzzo, but she's determined not to be out of line with supermarket and high-street prices on yardstick wines like Jacob's Creek and Spar claret.

Shelf-edge descriptors, and promotions such as the two wines for a fiver, have been successful in attracting customers to the delights of the Spar range. Aked has more plans on this front: a varietal promotion as well, and a 100 Days of Wine leading into 1997.

As busy trading controller for a large group, Aked can't just twiddle her thumbs and wait for things to happen. The amorphous structure of the Spar group means that stores aren't necessarily committed to buying from Aked HQ. In practice they do, and in a short space of time Aked has increased the proportion of wines supplied by her to Spar stores from 60 to 80 per cent.

She is helped in this by the Spar Wine Club. With 450 of the licensed outlets members, the club helps Aked create a forum for staff who are interested in wine. With the focus on wines in the £3.49–£4.99 price range, staff are given the incentive to sell better wines, while standard-bearers such as Rosemount and the Grans Fassian Mosel Riesling 'give the staff something to hang their hats on'.

Until this year Aked has done the demanding job on her own. Now she's to be joined by a buying assistant, Jo Power, and another new recruit, Stuart Croucher. The luxury of a three-person wine department (plus two stock controllers) should allow her the freedom to work on improving the basics further, and to get out and about a bit more. Her aim is to provide retailers with a better service and take the range to 200 lines (175 different wines) by May 1997. We've not heard the last of Spar – or of Liz Aked.

White

Under £3

BULGARIA

Spar Bulgarian Country White, Slaviantzi   13/20
Dry 🍶🍶 ▮
A blend of Muskat and Ugni Blanc, made in an aromatic, cool-fermented, modern style, this is a good, floral, summery white.

PORTUGAL

Dona Elena, Co-operativa de Benfica, Ribatejo   14/20
Dry 🍶🍶🍶 ▮
Characterful, fresh, faintly resinous southern Portuguese white, with a spicy tang and ripe, Iberian fruit characters.

£3–5

AUSTRALIA

Four Winds White   12/20
Off-dry ▮
Confected, honeyed, flattish Aussie white made from unspecified grapes. Overblown.

1995 Jacob's Creek Dry Riesling   14/20
Off-dry 🍶 ▮
Boiled lemon-and-lime sweets-style Riesling from Orlando, made in an easy-drinking, commercial style with pronounced sweetness. Dry it isn't.

CHILE

1995 Chilean Chardonnay, Canepa, Rancagua   15/20
Dry 🍶🍶🍶 ▮
Tangy, crisp, extremely well-made Chilean white from the Canepa winery, showing flavours of melon and toast, underpinned by fresh acidity.

CZECH REPUBLIC

Spar Moravian Vineyards   14/20
Dry 👜👜👜 🍶
From the little-known (except to the people who live there) Velke Pavlovice region, this is a well-made, unusual, white-pepper and ginger-scented dry white blend of Olaszriesling and Müller-Thurgau.

FRANCE

Spar French Country White, Vin de Pays de l'Hérault, 1 litre
                                                     12/20
Dry 🍶
Soft, basic, baked-apple southern French quaffer in a litre bottle. Lacks a bit of zip.

1994 Gemini Sauvignon Blanc   13/20
Dry 👜 🍶
Stylishly packaged (if you like brash labels), this is an attempt at a modern white Bordeaux in form and content. Tart and rather light on Sauvignon character.

1995 Spar Chardonnay, Vin de Pays d'Oc, Cuxac   14/20
Dry 👜👜👜 🍶
Crisp, good-value, unoaked Chardonnay from the Cuxac co-operative, with fresh grapefruit and honeydew melon characters.

1995 James Herrick Chardonnay, Vin de Pays d'Oc 15/20
Dry 👜👜 🍶
Elegant, minerally Chardonnay from Englishman James Herrick's southern French vineyards near Narbonne, showing restrained spicy oak and melony fruitiness.

GERMANY

Spar Hock   13/20
Medium sweet 👜 🍶
Decent, floral Hock, which is fresher than many high-street examples.

Spar Rheinhessen Liebfraumilch   11/20
Medium sweet 🍶
Same price, but flatter, soupier and less interesting than the Hock.

ITALY

Spar Sicilian Vino da Tavola 14/20
Dry 🍾🍾 ▯
Weighty, fresh, nutty Sicilian white with considerable richness for a sub-£3.50 quaffer.

Spar Soave 13/20
Off-dry 🍾 ▯
Fresh, sweetish, apple and pear-flavoured Veneto white, which has crept into Spar's top-ten best-sellers this year.

Spar Rondolle Bianco 14/20
Dry 🍾🍾 ▯
Ripe, zesty, unoaked Puglian blend of the local Bombino and Chardonnay, showing characterful greengage flavours and a twist of acidity.

NEW ZEALAND

1994 Cook's Hawkes Bay Sauvignon Blanc 14/20
Dry 🍾 ▯
Tangy, well-made green-bean and grapefruit-style Sauvignon Blanc from New Zealand's North Island, with a slightly lean finish.

SOUTH AFRICA

1995 South African Classic White, Madeba 14/20
Dry 🍾🍾 ▯
A blend of Chenin Blanc and Colombard from the warm-climate region of Robertson, this is a zesty, dry, citrus fruity Cape white.

Paarl Heights Colombard 14/20
Dry 🍾🍾 ▯
Boiled-sweets-like Cape Colombard with refreshingly crisp, grapefruity flavours.

Paarl Heights Chenin Blanc 15/20
Dry 🍾🍾🍾 ▯
Fresh, grassy Cape Chenin Blanc from the Boland Wynkelder co-operative, with appealing ripe pear flavours and carbon dioxide spritz.

Sable View Chardonnay
Dry ▮

13/20

From the giant Stellenbosch Farmers Winery group, this is a clean, oak-chipped Cape white with rather dilute fruit flavours.

SPAIN

Spar Valencia Dry
Dry 💰 ▮

13/20

Made from the indigenous Merseguera grape, this is a clean, cool-fermented Spanish white with a zingy orange-peel bite.

Spar Valencia Medium
Medium dry ▮

12/20

Sweetened-up, commercial Valencia white made from the Merseguera grape. We prefer the crisper, dry version.

Spar Valencia Sweet
Medium sweet ▮

12/20

Sugary, decently made Valencia white from the Gandia winery. Spain's answer to Liebfraumilch.

£5–8

FRANCE

1994 Spar Viognier Cuxac, Vin de Pays d'Oc
Dry 💰 ▮

14/20

Rather muted, southern French Viognier, from the Cuxac co-operative, which has lost its primary fruit aromas.

GERMANY

1992 Grans Fassian Riesling, Mosel
Medium dry 💰💰💰 ▮

16/20

Stylish, elegantly balanced Mosel Riesling just starting to develop the kerosene character of maturity, and cut by green-apple acidity and lovely fruitiness.

Red

Under £3

BULGARIA

Bulgarian Country Red, Cabernet Sauvignon/Cinsault, Russe

13/20

Medium-bodied 🜲🜲 ▮
Vibrantly coloured Bulgarian blend of Cabernet Sauvignon and Cinsault, with some oak character and rustic raspberry fruit.

PORTUGAL

Dona Elena, Co-operativa de Benfica, Ribatejo 13/20
Medium-bodied 🜲🜲 ▮
Decently made, robust, damson-fruity southern Portuguese red, interpreting traditional grape varieties in a modern style.

£3–5

AUSTRALIA

Four Winds Red, Normans 11/20
Medium-bodied ▮
Simple mint-humbug-style red, which should be scattered to the four winds.

1994 Jacob's Creek Dry Red 13/20
Medium-bodied ▮
Minty, ripe, faintly medicinal, best-selling Aussie blend of Shiraz and Cabernet Sauvignon, let down by a rasp of added acidity.

BULGARIA

1993 Spar Bulgarian Merlot/Gamay 12/20
Medium-bodied ▮
Rather rasping, high-acid Bulgarian blend, which fails to taste of either Merlot or Gamay.

CHILE

1994 La Fortuna Malbec, Lontue 15/20
Medium-bodied 👝👝 |
Clove-spicy, aromatic, richly fruity Chilean Malbec with good structure and length and elegant tannins for a sub-£5 wine.

1995 Chilean Cabernet Sauvignon, Maipo 14/20
Medium-bodied 👝👝 |
Still youthful, this is a firm Chilean Cabernet Sauvignon with oodles of cassis fruit. Needs time to soften, though.

1994 Chilean Merlot, Rancagua 15/20
Medium-bodied 👝👝👝 |
Succulent, fleshy Chilean Merlot from the Rancagua region, with ripe, black-cherry fruitiness and very fresh acidity.

CZECH REPUBLIC

Spar Moravian Vineyards 13/20
Medium-bodied 👝👝 |
A blend of Frankovka and Vavrinecke grapes made by Aussie Nick Butler, showing attractive white-pepper notes and soft, herbaceous fruit.

FRANCE

Spar French Country Red, Vin de Pays de l'Hérault, Val d'Orbieu, 1 litre 13/20
Medium-bodied 👝 |
Robust, quaffable southern French picnic plonk in a litre bottle, with a smidgeon of Mediterranean spice.

Spar Claret, Rolland et Cie 14/20
Medium-bodied 👝👝 |
Young, juicy, well-made basic claret with commendable character and freshness filled out by firm tannins.

1994 Gemini Merlot, Vin de Pays d'Oc 13/20
Medium-bodied 👝 |
Extracted Languedoc-Roussillon Merlot in a pseudo-Australian package, with some redeeming grassy fruitiness.

ITALY

Spar Valpolicella

13/20

Light-bodied 👜👜 🍶

Soft, clean, cherry fruity Veneto red, which is deservedly in Spar's top-ten best-sellers.

Spar Rondolle Rosso

14/20

Medium-bodied 👜👜 🍶

A modern, fruit-laden Puglian *rosso* made from the Negroamaro and Cabernet Sauvignon grapes, with flavours of cherry and ripe plum and softly textured tannins.

1994 Spar Montepulciano d'Abruzzo, Cantina Tollo

14/20

Medium-bodied 👜👜👜 🍶

Smooth and characterful, especially for an often rustic style, this Adriatic red is a fruity pasta-enhancer with an almondy edge.

1994 Spar Chianti, Frescobaldi

15/20

Medium-bodied 👜👜👜 🍶

Fresh, invigorating, Sangiovese-based red from the house of Frescobaldi, with lively cherry fruitiness and a backbone of tannin.

SOUTH AFRICA

1993 South African Classic Red, Madeba

12/20

Medium-bodied 🍶

Pruney, dried-out, warm-climate Cape blend from the Madeba winery.

1995 Paarl Heights Red, Boland Wynkelder

14/20

Medium-bodied 👜👜 🍶

Fresher, juicier proposition deliberately made in a modern, softly fruity style with the faintest hint of oak character.

1993 Sable View Cabernet Sauvignon

12/20

Medium-bodied 🍶

Farmyardy, old-fashioned Cape red from Stellenbosch Farmers Winery, with rustic tannins and neutered fruit character.

SPAIN

Spar Valencia Red   13/20
Light-bodied 👛👛 🍷
Made from the local Bobal grape, this raspberry fruity Iberian red is Spain's
answer to Valpolicella.

Spar Valdepeñas, Felix Solis   12/20
Medium-bodied 🍷
Made entirely from the Cencibel grape, this is a dilute, agricultural tinto that
you'd only drink on an 18–30s' holiday.

Campo Rojo Cariñena   12/20
Full-bodied 🍷
Cooked, raisiny Spanish plonk with added splinters and dry tannins.

£5–8

AUSTRALIA

1993 Hardy's Bankside Shiraz, S.E. Australia   16/20
Full-bodied 👛👛👛 ➖
Dense, richly textured, cinnamon-tinged cross-regional Shiraz from Australia's
number two, BRL-Hardy. Attractively spicy with a firm backbone of tannin.

NEW ZEALAND

1994 Cook's Hawkes Bay Cabernet Sauvignon   13/20
Medium-bodied 🍷
There's far too much oak in this weedy Kiwi Cabernet Sauvignon for our liking.
Poverty Bay would be more like it.

Rosé

£3–5

FRANCE

1994 Spar Rosé de Syrah, Vin de Pays d'Oc, Val d'Orbieu   14/20
Dry 👓 🍾
Pleasantly dry, redcurrant fruity southern French rosé from the sprawling Val d'Orbieu group.

Fortified

£5–8

PORTUGAL

1989 Spar Old Cellar Late Bottled Vintage Port, Smith Woodhouse
15/20
Full-bodied 👓👓 🍾
Peppery sweet, well-made Late Bottled Vintage Port, with raisiny richness and a fiery bite.

Tesco ☆☆☆(☆)

Address: Old Tesco House, Delamare Road, Cheshunt, Herts EN8 9SL

Telephone/fax: 01992 632222; 01992 658225

Number of branches: 553 (including 507 Tesco supermarkets, 25 Metro, 11 Tesco Express, 1 Tesco Vin Plus in Calais, 2 Tesco pharmacies, 7 Tesco Home 'n' Wear)

Opening hours: 9.00am to 8.00pm Monday to Thursday; 9.00am to 9.00pm Friday; 8.00am to 8.00pm Saturday; 10.00am to 4.00pm Sunday

Credit cards accepted: Access, Visa, Switch

Discounts: 5 per cent on six bottles

Facilities and services: Tesco Clubcard; Tesco Direct (see text for details); in-store tastings

Special offers: Wines of the month; May Wine Festival promotion

Top ten best-selling wines: Bulgarian Country White; 1995 Frascati Superiore; Hock Deutscher Tafelwein; Liebfraumilch Pfalz; Lambrusco Bianco 4 per cent Light; South African Dry White Wine 3-litre box; Reka Valley Bulgarian Cabernet Sauvignon; French Red Country Wine; 1994 Chianti Classico, San Casciano; Tesco Cava

Range:

GOOD: Italy, Australia, South Africa, Champagne

AVERAGE: Bordeaux, Rhône, Loire, white Burgundy, regional France, Spain, Portugal, Eastern Europe, Germany, New Zealand, United States, Chile

POOR: Alsace, Beaujolais, red Burgundy

UNDER-REPRESENTED: None

If size is everything, then Tesco's got it. With a grand total of 837 wines, Tesco is proud of the fact that its range of wines is the biggest by far among the supermarkets. Since the takeover of William Low in Scotland, Tesco can flex its bulging muscles still further after overtaking Sainsbury's as Britain's biggest

Tesco

drinks purveyor. One in every eight beers, wines and spirits sold in the high street or out-of-town superstore is now a Tesco purchase.

The all-female wine-buying team under the Jaguar-driving Stephen Clarke clearly enjoys its globetrotting remit, but could the the size of Tesco's range be a little bewildering for customers? Not so, according to Tesco PR/technical controller, Janet Lee. 'Tesco customers appreciate the choice, and it's not confusing for them. We're not preaching to the converted. With information on back labels, in leaflets, and on the new wine list, it's part of our role to educate our customers.'

We wondered last year how Tesco intended to help customers pick their way though the bewilderingly large range. The experiment with in-store advisers has been successful, says Lee, but there are still only 21 such advisers to help customers pick and choose and handle the in-store tastings. Why not more? 'It's not that easy to get people of the right calibre to do the job properly,' says Lee.

Tesco has been hyperactive this year on the promotions front, with a regular red, white and fizz of the month, plus a guest beer and a Port of the month (should go down a storm). In May Tesco held its second wine festival, which was more focused this year than last. It included, among others, a handful of £2.99 bargains from Argentina, which subsequently fed their way onto the main wine list. In all, the festival added up to a merry 1,200 days of in-store tastings.

Euro '96 gave Tesco the chance to sport a different wine from each of the participating countries, which was all very well if you managed to time your shopping for a French, Spanish or Italian day, but a little less exciting for the Germany v. England semi-final. Meanwhile, a discount of 5 per cent on every six-bottle purchase (excluding fortified wines), plus an itsy free wine carrier with every half-dozen, no doubt added to the foot traffic.

Big Brother may not be watching you, but at Tesco he's certainly doing his best to tempt you to buy his wines, using just about any modern medium at his disposal. The introduction of Club Card in February 1995 has enabled Tesco to use the data collected to target different groups. The Club Card magazine, for instance, is mailed to homes quarterly, focusing on young families, students and 'empty nesters', among others.

Tesco Recipe Collection, a glossy monthly featuring gastro-porn, such as desserts topped with whipped cream and dusted with icing sugar, has been re-launched and, presumably along with many of its readers' waistlines, has expanded. While the recipes and certainly the photos appear to be designed to torture weight-watchers, this glossy also features wine writers (not Grapevine's, we hasten to add) waxing poetic about Tesco lager, Woodpecker cider and Kentucky Bourbon, or whatever editor Maggie Bright deems appropriate for the month in question.

Since we reported last year on the unveiling of Tesco's mail-order wines at Madame Tussaud's, and the uncanny resemblance of the Wine Select range to the lifeless waxwork dummies surrounding it, the range has been revamped as Tesco Direct; 50 or so wines are now available for self-selection to some 35,000 customers by mail, phone or via the Internet (http://www/tesco.co.uk/direct), with delivery at £4.25 for one case, or free for two cases or more.

France is still the biggest-selling country by far at Tesco, with around 30 per cent of wine sales, followed by Italy with just over 10 per cent. The French wine buyers, Sarah Marsay and Judith Candy, have put a lot of effort into the south of France, as well as in projects to improve the quality of staples such as Tesco's basic Muscadet and Rosé d'Anjou. After a quiet year, Germany in third place and Eastern Europe in sixth present a considerable challenge for the two newcomers to the buying team, Ruth Traylor and Helen Robinson.

Not surprisingly, the biggest growth areas at Tesco are in New World wines. With 88 Australian wines on the list, Tesco sells more Aussie wine than any other retailer, with the possible exception of Oddbins. And not just bog-standard Australian Chardonnay or Shiraz. To give the Australian map a bit of local colour, buyer Anne-Marie Bostock has added six excellent new regional varietals to the range. Tesco is also good at shifting high-quality Australian classics such as Tim Adams' Clare Valley Semillon and Pam Dunsford's brawny Chapel Hill Shiraz from McLaren Vale.

Australia apart, Chile and South Africa have been the biggest growth areas over the past year in the New World. And to its list of exotic but not hugely relevant outposts of the winemaking world, which last year included Canada and Brazil, Tesco has this year brought the delights of Uruguayan and Peruvian wine to its adventurous customers.

Buying controller Anne-Marie Bostock has made it her personal mission to do something about the high incidence of cork taint, which is reckoned to spoil at least one in 20 wines. Already Tesco has experimented with plastic corks on a handful of wines. This time Bostock is determined to go one step further and try out screwcaps in a special promotion in the autumn. It's widely believed that screwcaps are the most effective seal for a bottle, but customers who enjoy the ceremony of pulling the cork still need convincing.

So all in all, no complaints from us over the size of the wine range, customer service and energy for continuing innovation at Tesco. But the jarring note that struck us last year has not gone away. Our tasting at Tesco this year was one of the least impressive in our tasting calendar, quite simply because there were too many indifferent wines. As we said last year about Tesco's range: when it's good, it's very good, but when it's poor, it's simply not up to scratch. Chopping out the dead wood and reducing the list to a more manageable size would be a good start.

White

Under £3

BULGARIA

Tesco Bulgarian Country White, Pomorie 13/20
Off-dry 🍷🍷 ▯
A blend of Ugni Blanc and Muscat, this is a slightly sweetened, mellow Bulgarian white with pleasantly grapey, lime-zesty flavours.

GERMANY

Hock, Deutscher Tafelwein, Rhein, Maas Nathan 11/20
Medium sweet ▯
Dull, sugary, German white, which would not have amused Queen Victoria.

Liebfraumilch, Pfalz, Qualitätswein 10/20
Medium sweet ▯
Bitter-sweet, undistingished German sugar water, which makes a mockery of the quality-wine designation.

HUNGARY

Tesco Reka Valley Hungarian Chardonnay 13/20
Off-dry 🍷🍷 ▯
From the almost unpronounceable region of Szekszard (try sex-art), this is a sweetish, clean, baked-apple-like Chardonnay with a tangy aftertaste.

ITALY

Lambrusco Bianco, 4 per cent, Light 12/20
Sweet 🍷 ▯
Rather hollow, lemonade-like Italian sweetie with a curious vanilla-pod character. At least it's fresh.

£3–5

ARGENTINA

Picajuan Peak Chardonnay   14/20
Dry 🍷🍷 |
The Argentine source of this rich, tropically fruity Chardonnay may be tucked away in the small print, but it's a promising first base for Mendoza winery, La Agricola. We found the oak just a little bitter on the finish.

AUSTRALIA

1995 Jacob's Creek Semillon/Chardonnay, South Eastern Australia   14/20
Off-dry 🍷 |
Ever-reliable, deservedly popular Aussie white blend from the Barossa-based Orlando Winery, in which the herby, lemony character of the Semillon grape is distinctively refreshing.

1995 Jacob's Creek Chardonnay, Orlando   14/20
Off-dry 🍷 |
One of the biggest-selling wines in Britain. And you can see why this commercial, sweetish, toasty-oaky Chardonnay is so popular.

1995 Lindemans Bin 65 Chardonnay   15/20
Off-dry 🍷🍷 |
Toffee and pineapple-fruity Aussie super-blend from winemaker Phillip John. In a short vintage, he's maintained the Bin 65 hallmark of ripeness and approachability.

1995 Penfolds Koonunga Hill Chardonnay   16/20
Dry 🍷🍷🍷 |
Classy, complex, barrel-fermented Aussie Chardonnay with butter and toffee-fudge richness balanced by beautifully judged, refreshing acidity.

1994 Tesco Hunter Valley Semillon   15/20
Dry 🍷🍷 |
Extremely well-selected Hunter Valley Semillon with classic ageworthy flavours of lemon peel and weighty, textured richness, underpinned by cleansing acidity.

1994 Tesco Clare Valley Riesling   16/20
Dry 🍾🍾🍾 |

Toasty, complex, richly proportioned Clare Valley Riesling from Jane Mitchell, one of the Clare Valley's best producers, with good concentration and fresh lime-zest notes. A regional classic that lives up to its billing.

AUSTRIA

1995 Lenz Moser Grüner Veltliner   14/20
Bone dry 🍾🍾 |

White-pepper and celery-like Austrian dry white made from the central European Grüner Veltliner grape. Characterful stuff, with good weight and sharp acidity.

BRAZIL

Tesco Brazilian Chardonnay/Semillon   11/20
Dry |

The brightly coloured label is the best thing about this tart, unbalanced, oak-chipped blend of undistinguished Chardonnay and Semillon. Dont start the carnival with this one.

CHILE

1996 Santa Ines Sauvignon Blanc, Maipo Valley   14/20
Dry 🍾🍾 |

Crisp, grapefruity, piercingly fresh Maipo Valley Sauvignon Blanc from the up-and-coming Santa Ines winery. No mistaking the grape variety here.

1995 Errázuriz Chardonnay   15/20
Dry 🍾🍾 |

A refreshingly fruity, well-packaged blend of Chardonnay, mainly from Curicó with 14 per cent of the grapes from the Casablanca Valley. Nicely judged oak adds complexity to the citrusy flavours.

FRANCE

1995 Marsanne, Domaine de Montaubéron, Vin de Pays des Côtes de Thongue · · · · · · · 15/20
Bone dry 🍷🍷🍷 ▯
Rich, well-made, pear-like Languedoc white from the shores of the Mediterranean, with spicy notes and a backbone of acidity.

1995 Chardonnay Reserve, Maurel Vedeau · · · · · · · 13/20
Dry ▯
Somewhat confected, boiled-sweets-like southern French Chardonnay, in which oak treatment leaves a faintly bitter taste in the mouth.

1995 Tesco White Burgundy, Cave de Viré · · · · · · · 14/20
Dry 🍷 ▯
Slightly coarse, apple-core-like white Burgundy from the Viré co-operative. At £4.59, Chardonnay from Chile or South Africa is generally a better bet.

1993 Gaston Dorléans Vouvray Demi-Sec, F. Bourillon · · · · · · · 13/20
Medium sweet ▯
Unbalanced, sweetish, honeyed Loire Chenin Blanc from an average vintage. Finishes with a rasp of acidity.

HUNGARY

1995 Badger Hill Dry Furmint · · · · · · · 14/20
Bone dry 🍷🍷 ▯
Spritzy, fresh, crisply turned out Hungarian white, showing the assertive dryness of the Tokay region's Furmint grape.

ITALY

1995 Frascati Superiore, GIV · · · · · · · 13/20
Dry 🍷 ▯
Basic, baked, southern Italian white, which finishes abruptly. Should be a lot fresher.

Colli Amerini Bianco · · · · · · · 14/20
Dry 🍷🍷 ▯
Weighty, nutty Umbrian white with a honeyed texture and good character for a sub-£5 Italian white.

1995 Tesco Verdicchio Classico   15/20
Dry 👛👛👛 ▮
Spritz-fresh, herbal, central Italian white with attractive honey and white-pepper notes and good length. Excellent value at under £4.

Tesco Chardonnay del Trentino   14/20
Dry 👛👛 ▮
Refreshing, apple-fruity Alpine Chardonnay, with decent buttery richness and a tang of grapefruity acidity.

1995 Pipoli Chiaro Aglianico Bianco   15/20
Dry 👛👛👛 ▮
Super-modern Basilicata white made from the characterful Aglianico grape, showing cool-fermented flavours of pear and quince and a zesty aftertaste.

NEW ZEALAND

Tesco New Zealand Dry White Wine   14/20
Dry 👛👛 ▮
Grapey, orange-blossom-scented New Zealand blend of mainly Müller-Thurgau with pleasantly soft, peachy fruitiness. Tesco's answer to the popular Nobilo's White Cloud.

Tesco New Zealand Sauvignon Blanc   14/20
Bone dry 👛👛 ▮
Very tart, elderflower and artichoke-like New Zealand Sauvignon Blanc from the Gisborne region of North Island. Bracing stuff.

Tesco New Zealand Chardonnay, Gisborne   14/20
Dry 👛 ▮
Oak and toffee-fudge-like New Zealand Chardonnay with an abundance of splinters and some underlying buttery richness.

SOUTH AFRICA

Tesco Cape Chenin Blanc   13/20
Off-dry 👛 ▮
Cool-fermented, pleasantly fresh, if simple, Cape white made from the ubiquitous Chenin Blanc, aka Steen.

Tesco Franschhoek Semillon   14/20
Dry 👛👛 ▮
Soft, lightly toasty Cape Semillon from one of South Africa's cooler wine regions, with refreshing lemony acidity.

Tesco South African Chardonnay/Colombard   13/20
Off-dry 👛 ▮
This sweetish, pear-droppy Cape blend from the warm-climate Robertson district made by Australian John Worontschak is closer to fruit juice than wine.

Tesco Barrel-Fermented Chenin Blanc   15/20
Dry 👛👛👛 ▮
Fresh, oak-fermented, lees-aged Chenin Blanc made by flying winemaker Kym Milne. Smoky, weighty white with excellent intensity of flavour for a sub-£4 wine.

1995 De Wetshof Rhine Riesling   15/20
Dry 👛👛 ▮
Zesty, fresh Cape Riesling from Danie de Wet, who's better known for his outstanding Chardonnays. Aromatic, but nicely restrained on the palate.

1995 Van Loveren Special Late Harvest Gewürztraminer, half-bottle   13/20
Sweet 👛 ▮
Soft, gooey, tinned lychee-like Cape sticky with a marshmallow middle and an aggressively acidic bite.

UNITED STATES

1995 Tesco California Chardonnay   14/20
Off-dry 👛 ▮
Smoky-oaky, butterscotch-style Chardonnay from the Stratford winery. A touch confected perhaps, but this has plenty of banana and boiled-sweets flavours and reasonable weight.

£5–8

AUSTRALIA

1994 Preece Chardonnay 1994, Mitchelton   15/20
Dry 👝👝 ▯
Lightly oaked, elegant, green olive-like Victorian Chardonnay with fresh, cool-climate acidity and good length of flavour.

1994 Ironstone Semillon/Chardonnay, Margaret River   16/20
Dry 👝👝👝 ▯
From the Margaret-based Cape Mentelle winery, this is a pithy, herby, grapefruity blend of Semillon/Chardonnay, with intensity of flavour and a zing of carbon dioxide gas.

1995 Tesco McLaren Vale Chardonnay   15/20
Dry 👝👝 ▯
Richly oaked, tropical fruity South Australian Chardonnay, which is subtler than it appears on first acquaintance, but is still a generous, buttery white.

AUSTRIA

1994 Lenz Moser Prestige Beerenauslese   15/20
Very sweet 👝👝 ▯
From the lake-influenced Burgenland region, this is an intensely sweet raisin and fig-like Austrian dessert wine, with flavours of honey, toffee and dried fruits.

CHILE

1994 Errázuriz Barrel-Fermented Chardonnay Reserva   16/20
Dry 👝👝👝 ▬
Complex, refreshing, Chilean reserve Chardonnay from the Curicó region, showing well-judged barrel-fermented characters, a touch of butterscotch and flavoursome citrus fruitiness.

FRANCE

1995 Pouilly Fumé, Fouassier   15/20
Dry 💰 ▮
Light, nettley Pouilly Fumé with crisp acidity and underwhelming fruit flavours.

1994 Domaine Saint James Viognier   14/20
Dry 💰 ▮
Decent, if rather dilute, southern French Viognier from Henri Gualco, who pioneered plantings of the Rhône's fashionable white grape in the south of France. There are better examples on the market.

1994 La Porcii Chardonnay   13/20
Dry ▮
Overblown, over-oaked Languedoc Chardonnay with a fancy name. Time for the 1995 vintage, we feel.

1994 Montagny Premier Cru, Oak-Aged, Buxy   13/20
Dry ▮
Oaky, stewed-apple-like Côte Chalonnaise white Burgundy from the Buxy co-operative. Rather flat and old-fashioned.

NEW ZEALAND

1995 Villa Maria Private Bin Sauvignon Blanc   15/20
Dry 💰💰 ▮
Crisp, green-bean-like Kiwi Sauvignon Blanc from South Island's Marlborough region, showing something of the leanness of the 1995 vintage.

1993 Stoneleigh Chardonnay, Marlborough   14/20
Dry ▮
Ageing butter and toffee-fudge New Zealand Chardonnay with austere acidity. Almost mature and Chablis-like, but the balance doesn't quite work here.

SOUTH AFRICA

1995 Schoone Gevel Chardonnay, Wyn Van Oorsprong   15/20
Dry 💰 ▮
From a producer whose name sounds like an orthopaedic mattress, this is a fresh, lemony Cape Chardonnay marred by heavy-handed oak. Almost very good.

Over £8

SOUTH AFRICA

South African Dry White Wine, 3-litre winebox   12/20
Dry 🍾
Very basic, pear-droppy white with varnishy, nail-polish-remover notes.

Red

Under £3

BULGARIA

Tesco Reka Valley Bulgarian Cabernet Sauvignon   13/20
Medium-bodied 💰💰 🍾
Smooth, oak-chippy Cabernet Sauvignon from the Suhindol region. An attempt at a modern style, which is on the right lines.

FRANCE

Tesco Domaine de Beaufort, Minervois   13/20
Medium-bodied 💰💰 🍾
Spicy, characterful Languedoc *rouge* with rustic rosemary and cherry fruitiness and an astringent aftertaste.

Tesco French Country Wine, Vin de Pays de l'Aude   13/20
Medium-bodied 💰💰 🍾
Robust, chunky, southern French *vin de pays* red with plenty of tannin and grip, but insufficient fruit.

HUNGARY

Tesco Reka Valley Hungarian Merlot, Szekszard   13/20
Medium-bodied 🛍🛍 ▮
Plummy, peppery, freshly fruity Hungarian Merlot with easy-drinking tannins
and a green-pepper tinge.

ROMANIA

Romanian Cellars Pinot Noir/Merlot, Dealul Mare   13/20
Medium-bodied 🛍🛍 ▮
Chocolatey, oak-chippy, Romanian blend of Pinot Noir and Merlot, with an
attractively sweet core of strawberry and plum fruitiness and a rustic bite.

Romanian Cellars Pinot Noir   13/20
Medium-bodied 🛍🛍 ▮
You wouldn't confuse this young Romanian red with a Gevrey-Chambertin, but
it's an honest, chunky Pinot Noir with some spicy oak character.

£3–5

ARGENTINA

Picajuan Peak Bonarda, La Agricola   14/20
Medium-bodied 🛍🛍 ▮
It's good to see a supermarket listing a wine made from Bonarda, Argentina's
attractive, quaffable red grape variety. This soft, but meaty, good-value number
is typical of the style.

Picajuan Peak Sangiovese   14/20
Medium-bodied 🛍🛍 ▮
Throat-warming, soft, spicy red with chunky, Mediterranean-style tannins from
La Agricola, one of Argentina's most open-minded wineries.

AUSTRALIA

1994 Hardy's Nottage Hill Cabernet Sauvignon/Shiraz   13/20
Medium-bodied ▮
A basic, faintly medicinal, cordial-like Aussie blend. Hardy's usually makes better
wine than this.

1994 Rawson's Retreat Bin 35 Cabernet/Shiraz 14/20
Full-bodied 💰 ▮

A minty, sagey Aussie blend of Cabernet Sauvignon and Shiraz, in which dry oakiness dominates the sweet blackcurrant fruit. We prefer the Rawson's white.

AUSTRIA

1994 Lenz Moser Blauer Zweigelt, Neusiedlersee 14/20
Light-bodied 💰💰 ▮

From a country that's not renowned for its red wines, this is a cherryish, lightly fruity Burgenland quaffer made from the local Blauer Zweigelt grape.

BULGARIA

1990 Tesco Bulgarian Cabernet Sauvignon Reserve, Rousse 13/20
Medium-bodied 💰 ▮

Surprisingly deeply coloured for a 1990, this is a chewy, splintery attempt at a modern style, with a harsh acidified aftertaste.

CHILE

1996 Santa Ines Cabernet Merlot, Maipo Valley 15/20
Medium-bodied 💰💰💰 ▮

Deeply coloured, softly textured, blackcurrant fruity Chilean blend of Cabernet Sauvignon and Merlot with good structure and fine-grained tannins.

Tesco Chilean Cabernet Sauvignon, Curicó 14/20
Medium-bodied 💰💰 ▮

Grassy, chocolatey Chilean Cabernet Sauvignon with pleasantly juicy blackcurrant fruit and faintly rustic tannins.

1995 Errázuriz Merlot, Curicó 15/20
Medium-bodied 💰💰 ▮

A luscious, juicy, Chilean Merlot made by Kiwi Brian Bicknell before his return to New Zealand. Finishes with a pleasantly grassy tang.

1995 Santa Carolina Merlot Reserva, San Fernando Valley 13/20
Medium-bodied 💰 ▮

Oaky, slightly hollow, San Fernando Valley Merlot from Santa Carolina winemaker, Pilar Gonzalez. For the same price we'd rather drink the Errázuriz.

FRANCE

1995 Equus Bergerac Rouge, Yves Pagès   13/20
Medium-bodied 🛍 ▮
Stylishly packaged Dordogne blend of Merlot and Cabernet Sauvignon, which smells better than it tastes. Pleasantly grassy on the nose, but rather hollow and extracted on the palate.

Tesco Fitou, Mont Tauch   12/20
Full-bodied ▮
Raisiny, old-fashioned Fitou with dry, gum-puckering tannins. Not one of the Mont Tauch co-operative's greatest hits.

1993 Cabardès, Domaine de Jouclary   14/20
Medium-bodied 🛍🛍 ▮
Mint and sage aromas and ripe, full-flavoured fruit reminded us of Italy's Puglia in this characterful southern French red.

1994 Domaine de la Sansoure, Corbières, Mont Tauch   14/20
Full-bodied 🛍🛍 ▮
Gutsy, rosemary-scented Languedoc rouge with a core of sweet blackberry fruit and robust, drying tannins.

1995 Domaine du Soleil Merlot, Vin de Pays de l'Aude   13/20
Medium-bodied 🛍 ▮
Light, stalky Cabernet Franc-like Merlot from the Languedoc-Roussillon region. From such a warm climate, you'd expect a bit more fruit intensity from this red. Suitable for vegans and vegetarians.

1993 Tesco Les Domaines Château Saint Louis La Perdrix, Costières de Nîmes   14/20
Medium-bodied 🛍 ▮
Structured, mature Provençal red from the Costières de Nîmes appellation. Spicy, tarry red with Syrah-like aromas and fresh acidity.

1994 Château Maurel Fonsalade Oak-Aged, Saint Chinian   14/20
Full-bodied 🛍 ▮
Produced from Grenache, Syrah, Cinsault and Carignan, this is a robust, if over-oaked, Saint Chinian, whose chocolatey-sweet fruitiness would taste better without all those splinters.

1994 Baron De La Tour Fitou, Elévé en Fût de Chêne   15/20
Full-bodied 👝👝 ▦–

Oak-matured, Syrah-influenced Fitou with good chocolate and blackberry fruit characters and a backbone of tannins and Mediterranean spice.

1994 Domaine Georges Bertrand Corbières, Cuvée Spéciale, Vieilli en Fûts de Chêne Merrain   15/20
Full-bodied 👝👝 🍶

A wee bit on the oaky side, this domaine-bottled Corbières has a lot of spice and powerful fruit richness to soak up the barrel staves.

1995 Château du Bluizard, Beaujolais-Villages   12/20
Medium-bodied 🍶

Basic, soupy Beaujolais-Villages with charmless tannins and barely identifiable Gamay fruitiness.

ITALY

1994 Chianti Classico, San Casciano   14/20
Medium-bodied 👝👝 🍶

The most interesting of Tesco's top-ten best-sellers, this is a refreshingly drinkable Chianti, with warming alcohol and cherry fruitiness.

Tesco Valpolicella, Cantina Sociale di Soave   13/20
Light-bodied 👝👝 🍶

Made at the reliable Soave co-operative, this is a tartly fruity, decently made Veneto glugger, with light summer-pudding fruit flavours and acidity.

MEXICO

1993 Tesco Mexican Cabernet Sauvignon, L.A. Cetto   12/20
Full-bodied 🍶

From Mexico's Pacific-influenced Baja California peninsula, this is a sweet, drying, almost Portuguese-like red, whose best days are behind it.

1993 Petite Sirah, L.A. Cetto   14/20
Full-bodied 👝 🍶

From the same winery, this is a much more vibrantly fruity Mexican red, with baked, damson-skin characters and robust, chewy tannins.

NEW ZEALAND

Tesco New Zealand Cabernet Sauvignon, Huapei   11/20
Light-bodied
Light, earthy Kiwi red, showing green oak character and a tart, acidic finish.

1994 Cooper's Creek Hawkes Bay Merlot   15/20
Medium-bodied
Oaky, well-made, Hawkes Bay Merlot with smooth tannins and green-edged flavours.

SOUTH AFRICA

Tesco Paarl Cabernet Sauvignon   13/20
Full-bodied
Minty, blackcurrant-pastille-like Cape Cabernet from Paul and Hugo de Villiers, with a baked rusticity typical of many South African reds.

1995 Maskam, Vredendal, Olifants River   14/20
Full-bodied
A Cape blend of Ruby Cabernet, Cabernet Sauvignon and Merlot aged in French oak barrels, this is a charry, decently made, if somewhat hollow, Olifantsriver red.

1994 Schoone Gevel Merlot, Wyn Van Oorsprong   15/20
Medium-bodied
Green-pepper fruity, vanilla oaky Cape Merlot with succulent tannins and considerable complexity for a sub-£5 red. Oorsprong Dutch Technique, as it were.

1994 Tesco South African Shiraz/Cabernet Sauvignon   14/20
Full-bodied
The best of the wines that John Worontschak has made for Tesco, this Robertson blend of Shiraz and Cabernet Sauvignon is ripe and sweetly fruity, with a coating of smoky oak chips.

Tesco Beyers Truter Pinotage   15/20
Full-bodied
Inky-purple, richly perfumed Cape Pinotage from the acknowledged master of the style – Beyers Truter of the Kanonkop winery – showing plenty of spicy American oak and succulent raspberry fruit flavours, although it finishes a teeny bit dry.

SPAIN

Tesco Viña Mara, Rioja Alavesa   13/20
Full-bodied 💰 ▮

Damson fruit-dominated, faintly pongy Rioja with a hint of oak character and coarse, chewy tannins.

1994 Marqués de Griñon Rioja   15/20
Medium-bodied 💰💰 ▮

Made entirely with Tempranillo grapes from the Rioja Alavesa, this is an elegant, well-judged marriage of oak and soft, strawberry fruitiness at a pretty good price.

UNITED STATES

Tesco Californian Zinfandel, Stratford   13/20
Full-bodied 💰 ▮

Cooked, blackberry jam-like California red made from the in-vogue Zinfandel grape. Too coarse and alcoholic for its own good – or yours.

£5–8

AUSTRALIA

1993 Penfolds Bin 128 Shiraz, Coonawarra   16/20
Full-bodied 💰💰💰 ▬▬

Proving that it doesn't only make cross-regional blends, this silky, milled pepper-style Shiraz from Penfolds brings out the elegance and cool-climate freshness of Coonawarra reds.

1993 Ironstone Cabernet/Shiraz   16/20
Medium-bodied 💰💰💰 ▬▬

Rich, concentrated, sweetly blackcurranty Western Australian blend of Cabernet and Shiraz from Margaret River's Cape Mentelle winery, showing a fresh, herbaceous bite and plenty of stuffing.

1993 Barossa Valley Merlot   16/20
Medium-bodied 👜👜👜 🍾

Full-flavoured, coffee-bean oaky, sumptuously textured Barossa Valley Merlot, which manages to combine ripe mulberry fruit flavours with a silky, green-pepper undertone.

1994 Coonawarra Cabernet Sauvignon   15/20
Medium-bodied 👜👜 🍾

From Tesco's excellent range of Australian regional wines, this is a well-structured, but elegant Coonawarra Cabernet Sauvignon, with pleasantly refreshing blackcurrant fruitiness and good varietal character.

CHILE

1994 Carmen Cabernet Sauvignon, Central Valley   15/20
Medium-bodied 👜👜 🍾

An elegant, oak-aged, blackcurrant-pastille-style Chilean Cabernet Sauvignon made by star winemaker Alvaro Espinoza. Should be closer to £5 than £6.50.

FRANCE

1992 Chinon, La Baronnie Madeleine, Couly Dutheil   15/20
Medium-bodied 👜👜 🍾

Light, grassy Loire Valley Cabernet Franc from négociant Couly Dutheil, which, as you'd expect for a 1992, is beginning to fade a little. All the same, there's some elegant sweet fruit character on the palate.

1993 Le Moulin de Saint François Corbières, Gérard Bertrand
16/20
Full-bodied 👜👜👜 🍷

A classy, angostura bitters-scented, oak-aged blend of Grenache, Carignan, Syrah and Mourvèdre from grower Gérard Bertrand, showing excellent concentration, smooth tannins and Mediterranean character.

1994 Beaumes de Venise, Côtes du Rhône Villages   15/20
Full-bodied 👜👜 🍾

From the local co-operative better known for its sweet fortified Muscat, this is a well-made, peppery Côtes du Rhône Villages red with attractive Syrah-like freshness.

1993 Domaine de la Machotte, Gigondas   15/20
Full-bodied 🛍🛍 ▮
A southern Rhône blend of Grenache, Mourvèdre and Syrah with heady, peppery aromas and initially sweet raspberry fruity flavours, followed by robustly chewy, dry tannins.

1993 Crozes-Hermitage, Cave de Tain   13/20
Medium-bodied ▮
From a difficult northern Rhône vintage, this is a lean, faintly medicinal Syrah, which doesn't quite live up to the Baudelaire poem quoted on the label. *L'âme du vin?* Perhaps not.

1995 Saumur-Champigny, Thierry Germain   15/20
Medium-bodied 🛍 ▮
Firm, grassy, cherry fruity Cabernet Franc from the Loire's most fashionable red wine appellation. Should be a bit more concentrated, given the vintage.

ITALY

1991 Chianti Classico Riserva, San Casciano   14/20
Medium-bodied 🛍 ▮
Rapidly maturing, licorice and almond-scented Chianti with a core of savoury Sangiovese fruit and a drying herbal finish. Drink up.

1993 Rosso di Montalcino, Cantine Leonardo da Vinci   15/20
Medium-bodied 🛍🛍 ▮
Savoury, leathery southern Tuscan red with more concentration than you'd expect from Brunello's lighter cousin, and a firm backbone of savoury tannins.

SOUTH AFRICA

1994 Fairview Merlot   15/20
Full-bodied 🛍🛍 ▮
Made by innovative cheese-and-wine specialist Charles Back, this is an oaky, chocolatey, full-bodied Merlot with a solid backbone of tannins.

Over £8

AUSTRALIA

1993 Rosemount Estate Coonawarra Show Reserve Cabernet Sauvignon   16/20
Full-bodied 👜 ▮

Nicely maturing, coffee-bean oaky Coonawarra Cabernet Sauvignon with sweet, succulent cassis fruitiness and smooth tannins.

1994 Chapel Hill McLaren Vale Shiraz   17/20
Full-bodied 👜👜👜 ▬▬

Made by Pam Dunsford, one of McLaren Vale's leading figures, this is an extremely flavoursome, peppery Shiraz matured in spicy, coffee-bean American oak, with smooth, fine-grained tannins. A classy drop from a winery whose wines get better with every vintage.

1993 Chapel Hill McLaren Vale/ Coonawarra Cabernet Sauvignon   17/20
Full-bodied 👜👜👜 ▬▬

A blend of mainly McLaren Vale with 30 per cent Coonawarra grapes from Pam Dunsford, this is an elegant, vanilla oaky Cabernet, which neatly combines the blackcurranty intensity of Coonawarra with the smoothness of McLaren Vale fruit.

FRANCE

1990 Louis Jadot Beaune Premier Cru   15/20
Medium-bodied 👜 ▮

Solid, négociant-style red Burgundy with lots of oak and a warm rasp of alcohol. Hardly *premier cru*-worthy.

1992 Châteauneuf-du-Pape, Le Chemin des Mulets, Jean-Pierre and François Perrin   15/20
Full-bodied 👜 ▮

Blended by the Perrins of Château de Beaucastel, this heady Grenache/Syrah-based red is fairly concentrated stuff for a 1992, but needs drinking up all the same.

Sparkling

£5–8

FRANCE

1991 Tesco Crémant de Bourgogne, Cave de Viré   15/20
Dry 🍾🍾🍾 ▮
Buttery, toasty, Chardonnay-fruity Burgundian fizz from the Viré co-operative.
Good-value Champagne-substitute, with attractive bottle-aged characters.

ITALY

Villa Pigna Sparkling Riserva Extra Brut, Fratelli Rozzi   15/20
Dry 🍾🍾🍾 ▮
Surprisingly complex for an Italian Champagne-method fizz, this is a rich,
creamy, Pinot Noir-like sparkler with a refreshingly dry finish.

SOUTH AFRICA

Tesco South African Sparkling   12/20
Off-dry ▮
Made by Australian John Worontschak, this is a tart, cabbagey, slightly
sweetened Cape fizz, whose colourful label promises more than it delivers.

SPAIN

Tesco Cava Brut   14/20
Dry 🍾🍾 ▮
Fresh, lemony, youthful Catalan fizz made in a fruity, up-front style.

Over £8

AUSTRALIA

1993 Green Point, Domaine Chandon   16/20
Dry 🛍🛍🛍 ❙
The red fruit character of the Pinot Noir grape is abundantly apparent in this Victorian-based blend of Pinot Noir and Chardonnay from the thinking woman's winemaker, Dr Tony Jordan. As you might expect from a Moët et Chandon-owned subsidiary, this is a good substitute for Champagne.

FRANCE

Tesco Champagne Premier Cru Brut   16/20
Dry 🛍🛍🛍 ❙
Rich, honeyed, commendably mature own-label Champagne, with strawberry fruity Pinot Noir characters and a soft cushion of bubbles.

1985 Tesco Vintage Champagne, Premier Cru, Cave de Chouilly
15/20
Dry 🛍 ❙
Toasty, green-tinged Vintage Champagne from the Chouilly co-operative, with a faintly bitter aftertaste.

NEW ZEALAND

Lindauer Special Reserve NV   15/20
Dry 🛍🛍 ❙
Frothy, dry Kiwi blend of Pinot Noir and Chardonnay, with youthful fruit flavours and good weight.

Deutz Marlborough Cuvée   15/20
Dry 🛍🛍 ❙
Elegantly aromatic South Island fizz, which promises slightly more than it delivers on the palate. Youthful, crisp and tangy, but lacking a third dimension of complexity. We enjoyed last year's blend rather more.

SOUTH AFRICA

1992 Simonsig Kaapse Vonkel   13/20
Dry 🍾

Earthy, rubbery, old-fashioned Cape fizz with coarse bubbles. A wine that's been better in the past.

The Thresher Group

Including:

Thresher Wine Shops ☆☆☆(☆)
Wine Rack ☆☆☆☆
Bottoms Up ☆☆☆☆(☆)

Address: Sefton House, 42 Church Road, Welwyn Garden City, Herts AL8 6PJ

Telephone/fax: 01707 328244; 01707 371398

Number of branches: 84 Bottoms Up, 119 Wine Rack, 817 Thresher Wine Shops, 390 Drinks Cabins, 124 Huttons, 1 Home Run

Opening hours: Minimum trading hours: 10.00am to 10.30pm Monday to Saturday; 10.00am to 10.00pm Sunday; Huttons open from 8.00am

Credit cards accepted: Access, Visa, Switch, American Express

Discounts: On cases of table wine (including sparkling wine) under £120: 10 per cent at Bottoms Up, 5 per cent at Wine Rack and Thresher Wine Shops. On cases of table wine (including sparkling wine) over £120: 10 per cent at all three. On mixed cases of Champagne: 15 per cent (10 per cent off six if under £120) at Bottoms Up, seven for the price of six at Wine Rack and 10 per cent on cases over £120 at Thresher Wine Shops. Also special discounts for club members

Facilities and services: Glass loan; home delivery; in-store tastings every Friday and Saturday at Bottoms Up and Wine Rack, occasionally at Thresher Wine Shops; clubs: Cellar Key and Exclusively Alsace (Wine Rack), Imbibers (Bottoms Up), Wine with Food Club (Thresher Wine Shops)

Special offers: Wine Buyer's Guarantee in Thresher Wine Shops (take it back if you don't like it and replace it with something else); Drinks Direct Gifting Service (any bottle delivered within mainland UK for £9.99 plus store price, or £5.99 within two days) – for orders ring 0800 23 22 21; Bottoms Up 'Try before you Buy' and Bottoms Up price guarantee: buy any wine cheaper by the case within seven days of purchase, and it will refund the difference and add a free bottle of the same wine

The Thresher Group

Top ten best-selling wines:

Thresher Wine Shops

Penfolds Bin 21; Jacob's Creek Shiraz/Cabernet; Liebfraumilch Gustav Prinz; Bulgarian Cabernet Sauvignon; Lambrusco Bianco; Bulgarian Russe Red; Jacob's Creek Semillon/Chardonnay; Domaine du Tariquet; Bulgarian Country Wine; Albor Tinto

Range:

GOOD: Alsace, Bordeaux, regional France, Italy, Spain, Germany, Portugal, South Africa, Australia, New Zealand, Chile, Champagne and sparkling wines

AVERAGE: Burgundy, Beaujolais, Loire, Eastern Europe, California

POOR: Rhône

UNDER-REPRESENTED: None

Wine Rack

Domaine du Tariquet; Penfolds Bin 21; Jacob's Creek Shiraz/Cabernet; Albor Tinto; Tollana Dry; Jacob's Creek Semillon/Chardonnay; Lindauer; Penfolds Bin 35; Vin de Pays du Gers; Seppelt Great Western

Range:

GOOD: Alsace, Bordeaux, Burgundy, regional France, Italy, Spain, Germany, Portugal, South Africa, Australia, New Zealand, Chile, Champagne and sparkling wines

AVERAGE: Beaujolais, Loire, Eastern Europe, California

POOR: Rhône

UNDER-REPRESENTED: None

Bottoms Up

Jacob's Creek Shiraz/Cabernet; Jacob's Creek Semillon/Chardonnay; Domaine du Tariquet; Tollana Dry White; Vin de Pays du Gers; Pinot Grigio Fiordaliso; Penfolds Bin 21; Albor Tinto; Bulgarian Cabernet Sauvignon; Lindauer

Range:

GOOD: Alsace, Bordeaux, Burgundy, regional France, Italy, Spain, Germany, Portugal, South Africa, Australia, New Zealand, Chile, Champagne and sparkling wines

AVERAGE: Beaujolais, Loire, Eastern Europe, California

POOR: Rhône

UNDER-REPRESENTED: None

So farewell, then, Thresher Drinks Stores. And goodbye to Food and Drink Stores from Thresher, too. After the latest bout of restructuring, the only trace of the 'T' word in the high street will be in the 'signage', as marketing bods call it, and in hand-outs for Thresher Wine Shops.

What's going on here? Have brewers Whitbread succumbed to the twin pressures of cross-Channel shopping and the seemingly inexorable supermarket growth and thrown in the bar towel? Have they, heck. The Thresher name may be dispensable, but its gradual disappearance is all part of a strategy designed, in the words of Thresher's niche-retailing oracle, Tim Waters, 'to maximise our opportunities in every locality'.

Waters and his marketing colleagues have seen the future, and it's all about segmentation. Horrible word it may be, but this is arguably the only way to run a 1,500-store leviathan as a flexible, modern off-licence chain. Sufficiently adaptable, in other words, to satisfy customers with the right mix of wines and other products.

To sell wine in any volume these days it's apparently not enough to put a few bottles on a shelf and stand back. Several other factors determine a store's place in the great chain of off-licence being: location, size, staff, the competition and, above all, the shape and depth of local customers' pockets. Enter segmentation and other gimmicks.

In an attempt to claw back some of the business lost to supermarkets and cross-Channel outlets, Thresher has sought to breathe some life into its ailing Drinks Stores – first by plugging them into the National Lottery and then by converting them into snappier-sounding Drinks Cabins, staffed – one would imagine – by men in raccoon hats.

A name change has also occurred at Thresher's Food and Drink convenience stores, now re-christened Huttons – not, we are assured, in deference to the editor of *The Observer*. And, still with new names, the Bottoms Up concept has been taken a step further with the opening of something called Booze Barn. (Who thinks up these names?)

Booze Barn is a giant retail park site of 10,000 square feet located at Staples Corner, off London's North Circular Road, where customers can buy in bulk or by the single bottle. Could Booze Barn be the future of wine retailing? Ask Tony Mason, of Majestic Wine Warehouses.

In its flagship Bottoms Up stores this year, Thresher has worked on its Champagne range and added special parcels of wines from Spain and red Bordeaux. In addition, you can 'try before you buy' any bottle under £10.

The Thresher Group

Sounds good to us. And Bottoms Up still has the sharpest range of discounts across the Thresher board.

With a new focus on South Africa, and Master of Wine Jo Standen's crusade to employ better managers, Wine Rack is changing at an even faster rate. The generally younger, more enthusiastic staff have helped to lighten the feel of what was sometimes perceived as a rather stuffy corner of the Thresher empire.

Down on the stripped wooden floors of Bottoms Up, Wine Rack and Thresher Wine Shops, sales of New World wines continue to lead the way. Indeed, when the Thresher board were recently given a briefing by their experienced head buyer Kim Tidy, they were staggered to learn that the New World now accounts for 40 per cent of wine sales at Thresher. Australia and California are still out in front, but South Africa and Chile are yapping at their heels, with New Zealand and Argentina bringing up the rear.

If Oddbins was once dubbed 'Ozbins', for its extensive Australian range, Wine Rack may yet earn the sobriquet 'Capebins'. South Africa was the country that Thresher chose this year to give Wine Rack a major face-lift. Lucy Warner's Cape crusade has brought 50-odd new wines to the range from a mix of co-operatives, estates and giant companies.

With a number of wines specially made for Thresher by Aussie winemaker Kym Milne, the hit rate is high, although a rump of dull KWV wines seems as hard to eradicate as memories of apartheid in some quarters. All 52 wines (some just small but high-quality parcels from Thelema, Stellenryck, Glen Carlou and Hamilton Russell) have gone into Wine Rack, with 32 in Bottoms Up and 20 in Thresher Wine Shops.

Why such saturation plundering of the Cape? Hadn't Thresher seen past over-enthusiasms such as Alsace and New Zealand come to grief? 'To an extent, that's true,' admits chief buyer Kim Tidy. 'But if you don't take risks and never experiment, you'll never learn. Someone was going to major on South Africa, and there had been rumours of volume shortages, so it seemed a good idea to secure sources of supply. We thought customers would go for it.'

To help get the South African ball rolling, Thresher enlisted the support of Wines of South Africa, whose Jane Hunt gives masterclasses, and high-profile producers such as Jeff Grier, of the excellent Villiera Estate.

Thresher has learnt from its mistakes. Two years ago, football-mad buyer Jon Woodriffe (who's since moved to Penfolds) did a lot of work developing the Chilean range. Nevertheless, sales at first failed to match expectations. This was not the fault of the wines, many of which were excellent, but because the labels didn't look good and there was no proper focus in the stores. But when the range was extended and re-packaged, things improved. Thresher sold 120,000 cases of Chilean wine last year – almost as many as it sold from South Africa.

Having taken two bites at the Chilean cherry, Thresher has become a little more cautious. The groundwork for the launch of a small new range of Argentine wines has been well prepared. Six new wines have been selected from Peñaflor, La Agricola and others, and a competition has been launched to find a suitable name. La Mano de Dios, perhaps?

Although the focus of the Thresher wine range has radically shifted towards the New World over the past couple of years, it's not all one-way traffic. Thresher's sartorially-challenged Bordeaux buyer, Julian Twaites, keeps plugging away at finding suitable value-for-money *petits châteaux*, mainly from the less fashionable (or expensive) districts, such as the Côtes de Bourg and Côtes de Blaye.

'Bordeaux still has plenty to offer in the traditional style,' says Twaites. 'It doesn't need to be Australianised.' Perhaps not, but after a run of dreary vintages, a bit of Australian weather would do nicely, thank you. White Bordeaux, meanwhile, has lost its allure for Thresher customers.

Even before Jürgen Klinsmann and his mates came to Euro '96, Germany was continuing to lose its hold on the market. Thresher made an attempt to stem the ebbing tide, with a German promotion in the summer and a creditable, if not entirely successful, attempt to make a modern, fruity, New World-influenced German wine called Solus (mind how you pronounce this one).

At the same time, Thresher has listed 13 well-chosen estate wines, some of which are excellent. Sadly for Thresher's eccentric PR mouthpiece, David Howse, his suggestion that the promotion be called 'Get Schloss'd' was rejected.

Spain is the one traditional area that continues to do well at Thresher, mainly because it has put a lot of effort into its range. The reds from Raimat and Martinez Bujanda are hard to beat. And with Portugal bolstered by some excellent new wines from Peter Bright, the future for the Iberian peninsula at Thresher looks fine and dandy.

Partly as a result of the shift towards the New World, Thresher has delisted some of the wines from smaller, independent estates in the 60-strong Languedoc-Roussillon range. This seems a pity, but Lucy Warner says that Thresher intends to do more buying in the south of France in 1997. The Rhône, meanwhile, remains a problem area. 'There is no traditional base of Rhône enthusiasts,' says Warner. 'So it's very difficult to sell.'

Other parts of the range have performed rather better. In fact, in a struggling off-licence sector, Thresher managed to increase its wine sales by 9 per cent last year. Not surprisingly, Thresher is bullish about its performance as Britain's most powerful and dynamic off-licence chain.

Ruthlessly culling under-performing shops (57 stores, according to news reports, although some say as many as 300 will be sold in the end), Thresher has opened 50 new stores this year, with plans for a further 50 or so in the pipeline. It may not have succeeded in hoovering up Oddbins, as it seemed about to do at one point in mid-1996, but the marketing department, the buyers and, most important of all, the store managers have plenty of things to be getting on with.

All wines are available in Thresher Wine Shops (TWS), Wine Rack (WR) and Bottoms Up (BU), unless otherwise indicated.

White

Under £3

HUNGARY

Butler's Blend, Hungarian Muscat/Riesling 13/20
Dry 👛👛 🍾
Spicy, aromatic blend of Muscat and Riesling from the Kiskoros region south of Budapest. Drier than you'd expect, and attractively summery.

SPAIN

Casa Rural White, Viticultores de Padres 14/20
Bone dry 👛👛👛 🍾
Clean, zesty, apple-fresh Spanish white with commendable dry fruitiness. Excellent tapas-bar white.

£3–5

AUSTRALIA

1995 Tollana Dry White 14/20
Off-dry 👛👛 🍾
An appealing Aussie cheapie hiding its Riesling origins behind a non-committal 'dry white' label. Tangy, fresh and sweetish.

1995 Tollana Medium Dry   13/20
Medium dry 👜 ▮
Confected, barley-sugar-like white made from Tollana knows what. Mawkish stuff.

1995 Red Cliffs Estate Riesling/Traminer, Victoria   14/20
Off-dry 👜👜 ▮
Australia's fruity response to Alsace's Edelzwicker, this is an aromatic blend of Riesling and Gewürztraminer, attractively priced at under £4.

1995 Red Cliffs Estate Colombard/Chardonnay   14/20
Dry 👜 ▮
A good commercial blend of Colombard and Chardonnay from Mildura in Australia's irrigated heartland. Should be under £4.

1995 Rawson's Retreat Bin 21 Semillon/Chardonnay/Colombard
    15/20
Dry 👜👜👜 ▮
Lime-fresh, ice cream soda-like blend of Semillon, Chardonnay and Colombard from Australia's biggest winery, Penfolds, proving that big-volume wines can show character in the right hands. Super stuff.

1994 Bridgewater Mill Riesling Clare Valley   13/20
Off-dry 👜 ▮
Clumsy, over-sulphured Clare Valley Riesling from Petaluma's obsessive and usually brilliant Brian Croser. Unfocused, sweetish and ageing.

BULGARIA

1995 Twin Peaks Chardonnay/Rikat, Russe   13/20
Off-dry 👜 ▮
New-style, boiled-sweety Bulgarian blend with easy-drinking fruit, from the Russe winery.

1995 Targovischte Chardonnay, Domaine Boyar   13/20
Off-dry 👜👜 ▮
Clean, boiled-sweet-style Bulgarian Chardonnay with a New World bent, showing further progress for Bulgarian whites.

1995 Targovischte Barrel-Fermented Chardonnay   14/20
Dry 👜👜 ▮
Splintery, gassy, crisp Bulgarian white, which is moving in the right direction but hasn't quite reached its destination.

CHILE

1995 Las Colinas Semillon/Sauvignon, Santa Carolina   14/20
Dry 💰💰 🍾
Crisp, fresh, lime-zesty Chilean blend of Semillon and Sauvignon Blanc, made for Thresher by the team of Pilar Gonzalez and Ignacio Recabarren. More Riesling than Bordeaux blend in style.

1995 Las Colinas Semillon, Lontue   15/20
Dry 💰💰💰 🍾
Weighty, intensely herbal, creamy Chilean Semillon with good concentration of fruit sweetness, from travelling Frenchman, Jacques Lurton

1994 Las Colinas Riesling, San Pedro   13/20
Off-dry 💰 🍾
Confected lime-sherbet-like Chilean Riesling from Jacques Lurton, with added sweetness.

1995 Santa Carolina Chenin Blanc   15/20
Dry 💰💰 🍾
If you've always found Loire Chenin Blanc on the austere side of the torture rack, this soft, peach and aniseed-scented Chilean white might be more to your liking.

1995 Las Colinas Chardonnay, Lontue   14/20
Dry 💰 🍾
Well-made, tropical fruit and oak-chip-style Chardonnay from Jacques Lurton at the San Pedro winery. Fine, but a bit simple.

1995 Trio Chardonnay, Casablanca   16/20
Dry 💰💰💰 🍾
A strong contender for the title of Chile's best sub-£5 Chardonnay, this rich, mealy, complex Chablis-meets-California-style white reflects well on Concha y Toro's winemaker, Ignacio Recabarren, and the cool-climate vineyards of Casablanca. Shame about the dog's dinner packaging.

1996 Santa Carolina Sauvignon Blanc Nouveau, Lontue   14/20
Dry 💰💰 🍾
Fresh, nettley essence of young Chilean Sauvignon Blanc, at a starter bottle price of around £4.

FRANCE

1995 Muscadet Côtes de Grand Lieu sur lie, Vignerons de la Noëlle   15/20
Bone dry 👛👛 |
Fresh, weighty, bone-dry *sur lie* Muscadet from a recently introduced sub-appellation.

1994 Acacias, Terret, Vin de Pays des Côtes de Thau, Paul Boutinot   12/20
Dry |
Dull, unbalanced, southern French white made from the Vermouth grape, Terret. Try a taste of Martini instead.

1995 Domaine du Tariquet, Vin de Pays des Côtes de Gascogne
14/20
Off-dry 👛👛 |
Côtes de Gascogne has crept up in price recently, but this grapefruity Ugni Blanc-based blend is a refreshing, attractively fruity quaffer.

GERMANY

1995 Liebfraumilch, Regional Classics   12/20
Medium sweet |
Thresher has been so busy in other parts of the world that it appears to have neglected its basic Lieb. To call this simple German blend a regional classic is like calling Des O'Connor an operatic tenor.

1995 Solus, Rheinhessen, Langenbach   13/20
Medium sweet 👛 |
Fresh, fruity, modern German white made from the usual Rheinhessen suspects. A grapey but still sugary style, which is at least fruitier than the Lieb.

HUNGARY

1995 Gyöngyös Estate Chardonnay, Hugh Ryman   14/20
Dry 👛👛 |
Fresh, zingy, lightly oaked, greengage-style Hungarian Chardonnay from Hugh Ryman. A vast improvement on recent disappointing vintages.

1995 Gyöngyös Sauvignon Blanc, Hugh Ryman   14/20
Dry 👝👝 🍶
A good vintage for Hungarian whites has helped to boost the aromatic intensity of the Sauvignon Blanc grape in this lemon zesty, crisp, dry white.

1994 Cool Ridge Barrel-Fermented Chardonnay, Nagyrede   16/20
Dry 👝👝👝 🍶
Possibly the best white that Kym Milne has made in Eastern Europe, this rich, harmonious, oak-fermented Chardonnay has the peachy ripeness of a New World style balanced by near-Burgundian complexity and finesse. And all this for under a fiver.

ITALY

1995 Pinot Grigio Fiordaliso, Vino da Tavola, GIV   15/20
Dry 👝👝 🍶
Soft, slightly nutty, ripe pear-like Veneto Pinot Grigio from the cutting-edge winery, Gruppo Italiano Vini.

1995 Cortese del Piemonte, Contea di Castiglione   16/20
Dry 👝👝👝 🍶
A really enjoyable Piedmontese white made by the original Aussie flying wine-maker, Martin Shaw, with lime and pear fruit aromas and a surprising amount of concentration for an Italian white under £5.

NEW ZEALAND

1995 Kapua Springs Medium Dry White   13/20
Off-dry 👝 🍶
Surprisingly drinkable for a sub-£4 New Zealand white from the difficult 1995 vintage, this fruity, sweetish, floral blend is a decent southern hemisphere alternative to Liebfraumilch.

1995 Villa Maria Private Bin Sauvignon Blanc, Marlborough   15/20
Dry 👝👝 🍶
Tart, catty Kiwi Sauvignon from the Marlborough region. One of the better-value, commercial whites produced in New Zealand in 1995.

PORTUGAL

1995 Bright Brothers Fernão Pires/Chardonnay, Ribatejo   15/20
Dry 🛍🛍🛍 ▯

Full-bodied, fragrant, modern-style Portuguese white made by resident Australian Peter Bright, combining the indigenous Fernão Pires with the ubiquitous Chardonnay. A rich, spicy, lightly oaked blend. Good, if not quite as thrilling as last year's *Grapevine* wine of the year.

SOUTH AFRICA

1995 Winelands Bush Vine Chenin Blanc   15/20
Dry 🛍🛍 ▯

Only a relatively small proportion of the Cape's widespread Chenin Blanc is old vine material. This well-made, sumptuously juicy white from Kym Milne is an example of what low yields and venerable vineyards can achieve.

1995 Villiera Oaked Chenin Blanc (WR/BU)   16/20
Dry 🛍🛍🛍 ▯

Another example of Chenin Blanc at its most interesting (a rare phenomenon), this time from Jeff Grier's Villiera estate in Paarl. Creamy, spicy, subtly oaked white with honeyed richness and concentration.

1996 Stellenbosch Dry White   14/20
Off-dry 🛍🛍 ▯

Made from the unusual Crouchen Blanc grape at the Welmoed winery by Kym Milne, this is a ripe pear and banana-like, cool-fermented white with refreshing crispness.

1996 Winelands Medium Dry   14/20
Medium dry 🛍🛍 ▯

Grapey, attractively balanced blend of Chenin Blanc, Crouchen Blanc and the aromatic Muscat, this is a crowd-pleasing Cape quaffer, which needs to be well-chilled.

1995 Hartenberg Weisser Riesling (WR)   15/20
Off-dry 🛍🛍 ▯

Opulent, almost Alsace-like Cape Riesling, with marked petrolly undertones and a soft, floral sweetness. A welcome alternative to Chenin Blanc, Chardonnay and Sauvignon.

1996 Winelands Sauvignon Blanc (WR/BU)   15/20
Dry 💰💰💰 🍷
Another characterful white from the talented Kym Milne, this is an elderflower-scented, Marlborough taste-alike with lively acidity and assertive green bean flavours.

SPAIN

1995 Viña Calera Sauvignon Blanc   15/20
Dry 💰💰 🍷
Arguably Spain's best Sauvignon Blanc. Not hard, mind, but this collaboration between Hugh Ryman and Rueda's Marqués de Riscal of Rioja is a gooseberry and grapefruit-style, unoaked white of pleasing intensity.

UNITED STATES

1995 Kings Canyon Chardonnay   13/20
Off-dry 🍷
Hefty, alcoholic, toffee-fudge-like California Chardonnay from Englishman Hugh Ryman.

£5–8

AUSTRALIA

1995 Samuel's Bay Colombard, Barossa Valley   15/20
Dry 💰 🍷
Greengage and plum-scented, unoaked Colombard from wise-cracking Adam Wynn. Good-quality fruit and attractively fresh acidity, but a little pricey at £5.99.

1995 Rosemount Lightly Oaked Semillon   16/20
Dry 💰💰 🛢
Rich, refreshing, Aussie Semillon with flavours of lemon curd and a hint of oak. Zesty, crisp and well-crafted. Thanks for toning down the oak, guys.

FRANCE

1995 Clos de la Fine Muscadet sur lie, Luc et Andrée-Marie Choblet 16/20
Bone dry 🍷🍷🍷 ▌

Bracingly fresh, grower's Muscadet with remarkable intensity and a characterful *sur lie* prickle of lees-derived petillance.

1995 Domaine Laroche Bourgogne Chardonnay, Tête de Cuvée (WR/BU) 15/20
Bone dry 🍷🍷 ▌

From leading Yonne négociant Laroche, this tastes like declassified Chablis. Crisp, dry Chardonnay with an appealing, minerally tang.

1994 Tokay Pinot Gris Réserve, Cave de Turckheim 15/20
Dry 🍷🍷 ▌

The Turckheim co-operative produces some of the best-value white wines in Alsace, as this delicately spicy, peachy, full-bodied Tokay Pinot Gris amply demonstrates.

GERMANY

1994 Forster Pechstein Riesling Kabinett, Rheinpfalz, Reichsrat Von Buhl 17/20
Medium sweet 🍷🍷🍷 ▬

An extremely intense, richly concentrated Rheinpfalz estate Riesling, combining ripe pear and tropical citrus fruit flavours in a beautifully balanced, harmonious whole.

1993 Ruppertsberger Linsenbusch Riesling Spätlese, Rheinpfalz, Winzerverein Hoheburg 16/20
Sweet 🍷🍷🍷 ▬

Pure, elegant Rheinpfalz Riesling with sweet-and-sour lemony acidity and white-pepper notes adding up to a really flavoursome, characterful white at around £6.

1992 Dalsheimer Steig Siegerrebe Auslese, Rheinhessen, Weingut Schales 17/20
Sweet 🍷🍷🍷 ▬

Made from the Siegerrebe grape, a crossing of aromatic Gewürztraminer with Madeleine Angevine, this is an astonishingly rich and spicy, concentrated dessert white, with sumptuous apricot and mandarin orange fruitiness and a long aftertaste.

NEW ZEALAND

1994 Church Road Chardonnay, Hawkes Bay, Montana   16/20
Dry 🍾🍾🍾 ➡️

From Montana's McDonald winery in North Island's Hawkes Bay, this attractively toasty, cinnamon-spice and citrus fruit Chardonnay has established itself as one of New Zealand's best. There's a difference at McDonalds you'll enjoy.

1995 Selaks Sauvignon Blanc, Marlborough   15/20
Dry 🍾🍾 ▯

A typically assertive Marlborough style from Auckland winery Selaks, with tart, green-pepper and capsicum aromas and flavours and an austere nip of acidity .

1995 Palliser Estate Sauvignon Blanc, Martinborough   15/20
Dry 🍾 ▯

One of the more interesting Kiwi Sauvignon Blancs produced in 1995, this is still on the green and one-dimensional side, especially given this Martinborough winery's excellent record.

SOUTH AFRICA

1995 Stellenryck Sauvignon Blanc (WR)   15/20
Dry 🍾 ▯

Sourced from the sprawling Bergkelder group, this top-of-the-range Sauvignon Blanc is a rich, gooseberry fruity white with a touch of smoky complexity. A little pricey at £7 or so.

1995 Stellenryck Chardonnay (WR)   14/20
Dry ▯

Unreconstructed Cape Chardonnay with uneven, charred oak and an awkward imbalance of fruit and acidity.

1995 Villiera Sauvignon Blanc (WR/BU)   16/20
Dry 🍾🍾🍾 ▯

One of the best-value New World Sauvignons at little more than £5, this is a ripe, intensely melon-fruity white with assertively aromatic, elderflower notes.

1995 De Wetshof Chardonnay d'Honneur (WR/BU)   16/20
Dry 🍾🍾🍾 ▬
The top Chardonnay from Danie de Wet's impressive Robertson winery, this is a tightly focused, barrel-fermented white, with well-integrated oak nuttiness and the concentration of fruit to age in bottle for a good year or three.

1995 Villiera Gewürztraminer   16/20
Off-dry 🍾🍾🍾 ▬
One of the few Gewürztraminers produced in the southern hemisphere, this is a lightly spicy, elegant white with a relatively restrained (for Gewürz) lychee fruit character.

Over £8

FRANCE

1995 Saint Véran, Domaine des Deux Roches, Les Terres Noires (WR/BU)   17/20
Dry 🍾🍾🍾 |
Intensely spicy, highly concentrated Mâconnais white Burgundy from one of the best domaines in Saint Véran. A crisp, abundantly fruity expression of the Chardonnay grape.

1994 Chablis Premier Cru, Fourchaume, Château de Maligny (WR/BU)   17/20
Dry 🍾🍾🍾 |
A stocking-filler Chardonnay specially priced at just under a tenner for Christmas 1996. Buttery and softly textured, but lifted by bone-dry crispness, this is classic, premier cru Chablis.

1994 Puligny-Montrachet, Louis Carillon (WR/BU)   17/20
Dry 🍾🍾 ▬
A stylish, tightly focused village white Burgundy from the well-respected Carillon family. This needs another year or so in bottle to develop into a classic.

1991 Chablis Premier Cru, Côte de Léchet, Defaix   17/20
Bone dry 🍾🍾 ▬
From an estate that specialises in age-worthy Chardonnays, this is a structured, intriguingly mature *premier cru* Chablis, which combines buttery richness with an intense streak of fresh acidity.

SOUTH AFRICA

1995 Hamilton Russell Chardonnay, Walker Bay (WR)   16/20
Dry 🍾🍾 ●━

Consistently among South Africa's best Chardonnays, this cool-climate, barrel-fermented white is an elegant, butterscotchy, cinnamon-spicy number with perfectly poised acidity and the concentration to age.

Red

Under £3

BULGARIA

1995 Iambol Cabernet Sauvignon   14/20
Medium-bodied 🍾🍾🍾 ▮

Modern-style Bulgarian glugger with the emphasis on blackcurrant and cherry fruit flavours. The tannins are a mite rustic.

SPAIN

Casa Rural Red Tinto, Viticultores de Padres   13/20
Medium-bodied 🍾🍾 ▮

An honest, well-made tapas-bar red with a suitably bucolic name and label.

£3–5

AUSTRALIA

Tollana Red, South Eastern Australia   13/20
Medium-bodied 🍾 ▮

Pretty basic, jammy Australian red blend with added acidity and insufficient fruit character. A wine struggling to meet a price point.

1994 Tollana South Australia Shiraz/Cabernet   14/20
Medium-bodied 💰 🍷
A small step in price, and a small leap in quality from the basic Tollana Red. At least this wine has some sweet blackcurrant fruit to it.

BULGARIA

1990 Iambol Cabernet Sauvignon Special Reserve   14/20
Medium-bodied 💰💰 🍷
In contrast to the youthful fruit of the sub-£3 Iambol red, this is an assertively oaky Cabernet Sauvignon, which has developed into something interesting after half a dozen years in bottle.

CHILE

1996 Las Colinas Merlot   15/20
Medium-bodied 💰💰 🍷
Juicy, brambly, sweetly fruity Chilean red made from the fashionable Merlot grape. We could drink a lot of this.

1995 Trio Merlot   16/20
Medium-bodied 💰💰💰 🍷
The aromas were a little funky when we tasted it, but the fruit quality of this newly released red from Concha y Toro is remarkable in a wine under a fiver. Intense cassis fruit and fine-grained tannins are the hallmarks here. Shame about the silly bottle.

1994 Trio Cabernet Sauvignon, Concha y Toro   15/20
Medium-bodied 💰💰 🍷
Not quite as fine as the Trio Merlot (maybe it's because it's a year older), but this is still a well-made blackcurrant-pastille-like red, with commendable intensity of fruit and a dry aftertaste.

FRANCE

1995 Figaro, Vin de Pays de l'Hérault   13/20
Medium-bodied 💰 🍷
A Languedoc blend of Grenache and Carignan from the Villeveyrac co-operative, this is a soft, carbonic-maceration-style red with a hottish finish.

1995 Fitou, Réserve Spéciale   14/20
Full-bodied 🍷🍷 |
Same grape varieties, same region, but a better class of wine. Warm, spicy, robust red from one of France's best co-operatives.

Côtes du Rhône Regional Classics   13/20
Medium-bodied 🍷 |
Lightly peppery, softly fruity southern Rhône blend with a dry aftertaste.

Claret, Bordeaux, Regional Classics, Peter Sichel   12/20
Medium-bodied |
Basic, overpriced, rasping red Bordeaux. If this is a regional classic, perhaps Bordeaux should consider switching to potato farming.

1995 Coteaux du Tricastin, Domaine de Montine   15/20
Full-bodied 🍷🍷 ☞
White-pepper and plum-scented southern Rhône red, with fresh acidity and a backbone of youthful tannins.

ITALY

1994 Alasia Dolcetto d'Asti   14/20
Medium-bodied 🍷 |
Black-cherry fruity Piedmontese quaffer made by Aussie Martin Shaw at the Araldica co-operative. Should be £1 cheaper.

PORTUGAL

Ramada Red, Vinho Regional Estremadura, José Neiva   11/20
Medium-bodied |
Sweetish, tomato-skin-style Portuguese plonk, which lacks the right sort of Iberian character.

1994 Fiuza Oak-Aged Cabernet Sauvignon   16/20
Medium-bodied 🍷🍷🍷 |
Elegant, almost New Zealand-like Cabernet Sauvignon, which is remarkable given that the wine was made in the warm Portuguese south. Fine tannins, smoky oak and green-pepper fruitiness make this restrained red a brilliant alternative to red Bordeaux.

1995 Bright Brothers Douro Red 16/20
Full-bodied 🜂🜂🜂 ▬

Hugely concentrated, violet-scented, chocolate and plum-like Douro Valley blend from the irrepressible Peter Bright. On the chunky side, but there's a core of succulent fruit that shines brightly.

ROMANIA

1995 Vampire's Leap Cabernet Sauvignon 13/20
Full-bodied 🜂 |

A blood-red attempt at a toothsome modern style from Romania – hence the Transylvanian link. Too extracted and dry for its own good, but at least it's moving towards the twentieth century.

1995 Vampire's Leap Merlot 13/20
Full-bodied 🜂 |

Another full-bodied, as it were, Romanian red, made by Stephen Donnelly for the Hanwood Group, showing beetrooty fruit characters and bitter aggressive tannins. Fangs for the memory.

SOUTH AFRICA

Boschendal Le Pavillon 15/20
Medium-bodied 🜂🜂 |

A non-vintage blend of Merlot, Cabernet, Syrah and Pinotage, with sage and mint-like aromas and an abundance of juicy blackcurrant fruit.

1993 KWV Roodeberg 11/20
Medium-bodied |

Cooked, sweetish, red plonk from KWV, in the old-fashioned South African tradition.

1995 Winelands Cinsault/Tinta Barocca 15/20
Medium-bodied 🜂🜂🜂 |

An aromatic, super-charged Mediterranean-style blend from Aussie Kym Milne, showing exuberantly ripe, strawberry and plum fruitiness and juicy sweet tannins. A wine with considerable oomph.

1995 Winelands Pinotage 16/20
Full-bodied 🜂🜂🜂 ▬

Another Kym Milne stunner, proving that he can turn his hand to South Africa's indigenous Pinotage grape as well as any local. This is a raspberry sweet, deftly oaked, spicy red with lovely perfume and excellent length of flavour.

SPAIN

Copa Real Tinto   14/20
Medium-bodied 👜👜👜 ▮
Juicy, up-front, unoaked Spanish blend with attractively strawberryish fruit.

Copa Real Plata Tinto   13/20
Medium-bodied 👜 ▮
The same thing with a few added splinters, for an extra 60 pence. Now you know the price of oak chips.

1994 Baso Navarra Garnacho   14/20
Medium-bodied 👜 ▮
From Telmo Rodriguez of the Remelluri estate in Rioja, this is a softly fruity Garnacha, or Garnacho if you prefer, which is beginning to lose its bloom.

1993 Fuente del Ritmo   13/20
Full-bodied ▮
Dry, coconutty La Mancha Tempranillo made by Californian Ed Flaherty. A rather rustic Rioja clone.

1995 Valdemar Tinto , Martinez Bujanda   16/20
Medium-bodied 👜👜👜 ▮
Vibrant young Tempranillo from one of Rioja's most forward-looking bodegas, with cherry and raspberry fruitiness unmolested by oak. As good as you'll get in this style.

1994 Marqués de Griñon Rioja   15/20
Medium-bodied 👜👜 ▮
Made entirely with Tempranillo grapes from the Rioja Alavesa, this is an elegant, well-judged marriage of oak and soft, strawberry fruitiness at a pretty good price.

El Mesón Rioja, CVC   15/20
Medium-bodied 👜👜 ▮
A silky, elegant, attractively oaked Pinot Noir-like Rioja with sweetly mature vanilla and raspberry fruitiness.

£5–8

AUSTRALIA

1994 Rosemount Estate Merlot, South Australia (WR/BU)   15/20
Medium-bodied 🛍 ❗

Intense, minty, youthful Australian Merlot showing freshness, vigour and restrained oak. Should be under a fiver.

1994 Samuel's Bay Malbec, Padthaway   16/20
Medium-bodied 🛍🛍🛍 ❗

Sage and ginger spice aromas characterise this unoaked and innovative Padthaway interpretation of south-west France's Malbec grape. We enjoyed this exuberantly fruity wine a year ago and we haven't changed our minds.

FRANCE

1993 Côtes du Rhône, Château du Grand Prébois   15/20
Full-bodied 🛍🛍 ❗

Super-ripe, chocolate and raisin-like Côtes du Rhône with masses of Grenache fruit and heady alcohol. Impressive stuff that could easily pass for a Côtes du Rhône Villages.

1992 André Lurton Oak Aged Claret   15/20
Medium-bodied 🛍🛍 ❗

Highly drinkable for a 1992, this is a ripeish Right Bank-style claret based on the supple Merlot grape, with oak influence for good measure.

1993 Château Suau, Premières Côtes de Bordeaux (Unoaked)
14/20
Medium-bodied 🛍 ▬

An unoaked Premières Côtes claret from grower Aldebert-Bonnet, which shows the leanness of the 1993 vintage.

1991 Château Suau, Premières Côtes de Bordeaux   15/20
Medium-bodied 🛍🛍 ❗

Same producer, but more flesh, oak and fruit. A good Christmas lunch claret.

1994 Château Sauvage, Premières Côtes de Bordeaux   14/20
Medium-bodied 🍷 ▯

A pleasant modern blend of 60 per cent Merlot, 30 per cent Cabernet Sauvignon and 10 per cent Cabernet Franc, which is a little light on fruit for a 1994.

1993 Château Bonnet Rouge, Bordeaux   15/20
Medium-bodied 🍷🍷 ▯

With more pronounced new oak than his oak-aged claret blend, André Lurton's own château red is lively and redolent of cassis fruit. Finishes on the dry side.

1994 Château Langoiran, Premières Côtes de Bordeaux   16/20
Medium-bodied 🍷🍷 ▭

This is a bit more like it, showing stuffing, fruit concentration and spicy oak. The sort of forward, supple claret that the Premières Côtes ought to be producing in greater volume.

1993 Château Lamarche, 'Lutet', Bordeaux Supérieur   16/20
Medium-bodied 🍷🍷🍷 ▯

Blessed with a bottle that's so heavy you can barely lift it off the table, this is an ultra-modern, coffee-bean oaky red Bordeaux with plenty of stuffing, fleshy texture and ripe fruit flavours. Good value at around £7.

NEW ZEALAND

1994 Montana Cabernet Sauvignon   15/20
Medium-bodied 🍷🍷 ▯

A grassy, black-cherry fruity Marlborough and Hawkes Bay blend of Cabernet Sauvignon, with a dollop of Merlot attractively fleshed out with some spicy coffee-bean oak. Good value at just over £5.

SOUTH AFRICA

1995 Beyerskloof Pinotage (WR/BU)   16/20
Full-bodied 🍷🍷🍷 ▭

Chunky, vibrantly coloured, oak and raspberry fruity Pinotage from Kanonkop winemaker, Beyers Truter. Plenty of character, as you'd expect from South Africa's most distinctive red grape variety.

1995 Delheim Pinotage (WR)   15/20
Full-bodied 👝👝 ➖

A powerfully structured, concentrated Cape Pinotage with cedary oak and notes of ginger and blackberry fruit. A muscular red that will reward patience.

1995 Warwick Pinotage (WR)   17/20
Full-bodied 👝👝👝 ➖

From Canadian Norma Ratcliffe's outstanding Stellenbosch winery, this is an inky, dense, complex Pinotage with surprisingly fine-grained tannins and chocolatey flavours. Again a wine for patient cellaring.

1994 Villiera Merlot (WR)   16/20
Medium-bodied 👝👝 ➖

Stylish, elegantly oaked, almost Saint Emilion-like Cape red from Jeff Grier's Villiera Estate, showing fleshy, concentrated blackcurrant fruit flavours, sweet vanilla oak and fresh, balancing acidity.

1994 Villiera Cabernet Sauvignon (BU)   16/20
Medium-bodied 👝👝👝 ➖

Made from new clone Cabernet Sauvignon, the mintiness and ripe juiciness of the variety comes through beautifully on this stylishly balanced, modern Cape red. We've yet to have a disappointment from Villiera.

SPAIN

1993 Conde de Valdemar Rioja Crianza   16/20
Medium-bodied 👝👝👝 ➖

Skilfully oaked, fruit-steered, modern Rioja with intense aromas and flavours and excellent balance from a winery that rarely disappoints.

1991 Viña Amezola Rioja Crianza   14/20
Medium-bodied 👝 ❘

A Rioja blend of Tempranillo and the rare Mazuelo grape aged in French and American oak. The fruit is too light for the weight of oak.

1991 Barón de Ley, Rioja Reserva   16/20
Medium-bodied 👝👝👝 ➖

Oaky, Cabernet Sauvignon-influenced Rioja Reserva, which is just getting into its stride. An attractively fruity, well-oaked red with considerable complexity.

1991 Conde de Valdemar Reserva Rioja   17/20
Medium-bodied 🍷🍷🍷 ▮

Mature, top-quality, estate-bottled Rioja with gamey, aniseedy concentration and finely judged oak. A stunner.

Over £8

FRANCE

1994 Terroir de Tuchan Fitou (BU)   15/20
Full-bodied 🍷 ▬▬

The top wine from the Mont Tauch co-operative is an ambitiously priced but extremely well-made Syrah-based Fitou, enhanced by new oak ageing and old vine concentration.

1994 Nuits Saint Georges, Domaine de l'Arlot   15/20
Medium-bodied 🍷 ▮

Ripe, abundantly oaked New World-style Pinot Noir, with raspberry fruitiness and a dry, splintery finish.

1992 Château Yon-Figeac, Saint Emilion Grand Cru (WR/BU)
16/20

Medium-bodied 🍷🍷 ▮

Mocha-like oak flavours are the dominant feature of this supple, Merlot-based claret. Good but pricey, especially given the mediocre vintage.

NEW ZEALAND

1994 Church Road Cabernet Sauvignon/Merlot, Hawkes Bay, Montana   16/20
Medium-bodied 🍷🍷🍷 ▮

Supple, elegant, cool-climate Bordeaux blend, which would outperform most *cru bourgeois* claret. Nicely oaked and firmly structured.

1994 Martinborough Vineyards Pinot Noir   16/20
Medium-bodied 🍷🍷🍷 ▮

Wild strawberry fruit and a broad attack of flavours make this cleverly oaked, spicy Kiwi Pinot Noir one of the the best red Burgundy alternatives from the southern hemisphere.

SPAIN

1989 Conde de Valdemar Rioja Gran Reserva   17/20
Medium-bodied 👜👜👜 ❚
Another brilliant wine from Martinez Bujanda, made from Tempranillo and
Mazuelo grapes from vineyards in the Rioja Alavesa and Rioja Alta. Sweetly
fruity and almost Burgundian in its complexity, this is a modern classic.

1989 Martinez Bujanda Rioja Reserva (BU)   17/20
Medium-bodied 👜👜👜 ➡
Intensely concentrated, structured Rioja reserva with vigorous fruit, vanilla oak
and tannins in succulent harmony. Rioja doesn't get much better than this.

1990 Martinez Bujanda Garnacha Reserva (BU)   16/20
Full-bodied 👜👜 ❚
Closer to Châteauneuf-du-Pape in style, thanks to a large proportion of
Garnacha (aka Grenache) grapes. Raisiny, heady, chewy stuff.

Rosé

£3–5

FRANCE

1995 Fortant Rosé Sec Cabernet   14/20
Off-dry 👜👜 ❚
Light, thirst-quenching, redcurrant and strawberry fruity Languedoc rosé from
pasta magnate Robert Skalli. Drink it well-chilled.

Sparkling

Over £8

AUSTRALIA

1992 Croser Brut 16/20
Dry 🍷🍷🍷 ▮
With its distinctive, savoury-yeasty aromas, this tangy, complex, Adelaide Hills fizz could only be Croser. Elegant, characterful stuff from the eponymous Brian Croser.

1993 Green Point, Domaine Chandon 16/20
Dry 🍷🍷🍷 ▮
The red fruit character of the Pinot Noir grape is abundantly apparent in this Victorian-based blend of Pinot Noir and Chardonnay from the thinking woman's winemaker, Dr Tony Jordan. As you might expect from a Moët et Chandon-owned subsidiary, this is closer to Champagne in style than the Croser.

FRANCE

Jean de Praisac Brut Champagne 16/20
Dry 🍷🍷🍷 ▮
Malty, mature, strawberryish Champagne with an abundance of Pinot grape flavours. Hard to beat at under £12.50.

Le Mesnil Blanc de Blancs Champagne 16/20
Bone dry 🍷🍷🍷 ▮
Toasty, dry, honeycomb-like Champagne made entirely from the Chardonnay grape, with a refreshing dry finish.

Drappier Carte d'Or Brut Champagne 16/20
Dry 🍷🍷 ▮
You can almost taste whole strawberries in this deliciously full-flavoured, Pinot-dominated négociant Champagne. We'd be happy to drink a lot of this any time, anywhere.

1988 Veuve Clicquot Rich Reserve Champagne (WR/BU)   15/20
Medium sweet 🍷 ▮
We may be old-fashioned, but we'd rather not drink our Champagne sweet.
This is a good example of its style, provided that you want to drink Champagne
and eat Madeira cake at the same time.

NEW ZEALAND

Lindauer Special Reserve NV   15/20
Dry 🍷🍷 ▮
Frothy, dry Kiwi blend of Pinot Noir and Chardonnay, with youthful fruit
flavours and good weight.

Deutz Marlborough Cuvée   15/20
Dry 🍷🍷 ▮
Elegantly aromatic South Island fizz, which promises slightly more than it
delivers on the palate. Youthful, crisp and tangy, but lacking a third dimension of
complexity. We enjoyed last year's blend rather more.

Unwins ☆☆(☆)

Address: Birchwood House, Victoria Road, Dartford, Kent DA1 5AJ

Telephone/fax: 01322 272711; 01322 294469

Number of branches: 310

Opening hours: 9.00am to 10.00pm Monday to Saturday; 12.00pm to 3.00pm and 7.00pm to 10.00pm Sunday

Credit cards accepted: Access, Visa, Switch, Delta, Master Card, American Express, Diners Club, Transax

Discounts: Five per cent on 6 bottles of table and sparkling wines (may be mixed); 10 per cent on 12 bottles of table and sparkling wines (may be mixed); 12.5 per cent on 12 bottles of Champagne; 12.5 per cent on all other orders over £200

Facilities and services: Free glass loan; in-store tastings; mail order; gift vouchers; monthly accounts; home delivery (most branches)

Top ten best-selling wines: Encanto Red; Encanto White; 1994 Frascati Superiore Tullio San Marco; Lambrusco Bianco (4 per cent); Stockmans Bridge White; Stockmans Bridge Red; 1995 Jacobs Creek Semillon/Chardonnay; 1995 Mauregard Petit Château White; 1994 Fitou; 1994 Mauregard Petit Château Red

Range:

GOOD: Red Bordeaux

AVERAGE: Australia, White Bordeaux, Burgundy, Rhône, Loire, regional France, Alsace, Italy, Spain, Portugal, Chile, Austria, New Zealand, Champagne and sparkling wines, Port

POOR: South Africa, Beaujolais, French Vins de Pays, Germany, Bulgaria, Hungary, United States

UNDER-REPRESENTED: Argentina, and bits of all the above, except red Bordeaux

Bucking the trend of high-street off-licence closures, Unwins, aged 153, took its tally of shops from 298 to 310 last year. Ten of the new shops were conversions of the Cooks chain, based in Suffolk and Essex. A further two shops opened in Calne and Petersfield. And at the time of writing, Unwins was anticipating the opening of a new Bottoms-Up-sized 'superstore' in Sawbridgeworth. Dynamic or what?

Conduct a vox pop to find the word that best describes this curious high-street survivor, and 'dynamic' would probably not feature in the top ten. Bigger than Davisons or Fuller's, Unwins is by some distance the largest of the independently owned high-street chains. It has 25 shops in London, with the rest dotted about the shire counties in places like Stansted Mountfitchet, Thundersley and Buntingford. While other chains battle it out in the crowded high streets, Unwins takes a commuter-belt back seat.

Owning a substantial amount of its own properties helps to shield Unwins from the tooth-and-claw unpleasantness of high-street life. The Dartford-based chain has a loyal and friendly staff too, prepared to work long hours to serve toing and froing commuters. But if it has the wherewithal to expand, why does Unwins still feel like a Network South-East train waiting for the signals to change between East Wittering and Peacehaven?

According to Bill Rolfe, Unwins' special purchasing and marketing director, 'Customers see us as a shop they can use where they feel comfortable. We're not just a wacky company, but a comfortable retailer for nice people' (Oddbins customers, please note). 'We haven't neglected tradition,' adds Rolfe, 'but we recognise that it's a fast-moving environment and that we need to keep abreast of fashion.'

In the last two years we have noticed signs of Unwins emerging from its torpor. Prices have become more competitive, and promotions have been introduced, along with a slogan-bearing T-shirt. A handful of new wines from Australia showed evidence of a fresh approach to the wine range. But while strong in the traditional areas of Bordeaux and Port, Unwins remained palpably weak in other areas, especially the two fastest-developing countries of the New World, Chile and South Africa.

Never having encountered Unwins' wine buyer, Gerald Duff, in the three previous incarnations of *Grapevine*, we were on tenterhooks this year. Recognising that the expanding world of wine has become too much even for his broad shoulders, Duff has enlisted the beer buyer, the spirits buyer and the sweets and fags buyer to help out. The Italian and Iberian range devolve to ex-beer buyer Bill Rolfe, Eastern Europe to spirits buyer, 'Lucky' Jim Wilson, and fortified wines to Jim Dobson.

Where have Duff's efforts been concentrated this year? Well, he took two trips to the Languedoc-Roussillon and liked it so much that he returned for a third bite of the cherry in January. The fruits of these jaunts will be nine or ten new southern French wines 'in small parcels'.

Unfortunately, the parcels appear to have been held up in the post, so the *Grapevine* team has yet to taste and report on the fruits of Duff's Midi adventure. Now that he has developed a taste for travel, he plans to add exponentially to his air-miles tally this year with trips to South Africa, Australia and 'hopefully', California.

The conscious decision to move more into line with their competitors has resulted in a squeeze on Unwins' profit margins, but sales have still grown by 8 per cent in volume. A snapshot of sales shows the growing popularity of New World wines, which over a two-month period rose to account for 22 per cent, compared with the previous year's 16 per cent. New premium wines from Australia, and a handful from Chile, New Zealand and California, show that there is something positive in the Dartford air.

Chile has been a big success at Unwins, with excellent wines from the outstanding Canepa winery. Sales indicate a reversal of the decline in French wines, in particular a move back to Bordeaux and *vins de pays*. It's been a good year at Unwins for Portuguese reds, but less so for Italy, which 'has taken a battering' due to hefty price increases.

Despite research that apparently shows that Unwins' customers, like policemen, are getting younger, there is still a bland-leading-the-bland feel about the Unwins wine range, which lists 415 table wines, 50 sparkling wines and 40 fortified. Lavish adverts for Veuve Clicquot, Burgundy négociant Bichot and Australia's Lindemans adorn the pages of the glossy but uninspiring wine list, which curiously features a bottle of Premium Export lager and a bottle opener on its cover.

As far as we can make out, it's more of the same from Burgundy, Beaujolais, the Rhône, Loire, Italy, Spain and Germany, and the South African range is still dominated by KWV. There are also too many bulk buys – take five and we'll give you a good price, Gerald – from individual merchants and importers.

The Unwins team does not feel – and we agree – that it has cracked the trade-off between what's safe and the kind of adventurous stuff that it needs in order to give customers more choice and excitement. Certainly Gerald Duff talks a good range. This year will be the test of how much the D'Artagnan of Dartford and his three musketeers can translate rapier thrusts into serious action. *En garde!*

White

Under £3

SPAIN

Encanto, Vino de la Zona de Betanzos   11/20
Off-dry |
We've no idea where Betanzos is, but we think it's an industrial estate somewhere outside Toledo. A top-ten best-seller at Unwins, which has more to do with its sub-£3 price tag than the fat, stewed apple flavours in the bottle.

£3–5

AUSTRALIA

Stockmans Bridge Dry White, Southcorp   13/20
Off-dry 🝆 |
Not as dry as the label would have you believe, but this soft, crowd-pleasing Aussie white is a decent, sweetish barbecue glugger.

1995 Jacob's Creek Semillon/Chardonnay, South Eastern Australia   14/20
Off-dry 🝆 |
Ever-reliable, deservedly popular Aussie white blend from the Barossa-based Orlando winery, in which the herby, lemony character of the Semillon grape is distinctively refreshing.

CHILE

1996 Canepa Sauvignon Blanc   15/20
Dry 🝆🝆🝆 |
Zesty, ultra-fresh Chilean Sauvignon Blanc made by the lugubrious Andres Ilabaca and showing lemon and gooseberry-like fruit flavours.

FRANCE

1995 Château Bel Air L'Espérance, Mauregard, Bordeaux   14/20
Dry 👛👛 ▌
Made by Yvon Mau, a company that supplies Unwins on an extensive basis, this blend of Sémillon, Muscadelle and Sauvignon is clean, zesty and pleasantly fruity.

1995 Domaine Lanine, Vin de Pays des Côtes de Gascogne, Grassa   14/20
Dry 👛👛 ▌
Zippy, apple and grapefruit-style Gascon white, which marks the rejuvenation of the Grassa name. Light and bright and interesting to drink.

HUNGARY

1995 Gyöngyös Estate Chardonnay, Hugh Ryman   14/20
Dry 👛👛 ▌
Fresh, zingy, lightly oaked, greengage-style Hungarian Chardonnay from Hugh Ryman. A vast improvement on recent disappointing vintages.

1995 Gyöngyös Sauvignon Blanc, Hugh Ryman   14/20
Dry 👛👛 ▌
A good vintage for Hungarian whites has helped to boost the aromatic intensity of the Sauvignon Blanc grape in this lemon-zesty, crisp, dry white.

ITALY

1995 Frascati Superiore, Tullio   12/20
Dry ▌
Flat, flavour-challenged, undistinguished Roman white, which should be thrown to the lions.

1995 Verdicchio Del Jesi Classico, Vigneti Mancini   15/20
Dry 👛👛 ▌
Buttery, nutty, almost Soave-like Verdicchio from the Marches region of Italy's Adriatic coast. We just lurve the lampshade bottle.

NEW ZEALAND

Waimanu Dry White, Corbans   10/20
Off-dry 🍶
Distinctly musty Kiwi white with marked acidity and tart, sweetish lemon-meringue flavours. New Zealand struggles to make palatable wine under £4.

£5–8

AUSTRALIA

1994 Maglieri Riesling, McLaren Vale   16/20
Dry 🍶🍶🍶 ▬
A classic Australian Riesling with fresh lime and tropical fruit flavours and notes of nut and Mosel-like kerosene. A weighty, beautifully balanced Aussie white.

1994 Tyrrells Old Winery Semillon, Hunter Valley   14/20
Dry 🍶 🍶
Curiously light in alcohol for Australia's Hunter Valley, this is a broad, pleasantly oaked, refreshing Semillon from one of the region's best-known wineries.

1995 Penfolds Barossa Valley Semillon/Chardonnay   16/20
Dry 🍶🍶🍶 🍶
Neville Falkenberg, Penfolds' white winemaker, has produced a deliciously restrained Barossa Valley blend with peach and citrus fruit flavours underscored by lightly smoky oak. Excellent stuff at under £6.

1993 Saltram Mamre Brook Chardonnay, South Australia   14/20
Dry 🍶 🍶
Golden-coloured, toffee-fudge-like Chardonnay with hefty oak and ripe, pineapple fruitiness. They don't make 'em like this any more. Maybe just as well.

1995 Rothbury Estate Chardonnay, Hunter Valley   16/20
Dry 🍶🍶🍶 🍶
A Hunter Valley style that no longer wears its flavours on its sleeve – and shirt-front. More delicate than in the past, this balances vanilla oak, ripe buttery fruit and crisp acidity in a highly drinkable style.

FRANCE

1994 Château Ducla, Entre-Deux-Mers, Yvon Mau   15/20
Dry 🍷 ▮

A Bordeaux blend of Semillon and Sauvignon made in a modern idiom. Fresh, grassy fruitiness and a degree of complexity. Should be under £5.

1993 Domaine du Tariquet, Vin de Pays des Côtes de Gascogne, Cuvée Bois, Grassa   16/20
Dry 🍷🍷🍷 ▮

Yves Grassa's top, barrel-fermented white is the best wine we know of in Gascony. An aged, super-ripe, melon and grapefruit-like blend, with a sheen of restrained new oak. Well worth a punt at under £6.

NEW ZEALAND

1995 Villa Maria Private Bin Chardonnay, Gisborne   16/20
Dry 🍷🍷🍷 ▮

From George 'The Ventriloquist' Fistonich's Auckland winery, this is a North Island Chardonnay, which appears to have evaded the difficult vintage conditions that hit the South. Elegant, citrus-fruity Kiwi Chardonnay with a grace note of oak.

SPAIN

1995 Raimat Chardonnay, Costers del Segre   14/20
Dry 🍷 ▮

Unoaked, Catalan Chardonnay from a modern, New World-influenced winery near Lerida, showing sweetish, banana-like fruit and tart acidity.

UNITED STATES

1994 Sutter Home Chardonnay, California   15/20
Off-dry 🍷🍷 ▮

A well-made and well-priced California Chardonnay from a company that specialises in sticky Blush wines. Ripe, sweet and buttery with toffee-fudge undertones and spicy oak.

1993 Montevina Chardonnay, California
Dry 🍷 ▮

14/20

Full, oaky, slightly overblown California Chardonnay with a Clint Eastwood fistful of alcohol and some pleasantly buttery fruit.

Over £8

AUSTRALIA

1993 Saint Hubert's Chardonnay, Yarra Valley
Dry 🍷🍷 ▮

16/20

Mature, cool-climate Chardonnay from Australia's painterly Yarra Valley. A concentrated, well-made, richly oaked dry white, which needs to be drunk sooner rather than later.

1995 Tyrrells Vat 47 Pinot-Chardonnay, Hunter Valley
Dry 🍷🍷🍷 ▬▬

17/20

£12 may seem a lot to pay for an Aussie Chardonnay, but this pioneering Hunter Valley is straight out of the top flight. It's a crafted, complex white, with butterscotch notes derived from the stirring of the lees in the barrel and malolactic fermentation. Classy stuff.

FRANCE

1988 Gewürztraminer Réserve, Trimbach
Dry 🍷🍷🍷 ▮

17/20

Typical of the Trimbach style, this is a subtle, elegant Alsace white, which restrains even the exuberance of the Gewürztraminer grape. Mature, but still remarkably fresh and floral-scented.

Red

Under £3

SPAIN

Encanto Tinto, Vino de la Zona de Betanzos   11/20
Medium-bodied 🍷
Cooked, earthy plonk, which made us reach for the nearest *cerveza*.

£3–5

AUSTRALIA

Stockman's Bridge Red, Southcorp   14/20
Medium-bodied 💰💰 🍷
Berry-fruity Aussie blend from the Southcorp group, with soft, juicy tannins and minty, cherryish flavours.

1994 Lindemans Bin 45 Cabernet Sauvignon, South East Australia   14/20
Medium-bodied 💰 🍷
Simple, fruity, mint and blackcurrant juice-style red with a smattering of oak character. A neophyte's Aussie Cab.

1994 Hardy's Nottage Hill Cabernet Sauvignon/Shiraz 13/20
Medium-bodied 🍷
A basic, faintly medicinal, cordial-like Aussie blend. Hardy's usually makes better wine than this.

CHILE

1995 Concha y Toro Merlot, Rapel Valley   15/20
Medium-bodied 💰💰 🍷
Juicy, fruit-laden Rapel Valley Merlot with pure, cassis characters and soft-textured tannins. Short on complexity, but long on flavour.

FRANCE

1994 Fitou, Mont Tauch   14/20
Full-bodied 💰💰 ▮
Thyme and angostura-bitters-like, traditional Languedoc blend based on the Carignan grape. Good autumnal red from the Mont Tauch co-operative, with a faintly rustic finish.

1994 Château Girolatte, Mauregard, Bordeaux   15/20
Medium-bodied 💰💰 ▮
Dominated by the Merlot grape, which lends succulence to this classic Bordeaux blend, this is a well-made, freshly fruity claret from the Yvon Mau stable.

1992 Domaine de Caunettes Hautes, Cabardès   15/20
Medium-bodied 💰💰 ▮
From a VDQS area just north of the medieval, tourist-clogged town of Carcassonne, this is a grassy, mature Cabernet Franc-like red, attractively unoaked for maximum fruit impact.

ITALY

1995 Montepulciano d'Abruzzo, Miglianico   12/20
Medium-bodied ▮
Hollow, rustic, southern Italian *rosso* with the dilution characteristic of a dodgy vintage.

MEXICO

1993 L.A.Cetto Petite Sirah   14/20
Full-bodied 💰 ▮
Chunky, extracted Mexican red from the Baja California peninsula, with peppery spice, sun-baked fruit and rather overworked tannins.

1993 L.A.Cetto Cabernet Sauvignon   15/20
Full-bodied 💰💰 ▮
Central America's answer to Puglia or the Languedoc, this is a raisin-rich, slightly cooked Cabernet Sauvignon with plenty of sweet fruit and hefty oak.

PORTUGAL

1995 Terras de Xisto, Vinho Regional Alentejo   15/20
Medium-bodied 👜👜👜 ▮

Ripe, softly textured Portuguese red with cedarwood oak and forward strawberry fruitiness. A bargain at under £4.

UNITED STATES

1993 Sutter Home California Cabernet   14/20
Medium-bodied 👜👜 ▮

Pleasantly ripe, commercial, green-pepper-style California Cabernet Sauvignon with sweet, lollipop-like fruit and palate-charming tannins.

£5–8

AUSTRALIA

1995 Tyrrells Old Winery Pinot Noir   13/20
Medium-bodied ▮

Unappealing, jammy, warm-climate Pinot Noir, which seems to go down better in Australia than it does in Tooting.

1993 Penfolds Bin 128 Shiraz, Coonawarra   16/20
Full-bodied 👜👜👜 ➡—

Proving that it doesn't only make cross-regional blends, this silky, milled pepper-style Shiraz from Penfolds brings out the elegance and cool-climate freshness of Coonawarra reds.

FRANCE

1995 Bourgueil, Les Barroirs, Couly-Dutheil   15/20
Light-bodied 👜👜 ▮

Approachable, lead-pencil and green-pepper-scented Bourgueil from the reliable négociant firm of Couly-Dutheil. Fresh, fragrant and fruity with the unmistakable character of Loire Cabernet Franc.

1994 Crozes-Hermitage, Louis Mousset   14/20
Medium-bodied 💰 ▮

A lightish, easy-drinking Syrah blended by the southern Rhône négociant firm of Louis Mousset. From a good vintage such as 1994, this should have more stuffing.

1990 Château de Crouseilles, Madiran, Les Vignerons du Vic Bilh
15/20

Full-bodied 💰💰 ▮

A mature, vanilla-oaky Tannat showing the grape's characteristic bite, rusticity and capacity to age. An ambitious and successful co-operative red.

SPAIN

1991 Raimat Tempranillo   14/20
Medium-bodied ▮

No shortage of smoky, coconutty American oak and sweetly ripe strawberry fruitiness here. But we found the wine a bit gawky and confected.

UNITED STATES

1991 Columbia Crest Merlot, Columbia Valley   15/20
Full-bodied 💰 ▭–

Showing pronounced aromatic oak, chewy tannins and some maturity, this Washington State Merlot, with its chocolate and green-pepper flavours, is beginning its descent, as American Airlines might put it. Chocks away!

Over £8

AUSTRALIA

1993 Tyrrells Vat 8 Shiraz/Cabernet Sauvignon, Hunter Valley
16/20

Full-bodied 💰💰 ▭–

Tyrrells is rather better at Shiraz/Cabernet Sauvignon blends than it is at Pinot Noir, if this spicy, minty, complex Hunter Valley blend is anything to go by. A wine with a lot in reserve, although pricey at nearly £15.

1993 Maglieri Shiraz, McLaren Vale   16/20
Full-bodied

Sweet, American oaky, mint-humbug-style Shiraz from the sculpted, undulating hills of McLaren Vale. A lush, velvety red.

FRANCE

1992 Château du Périer, Médoc, Cru Bourgeois   15/20
Medium-bodied

Soft cedary fruit and vanilla oak make this forward *cru bourgeois* claret a very acceptable drink, despite the leanness of the rain-drenched vintage.

1992 Château Segonnes, Margaux   13/20
Medium-bodied

The second wine of Margaux Second Growth Château Lascombes, from a second-rate vintage. That's enough seconds (Ed.).

1992 Château Grand Lartigue, Saint Emilion Grand Cru 13/20
Medium-bodied

A rather stringy claret, which smells like the inside of a church hymn book. No-one ever said that 1992 was a conventional vintage.

ITALY

1991 Barbaresco, Giordano   13/20
Full-bodied

The tannins are taking over the fruit on this ageing Piedmontese Nebbiolo from the merchant house of Giordano.

LEBANON

1989 Château Musar, Bekaa Valley   12/20
Full-bodied

Raisiny, old-fashioned, over-alcoholic, vinegary Lebanese red, which barely survived the ravages of war. A curiosity that has had its day, but remains popular with fogeys, young and old.

PORTUGAL

1991 Quinta da Foz, de Arouce, Vinho Regional Beiras   16/20
Full-bodied 👜👜 ♦
An inky, quintessentially Portuguese red, with lashings of black cherry and chocolate fruit encased in robust tannins and splintery oak. One of the Iberian Peninsula's best reds, optimistically priced at nearly £11.

Sparkling

£5–8

AUSTRALIA

1992 Seaview Pinot Noir/Chardonnay   15/20
Dry 👜👜 ♦
From the Penfolds stable, this is a beer-yeasty, Champagne-method blend of Pinot Noir and Chardonnay with mature, old-style fruitiness and a nutty aftertaste.

FRANCE

Crémant d'Alsace 'Mayerling' Brut, Turckheim Co-operative 15/20
Dry 👜👜 ♦
Clean, well-made, slightly neutral Alsace fizz based on the Pinot Blanc grape, showing a touch of bready, bottle-mature character.

SPAIN

Cava Brut, Codorniu   14/20
Dry 👜👜 ♦
Fresh, zippy Catalan Champagne-method fizz from the Spanish Cava giant, Codorniu.

Over £8

FRANCE

Duchatel Champagne Brut   13/20
Dry 🏷 🍾
Unwins has been buying Champagne from Duchatel since 1874. Why? This is a light, rather characterless fizz, which at least has the virtue of being cheap. If you call that a virtue with Champagne.

Vouvray Tête de Cuvée Brut, Cave des Viticulteurs du Vouvray
15/20
Dry 🏷🏷 🍾
A big-bubbled, appley Loire frother with typical honeyed Chenin Blanc fruit flavours and a creamy, mouth-filling mousse.

Nicolas Feuillatte Champagne Brut, Premier Cru   16/20
Dry 🏷🏷 🍾
A much-improved, widely available, malty Brut fizz whose ample dose of reserve wine and Pinot Noir fruit make it one of the better-value high street Champagnes at around £15 a bottle.

Fortified

£3–5

FRANCE

1994 Rivesaltes Vintage, Mont Tauch, 50 cl.   15/20
Full-bodied 🏷🏷 🍾
A fiery fortified red made from 40-year-old Grenache vines, this sweet and strong, raisin and toffee-like Vin Doux Naturel from the Roussillon region is a youthful alternative to Ruby Port.

Victoria Wine ☆☆☆(☆)

Including:
Victoria Wine Cellars ☆☆☆☆

Address: Dukes Court, Dukes Street, Woking, Surrey GU21 5XL

Telephone/fax: 01483 715066; 01483 755234

Number of branches: 1,545, including 62 Victoria Wine Cellars and 184 Haddows in Scotland, plus Victoria Wine in Cité de l'Europe, Calais

Opening hours: Varies according to location, but majority of stores open 10.00am to 10.00pm Monday to Saturday; hours on Sunday vary, depending on location

Credit cards accepted: Access, Visa, American Express

Discounts: 10 per cent on mixed cases of light and sparkling wine; 5 per cent on cases of beer; 7 for the price of 6 on Champagnes and sparkling wines over £5.99; 10 per cent discount on unmixed cases of beer and lager at Victoria Wine Cellars

Facilities and services: By-the-case sales; glass loan free with larger orders; home delivery on a local basis by arrangement; in-store tastings in selected shops on an occasional basis – more frequently in Wine Shops and Victoria Wine Cellars; Post Haste nationwide delivery service (Freephone 0800 526464)

Special offers: Monthly promotions of two bottles for £5

Top ten best-selling wines: Liebfraumilch Victoria Wine; Sansovino Lambrusco Bianco, Chiarli; Victoria Wine French Dry White, Vin de Pays d'Oc; Hardy's Stamps of Australia Semillon/Chardonnay; Victoria Wine French Red Vin de Pays d'Oc; Claret Victoria Wine; Ed's Red La Mancha; Jacob's Creek Shiraz/Cabernet; Hardy's Stamps of Australia Shiraz/Cabernet; Clearsprings Cape Red. (The top ten varies across the segments and depends on the time of the year and the promotion, but the above shows a typical month and gives an indication of the countries/styles featured)

Victoria Wine

Range:

GOOD: Regional France, Bordeaux, Chile, Argentina, Australia, New Zealand, sparkling wines, Sherry and Port

AVERAGE: Burgundy, Rhône, Beaujolais, Loire, Alsace, Germany, Portugal, Spain, Italy, Eastern Europe, South Africa, United States, Champagne

POOR: None

UNDER-REPRESENTED: England

'We're the best,' trumpeted a headline in *Trailblazer,* the staff newspaper of the Victoria Wine Company, as it's known down Woking way. Had the sub-editor chosen to overlook Bottoms Up, Wine Cellar, Wine Rack, Fuller's and Oddbins, Victoria Wine's increasingly strong competition in the high street? Apparently not. The headline referred to a survey carried out by the Arnold Schwarzenegger-sounding Total Research, which placed Victoria Wine ahead of Oddbins in an interviewees' dream shopping centre, alongside Marks & Spencer, Boots and W.H. Smith.

Britain's largest off-licence chain (10 stores ahead of the Thresher Group on current figures) is clearly regarded as an integral part of the local retail scene by many customers. But recognition is not the same thing as sales. As anyone who has recently looked at a shopping arcade will know, the living isn't easy in the high street these days, even in summer time.

Richard Lowe, Victoria Wine's bright, Stoke City-supporting buying and marketing director, is adamant that 'We're the most profitable chain in the high street in terms of sales per square foot.' Nevertheless, he thinks there will be further rationalisation among specialist booze chains over the coming years and suggests that, 'In the longer term we may not regard high street retailing as our core business.'

The solution, he says, is direct delivery, a market that already contains two impressive operations in The Wine Society and Direct Wines, but in which, crucially, the supermarkets are weak. 'It's a big opportunity for us to use our brand name,' adds Lowe. 'We've got huge national coverage already, so we're used to shifting wine around the UK.'

Post Haste, a nationwide delivery service, is already up and strolling. But, for the time being, the high street remains Victoria Wine's main focus. The two-year-old merger with Augustus Barnett has been digested (although some local shops retain the old Augustus Barnett awnings) and new shops continue to open. The number of Victoria Wine Cellars, the chain's upmarket stores, has increased from 45 to 62 and there are plans to open another five to ten a year between now and the millennium. Overall, according to planning manager

Mark Davis, 'We intend to buy 50 new shops and close around 20 each year, as we recycle the estate.'

One surprising area of expansion is in the Czech Republic, where Victoria Wine opened its first store in August 1996 in partnership with Drinks, one of the Czech Republic's largest wine and spirits wholesalers. A further four stores were due to follow by early 1997 and Victoria Wine has plans for 95 more over the next five years. It has also made a real success this year of its Calais store, housed in the Cité de l'Europe shopping centre (discussed in greater detail in our section on cross-Channel wine).

Back in the UK, the wine department has been through a number of changes this year. Rosemary Neal and Joanne Convert have left, to be replaced by buying manager Tina Hudson and up-and-coming buyer Paul Stacey from Waitrose. The three-man buying team now consists of senior wine buyer Thomas Woolrych, wine development manager and Master of Wine Hugh Suter and newcomer Stacey, all of whom report to Hudson.

As far as the shops are concerned, Victoria Wine has resisted the temptation of 'segmentation', a mania that has gripped Thresher and Greenalls Cellars over the last two years. Unofficially, its stores are divided into three categories – Victoria Wine Cellars, Wine Shops and Neighbourhood Drinks Stores – but only Cellars advertises the fact on its fascias. 'Our research says that we've got far better brand awareness than Thresher,' says Richard Lowe, 'so what would be the point in segmenting the estate?'

One new idea, still under the Victoria Wine name, is a wine warehouse-style operation in the south and west of England. There are plans for two of these by early 1997, one in London and one in Bristol, with the focus 'on the middle market', according to Lowe, with lots of lager and, we assume, Liebfraumilch. To a certain extent the model here is Majestic, although the Victoria Wine stores will be 'bigger and less highbrow'.

Victoria Wine itself has been 'about level on wine sales' over the last 12 months. But, notwithstanding its name, the chain isn't only dependent on wine. 'There are 3.2 million customers a week in our stores and a lot of them come in to buy 20 Embassy,' says Lowe. 'I don't see anything wrong with that. Cigarettes help to keep some of our city-centre shops open.'

In fact, only 65 per cent of Victoria Wine's turnover comes from wines, beers and spirits. The rest is down to tobacco, snacks, confectionery and soft drinks. Oh, and lottery tickets. Victoria Wine has 130 lottery centres and would like to have more. 'It's low-margin, high-turnover business,' says Lowe, 'a bit like cigarettes.'

What about wine? How does someone who's come in to buy a bottle of Champagne feel about a lottery-ticket queue. 'We wouldn't want to do anything that would get in the way of selling wine,' says Mark Davis. 'It's the most profitable thing we do. Your authority as a drinks retailer is linked to your authority as a wine retailer.'

As it happens, the wine range is pretty good at Victoria Wine, especially at Cellars, which gets the full 600-strong line-up. The new buying team is the strongest that the chain has ever had, and impressive new wines have been listed from Italy and Spain since Stacey's arrival.

Victoria Wine has also benefited from the talents of the remarkably modest Hugh Suter, who realised a long-term ambition in 1995 by making wine in the Loire and California. 'I'd made wine thousands of times in my head,' says Suter, 'but it was great to get my hands dirty.' The first five Suter wines are very promising, particularly the pair from California, and he intends to make more in 1996 and 1997.

Suter's and his fellow buyers' work has also borne (tropical) fruit in Chile and Argentina, where Victoria Wine's range is one of the best in the high street. Other areas of concentration this year have included Eastern Europe and South Africa, with Portugal the next country in line for a revamp. Germany, meanwhile, has been put in cold storage, with many of the best estate wines on the list offered as bin ends.

Overall, France is the dominant country, with just over a quarter of sales, but Australia (16.7 per cent) and South Africa (8.3 per cent) are very strong too. The slightly depressing thing about Australia is that Victoria Wine's position has been achieved without listing interesting parcels from smaller estates. 'We do best with wines from Orlando, Penfolds and Hardy's,' says Suter. 'We've tried to sell things like Katnook, but it's like pushing water uphill.'

The problem with Victoria Wine, as with any large chain, is that it can be hard to find the best wines, especially in Neighbourhood Drinks Stores and their Scottish equivalent, Haddows, which stock only 25 per cent of the total range. Nevertheless, the 800 Wine Shops sell 450 wines and Cellars, as already mentioned, takes the lot. So there's a good chance that you'll find our favourite wines in your local Victoria Wine.

The other drawback is that the stores themselves vary enormously in terms of appearance, depending almost entirely on location. Some are smart and wine-friendly; others are like something out of a war zone, with bandit screening and security cameras. When Total Research asked its survey respondents about Victoria Wine, they must have had the former stores in mind. Mind you, Arnold Schwarzenegger would make a pretty daunting off-licence manager for thieves in the less salubrious parts of Britain. Hasta la vista, baby!

Wines marked with an asterisk (*) are available at Victoria Wine Cellars only. The full range is available in Victoria Wine's Cité de l'Europe store (see page 594 for further details).

White

Under £3

FRANCE

Le Midi Blanc, Vin de Pays de l'Aude   12/20
Dry 🝑 ▮
Tart, appley, unobjectionable southern French plonk for mad dogs and Englishmen.

GERMANY

1995 Liebfraumilch, Victoria Wine   13/20
Medium sweet 🝑🝑 ▮
Soft, grapey, decently fresh Müller-Thurgau-based white with rose-petal aromas and good zest. Still one of the best Liebs in the high street.

ITALY

Sansovino Lambrusco Bianco, Chiarli, 8 per cent   `   13/20
Sweet 🝑🝑 ▮
Lambrusco for grown-ups, if such a thing exists, with ripe pear characters and a lemonadey froth.

£3–5

ARGENTINA

1995 Lurton Chenin Blanc, Mendoza   14/20
Dry 🝑🝑🝑 ▮
Spicy, flavoursome, weighty Argentine white from Frenchman Jacques Lurton, showing honeyed richness and good acidity.

AUSTRALIA

1996 Brokenback Ridge Semillon/Chardonnay, Southcorp   14/20
Dry 👜👜 ▮
Smoky, slightly unbalanced Aussie blend of Semillon and Chardonnay from the Southcorp Group, in which the oak chips are dominating the fruit at the moment. Still, a pleasant enough drink.

1995 Hardy's Stamps of Australia Semillon/Chardonnay   14/20
Dry 👜👜 ▮
A top-ten best-seller at Victoria Wine, this is a reliably quaffable Aussie white from the BRL-Hardy operation, with tropical fruit flavours and a touch of oak chip for extra weight.

*1995 Hardy's Nottage Hill Riesling   16/20
Off-dry 👜👜👜 ▮
The best of Hardy's Nottage Hill range by far, this is an intensely aromatic, lime and citrus fruity South Eastern Australian Riesling, with excellent weight, body and soul. They even have the courage to package it in a flute bottle.

1995 Deakin Estate Chardonnay, Victoria   14/20
Off-dry 👜 ▮
Super-ripe, pineapple-chunk and butterscotch-style Chardonnay from Australia's Riverina district. Heavier than in previous vintages.

CHILE

1995 Altura Chardonnay, Viña Tocornal   12/20
Dry ▮
Basic, rather bitter Chilean Chardonnay from the country's biggest winery, Concha y Toro. Time for the 1996.

1995 Cono Sur Gewürztraminer   15/20
Dry 👜👜👜 ▮
One of the few Gewürztraminers produced outside Europe, this is a refreshing, elegant white with Turkish Delight and lychee characters typical of the grape.

FRANCE

Victoria Wine French Dry White, Vin de Pays d'Oc, Skalli   13/20
Dry 🛍 ▪

Clean, modern, well-made southern French blend with soft, spicy Mediterranean fruit flavours.

1995 Chardonnay, Galet Vineyards, Vin de Pays d'Oc, Meffre 15/20
Dry 🛍🛍🛍 ▪

Stylishly packaged Midi Chardonnay made in a New World style by Thierry Boudinaud of Gabriel Meffre. Mealy, elegantly balanced and fresh, with melon fruitiness.

1995 Bois de Lamothe, Côtes de Duras Blanc   15/20
Dry 🛍🛍🛍 ▪

Flavoursome, south-western French blend of Sauvignon Blanc and Semillon, with the grapefruity freshness of the former and the herbal weight and texture of the latter.

1995 Domaine de la Roulerie, Muscadet de Sèvre et Maine sur Lie   15/20
Dry 🛍🛍 ▪

Made by Victoria Wine's resident Master of Wine, Hugh Suter, this partially oak-fermented *sur lie* Muscadet is a weighty, refreshing, ultra-modern Loire white with understated vanilla notes.

1995 Domaine du Pré Baron, Sauvignon de Touraine   15/20
Bone dry 🛍🛍 ▪

Subtle, nettley, crisply proportioned Loire Sauvignon Blanc, which shows the quality of the 1995 vintage.

*1995 Roussanne Barrel Reserve, Galet Vineyards, Vin de Pays d'Oc   15/20
Dry 🛍🛍 ▪

Oak-influenced southern French white made from the rare Roussanne variety by Thierry Boudinaud and showing appealing oak, herbal spiciness and medium length of flavour.

1995 La Langue, Domaine Sainte Madeleine, Oaked Chardonnay, Vin de Pays d'Oc   14/20
Dry 🛍 ▪

Golden-hued, oak-fermented southern French Chardonnay with buttered toffee flavours and ripe, if somewhat clumsy, fruit richness.

1995 Philippe de Baudin, Sauvignon Blanc   15/20
Dry 👜👜 🍾

A full, come-hither, southern French Sauvignon Blanc from Aussie giant, BRL-Hardy. Ripe and rich, with flavours of passion fruit and gooseberry and a tangy acidity for balance.

GERMANY

1994 Bornheimer Adelberg Kabinett, Kendermann   13/20
Medium sweet 👜 🍾

Honeyed, grapey, Rheinhessen white, which is a quarter-step up from most Liebfraumilch.

HUNGARY

1995 Chapel Hill Rheinriesling, Balatonboglar   14/20
Dry 👜👜 🍾

A little lacking in the characteristic aromas of the Riesling grape perhaps, but this dry, white-peppery Hungarian white from Kym Milne is a zippy, characterful buy at just over £3.

ITALY

1995 Esino Bianco DOC   13/20
Dry 👜 🍾

Grassy, green-olive-like Italian quaffer from the Marche region, with simple, rather dilute flavours of apple and pear.

1995 Villa Romana Frascati Superiore, Colli di Catone   15/20
Dry 👜👜👜 🍾

Aromatic, weighty, well-made Roman white with notes of nut and resin and a fresh acidity for extra lift. Characterful stuff – shame about the naff package.

1995 Le Vele, Verdicchio dei Castelli di Jesi Classico, Tordiruta
15/20
Dry 👜👜 🍾

Fresh, cool fermented central Italian white made in a zesty, modern, New World style, with ripe pear fruitiness and a grapefruity tang.

NEW ZEALAND

1995 Cook's Chardonnay, Gisborne   15/20
Dry 👝👝 🍾

Commercial, well-made, North Island Chardonnay with spicy, peachy fruitiness and crisp, lemony acidity.

SOUTH AFRICA

1996 Kumala Semillon/Chardonnay   14/20
Dry 👝👝 🍾

Attractive, ripe pear and boiled-sweets-style Cape blend from a winery that is producing some of the best sub-£4 wines in South Africa at the moment.

1996 Agulhas Bank Chardonnay, Savanha   13/20
Dry 🍾

Light, rather green Cape Chardonnay with dilute fruit flavours and a touch of oak chip. Should be at least 50 pence cheaper.

1993 Van Loveren Gewürztraminer Late Harvest   15/20
Sweet 👝👝👝 🍾

Stunningly priced at under £5, this is a rich, weighty, late-picked Robertson Gewürz with a pot-pourri of rose-petal and lanolin spice and masses of sweet flavour.

UNITED STATES

1995 Mohr Fry Ranch Sauvignon Blanc, Lodi   15/20
Dry 👝👝👝 🍾

Ripe grapefruit and melon-style Sauvignon Blanc, with miles more flavour and varietal character than most Californian examples of the Loire's aromatic white grape.

1995 Ranch Series Chardonnay, San Joaquin County   15/20
Dry 👝👝 🍾

Another highly drinkable wine made by Victoria Wine's Hugh Suter, this is a smartly turned-out, lightly oaked, buttery-rich Californian Chardonnay, which is a great deal better than most sub-£5 West Coast whites.

£5–8

AUSTRALIA

1995 Basedow Chardonnay, Barossa Valley   16/20
Dry 🍾🍾 ▐
Deeply coloured, intensely oaky Barossa Valley Chardonnay, which is short on
subtlety, but long on sweet vanilla, cinnamon and burnt-butter characters. A big
improvement on the 1994, which may still be around in some stores.

CHILE

1995 Caliterra Casablanca Chardonnay   16/20
Dry 🍾🍾🍾 ▐
One of Chile's leading Chardonnays, this Casablanca-sourced white from Brian
Bicknell is a crisp, grapefruity, subtly oaked style with a Pacific-influenced, cool-
climate tang.

FRANCE

1995 Château Laribotte, Oaked Bordeaux   16/20
Dry 🍾🍾🍾 ▐
Smoky, Graves-like white from the excellent house of Ginestet, with super-fresh
grapefruit and lemongrass flavours and oak-aged complexity. Lovely stuff.

*1995 La Langue, Chardonnay/Viognier, Vin de Pays d'Oc   14/20
Dry 🍾 ▐
Flavoursome, if rather pricey, Languedoc blend of France's two most
fashionable grape varieties, showing fresh apricot notes and citrus-fruit acidity.
A little light.

1995 Mâcon Vinzelles, Les Cailloux Blancs   16/20
Dry 🍾🍾🍾 ▐
Rich, complex, co-operative-bottled Mâcon white with masses of buttery
flavour, well-judged oak and fresh acidity, made by South African Jean-Luc
Sweerts. They ought to give him the keys of Mâcon for this one.

---

*1995 Fat Bastard Chardonnay, Vin de Pays d'Oc   15/20
Dry 🍾🍾 ▯

A ripe, attractively oaked New World-influenced southern French Chardonnay from Thierry Boudinaud, with throat-warming alcohol and peachy fruitiness. Not to be confused with Bâtard-Montrachet.

SOUTH AFRICA

1995 De Wetshof, Lesca Chardonnay   16/20
Dry 🍾🍾🍾 ▯

Named after Danie De Wet's charming wife, Lesca, this is a rich, leesy, refreshingly tangy Robertson Chardonnay, with subtle butterscotch characters and excellent balance.

*1996 Springfield Special Cuvée Sauvignon Blanc   16/20
Dry 🍾🍾🍾 ▯

Concentrated, nettley, Loire Valley-style Sauvignon Blanc, which shows the progress that South Africa's white wines have made in the last two vintages. Stylish, elegantly fruity stuff that could easily be mistaken for a Sancerre.

Over £8

FRANCE

1995 Pouilly Fumé, Domaine Seguin   17/20
Bone dry 🍾🍾🍾 ▭—

Intense, minerally, flinty Loire Sauvignon Blanc with excellent concentration and stylish length of flavour. Classic Pouilly Fumé.

*1992 Chablis, Premier Cru, Mont de Milieu, La Chablisienne
                                                             17/20
Bone dry 🍾🍾 ▭—

Structured, abundantly oaked *Premier Cru* Chablis, with multi-dimensional flavours, lemony acidity and understated toffee and vanilla richness.

NEW ZEALAND

*1994 Corbans Private Bin Gisborne Chardonnay   16/20
Dry 🍾🍾 ▯
Pineapple and tropical citrus fruity Chardonnay, withe ripe mango characters lifted by fresh acidity and smooth, toasty oak.

SOUTH AFRICA

*1995 Longridge Chardonnay, Stellenbosch   16/20
Dry 🍾🍾🍾 ▯
Restrained, well-proportioned South African Chardonnay with understated toasty oak and vanilla-fudge notes and a refreshing acidity. An encouraging, modern-style Cape white.

UNITED STATES

*1994 Laguna Ranch Chardonnay, Gallo   16/20
Dry 🍾🍾 ▯
From the producers of Hearty Burgundy and Thunderbird, this is a stylish attempt at a modern, white Burgundy-style Chardonnay, with classy, toasty vanilla oak, caramel notes and cool-climate intensity of flavour.

Red

Under £3

FRANCE

Le Midi Rouge, Vin de Pays de l'Aude, Val d'Orbieu   13/20
Medium-bodied 🍾🍾 ▯
Faintly spicy, chunky Languedoc red from the enormous Val d'Orbieu operation. Decent plonk.

£3–5

ARGENTINA

1995 Balbi Malbec   14/20
Full-bodied 👜👜 ⸯ
Good-value Argentine red with plenty of oak and sweet chocolate and blackberry fruitiness. Finishes with a rough-edged bite.

1995 Balbi Cabernet Sauvignon   15/20
Medium-bodied 👜👜 ⸯ
Ripe, intensely blackcurranty, sweetly oaked Argentine Cabernet Sauvignon from the go-ahead Balbi winery. A stylish red in a stylish package.

AUSTRALIA

1994 Jacob's Creek Shiraz/Cabernet   13/20
Medium-bodied ⸯ
Minty, ripe, faintly medicinal best-selling Aussie blend of Shiraz and Cabernet Sauvignon let down by a rasp of added acidity.

1995 Hardy's Stamps of Australia Shiraz/Cabernet   14/20
Medium-bodied 👜 ⸯ
Sweetish, ginger-spicy Aussie blend of Shiraz and Cabernet Sauvignon with simple mint-humbug flavours.

CHILE

1995 Altura Cabernet Sauvignon, Viña Tocornal   14/20
Medium-bodied 👜👜👜 ⸯ
Juicy, unoaked, well-priced Chilean Cabernet Sauvignon from Concha y Toro, with medium-weight tannins and sweet cassis fruitiness. A bargain at just over £3.50.

1995 Cono Sur Merlot   15/20
Medium-bodied 👜👜👜 ⸯ
Inky, purple-hued Merlot with masses of sweet, brambly fruit, supple tannins and a hint of green pepper. Very moreish.

1995 Merlot/Malbec, Concha y Toro   14/20
Medium-bodied 👜👜 ▯
Spearminty, pungently fruity blend of Merlot and Malbec, with a drier finish than
the more luscious Cono Sur Merlot.

1995 Canepa Zinfandel   15/20
Medium-bodied 👜👜👜 ▯
From Andres Ilabaca, this is one of Chile's few Zinfandels, showing soft, sweet,
raspberry and tobacco-pouch aromas and spicy, peppery flavours.

1995 Casablanca Cabernet Sauvignon, Miraflores Estate   16/20
Medium-bodied 👜👜👜 ▯
Exuberant, intensely aromatic cassis fruit and American oak-aged spiciness
make this elegant, but firmly structured Cabernet Sauvignon from Ignacio
Recabarren an excellent buy at under £5.

FRANCE

Victoria Wine French Red, Vin de Pays d'Oc, Skalli   13/20
Medium-bodied 👜 ▯
Chewy, sweetish, southern French *rouge* with a fiery, tannic bite, from the Skalli
winery in Sète.

1995 Grenache/Syrah, La Baume, Vin de Pays d'Oc   14/20
Medium-bodied 👜👜 ▯
Juicy, gluggable, carbonic maceration-style blend from BRL-Hardy's winery near
Béziers, with chunky blackberry fruit and a refreshing twist of acidity.

1995 La Langue, Merlot, Vin de Pays d'Oc   15/20
Medium-bodied 👜👜👜 ▮
Smooth, green-pepper-scented Merlot from Delta Domaines, showing supple
blackcurrant fruit balanced by medium-weight tannins.

Claret, Victoria Wine   14/20
Medium-bodied 👜👜 ▯
Firm, chunky, youthful Merlot-based claret from négociant Calvet, which is a lot
more approachable than most sub-£4 red Bordeaux.

1994 La Langue, Domaine Saint Benoît, Vin de Pays d'Oc   16/20
Full-bodied 👜👜👜 ▯
An aromatic Midi blend of Syrah, Grenache and Merlot, with lovely, succulently
sweet, spicy fruit in the mould of a Crozes-Hermitage.

---

*1994 La Langue, Domaine Sainte Madeleine, Syrah 14/20
Full-bodied 🏆 🍾

One grape, one dimension and too much extraction. Nothing like as good as the Domaine Saint Benoît.

1995 Montpeyroux, Coteaux du Languedoc Rouge, Meffre 14/20
Full-bodied 🏆

Powerful, chunky, black-cherry fruity Languedoc blend of mainly Carignan with Grenache and Syrah, showing firm, rustic tannins and a touch of oak sweetness.

1995 James Herrick, Cuvée Simone, Vin de Pays d'Oc 16/20
Full-bodied 🏆🏆🏆 ▬

Named after his Californian wife, Simone, James Herrick's first Languedoc venture into red wine is a triumph, showing tarry, aromatic Syrah characters, fleshy, sweet fruit and southern spiciness. Still chunky, but should soon soften into a memorable sub-£5 red.

1995 Grenache Vieilles Vignes, La Baume, Vin de Pays d'Oc 14/20
Full-bodied 🏆

Peppery, broad, raspberry and damson fruity old-vine Grenache from BRL-Hardy, which is let down by drying tannins.

ITALY

1994 Valpolicella Classico, Vigneti in Marano, Pasqua 15/20
Medium-bodied 🏆🏆🏆

Thirst-quenching, concentrated, single vineyard Valpolicella, with cherry and plum fruit flavours and refreshing acidity. Proof that Valpol under £5 needn't be light and insipid.

NEW ZEALAND

1994 Timara Cabernet/Merlot, Montana 13/20
Medium-bodied

Coffee-bean oaky, herbaceous New Zealand red from Montana, with a thin, weedy finish.

SOUTH AFRICA

Clearsprings Cape Red   11/20
Full-bodied ▮
Sweetish, faintly grubby Cape red with hefty alcohol and drying tannins.

1995 Kumala Cinsault/Pinotage   15/20
Full-bodied 👜👜👜 ▮
A well-made, warm-climate blend of Cinsault and the indigenous South African
Pinotage. Sweetly ripe, red fruit flavours, with a characterful slice or three of
baked banana.

1995 Cape View Merlot   15/20
Medium-bodied 👜👜👜 ▮
Chocolatey, sweetly oaked South African Merlot from Aussie Kym Milne,
showing ripe cassis fruit and soft, supple tannins.

SPAIN

1994 Ed's Red, La Mancha   13/20
Medium-bodied 👜 ▮
Smoky, chewy, splintery La Mancha red made from the Tempranillo grape. The
Ed in question is Californian winemaker, Ed Flaherty, not our editor, Mandy
Greenfield.

£5–8

AUSTRALIA

1994 Basedow Bush Vine Grenache, Barossa   14/20
Full-bodied 👜 ▮
Oak, oak and more oak is the dominant flavour in this rather chewy Barossa
Valley Grenache. Barely worth one in the bush.

1993 Hardy's Bankside Shiraz   16/20
Full-bodied 👜👜👜 ▮
Dense, richly textured, cinnamon-tinged cross-regional Shiraz from Australia's
number two, BRL-Hardy. Attractively spicy with a firm backbone of tannin.

1994 Basedow Shiraz, Barossa   16/20
Full-bodied 👜👜👜 ▬
Sweetly oaked, licorice-spicy Barossa Shiraz with lots of minty, blackberry fruit
and character. Good value at under £7.

CHILE

*1995 Cono Sur Pinot Noir Reserve   16/20
Medium-bodied 👜👜👜 ▬
It's a shame that rangy Ed Flaherty has moved to the Errázuriz winery, because
this is his best-ever Pinot Noir Reserve, made like a modern Côte de Beaune
red Burgundy with attractively spicy oak, wild strawberry fruitiness and
medium-weight tannins.

*1994 Caliterra Reserva Cabernet Sauvignon, Maipo Valley   16/20
Medium-bodied 👜👜👜 ▬
Sage and blackcurrant essence-like Chilean Cabernet Sauvignon, with ripe,
structured, berry fruit flavours, well-handled oak and the concentration to age.

FRANCE

*1993 Domaine de la Baume Merlot, Vin de Pays d'Oc   16/20
Full-bodied 👜👜👜 ▬
An intensely oaky, hugely coloured, sage-scented Midi Merlot with the structure
and blackcurrant fruit intensity to age for at least a couple of years. An
Australian-style wine made by French-based Australian winemakers.

1993 Valréas, Domaine de la Grande Bellane, Côtes du
Roussillon Villages   15/20
Full-bodied 👜👜 |
An organic blend of mainly Syrah with 25 per cent Grenache, this is a spicy,
peppery, clove-like Roussillon red with ripe raspberry fruit and robust tannins.

*1995 Saint Nicolas de Bourgueil , Les Aisselières, Couly-Dutheil
                                                                   13/20
Medium-bodied |
Rather austere Loire Cabernet Franc from the small, river-bank appellation of
Saint Nicolas de Bourgueil. We prefer Couly-Dutheil's Chinons to this chewy,
fruitless number.

1995 Château de l'Abbaye de Sainte Ferme, Bordeaux Supérieur
15/20

Medium-bodied 💰 ➖

Ripe, cassis fruity, well-structured claret from the generally impressive 1995 vintage. An authentic grower's red, which is still in short trousers.

*1995 Château du Hureau, Saumur-Champigny, Vatan   16/20
Medium-bodied 💰💰💰 ➖

Succulent, youthful, concentrated Cabernet Franc from one of the Loire's most fashionable appellations, with stylish oak and smooth black-cherry fruitiness.

ITALY

1993 Barbaglio, Rosso del Salento   15/20
Full-bodied 💰💰 ▯

Baked, raisiny, strappingly alcoholic Puglian red with rosemary aromas, fresh acidity and chunky, chocolatey fruit characters. A powerful winter warmer.

1994 Argiolas, Costera, Cannonau di Sardegna   16/20
Full-bodied 💰💰💰 ➖

Tarry, massively oaked, powerfully structured Sardinian red made from the local Cannonau grape, otherwise known as Grenache. Leafy, complex stuff.

SOUTH AFRICA

1995 Beyerskloof Pinotage   16/20
Full-bodied 💰💰💰 ➖

Chunky, vibrantly coloured, oak and raspberry fruity Pinotage from Kanonkop winemaker, Beyers Truter. Plenty of character, as you'd expect from South Africa's most distinctive red grape variety.

1995 Fairview Cabernet Sauvignon   15/20
Full-bodied 💰 ➖

Tight, dry, chewy Cape Cabernet Sauvignon, which may soften with another year in bottle. We certainly hope so.

UNITED STATES

*1993 Kenwood Zinfandel, Sonoma Valley   17/20
Full-bodied 💰💰💰 ➖

Spicy, intense, cinnamon oaky Sonoma Valley Zinfandel, with smooth tobacco and blackberry fruit flavours and excellent concentration.

Over £8

AUSTRALIA

1993 Penfolds Cabernet Sauvignon Coonawarra   16/20
Full-bodied 👛👛 🍾
Purple-hued, deeply concentrated Penfolds Cabernet Sauvignon from Australia's leading red wine region, with masses of in-your-face oak and sweet, succulent blackcurrant and vanilla fruitiness. A formula that works.

FRANCE

*1992 Château de Villegeorge, Haut-Médoc   16/20
Medium-bodied 👛 🍾
Commendably concentrated for a 1992 Médoc red, with modern coffee-bean oak and supple vanilla and blackcurrant fruitiness.

*1993 Château La Salle de Poujeaux, Moulis   15/20
Medium-bodied 👛 🍾
The second wine of Château Poujeaux, one of the best *crus bourgeois* in Bordeaux, this is a firm, structured claret, which ought to be £3 cheaper, given the rather average vintage.

ITALY

1990 Chianti Classico Riserva, Viacosta, Rodano   15/20
Medium-bodied 👛 🍾
Oaky, structured, mature Chianti Classico from an excellent vintage, with leafy, almondy flavours and dry tannins. Drink up.

UNITED STATES

*1991 Frei Ranch Merlot, Gallo   15/20
Medium-bodied 🍾
The changing face of the world's largest winery is represented by this sweetly oaky, if somewhat dilute, chewy Sonoma Valley Merlot. Rather expensive at around £11 but a pace in the right direction.

Rosé

£3–5

FRANCE

1995 Château la Jaubertie Rosé, Bergerac   14/20
Dry 🍷 |
Deeply coloured, *clairet-style* Bergerac rosé from Hugh Ryman's Château la Jaubertie, with soft redcurrant and rhubarb fruit and a dry finish.

Sparkling

£5–8

SOUTH AFRICA

Graham Beck Brut   15/20
Dry 🍷🍷🍷 |
Soft, malty, flavoursome Cape fizz made from Pinot Noir and Chardonnay grapes, with partial barrel-fermentation for added complexity.

Over £8

AUSTRALIA

*1993 Green Point Rosé   16/20
Dry 🍷🍷🍷 |
Delicate, onion-skin-hued rosé with Pinot Noir-dominated fruit flavours, good structure and a stylish mousse. Dr Tony Jordan is producing increasingly complex wines at Moët et Chandon's Yarra Valley winery.

FRANCE

*Cuvée Trésor, Bouvet-Ladubay   16/20
Dry 🍾🍾🍾 ▮
Stylish Saumur sparkler with plenty of appley aromas and honeyed richness,
fresh tangy acidity and considerable length of flavour. About as good as Loire
sparkling wine gets.

*Pol Roger White Foil Champagne   18/20
Dry 🍾🍾🍾 ▮
One of our favourite non-vintage Grandes Marques – which puts us in the
company of Sir Winston Churchill, no less – this is an elegant, bready,
honeycomb and strawberry-scented Champagne with superb balance and
length of flavour.

Fortified

£3–5

SPAIN

Oloroso Seco, Sanchez Romate, half-bottle   16/20
Dry 🍾🍾 ▮
Caramel and crème brûlée aromas, and almond and ground-coffee flavours,
make this a characterful, genuinely dry Sherry with tangy acidity.

£5–8

PORTUGAL

*Noval Extra Dry White Port   15/20
Off-dry 🍾 ▮
Creamy, nutty white Port from the French-owned Quinta do Noval. with
warming 20 per cent-plus alcohol and a lift of Portuguese spice.

Over £8

PORTUGAL

*Calem 20 Year Old Port   15/20
Full-bodied   🍷   ⬦
Old-fashioned, spirity tawny from an independent, Portuguese-owned Port house, with sweet raisin and chocolate fruit and a drying finish.

Waitrose ☆☆☆☆(☆)

Address: Doncastle Road, Southern Industrial Area, Bracknell, Berkshire RG12 8YA

Telephone/fax: 01344 424680; 01344 860428

Number of branches: 115 (by the end of 1996)

Opening hours: 8.30am to 6.00pm Monday and Tuesday; 8.30am to 8.00pm Wednesday and Thursday; 8.30am to 9.00pm Friday; 8.30am to 6.00pm Saturday; selected branches open 10.00am to 4.00pm Sunday

Credit cards accepted: Access, Visa, Switch, Delta, Master Card, Waitrose and John Lewis account cards

Discounts: Wines-of-the-month discount of 12 bottles for the price of 11 (without 5 per cent discount) or 5 per cent discount on a whole case of wine, including Champagne and fortified wines

Facilities and services: Free glass loan against returnable deposit of £5; home delivery through Waitrose Direct (Freephone 0800 413331); occasional in-store tastings

Special offers: *En primeur* and special case offers through Waitrose Direct

Top ten best-selling wines: 1995 Vin de Pays du Gers, Le Pujalet; 1995 Côtes du Roussillon; 1994 Sâmburesti Romanian Pinot Noir; 1995 Domaine de Fontanelles Sauvignon Blanc, Vin de Pays d'Oc; Fitou, Mont Tauch; 1994 Orchard Hill Dry Country White; 1995 Chardonnay, Vin de Pays du Jardin de la France; 1995 Les Trois Couronnes Rouge, Vin de Pays de l'Hérault; 1995 Domaine de Rose Syrah/Merlot, Vin de Pays d'Oc; 1995 Bergerac Blanc, Marquis de Beausoleil, Yvon Mau

Range:

GOOD: Bordeaux, Burgundy, regional France, Eastern Europe, Germany, Argentina, Chile, Australia, South Africa, Champagne and sparkling wines, Sherry and Port

AVERAGE: Rhône, Beaujolais, Alsace, Loire, England, Italy, Spain, New Zealand

POOR: None

UNDER-REPRESENTED: United States, Portugal

Waitrose

'We're in a state of flux, and have been for some time,' Julian Brind, Waitrose's patrician head of wines, beers, spirits and soft drinks, told us this year. 'We've been up against it.' What was worrying the foxtrotting, tennis-mad Brind? Was it the small Italian vintage? Was it prices in Australia? Was it his department's standing in the monthly league tables published in *The Gazette*, the John Lewis Partnership's quirky in-house journal?

The answer was the dwindling number of Waitrose wine specialists. With the departure of Neil Sommerfelt to International Wine Services and the retirement of David Grandorge, Waitrose's proudly touted quintet of Masters of Wine had been reduced to three (David Gill, Dee Blackstock and Brind himself) by the summer of 1996. Add the loss of Paul Stacey, a promising trainee buyer who moved to Victoria Wine, and Waitrose's wine-buying resources were severely depleted. When we met in early August, Brind was on the verge of an important Alan Shearer-like signing to bring the MW count back up to four. But details were still under padlock, reinforced chain and key.

Where some wine departments would implode with the pressure of it all, the Waitrose team seems to have adapted comfortably to the situation. The only problem, as far as Brind is concerned, is that the revamp of the Spanish and Portuguese ranges has had to be postponed for a while longer.

Otherwise, it's been pretty much business as usual on the wine-buying front. The Waitrose range of 500-odd wines evolves slowly, rather than with a rush or a flurry of new acquisitions. In part, this is because it already outperforms the supermarket competition, but also because, as Brind puts it, 'There aren't any new and exciting places to discover. We look at every area we deal with and try to make improvements.' Brind has no plans to boost the list to a strapping 800 wines because, he says, 'It's over the top. It just confuses the public.'

If this makes Waitrose sound staid and predictable, it shouldn't do. The range is as interesting and original as ever, with particular strengths in Eastern Europe, where David Gill has done excellent work building on his time at Bulgarian Vintners, Chile, South Africa, Australia, Germany and especially France. It is also remarkably consistent. Poor wines are rare at Waitrose, and when they do surface they tend to be at the cheaper end of the range.

Not that Waitrose's customers are obsessed with bargain-basement wines. The average bottle sale is an impressive £4.75 and the top-ten best-sellers list is remarkably free of the dreaded trio of Lambrusco, Liebfraumilch and Hock. 'We sell very little cheap German wine,' says Brind, 'but we do well with the stuff over £4. Our customers aren't as price-oriented as most. We're lucky because our stores tend to be in areas with ABC1 shoppers, who've got a bit more money to spend.'

The refusal to take the cost-cutting path also extends to Waitrose's four wines of the month. 'We don't reduce the prices any more,' explains Brind, 'because we found it didn't make much difference to sales. What we're doing by selecting four wines is reducing the choice. People thank us for that.' So, no £1.99 specials at Waitrose, although the wines are offered on a 12-for-11 basis.

The absence of cheap wines hasn't affected Waitrose's performance. In fact, despite the staffing shortages, Waitrose has had a bumper year, with sales up 25 per cent in value. When he opens his copy of *The Gazette* each week, Brind can be proud that wine is the best-performing department within the John Lewis empire. 'We're doing better than any other supermarket, too,' he claims.

Waitrose is outperforming the market in France, Australia, South Africa, New Zealand and South America, which suggests a New World bias among its customers. Nearly 19 per cent of sales are accounted for by the last four areas. 'Our old customers are being more adventurous,' says Brind, 'but we're still French-led.'

They certainly are. France is only one of 30-odd countries featured on the Waitrose list, but it gets number-one billing. It takes a whopping 40 per cent of the retail tarte, nearly 15 per cent ahead of the national average, with one of the best ranges in the country. In line with its competitors, Waitrose has turned its attention to the Languedoc-Roussillon in recent vintages, but it hasn't neglected the classic areas of Bordeaux, Burgundy, the Rhône, Alsace and Champagne.

So confident is Waitrose of its ability to sell top French wines that it is about to launch a new 'super-fine' range of wines like First and Second Growth clarets in store – and this at a time when most supermarkets are using their fine-wine racks for firewood. 'We feel that 20 or so really fine wines will add interest to the wine department,' says Brind.

The classics notwithstanding, this year has witnessed one important innovation: in-store tastings. Since January 1996 a total of 46 branches have been holding tastings at least four days a week, run by an outside agency. The wines on tasting can increase their sales by as much as 2,000 per cent, according to Brind, but he acknowledges that the whole exercise is still very expensive. 'Customers like them, so we'll continue to do them,' he says.

Waitrose's mail-order arm, Findlater, Mackie, Todd, has also been through a few changes in the last 12 months. FMT, or Waitrose Direct as it's been re-christened, now lists the entire Waitrose range, rather than a specially chosen selection, although 50 or so small-volume lines, such as Thelema Chardonnay from South Africa and California's Niebaum-Coppola Cabernet Franc, are not sold through the Waitrose stores. Waitrose Direct also offers wines, such as the 1995 Bordeaux, *en primeur*.

Learning to run a mail-order business has not been easy for Waitrose. 'We took over a company that wasn't going anywhere,' says Brind, 'and it's taken us two years to learn the mail-order ropes.' From a small base, the list is now 'beginning to motor'. Brind's hunch is that the whole operation will be so successful that 'Eventually the stores will start to complain that so much is being sold direct.'

Waitrose Direct provides access to the wine range for people who live north of Leicester, Birmingham and Norwich – the perimeter-fence of the John Lewis retail business. This is a boon for northern-based readers of *Grapevine*. Waitrose still has work to do in Spain and Portugal, but its list remains one of the best, if not the best, in the supermarket sector.

Did we say supermarket sector? With characteristic independence of mind, Brind says that he doesn't see Waitrose as part of the supermarket jungle. 'We've always done our own thing,' he says. Long may Waitrose plough its solo furrow – with or without a fifth Master of Wine.

White

Under £3

FRANCE

1995 Bergerac Blanc   13/20
Dry 👛👛 ▮
Bordeaux négociant Yvon Mau has here produced a soft, quaffable, unoaked white with sharp acidity.

1995 Boulder Creek, Vin de Pays de Vaucluse   13/20
Dry 👛👛 ▮
Despite the silly Wild West-style name, this southern Rhône quaffer is a decent apple and pear fruity, cleanly made white.

HUNGARY

1994 Orchard Hill Dry Country White   13/20
Off-dry 👛👛 ▮
Soft, spicy blend of Olaszrizling and Gewürztraminer from northern Hungary. One of Waitrose's cheapest whites – and it shows.

1995 Chapel Hill Irsai Oliver 14/20
Dry 👜👜👜 🍾

A good example of the new-wave whites emerging from Hungary at the moment, Kym Milne's massively aromatic, zesty Irsai Oliver is a classic, floral aperitif.

£3–5

ARGENTINA

1994 Alamos Ridge Chardonnay, Mendoza 15/20
Dry 👜👜 🍾

Pineapple and melon fruity Chardonnay from the progressive Catena winery, with well-judged vanilla oak and hints of toffee and crème caramel.

AUSTRALIA

1996 Currawong Creek Semillon/Chardonnay 13/20
Dry 👜 🍾

Fresh, if rather confected, young white with marked acidity and a gassy spritz. A bit thin given its £4 price tag.

1994 Houghton Wildflower Ridge Chenin Blanc 15/20
Dry 👜👜 🍾

Honeysuckle-scented, richly flavoured Chenin Blanc from Western Australia's largest winery. A ripe, passion fruity white with lively acidity.

1996 Ridgewood Trebbiano, South Eastern Australia 14/20
Dry 👜👜 🍾

Softly fruity Aussie interpretation of a widely planted (and normally neutral) Italian grape, with ripe pear flavours and a rounded texture.

1996 Hardy's Southern Cross Semillon/Chardonnay 15/20
Dry 👜👜👜 🍾

Well-made, tropically fruity Aussie blend with good balance and refreshing acidity. The 1996 vintage from Down Under looks promising.

1996 Waitrose Australian Riesling/Gewürztraminer, Angove's

14/20

Off-dry 👜👜 ▮

A soft, perfumed blend of the two aromatic varieties, Riesling and Gewürztraminer, this is a grapy, rose-petal spicy white at a good price. The label might give you a few sleepless nights.

CHILE

1996 Montenuevo Sauvignon Blanc 14/20
Dry 👜👜 ▮

Smoky, gun-flinty Chilean Sauvignon Blanc from the reliable Canepa winery, with zippy spritz and acidity.

1995 Caliterra Chardonnay, Curicó 15/20
Dry 👜👜 ▮

Sweet, tropical fruity Chilean Chardonnay with a soft texture and ripe peach and banana flavours.

ENGLAND

1993 Chiltern Valley Medium Dry 15/20
Dry 👜👜 ▮

Nettley, weighty, mature (but still remarkably fresh) English white with attractively smoky undertones and lots of flavour.

FRANCE

1995 Vin de Pays du Gers, Le Pujalet 14/20
Dry 👜👜👜 ▮

From the Plaimont co-operative, this is a zesty, refreshing Gascon white with grapefruit characters and a clean spritz.

1995 Domaine de Fontanelles Sauvignon, Vin de Pays d'Oc 15/20
Dry 👜👜👜 ▮

Fresh, elegant, grapefruity southern French Sauvignon Blanc from the Foncalieu winery, with a lemon-zest finish.

1995 Chardonnay, Vin de Pays du Jardin de la France, Pierre Guéry
12/20

Dry

Gluey, rather tart Loire white, which tastes more like Chenin Blanc than Chardonnay.

1995 Waitrose Muscadet, Pierre Guéry
13/20

Dry

Clean, but rather basic Muscadet, which should be more interesting given the excellent 1995 vintage in the Loire.

1995 Côtes du Lubéron
15/20

Dry

Refreshing, very well-made southern Rhône white made in a modern style with mealy, ripe pear fruitiness and crisp acidity. A bargain at just over £3.50.

1995 Mâcon-Villages Chardonnay
14/20

Dry

Decent, if unexceptional, old-style Mâcon-Villages, with notes of nut and butter and restrained Chardonnay fruit.

1995 Chardonnay, Maurel Vedeau, Vin de Pays d'Oc
16/20

Dry

Spicy, sumptuous, New World-influenced southern French Chardonnay, which knocks spots off most Mâconnais whites at the same price. Very complex for a sub-£5 white.

1995 James Herrick Chardonnay, Vin de Pays d'Oc
15/20

Dry

Elegant, minerally Chardonnay from Englishman James Herrick's southern French vineyards near Narbonne, showing restrained, spicy oak and melony fruitiness.

1995 Cuckoo Hill Viognier, Château de Raissac, Vin de Pays d'Oc
16/20

Off-dry

Nick Butler has had a huge impact on the quality of the wines made at the Languedoc's Château de Raissac since leaving Hungary. This ripe honeysuckle and peach-like example of southern France's most sought-after grape is a flavoursome, beautifully balanced stunner.

1995 Pinot Blanc d'Alsace, Blanck Frères   15/20
Dry 🍾🍾🍾 ▮

This Pinot Blanc de Blanck, as it were, is extremely well-priced for an Alsace white, showing weighty, peachy, lightly spicy fruitiness and more character than you normally see from the grape.

1995 Cuvée d'Alban, Barrique-Fermented, Dulong, Bordeaux
15/20

Dry 🍾🍾🍾 ▮

A poor person's white Graves from the house of Dulong, this is a smoky, textured, well-made white Bordeaux with a lot to say at under £4.

GERMANY

1995 Waitrose Morio-Muskat, Pfalz   14/20
Medium 🍾🍾 ▮

White-pepper and grapefruit-scented white with a sherbet lemon tang. The acceptable face of cheap German wine.

GREECE

1994 Kouros Patras   14/20
Dry 🍾🍾 ▮

With its peculiar wrap-around label, this Peloponnesian white made from the native Rhoditis grape is a fresh, well-made and even stylish change from the mediocrity of Retsina.

HUNGARY

1995 Lakeside Oak Chardonnay, Balatonboglar   14/20
Dry 🍾🍾 ▮

Smoky oaky, Islay malt whisky-scented Hungarian Chardonnay from Aussie Kym Milne. Fresh and typically well-crafted.

1994 Dry Furmint, Disznoko, Tokay   16/20
Bone dry 🍾🍾🍾 ▮

Characterful, tea-leafy, bitingly dry white from Hungary's top wine region, with underlying honeyed opulence. Exciting stuff.

ITALY

1995 Chardonnay Vino da Tavola delle Tre Venezie, Vallade 14/20
Dry 🍷🍷 🍶
Spicy, tangy, well-balanced northern Italian Chardonnay, unoaked for maximum fruit impact. Highly affordable at under £3.50.

1995 Waitrose Nuragus di Cagliari, Dolianova 15/20
Dry 🍷🍷🍷 🍶
Water-white, crisply fruity Sardinian quaffer made from the local Nuragus grape and showing notes of greengage and a nutty tang.

1995 Soave Classico, Vigneto Colombara, Zenato 15/20
Dry 🍷🍷 🍶
Well-packaged, concentrated Veneto white with a zesty spritz and nicely rounded fruit flavours.

NEW ZEALAND

1996 New Zealand Dry White, Villa Maria 14/20
Off-dry 🍷🍷 🍶
An early indication of the improved quality of the 1996 vintage in New Zealand, this is an attractively fruity, forward Müller-Thurgau, with grapey sweetness balanced by crisp acidity.

SOUTH AFRICA

1995 Culemborg Chenin Blanc, Paarl 14/20
Dry 🍷🍷 🍶
Well-made, aromatic, honeyed Cape Chenin with guava-fruit character and good concentration for a sub-£3.50 white.

1996 Bellingham Sauvignon Blanc, Paarl 15/20
Dry 🍷🍷 🍶
Light, spritzy, green-bean-style Cape Sauvignon Blanc with good varietal character and plenty of flavour.

£5–8

AUSTRALIA

1996 Saint Huberts Sauvignon Blanc, Yarra Valley   15/20
Dry 🍷 |
Elegant, grassy Sauvignon Blanc from one of Australia's leading cool-climate regions, showing tangy acidity, good varietal character and plenty of flavour.

1995 Moondah Brook Verdelho, Western Australia   15/20
Dry 🍷🍷 |
Fresh, characterful, passion fruity Western Australian white made from Madeira's Verdelho grape. Distinctive stuff.

1994 Saltram Mamre Brook Chardonnay, South Australia   16/20
Dry 🍷🍷🍷 |
Broad, tropical fruity Aussie Chardonnay with excellent oak integration and rich flavours of caramel and vanilla.

1995 Basedow Chardonnay, Barossa Valley   16/20
Dry 🍷🍷 |
Deeply coloured, intensely oaky Barossa Valley Chardonnay, which is short on subtlety, but long on sweet vanilla, cinnamon and burnt-butter characters. A big improvement on previous vintages.

FRANCE

1995 Tokay Pinot Gris d'Alsace, Cave de Beblenheim   15/20
Dry 🍷🍷 |
Weighty, concentrated Alsace white with ripe, peachy fruitiness and plenty of alcohol.

Waitrose Gewürztraminer d'Alsace   15/20
Dry 🍷🍷 |
Full-bodied, pungently spicy Alsace Gewürz, with enough acidity to cut through the lychee-like opulence.

1990 Château Tour Balot, Premières Côtes de Bordeaux   13/20
Sweet

Gluey, old-fashioned Premières Côtes sticky with tart acidity and a surprising lack of concentration for a 1990.

1992 Château La Caussade, Sainte-Croix-du-Mont   16/20
Sweet

Elegant, honeyed, oak-influenced Sauternes substitute made from 75 per cent Semillon and 25 per cent Sauvignon Blanc and showing a hint of the much sought-after (in sweet wines) botrytis character.

GERMANY

1995 Ockfener Bockstein Riesling, Dr Wagner   16/20
Medium

Super-fresh, sweet-and-sour Mosel white with pure Riesling fruit flavours and thirst-quenching acidity. Classy stuff at just over £5.

1989 Avelsbacher Hammerstein Riesling Spätlese   15/20
Medium sweet

Mature, petrolly Mosel Riesling with ripe apple fruitiness and assertive acidity.

NEW ZEALAND

1996 Lawsons Dry Hills Sauvignon Blanc, Marlborough   17/20
Dry

Intense, tightly focused Kiwi Sauvignon Blanc from the promising 1996 vintage, combining the flintiness of a good Pouilly-Fumé and the tropical, gooseberry fruitiness of Marlborough at its characterful best.

1995 Villa Maria Chardonnay, Gisborne   15/20
Dry

Fresh, pineapple-chunky Gisborne Chardonnay from New Zealand's difficult 1995 vintage, with elegantly handled oak and zingy acidity.

SOUTH AFRICA

1995 Klein Constantia Chardonnay, Constantia   15/20
Dry

Old-fashioned, buttered-toast-style Cape Chardonnay with the full toffee-fudge monty of Burgundian techniques.

USA

1994 Fetzer Sundial Chardonnay   14/20
Off-dry 🍯 ▮

Basic, toffee popcorn-like California Chardonnay from Mendocino County's Fetzer winery. One for consumers with a sweet tooth.

Over £8

AUSTRALIA

1993 Arrowfield Show Reserve Botrytis Riesling, Cowra, 37.5 cl
15/20

Very sweet 🍯 ▮

Deeply coloured, botrytis-intense Aussie sticky with flavours of honey and candied orange peel. A one-glass wine.

FRANCE

1995 Chablis, La Chablisienne   16/20
Dry 🍯🍯 ▭▬

Youthful, restrained, fruit-dominated Chablis from the excellent local co-operative. A few more months in bottle should allow the wine's minerally flavours to develop nicely.

HUNGARY

1988 Tokaji Aszu, 5 Puttonyos, 50 cl   16/20
Very sweet 🍯🍯🍯 ▭▬

Golden-hued, stem-ginger and raisin fruity dessert white from Hungary's famous Tokay region. Fresh acidity prevents the wine from cloying.

Red

Under £3

BULGARIA

1995 Merlot/Gamza, Pleven   13/20
Medium-bodied 🛍🛍 ▌
Light, peppery, strawberry jam-like blend of Merlot and Bulgaria's native Gamza grape.

FRANCE

1995 Les Trois Couronnes, Vin de Pays de l'Hérault   12/20
Medium-bodied 🛍 ▌
Basic, chewy Languedoc plonk, which reflects its lowly price tag.

1995 Domaine de Rose Syrah/Merlot, Vin de Pays d'Oc   14/20
Medium-bodied 🛍🛍🛍 ▌
With its attractive 'New' Labour rose label, this deeply hued, softly fruity Languedoc blend is a juicy, blackcurrant quaffer at a good price.

£3–5

AUSTRALIA

1996 Waitrose Australian Malbec/Ruby Cabernet   14/20
Medium-bodied 🛍🛍 ▌
We're not sure about the acid-trip label, but this is a juicy, attractively oaked blend of the unusual (for Australia) Malbec and Ruby Cabernet, with simple fruit flavours and smooth tannins.

1996 Hardy's Southern Creek Shiraz/Cabernet   13/20
Medium-bodied 🛍 ▌
Oak, mint humbug and fruit juice-style Aussie quaffer from the BRL-Hardy giant. Short on subtlety.

CHILE

1995 Las Cumbres Dry Red, Viña Tocornal   14/20
Medium-bodied 👜👜 ▯
Lively, claret-busting, blackcurrant pastille-style Chilean red, which finishes a little dry. Still, not bad at just over £3.

1994 Santa Carolina Malbec   15/20
Medium-bodied 👜👜👜 ▯
Intense, peppery Chilean red made by Pilar Gonzalez at the Santiago-based Santa Carolina winery. A tarry, sagey Malbec with masses of sweet fruit and flavour.

1995 Isla Negra Chilean Red   14/20
Medium-bodied 👜👜 ▯
From Chile's largest winery, Concha y Toro, this is a youthful, oak-influenced Cabernet Sauvignon with vibrant cassis fruitiness and hardening tannins.

FRANCE

1995 Côtes du Roussillon, Jeanjean   13/20
Full-bodied 👜 ▯
Youthful, baked, sweetish Roussillon rouge with chewy tannins and an earthy bite.

Fitou, Mont Tauch   13/20
Full-bodied 👜 ▯
Spicy, robust, warm-climate Fitou with dryish tannins from the normally reliable local co-operative. A wine that should be 50 pence cheaper.

Waitrose Good Ordinary Claret, Bordeaux   13/20
Medium-bodied 👜 ▯
Plonky, rather basic Bordeaux Rouge with chewy tannins. Ordinary just about sums it up.

1995 Waitrose Beaujolais, Cave de Bully   13/20
Light-bodied 👜 ▯
Light, attenuated Gamay with confected raspberry fruit flavours.

1994 Château Saint-Maurice, Côtes-du-Rhône   14/20
Medium-bodied 💰 ▮

A classic blend of Grenache, Cinsault and Syrah with ripe, raisiny, warm-climate fruit flavours and an alcoholic punch of dry tannin.

1994 Domaine de Cantemerle, Côtes-du-Rhône Villages   15/20
Full-bodied 💰💰 ▬

Made by New World oenologists, Jean-Luc Sweerts and Mark Robertson, this is a more intense, sweetly fruity southern Rhône blend, with the heady, brown-sugar notes of the Grenache grape.

1995 Domaine des Salices Syrah, Vin de Pays d'Oc, Jacques Lurton   14/20
Medium-bodied 💰💰 ▮

Meaty, fruity, softly textured southern French Syrah with a harsh, acidified finish.

1995 Merlot/Cabernet Sauvignon, Vin de Pays d'Oc, Martine Moulin   13/20
Medium-bodied 💰 ▮

A solid, if dour, claret alternative from the Midi. Rather chewy.

1995 Domaine des Fontaines Merlot, Vin de Pays d'Oc   14/20
Medium-bodied 💰💰 ▮

Merlot on its own is often a better bet than a Merlot/Cabernet Sauvignon blend, if you're spending less than £3.50. This aromatic, smoothly textured red proves the point.

1995 L'Enclos Domeque Mourvèdre/Syrah, Vin de Pays d'Oc
     14/20

Medium-bodied 💰💰 ▮

Richly coloured, inky-purple Midi blend of Mourvèdre and Syrah with chunky tannins and sweet, crushed raspberry fruit. Suitable for vegetarians and vegans – both rare breeds in France.

1995 James Herrick, Cuvée Simone, Vin de Pays d'Oc   16/20
Full-bodied 💰💰💰 ▬

Named after his charming Californian wife, Simone, James Herrick's first Languedoc venture into red wine is a triumph, showing tarry, aromatic Syrah characters, fleshy, sweet fruit and southern spiciness. Still chunky, but should soon soften into a memorable sub-£5 red.

1994 Cahors, Cuvée Reservée, Côtes d'Olt   13/20
Full-bodied 🖐 ▮
Meaty, chunky, drying Malbec-based south-western French red, with a bitter almond aftertaste.

ITALY

1993 Waitrose Monica di Sardegna   14/20
Full-bodied 🖐🖐 ▮
Characterful, raisin and soft leather-scented Sardinian pasta-basher, showing intense Mediterranean spice and dry tannins.

1995 Montepulciano d'Abruzzo, Umani Ronchi   14/20
Full-bodied 🖐🖐 ▮
Gamey, chocolatey, ripe plum-like Abruzzo quaffer, with savoury tannins and good bite for a sub-£4 red.

1994 Sangiovese, Vino da Tavola di Toscana, Fiordaliso, GIV 14/20
Medium-bodied 🖐🖐 ▮
Sweetly fruity, modern Tuscan red from Veneto giant, GIV. The character of the Sangiovese grape really comes through on the palate.

1995 Waitrose Chianti   13/20
Medium-bodied 🖐 ▮
Decent trattoria Chianti, whose restrained fruit flavours are indicative of a difficult vintage in Italy.

1995 Negroamaro del Salento, Le Trulle, Vino da Tavola   13/20
Medium-bodied 🖐 ▮
On the light side for a Puglian Negroamaro, this is a herbal, raspberry fruity *rosso* padded out with drying oak character.

ROMANIA

1994 Sâmburesti Pinot Noir   13/20
Medium-bodied 🖐 ▮
Soupy, sweetish, rough-edged Romanian Pinot Noir, which tastes old and leathery for a two-year-old wine.

SOUTH AFRICA

1995 Merwida Ruby Cabernet, Worcester 15/20
Medium-bodied 🍷🍷🍷 ▮

Ripe, mulberry fruity, intensely juicy Ruby Cabernet from the warm-climate region of Worcester, showing full but well-managed tannins and considerable length of flavour.

1996 Athlone Pinot Noir, Sonop 11/20
Full-bodied ▮

Rubbery, unbalanced, vinegary Pinot Noir from a country that struggles to produce anything drinkable from Burgundy's famous red grape.

SPAIN

1995 Las Lomas Tempranillo/Cabernet Sauvignon, Valencia 12/20
Full-bodied ▮

Cheap, plonkish Valencian blend of Tempranillo and Cabernet Sauvignon, with clumsy acidity and a stave or two of oak character.

1994 Fuente del Ritmo Tempranillo, La Mancha 14/20
Medium-bodied 🍷🍷 ▮

The 'fount of rhythm' might sound like a Tantric sex manual, but this oaky Spanish Tempranillo from the flat central plain, or meseta, is a quaffable, if splintery, alternative to Rioja. Not quite sex in a bottle, Sting.

USA

1993 Cartlidge & Browne Zinfandel, California 14/20
Full-bodied 🍷 ▮

Sweet, tobacco-ish, raspberry fruity introduction to California's semi-indigenous wine style, with plenty of alcohol and a licoricey bite.

£5–8

AUSTRALIA

1994 Browns of Padthaway Cabernet Sauvignon, Family Reserve
17/20

Full-bodied 💰💰💰 ➖
From grower Donald Brown (not to be confused with Brown Brothers of Milawa), this is a deeply coloured, richly concentrated, silky-sweet Cabernet Sauvignon with the power and cassis intensity to age. A real artery-stripper.

1994 Château Reynella Basket Pressed Shiraz   15/20
Full-bodied 💰 ➖
Massively oaked, termite friendly McLaren Vale Shiraz, with astringent tannins dominating the plum and blackberry fruit characters.

1996 Yaldara Grenache, Whitmore Old Vineyard   16/20
Full-bodied 💰💰 ➖
Concentrated, powerfully alcoholic, liquid summer-pudding-like old-vine Grenache from South Australia's Barossa Valley. Spine-tingling stuff.

1994 Tatachilla Merlot, Barossa Valley and McLaren Vale   15/20
Full-bodied 💰 ▮
Coffee-bean oaky, blackberry essence-style Merlot blend from two of South Australia's best red-wine regions. The oak is the dominant feature here, drying the sweet, ripe fruit a little.

FRANCE

1994 Château Ségonzac, Premières Côtes de Blaye   15/20
Medium-bodied 💰💰 ➖
Firm, modern, well-oaked claret from the Blaye hills, opposite the Médoc, showing the plumpness of the Merlot grape variety and a drying finish.

1994 Château Chicane, Graves   16/20
Medium-bodied 💰💰 ➖
A wine for Damon Hill and Murray Walker, this is a lively, cedary Graves blend of Cabernet Sauvignon, Merlot and Malbec with a racy, refreshing aftertaste.

1994 Crozes-Hermitage, Caves des Clairmonts   15/20
Medium-bodied 🍴🍴 ⧫

Attractively peppery, aromatic northern Rhône Syrah from the tiny Clairmonts co-operative, with juicy blackberry fruit and fresh acidity.

ITALY

1993 Salice Salentino Riserva, Cosimo Taurino   15/20
Full-bodied 🍴🍴 ⧫

Rich, savoury, raisiny, southern Italian *rosso* with lots of sweet, pruney fruit and alcohol. A good barbecue red.

SOUTH AFRICA

1996 Diemersdal Pinotage, Coastal Region   15/20
Full-bodied 🍴🍴 ▬

Juicy, ripe, bubble-gum and banana-like Cape Pinotage with oodles of sweet raspberry fruitiness and relatively approachable tannins.

1994 Delheim Cabernet Sauvignon, Stellenbosch   14/20
Full-bodied 🍴 ▬

Green-pepper-scented, substantially splintery Stellenbosch Cabernet Sauvignon with sweet fruit and a counterpoint of drying tannin.

1993 Klein Constantia Cabernet Sauvignon, Constantia   16/20
Full-bodied 🍴🍴 ⧫

Mature, structured, cool-climate (for South Africa) Cabernet Sauvignon, with sweet vanilla oak and blackberry fruit complexity.

1992 Warwick Merlot, Stellenbosch   16/20
Full-bodied 🍴🍴 ⧫

Subtle, elegant, fine-grained Merlot from Canadian Norma Ratcliffe's Stellenbosch winery. Good fruit concentration, well-integrated oak and refreshing acidity make this a complex, mature drop.

1993 Warwick Cabernet Franc, Stellenbosch   16/20
Full-bodied 🍴🍴 ⧫

Flavoursome, characterful Stellenbosch red with leafy, green-pepper fruitiness and elegant tannins. An intensely flavoured Cape equivalent of a good Saint Emilion.

1995 Clos Malverne Pinotage Reserve, Stellenbosch   17/20
Full-bodied 🝢🝢🝢 ➡
Extremely rich, chunky Cape Pinotage made from 30-year-old vines in
Stellenbosch. Spicy oak and intensely juicy blackberry fruit make this an
excellent introduction to a celebrated indigenous style.

SPAIN

1993 Cosme Palacio Rioja   15/20
Medium-bodied 🝢🝢 |
Complex, peppery, vanilla oaky Rioja, with wild strawberry fruitiness and a
sweet, leathery back palate.

Over £8

FRANCE

1993 Chorey-lès-Beaune, Domaine Maillard   16/20
Medium-bodied 🝢🝢🝢 |
Stylish, modern, spicily oaked village red Burgundy from a consistently reliable
estate. Showing the structure of the excellent 1993 vintage, it needs another
year or two to reach its peak. But don't be afraid to drink it now.

1990 Château Sergant, Lalande de Pomerol   17/20
Medium-bodied 🝢🝢🝢 |
Mature, gamey Merlot from a Pomerol satellite in one of the finest vintages of
the last decade. Silky, concentrated fruit flavours and delicious length of flavour
make this a perfect Christmas claret.

1993 Mercurey, La Framboisière, Faiveley   16/20
Medium-bodied 🝢🝢🝢 ➡
Aptly named, well-structured, raspberry fruity Côte Chalonnaise red Burgundy
from the respected négociant house of Faiveley. Excellent value at under £10.

1994 Clos Saint Michel, Châteauneuf du Pape, Guy Mousset
17/20
Full-bodied 🝢🝢🝢 |
Heady, sumptuously fruity, Grenache-based Châteauneuf, with masses of spice
and angostura bitters character, lifted by fresh acidity. Benchmark stuff.

SPAIN

1986 Campillo Gran Reserva Rioja 17/20
Medium-bodied 🝞🝞🝞 ▮
Garnet-hued, well-structured Gran Reserva Rioja made entirely from the Tempranillo grape, a fact that explains the wine's longevity and concentration. Lovely, sweetly mature Rioja at under £10.

Rosé

£3–5

SOUTH AFRICA

1996 Culemborg Blanc de Noirs 13/20
Off-dry 🝞 ▮
Sweetish, gluggable, strawberry fruity rosé, which, despite what the label says, is not a Blanc de Noirs.

Sparkling

£5–8

FRANCE

Waitrose Blanquette de Limoux Brut 15/20
Dry 🝞🝞 ▮
Frothy, big-bubbled sparkler from the Languedoc's Limoux region, showing a touch of bottle-developed complexity.

Waitrose Saumur Brut   15/20
Dry 🍾🍾 ▮
Well-made, Chenin Blanc-based Loire fizz with crisp apple fruitiness, assertive acidity and a fine mousse.

Clairette de Die, Tradition   14/20
Medium sweet 🍾 ▮
Grapey, marmaladey, sweetish southern French fizz, which tastes a bit like Asti Spumante.

SOUTH AFRICA

1992 Krone Borealis Brut   14/20
Dry 🍾 ▮
Youthful, rather unbalanced Cape fizz with some brioche-like characters but insufficient bottle-aged complexity.

SPAIN

Waitrose Cava Brut   13/20
Off-dry 🍾 ▮
Tangy, slightly earthy Catalan fizz with rather coarse, youthful bubbles and lemony fruit.

Over £8

FRANCE

Bredon Brut Champagne NV, F. Bonnet   13/20
Dry ▮
Waitrose's price-fighting Champagne is a rather coarse, unripe sparkler with tart acidity. The New World offers much better value at this price.

Waitrose Blanc de Noirs NV, A. Bonnet   17/20
Dry 🍾🍾🍾 ▮
For an extra 50 pence, you can buy a bottle of this malty, fresh, Pinot-based Champagne from the southerly Aube region. Consistently among the leading supermarket own-label Champagnes.

Waitrose Brut NV, F. Bonnet   15/20
Dry 🍾🍾 🍾
Sweetish, well-made own-label fizz, with good depth of flavour from added reserve wine. Still good value at under £13.

Waitrose Blanc de Blancs NV   17/20
Dry 🍾🍾🍾 🍾
Rich, bready, all-Chardonnay Champagne with a mouth-filling mousse and lots of buttery flavours.

Waitrose Brut Rosé NV, Caves Auboises   15/20
Dry 🍾🍾 🍾
Bronze-pink, Pinot Noir Champagne from the southerly Aube region, with youthful, tangy strawberry fruit flavours and refreshing acidity.

1989 Waitrose Brut Vintage, Marne et Champagne   16/20
Dry 🍾🍾🍾 🍾
A wine that is just getting into its stride, this is an intense, tightly structured vintage Champagne showing promising complexity for a comparatively young fizz.

Fortified

£5–8

ITALY

1994 Passito di Pantelleria, Pellegrino, 37.5 cl   15/20
Very sweet 🍾🍾 🍾
Spicy, brandy-snap and orange peel-flavoured Italian sticky, with well-judged fortification and fresh acidity.

SOUTH AFRICA

1979 White Jerepigo, Cavendish Cape   16/20
Very sweet 🍶🍶 ▬

From a seemingly bottomless vat of Cape fortified wine, this is a complex, intensely sweet cross between a mature white Port and a Madeira. An unusual, viscously rich one-off, from the days when men were men and the impalas were frightened.

SPAIN

Waitrose Solera Jerezano, Dry Oloroso, Diego Romero   17/20
Dry 🍶🍶🍶 ▮

Rich, dry, authentic Oloroso with flavours of almond and burnt toffee lifted by tangy acidity. Impossible to beat for value for money, at just over £5.

Over £8

PORTUGAL

Waitrose Ten-Year-Old Tawny, Skeffington Vinhos   16/20
Full-bodied 🍶🍶🍶 ▬

Fiery, peppery, chocolatey Tawny, with good maturity and concentration for a ten-year-old wood-aged Port.

The *Grapevine* Guide to Independent Wine Merchants

Introduction

Last year, we remedied an oversight from earlier editions of *Grapevine* by including a dozen independent wine merchants. This year we've gone a significant stage further. We've added 30 more independents whom we think offer the best range of wines and service in the country.

With little promotional budget and often only a single shop window in which to advertise their wares, the independents have to rely on a mouth-watering wine list and close contact with customers to communicate their strengths. They may not be able to match the economies of scale commanded by the big boys, but the independents have various aces to play in the game of selling wine.

Quality over quantity

The wines themselves, for starters. The supermarkets have tried – and largely failed – to sell what might loosely be called fine wines. Waitrose and Marks & Spencer apart, most have taken a machete to their dusty wooden wine racks. You may have to pay a bit more for a hand-crafted Burgundy, Barolo or California Cabernet Sauvignon, but wines of character and personality, whether from dour *paysans* or charismatic growers, are an independent's *raison d'être*.

The in-depth knowledge gained from years of combing local vineyards on and off the beaten track gives the specialists the edge in experience and enthusiasm. As Alistair Marshall of Adnams puts it: 'We're trying to shorten the distance between the person who makes it and the person who drinks it.'

All merchants great and small

Like the wines they sell, independents don't conform to a set standard or stereotype. They may be generalists, like Lay & Wheeler, Connolly's and Justerini & Brooks, or specialists in countries or regions. They may be traditional, like Berry Brothers & Rudd or Corney & Barrow, but you don't have to be chalk-striped, titled or pensioned-off to be on a wine merchant's mailing list. Try going to a tasting put on by the likes of Bibendum, or take a peek at the youthful Noel Young's list. If wine merchants, like policemen, are getting younger, then so are their customers.

Independent wine merchants are often substantial operations, like Tanners or Lay & Wheeler. They may not even, technically, be independent at all.

Independent Wine Merchants

Justerini & Brooks, for instance, the posh St James's Street merchant, is in fact umbilically linked to its corporate parent, Grand Metropolitan.

But there's an increasing number of urban, suburban and country-based lone rangers. Howard Ripley and Adam Bancroft, for instance, exemplify the committed one-man merchant. They may not be greedy or ambitious, but they have an excellent idea of what they like, along with a shrewd idea of their customers' tastes. Firms such as Chippendale Fine Wines or Vin du Van may sound like music-hall acts, but in their own idiosyncratic way, they're equally serious about what they do.

The virtues of specialisation

Another independent wine merchant ace is specialisation. No high-street retailer can match Valvona & Crolla for wall-to-wall Brunello di Montalcino; the Australian Wine Club for its regional diversity; or Gauntley's of Nottingham for its Rhône-studded list. Equally, the more traditional merchants carry stocks of older, ready-for-drinking vintages that simply can't be found in the high street.

Independents vary widely in their focus. Farr Vintners and Reid Wines are best known for their fine and rare wines. The bulk of Connolly's business in Birmingham is selling to restaurants, hotels and wine bars. One merchant, Halves in Ludlow, devotes his entire business to selling half-bottles. And while a handful, such as Valvona & Crolla in Edinburgh, sell exclusively retail, others, including the Australian Wine Club, sell by mail order only.

Between the two, many independents rely on mixing retail sales with mail order, selling to restaurants and hotels, perhaps even with a fine-wine or broking agency attached. Increasingly, they'll get involved at the sharp end, cutting out the middleman and becoming importers themselves. With first-hand knowledge of the product, they can often give customers the advantage of a better deal and better service.

The growth of mail order

Retail outlets can be shop windows for wine lists, but despite the continued existence of the likes of Eldridge Pope, with a dozen retail outlets dotted about the West Country, mail order is an expanding area for a number of independent wine merchants. East Anglia's Thomas Peatling, for instance, which sold most of its shops to Victoria Wine this year in order to concentrate on its mail-order side, Peatlings Direct.

The importance of mail order is reflected in an increasing interest from supermarkets in this aspect of the independents' business. Electronic data-gathering, with systems such as Epos, allows them to target wine customers according to their preferences and spending power. Waitrose has turned its acquisition of the merchant Findlater, Mackie, Todd into a growing mail-order business; Tesco is threatening to make its entire range of 800-plus wines available to its customers; while Sainsbury's and Marks & Spencer have dipped their toes into the mail-order water, too.

The threat of the supermarkets

'There are so many out-of-town shopping malls ringing the city that the supermarkets are really squeezing the independents in Edinburgh,' says Philip Contini of Valvona & Crolla. Over and above supermarket saturation, the independents are also having to cope with the improved wine ranges in the high street. According to Master of Wine David Gleave of Enotria Winecellars: 'It's becoming more and more difficult for the independents, given what the supermarkets and high-street chains are offering.'

But supermarkets have helped to make wine drinking popular. And when neophyte drinkers' palates mature, the independent wine merchants are there to supplement their everyday drinking with something special. For some merchants too, such as Bibendum and Enotria Winecellars, supplying supermarkets and high-street chains is part and parcel of the business.

Service with a smile

Whether the merchant is in the traditional or modern camp, personal service and good relationships with customers set the independents apart. There may be in-store advisers in some of the bigger supermarkets, and some, such as Sainsbury's, are committed to upping the service element. But trained staff and even informative back labels are no substitute for the personal touch.

With a much wider selection than the supermarkets, the likes of Oddbins, Bottoms Up, Victoria Wine Cellars and Greenalls Wine Cellars can rival the independents in some areas, but levels of service are still not comparable. The successful independent is better at personal service because it has to be.

Customers are no longer prepared to put up with the out-to-a-long-lunch attitude of yesteryear. Increasingly, the wine merchant's bank balance depends on dispensing expertise and common-sense advice in a friendly manner, about what to drink with what, or the optimum moment for opening a particular wine.

The booze cruise

The independents are mixed in their views about the threat of the cross-Channel booze cruisers and bootlegging. Richard Tanner, chairman of the ultra-respectable Midlands firm of Tanners, was aghast to find himself at a party given by one of his customers during the year in which he was casually informed that the booze on offer came, not from him, but from a bootlegger.

According to Alistair Marshall of Adnams, 'The independents are suffering

Independent Wine Merchants

from cross-Channel shopping, but although we're seeing more black-market stuff about, nothing's being done and it's growing.' Possibly, but Bibendum, among others, reports that there's little overlap between its type of business and the plonk that most people bring back from the cross-Channel ports.

The *en primeur* game

Offering a new vintage before it's been bottled, known as *en primeur*, became a staple of independent business in the 1980s. Starved of good harvests in the classic regions of France until this year, the independents have at last had something to get excited about with the 1995 vintage in France.

Hype apart, 1995 Bordeaux *en primeur* offers from independent wine merchants were more voluminous than they've been since the great 1990 vintage. Even Christie's, the upper-crust St James's auctioneer, got its lily-white hands grubby by offering Bordeaux *en primeur* for the first time.

Burgundy, too, had an excellent vintage in 1995, and while you won't see huge quantities of premier cru Vosne-Romanée or Chassagne-Montrachet in the high street, look out for the fruits of what could be a thrilling vintage offered by independent wine merchants in the early half of 1997.

And with the millennium rapidly approaching, there will be a number of interesting deals on vintage Champagnes, especially the excellent 1990 vintage, disgorged just in time for the party. Let's hope there are as many independents around then as there are today to help fuel the celebrations.

Adnams

Address: The Crown, High Street, Southwold, Suffolk IP18 6DP

Telephone/fax: 01502 727220 (general enquiries); 01502 727222 (mail order); 01502 727223

Number of branches: 3

Opening hours: Southwold Wine Shop: 10.00am to 7.30pm Monday to Saturday; Norwich Grapevine: 9.00am to 9.00pm Monday to Saturday; Cellar and Kitchen Store, 10.00am to 6.30pm Monday to Saturday; mail order: 9.00am to 5.00pm Monday to Friday, and 9.00am to 12.00am Saturday

Credit cards accepted: All but American Express

Discounts: 5 per cent on orders of six cases or more

Facilities and services: Advice; cellarage; gift packs; wine search (for wines not on list); corporate supply; wine list compilation; lectures and tutored tastings

Mail order: Free delivery to any mainland UK address on any order over £100, or for two cases or more

Area(s) of specialisation: 'Everything,' according to Adnams, but especially good, we reckon, in Spain, Italy, France, Germany and Australia.

From a small, painterly outpost on the Suffolk coast, Adnams sets out to colonise the world afresh each year, dispatching employees to every corner of the vinous globe, camera and pen in hand. The result is one of the most individual lists in the country, guided and prodded by the controlling talent of the ear-ringed chairman of the board, Simon Loftus.

The key words here are quirkiness and enthusiasm. There are times when you might not like an Adnams' selection, but it's hard to fault the passion behind its inclusion in the range. Adnams' buying staff are pioneers, not content with picking me-too brands and safe choices. They like to venture to off-the-map places in regions such as Galicia and southern Italy, returning with hand-selected gems from new producers. We, and their customers, are glad they do.

Adnams is the place for the mail-order wine lover with a taste for the exotic. It is also to be praised for its willingness to champion unfashionable grapes, such as Riesling, for peculiar wine styles, for its breathless regular offers and, most of all, for its list, which we rate as the best illustrated and most informative in the country. Oh, and its beers aren't bad, either.

White

£3–5

CHILE

1995 Libertador Chardonnay, Curicó, Mitjans 15/20
Off-dry 💰💰💰 ▮

The Libertador in question is not Adnams' chairman Simon Loftus, but the amusingly named Chilean national hero, Bernardo O'Higgins. And the wine behind the label is none other than a Valdivieso Chardonnay, showing sweetish, spicy citrus-fruit flavours and a stylish sheen of oak.

ITALY

Bianco di Kuddia, Zibibbo Secco, Enopolio di Pantelleria 15/20
Dry 💰💰 ▮

Dry, warm-climate, baked-apple and stem-ginger-like Muscat with idiosyncratic flavours and orange-peel zest. A typically off-the-wall Adnams' selection.

SPAIN

Basa, Rueda 15/20
Dry 💰💰 ▮

Clean, well-made, grapefruit tangy Rueda blend of Verdejo with a little Viura and Sauvignon for added interest, made to Adnams' specifications by Telmo Rodriguez of Rioja's Remelluri estate.

£5–8

AUSTRALIA

1995 Canoe Tree Colombard/Chardonnay, Murray Valley 15/20
Dry 💰💰 ▮

Ripe, honeyed, but refreshing Murray Valley blend of Colombard and Chardonnay with the acidity of the Colombard grape slicing like a sharp penknife through the peachiness of the Chardonnay.

FRANCE

1994 Domaine de Bosc, Muscat Sec Perlé, Vin de Pays d'Oc
15/20

Dry 👜👜 🍶

Naturally vivacious, floral, perfumed dry Muscat from Pierre Bésinet, with a hint of bitterness derived, we reckon, from an overnight maceration on the grape skins.

1994 Château Le Chec, Graves
16/20

Dry 👜👜👜 🍶

A stylish, oak-fermented, well-priced white Graves from Christian and Sylvie Auney, with beeswax notes and fresh, herby Semillon flavours to complement the spicy oak.

1994 Château Sainte Estève d'Uchaux, Côtes du Rhône, Gérard et Marc Français
16/20

Dry 👜👜👜 🍶

Beeswax and aniseed aromas and ripe herb and fresh pear flavours make this grower's white one of the best Côtes du Rhône *blancs* we've had at the price this year.

GERMANY

1995 Domdechant Werner Hochheimer Kirchenstuck Riesling, Rheingau
17/20

Medium dry 👜👜👜 ➤

From the eastern end of the Rheingau, Franz Werner's soft, ripe, extremely stylish Riesling is delicately infused with flavours of ripe apricot and tangy grapefruit. A bargain at under £8.

SPAIN

1995 Abadia Da Cova, Ribera Sacra, Albarinho
17/20

Bone dry 👜👜👜 ➤

From a vineyard situated on the slopes above the River Miño, this is a peach and ripe pear-like, unoaked Galician white, with superb concentration and fresh acidity. A good-value introduction to one of Spain's most sought-after wine styles.

Over £8

FRANCE

1992 Domaine du Closel, Savennières, Clos du Papillon, Madame de Jessey   16/20
Bone dry 🪙🪙 ▮
For aficionados of the weird and wonderful, this dry, baked-apple and honey-like Chenin Blanc is a stylish, characterful, if rather austere treat. Concentrated stuff, which, believe it or not, is good value for a Savennières, at just over £8.50.

1992 Vouvray Sec, Domaine des Aubuisières, Cuvée Victor
                                                              16/20
Dry 🪙🪙 ▮
Another Loire Chenin Blanc from the 1992 vintage, showing greater opulence and honeyed weight, this excellent dry Vouvray from grower Bernard Fouquet is a classic introduction to the Loire's most interesting white grape.

Red

£3–5

FRANCE

1994 Domaine Michel, Vin de Pays de Vaucluse   14/20
Medium-bodied 🪙 ▮
Basic, plum and raspberry fruity southern Rhône red with juicy flavours and rasping tannins and acidity.

PORTUGAL

Piornos, Cova da Beira, Vinho de Mesa Tinto   15/20
Medium-bodied 🪙🪙🪙 ▮
A chunky, sagey Portuguese co-operative blend of Rufete, Jaen and Bastardo, with sweet, wild blackberry fruitiness and a hint of Iberian spice. Light, refreshing, good-value Portuguese quaffer at under £4.

SPAIN

1995 Baso Garnacha, Navarra   13/20
Medium-bodied 🍾
Raspberry and plum-jam-like, unoaked Navarra Garnacha from Telmo
Rodriguez, with coarse, drying tannins on the aftertaste.

1994 Lar de Barros, Extremadura, Vino de la Tierra   14/20
Full-bodied 💰 🍾
Farmyardy, extracted, unoaked Tempranillo from Spain's western border with
Portugal, showing drying rustic tannins and fungal notes.

£5–8

CHILE

1994 Libertador Cabernet/Merlot   15/20
Medium-bodied 🍾🍾💰 ➖
Ripe cassis-fruity Lontue Valley blend of Cabernet Sauvignon and Merlot from
the Valdivieso winery, with sweet chocolatey oak and supple tannins. Still
youthful, but extremely drinkable now.

FRANCE

1995 Château du Grand Moulas, Côtes du Rhône   16/20
Full-bodied 🍾🍾🍾 ➖
Consistently among the best Côtes du Rhône producers, Mark Ryckwaert
makes excellent-value, spicily rich reds, blending mainly Grenache with 20 per
cent Syrah to superb effect. This example from the extremely promising 1995
vintage is still vigorously youthful and packed with blackberry fruit
concentration. A super winter warmer.

1994 Carignanissime, Minervois   15/20
Full-bodied 💰 🍾
From Patricia and Daniel Domergue, this old-vine Carignan (there's not much
recently planted Carignan around) is redolent of pot-pourri and herbs, with
sweet, unfiltered, blackberry fruit flavours and muscular Mediterranean tannins.

ITALY

1995 Villa Dorata, Eloro Rosso   16/20
Full-bodied 🍷🍷🍷 ▄▬
Made in Sicily at a small co-operative near the ruins of Syracuse, entirely from the Nero d'Avola grape, this is a thirst-quenching angostura bitters-scented and damson fruity red with considerable gluggability.

1993 Rosso Conero, Fattoria Le Terrazze   15/20
Full-bodied 🍷🍷 ▮
From Italy's Marche region, this is a smoothly textured, blackberry fruity red with vibrant acidity and pleasantly robust tannins. Not particularly complex, but packs a considerably fruity punch.

1992 Primitivo di Manduria Rosso   15/20
Full-bodied 🍷🍷 ▮
Made from Puglia's Primitivo grape, which may or may not be connected to California's Zinfandel (answers on a postcard to Simon Loftus), this is a cooked, hefty, alcoholic red with enough blackberry jam sweetness and character to make it a thought-provoking buy at just under £6.

Over £8

AUSTRALIA

1994 Tim Gramp McLaren Vale Grenache   16/20
Full-bodied 🍷🍷 ▄▬
Chunky, sweetly oaked, robustly alcoholic McLaren Vale Grenache with mint and black fruit flavours and excellent, old-vine concentration. An Australian challenge to Châteauneuf-du-Pape.

FRANCE

1993 Givry Premier Cru, Les Grands Pretans, Xavier Besson
16/20

Medium-bodied 🍷🍷 ▄▬
Modern-style Côte Chalonnaise red Burgundy, with lots of colour, spicy new oak and well-structured raspberry fruit complexity. Good value for under £10.

Rosé

£3–5

FRANCE

1995 Rosé de Saignée, Domaine des Terres Noires, Vin de Pays de l'Hérault   14/20
Dry 🌢🌢 ▯
Decent, fruity southern French rosé made using the *saignée* method (running off the juice after a short contact with the skins), with soft, rosehip and raspberry fruit flavours and a pleasingly dry finish.

Australian Wine Club

Address: 21a Southlea Road, Datchet, Slough SL3 9BX

Telephone/fax: 01853 594 924l; 01753 591 369 (Freephone order line: 0800 716 893)

Number of branches: Mail-order only

Opening hours: 9.00am to 6.00pm Monday to Friday; 9.00am to 2.00pm Sunday

Credit cards accepted: Access, Visa, American Express

Discounts: To Wine Plan subscribers

Facilities and services: 'None spring to mind,' apparently, but we're rather fond of Roy, the delivery man; one major consumer tasting each year in central London

Mail order: Free delivery to any mainland UK address; minimum purchase 12 bottles – may be mixed or unmixed

Area of specialisation: Australia

The move a year ago from a dingy basement under the Strand to the Datchet hydrangea belt has allowed the unruly trio of Craig Smith, Mark Manson and Master of Wine Phil Reedman to concentrate on what they do best: sell large quantities of Australian wine from good to very good estates, such as St Hallett, Tim Adams, Heritage, Veritas, Willows, Primo Estate and Chapel Hill. Strand regulars may bemoan the loss of a great place to drink the occasional Coopers' Ale, but Smith and his cohorts claim to be a lot happier in the country, thank you.

The prices are not always the cheapest, but the level of service and the down-the-telephone banter are excellent. Mail-order customers are kept in thrall via monthly newsletters and irreverent, punchy tasting notes. This is often the best (and first) place to snap up new releases of hard-to-find wines like St Hallett Old Block and Tim Adams The Fergus. The AWC also sells quite a bit of wine to Tesco and Thresher – both of which provide the chance to buy individual bottles before you commit yourself to a case purchase (and the obligatory insults) from Datchet.

The only snag, as far as we're concerned, is that close relations with a regular line-up of producers mean that the AWC seems on occasions to buy wines irrespective of local vintage conditions. Otherwise, this is the best place to buy mail-order Aussie wines in Britain, with a relaxed, but highly professional, approach to the subject.

White

£5–8

AUSTRALIA

1996 St Hallett Poachers Blend   14/20
Off-dry 🍷 ▌
Clean, cool-fermented, pear-drop fruity Barossa white, with a touch of melon-like sweetness and an acid-drop tang.

1996 Primo Estate Colombard   15/20
Dry 🍷🍷 ▌
From Joe Grilli's little Italian corner of the Adelaide plains, this is an unoaked, appealingly drinkable, grapefruity white made from the Colombard grape, with good concentration and lemony acidity. Like a Gascon white on steroids.

1994 Buckley's Semillon   16/20
Dry 🍷🍷🍷 ▌
Blended for the Australian Wine Club's reliable Buckley's label, this is a weighty, rich and smoky Barossa Semillon with broad, honey and ice cream-soda characters and excellent concentration.

1995 St Hallett Chardonnay   16/20
Dry 🍷🍷 ▌
Made by Neil Dodderidge, formerly of Mountadam, the 1995 represents a change in style for St Hallett's Chardonnay. French oak fermentation and restrained stone fruit characters have resulted in an elegant Chardonnay for Barossa Valley. A promising new departure.

1996 Allandale Chardonnay, Hunter River   15/20
Dry 🍾🍾 ▯

A step up from the rather charry-oaky 1994, this is a spicy, melon-like Hunter Valley Chardonnay with sweet vanilla French and American oak characters and warming alcohol.

1995 Tim Adams Riesling   16/20
Dry 🍾🍾 ➖

From the small 1995 Clare Valley vintage, this is a restrained lime fruity Riesling from Tim 'Bonecrusher' Adams, which doesn't quite have the excitement and fruit concentration of the 1994, but should develop interesting nut and kerosene notes in bottle.

1994 Primo Estate Botrytis Riesling, Eden Valley, half-bottle
                                                           15/20

Very sweet 🍾 ▯

Botrytis-inoculated Eden Valley Riesling made by Joe Grilli, with lusciously ripe lemon and lime fruit flavour and honeyed sweetness. Flavoursome, if lacking complexity.

Over £8

AUSTRALIA

1995 Petaluma Riesling, Clare Valley   17/20
Dry 🍾🍾🍾 ➖

From the same Clare Valley region as the Tim Adams Riesling, Brian Croser's lime-zesty version is a richly concentrated and typically elegant white, which will age for at least five years in bottle.

1995 Tim Adams Semillon, Clare Valley   15/20
Dry 🍾 ▯

Not as stunning as the super-concentrated 1994, but this smoky, lemon-zesty white still has the hallmarks of a good Clare Valley Semillon.

1993 Ashton Hills Chardonnay, Adelaide Hills   17/20
Dry 🍾🍾🍾 ▯

From Stephen George's cool-climate vineyards near Adelaide Hill's Mount Lofty, this is an intense toffee-fudge and citrus fruit-style Chardonnay with hand-crafted complexity and deftly handled oak. Thrilling stuff.

1993 Wignalls Chardonnay   15/20
Dry 🍷 ▮

A golden-coloured, ripely textured Chardonnay from Albany in Australia's cool-climate south-western corner, with a thick coating of oak and a surprisingly hefty whack of alcohol. A little clumsy by winemaker John Wade's normally exalted standards.

Red

£5–8

AUSTRALIA

1995 Buckley's Clare Valley Malbec   15/20
Medium-bodied 🍷 ▮

Sage and mint aromas and sweet, spicy damson and licorice fruitiness are let down by a rather light, hollow middle.

1994 St Hallett Cabernet/Merlot, Barossa Valley   15/20
Medium-bodied 🍷 ▮

Winemaker Stuart Blackwell has dropped Cabernet Franc from his Bordeaux blend for the 1994 vintage. Otherwise this is a chip off the St Hallett block, with soft, red-berry fruitiness, fine-grained tannins, sweet oak and a lightish finish.

1993 David Traeger Shiraz, Victoria   15/20
Medium-bodied 🍷 ▮

A peppery, refreshing, medium-bodied Victorian Shiraz from David Traeger's vineyards in the Goulburn Valley. A lot of oak for the weight of fruit.

1995 RBJ Theologicum Mourvèdre/Grenache, Barossa Valley 14/20
Full-bodied 🍷 ▮

Alcoholic, raspberry fruity, southern Rhône-style blend, which is light on fruit for a wine with 14 per cent alcohol. Not the Holy Grail.

1995 Blaxland Mourvèdre/Grenache   15/20
Full-bodied 👜👜 |
Made from the same two Barossa Valley grapes, this throat-warming, robustly
fruity blend is a bit more like it, with masses of pepper and blackberry fruit, and
tarry oak and tannins. Strapping stuff.

Over £8

AUSTRALIA

1994 Chapel Hill McLaren Vale Shiraz   17/20
Full-bodied 👜👜👜 ■-
Made by Pam Dunsford, one of McLaren Vale's leading figures, this is an
extremely flavoursome, peppery Shiraz matured in spicy, coffee-bean American
oak with smooth, fine-grained tannins. A classy drop from a winery whose
wines get better with every vintage.

1993 Chapel Hill McLaren Vale/Coonawarra Cabernet Sauvignon
17/20

Full-bodied 👜👜👜 ■-
A blend of mainly McLaren Vale with 30 per cent Coonawarra grapes from
Pam Dunsford, this is an elegant, vanilla oaky Cabernet, which neatly combines
the blackcurranty intensity of Coonawarra with the smoothness of McLaren
Vale fruit.

1994 Primo Estate, Joseph Cabernet Sauvignon/Merlot, Moda
Amarone   17/20
Full-bodied 👜👜👜 ■-
Made by the sports-car driving Joe Grilli, this is an extremely rich, concentrated,
vanilla oaky red from the Adelaide Plains, made from 80 per cent Cabernet
Sauvignon and 20 per cent Merlot, adopting the Italian method of drying the
grapes to concentrate fruit sugar, flavour and acidity. Australia's answer to
Amarone della Valpolicella.

1994 Bowen Estate Coonawarra Cabernet Sauvignon/Merlot/
Cabernet Franc   15/20
Medium-bodied 👜 |
Less alcoholic than the 1993, this Coonawarra Bordeaux-style blend from
Doug and Joy Bowen is minty and blackcurranty, if slightly sharp on the finish.

1994 Bowen Estate Coonawarra Shiraz   16/20
Full-bodied 👛👛 ▬
Densely coloured, milled pepper-scented Coonawarra Shiraz from growers Doug and Joy Bowen, with the cool-climate elegance we expect from a Coonawarra red. Needs time to develop complexity in the bottle.

1995 Allandale Hunter River Valley, Matthew Shiraz   14/20
Full-bodied 👛 🍾
Sweet, spicy, mulberry fruit aromas are the best feature of this youthful Hunter Valley Shiraz, but we found the acidification a little clumsy and the tannins rather astringent.

1993 St Hallett Old Block Shiraz   16/20
Full-bodied 👛👛 ▬
An Australian red which (just about) deserves its cult status for its surprisingly elegant balance and fruit richness. Spicy American oak and blackberry and raspberry fruit concentration with supple, fine-textured tannins, which will age well over the next five years.

1995 Tim Adams The Fergus   17/20
Full-bodied 👛👛 ▬
Made predominantly from Grenache with small amounts of Cabernet Franc, Shiraz and Malbec, this is a ginger and pepper-spicy Clare Valley blend with masses of powerful alcohol and raspberry, plum and damson fruit. The best red wine we've had yet from Tim Adams.

Sparkling

£5–8

AUSTRALIA

Tim Adams Sheoaks Brut NV   14/20
Dry 👛 🍾
Soft, toasty, large-bubbled Clare Valley fizz from Tim Adams, with coarse buttery flavours cut by lemon-zest acidity. Rather pointless.

Avery's

Address: Orchard House, Southfield Road, Nailsea, Bristol BS19 1JD

Telephone/fax: 01275 811100; fax 01275 811101

Number of branches: 2

Opening hours: 10am to 7 pm Monday to Saturday

Credit cards accepted: Visa, Master Card

Discounts: By negotiation on special orders

Facilities and services: Glass hire; tutored tastings; group tastings; delivery; storage of customers' reserves; sale of customers' reserves at auction; newsletters and *en primeur* offers; in-store tastings in Culver Street Wine Cellars, Bristol; monthly newsletters and special offers; quarterly 'Automatically from Avery's' mixed cases of wine; the Avery's Bin Club

Mail order: Free delivery free to any mainland UK address for two cases or more; otherwise, £5.50 per consignment

Area(s) of specialisation: Burgundy, Bordeaux, the New World, Port

With a broad selection from its 1,000-strong list, Avery's new Culver Street Wine Cellars have been 'a great success', reports Master of Wine John Avery in the Bristol-based company's 1996 wine list. The new premises are the first stage in a major programme of modernisation for one of the country's most traditional merchants, which made its name from nearly two centuries of bottling claret and Burgundy in its Bristol cellars.

The lower level of cellars has been opened for parties and corporate events and the retail site at 7 Park Street shifted to No. 8 opposite, allowing more space to display wines for customers who want to buy by the bottle. Relocating the offices and warehouse to Nailsea, meanwhile, has resulted in the more effective management of stock and the ability to store customers' reserves in a temperature-controlled warehouse. A priority for 1996, says John Avery, is to speed up delivery, not just to Bristolians but nationwide.

Thanks to John Avery's pioneering interest in the New World, the company has brought Tyrrells of Australia, Nobilo of New Zealand, Norton of Argentina and Klein Constantia of South Africa to its customers, along with Swanson, Sonoma-Cutrer and Far Niente of California, Inniskillin of Canada, and Echeverria of Chile. The addition of Somontano's smart Enate wines has brought some much-needed *pzazz* to the Spanish range, although the Bordeaux and Burgundy sections still have a resolutely old-fashioned air.

As we mentioned last year, Avery's cosy relationship with some of its suppliers occasionally leads to what looks like buying on auto-pilot. We're still not convinced by South Africa's Rustenberg or Remoissenet in Burgundy. On the other hand, the acquisition of Enate and the improvements at Undurraga in Chile, along with a shower of newsletters and regular offers, augur well for an increasingly dynamic future for Avery's.

White

£3–5

NEW ZEALAND

1995 Nobilo White Cloud   14/20
Off-dry 👛👛 🍾
A Kiwi white that never lets you down. This zesty, off-dry blend of Müller-Thurgau with a dollop of Sauvignon Blanc for aromatic freshness is a good introduction to New Zealand wine.

£5–8

AUSTRALIA

1995 Opal Ridge Unoaked Chardonnay, South Australia
                                                           14/20

Off-dry 👛 🍾
Tropical fruity, unoaked Murray River Valley Chardonnay, aptly named for its opulently sweetish Opal Fruits characters.

CANADA

1994 Inniskillin Chardonnay, Niagara   15/20
Dry 🍾 ▮

From one of the few decent wineries in Canada, this is a lemony fresh, if rather lean, almost Chablis-like Niagara Peninsula Chardonnay aged in French oak, with tongue-tingling spritz.

CHILE

1995 Echeverria Chardonnay Reserva   15/20
Dry 🍾🍾 ▮

Made by former World Bank economist-turned-winemaker Roberto Echeverria, this is an elegant, concentrated, delicately oaked Chilean Chardonnay with fresh, lightly buttered fruitiness and a citrusy tang.

FRANCE

1994 Domaine de Perches, Mauzac, Vin de Pays des Côtes du Tarn   15/20
Dry 🍾🍾 ▮

From English growers Nicholas and Charlotte Fraser, this is a richly fruity Gaillac white made from the local Mauzac grape, with flavours of ripe pear and refreshing acidity. An extra year in bottle has allowed the wine's flavours to develop.

1994 Avery's Fine White Burgundy, Mâcon Péronne, Cave de Lugny   13/20
Dry ▮

After dumping on Avery's Fine White Burgundy last year, we hoped to see an improvement from the 1994 vintage, but the winemaking is as old-fashioned as ever. Gluey tartness and a bitter apple-core finish. 'Fine' is a considerable overstatement.

NEW ZEALAND

1995 Nobilo Poverty Bay Chardonnay   15/20
Dry 🍾🍾 ▮

If you've ever taken a BA flight, you may have met this highly commercial, flavoursome North Island white in a quarter-bottle. It's sweet and spicily oaked, with cool-climate melon and citrus fruit characters. Beam us up!

1994 Nobilo Gisborne Chardonnay   16/20
Dry 🍷🍷🍷 |

Still in New Zealand's North Island, but this time with the 1994 vintage, this is a buttery, sweetly oaked Chardonnay with nutmeg spice, grapefruity acidity and an extra dimension of flavour.

SPAIN

1995 Enate Blanco, Somontano   14/20
Dry 🍷 |

From the ultra-modern Enate winery, this is a stainless-steel blend of 60 per cent Chardonnay and 40 per cent Macabeo, made by Jesus Artajona. A fresh, appley, slightly neutral white with lively acidity, at just over £5.

Over £8

FRANCE

1995 Sancerre Domaine de la Moussière, Alphonse Mellot
                                                            15/20
Dry 🍷 |

From the eccentric Alphonse Mellot, who also owns one of the best restaurants in the village of Sancerre, this is a well-made, minerally Sauvignon Blanc with fresh acidity. We think it lacks a third dimension, however.

1992 Givry Blanc, Domaine Thénard, Remoissenet   16/20
Dry 🍷🍷 |

Made at a leading Côte Chalonnaise estate by Avery's long-term white Burgundy supplier, Remoissenet, this is a fogey-friendly, old-fashioned Chardonnay with crisp acidity and concentrated, honeyed, nutty weight.

SOUTH AFRICA

1995 Hamilton Russell Chardonnay, Walker Bay   16/20
Dry 🍷🍷 ▭

Consistently among South Africa's best Chardonnays, this cool-climate, barrel-fermented white is a rich, butterscotchy, cinnamon-spicy number with perfectly poised acidity.

SPAIN

1994 Enate Chardonnay, Barrel-Fermented, Somontano   16/20
Dry 👜👜 ⧉

Vying with Torres' Milmanda for the title of Spain's best Chardonnay, this is a complex, barrel-fermented Somontano white with an amusing, childish scrawl of a label. It's an elegant, crafted style, which uses barrel-fermentation, cinnamon oak and contact with the wine's fermentation lees to extract every ounce of complexity from the Chardonnay grape.

UNITED STATES

1993 Clos du Val Chardonnay, Carneros, Napa Valley   17/20
Dry 👜👜👜 ⧉

Made by long-term California resident, Frenchman Bernard Portet, this is a stylish, nicely balanced Chardonnay from the Carneros region, which borders San Francisco's San Pablo Bay. A full-bodied, well-crafted Chardonnay with buttery, leesy richness and fresh cool-climate intensity.

Red

£3–5

CHILE

1995 Undurraga Merlot   15/20
Medium-bodied 👜👜 ⧉

From a winery that's made enormous strides in the last two vintages, this is a good, juicy, green-pepper-style Colchagua Valley Merlot, made with the fruit-conscious British palate in mind.

£5–8

AUSTRALIA

1993 Opal Ridge Cabernet/Shiraz, South Australia   14/20
Medium-bodied 💰 ▯

Minty, smooth, faintly tobaccoey Aussie blend of Cabernet Sauvignon and Shiraz, which is drinkable enough, but ought to be £1 cheaper.

SOUTH AFRICA

1990 Klein Constantia Cabernet Sauvignon   15/20
Full-bodied 💰💰 ▯

From the cool Constantia hills behind Cape Town, this French oak-aged Cabernet Sauvignon has more elegance and cassis fruit intensity than many Cape reds, but we feel the oak is starting to desiccate the wine. So drink soon.

1990 Klein Constantia Marlbrook   16/20
Full-bodied 💰💰 ▯

From the same estate in the same vintage, this is a richer, riper, better-balanced red with plum and blackcurrant fruit characters, but still firmly structured, oaky tannins.

SPAIN

1994 Enate Tinto   14/20
Medium-bodied 💰 ▯

A blend of Moristell and Tempranillo from the cool-climate region of Somontano, this is a simple cherry fruity red with a touch of oak, but no great depth.

1993 Enate Tempranillo Cabernet Sauvignon, Crianza   15/20
Medium-bodied 💰 ▯

A Navarra-pioneered blend of Tempranillo and Cabernet Sauvignon, which has been adopted by neighbouring Somontano's Enate to good effect, this is dry and on the chewy side with pronounced oak flavours, but the underlying blackcurrant fruit quality is good.

Over £8

UNITED STATES

1992 Clos du Val Cabernet Sauvignon, Napa Valley   17/20
Full-bodied 🍷 ➖
Frenchman Bernard Portet, whose family hails from Bordeaux, is at his confident best working with Cabernet Sauvignon. This silky, but structured, age-worthy California red has superb cassis and cedary oak characters, and will benefit from another five to ten years in bottle.

1993 Swanson Napa Valley Merlot   16/20
Full-bodied 🍷 ➖
Merlot is California's hottest red grape – to use the California parlance – at the moment, which may explain the ambitious £15 price tag here. The wine is youthful, oaky, black-cherry spicy and concentrated, but a shade on the dry and extracted side.

Sparkling

Over £8

FRANCE

Avery's Special Cuvée Champagne   14/20
Dry 🍷 ❘
Youthful, sharpish, appley fizz with insufficient bottle development for our taste. Tuck away for a year at least for the fruit to round out.

Fortified

£5–8

UNITED STATES

Essencia Orange Muscat, Quady   13/20
Very sweet 🍾

From dessert-wine nut, Andrew Quady, this candied orange-peel-style sticky is California's rather overpriced answer to Moscatel de Valencia. One for lovers of trifle.

Bibendum

Address: 113 Regent's Park Road, London NW1 8UR

Telephone/fax: 0171 722 5577; 0171 722 7354

Number of branches: 1

Opening hours: 10.00am to 6.30pm Monday to Thursday; 10.00am to 6.30pm Friday; 9.30am to 5.00pm Saturday

Credit cards accepted: Visa, Switch, Master Card, American Express

Discounts: Not available

Facilities and services: Comprehensive party service; cellaring service; fine wine desk; gift service; corporate service; regular in-store tastings, both tutored and untutored

Mail order: Free delivery to any mainland English and Welsh address (minimum order one case); for London addresses, delivery within 24 hours; for all other addresses within mainland England and Wales, delivery usually within three days; delivery service to other parts of the UK also available on request

Area(s) of specialisation: A good generalist, with particular strengths in Italy, France, Australia, South Africa and South America; also good on fine wines

It's hard to visit a wine region these days without bumping into Simon 'Air Miles' Farr. The bespectacled taster seems to spend half his year charging between the two hemispheres – blending a wine here, advising a producer there and unearthing new goodies for Bibendum's busy collage of a list.

Farr also finds time to run one of the busiest events' calendars in the wine trade. The Primrose Hill merchant's tutored tastings, chaired by Farr and sidekick Willie Lebus, are some of the best in the capital, and its annual Bordeaux and Burgundy *en primeur* evenings are an enjoyable scrum of fine wine and North London gossip.

Bibendum is the epitome of a modern wine merchant, despite a young fogeyish veneer. It sells large quantities of wine to high-street chains and supermarkets and acts as a front-line agent for producers in Europe and the New World, steering them towards more modern, consumer-friendly styles. It may not have the quirkiness of an Adnams, or the strength in depth of a Lay & Wheeler, but, in a little over a decade, it's established itself as one of the liveliest, most open-minded wine merchants in the land.

White

£5–8

AUSTRALIA

1995 Deakin Estate, Alfred Chardonnay   14/20
Dry 🌢 ▯
Smoky, bacon-rind oak and melon and pineapple fruit are the dominant flavours in this Chardonnay from Mildura's Wingara group. The oak gives the wine a faintly bitter twist.

FRANCE

1995 La Serre Chardonnay, Vin de Pays d'Oc   15/20
Dry 🌢🌢🌢 ▯
Blended with Val d'Orbieu by Bibendum buyer and world traveller extraordinaire Simon Farr, this is an elegant, melony, full-flavoured Languedoc Chardonnay with a delicate brushstroke of oak.

1995 Domaine du Colombier, Crozes-Hermitage Blanc
16/20
Dry 🌢🌢 ▭▬
Modern, mealy, barrel-matured northern Rhône white with minerally fruit richness, vanilla oak and alcohol sweetness.

ITALY

1995 Verdicchio dei Castelli di Jesi Classico, M. & G. Brunori
16/20
Bone dry 🌢🌢🌢 ▯
White-pepper-scented, flavoursome Verdicchio with a crisp bite of lime citrus fruitiness, a zesty prickle of gas and excellent length of flavour.

NEW ZEALAND

1995 Lawson's Dry Hills Gewürztraminer, Marlborough   17/20
Dry 🍷🍷🍷 ▮
Rich and concentrated, especially for a wine from the generally mediocre 1995 in New Zealand, this deep straw-hued Alsace taste-alike from Claire Allen is packed with honey and rose-petal characters and a pleasingly dry finish.

SOUTH AFRICA

1995 Tharakkoma Colombard, Olifants River   15/20
Dry 🍷🍷🍷 ▮
Ripe weighty, warm-climate Colombard from the Olifants River region, with fresh pear flavours and lively acidity. Reassuringly free of boiled-sweets characters.

Over £8

FRANCE

1995 Sancerre, Le Manoir, Vieilles Vignes, André Neveu   17/20
Dry 🍷🍷 ▮
Super-ripe, honeyed Sancerre with old-vine concentration and refreshing acidity. Its idiosyncratic character might surprise Sancerre purists, but this is a weighty, flavoursome and unusual Loire Sauvignon.

1994 Puligny-Montrachet, Jean-Marc Boillot   17/20
Dry 🍷 ➡
Powerful, sweet oak-dominated village Puligny from Pommard-based grower, Jean-Marc Boillot, with forward, honeyed richness and a firm backbone of acidity. Pricey at nearly £30.

1994 Chablis Premier Cru, Mont de Milieu, Louis Pinson   18/20
Bone dry 🍷🍷🍷 ➡
Traditional, but beautifully defined *premier cru* Chablis from grower Louis Pinson, with minerally intensity of flavour, creamy texture and firm acidity. A bargain at £11.

ITALY

1994 Tocai Colli Orientali del Friuli, Marina Danielli   16/20
Dry 🏺🏺 ▮

Angelica and marzipan, spicy north-eastern Italian white, with lime and green-apple crispness and masses of weight and character from grower Marina Danielli.

UNITED STATES

1994 Morgan Winery Sauvignon Blanc, Sonoma   17/20
Dry 🏺🏺🏺 ▬

A stylish, Graves-style Sonoma County blend of barrel-fermented Sauvignon Blanc with 14 per cent Semillon, with an exotic guava and grapefruit tang.

Red

£5–8

FRANCE

1992 Château Brandeau, Côtes de Castillon   15/20
Medium-bodied 🏺🏺 ▮

Made by English winemakers Fern King and Andrea Gray, this is an organic, Merlot-based Right Bank claret, with lots of character and substantial weight of fruit for a 1992.

ITALY

1993 La Rosa Bianca Vino di Tavola Rosso, Podere Il Palazzino
15/20

Medium-bodied 🏺🏺 ▮

A soft, easy-drinking, cherryish Tuscan blend, with enough savoury fruit and tannin to make it obviously Italian. A rosa that grows on you. Good value at just over £5.

Over £8

ARGENTINA

1994 Catena Malbec, Mendoza   17/20
Full-bodied 🛍️🛍️🛍️ ▬

Concentrated, mulberry fruity Mendoza Malbec from Nicolas Catena's Esmeralda winery, showing fine-grained, elegant tannins and savoury, herbal flavours with the weight and acidity to age.

FRANCE

1993 Domaine de Font-Sane, Gigondas   17/20
Full-bodied 🛍️🛍️🛍️ ▮

From grower Véronique Peysson, this is a dense, warmly spicy, massively structured, Grenache-based red, which outstrips many a Châteauneuf-du-Pape for sheer power and pizazz. Southern Rhône at its characterful best.

1995 Morgon, Marcel Lapierre   16/20
Medium-bodied 🛍️🛍️ ▬

Made by Marcel Lapierre, a highly individual Morgon grower who uses little or no sulphur in his wines, this is a rich, peppery, intensely fruity, unfiltered Gamay, whose firm structure makes it closer to a top Côtes du Rhône than a Beaujolais. About as good as Beaujolais gets.

1992 Nuits Saint Georges, Jean Chauvenet   17/20
Medium-bodied 🛍️🛍️🛍️ ▮

Characterful, farmyardy red Burgundy from grower Jean Chauvenet, whose wild strawberry fruit and gamey flavours make it a pleasure to drink now and a comparative bargain at under £17. Authentic, concentrated Pinot Noir.

ITALY

1991 Barbera d'Alba Vigna Clara, Eraldo Viberti   16/20
Medium-bodied 🛍️🛍️ ▬

Oaky, structured, black-cherry and plum-skin fruit Piemontese Barbera, made in an Angelo Gaja-influenced new-wave style with vibrant, tongue-tingling acidity.

NEW ZEALAND

1994 Te Kairanga Pinot Noir Reserve   16/20
Medium-bodied

Ripe, mulberry fruity Pinot Noir from North Island's Martinborough region, with plenty of alcohol and sweet, smooth-textured flavours.

SOUTH AFRICA

1994 De Trafford Merlot, Stellenbosch   17/20
Full-bodied

Substantially oaked, concentrated, well-structured Stellenbosch Merlot, with masses of colour, black-cherry and cassis fruit and ripe, silky tannins. The sweet vanilla oak complements the fruit beautifully in this classy Cape red. One of the best reds we've ever tasted from South Africa.

UNITED STATES

1993 Elyse Wine Cellars Zinfandel Morisoli Vineyard, Napa Valley   17/20
Full-bodied

Pepper, crushed raspberry and tobacco-leaf aromas from Elyse's Morioli Vineyard at Rutherford in Napa, with lovely sweet-plum fruitiness and well-judged, sweet American oak to follow.

1994 Acacia Pinot Noir, Carneros   17/20
Medium-bodied

From one of the best recent vintages in Carneros, Pinot Noir buff Larry Brooks has produced a well-structured, elegantly oaked, black-cherry and raspberry fruity red with the backbone to age for another two to five years.

Sparkling

Over £8

FRANCE

Champagne Albert Beerens, Reserve NV   16/20
Dry 🍾🍾🍾 ▯

Good-value, Pinot Noir-fruity Aube-region Champagne with a soft, creamy mousse, plenty of elegant strawberry fruit flavours and good, cleansing acidity.

Fortified

Over £8

PORTUGAL

Niepoort Senior Fine Old Tawny Port   17/20
Full-bodied 🍾🍾🍾 ▬

From Dirk Niepoort's family-owned Port house, this is a fragrant, intensely concentrated, mature, nutty tawny with a sophisticated dry finish and spicy depth.

Bordeaux Direct

Address: New Aquitaine House, Paddock Road, Reading, Berkshire RG4 5JY

Telephone/fax: 0118 9481718; 0118 9471928

Number of branches: 5

Opening hours: 9.00am to 7.00pm Monday to Friday; 9.00am to 5.00pm Saturday; 10.00am to 4.00pm Sunday

Credit cards accepted: Access, Visa, Switch, American Express, Diners Club

Discounts: On all case purchases

Facilities and services: Free glass loan from retail outlets; cellaring service for customers' wines to be introduced in 1997; regular in-store tastings throughout the year, plus bottles always open for tasting; monthly special offers to selected customers

Mail order: Delivery to a single addess at £3.99 per order; delivery lead time up to 21 days

Area(s) of specialisation: Bordeaux, French regional wines

Bordeaux Direct, as its name suggests, started off as a mail order-cum-retail operation in 1969, with particular expertise in the wines of the Gironde. Founder Tony Laithwaite used to source wines himself and ship them home in the back of a van.

Things have changed a bit since then. Bordeaux Direct is now the largest mail-order operation in the country, with sales of over 800,000 cases and a turnover of £40m. It has also cast its gaze beyond Bordeaux, first to other parts of France and more recently to the New World. Bordeaux Direct can take the credit, too, for pioneering the concept of flying winemakers, by introducing Australian oenologists to sleepy southern French co-operatives in the mid-1980s.

Today the list runs to 460 wines, most of them exclusive, and available by the bottle from Bordeaux Direct's five retail shops as well as by the mail-order case. Prices are not always cheap (a *vin de table* at £5.39 a bottle is hardly a snip), but the basic quality of the wines is extremely good. There are also six full-time wine advisers to give advice over the telephone.

The same quality is apparent in the educational literature that Bordeaux Direct consumers receive each month, including information packs and helpful tasting notes. Selling most of its wines direct means that the Reading-based company can choose wines that 'might look a bit weird on the shelf', according to managing director, Greg Hodder, 'but which have a great story behind them. We're selling a bit of theatre.'

White

£5–8

AUSTRALIA

1996 Yarrunga Field Bin 303, Special Reserve, South Eastern Australia   15/20
Dry 👛👛 ▮
Fresh, peachy, cross-regional Australian blend with well-judged vanilla oak character, ripe, richly textured flavours and restrained tropical fruitiness.

FRANCE

1995 Château Haut Reygnac, Entre Deux Mers, Haut Benauge
16/20
Dry 👛👛👛 ▮
Modern, ultra-clean, well-crafted white Bordeaux with ripe pear notes and well-rounded fruitiness. Highly drinkable.

1995 Le Bois de Combelle Chardonnay, Vin de Pays des Coteaux de l'Ardèche   14/20
Dry 👛 ▮
Refreshing, well-made, unoaked Ardèche Chardonnay with cool-fermented fruit character but insufficient depth for a Chardonnay at £6.

1995 Domaine des Cassagnoles, Vin de Pays des Côtes de Gascogne   16/20
Dry 🗤🗤 ▮

Flavoursome, highly aromatic, grapefruit-zest-style Gascon, with crisp, appley freshness and good weight. Much better than bog-standard Vin de Pays des Côtes de Gascogne, but so it should be at over £6.

1995 Laithwaite Semillon, Oak-Aged, Bordeaux   16/20
Dry 🗤🗤🗤 ▮

Named after Bordeaux Direct's founder, Tony Laithwaite, this is a smoky, attractively textured, herbal Semillon with a lemongrass tang from the promising 1995 vintage in Bordeaux.

1995 Domaine des Verchères, Bourgogne   15/20
Dry 🗤🗤 ▮

Highly palatable, modern-style domaine-bottled white Burgundy showing elegant vanilla oak and citrus fruit intensity. A good house-white Burgundy.

UNITED STATES

1995 CK Cellars Chardonnay, Saint Helena, California   16/20
Dry 🗤🗤 ▮

A rich, but well-balanced, California Chardonnay with restrained smoky oak, lemon butter and a hint of tropical fruitiness. This is a lot less gooey than most sub-£10 California Chardonnays.

Over £8

AUSTRALIA

1994 Rovalley Ridge Chardonnay, Bin 102, Barossa Valley   17/20
Dry 🗤🗤🗤 ▮

Come-hither, toffee-fudge aromas and ripe melon fruit flavours are beautifully balanced by excellent, fresh acidity in this full-flavoured, characterful Barossa Valley Chardonnay from Miranda Wines.

FRANCE

1995 Vouvray Réserve, Champalou   17/20
Medium dry 👜👜👜 ☛
From the excellent 1995 vintage, this is a classic demi-sec style of Vouvray, with honey and ripe Cox's apple notes and an elegant bite of refreshing acidity for the perfect balance.

1995 Domaine Emmanuel Dampt, Vieilles Vignes, Chablis   18/20
Bone dry 👜👜👜 ☛
Super-ripe, honeyed, deliciously aromatic Chablis with sumptuous old-vine concentration and a steely backbone of acidity. Super stuff.

Red

£3–5

PORTUGAL

1995 Vega, Vinho de Mesa Tinto   13/20
Full-bodied 🍾
Basic, raisiny Portuguese *tinto* with sweet, jammy fruit and rustic tannins. The only duffer we've tasted from Bordeaux Direct this year.

£5–8

AUSTRALIA

1994 Hamilton Ridge Shiraz, Barossa Valley, Peter Lehmann
16/20

Full-bodied 👜👜👜 ☛
From Peter Lehmann, the man who personifies the heart and soul of the Barossa, this is a pure fruit-steered Shiraz with throat-warming alcohol and essence of blackberry fruitiness and sweet vanilla oak.

CHILE

1995 La Finca Cabernet Sauvignon   15/20
Medium-bodied 🍷 ▮

An ambitious Chilean red from the Colchagua Valley in its first vintage, showing juicy raspberry and blackcurrant fruit characters, some spicy oak and a bite of dry tannin. Interesting, but ought to be £1.50 cheaper.

FRANCE

Pigassou, Vin de Table   15/20
Full-bodied 🍷🍷 ▮

Inky, juicy, smoothly balanced southern French *vin de table* which, despite its humble appellation, is a ladder up from plonk. Concentrated, robust, blackberry fruity red. Shame it's not under £5.

1995 Le XV du Président, Côtes du Roussillon Villages   16/20
Full-bodied 🍷🍷🍷 ▮

A wine that sounds like a Jacques Chirac rugby club *cuvée*, but would be wasted on your average front-row forward, this is a smart, co-operative-sourced, hillside Roussillon red with a whacking 15 per cent alcohol, ripe juicy red fruits and plenty of garrigue spice.

1991 Château de Calce, Côtes du Roussillon   15/20
Full-bodied 🍷 ▮

Also from the Roussillon region near France's Pyrenean border with Spain, this is in a more traditional style, with angostura bitters aromas, a core of sweet fruit and chewy, leathery tannins.

ITALY

1995 Farnese Signifero, Montepulciano d'Abruzzo   15/20
Full-bodied 🍷🍷 ▮

From the Abruzzi's Moro Valley region, this is a well-made, cherryish, modern Montepulciano, with easy-drinking tannins and refreshing acidity.

1995 La Situlia Merlot, Trentino   15/20
Medium-bodied 🍷🍷 ▮

Grassy, lightly oaked northern Italian Merlot with refreshing balance of lively damsony acidity and sweet cassis fruitiness. Elegantly styled, well-packaged, good Right Bank claret alternative.

SOUTH AFRICA

1991 Goede Hoop, Stellenbosch 16/20
Full-bodied 🍾🍾🍾 ▯

Traditional Pinotage-like Stellenbosch red from the sprawling Bergkelder group, with good, sweet fruit concentration and mature leathery tannins. One of the Bergkelder's best reds.

SPAIN

1995 Castillo Labastida, Rioja 16/20
Medium-bodied 🍾🍾🍾 ▯

Juicy, concentrated, fruit-dominated co-operative-sourced Rioja, with vibrant, youthful strawberry and blackcurrant fruit intensity.

Over £8

FRANCE

1994 Château La Clairière Laithwaite, Côtes de Castillon 16/20
Medium-bodied 🍾🍾 ▭▬

Well-structured modern, Merlot-based claret made for keeping, with deep-hued cassis fruit, spicy new oak and ripe, succulent tannins.

1994 Château d'Escurac, Médoc, Cru Bourgeois 15/20
Medium-bodied 🍾🍾 ▭▬

A contrast in style with Bordeaux's Left Bank, this is an age-worthy, traditional Médoc *cru bourgeois*, with a sweet core of Cabernet Sauvignon-based fruit and robustly chewy tannins.

1990 Fixin Premier Cru, Clos du Chapitre, Domaine Marion
15/20

Medium-bodied 🍾 ▯

Good, honest, northern Côtes de Nuits Pinot Noir, with masses of colour and richness and a rustic rasp of dry tannin and acidity.

1988 Château Lagrange, Saint Julien 17/20
Medium-bodied 🍾🍾 ▭▬

From the under-rated 1988 vintage, this is a focused, tightly structured Saint Julien from Suntory-owned Château Lagrange, with stylish, cedary aromas and maturing leaf and chocolate fruit characters.

Eldridge Pope

Address: Weymouth Avenue, Dorchester, Dorset DT1 1QT

Telephone/fax: 01305 251251; 01305 258155

Number of branches: 12

Opening hours: 9.30am to 5.30pm Monday to Saturday

Credit cards accepted: Visa, Master Card, American Express

Discounts: Case discounts

Facilities and services: In store tastings; local delivery; glass hire; cellarage; wine advice; *en primeur* and other special offers; bin-end sales

Mail order: Telephone 01305 258347 at Head Office for details

Area(s) of specialisation: France and, increasingly, Australia and South Africa

If you've heard of Eldridge Pope, it's probably because your thirst has been quenched at some stage by one of its West Country brews. Royal Oak, Hardy County and a variety of other ales are the staple fare of this Dorchester-based brewer, pub-owner and wine retailer.

In fact, with a thriving mail-order business and 12 retail shops dotted about West Country market towns such as Sherborne, Shaftesbury and Wincanton, about one-third of Eldridge Pope's turnover comes from wine. The shops include four wine libraries in Bristol, Exeter and London, where you can sip on a bottle drawn from the helpful, address-book-style Eldridge Pope list at cost price – an excellent idea, if only the limited fare were a bit more interesting and the early closing time didn't leave you gasping just when you most wanted a drink.

Since Master of Wine Joe Naughalty went into semi-retirement last year, the staunchly French-orientated list has been taken over by Sue Longman. Despite Eldridge Pope's traditional strengths in mature clarets and Burgundies, not to mention fine German estate wines and its distinctive selection of French country wines, Kinahan is clearly keen to steer Eldridge Pope in the direction of good-value wines from the New World, in particular Chile, South Africa and Australia.

The Eldridge Pope list nods towards Italy and Spain – just about anywhere that isn't traditional, in fact – rather than bending over backwards to stock the sort of interesting wines to be found in the treasure trove of its French section. 'The fact remains,' says chairman Christopher Pope, 'that when God made the world, his most loving finger paused on the soil and climate of parts of France.' Now there's a challenge for the new wine-buyer.

White

£3–5

FRANCE

1994 Domaine Loubadère, Gros Manseng, Cuvée Coup de Coeur, Vin de Pays des Côtes de Gascogne   15/20
Off-dry 👛👛 ▮
Rich, ripe, sweetish Gascon white made from the superior Pyrenean Gros Manseng grape, with ripe, passion fruit flavours and a pleasant grapefruity tang.

£5–8

AUSTRALIA

1994 Chardonnay, Eden Crest Vineyard, Eden Valley   16/20
Off-dry 👛👛👛 ▮
Sweetish, toffee and pineapple-chunk-like Chardonnay, which tastes more like a powerful Barossa Valley white than a cool-climate Eden Valley style. Punchy, flavoursome stuff at around £6, from Marjorie and James Irvine.

FRANCE

1995 Jurançon Sec, Grain Sauvage   15/20
Dry 👛👛 ▮
Made at the local Jurançon co-operative from Gros and Petit Manseng grapes, this is a waxy, honeyed, characterful Pyrenean white with tropical, but fresh, guava fruit flavours.

1989 The Chairman's Rich, Old-Fashioned Dessert Wine, Château de Berbec   13/20
Sweet

Mawkishly sweet, barley-sugar-flavoured Premières Côtes Bordeaux sticky for grown-ups (presumably including the chairman) who enjoy toffee apples. 'Old-fashioned' just about sums it up.

1993 The Chairman's White Burgundy, Antonin Rodet   14/20
Dry

Innocuous, but cleanly made house-white Burgundy from Mercurey-based négociant, Antonin Rodet. The chairman could almost certainly find something with a bit more flavour than this.

SOUTH AFRICA

1995 Dieu Donné Chardonnay   15/20
Dry

Fresh, citrus fruit, toffee-fudge and bacon-rind-style Cape Chardonnay with soft texture and a refreshing tang of acidity. Decent enough, if lacking a bit of complexity.

Over £8

FRANCE

1993 Savennières, Clos du Papillon, Baumard   17/20
Bone dry

From the tiny appellation of Savennières, this is a white-pepper-scented, ripely textured Chenin Blanc with good ageing potential and considerable finesse and length of flavour.

1995 Pouilly Fumé, Vieilles Vignes, Domaine François Tinel   17/20
Bone dry

Intense, minerally, super-crisp Sauvignon Blanc with genuine old-vine richness and concentration, and a nettley undertone. Super stuff from the superior 1995 vintage.

1993 Chablis Premier Cru, Montée de Tonnerre, Domaine Jean Durup 15/20
Dry 👝 ▮

For a *premier cru* Chablis from one of the village's best vineyard sites, this is a little short of stuffing and character. It's pleasantly fresh, fruity and crisp, but lacks the complexity of great white Burgundy.

NEW ZEALAND

1995 The Chairman's Exuberantly Fruitful New World Sauvignon, Nelson 16/20
Dry 👝👝 ▮

Bottled for Eldridge Pope chairman, Christopher Pope, by Nelson's Redwood Valley winery, this is an elegant, gooseberryish Kiwi Sauvignon Blanc with soft, elderflower notes.

Red

£3–5

FRANCE

Reynier Rouge, Vin de Table, Antonin Rodet 14/20
Medium-bodied 👝👝 ▮

Good-value, exuberantly juicy, red quaffer from négociant Antonin Rodet, with robust plum and black-cherry fruitiness.

1994 Château Lamargue, Costières de Nîmes 14/20
Full-bodied 👝 ▮

A Provençal red that starts out sweet, succulent and spicy, but finishes up on the dry and chewy side.

£5–8

AUSTRALIA

1994 Clancy's, Barossa Valley, Peter Lehmann   16/20
Full-bodied 🗯🗯🗯 ▬►

A blend of Shiraz, Cabernet Sauvignon, Merlot and Cabernet Franc from Barossa personality Peter Lehmann, showing masses of ripe, minty, blackberry fruit and sweetly toasted American oak. Like its maker, a wine with plenty of personality.

FRANCE

1994 Abbaye de Valmagne, Coteaux du Languedoc, Gaudart d'Allaines   15/20
Full-bodied 🗯🗯 ▮

Ripe, southern French blend of Syrah, Mourvèdre and Grenache, with plenty of alcohol and smooth, robustly spicy fruitiness.

1993 Chairman's Traditional Mature Claret, Haut Médoc   16/20
Medium-bodied 🗯🗯🗯 ▬►

You may choose to differ with the chairman's description of 'mature' for a 1993 claret, but this Haut Médoc from Château Larose Trintaudon has plenty of succulent, grassy fruitiness, with good concentration and still youthful tannins.

1994 The Chairman's Red Burgundy, Labouré-Roi   15/20
Medium-bodied 🗯🗯 ▮

Light, raspberry fruity, thirst-quenching red Burgundy from the Nuits Saint Georges-based house of Labouré-Roi. A little simple, but there's some honest Pinot Noir flavour on show here.

SOUTH AFRICA

1992 Backsberg Cabernet Sauvignon, Paarl   14/20
Full-bodied 🗯 ▮

Smooth, modern Cape Cabernet Sauvignon from the father-and-son duo of Sydney and Michael Back, with lightly sweet, blackcurrant fruit and the rather rubbery twang typical of many South African reds.

Over £8

FRANCE

1993 Châteauneuf-du-Pape, Domaine de Montpertuis, Cuvée Classique, Paul Jeune   15/20
Full-bodied 👛 🍾
Well-made, violet-scented, old-style Châteauneuf-du-Pape with swingeing alcohol and chunky dry tannins.

UNITED STATES

1993 Pinot Noir, Gundlach Bundschu, Sonoma Valley   15/20
Medium-bodied 👛 🍾
Warm-climate, raspberry jam-like California Pinot Noir, with smooth tannins and smart vanilla oak, from the winningly named Gundlach Bundschu winery.

Sparkling

£5–8

FRANCE

Cuvée de l'Ecusson Brut, Bernard Massard   13/20
Off-dry 🍾
Medium-priced Luxembourg-bottled Eurofizz with coarse flavours, big bubbles and soupy sweetness. Should be £2 cheaper.

Over £8

FRANCE

Champagne Reynier Brut   15/20
Dry 🍷🍷 🍾
Youthful, malty, Pinot-based house Champagne with appealing strawberry fruit flavours and a fresh, tangy mousse.

1990 The Chairman's Champagne Blanc de Blancs   15/20
Dry 🍷 🍾
Mature, honeyed, all-Chardonnay Champagne, whose toasty aromas are its best feature. On the palate, the fruit and acidity are slightly out of kilter.

Enotria Winecellars

Address: 153–5 Wandsworth High Street, London SW18 4JB

Telephone/fax: 0181 871 2668; 0181 961 8773

Number of branches: 1

Opening hours: 10.00am to 7.00pm Monday to Saturday

Credit cards accepted: Access, Visa, Switch, Delta, Master Card

Discounts: 5 per cent collection discount on orders over 12 bottles; 'discretionary' on larger orders

Facilities and services: Autumn and spring tutored tasting series; free Saturday tastings; advice; free glass loan; frequent case offers and selections

Mail order: Free delivery of one case or more within the M25, or two cases or more elsewhere on the UK mainland; otherwise £5; allow 48 hours for delivery

Area(s) of specialisation: Italy, but increasingly impressive in Australia and France

A year ago we expressed a degree of concern at the takeover of Italian specialists Winecellars by the enormous Enotria operation, suggesting that the influence of white truffle-loving magnate Remo Nardone might not be entirely beneficial to the reputation and individuality of the Wandsworth-based merchant.

As it happens, we appear to have been unnecessarily pessimistic. The extra financial clout has given Enotria Winecellars' talented buyer, River Café regular and Master of Wine David Gleave, the chance to go out and source new agencies in France and the New World, such as Domaine de la Janasse in the Rhône, Didier Champalou in Vouvray, Mont Gras in Chile, and Kunde, J. Lohr and Sonoma Pacific in California. This has meant that, as well as possessing the best Italian list in the country, Enotria Winecellars has developed a strong supporting cast of wines from other places.

For the time being, the Wandsworth shop remains a delight for Italophiles (it's worth a visit just to buy olive oil), but mail order is an increasingly important part of the business. In fact, the plan is to replace the annual list with a mail-order newsletter every four to six weeks. Some of us may lament the loss of the distilled wisdom of David Gleave, the country's leading expert on Italian wines, but if mail order helps to alert more buyers to the delights of Allegrini, Felsina Berardenga and Pieropan, we shan't complain. Provided there's still enough left for us...

White

£3–5

CHILE

1995 Chardonnay, Mont Gras   14/20
Off-dry 🍷 🍾
Well-made, if rather sweet, Chardonnay from an ultra-modern winery in Colchagua, with soft, smoky vanilla oak and an alcoholic backbite. Made with the North American palate in mind.

HUNGARY

1995 Château Megyer Tokaji Furmint   16/20
Bone dry 🍷🍷🍷 ►
Characterful, restrained, lightly honeyed, austere dry white from Hungary's Tokay region, with a biting acidity that would cut through the richest of white fish sauces.

£5–8

AUSTRALIA

1994 Riesling, Skillogallee, Clare Valley   16/20
Dry 🍷🍷🍷 🍾
Lemon-curd-scented Clare Valley Riesling from winery-cum-restaurant Skillogallee. Like a cross between a Riesling and a Semillon, showing lime-zest fruit flavours and a full-bodied, herbal twist. One of the best Clare Valley Rieslings.

ITALY

1995 Alasia Chardonnay, Piemonte   15/20
Dry 👜👜 ▯
Fresh, elegant, melony, north-western Italian Chardonnay, which is the result of
a collaboration between Australian winemaker Martin Shaw and the go-ahead
Araldica co-operative. Unoaked for optimum fruitiness.

1995 Alasia Arneis, Langhe   16/20
Dry 👜👜👜 ▯
From the same fruitful partnership, this is an extremely characterful, perfumed
interpretation of Piemonte's native Arneis grape variety, with ultra-crisp,
lemony acidity and 25 per cent barrel fermentation for added weight and
complexity.

SOUTH AFRICA

1995 Stormy Cape Chenin Blanc   15/20
Dry 👜👜 ▯
Fresh, spritzy, well-made Cape Chenin Blanc with flavours of ripe passion fruit
and a grapefruity twist.

Over £8

AUSTRALIA

1995 Sauvignon Blanc, Shaw and Smith   16/20
Dry 👜 ▯
Exotic, citrus fruity Australian Sauvignon from Martin Shaw and Michael Hill-
Smith, whose cool-climate origins (the wine, not the winemaking cousins, that
is) have resulted in a wine of delightful grapefruity intensity and tangy acidity. A
much better bet than most Kiwi Sauvignon Blanc from the 1995 vintage.

FRANCE

1994 Chablis Premier Cru, Vaucoupin, Jean-Pierre Grossot   18/20
Dry 👜👜👜 ▬▬
Classic, minerally, assertively dry *premier cru* Chablis from grower Jean-Pierre
Grossot, streaked with honey and butter and superb cool-climate intensity.

1994 Mâcon Charnay Vieilles Vignes, Domaine Manciat Poncet
17/20

Dry 🍾🍾🍾 ▬

Remarkably concentrated for a Mâcon Villages, this is a textured, stylishly oaked southern Burgundian Chardonnay with hazelnutty characters and the kind of weight you'd expect from a good village Meursault. Nothing poncet about this find.

1995 Condrieu, La Côte, Cuilleron
19/20

Dry 🍾🍾🍾 |

A wine whose fabulous aromas of honeysuckle and ripe apricot make you want to plunge your nose into your glass and hold it there all day. From young grower Yves Cuilleron, this is stunningly concentrated, essence of Viognier at its sensual best. Even at £23 a bottle, this is good value for money.

ITALY

1995 Pinot Grigio, Eno Friulia
16/20

Bone dry 🍾🍾 |

From the Puiatti family in Italy's north-eastern corner, this water-white Pinot Grigio is super-fresh, nutty and surprisingly unoaked, with a delicate apricot tang.

1994 Soave Classico Superiore, Vigneto La Rocca, Pieropan
17/20

Bone dry 🍾🍾🍾 |

A connoisseur's Soave from the house of Pieropan, with deliciously fresh, intensely buttery concentration, weight and terrific length of flavour, finishing with a nutty tang. Soave doesn't get any better than this.

UNITED STATES

1995 Kunde Chardonnay, Sonoma Valley
17/20

Dry 🍾🍾🍾 |

From a family of Sonoma Valley growers that has recently started to bottle its own wine, this is a restrained, stylishly oaked, unfiltered Chardonnay, with elegant notes of butterscotch and honey. Better balanced than most California Chardonnays at the price.

Red

£3–5

CHILE

1995 Merlot, Mont Gras   15/20
Medium-bodied 👜👜 🍷
Smooth, grassy, softly textured Colchagua Merlot from Hernan Gras's newly established winery near Santiago.

£5–8

ITALY

1995 Valpolicella Classico, Allegrini   16/20
Medium-bodied 👜👜👜 🍷
A blend of Corvina and Rondinella grapes from the quality-conscious Allegrini family, made in a characterful, modern style, with youthful black-cherry flavours and a pleasingly refreshing dry finish. Dangerously drinkable stuff.

UNITED STATES

1995 Wildflower Gamay, J. Lohr   15/20
Medium-bodied 👜 🍷
Lusciously vibrant, Day-Glo-ruby Monterey Gamay, with sweetly juicy raspberry fruit and thirst-quenching acidity. Thoroughly gluggable, if rather simple for an £8 wine.

Over £8

AUSTRALIA

1993 Zema Estate Coonawarra Cabernet Sauvignon   16/20
Medium-bodied 👜 🍷
Deeply coloured, elegantly structured Coonawarra Cabernet with mulberry fruit flavours and rather austere acidity. Sweetly oaked, but a little short of stuffing.

1994 Mount Langhi Ghiran, Shiraz   16/20
Full-bodied 👜👜 ▬

Intense, mint and freshly milled pepper-like Victorian Shiraz with a tightly bound core of spicy blackberry fruit. Success in recent vintages has encouraged the owners to push the price over the £10 mark.

FRANCE

1993 Chambolle Musigny Premier Cru, Les Chatelots, Ghislaine Barthod   17/20
Medium-bodied 👜👜 ▬

From the excellent 1993 vintage, this is a structured, youthful Chambolle *premier cru* with loganberry and red-cherry fruitiness, smooth vanilla oak and considerable dry tannins on the finish. One to keep.

1994 Crozes-Hermitage, Domaine Combier   16/20
Full-bodied 👜👜 ▬

Beautifully made, organically grown northern Rhône Syrah in a stylish package. Densely aromatic, blackberry spicy aromas with chocolatey richness, sweet oak and substantial structure.

1994 Domaine de la Janasse, Cuvée Chaupin, Châteauneuf-du-Pape   17/20
Full-bodied 👜👜 ▬

From the youthful Christophe Sabon, this is a rich, heady, ultra-modern Châteauneuf-du-Pape with a densely structured core of tannin, excellent Grenache fruit sweetness and a peppery injection of Syrah.

ITALY

1993 Chianti Classico, Felsina Berardenga   17/20
Medium-bodied 👜👜👜 |

Concentrated, beautifully judged, Sangiovese-based Tuscan red with finely textured, cedary oak, masses of colour and savoury, plum-skin fruitiness. As complex as you'll get from a straight Chianti Classico.

1993 Pomino Rosso, Fattoria di Petrognano, Chianti Rufina   16/20
Medium-bodied 👜👜 ▬

Ultra-modern, deeply coloured, oak-influenced Tuscan blend of Cabernet Sauvignon and Sangiovese, with savoury blackberry fruitiness and the lively acidity you'd expect from an Italian red.

UNITED STATES

1994 Bearboat Pinot Noir   16/20
Medium-bodied 🍖 ▮

Made by the producers of Sonoma Pacific sparkling wine, this is a rich, concentrated, if alcoholic, Russian River Pinot Noir, with attractive raspberry fruit and no shortage of sweet smoky oak. Pricey at £20.

Justerini & Brooks

Address: 61 Saint James's Street, London SW1A 1LZ

Telephone/fax: 0171 493 8721; 0171 499 4653

Number of branches: 2, London and Edinburgh (45 George Street, Edinburgh EH2 2HT)

Opening hours: 9.00am to 5.30pm Monday to Friday

Credit cards accepted: Access, Visa, American Express, Diners Club, Connect Card

Discounts: Contact head office for case-rate details

Facilities and services: Selected Cellar Plan and Personal Cellar Plan for laying down wine; broking; storage; regular *en primeur* offers; in-store tastings

Mail order: 8–10 mail-order offers each year posted to all customers; free delivery to any mainland UK or Northern Ireland address for two cases or more

Area(s) of specialisation: Bordeaux, Burgundy, Germany

With its close links to J & B Rare, its eight royal seals, and smart St James's Street address, Justerini & Brooks has the delivery van to make your neighbours go green with envy. Even the driver comes wearing a jacket and tie. Before you order, make sure though that you've perused the list well in advance, because although the selection of grower's wines is second to none, so are the prices. In fact, if value for money is your top priority, J & B is not your wine merchant.

Justerini's buyer, Hew Blair, rightly prides himself on J & B's list, with each page loudly trumpeting 'the fine wines of Justerini & Brooks'. The major strengths of the Justerini list lie in the traditional regions of France and Germany. But wines such as California's Chalk Hill and Saintsbury, Scotchman's Hill, Neil Paulett and Cape Mentelle from Australia, South Africa's Thelema and Kanonkop and New Zealand's Ata Rangi, Palliser and Dry River show that J & B doesn't think that fine wines are confined within the borders of Western Europe.

J & B's smart shop-fronts in London and Edinburgh are the window dressing for a largely mail-order business to its well-heeled private customers, described by Hew Blair as 'combining the enjoyment of fine wine and the possession of substantial amounts of spare cash'. But, just to show that it hasn't entirely overlooked value for money, Hew Blair has developed an affordable southern French and country wine range too, with excellent wines such as Château Tour des Gendres and Domaine du Vieux Chêne.

White

£5–8

FRANCE

1994 Mâcon-Uchizy, Domaine Talmard   16/20
Dry 🍒🍒🍒 ▮
From Paul and Philibert Talmard, this is a ripe, ginger-spicy southern Burgundian Chardonnay with grapefruit and melon-like fruitiness to the fore and stylish, dry acidity. Excellent grower's Mâcon.

Over £8

AUSTRALIA

1994 Scotchman's Hill Chardonnay   17/20
Dry 🍒🍒🍒 ▬
From the Bellarine Peninsula south of Melbourne, this is an elegant, but powerful, butterscotchy, Victorian Chardonnay, with ripe melon and citrus fruit characters and a complex, tapering finish.

FRANCE

1995 Pouilly Fumé, Serge Dagueneau   15/20
Dry 🍒 ▮
An atypical Pouilly Fumé with flavours of ripe pears and an inappropriate boiled-sweets character. A little disappointing at £9 a bottle.

1994 Chablis, Laurent Tribut   16/20
Bone dry 🜊🜊 ❘

Classic grower's Chablis from Laurent Tribut, showing the stylish acidity and balance of the 1994 vintage. Characterful, creamy, lightly honeyed Chardonnay with a sharpened guillotine blade of acidity. For peasants, rather than aristocrats – provided they can afford the £9.50 price tag.

1994 Saint Romain, Sous Le Château, Coste Caumartin   17/20
Bone dry 🜊🜊🜊 ▬

From the hillside village of Saint Romain, behind the better-known communes of Meursault and Puligny-Montrachet, this is a tightly focused, extremely well-made Chardonnay with finely crafted oak influence and piercingly austere, citrus fruit characters. Should age well for at least five years.

1993 Chassagne Montrachet Premier Cru, Les Chenevottes, Jean-Noël Gagnard   17/20
Bone dry 🜊🜊 ▬

With its smoky-bacon nose and austere acidity, this *premier cru* Chassagne from one of the village's most reputable domaines is too tightly wound to drink at the moment, but will develop into something pretty special over the next three to five years. Structured, concentrated stuff.

1994 Riesling, Clos des Capucins, Cuvée Sainte Catherine II, Domaine Weinbach   18/20
Off-dry 🜊🜊🜊 ▬

Ripe, rich, intensely concentrated Alsace Riesling from Colette Faller, with minerally, lime-zest characters and a sickle of acidity. Alsace Riesling doesn't get any better than this.

GERMANY

1994 Brauneberger Juffer-Sonnenuhr, Riesling Spätlese, Fritz Haag   17/20
Medium sweet 🜊🜊 ▬

Refreshing, delicate, exquisitely balanced young Riesling from the leading Mosel estate of Fritz Haag, with a green-apple tang and well-judged fruit sweetness. Should develop well over the next two to five years.

UNITED STATES

1993 Chalk Hill Chardonnay   16/20
Dry 🝔🝔 ▮

A hugely rich, Sonoma County tilt at a Meursault-style Chardonnay from Francophile Dave Remy, with textured, hazelnut and buttered-toast characters, and New World ripeness and concentration.

Red

£3–5

SOUTH AFRICA

1995 Fairview Kopland Zinfandel/Cinsault   15/20
Full-bodied 🝔🝔 ▬

One of the few sub-£5 wines at Justerini & Brooks, this is a sumptuously oaky, abundantly spicy blend of Zinfandel and Cinsault, with plum and raspberry fruitiness and pleasantly robust, peppery tannins, from Charles Back's innovative Paarl-based winery.

£5–8

FRANCE

1994 Morgon, Château de Raousset   15/20
Medium-bodied 🝔 ▬

Structured, traditional Gamay from one of the best of the *cru* villages in Beaujolais, this is an almost Pinot Noir-like red with a solid core of raspberry fruit and dry, oak-derived tannins.

1992 Côtes du Rhône, La Haie aux Grives, Domaine du Vieux Chêne   16/20
Full-bodied 🍾🍾🍾 ▬▬

From growers Jean-Claude and Beatrice Bouche, this is a concentrated, extremely well-made Côtes du Rhône with masses of aroma, fruit and peppery intensity. An excellent red, especially given the vintage conditions in 1992.

1994 Merlot, Domaine du Vieux Chêne, Vin de Pays de Vaucluse
14/20

Medium-bodied 🍾 ⏐

From the same producers, this is a decent, soft and smoothly textured blackberryish southern Rhône Merlot, with well-handled oak maturation and a slightly tart finish.

Over £8

AUSTRALIA

1993 Leconfield Cabernet Sauvignon, Coonawarra   16/20
Full-bodied 🍾🍾 ⏐

Solid, four-square Coonawarra Cabernet Sauvignon with masses of coffee-bean oak, mint and cassis fruit, with mildly astringent, chunky tannins for backbone.

FRANCE

1990 Chinon, Cuvée des Varennes du Grand Clos, Charles Joguet
17/20

Medium-bodied 🍾🍾🍾 ⏐

Elegant Cabernet Franc from one the Loire's best red winemakers, Charles Joguet, with pure, ripe cassis sweetness and refreshing acidity. An excellent expression of Cabernet Franc. Drink up.

1990 Château Fourcas-Loubaney, Cru Bourgeois, Listrac-Médoc
16/20

Medium-bodied 🍾🍾 ⏐

Youthful, coffee-bean oaky *cru bourgeois* claret from the excellent 1990 vintage, with attractively ripe blackcurrant fruit flavours. This has softened since we tasted it a year ago into an appealing Listrac classic.

1989 Château Beauséjour-Duffau-Lagarrosse, Premier Grand Cru Classé, St Emilion 16/20
Medium-bodied 🍷 🍾
Still powerful, still extracted, still deeply-coloured St Emilion from the much-acclaimed bicentenary vintage, this £35 blockbuster is still developing as the tannins start to soften and mature. We may just have to taste it again next year.

1991 Nuits Saint Georges, Robert Chevillon 17/20
Medium-bodied 🍷🍷🍷 🍾
Untamed grower's village Burgundy with ripe *fraises du bois* fruit and gamey sweetness supported by firm, dry, well-structured tannins. The sort of Pinot Noir that the New World would love to emulate.

1992 Saint Aubin Premier Cru, Les Frionnes, Henri Prudhon 16/20
Medium-bodied 🍷🍷🍷 🍾
A contrast in style, this is a modern, spicily oaked, strawberry fruity Pinot Noir, which is pleasantly fruity without the complexity of the Nuits Saint Georges.

1991 Savigny Premier Cru, La Dominode, Bruno Clair 17/20
Medium-bodied 🍷🍷🍷 🍾
From one of Burgundy's leading young growers, this is a richly coloured, firmly structured Pinot Noir with chocolatey, plum-like fruitiness and real concentration. A lot of poke for your francs.

1994 Crozes-Hermitage, Château Curson, Domaine Pochon 16/20
Full-bodied 🍷🍷 🍾
Modern-style, heavily oaked Crozes-Hermitage with rich, intense blackberry fruit concentration, made in a wanna-be Hermitage mould and showing a lot of stuffing for a supposedly simple Crozes-Hermitage.

1990 Saint Joseph, Les Grisières, André Perret 17/20
Medium-bodied 🍷🍷🍷 🍾
André Perret is one of the best growers in Condrieu. It might be auto-suggestion, but this stylish, 1990 northern Rhône Syrah with its sweet, blackberry fruit and stylish vanilla oak smells a little like Viognier. Lovely stuff.

1991 Côte-Rôtie, René Rostaing 18/20
Full-bodied 🍷🍷🍷 🍾
Powerfully aromatic, meaty, full-flavoured Syrah from an under-rated vintage in the northern Rhône. It's drinkable now, but this extremely rich and smoky, blackberry-fruity Côte Rôtie will age for another few years yet.

Lay & Wheeler

Address: Gosbecks Road, Gosbecks Park, Colchester, Essex CO1 9JT

Telephone/fax: 01206 764446; 01206 560002

Number of branches: 1, The Wine Centre, Colchester

Opening hours: 9.00am to 7.00pm Monday to Saturday; 10.00am to 4.00pm Sunday

Credit cards accepted: Visa, Master Card, American Express

Discounts: Wholesale terms for 5-case (mixed) orders; collection discount £3 per case

Facilities and services: Wine workshops; *en primeur* offers; bin-end sales; bi-monthly customer newsletter; wine racks; sale or return; free glass loan; ice; additional party equipment (ice buckets, punchbowls etc.); waiter service and food for cocktail parties; gift vouchers; in-store tastings; cellarage

Mail order: Nationwide; call Lay & Wheeler for terms and details

Area(s) of specialisation: Good everywhere, but with strengths in Bordeaux, Burgundy, Rhône, Alsace, Loire, Germany and Australia

At first glance the predominantly male, suit-wearing dramatis personae smiling out from the front pages of Lay & Wheeler's traditional wine list could be mistaken for the management of a small, suburban building society. If Lay & Wheeler were to enter a competition for Britain's most dependable, friendly and informative company, it would almost certainly run off with the award. The personnel are a major key to Lay & Wheeler's success. The mouth-wateringly extensive wine list is the other.

Enquire within, and behind the holiday snapshots of anonymous vineyards and growers cut off at the knees you'll find one of the best-endowed wine lists, perhaps the best-endowed list, in fact, in the country. This family-owned Colchester company prides itself on personal service and, with the long-suffering bedside manner of a faithful family retainer, paterfamilias Richard Wheeler oozes solicitude for his long-standing customers.

Lay & Wheeler may be a traditional merchant with its feet firmly in the classic regions of Bordeaux, Burgundy, Port and Champagne, but the company has not been slow to nose its way into value-for-money nooks in the south of France and the brave New World of Australia, California, South Africa, Chile and New Zealand. As we mentioned last year, its wine workshops are among the most informative in the country, often tutored by high-profile visiting winemakers keen to be part of Colchester's extended family.

White

£3–5

FRANCE

1995 Vin de Pays des Côtes de Gascogne, Cépage Colombard

14/20

Dry 🍷🍷 ▮

Tangy, fresh, well-made Gascon white from the superior Colombard grape made at the modern Plaimont co-operative. Crisp and pleasantly drinkable.

£5–8

FRANCE

1995 Marquise de Bairac Chardonnay, Vin de Pays d'Oc   15/20

Dry 🍷🍷 ▮

A stylish, well-made Languedoc-Roussillon alternative to Mâcon Blanc, with peach and citrus fruit flavours and a tangy, lightly smoky aftertaste.

1995 Quincy, Jean-Michel Sorbe   16/20

Bone dry 🍷🍷 ▮

Restrained, crisply elegant Loire Sauvignon Blanc from the benchmark 1995 vintage, made in a nettley, mini-Sancerre mould with good length and acidity.

1995 Château Pierrail, Bordeaux, Jacques Demonchaux   15/20
Dry 🍷🍷 🍾
Assertively aromatic blend of Sauvignon Blanc and Sauvignon Gris from Jacques Demonchaux's highly reliable Bordeaux château, with lemon-zesty flavours and a refreshing zip of acidity.

1994 Alsace Pinot Blanc, Vieilles Vignes, François et Felix Meyer
16/20
Dry 🍷🍷 🍾
Made at an impressive family winery in Alsace by the New World-trained Felix Meyer, this is a commendably characterful, peachy Pinot Blanc with appealing honeyed richness balanced by good, fresh acidity.

NEW ZEALAND

1995 Mount Riley Sauvignon Blanc, Marlborough   14/20
Off-dry 🍷 🍾
Tinned pea and sweetcorn-like New Zealand Sauvignon Blanc, well priced at under £6, with a touch of sweetness to round out the harsher edges of the 1995 vintage.

SOUTH AFRICA

1995 Rosenburg Sauvignon Blanc/Chardonnay   14/20
Dry 🍷 🍾
Youthful, gassy but rather dilute Cape blend of Sauvignon Blanc and Chardonnay, which appears to have suffered from high yields in the vineyard. Ought to be at least £1 cheaper.

Over £8

UNITED STATES

1993 Monticello Corley Family Vineyards, Napa Valley   15/20
Dry 🍷 🍾
Barley-sugar and toffee-fudge-style, barrel-fermented Napa Valley Chardonnay with a massive 14 per cent whack of alcohol and lees-derived, burnt-butter notes. A big, old-fashioned mouthful.

Red

£5–8

FRANCE

1992 Lirac, Les Queyrades, André Mejan   15/20
Full-bodied �· ▮
In a difficult vintage, André Mejan has succeeded in extracting plenty of sweet, alcoholic, strawberry fruitiness with peppery, drying tannins.

SPAIN

1994 Señorio de Nava, Tinto Joven, Ribera del Duero   15/20
Medium-bodied 🎚🎚 ▭—
Juicy, youthful, licoricey, all-Tempranillo red, which shows how good the fruit quality can be in Spain's up-and-coming Ribera del Duero region. Made for early consumption, but with a considerable tannic bite. The label doesn't do the wine justice.

Over £8

AUSTRALIA

1992 Reynolds Cabernet Sauvignon, New South Wales   15/20
Full-bodied 🎚 ▭—
Over-oaky, astringent Hunter Valley Cabernet Sauvignon with sweet licorice and coconutty American oak flavours predominating. Cabernet Sauvignon is not the Hunter Valley's best ambassador.

1993 Henschke Keyneton Estate Shiraz/Cabernet Sauvignon/ Malbec, Barossa Valley   17/20
Full-bodied 🎚🎚🎚 ▭—
Deeply coloured, sweetly oaked, aromatically complex Barossa blend of mainly Shiraz and Cabernet Sauvignon, with mulberry and cassis fruit, well-judged vanilla oakiness and smooth tannins. Well up to the usual high standards of Australia's top red wine estate.

AUSTRIA

1994 Heinrich Blauer Zweigelt   16/20
Medium-bodied 👜👜 🍾

Named after the Austrian professor who crossed Blaufränkisch with the Saint Laurent grapes, Blauer Zweigelt is one of Austria's most characterful red varieties. This example from grower Gernot Heinrich is an elegantly peppery, mulberry fruity red with concentrated flavours and sweet vanilla notes.

FRANCE

1995 Domaine de la Voûte des Crozes, Côte de Brouilly   16/20
Medium-bodied 👜👜 ➡

From Lay & Wheeler's excellent selection of *crus* Beaujolais, this is a dense, chocolatey, strawberry fruity Gamay from grower Nicole Chanrion, with the Burgundian structure and acidity we expect from a good Côte de Brouilly.

Bourgogne Rouge, Cuvée Fûts de Chêne, Les Vignerons d'Igé
15/20
Medium-bodied 👜 🍾

A fixture on the Lay & Wheeler list since 1989, this Mâconnais co-operative red Burgundy is an honest, characterful, if over-oaked Pinot Noir with a rustic dry finish.

1990 Château de Plassan, Premières Côtes de Bordeaux   16/20
Medium-bodied 👜👜 ➡

Fleshy, chocolatey, modern-style Bordeaux from the Premières Côtes, with sweet, coffee-bean oak, plenty of weight and flavour and a slightly drying finish.

1993 Chateau Charmail, Haut-Médoc, Cru Bourgeois   15/20
Medium-bodied 👜 ➡

Mocha and chocolate-scented, assertively oaky *cru bourgeois*, made with the American palate in mind. There's plenty of good fruit here, but it's rather smothered by the splinters at the moment.

ITALY

1993 Fattoria di Geggiano, Chianti Classico, Siena   16/20
Medium-bodied 👜👜 🍾

Aromatic, structured, black-cherry fruity Chianti Classico with masses of individuality and honest rusticity.

Sparkling

Over £8

UNITED STATES

1991 Schramsberg Blanc de Blancs   15/20
Dry 👛 🍾
From Jack and Jamie Davies, this is a ripe, richly toasty California blend of Chardonnay with a little Pinot Blanc, which starts out along the right lines, but finishes somewhat abruptly.

Lea & Sandeman

Address: 301 Fulham Road, London SW10 9QH

Telephone/fax: 0171 376 4767; 0171 351 0275

Number of branches: 3, Fulham Road; 211 Kensington Church Street, London W8 7LX (0171 221 1982); and 51 High Street, Barnes, London SW13 9LN (0181 878 8643)

Opening hours: 9.00am to 8.30pm Monday to Friday; 10.00am to 8.30pm Saturday

Credit cards accepted: Access, Visa, Master Card, American Express

Discounts: Single bottle sales with discounts on cases, including mixed cases

Facilities and services: Glass loan; cellarage through Elephant Storage; party service; *en primeur* offers; wine advice

Mail order: Free delivery in central London (or close to the shop in Barnes) for a case or more, and on any order over £150 anywhere else in mainland UK south of Perth; elsewhere, or in smaller quantities, by arrangement (usually deliver free to the Isles of Scilly)

Area(s) of specialisation: France, Italy

Wannabe workout freak Charles Lea and motorcycling Patrick Sandeman boldly set out their first Fulham Road store in November 1988. The venture has been an evident success. With the acquisition of the Barnes Wine Shop last year, the well-spoken duo have extended their London fine-wine business to three well laid-out shops. Only one-third of Lea & Sandeman's business is retail, however. The bulk is mail order.

Charles and Patrick, not to mention Rupert and Monty, are the people to seek out for top-quality, carefully selected growers' wines from the classic regions of France and Italy, as well as regular *en primeur* offers of claret and Burgundy. Both Sandeman and Lea are self-confessed traditionalists, and although Charles Lea has admitted that he's not desperately keen on the stuff from Down Under, more than a token presence of Australian, Kiwi, Californian, South African and Argentine wines has sneaked its way onto the posh premises in Fulham Road, Kensington Church Street and Barnes.

Lea & Sandeman prides itself on buying parcels of wine that are too small to sell in high-street off-licence chains. Even though the Fulham Road shop has to compete with an Oddbins opposite, customers obviously enjoy the personal touch and the boyish enthusiasm of the Lea & Sandeman staff.

In a high street that is increasingly concertina-like in its concentration, it's encouraging to find a range which, although not inconsiderably priced – as John Major might put it – is never short on personality. Coupled with its slightly old-fashioned, Harrovian-style service, Lea & Sandeman deserves recognition for keeping the flame of quality and individuality burning brightly.

White

£5–8

FRANCE

1995 Touraine Sauvignon, Domaine des Cabotières, Joël Delaunay   15/20
Bone dry 👜👜 ▮
Light, assertively dry Touraine Sauvignon with delicate, nettley flavours and ripe, softly textured fruit.

1995 Château de Lascaux, J.-B.Cavalier   16/20
Dry 👜👜👜 ▮
Spicy, full-flavoured, unoaked blend of Viognier, Grenache Blanc and Rolle, with notes of nutmeg, buttered toast and zesty acidity. Intriguing stuff.

ITALY

1995 Garbi, Vino da Tavola delle Marche   15/20
Dry 👜 ▮
Spritzy, fresh, if rather neutral blend of Trebbiano and Chardonnay from the Marche region, with tangy weight and the faintest bitter twist.

Over £8

FRANCE

1995 Sancerre, Domaine Delaporte   17/20
Bone dry 👛👛 ▬
From Vincent and Jean-Yves Delaporte's vineyard in Chavignol, this is a crisp, minerally, apple-fresh Sancerre with considerable intensity and length of flavour. Delicious stuff.

1994 Savennières, Clos de Coulaine, Papin-Chevalier   16/20
Dry 👛👛 ▬
Characterful, flavoursome Chenin Blanc with notes of honey and fresh pear and a touch of residual sweetness to round out the acidity.

1994 Rully Premier Cru, La Pucelle, H. and P. Jacqueson   16/20
Dry 👛👛 ▬
From the best white wine appellation in the Côte Chalonnaise, this is a rich, still youthful, oak-fermented Chardonnay with nutty flavours, weight and concentration underpinned by steely acidity.

1993 Bourgogne Blanc, Domaine Charles et Rémi Jobard   17/20
Dry 👛👛👛 🍾
From Meursault-based growers Charles and Rémi Jobard, this looks expensive at around £10 for a basic white Burgundy, but then this is no ordinary Bourgogne Blanc. If this weighty, hazelnutty, beautifully balanced Chardonnay is declassified Meursault, we'd love to see the real thing.

1994 Coteaux du Layon Beaulieu, Papin-Chevalier   18/20
Very sweet 👛👛👛 ▬
Golden-hued, botrytis-affected Loire sticky with the almost viscous concentration of crystallized apricot and mandarin orange and delightful, balancing acidity. Good value, even at £15.

ITALY

1995 Le Terrazze della Fattoria di Manzano, Vino da Tavola Toscano   16/20
Dry 👛👛 🍾
Modern, oak-scented, international-style blend of Sauvignon Blanc, Chardonnay and Grechetto, which combines the three grapes to good effect in a nutty Graves-like white with a zippy, refreshing tang of acidity.

1995 Con Vento, Tenuta del Terriccio   17/20
Dry 🍷🍷🍷 ▍

There may only be 4 per cent Gewürztraminer in this Sauvignon Blanc-dominated blend, but the aromatic ginger spiciness of the grape is very much in evidence on the nose and palate. A smart Livornian coast table wine with well-defined acidity and delightful flavours of greengage and pear. One for Sister Wendy.

1990 Vin Santo, Fattoria Le Pupille, Vino da Tavola Toscana, 50cl.
                                                           16/20

Very sweet 🍷🍷 ▬▬

Almost Sherry-like, sweet Tuscan curiosity with raisin and date-like fruit and a Seville orange tang on the finish. Very concentrated stuff, if rather old-fashioned.

Red

£5–8

FRANCE

1992 Les Chemins de Bassac, Pierre Elie, Vin de Pays d'Oc, Isabelle et Rémi Ducellier   16/20
Medium-bodied 🍷🍷🍷 ▍

Stylish, Languedoc blend of Syrah, Grenache, Cabernet Sauvignon and even a splash of Pinot Noir. A well-structured but highly drinkable red with some blackcurrant fruitiness adding a claret-like sheen.

1992 Château Le Roc, Côtes du Frontonnais, Cuvée Réservée, Famille Ribes   16/20
Full-bodied 🍷🍷 ▍

Milled pepper-scented, almost Syrah-like southern French blend with mature blackberry fruitiness and robust, throat-warming tannins.

1994 Domaine Piquemal, Cuvée Pierre Audonnet, Vin de Pays des Côtes Catalanes   15/20
Full-bodied 👛👛 🍾–

Robustly tannic, oaky, modern, cinnamon-tinged blend of Merlot, Grenache, Cabernet Sauvignon and Carignan from Pierre Piquemal. Flashily modern, if a little bit short of Mediterranean soul.

1994 Domaine d'Aupilhac, Montpeyroux   16/20
Full-bodied 👛👛 🍾–

Super-rich, intensely weighty, bitter-chocolate Coteaux du Languedoc blend of Syrah, Grenache, Mourvèdre, Carignan and Cinsault, with tobacco-ish, firm tannins. Stash this away for a year or so.

1994 Lirac, Domaine de la Mordorée, Delorme   16/20
Full-bodied 👛👛 🍾–

Intense, muscular, blackberry-scented southern Rhône Grenache/Syrah blend, with chunky dry tannins and masses of concentrated, sweet fruit. A wine with a long way to go.

Over £8

AUSTRALIA

1992 Pike's Clare Valley Cabernet Sauvignon   16/20
Medium-bodied 👛👛 🍾–

Australian wines are a comparative rarity at French and Italian specialists Lea & Sandeman, so it's good to see this on the list; an Aussie red from a good Clare Valley grower. This cassis and mint Cabernet Sauvignon, blended with Cabernet Franc and Merlot and aged in French oak, is a successful Australian attempt at a Bordeaux style.

FRANCE

1995 Saint-Nicolas-de-Bourgueil, La Source, Yannick Amirault
17/20

Medium-bodied 👛👛👛 🍾–

Textbook Loire Cabernet Franc from the impressive 1995 vintage, with smooth, fine-grained tannins, ripe cherry fruit flavours and attractive green-pepper freshness. One of the best Loire reds we've tasted this year.

1993 Mercurey Premier Cru, Les Velay, Domaine de la Monette, Paul-Jean Granger
16/20
Medium-bodied 👜👜 ▬▬

Forward, attractively balanced Côte Chalonnaise red Burgundy with appealing raspberry fruit sweetness, delicate spicy oak and refreshing acidity for length and finesse.

1991 Vosne Romanée, Mugneret-Gibourg
16/20
Medium-bodied 👜 ▮

We loved the wild strawberry aromas of this concentrated, well-structured Côte de Nuits Pinot Noir, but found the tannins a little too dry and rustic on the gums for total satisfaction.

ITALY

1992 Querciabella, Chianti Classico
17/20
Full-bodied 👜👜👜 ▬▬

From an ultra-modern winery in the town of Greve, this is an extremely impressive, characterful Chianti, especially for a 1992, with sagey, savoury notes and a sweet middle palate of plum and black-cherry fruit.

1992 Vigna Sant'Anna, Vigna Il Vallone, Simona Fabroni Ruggeri
16/20
Medium-bodied 👜👜 ▮

A super-Tuscan blend of 70 per cent Sangiovese with 30 per cent Cabernet Sauvignon aged in French oak for ten months, this is a modern-style, vanilla oaky Tuscan red with good fruit concentration, but a few too many splinters, given the vintage. Chianti for Bordeaux lovers.

1993 Olimpo Vigneti di Levrara, Cabernet Sauvignon, Valdadige, Altariva
15/20
Medium-bodied 👜 ▮

From Italy's northernmost, alpine Alto Adige close to the border with Austria, this designer-packaged, green-pepper-tinged Cabernet Franc-like red is Italy's answer to Bourgueil or New Zealand's South Island.

Rosé

£5–8

FRANCE

1995 Château de Lascaux, Coteaux du Languedoc, J.-B. Cavalier
15/20

Dry 🍷🍷 ▮

A serious, dry, Languedoc rosé blend of Syrah and Grenache, with weighty, redcurrant fruitiness and a sophisticated finish.

Thomas Peatling

Address: Westgate House, Bury St Edmunds, Suffolk IP33 1QS

Telephone/fax: 01284 755949; 01284 705795

Number of branches: 3

Opening hours: 9.00am to 5.00pm Monday to Saturday

Credit cards accepted: Access, Visa, Switch, American Express

Discounts: 5 per cent on case quantities of individual wines

Facilities and services: Free glass loan; free local delivery; cellarage; regular in-store tastings; annual wine festival on 2 November 1996; regular monthly Peatlings Direct leaflets, offering six to ten mixed cases at special prices

Mail order: Peatlings Direct: full range available to UK mainland; delivery £4.50 per single case, two cases or more delivered free. Telephone 01284 714466; fax 01284 705795; manager: Michael Newell

Area(s) of specialisation: Bordeaux, vintage Port.

If you're wondering why the number of Thomas Peatling wine shops has been trimmed this year, from 26 to a mere rump in Bury St Edmunds, Colchester and Long Sutton, the answer is that the East Anglia-based merchant sold off all but three of its retail shops to Victoria Wine in 1996 in order to concentrate on its wholesale and mail-order business.

As a result of the switch in company policy, the mail-order side, Peatlings Direct, has been expanded, trebling its turnover during the past year. The stylish, almost telephone-directory list has also been upped a gear to include copious, and often mouth-watering tasting notes on a vast selection of wines, including a fair number of the humbler wines in the Peatling's pantheon. Bottling some of its own wines makes Peatlings one of the best-priced independent merchants in the country.

Master of Wine Robin Crameri, who buys the Peatlings wines, has put together a bold, often idiosyncratic range of wines, mixing domaine-bottled Burgundies and well-picked clarets with a slowly improving New World range. Now that the mail-order operation has become its central focus, Peatlings may finally get the audience beyond the boundaries of East Anglia that it deserves for its extremely competitive selection of Ports, Burgundies, Spanish wines, German Rieslings and clarets.

White

£3–5

FRANCE

1995 Sauvignon de Touraine, Les Arachis du Château 14/20
Dry 👛👛 🍷
Decent, basic, lightly nettley Loire Valley Sauvignon Blanc, which is good value at under £4.

1995 Muscadet de Sèvre et Maine sur lie, Les Placelières 15/20
Bone dry 👛👛 🍷
Fresh, ultra-tangy *sur lie* Muscadet, which once again confirms the quality of the 1995 vintage.

NEW ZEALAND

1995 Sauvignon Blanc, Steepleview, Marlborough 14/20
Dry 👛👛 🍷
Well done Thomas Peatling, for selling a pleasantly elderfloral New Zealand Sauvignon Blanc at under £4, even if it is a shade on the dilute side.

£5–8

AUSTRALIA

1995 Dennis Chardonnay, McLaren Vale 15/20
Dry 👛 🍷
The Dennis in question is Peter Dennis, and not the hero of the *Beano*. This is a well-made, French-oak-fermented McLaren Vale Chardonnay, but the splinters have got the upper hand at the moment.

SOUTH AFRICA

1995 Hilltop Chardonnay, Cyril and Charles   16/20
Dry 🍾🍾🍾 ▮

A well-priced Cape Chardonnay with restrained vanilla oak and intense citrus fruit characters against a background of toffee and butterscotch notes. Plenty of flavour and complexity for under £6 from the intriguingly named duo, Cyril and Charles.

Over £8

AUSTRALIA

1995 The Jim Jim Hanging Rock Winery Sauvignon Blanc, Victoria   17/20
Dry 🍾🍾🍾 ▮

Made in Victoria's cool-climate Macedon Mountain region, this is one of Australia's most elegant Sauvignon Blancs, with crisp, blackcurrant-leaf aromas and a grapefruity, well-rounded tang.

FRANCE

1994 Pouilly-Fuissé, Vieilles Vignes, Domaine Cordier   16/20
Dry 🍾🍾 ▬

A smartly packaged old-vine Pouilly-Fuissé, in which the constituent parts of coconutty oak, buttery fruit and marked acidity have not yet quite come together. We'd like to see the wine in another year.

UNITED STATES

1994 Gallo Laguna Ranch Chardonnay, Sonoma   16/20
Dry 🍾🍾 ▮

From the producers of Hearty Burgundy and Thunderbird, this is a stylish attempt at a modern, white Burgundy-style Chardonnay, with classy, toasty vanilla oak, caramel notes and cool-climate intensity of flavour.

Red

Under £3

FRANCE

Côtes du Roussillon Villages   14/20
Full-bodied 🍶🍶🍶 ▮
By shipping and bottling this robustly spicy Côtes du Roussillon itself, Thomas Peatling has managed to limbo under the magic £3 barrier, which seems to defeat almost every other independent merchant in the country.

£3–5

FRANCE

1994 Coteaux du Languedoc Syrah   14/20
Full-bodied 🍶🍶🍶 ▮
Robust, chocolatey Languedoc Syrah, chosen and bottled by Thomas Peatling, with some good blackberry fruit at the price and a rustic bite on the finish.

£5–8

FRANCE

1995 Moulin-à-Vent, Les Burdelines, Ghislaine Belicard   16/20
Medium-bodied 🍶🍶🍶 ▮
Closer to a light Saint Amour than a Moulin-à-Vent in style, this is a vibrant, thirst-quenchingly drinkable Gamay with attractive cherry and strawberry fruit notes. A real grower's Beaujolais with some style.

1993 Margaux   15/20
Medium-bodied 🍶🍶 ▬
Well-structured, serious Médoc red vinified at Château Labégorce Zédé, with blackcurrant fruit and something of the green-edged tannins of the vintage.

1992 Peatlings Pessac-Léognan   15/20
Medium-bodied 👛👛 ⏐
Unlikely to be declassified Château Haut-Brion, but this solid, dry, well-made
northern Graves red from a less than exciting vintage is an extremely well-
priced claret at under £7.

SOUTH AFRICA

1995 Hilltop Pinotage, Cyril and Charles   15/20
Full-bodied 👛👛 ⏐
From the music-hall duo of Cyril and Charles, this is a sweetish, banana and
strawberry fruity red with attractively chunky tannins. A good introduction to
South Africa's indigenous crossing of Cinsault and Pinot Noir.

SPAIN

1987 Viña Valoria, Rioja Reserva   13/20
Medium-bodied ⏐
Garnet-hued, almost tawny, ageing Rioja Reserva, in which the dry oak has long
ago subdued the fruit character.

Over £8

AUSTRALIA

1993 The Hanging Rock Winery Cabernet Sauvignon/Merlot
16/20

Medium-bodied 👛👛 ➡️
Intense, ginger and mint-like Victorian blend of Cabernet Sauvignon and
Merlot, with succulent fruit and refreshing acidity, from Victoria's cool Macedon
Mountains. One for the picnic hamper.

FRANCE

1988 Château Gruaud-Larose   15/20
Medium-bodied 👛 ➡️
Structured, but still comparatively youthful *cru classé* with the Cordier stamp of
sweet coffee-bean oak and farmyardy flavours. We're not sure the fruit will last
the course as the wine ages.

UNITED STATES

1992 Gallo Frei Ranch Cabernet Sauvignon, Sonoma   16/20
Full-bodied 🍷🍷 ▬

From Gallo's extensive new Sonoma Valley project, this Dry Creek Valley red is an intense, cassis-flavoured, deeply oaked blend of Cabernet Sauvignon with 15 per cent Cabernet Franc and 6 per cent Merlot. A step in a serious direction from the world's largest winery.

Rosé

£5–8

SPAIN

1994 Viña Valoria Rioja Rosado   13/20
Dry 🍷

Rosados from Rioja are rather rare and this dry, rather flat-footed *rosado* in a fancy bottle is unlikely to start a new trend.

Sparkling

Over £8

FRANCE

Brusson Père et Fils Champagne   15/20
Dry 🍷🍷

Reliable, sweetish house-Champagne with some toasty, bottle-aged character.

Fortified

£3–5

ITALY

Woodhouse Marsala   12/20
Medium sweet
Earthy-dry, rustic Sicilian fortified sticky made from Catarratto and Grillo grapes. Cheap and rather nasty.

SPAIN

Peatlings Manzanilla   16/20
Bone dry
Savoury, super-fresh, olive and almond-friendly Manzanilla from the house of Barbadillo, with a dry, flor-yeasty tang. Brilliant value at just over £4.

£5–8

FRANCE

Maury Vin Doux Naturel   13/20
Full-bodied
From one of the most beautiful villages in the Roussillon, this bog-standard, coarsely fortified sweetie gives little indication of the true quality of genuine Maury.

Over £8

PORTUGAL

Peatlings Crusted Port, Warre   16/20
Full-bodied
Shipped and bottled by Thomas Peatling in 1991, this non-vintage Douro Valley blend is a sweet, spicy, concentrated raisin and honey-like red with well-judged, fortifying spirit.

Tanners

Address: 26 Wyle Cop, Shrewsbury, Shropshire SY1 1XD

Telephone/fax: 01743 232400; 01743 344401

Number of branches: 4

Opening hours: 9.00am to 6.00pm Monday to Saturday; 10.00am to 4.00pm Sundays (in December)

Credit cards accepted: All major credit cards accepted, but Access and Visa preferred

Discounts: 5 per cent on collected wines of a case or more, 7.5 per cent on ten cases or more; for delivered orders, 2.5 per cent on three cases, 5 per cent on five cases, 7.5 per cent on ten cases

Facilities and services: Goods on sale or return; free glass loan; waiter service; valuation and purchase of rare and interesting wines; gift packs; gift vouchers; monthly payment cellar scheme; regular newsletters and offers

Mail order: Free delivery within local area and nationwide for orders of 12 or more bottles

Area(s) of specialisation: France (particularly the classic areas and the Languedoc-Roussillon), Germany, the New World.

Last year's winner of *Grapevine's* Independent Wine Merchant of the Year award continues to run one of the best family-owned specialists, offering everything from well-priced Languedoc-Roussillon reds to venerable Valdespino Sherries.

Although conservative by nature, Richard and son James Tanner are never afraid to embrace change. Their range of New World wines, for example, contains a number of top-notch wineries, such as C.J. Pask in New Zealand, Jim Barry in Australia and Vriesenhof in South Africa. But France remains the focus of the business, where domaine- and château-bottled wines are sourced with care.

The Tanners' list may not be as sumptuous or well-illustrated as some, but it's a tightly written, informative document, which pares waffle to the bone. The same focus is apparent in Talking Tanners, its regular newsletter, and in its unhurried approach to the traditional business of selling wine in general. Prices are extremely competitive across the board, service is polite and efficient, and (most important of all) the wines are some of the most reliable in the country. The epitome of a first-rate country wine merchant.

White

£3–5

FRANCE

1994 Tanners Sauvignon, Vin de Pays d'Oc, Jacques Lurton   15/20
Dry 👜👜 ▮
Made for Tanners by roving Frenchman Jacques Lurton, this is a ripe, gooseberry fruity, southern French Sauvignon with the easy-drinking approachability that is sometimes lacking in its northerly counterpart, Sauvignon de Touraine.

£5–8

FRANCE

1994 Chardonnay, Domaine de l'Aigle, Classique, Limoux   15/20
Dry 👜👜 ▮
From the cool-climate region of Limoux south-west of Carcassonne, this is a ripe, melony, barrel-fermented Chardonnay with considerable elegance and complexity, from one of the best domaines in what is primarily a sparkling wine appellation.

GERMANY

1994 Grauer Burgunder Spätlese Trocken, Weingut Schales, Rheinhessen   16/20
Off-dry

Scented, almost exotic Pinot Gris (Grauer Burgunder) with peach and pineapple notes and a zesty fresh, grapefruity tang.

UNITED STATES

1995 Ca' del Solo, Malvasia Bianco   15/20
Dry

From literary punster and media rent-a-quote Randall Grahm, this is a jasmine-scented, grapey, spritz-fresh Monterey dry white, which doesn't quite live up to its brilliant label or its £8 price tag.

Over £8

AUSTRALIA

1992 Coriole Semillon, McLaren Vale   16/20
Dry

Extremely characterful McLaren Vale Semillon, which is remarkably fresh for a 1992 and intriguingly redolent of sweet oak, ice cream soda and elderflower. At just over £8, this is a flavoursome, distinctive estate white.

FRANCE

1994 La Cuvée Passion du Château Bel Air, Bordeaux   16/20
Medium dry

New oak-fermented blend of Semillon and Sauvignon from the Entre-Deux-Mers, made in a modern Graves style with elegant vanilla oak, refreshing acidity and zesty, creamy, citrus-peel characters.

1993 Mâcon Clessé, Quintaine   17/20
Dry

From biodynamic purists Pierrette et Marc Guillemot in the hamlet of Quintaine, this is a stylish, richly endowed, beautifully judged Chardonnay with attractive honey and aniseed-like complexity and plenty of buttery, full flavour.

1992 Santenay, Le Saint Jean   16/20
Dry 👜👜 ▯

Ripely concentrated, old-style white Burgundy made in an idiosyncratic style by Vincent Girardin, one of the best growers in the predominantly red wine village of Santenay. Weird cheese-rind and honey characters make this a highly unusual buy.

GERMANY

1994 Ockfener Bockstein Riesling, Dr Heinz Wagner, Mosel Saar Rüwer   16/20
Medium sweet 👜👜 ▯

Pricey for a Qualitätswein at just over £10 perhaps, but this elegant, featherweight Mosel Riesling is a refreshingly juicy, apple-crisp white with stylish balancing acidity.

1995 Erdener Treppchen Riesling Auslese, Weingut Meulenhof
                    18/20

Sweet 👜👜👜 ▭▬

Peachy, intense, beautifully defined Mosel Riesling from a top vineyard site in the Mosel Valley, showing sumptuously juicy, primary fruit flavours, super concentration and fine balancing acidity.

Red

£3–5

FRANCE

1993 Domaine de Belvezet, Côtes du Vivarais, Christian Deschamps   13/20
Full-bodied 👜 ▯

Decent southern French quaffer based on the ubiquitous Grenache grape, with a touch of pepper and rustic tannins.

£5–8

FRANCE

1994 Domaine des Glauges, Coteaux d'Aix en Provence, Les Baux   16/20
Full-bodied 💰💰💰 |

A succulent, modern Provençal blend, with attractive garrigue spiciness, ripe strawberry fruit flavour and brown-sugar characters. At under £6, this is a southern star in the making.

1993 Madiran, Domaine Maureou, Patrick Ducournau   16/20
Full-bodied 💰💰💰 |

From talented young winemaker and bullfighting aficionado, Patrick Ducournau, this is surprisingly elegant for Madiran, showing coffee-bean oak and almost claret-like cassis fruitiness, with none of the tannic bitterness you so often get in the local Tannat grape. A bargain at £6.

1994 Domaine des Rochelles, Anjou-Villages, Jean-Yves Lebreton
15/20

Medium-bodied 💰 ▬

From the slopes of the Aubance tributary of the Loire near Angers, this is an intense, peppery expression of the Loire Valley's Cabernet Franc grape, with green-edged tannins and a drying finish that cries out for food to show at its best.

1994 Côte de Brouilly, Claude et Michelle Joubert   15/20
Medium-bodied 💰 |

From the hill that is one of northern Beaujolais's most picturesque landmarks, this is a forward, strawberry fruity Gamay with well-defined acidity and tannins.

Over £8

AUSTRALIA

1993 Jim Barry Macrae Wood Shiraz, Clare Valley   17/20
Full-bodied 💰💰💰 ▬

Made in one of the wettest vintages on record in the Clare Valley, this is a minty, spicy, oak-infused Shiraz, in which low-yielding vines have triumphed over the deficiencies of a watery vintage. An elegant Aussie Shiraz with finely textured tannins.

FRANCE

1994 Domaine Sainte Anne, Cuvée Notre Dame des Cellettes, Côtes du Rhône Villages   16/20
Full-bodied 🍷🍷 ▬

Made from a blend of Syrah, Grenache and Mourvèdre by Burgundian refugee Guy Steinmaier, this is a spicy, rich, concentrated, blackberry fruity Côtes du Rhône Villages with the structure to age. Finishes a little dry.

1993 Givry Premier Cru, Clos Salomon, Domaine du Gardin
15/20

Medium-bodied 🍷 ▬

From grower Gérard Mouton, this is a modern Côte Chalonnaise red Burgundy with spicy oak and light raspberry and cherry fruit flavours. Well made, but we feel that the fruit may fall away before the tannins.

1993 Gevrey Chambertin, Denis Mortet   17/20
Medium-bodied 🍷🍷🍷 ▬

From one of the best recent vintages in Burgundy, this village-level Pinot Noir from grower Denis Mortet has the concentration, sumptuous wild-strawberry intensity and stylish oak of a *premier cru* with the backbone to age.

ITALY

1991 Barolo Zonchera, Ceretto   16/20
Full-bodied 🍷🍷 ▮

Maturing, brick-red Nebbiolo with the classic tannic structure and acidity of Alba's best red grape variety and surprisingly delicate, almost Pinot Noir-like, game and strawberry flavours.

NEW ZEALAND

1994 Kemblefield Cabernet Franc, Hawkes Bay   16/20
Medium-bodied 🍷🍷 ▮

Made by Californians John Kemble and Kaar (yes, Kaar) Field, this Hawkes Bay Cabernet Franc out-Loires the Loire for grassy, cassis-sweet fruit flavours and appealing, oak-aged smoothness. One of New Zealand's more interesting, non-Pinot Noir red wines.

Sparkling

Over £8

FRANCE

Tanner's Champagne, Duval Leroy   16/20
Dry 🍶🍶🍶 ▮
From the Vértus-based house of Duval Leroy, this malty, youthful, Pinot-based fizz is one of the best-value own-label sparklers we've tasted from an independent wine merchant at around £13.

Fortified

Over £8

PORTUGAL

Henriques & Henriques, Madeira, Malmsey, 10-Year-Old   15/20
Sweet 🍶 ▮
Sweet-oaky and rather spirity Madeira made from the Malmsey grape with the cooked character typical of the style. Rather pricey at £17 a bottle, when you think of the value to be found in Jerez.

SPAIN

Valdespino Solera 1842, Oloroso Viejo Dulce   18/20
Off-dry 🍶🍶🍶 ▬▬
If you've always thought that Sherry belonged at the end of an ironing board or in a pulpit, we suggest that you try a bottle of this enormously complex, mature Oloroso from the talented Miguel Valdespino. Sweet-and-sour flavours of almond and date, with crème brûlée notes, make this a venerable wine that leaves you groping for superlatives.

Grapevine's Best of the Rest

John Armit Wines

Address: 5 Royalty Studios, 105 Lancaster Road, London W11 1QF

Telephone/fax: 0171 727 6846; 0171 727 7133

Number of branches: 1

Opening hours: 9.00am to 6.00pm Monday to Friday

Credit cards accepted: Access, Visa, Switch

Discounts: No

Facilities and services: Cellar planning; cellarage; wine broker; *en primeur* offers; wine investment advice; major annual tasting in October; regular tutored tastings; private customer tastings on request

Area(s) of specialisation: Bordeaux, Burgundy

Fashionable, West London wine merchant catering for the capital's glitterati. Particularly good for growers' Burgundies, clarets from the Left Bank négociant house of Jean-Pierre Moueix, boutique California wineries and, appropriately enough, the never knowingly undercharged Angelo Gaja from Piedmont. Also hosts an annual lunch or dinner with American wine guru Robert Parker.

Berry Brothers & Rudd

Address: 3 St James's Street, London SWIA IEG

Telephone/fax: 0171 396 9600; 0171 396 9609

Opening hours: 9.00am to 5.30pm Monday to Friday

Number of branches: 3

Also at: Berry's Wine Warehouse, Hamilton Close, Houndmills, Basingstoke, Hants RG21 6YB. Telephone/fax: 01256 23566; 24 hour answerphone service; 01256 479558. Opening hours: 10.00am to 5.00pm Monday to Wednesday; 10.00am to 8.00pm Thursday and Friday; 10.00am to 4.00pm Saturday

And: Terminal 3 Departures Lounge, Heathrow Airport. Telephone/fax: 0181 564 8361/3; 0181 564 8379. Opening hours: 6.00am to 10.00pm daily.

Credit cards accepted: Access, Visa, American Express, Diners Club, JCB (at Heathrow only)

Discounts: On orders of 3 cases or more

Facilities and services: Wine broking; cellar planning; glass hire; gift service; party orders; daily in-store tastings; regular customer tastings throughout the UK; private customer tastings in-store on request; free delivery to UK mainland on orders over £100; wedding list service; *en primeur* offers; newsletters

Mail order: Ask for carriage charges if order is less than £100

Area(s) of specialisation: Bordeaux, Germany, Port

Ultra-traditional St James's merchant with a mail-order business based in Basingstoke and an over-priced world traveller-friendly shop in Heathrow's Terminal Three. Good for traditional French wines, and remains one of the few independents committed to fine German estate wines. Recent moves into the New World, with wineries such as Qupé, Wirra Wirra, Thelema and Hunter's are encouraging.

D. Byrne & Co

Address: Victoria Buildings, 12 King Street, Clitheroe, Lancashire BB7 2EP

Telephone: 01200 423152

Number of branches: 1

Opening hours: 8.30am to 6.00pm Monday to Wednesday and Saturday; 8.30am to 8.00pm Thursday and Friday

Credit cards accepted: None

Discounts: None

Facilities and services: Sale or return; free glass loan; party planning; cellar planning; storage; free tastings every Saturday and free annual tasting each autumn

Mail order: By arrangement only

Area(s) of specialisation: Bordeaux

A local, family-owned institution run by brothers Andrew and Philip Byrne from a nineteenth-century shop in the heart of Clitheroe. Produces a huge, if rambling, 68-page list with nothing in the way of tasting notes or information to guide the punter. Perhaps they aren't necessary, as the Byrnes are usually on hand to dispense advice and (most Saturdays) to conduct tastings in their cellars. The sort of merchant every English town would be more than happy to have.

Chippendale Fine Wines

Address: 15 Manor Square, Otley LS21 3AP

Telephone/fax: 0943 850633; 0943 850633

Number of branches: 1

Opening hours: 10.00am to 5.45pm Monday, Tuesday, Thursday, Friday; 9.30am to 5.00pm Saturday

Credit cards accepted: Access, Visa, Switch

Discounts: 5 per cent case discount on orders of 1 to 5 cases; 7 per cent on orders of 6 cases or more; 'Discount Club' members receive a further 1 or 2 per cent case discount and also a 3 per cent discount on bottle prices

Facilities and services: Sale or return; free local delivery on orders of 6 or more bottles; free glass loan; party planning; weekly in-store tastings; tutored tastings on request; free 'Discount Club'

Mail order: Nationwide delivery; ask for carriage charges

Area(s) of specialisation: Australia, regional France

The author of one of the most amusing wine lists in the country, supplemented by regular, soapbox-style outpourings in monthly newsletters, Michael Pollard is an *écrivain manqué*, who appears to have one eye on Robin Yapp's title as the Marcel Proust of the British wine trade and the other on a book of Ogden Nash poems. His Otley-based operation is a one-man Punch and Judy show, with particular strengths in Australia, the south of France and, latterly, Argentina. An idiosyncratic delight.

Connolly's Wine Merchants

Address: Arch 13, 220 Livery Street, Birmingham B3 1EU

Telephone/fax: 0121 236 9269; 0121 233 2339

Number of branches: 1

Opening hours: 9.00am to 5.30pm Monday to Friday; 10.00am to 2.00pm Saturday

Credit cards accepted: Visa, Switch, Master Card, American Express

Discounts: 10 per cent discount on unmixed and mixed cases of wine when orders are paid by cheque or cash

Facilities and services: Free local delivery for one case or more; free glass loan; sale or return; regular tutored tastings, often featuring winemakers

Mail order: Orders accepted both by telephone and fax for single-bottle and case sales; ask for carriage charges

Area(s) of specialisation: France, Italy, California

A highly active Midlands wine merchant run by enthusiast and William McGonagall wannabe, Chris Connolly ('Said Mr Clever, "Don't despair, I'll get us out of trouble. Give those Connolly's chaps a ring, they'll be here at the double.'") Connolly's holds lots of tastings and wine-and-food evenings, with the emphasis on the New World. But the main treat is the chatty, well-chosen list, called The Book of Bacchus, which covers the world's wine regions in just the right depth and throws in a good range of malt whiskies and Riedel glasses for good measure.

Corney & Barrow

Address: 12 Helmet Row, London EC1V 3QJ

Telephone/fax: 0171 251 4051; 0171 608 1373

Opening hours: 9.00am to 6.00pm Monday to Friday

Number of branches: 4

Also at: 194 Kensington Park Road, London W11 2ES. Telephone/fax: 0171 221 5122; 0171 221 9371. Opening hours: 10.30am to 8.00pm Monday to Saturday; 11.00am to 2.00pm Sunday.

And: Belvoir House, High Street, Newmarket, Suffolk CB8 8OH. Telephone/fax: 01638 662068; 01638 560255. Opening hours: 9.00am to 6.00pm Monday to Saturday

And: Corney & Barrow with Whighams of Ayr, 8 Academy Street, Ayr KA7 1HT, Scotland. Telephone/fax: 01292 267000; 01292 265903. Opening hours: 9.30am to 5.30pm Monday to Saturday

And: Corney & Barrow with Whighams of Ayr, 26 Rutland Square, Edinburgh EH1 2BW. Telephone/fax: 0131 228 2233; 0131 228 2243. Opening hours: 9.00am to 6.00pm Monday to Friday

Credit cards accepted: Access, Visa, American Express

Discounts: By negotiation

Facilities and services: Cellarage; corporate services; gift packing; wine broker; regular in-store tastings; cellar planning; sale or return; advice for weddings; contactable on e-mail; *en primeur*; broking lists and newsletters

Mail order: Deliver throughout mainland UK; ask for carriage charges

Area(s) of specialisation: Bordeaux, Burgundy

The kind of place where it helps to have a double-barrelled surname to get onto the mailing list, Corney & Barrow is the City wine merchant par excellence. Its close links with the ultra-expensive Domaine de la Romanée-Conti and Château Pétrus are a good indication of the style of operation, but there are less expensive wines on the list, too. Those from négociant Olivier Leflaive are especially noteworthy.

Farr Vintners

Address: 19 Sussex Street, London SW1V 4RR

Telephone/fax: 0171 828 1960; 0171 828 3500

Number of branches: 1

Opening hours: 10.00am to 6.00pm Monday to Friday

Discounts: On orders over £2,000 ex. VAT

Facilities and services: Cellarage; advice; valuation

Mail order: Minimum order £500 ex. VAT; ask for carriage charges

Area(s) of specialisation: Fine and rare wines

Short of a bottle of 1961 Château Latour? Run out of 1988 Château d'Yquem? Then call Farr Vintners, Britain's leading fine and rare wine brokers, whose thriving business was rewarded with a Queen's Award for Export Achievement. (This gives you an indication of the international spread of Farr's customers.) At times, the owners are a little too dependent on scores given by American wine writer Robert Parker and *The Wine Spectator* when it comes to choosing wines, but there's no denying the depth of knowledge and expertise here. A minimum order of £500 keeps the hoi polloi – but not necessarily the Japanese, Americans and Swiss – away.

Gauntley's of Nottingham

Address: 4 High Street, Exchange Arcade, Nottingham NG1 2ET

Telephone/fax: 0115 950 0555; 0115 951 0557

Number of branches: 1

Opening hours: 9.00am to 5.30pm Monday to Saturday

Credit cards accepted: Access, Visa, Switch

Discounts: 5 per cent case discount

Facilities and services: Sale or return; free glass loan; free local delivery; gift boxes; in bond transfers and storage; tutored tastings

Mail order: Worldwide for single bottles and cases; ask for carriage charges

Area(s) of specialisation: Rhône, Alsace, Loire, Languedoc-Roussillon

The amazingly youthful John Gauntley is often to be found truffling through the vineyards of France in search of new wines from his beloved Rhône, Loire and Languedoc-Roussillon. We can't fault the man's choice of specialist regions, or his choice of growers within them. He's also branched out into top estates in Australia, California, New Zealand and South Africa. Not a place for claret lovers.

Gelston Castle Fine Wines

Address: Gelston Castle, Castle Douglas, Scotland DG7 1QE

Telephone/fax: 01556 503012; 01556 504183

Opening hours: 9.00am to 6.00pm Monday to Friday; 9.00am to 12.00pm Saturday; and 24-hour answerphone service

Number of branches: 2

Also at: 45 Warwick Square, London SW1V 2AJ. Telephone/fax: 0171 821 6841; 0171 821 6350. Opening hours: 9.00am to 6.00pm Monday to Friday; and 24-hour answerphone service

Credit cards accepted: None

Discounts: By arrangement on large orders

Facilities and services: Gift packing and delivery; cellarage; menu planning; in-store and private tutored tasting; fine-wine dinners and wine weekends organised; cellar planning and evaluation; fine-wine broking and auction sale/purchase

Mail order: Orders may be placed by telephone, fax and post; free delivery in mainland UK for orders over £150, otherwise a fixed charge per drop

Area(s) of specialisation: Burgundy, the Midi, Loire, *petits châteaux*, Bordeaux, Germany

In with a shout for the title of Scotland's best independent wine merchant, Alexander Scott's turreted operation produces a stylish, hugely informative wine list and sends out regular offers of off-beat wines from regions such as Jurançon, Lombardy and Tokay. Scott is strong in Burgundy and the Midi and was also one of the few merchants to take a sensible approach to the Bordeaux 1995 *en primeur* campaign.

Peter Green

Address: 37a/b Warrender Park Road, Edinburgh EH9 1HJ

Telephone/fax: 0131 229 5925; 0131 229 5925

Number of branches: 1

Opening hours: 9.30am to 6.30pm Monday to Friday; 9.30am to 7.00pm Saturday; 12.00pm to 5.00pm Sunday (December only)

Credit cards accepted: Access, Visa, Switch, Delta, Master Card

Discounts: 5 per cent case discount

Facilities and services: Free glass loan; free local delivery; gift packaging service; cellarage; regular in-store tastings; tutored tastings 9 times a year; frequent organised group tastings; *en primeur* offers; bin-end sales

Mail order: Delivery throughout the UK; ask for carriage charges

Area(s) of specialisation: Australia, New Zealand, South Africa, Chile, Argentina, and so on around the world in 80 days

Edinburgh's most catholic selection of wines is housed in Michael Romer's Warrender Park Road shop, which combines the feel of a traditional wine merchant with the stacked-high, browser-friendly ambience of a wine warehouse. The range is so big that it's bound to be stronger in some areas than others, but if you're looking for a bottle from Oregon, Argentina or Zimbabwe, the chances are that Peter Green will be able to help.

Haynes, Hanson & Clark

Address: 25 Eccleston Street, London SW1W 9NP

Telephone/fax: 0171 259 0102; 0171 259 0103

Opening hours: 9.00am to 7.00pm Monday to Friday; 10.00am to 6.00pm Saturday

Number of branches: 2

Also at: Sheep Street, Stow-on-the-Wold, Gloucestershire GL54 1AA. Telephone/fax: 01451 870 808; 01451 870 508. Opening hours: 9.00am to 6.00pm Monday to Friday; 9.00am to 5.30pm Saturday

Credit cards: Access, Visa, Switch, Master Card

Discounts: 10 per cent case discount on mixed and unmixed cases

Facilities and services: Free local delivery; free glass loan; ice; gift packing service; wine bins made to order; cellar planning

Mail order: Free delivery throughout the UK with orders of 5 cases or more, or over £450

Area(s) of specialisation: Burgundy

Drawing on the knowledge of Master of Wine and Burgundophile-in-chief, Anthony Hanson, whose book, *Burgundy*, is by far the best tome on the subject, Haynes, Hanson and Clark is one of a small handful of places to buy fine, limited-production wines from the Yonne and the Côte d'Or. If you enjoy Chablis from Raveneau, Volnay from De Montille, Chambolle-Musigny from Roumier or Meursault from François Jobard, this is the place to open your cheque book and close your eyes. H,H&C also does a good job in the Loire, Bordeaux, Beaujolais and California.

Laytons Wine Merchants

Address: 20 Midland Road, London NW1 2AD

Telephone/fax: 0171 388 4567; 0171 383 7419

Opening hours: 9.00am to 5.30pm Monday to Friday; 10.00am to 4.00pm Saturday

Number of branches: 4 (including 3 André Simon shops)

Also at: 50–2 Elizabeth Street, Belgravia, London SW1W 9PB. Telephone/fax: 0171 730 8108; 0171 730 9284. Opening hours: 9.30am to 7.00pm Monday to Saturday

And: 21 Motcomb Street, Knightsbridge, London SW1X 8LB. Telephone/fax: 0171 235 3723; 0171 235 2062. Opening hours: 9.30am to 6.30pm Monday to Friday; 10.00am to 1.00pm Saturday

And: 23 Elyston Street, Chelsea Green SW3. Telephone/fax: 0171 581 2660; 0171 581 1203. Opening hours: 9.30am to 7.00pm Monday to Saturday

Credit cards accepted: Access, Visa, American Express

Discounts: 'Rare', apparently

Facilities and services: Free delivery on orders over £150; wedding list service; gift delivery service; regular customer tastings in London, Oxford, Cambridge, Manchester, York and Leeds/Bradford

Mail order: National and international deliveries available; ask for carriage charges

Area(s) of specialisation: France, Italy

Run by the cricket-mad Graham Chidgey, the only wine merchant we know of to have scored a first-class century, Laytons is a traditional, pinstripes-and-braces merchant, which concentrates on Bordeaux and Burgundy. It specialises in breathless *en primeur* offers and fine-wine bin ends, sold through mail order and its three André Simon shops. Laytons house-Champagne is worth a detour.

Moreno Wines

Address: 2 Norfolk Place, London W2 1QN

Telephone/fax: 0171 706 3055; 0171 286 0513

Opening hours: 10.00am to 6.00pm Monday to Friday; 10.00am to 8.00pm Saturday

Number of branches: 2

Also at: 11 Marylands Road, London W9 2DU. Telephone/fax: 0171 286 0678; 0171 286 0513

Opening hours: 12.00pm to 10.00pm Monday to Wednesday; 10.00am to 10.00pm Thursday to Saturday; 12.00pm to 10.00pm Sunday

Credit cards accepted: Visa, Switch, Master Card

Discounts: 5 per cent on one to three cases; 10 per cent on over three cases

Facilities and services: Free local delivery; corporate account facilities; in-store and tutored tastings; Spanish wine club

Mail order: £7 per case within the UK

Area(s) of specialisation: Spain, South America

Hispanophiles who find tapas-bar fare as dull as Julio Iglesias tend to gravitate towards academic-turned-wine-merchant Manuel Moreno's quirky West London shops. Hand-selected bottles from estates such as Guelbenzu, Marqués de Alella and Valdespino, as well as a broad selection of older vintages from the likes of Vega Sicilia and La Rioja Alta, make this one of the two best Spanish specialists in the country. Chilean wines from Viña Casablanca and Viña Porta and the Argentine Vistalba are worth a punt, too.

Morris & Verdin

Address: 10 The Leathermarket, Weston Street, London SE1 3ER

Telephone/fax: 0171 357 8866; 0171 357 8877

Number of branches: 1

Opening hours: 8.00am to 6.00pm Monday to Friday

Credit cards accepted: None

Discounts: None

Facilities and services: Glass hire; tutored tastings; free delivery within inner London

Mail order: Orders taken both by telephone and letter

Area(s) of specialisation: Burgundy, California

When the 1995 Burgundy vintage is released onto the *en primeur* market in the spring of 1997, Morris & Verdin's Leathermarket base is the first place the *Grapevine* team will head for. Master of Wine Jasper Morris's mouth-watering selection of growers' wines, from good-value house red and white Bourgogne to *premier* and *grand cru* stunners from the likes of Bonneau du Martray, Dominique Lafon, Daniel Rion and Pousse d'Or is a delight for Burgundophiles. He also buys well in Bordeaux and acts as an agent for some increasingly good wines from California producers, such as Au Bon Climat, Qupé and Bonny Doon.

James Nicholson

Address: 27a Killyleagh Street, Crossgar, County Down, Northern Ireland BT30 9DG

Telephone/fax: 01396 830091; 01396 830028

Number of branches: 1

Opening hours: 10.00am to 7.00pm Monday to Saturday

Credit cards accepted: Access, Visa, Switch, American Express

Discounts: Between 7 and 10 per cent on mixed or unmixed cases of wine

Facilities and services: Sale or return; free glass loan; regular free in-store tastings and occasional themed or winemaker tastings; gift packs; cellarage and free delivery of 1 case or more within Northern Ireland; latest offers can also be found on the Internet

Mail order: 48-hour delivery service available throughout the UK

Area(s) of specialisation: Bordeaux, Burgundy, Germany, California

The best wine merchant in Northern Ireland, and one of the finest in the UK to boot, James Nicholson's Crossgar operation is the model of an independent specialist. Nicholson is proud of having earned 25,000 Air Miles in his search for new wines this year, and his first-rate palate and judgement are apparent on every page of his stylishly designed, ring-bound list. Nicholson's standing with winemakers ensures that many of the world's biggest names can be found tutoring tastings for the citizens of Crossgar and Kildare.

Christopher Piper Wines

Address: 1 Silver Street, Ottery-St-Mary, Devon EX11 1DB

Telephone/fax: 01404 814139; 01404 812100

Number of branches: 1

Opening hours: 9.00am to 1.00pm, 2.00pm to 5.30pm Monday to Friday; 9.00am to 1.00pm, 2.30pm to 4.30pm Saturday

Credit cards accepted: Visa, Delta, Master Card

Discounts: 5 per cent on mixed and unmixed cases; 10 per cent on orders of three cases or more

Facilities and services: Free glass loan; sale or return; in-store tastings; account facilities; cellarage; bi-monthly newsletter; *en primeur* offers

Mail order: Free local delivery on orders of three cases or more; free delivery throughout the UK on orders of six cases or more

Area(s) of specialisation: Beaujolais, French country wines, Burgundy

One of the few British wine merchants with a degree in oenology (and the experience of making Beaujolais at Château des Tours in Brouilly every year), Chris Piper is an opinionated and dynamic Devon wine merchant, whose 'Noble Rot' newsletter is always thought-provoking. His list is strong on Burgundy and Beaujolais, as you'd expect, as well as on the New World. And regular offers of traditional, *en primeur* wines ensure a strong West Country following.

Terry Platt

Address: Ferndale Road, Llandudno Junction, Gwynedd LL31 9NT

Telephone/fax: 01492 592971; 01492 592196

Opening hours: 8.30am to 5.30pm Monday to Friday

Number of branches: 2

Also at: World of Wine, 29 Mostyn Avenue, Craig-y-Don, Llanduduno LL30 1YS. Telephone: 01492 872997. Opening hours: 10.00am to 8.00pm Monday to Saturday; 12.00pm to 3.00pm Sunday

Credit cards accepted: Access, Switch, Master Card

Discounts: By negotiation

Facilities and services: Sale or return; glass hire; corporate gifts; valuations; wine list preparation; in-store tastings every Friday and Saturday

Area(s) of specialisation: A good generalist

The leading wine merchant in Wales and a regular award-winner, Jeremy (son of Terry) Platt offers a broad, generally well-chosen range with highlights in Burgundy, Beaujolais and Bordeaux and an increasing presence in Australia, California, New Zealand and South Africa. The weirdest wines on the list are Wales' very own Monnow Valley Vineyards (full marks for patriotism, boyo), but non-Gaelic speaking customers would be better served drinking Martinez Bujanda from Rioja, Quinta do Carmo from Portugal or Vavasour from New Zealand.

Raeburn Fine Wines

Address: 2–3 Comely Bank Road, Edinburgh EH4 1DS

Telephone/fax: 0131 332 5166; 0131 332 5166

Number of branches: 1

Opening hours: 9.00am to 6.00pm Monday to Saturday; 12.30pm to 5.00pm Sunday

Credit cards accepted: Access, Visa, Switch, Delta, Master Card

Discounts: 2.5 per cent on mixed cases; 5 per cent on unmixed cases

Facilities and services: Tutored tastings; corporate tastings; *en primeur* offers

Mail order: Available throughout the UK; ask for carriage charges

Area(s) of specialisation: Burgundy, Bordeaux, New World

Famous for setting up a wine business at the back of a family florist's, Zubair Mohamed is an uncompromising, quality-oriented Edinburgh merchant with the best growers' Burgundy list in Scotland and an eye for idiosyncratic estates in the New World, such as Joseph Swann, Warwick Estate and Moss Wood. Mohamed also has a well-chosen, eclectic selection from Italy, Spain and Germany and hosts regular dinners and tutored tastings. More fun than selling chrysanthemums, we reckon.

Reid Wines (1992) Ltd

Address: The Mill, Marsh Lane, Hallatrow, Bristol BS18 5EB

Telephone/fax: 01761 452645; 01761 453642

Number of branches: 1

Opening hours: 9.00am to 6.00pm Monday to Friday; weekends by arrangement

Credit cards accepted: Visa, Master Card, with a 3 per cent surcharge on the total cost of each order

Discounts: None

Facilities and services: Occasional in-store tastings; free local delivery; glass hire

Mail order: Ask for carriage charges

Area(s) of specialisation: Generalist, with an emphasis on fine and rare wines

Peppered with wine quotes and Bill Baker's humorous asides, Reid Wines' laconic but authoritative list is a good place to find rare and mature bottles snapped up at the auction houses and described with self-deprecating honesty. The 'fine and rare' tag shouldn't be overstated, however, as Reid Wines lists plenty of things from more recent vintages, too, including traditional Burgundy, Bordeaux and Rhône, as well as Calera, Clos du Val and Niebaum Coppola from California, Taltarni from Australia and Wairau River from New Zealand.

Howard Ripley

Address: 35 Eversley Crescent, London N21 1EL

Telephone/fax: 0181 360 8904; 0181 360 8904

Number of branches: 1

Opening hours: 9.00am to 10.00pm Monday to Friday; 9.00am to 1.00pm Saturday; 9.00am to 12.00pm Sunday

Credit cards accepted: None

Discounts: None

Facilities and services: Free glass hire; free local delivery; private tastings on request

Mail order: National and international delivery; ask for carriage charges; minimum order 1 case

Area(s) of specialisation: Burgundy

One man, one region. Dentist and wine merchant Howard Ripley's single-minded focus on top-quality, domaine Burgundy shows considerable commercial derring-do. But if you're interested in the finest names of the Côte d'Or, such as Ramonet, Leroy, Leflaive, Lafarge and Rousseau, and money isn't too tight to mention, this is a warren of the world's best Pinot Noirs and Chardonnays. We don't know how Ripley funds his fact- and wine-finding visits to the cellars of Vosne, Pommard and Chassagne-Montrachet, but perhaps gold fillings have something to do with it.

Roberson

Address: 60 Alpha Street, Slough SLI IQX

Telephone/fax: 01753 521336; 01753 576748

Opening hours: 9.00am to 6.00pm Monday to Friday

Number of branches: 2

Also at: 348 Kensington High Street, London WI4 8NS. Telephone/fax: 0171 371 2121; 0171 371 4010. Opening hours: 10.00am to 8.00pm Monday to Saturday

Credit cards accepted: Visa, Switch, Delta, Master Card, American Express, Diners Club

Discounts: 5 per cent on mixed cases; 10 per cent on unmixed cases

Facilities and services: Free local delivery; cellarage; free glass hire; in-store tastings every Saturday at the shop; regular tutored tastings; *en primeur*

Mail order: Ask for carriage charges

Area(s) of specialisation: A catholic list

The smartest, most overtly designed wine shop in the capital (and a useful watering hole during the annual London Wine Trade Fair), Cliff Roberson's emporium is stocked with one of the most eclectic ranges in the country. The place to go if you're looking for a single bottle of something truly special, Roberson's carries good stocks of mature and unusual wines, such as Jura whites, and expensive Burgundies and clarets. Expect to pay Kensington rather than Kennington prices, however.

Ubiquitous Chip

Address: 12 Ashton Lane, Hillhead, Glasgow G12 8SJ

Telephone/fax: 0141 334 5007; 0141 337 1302

Number of branches: 1

Opening hours: 12.00pm to 10.00pm Monday to Saturday

Credit cards: Access, Visa, Master Card, American Express, Diners Club

Discounts: 5 per cent case discount

Facilities and services: Free glass loan; ice; free local delivery; tutored tastings; gift vouchers

Mail order: Ask for carriage charges

Area(s) of specialisation: Good general specialist, with an interesting list of fine and rare wines and malt whiskies

The title of Arnold Wesker's play, *Chips with Everything*, lives on in the name of this popular Glasgow media haunt, which serves enjoyable food as well as having the best wine list in the city. Presented in a no-frills, printer paper format, the wine list is a palate-watering selection from traditional and out-of-the-way regions of France, as well as Italy, Spain and the New World.

Valvona & Crolla

Address: 19 Elm Row, Edinburgh EH7 4AA

Telephone/fax: 0131 556 6066; 0131 556 1668

Number of branches: 1

Opening hours: 8.00am to 6.00pm Monday to Wednesday and Saturday; 8.00am to 7.30pm Thursday and Friday

Credit cards accepted: Access, Visa, Switch, American Express

Discounts: 10 per cent on unmixed cases; 5 per cent on mixed cases

Facilities and services: Daily in-store tastings; regular informal and tutored tastings; regular wine and food events; free delivery in Edinburgh for orders over £30; free glass loan; sale or return

Mail order: Ask for carriage charges

Area(s) of specialisation: Italy

If you like Italian food and wine, it's hard to walk through Valvona & Crolla's Elm Row deli without salivating. The Contini family's famous shop is a showcase for the best of Italy – north, south and central – stocking wines, olive oils, hams, salamis and fresh pasta. This is a meeting place for Edinburgh's Italian community and assorted Italophiles, who come here for gossip, tutored tastings, dinners, cookery demonstrations and an annual fungi foray. It's also a great place to buy Italian wine, with good stocks of older vintages and the best of modern Brunello, Chianti, Amarone and Barolo, plus a growing range from Puglia and Sicily.

La Vigneronne

Address: 105 Old Brompton Road, London SW7 3LE

Telephone/fax: 0171 589 6113; 0171 581 2983

Number of branches: 1

Opening hours: 10.00am to 8.00pm Monday to Friday; 10.00am to 6.00pm Saturday

Credit cards accepted: Access, Visa, Switch, Delta, American Express, Diners Club

Discounts: 5 per cent case discount

Facilities and services: Gift packing service; regular tutored tastings; newsletter; *en primeur* offers; free delivery within the UK for orders of £250 inc. VAT and over

Mail order: Ask for carriage charges

Area(s) of specialisation: Regional France, especially Rhône, Alsace, Bandol, Madiran, Languedoc-Roussillon and old and rare wines

Master of Wine Liz Berry and husband, Mike, may have decamped to Provence on a semi-permanent basis (and who can blame them), but their retail shop and tasting programme are still thriving, helped by the Berrys' endless flow of new finds from France's less traditional regions. If you're more interested in Bandol and Bouzet than Bordeaux and Burgundy, this Old Brompton Road institution is a must.

Vinceremos

Address: 261 Upper Town Street, Bramley, Leeds LS13 3JT

Telephone/fax: 0113 257 7545; 0113 257 6906

Number of branches: 1

Opening hours: 8.45am to 5.45pm Monday to Friday; office occasionally open Saturday – telephone first; 24-hour answerphone service

Credit cards accepted: Visa, Switch, Delta, Master Card

Discounts: 5 per cent on 5 cases or more; 10 per cent on 10 cases or more; trade discounts available

Facilities and services: Free local glass loan; cellarage

Mail order: Nationwide delivery (except Isle of Wight); free delivery on orders of 5 cases or more and to Leeds LS postcodes

Area(s) of specialisation: Organic and vegetarian wines, Hungary, Morocco, Russia

Taking its name from a revolutionary song, Jerry Lockspeiser's politically correct shop has outgrown its original focus on organic and vegetarian wines to list bottles from such diverse sources as Morocco, Hungary and the Ukraine. A large part of the business goes through Bottle Green, which sells mainly Hungarian and Moroccan wine to British supermarkets and off-licence chains. But Vinceremos was where it all started, and it still has one of the best vegetarian ranges in the country. Look out, in particular, for James Millton's bio-dynamic Kiwi wines.

The Vine Trail

Address: 5 Surrey Road, Bishopston, Bristol BS7 9DJ

Telephone/fax: 0117 9423946; 0117 9423946

Number of branches: 1

Opening hours: 9.00am to 7.00pm Monday to Saturday; and 24-hour answerphone

Credit cards accepted: None

Discounts: 2 per cent on 5 cases or more; 3 per cent on 10 cases or more; 5 per cent on 25 cases or more; trade discounts negotiable

Facilities and services: Cellarage; sale or return; free glass loan; free local delivery; ice; gift packing service; regular tastings; tutored private tastings; special food and wine events; fine-wine broking

Mail order: Delivery throughout the UK; ask for carriage charges

Area(s) of specialisation: Small domaine wines, especially from the Rhône, Beaujolais, south-west France and Languedoc

Bristol-based accountant-turned-wine-merchant Nick Brookes is a one-man promotional board for La France Profonde, specialising in small domaine wines from off the beaten (vine) trail. His list is restricted to only 80-odd wines, but you get the impression that Brookes knows them all personally. Each comes with a tempting explanatory tasting note. The quality of the wines is high, with wines from domaines such as Perret in Condrieu, Château Thivin in Côte de Brouilly, Clos Thou in Jurançon and Brusset in Cairanne.

Vintage Roots

Address: Sheeplands Farm, Wargrave, Berkshire RG10 8DT

Telephone/fax: 0118 9401222; 0118 9404814

Number of branches: 1

Opening hours: 9.00am to 6.00pm Monday to Friday; answerphone service out of office hours

Credit cards accepted: Access, Visa

Discounts: 5 per cent on all orders of 5 or more cases

Facilities and services: Occasional in-store tastings

Mail order: Telephone for details

Area(s) of specialisation: Organic and biodynamic wines

Based at the appropriately bucolic Sheeplands Farm, Lance Pigott and Neil Palmer's organic wine business recently celebrated its tenth anniversary. We can see why it's done so well – most of the world's best organic and bio-dynamic wines are stocked here, from Huet and Domaine de Marcoux to Millton and Fetzer. The list is extensive, well-illustrated and shows a commitment to the organic cause, with useful symbols and information.

Vin du Van

Address: Colthups, The Street, Appledore, Kent TN26 2BX

Telephone/fax: 01233 758727; 01233 758389

Number of branches: 1

Opening hours: 9.00am to 6.00pm daily; 24-hour answerphone

Credit cards: Access, Visa, Master Card, Eurocard

Discounts: None

Facilities and services: Free glass loan; free local delivery; sale or return for functions; tutored tastings

Mail order: Orders taken by telephone only; delivery in the UK within 48 hours (except for the Highlands and Islands); ask for carriage charges

Area(s) of specialisation: Australia, New Zealand

Ian Brown's background as an advertising copywriter is gloriously apparent in his witty, crisply written list. Vying with Chippendale Fine Wines for the title of Britain's most eccentric wine merchants, Brown and his collection of cats focus almost exclusively on Australia and New Zealand. Prices are keen and the selection impressive, mixing the familiar with the esoteric.

Yapp Brothers

Address: The Old Brewery, Mere, Wiltshire BA12 6DY

Telephone/fax: 01747 860423; 01747 860929

Number of branches: 1

Opening hours: 9.00am to 5.00pm Monday to Friday; 9.00am to 1.00pm Saturday

Credit cards accepted: Access, Visa, Diners Club

Discounts: Various case discounts; ask for full details

Facilities and services: Daily in-store tastings; tutored tastings for groups, either at the Old Brewery or private venues; wine lunches at restaurants throughout Great Britain

Mail order: £5 surcharge on single case or less; next morning delivery for orders received before 10.00am (except Scottish Highlands)

Area(s) of specialisation: Rhône, Loire, Provence

The original one-man wine merchant, launched in 1969 by dentist and purple-tinged travel writer, Robin Yapp. Being first in the queue enabled Yapp to sign up most of the best growers in his specialist areas, such as Chave in Hermitage, Filliatreau in Saumur-Champigny, Clape in Cornas and Domaine de Trévallon in Les Baux de Provence. The business has grown over the years, but retains the quirky, cartoon-strewn list and characterful touches that made Yapp such an important pioneer.

Noel Young Wines

Address: 56 High Street, Trumpington, Cambridge CB2 2LS

Telephone/fax: 01223 844744; 01223 844736

Number of branches: 1

Opening hours: 10.00am to 9.00pm Monday to Saturday; 12.00pm to 2.00pm Sunday

Credit cards accepted: Visa, Master Card, Diners Club

Discounts: 10 per cent on mixed and unmixed cases; 7 per cent case discount when paying by credit card

Facilities and services: Sale or return; glass hire; free delivery within 25 miles; free tastings every Friday evening and all day Saturday; regular winemaker evenings; tutored tastings as advertised in the newsletter

Mail order: Both national and international; call for charges

Area(s) of specialisation: Fine and rare wines, Austria, New World, quality French

Frequented by thirsty dons and well-heeled students, Noel Young's Cambridgeshire shop has established its alarmingly youthful owner as one of the most interesting wine merchants in the east of England, since it opened three years ago. The information-packed list runs to nearly 900 wines, with strengths in regional France, Austria (the best selection in Britain by far), Italy and the New World.

The *Grapevine* Guide to Cross-Channel Shopping

'Ere we go again...

If you think watching football does funny things to people, you should stand in a Calais cash-and-carry on a bank holiday weekend. It is as close to the realisation of an Hieronymus Bosch painting as either of us wishes to get. Sweating day-trippers stuff their brimming trolleys with case upon case of flavourless beer and wine, straining to guide them to the check-out before the next ferry, Shuttle or hovercraft departs.

Why does cross-Channel shopping render normally sensible people practically brain-dead? Greed is the only possible answer, barely discouraged by the retailers themselves. Even the leaflet handed out at the comparatively upmarket Sainsbury's in Calais pictures a couple staggering away from the store beneath columns of beer and wine.

For many people, the only constraining factor on their purchases is how to get the booze back to the UK. 'I've seen a few people wondering what to do with the kids when they've over-bought by a couple of cases,' says James Oakley of Tesco Vin Plus. 'They end up perched on top of the wine.'

Calais, which remains one of the ugliest towns in northern France, has become the focus of the cross-Channel booze boom. One recent estimate is that we'll be buying 20 per cent of our drink in continental outlets by the end of the century. The flow of beer and wine (most of it from Calais) has trebled in the last three years, according to a report published by *Datamonitor*. And with the opening of the Channel Tunnel, even more people appear to be buying their beer and wine on the Continent.

Things may not be quite as manic as they were on that foam-splashed day in January 1993, when a million corks popped to the sound of 'Auld Lang Syne'. But cross-Channel shopping has become a way of life in Britain, and is likely to remain so. As Richard Harvey of La Maison du Vin in Cherbourg put it: 'The market has reached a certain level and I can't see that changing, unless there's a huge hike or drop in UK duty.'

Over the past year, the pound has picked up against the franc, hovering around the FF7.80 mark. This piece of good news is partially offset by last year's increase in French VAT to 20.6 per cent, but the slightly better exchange rate has made buying wine a more attractive activity than it was a year ago. 'In 1995, the rate was FF7.40,' says Katrina Thom of The Grape Shop in Boulogne and Calais, 'so we should start to see a big increase in people coming to France.'

There were a few hitches during the year, however. The removal of the British visitor's passport in January 1996, coupled with a dearth of deals from ferry companies and nauseating cross-Channel weather, saw sales slow momentarily in the early part of the year. But by March the electronic tills were buzzing again.

The duty game
Duty on alcohol did not change in the November 1995 budget, so the savings between France and the UK remain the same as a year ago. The Chancellor may not spare the off-licences, supermarkets and independent wine merchants of southern England for a second year running, especially given the estimated loss of £370m (in a May 1996 report by industry analysts Gordon-Maxwell Associates) per annum to the Treasury from legal and illegal imports of drink. Kenneth Clarke has admitted that the government lost £210m in VAT and duty on *legitimate* imports in 1995.

For its part, the Wine & Spirit Association says that duty rates should be cut to protect British industry and jobs. Quoted in the tabloid *Off Licence News*, chairman David Grant claimed that the cross-Channel exodus was costing the British drinks industry the equivalent of £1.3 billion a year in lost sales.

We're glad we don't work for the Treasury. Whatever happens in the November 1996 budget, at the time of going to press UK duty stands at £12.64 a case excluding VAT on table wines (compared to FF2.04 in France) and £18.06 a case on Champagne, sparkling wines (FF4.92 in France) and fortified wines with between 15 and 22 per cent alcohol. That's a saving (on duty alone) of just over £1 a bottle on table wine and £1.50 on fizz, Port, Sherry, Madeira and fortified Muscats.

So far, the prediction that Britain would follow the likes of Denmark, Canada and Ireland by cutting duty rates to stem cross-border sales, has not come true. The Treasury is still not convinced that lower duty rates would produce a corresponding increase in drink sales, and with it, revenue, despite the fact that the duty increases in the last budget have resulted in falling UK sales of whisky and beer.

Bootleggers and booze bandits
Customs and Excise have been more active in discouraging bootleggers this year. Illegal imports remain a substantial problem, but a seven-year jail sentence for an East London smuggler who'd illegally sold 350,000 cases of beer (the equivalent of eight Mount Everests) may act as a deterrent. The French authorities have also started to clamp down on the spivvier end of the business, particularly in Calais.

Life is getting harder for the bootlegger. The incidence of so-called booze bandits stealing illegally-imported alcohol on the south coast of England, before it has reached its final destination, is on the increase, too. Several gangs have lost their hauls to local criminals while sleeping in nearby bed-and-breakfast accommodation. Others have had their transit vans hijacked, according to a report in the *Independent on Sunday*. Autoglass in Dover had a busy year in 1996.

What's your limit?

The rules governing cross-Channel buying have not changed since last year. The first and most important thing to remember is that as long as you are buying wine for your own use (and that includes parties, weddings and other celebrations), you can bring as much booze into the country as the axle on your vehicle will bear.

If the alcohol is not for your consumption, or that of your family or friends, you are breaking the law by carrying smuggled goods. Bootlegged booze (the first smugglers used to hide drink inside their boots, apparently) is anything you plan to sell to someone else without paying duty. In 1995 the owners of Death Cigarettes lost a test case designed to show that they could run a business bringing tobacco across the Channel without having to pay duty. The courts nipped that idea in the bud, along with any plans that more enterprising members of the wine trade may have had to try the same thing with wine.

Customs can stop you while you're travelling and ask whether the wine or beer you're carrying is really for your own consumption. If you don't want them turning up at the wedding like the proverbial bad one-pence piece, carry some evidence of any impending celebration with you (a packet of streamers is unlikely to satisfy Her Majesty's Customs officers).

The limits – or, to use the jargon, Minimum Indicative Levels – are the point at which Customs start to ask if the goods cross the dividing line between personal and commercial use. The current limits are 90 litres of table wine (of which not more than 60 may be sparkling), 20 litres of fortified wine, 110 litres of beer and 10 litres of spirits. If you want to bring back more, the burden of proof is on you.

What and where to buy

The choice of wines, beers and spirits available to the cross-Channel shopper was boosted considerably by the opening of the Cité de l'Europe's vast portals two years ago. Tesco and Victoria Wine have added to the diversity of wines available in Calais, as has the arrival of The Grape Shop on the other side of town.

In the debit column, the last 12 months have seen the closure of The Grape Shop's Gare Maritime shop and La Maison du Vin in Saint Malo. Several of the wider, readies-only cash-and-carries have also gone to the wall. As a result, Calais arguably has less of a frontier-town feel to it these days.

It is a mite surprising that most cross-Channel shoppers still make for Calais' rough and ready retailers. They could do better. Boulogne is served by the Seacat, but no ferries, and Cherbourg by longer and more expensive crossings. But that shouldn't put anyone off for a second. Both towns are considerably more attractive than Bootleg City and contain at least one top-notch wine merchant.

Small can be more interesting, too. In the more enlightened outlets, such as The Grape Shop, Victoria Wine, Le Chais, Nicolas, Perardel, The Wine Society and La Maison du Vin, you can take your pick of estate wines and growers' Champagnes. You can even find a good range of wines from New World countries. But stumble into the wrong retailer and you're likely to encounter considerable variation in the quality and range of wines available.

Without wishing to be too chauvinistic, we still think it pays to buy from British-owned supermarkets like Tesco and Sainsbury's, although French outlets such as Leclerc, Auchan and Mammouth have some attractive deals on Grande Marque Champagnes and classed-growth claret.

In general, however, the French hypermarkets are struggling to keep up. Last year we felt that some of them had begun to tailor their wine ranges to British palates. This year we couldn't see any substantive further improvements, although the Dieppe branch of Mammouth has taken on a few non-French Sainsbury's wines to add diversity to its range.

The problem with French supermarkets is that they often seem to regard quality as a secondary issue. The day may come when the French hypermarkets prove a match for the likes of Sainsbury's or Tesco, but so far it's the British as a whole who have taken the cross-Channel initiative. Which is why this year, as last, we've decided to concentrate on what the British-owned retailers have to offer.

Santé!

So, all in all, this is a still a good time to buy wine in France. Significant savings can still be made, especially on cheaper wines, where the difference in duty represents a larger percentage of the price, and on Champagne. Things are not quite as exciting as they once were, however. Whereas differences of £1.50 a bottle were once routine, we reckon the gap between UK and French prices is narrowing, especially on more expensive wines and those from the New World. Pay in sterling and you can also get stung by the varying exchange rates given by different stores. The rule here is to ask before you hand over your pound notes. *Caveat emptor…*

Supermarket and Wine Shop Addresses (By Port)

Amiens
Nicolas, I Rue De Beauvais, 80000 Amiens (22 91 83 15)

Boulogne
Auchan, Route Nationale 42, 62200 Saint Martin Les Boulogne

Le Chais, Rue des Deux Ponts, 62200 Boulogne (321 31 65 42)

The Grape Shop, 85–7 Rue Victor Hugo, 62200 Boulogne (321 32 10 41 or 0171 924 3638 in the UK)

Intermarché, 62360 Pont de Briques (321 83 28 28)

Prix Gros, Centre Commercial de la Liane, 62200 Boulogne-sur-Mer (321 30 43 67)

Les Vins de France, 11 Rue Nationale, 62200 Boulogne (321 30 51 00)

The Wine Society, Rue Fressin, 62140 Hesdin (321 86 52 07)

Caen
Nicolas, 10 Rue Bellivet, 14000 Caen (231 85 24 19)

Calais
Bar à Vins, 52 Place d'Armes, 62100 Calais (321 96 98 31)

Le Chais, 40 Rue de Phalsbourg, 62100 Calais (321 97 88 56)

Eastenders, 14 Rue Gustave Courbet, 62100 Calais (321 34 85 24)

The Grape Shop, 40 Rue de Phalsbourg, 62100 Calais (321 85 99 64)

Intermarché, 42–6 Avenue Antoine de St-Exupéry, 62100 Calais (321 34 42 44)

Mammouth, Route de Boulogne, 62100 Calais (321 34 04 44)

Perardel, Zone Industrielle Marcel Doret, 190 Rue Marcel Dassault, 62100 Calais (321 97 21 22)

Pidou, Zone Industrielle Marcel Doret, 190 Rue Marcel Dassault, 62100 Calais (321 96 78 10), and Quai de la Loire, 62100 Calais (321 46 07 67)

Prix Gros, Route St-Omer, 62100 Calais (321 34 65 98)

J. Sainsbury Bières, Vins et Spiritueux, Mammouth Centre, Route de Boulogne, 62100 Calais (321 82 38 48)

Le Terroir, 29 Rue des Fontinettes, 62100 Calais (321 36 34 66)

The *Grapevine* Guide to Cross-Channel Shopping

Tesco Vin Plus, Unit 122, Cité de l'Europe, 62231 Coquelles (321 46 02 70 or 01992 632222 in the UK)

Victoria Wine Unit, 179 Cité de l'Europe, 62231 Coquelles (321 82 07 32)

The Wine & Beer Company, Rue de Judée, Zone Marcel Doret, 62100 Calais (321 97 63 00 or 0181 875 1900 in UK), and Unit 3A , ZA la Français, 62231 Coquelles (321 82 93 64)

Cherbourg
Auchan, Centre Commercial Cotentin, 50470 La Glacerie (233 88 13 13)

Continent, Quai de l'Entrepot, 50104 Cherbourg (233 43 14 11)

Leclerc, 5 Rue des Claires, 50460 Querqueville (233 03 55 43)

La Maison du Vin, 71 Avenue Carnot, 50100 Cherbourg (233 43 39 79 or 01929 480352 in the UK)

Wine & Beer Company, Centre Commercial Continent, Quai de l'Entrepôt, 50100 Cherbourg (233 22 23 22)

Deauville
Nicolas, 31 Rue De Breney, 14800 Deauville (280 49 94 04)

Dieppe
Intermarché, 76370 Rouxmesnil Bouteilles (235 82 57 75)

LC Vins, 1 Grande Rue, 76200 Dieppe (235 84 32 41)

Leclerc, 76370 Etran-Martin Eglise (235 82 56 95)

Mammouth (including Sainsbury's), Centre Commercial Belvédère, 76371 Dieppe (232 90 52 00)

Le Havre
Nicolas, Les Halles Centrales, Rue Bernardin St Pierre, 76600 Le Havre (235 42 24 63)

The Wine & Beer Company, 16 Quai Frissard, 76600 Le Havre (235 26 38 10)

Roscoff
Les Caves de Roscoff, Zone de Bloscon, Ateliers 7–9, 29680 Roscoff (298 61 24 10 or 0171 376 4639 in the UK)

Rouen
Nicolas, 18B Place Du Vieux Marché, 76000 Rouen (235 71 56 10)

The *Grapevine* Guide to Cross-Channel Shopping

USEFUL TELEPHONE NUMBERS

Brittany Ferries: 299 82 80 80 (France); 0990 360360 (UK)

Customs & Excise Single Market Unit: 0171 620 1313

Hoverspeed: 321 46 14 14 (France); Freephone: 0590 1777; 0304 240101 (UK)

P&O Ferries: 321 46 10 10 (France); 0181 575 8555 (UK)

Sally Line Ferries: 328 26 70 70 (France); 0800 636465 (UK)

Le Shuttle: 321 00 61 00 (France); 0990 353535 (UK)

Stena Sealink: 321 46 80 00 (France); 01233 647047 (UK and European head office)

The Grape Shop ☆☆☆☆

Address: 85–7, Rue Victor Hugo, 62200 Boulogne

Telephone: 00 33 321 32 10 41

Opening hours: 10.00am to 7.00pm seven days a week

Also at: 40, Rue de Phalsbourg, 62100 Calais. Telephone: 00 33 321 85 99 64. Opening hours: 9.30am to 7.00pm seven days a week (closed Tuesday in winter)

Managers: Managing director Martin Brown; director Katrina Thom

Payment methods: Access, Visa; sterling cheques and cash; French francs

Discounts: Quantity discounts by negotiation

In-store tastings: Yes

English spoken: Yes

Following the cross-Channel herd, Martin Brown has moved the focus of his business from Boulogne to Calais over the last year. The dockside portakabin in the Gare Maritime has closed down and been replaced by a larger shop in Calais' Rue de Phalsbourg. The site is half as big again as the Gare Maritime and allows The Grape Shop to store greater quantities of wine on site.

Tourists who still hanker for the tranquillity and comparative beauty of Boulogne can still visit The Grape Shop's original premises in the Rue Victor Hugo, but the selection is broader in Calais. 'There are huge numbers of people coming to Calais,' Katrina Thom told us a little wearily, 'and fewer and fewer coming to Boulogne. Boulogne's a nicer place, but it's a bit of a detour.'

The new Calais shop is a former freezer centre on the outskirts of town, selling an impressive 800-strong wine list from a massive range of countries, including Australia, Mexico, Moldova and England. But, despite the worldwide selection, France accounts for two-thirds of sales, with house-wines and Champagnes the big-volume lines.

The Calais shop did not open as early as Martin Brown had hoped, owing to French bureaucracy. The extra expenses involved put a severe strain on the business, and at the time of writing, debts were in the hands of an official administrator. There's only one thing to do, in our view – get yourself over to Calais and buy your wines from The Grape Shop, one of the most individual wine merchants on the Continent.

White

Under 20FF

FRANCE

1994 Colombard Bellefontaine Vin de Pays des Côtes de Gascogne   12/20
Off-dry 🍾 🍶
Basic appley Gascon white blended by Franco-Mancunian wine merchant, Paul Boutinot. Crisp acidity doesn't quite compensate for mawkish sweetness.

1995 Domaine de Papolle Colombard, Vin de Pays des Côtes de Gascogne, Peter Hawkins   14/20
Dry 🍾🍾 🍶
The best vintage yet from Englishman Peter Hawkins' Gascon estate, showing fresh, pear-drop and grapefruit characters and grassy, almost Sauvignon-like crispness.

1995 Domaine de San de Guilhem, Alain Lalanne, Vin de Pays des Côtes de Gascogne   11/20
Off-dry 🍶
Hard, sulphur-scented, roughly-handled white. Hardly worth boarding Le Shuttle for.

Cuvée Jean-Paul, Demi-Sec, Blanc de Blancs   12/20
Medium dry 🍶
Very basic, gluey French *vin de table* with what smells like cheap Chenin Blanc at its core. Very cheap, but not cheap enough.

20–30FF

FRANCE

1995 Château Bois de Favereau, Bordeaux Sauvignon, A. Pellegrue   14/20
Dry 💰💰💰 ▯

It may be the effect of the well-rated 1995 vintage, but this attractive, concentrated white Bordeaux tastes more like a Sémillon than a Sauvignon Blanc. A classic, quaffing dry white.

1995 Château Tour des Gendres, Bergerac Blanc Sec, Conti   15/20
Dry 💰💰💰 ▯

A grapefruity, New World-style interpretation of south-west France's typical white varieties, Sauvignon Blanc and Sémillon. Ripe, honeyed, textured white with a citrusy tang.

1995 Château Le Comte, Entre-Deux-Mers   14/20
Dry 💰💰 ▯

A ripe, modern-style white Bordeaux made entirely from the Sémillon grape with faultless, if slightly soulless, technique by Gironde-based Englishman, Hugh Ryman.

1995 Domaine Le Noble Chardonnay Vin de Pays d'Oc, A.M. Bousquet   16/20
Dry 💰💰💰 ▯

A lightly barrel-fermented Midi Chardonnay made from grapes grown near the Languedoc cathedral-city of Béziers by Englishman Hugh Ryman. Well-crafted with melon-like fruitiness and a delicate patina of sweet spicy oak.

SOUTH AFRICA

1995 Simonsig Sauvignon Blanc, Stellenbosch   14/20
Dry 💰💰 ▯

The Sauvignon Blanc character is a little muted in the aroma department, but the crisp, nettley fruitiness makes this estate-grown Cape dry white a refreshing aperitif.

30–50FF

AUSTRALIA

1994 Salisbury Estate Chardonnay/Semillon, Victoria 13/20
Off-dry

There's a hole-in-the-middle of this sweetish, banana-split confection from the Mildura-based Alambie company in Australia's irrigated heartland.

1994 Salisbury Estate Chardonnay, Victoria 14/20
Off-dry

Better than the Chardonnay Semillon, but this smoky, pineapple-chunk white blend is a bit of a winemaker's breakfast.

1994 Hollick Coonawarra Botrytis Riesling 13/20
Sweet

The bearded, veteran winemaker Ian Hollick is best known for his intense Coonawarra Cabernet Sauvignons, which are a lot better than this sticky, confected, marmaladey, botrytis white.

FRANCE

1994 Domaine Henri Clerc et Fils, Chardonnay, Bourgogne Blanc, Les Riaux 12/20
Dry

Appellation contrôlée is an expression of vineyard location rather than grape variety, according to the French authorities, so we're slightly surprised to see the C-word on the label of this dull, gluey, baked-apple white Burgundy. But then it hasn't got a lot else going for it.

1993 Riesling Vin d'Alsace, Coteaux du Haut-Konigsbourg, Claude Bléger 15/20
Dry

Dry, aromatic Alsace Riesling, showing more weight than most German examples, with attractive lime-like maturity and crisply appetising acidity.

1994 Viognier, Vin de Pays d'Oc, Hugh Ryman 14/20
Dry

This strongly smoky, sumptuously full Viognier has lost a little bit of the freshness it had a year ago, but remains a good introduction to a fashionable and often overpriced grape.

1985 Vouvray Vignobles Brisebarre, Demi-Sec   15/20
Medium sweet 👛👛 ▮
Mature, honeyed, tea-leafy Loire white with 12 years under its neck label.
Chenin Blanc at its best is one of the few white grapes capable of sustaining its
freshness in bottle for this length of time. A rare opportunity to buy mature
Vouvray.

1989 Coteaux du Layon, Domaine de la Bergerie   15/20
Sweet 👛👛 ▮
From the foggy banks of the Loire tributary, the Layon, this is a weighty, mature
Chenin Blanc from one of the best vintages of the last decade. We enjoyed the
wine, but felt it was one honeybee short of a hive.

50–80FF

AUSTRIA

1994 Grüner Veltliner, Ernst Kolbl, Ried Reipersberg   16/20
Dry 👛👛👛 ▮
Almost certainly the only Austrian white wine available in Calais, and perhaps
the first ever on French soil, this is a rich, white-pepper-scented, concentrated
example of the country's most planted and most interesting white grape
variety.

1984 Lenz Moser Trockenbeerenauslese   13/20
Sweet ▮
Toffee-sweet with a confected, tinned mandarin orange-segments flavour, this is
noteworthy only for the fact that it pre-dates the 'anti-freeze' scandal that
struck Austria in the mid-1980s.

FRANCE

1994 Chablis Domaine Le Verger, Cuvée Vieilles Vignes, Alain Geoffroy   13/20
Dry ▮
Lean, mean, unoaked Chablis, allegedly from old vines, which is unlikely to
convert New World wine aficionados to the delights of the Yonne.

1994 Bourgogne Chardonnay, Sylvain Dussort   14/20
Dry 🍷 ▮

An imbalance of appley fruit and acidity reminded us more of Burgundy's sharpish Aligoté grape than the better-known Chardonnay. There's a degree of concentration but we would have liked more at the price.

1991 Auxey-Duresses, Domaine Jean Pascal   16/20
Dry 🍷🍷 ▮

From Puligny-Montrachet-based grower Jean Pascal, this is a nutty, mature, richly oaked but authentic white Burgundy from one of the Côte d'Or's under-appreciated communes. A poor person's Puligny.

NEW ZEALAND

1994 Nautilus Marlborough Chardonnay   15/20
Dry 🍷 ▮

Made in New Zealand by independent Australian winery, Yalumba, this is on the rich side for a Kiwi Chardonnay, showing buttered popcorn character and aromatic oak. The wine's marked acidity lends a sweet-and-sour character.

SOUTH AFRICA

1993 Thelema Chardonnay, Stellenbosch   16/20
Dry 🍷🍷🍷 ▮

With a handful of exceptions, South Africa hasn't really mastered the art of fine Chardonnay. This is one of them. It's a finely judged, mountain-grown example, from the boyish Gyles Webb, combining citrus fruitiness and oak-aged complexity.

Over 80FF

FRANCE

1988 Domaine Daniel Defaix, Chablis Premier Cru, Vaillon
17/20

Dry 🍷🍷🍷 ▮

Nutty, pungently mature Chablis from a grower who specialises in venerable, unoaked styles. Creamy, concentrated Chardonnay intensity with intriguing, old-style complexity.

1992 Meursault, Sylvain Dussort
Dry 👛👛👛 ➡

17/20

If you want to experience really good Meursault from a top vintage, this rich, layered, buttery example with its spine of acidity and minerally complexity is a must. One of us even spent his own, hard-earned dosh on a bottle of this, so it must be good.

1993 Château La Rame, Ste Croix du Mont, 50 cl.
Sweet 👛👛 ➡

16/20

Not cheap at nearly 100 francs for a half-litre bottle, but this oaky Sauternes taste-alike with its white-pepper and peachy intensity is a highly elegant dessert wine style.

Red

20–30FF

FRANCE

1994 Château Tour des Gendres, Bergerac
Medium-bodied 👛👛 🍾

14/20

A modern, elegant, lead-pencil-scented red with the emphasis on fruit rather than tannin or oak. A simple, fruity alternative to red Bordeaux.

1994 Domaine Le Noble Cabernet Sauvignon, Vin de Pays d'Oc, Hugh Ryman
Medium-bodied 👛👛👛 🍾

15/20

Englishman Hugh Ryman and his team of winemakers have produced an excellent-value Cabernet Sauvignon from coolish-climate vineyards near Carcassonne in the Languedoc. With a hint of oak character, and structured but juicy fruitiness, this is *une affaire*, at around 15 francs.

30–50FF

AUSTRALIA

1994 Salisbury Estate, Cabernet/Shiraz, Victoria   13/20
Medium-bodied
Over-oaked, over-extracted and, thank goodness, over there.

1992 Salisbury Estate Show Reserve Cabernet Sauvignon

12/20

Medium-bodied
Hollow, basic and lacking in fruit. Australia can do a lot better than this. Perhaps it's showing too much reserve.

FRANCE

1993 Domaine Ogereau, Anjou-Villages   14/20
Medium-bodied
Cabernet Franc-based wines from the Loire Valley need ripe vintages such as 1989 and 1990 to produce their best. We enjoyed this wine a year ago, but now the leanness of the vintage has begun to poke through the splinters.

1993 Château de Sours, Bordeaux   14/20
Medium-bodied
Esme Johnstone's reds are not yet quite as good as his rosés or whites, but this is decent quaffing red Bordeaux from a mediocre vintage with green-pepper aromas and dry tannins.

1994 Sancerre, Domaine Croix Saint Ursin, Sylvain Bailly
13/20

Light-bodied
A very light, lean Loire red from which the Pinot Noir fruit appears to have done a runner.

1993 Menetou-Salon, Domaine Henry Pellé, Morogues
15/20

Medium-bodied
A much better indication of what the Pinot Noir grape can produce in the Loire Valley when the yields are low enough to deliver flavour. This is a delicate, mature red with silky tannins and an attractive red-fruits fragrance.

1992 Domaine Rotier, Gaillac, Renaissance   15/20
Medium-bodied 👜👜 ▮

Well, you learn something every day. We'd never heard of the Braucol grape variety, which makes up just under half the blend of this south-western French blend. But now that we have, we rather like its Cabernet-like character, which, with Syrah, gives the wine a distinctively fruity character to complement the chewiness of the oak.

1993 L'Esprit de Teyssier, Bordeaux Rouge   15/20
Medium-bodied 👜👜 ▮

The second wine of Saint Emilion-based Château Teyssier, this is what Conservative Party worthies might describe as a luncheon claret. With Merlot suppleness and vanilla oak sweetness, this is good quaffing Bordeaux rouge.

1994 Faiveley Bourgogne   13/20
Medium-bodied ▮

Dull, beetrooty, extracted and dry. Mmmm...

1992 Château Villerambert-Julien, Minervois, Cuvée Trianon
16/20

Full-bodied 👜👜👜 ▮

From Gary Lineker look-alike owner, Marcel Julien, this is a richly spicy, still youthful, Minervois red, which has so much peppery, blackberry fruitiness that it almost reminds you of a good Syrah-based red from the northern Rhône.

1992 Crozes-Hermitage, Bernard Chave   15/20
Medium-bodied 👜👜 ▮

Not the best Crozes in the world (we suggest you get hold of a bottle of Belle, Graillot, Combier or Pochon for the true Crozes experience), but this peppery, aromatic, new oaky Syrah is pretty good for a rather light vintage.

50–80FF

ARGENTINA

1989 Navarra Correas Pinot Noir   12/20
Medium-bodied ▮

From an Argentine winery that produces leafy, rather old-fashioned reds, this is a fruitless (in both senses of the word) stab at a Pinot Noir.

AUSTRALIA

1993 Robertson's Well Coonawarra Cabernet Sauvignon　　16/20
Medium-bodied 🍷🍷🍷 ➡

Produced by Mildara, who are better known in the Coonawarra region for their popular Jamieson's Run brand, this is a mint-flecked, deeply coloured Cabernet with plenty of American oak and cassis intensity. May the well never run dry.

1991 Grant Burge Merlot, Barossa Valley　　　　　　　15/20
Full-bodied 🍷🍷 ▮

A typically approachable, well-crafted red from one of the Barossa Valley's leading figures and vineyard holders. It's a ripe, supple, chocolatey style with well-judged oak and sweet fruit.

AUSTRIA

1994 Strohwein Zweigelt, Weinbau Prechtl, 37.5 cl.　　16/20
Medium-bodied 🍷🍷 ➡

Surprisingly low in alcohol at 9 per cent, this is an attractive, central European red made from one of Austria's most intriguing red varieties, and using the traditional technique of drying the grapes on straw to concentrate the lusciousness of flavour. This sweet, summer-pudding red is a real find in the wastes of the Calais docklands.

FRANCE

1989 Château de Panigon, Médoc, Cru Bourgeois　　　12/20
Medium-bodied ▮

Dry, rustic and starting to peg out.

1989 Château de la Huste, Fronsac　　　　　　　　　15/20
Medium-bodied 🍷 ▮

From the same bicentenary vintage, this chocolatey-sweet, Right Bank Merlot-based Bordeaux has retained far more of its fruitiness and oomph. Still, we reckon it's time to drink it.

1990 Château Dalem, Fronsac　　　　　　　　　　　16/20
Medium-bodied 🍷🍷🍷 ➡

1990 is generally a better-balanced vintage than its immediate predecessor, and this youthful, spicy-oaky red lives up to the harvest's reputation. It has the structure, concentration and tannic backbone to improve in bottle for at least another three years.

1993 Bourgogne Les Perrières, Simon Bize   16/20
Medium-bodied 👜👜👜 ➡–

From one of the best young growers in Burgundy, this straight Bourgogne Rouge is a bit more substantial, displaying appealing Pinot Noir fruitiness, good weight and well-handled oak ageing. The 1993 vintage was excellent for reds in Burgundy, and this wine lives up to it.

1993 Ladoix Les Carrières, Edmond Cornu   16/20
Medium-bodied 👜👜👜 ➡–

A rich, oaky, village red Burgundy, which once more demonstrates that in a vintage such as 1993, even comparatively humble vineyards are capable of excitement. The oak is quite marked but should settle with another year or two's bottle age.

1993 Côte de Nuits Villages, Naudin-Ferrand   14/20
Medium-bodied 👜 ➡–

Rustic, slightly astringent red for Burgundy lovers on a budget. If that's not an oxymoron.

1994 Saint Joseph, Le Grand Pompée (sic), Paul Jaboulet   14/20
Medium-bodied 👜 ▮

Saint Joseph produces the lightest reds in the northern Rhône, but in a good vintage like 1994 we would expect more power and stuffing. Fresh and attractive, but it didn't ring our bell.

ITALY

1990 Rocca Rubia Riserva, Carignano del Sulcis   16/20
Full-bodied 👜👜👜 ▮

A savoury-herby, raisiny Sardinian red made from the comparatively unfancied Carignan grape, indigenous to the Mediterranean. This shows that with careful handling and low yields, even the humble, spear-carrying Carignan can be worth more than a walk-on part.

UNITED STATES

1991 Willamette Valley Oregon Pinot Noir   13/20
Medium-bodied ▮

The Willamette Valley has been touted by Oregonians as the best area outside Burgundy to grow Pinot Noir, but they would say that, wouldn't they? Perhaps not the best example of what they can do, this is lean, extracted and over-oaked.

Over 80FF

FRANCE

1993 Chorey-lès-Beaune Les Beaumonts, Sylvain Dussort   16/20
Medium-bodied 🝿🝿 ▮

This completes a trio of good-value red Burgundies at The Grape Shop and represents an interesting contrast in style. The spicy, elegant character of the Pinot Noir grape in the Côte de Beaune is more approachable here.

1992 Corton-Bressandes Grand Cru, Edmond Cornu   17/20
Medium-bodied 🝿🝿 ▮

Seductively sexy red Burgundy from an excellent grower, this is complex, gamey and sweetly oaked, with all the elegance, concentration and silky fruitiness one expects from expensive *grand cru* sites.

ITALY

1991 Felsina Berardenga, Chianti Classico   17/20
Medium-bodied 🝿🝿🝿 ▮

Chianti's claims to make world-class reds are justified by producers such as Felsina Berardenga, who are fanatical about the relationship between low yields and high quality. Wonderfully aromatic musk and cedar-scented *rosso*, with remarkable depth and flavour for a straight Chianti Classico.

Rosé

Under 20FF

AUSTRIA

1995 Zweigelt Austrian Dry Rosé, Kolbl, Wienviertel   13/20
Medium dry 🝿🝿 ▮

A soft, slightly syrupy, off-dry Austrian rosé, which is easy to drink, especially at under 20 francs.

20–30FF

FRANCE

1995 Château Villerambert-Julien Cuvée Opéra, Minervois   15/20
Dry 🍶🍶🍶 ▮
From an estate that produces some of the best red wines in the Minervois, this
is a subtle, dry, full-bodied, redcurrant-fruity rosé with crunchy freshness.

1993 Château de Sours, Bordeaux Rosé   15/20
Off-dry 🍶🍶🍶 ▮
Ex-Majestic Wine Warehouses director, Esme Johnstone, has developed a
following for his modern, fruity rosés. So much so that one London wine
merchant (apparently) successfully offers them *en primeur*. If you bought this at
the time and still have some left, you've done well, because it's developed grassy
smoothness and the green-pepper flavour of the Cabernet Sauvignon grape in
bottle.

Sparkling

30–50FF

AUSTRALIA

Seaview Brut   13/20
Off-dry 🍶🍶 ▮
Sherbety, simple, sweetish Aussie fizz with youthful, exuberant fruitiness and
big, gob-stopper bubbles. For punters on a budget.

50–80FF

FRANCE

Crémant d'Alsace, Méthode Traditionnelle, Claude Bléger   14/20
Dry 💰💰 ▌

An Alsace sparkler that has developed some yeasty aroma and flavour with age, but has managed to retain some of its youthful, Pinot Noir-like fruitiness. An affordable Champagne alternative.

Maurice Lassalle Champagne Brut, Chigny-lès-Roses   14/20
Dry 💰 ▌

A youthful, malty Pinot Noir-dominated *premier cru* Champagne from a grower in the Aube region whose wines are a regular feature of The Grape Shop's list. Could do with a little more time in bottle.

Over 80FF

Michel Genet Champagne Chouilly Grand Cru, Blanc de Blancs
15/20

Dry 💰💰 ▌

Not quite as exciting as last year's *Grapevine* favourite, possibly because of recent problem vintages in the Champagne region, but Michel Genet's youthful, all-Chardonnay fizz is still a comparative bargain at under 100 francs.

Larmandier Bernier Champagne, Cramant Grand Cru, Blanc de Blancs   16/20
Dry 💰💰 ▌

Another all-singing, all-dancing, all-Chardonnay grower's Champagne from the Côte des Blancs, showing toasty elegance and typical Chardonnay finesse, rounded out by some reserve wine richness and weight. Classy stuff.

Georges Gardet Champagne, Chigny-lès-Roses, Brut Spécial
15/20

Dry 💰 ▌

With its crème caramel notes, golden colour and honeyed maturity, this Champagne, disgorged in 1994, mixes green-apple acidity with a touch of bitterness. Not quite as fresh as last year's stellar example.

1988 Drappier Grande Sendrée Champagne Brut   17/20
Dry 👜👜👜 🍾

The favourite Champagne of ageing rocker Alvin Stardust, we're reliably informed by star-struck Grape Shop director, Katrina Thom. If so, our Alv has excellent taste and an eye for a bargain. Creamy, complex, soft-moussed Champagne with fresh winkle-picking acidity.

Michel Genet Champagne Rosé   15/20
Dry 👜👜 🍾

A pale-bronze, strawberryish rosé from the reliable grower Michel Genet, with an elegant, dry tang of acidity.

Serge Mathieu Cuvée Rosé   16/20
Dry 👜👜👜 🍾

Another grower's rosé Champagne showing more weight and Pinot Noir-based succulence and power, fleshed out by a dose of reserve wine from earlier years for complexity.

La Maison du Vin ☆☆☆

Address: 71 Avenue Carnot, 50100 Cherbourg

Telephone/fax: 00 33 233 43 39 79; 00 33 233 43 22 69

Opening hours: 9.00am to 6.00pm seven days a week

Manager: Pascale Chapron

Payment methods: Access, Visa; Eurocheques; sterling; French francs

Discounts: Negotiable

In-store tastings: Yes

English spoken: Yes; also Japanese

Facilities and services: Delivery to terminal and marina

Master of Wine Richard Harvey's La Maison du Vin store in Cherbourg continues to cater for the yachting and Volvo set travelling to and from the West Country, with a well-chosen if restricted range of 150 wines from the New World and an oddball selection of mainly ex-pat Brits scattered through the vineyards of southern France.

His Saint Malo venture, which opened in May 1995, fared less well and closed in December. Harvey's optimism about the town being 'a major tourist destination' proved unfounded, at least as far as wine-buying tourists were concerned. A year on, he has a different view of Saint Malo. 'There's only one ferry a day from Portsmouth and a summer ferry from Poole. It didn't work because there wasn't enough traffic coming through. It's not a place people go to shop for the day.'

So *au revoir* to the Saint Malo store, which has been turned into an estate agents. But the Cherbourg shop continues to do well, sticking to a road-tested line-up of producers, such as Domaine de Papolle, Domaine de la Ferrandière, Château Richard and James Herrick. Sales are 70 per cent French (we're talking geography here, rather than the nationality of the producers), with bits and pieces from Australia (Great Western Brut is a best-seller), Chile, Argentina and South Africa.

White

Under 20FF

FRANCE

La Maison Blanc, Vin de Table   13/20
Dry 👛👛 🍶
Clean, basic, faintly honeyed, appley white priced with the bargain-hunter in
mind.

**1995 Domaine de Papolle, Vin de Pays des Côtes de Gascogne,
Peter Hawkins**   14/20
Dry 👛👛 🍶
This is a soft, pear-fruity blend of Colombard and Ugni Blanc, with refreshing
acidity, from Englishman Peter Hawkins' Bas-Armagnac Gascon estate. An
improvement on past vintages.

20–30FF

FRANCE

1994 Château Richard, Bergerac Sec, Richard Doughty   15/20
Dry 👛👛 🍶
A ripe, rich, late-picked, Sémillon-based south-western French blend from
English geologist Richard Doughty's Dordogne estate, with peachy notes and
good balancing acidity.

1995 Sauvignon, Domaine de la Ferrandière, Vin de Pays d'Oc
                                                              15/20
Dry 👛👛👛 🍶
From a vineyard whose ungrafted vines are flooded on a regular basis to keep
them free of the vine-pest phylloxera, this is a ripe, modern, extremely well-
made, tropical citrus fruity Sauvignon Blanc with more weight than the 1994.

1995 Chardonnay, Domaine de la Ferrandière, Vin de Pays d'Oc
14/20

Dry 🍾🍾 ▮

From the same Languedoc domaine, this is a soft banana and boiled-sweets-style quaffer, unoaked for optimum freshness. We prefer the zippiness of the Sauvignon.

1995 Domaine du Vieux Chai, Muscadet de Sèvre et Maine sur lie, Bideau-Giraud
15/20

Dry 🍾🍾🍾 ▮

Ripe, fresh, *sur lie* Muscadet with textured, weighty citrus fruit characters and a slight spritz from maturation on the grape lees.

30–50FF

FRANCE

1994 Château Bauduc Les Trois Hectares, Bordeaux Sec, David Thomas
16/20

Dry 🍾🍾🍾 ▮

Made by amusing Welshman David Thomas, this Graves-like, oaked white Bordeaux made almost entirely from 50-year-old Sémillon vines shows tremendous weight, flavour and zesty complexity for a wine at this price.

1994 Chardonnay, Domaine de l'Aigle, Classique, Limoux   15/20

Dry 🍾🍾🍾 ▮

From the cool-climate region of Limoux south-west of Carcassonne, this is a ripe, melony, barrel-fermented Chardonnay with considerable elegance and complexity, from one of the best domaines in what is primarily a sparkling wine appellation.

50–80FF

FRANCE

1995 Sancerre, Domaine des Clairneaux, Jean-Marie Berthier
17/20

Bone dry 🍷🍷🍷 ▬▬
Fresh, ultra-modern grower's Sancerre with crisp, tangy acidity and notes of new-mown grass and blackcurrant leaf tapering to a stylish finish.

Red

Under 20FF

FRANCE

La Maison Rouge, Vin de Table
13/20
Medium-bodied 🍷🍷 |
Sweetish, Beaujoloid house-red, as it were, with a hint of spice and plenty of easy-drinking red fruits gluggability.

1995 Fenouill, Domaine Salvat, Vin de Pays des Coteaux des Fenouillèdes
14/20
Medium-bodied 🍷🍷🍷 |
A chunky, spicily sweet and fruity southern French quaffer with good colour and character for a cheap, domaine-bottled Midi *rouge*. Worth paying the extra six francs to secure a bottle of this instead of Richard Harvey's La Maison house-red.

1994 Merlot, Domaine de la Ferrandière, Vin de Pays d'Oc   15/20
Medium-bodied 🍷🍷🍷 |
From regular supplier Jacques Gau, whose wines are among the most popular bottles at La Maison du Vin, this is a supple, unoaked Merlot in in a Côtes de Castillon claret mould, complete with a rustic dry aftertaste. Still, at under 20 francs, you can't expect Château Talbot.

1994 Cabernet Sauvignon, Domaine de la Ferrandière, Vin de Pays d'Oc   15/20
Medium-bodied 💰💰💰 🍷
From the same supplier, this is another well-priced claret taste-alike, with grassy, unoaked intensity and punchy tannins.

20–30FF

FRANCE

1994 Château Richard, Bergerac, Richard Doughty   15/20
Medium-bodied 💰💰💰 🍷
An organically grown Bergerac red from Richard Doughty's Dordogne vineyards, this is a dry, unoaked claret-like Bergerac red, with some attractive chocolatey undertones and a nip of tannin.

1994 Domaine des Roudène, Fitou   11/20
Full-bodied 🍷
Not a patch on the aromatic 1991 from the same domaine, this is a dry, and rather pongy, Fitou with little finesse.

1993 Château du Donjon, Cuvée Tradition, Minervois   13/20
Full-bodied 🍷
Cuvée Tradition sums up this dry, plonky, Minervois red, which should come with a toothpick taped to the bottle.

1993 Château Coujan, Saint Chinian, Guy et Peyre   12/20
Full-bodied 🍷
Traditional, rustic Languedoc *rouge*, which has lost its fruit intensity and gained a thwack of dry tannin and a faintly vinegary edge.

30–50FF

FRANCE

1994 Merlot, Domaine de Ribonnet, Vin de Pays du Comté Tolosan, Christian Gerber   13/20
Medium-bodied 💰 🍷
From Swiss producer Christian Gerber's southern French estate, this is a wine where pronounced, green-edged oak has rather subdued the fruity quality.

1994 Cabernet Franc, Domaine de Ribonnet, Vin de Pays du Comté Tolosan, Christian Gerber   14/20
Medium-bodied 🌡 ▬

Same producer, same domaine, but a different grape variety and vintage. The result is a sweetly oaked, better-balanced red with herbaceous varietal character and a drying finish.

1993 Château Martindoit, Premières Côtes de Bordeaux, David Thomas   13/20
Medium-bodied ▮

Green-edged, rather over-extracted Premières Côtes claret from Welshman David Thomas, typical of the difficult 1993 vintage.

1994 Château Rozier, Côtes de Francs   15/20
Medium-bodied 🌡🌡 ▮

Supple, attractively textured Right Bank claret with malty, pleasantly grassy fruit flavours and medium weight and length.

Rosé

20–30FF

FRANCE

1995 Château Hélène, Cuvée Pénélope, Gris de Gris, Corbières
    15/20

Dry 🌡🌡 ▮

From a domaine best known for its red wines, Marie-Hélène Gau has produced an elegantly dry, full-bodied rosé with redcurrant and raspberry fruit characters and highly refreshing acidity.

J. Sainsbury Bières, Vins et Spiritueux ☆☆☆

Address: Mammouth Centre, Route de Boulogne, 62100 Calais

Telephone: 00 33 321 34 04 44 (Mammouth, ask for Sainsbury's)

Opening hours: 9.00am to 8.00pm Monday to Saturday

Manager: Frank Galand

Payment methods: Access, Visa, American Express; sterling; French francs; Reward Card points are available

Discounts: None, but special offers on selected wines and beers

In-store tastings: Yes

English spoken: Yes

Opened on 27 April 1994, J. Sainsbury Bières, Vins et Spiritueux was the first British supermarket to dip a toe into the piranha-infested waters of cross-Channel shopping. It was a daring move to set out its store within a wine-writer's spitting distance of the vast Mammouth complex itself, but with only 3,000 square feet of space, its rather pokey little shop was devoted entirely to the sales of wines, beers and, as you may have guessed, spirits.

On our first two visits to JSBVS, it looked a little forlorn beside Mammouth, the obvious first port of call for booze-cruisers in search of the cheapest plonk and Stella Artois. Given the scope of Tesco's giant Vin Plus in Calais' modern shopping mall, the Cité de l'Europe, it was obvious that, if the venture was to prosper, JS would have to offer its British customers more in the way of temptation.

Perhaps someone at Stamford Street HQ reads *Grapevine*. When we went back for a snoop this year, JSBVS was considerably busier and had expanded its floorspace to 5,000 square feet to accommodate a bigger chunk of JS wines, including a better New World section. Sainsbury's also offer a selected range of non-French wines within the new Mammouth hypermarket at Dieppe, where only 2–3 per cent of customers are English, compared with 90 per cent in Mammouth Calais.

J. Sainsbury Bières, Vins et Spiritueux

There are still drawbacks to shopping at JSBVS, however. On occasions savings barely cover the difference in duty and there are signs of old stock (still on the 1994 vintage of the James Herrick Chardonnay, when retailers in the UK have already moved to the 1995). But JSBVS appears to be on its way at last. The only problem is that we're not quite sure where.

For details of the wines available in Calais, see the main Sainsbury's entry on pages 276–299.

Tesco Vin Plus ★★★☆

Address: Unit 122, Cité de L'Europe, 62231 Coquelles

Telephone: 00 33 321 46 02 70

Opening hours: 9.00am to10.00 pm Monday to Saturday; closed Sunday except towards Christmas and Easter Sunday

Manager: James Oakley

Payment methods: All major credit cards; Eurocheques; sterling; French francs

Discounts: None

In-store tastings: Yes

English spoken: Yes

Even after Sainsbury's recent expansion of its Mammouth-complex store, Tesco's impressive Vin Plus emporium, at the Cité Gourmande end of Calais' very own shopping mall, remains five times the size of its puny rival down the road. We said last year that Tesco Vin Plus was the biggest off-licence in the Channel ports, possibly Europe, and no-one has yet taken us to task – or to court – over it.

With1,500 products, three-quarters of Tesco's Vin Plus business comes from its 1,000-strong wine list, including the entire UK Tesco range, plus a selection of wines such as Bordeaux *petits châteaux*, exclusive to Vin Plus. Thanks to the improved exchange rate this year, Tesco Vin Plus has been a lot busier. In fact, just about the only thing that keeps the volume of purchases down, says manager James Oakley, is the size of customers' cars.

At first, customers were almost entirely Brits indulging their passion for browsing, but now the French, with their predilection for classy clarets and single malt whiskies and, apparently, Martini, have added considerably to the weight of traffic clogging Vin Plus' spacious aisles. The I-speak-your-weight-style machines, which instantly convert the French franc price into its sterling equivalent, continue to offer an amusing diversion, even if they do remind you that savings on a bottle of wine usually amount to little more than the duty and VAT.

Tesco Vin Plus stocks the full Tesco range, as well as a range of exclusive wines, a selection of which is listed below. For other Tesco wines see pages 331–354.

White

Under 20FF

FRANCE

1995 Cépage Chardonnay, Vin de Pays du Jardin de la France, Les Chais du Comte   13/20
Off-dry 👜👜 ▮
Lemony, unoaked Loire Chardonnay with a spoonful of sugar to help the medicine go down.

20–30FF

FRANCE

1993 Riesling Heimburger, Réserve Particulière, Beblenheim
15/20

Dry 👜👜👜 ▮
Soft, weighty, lime-scented Alsace Riesling with plenty of body, fresh acidity and an attractive, tapering aftertaste. A good buy at just under 30 francs.

30–50FF

FRANCE

1994 Sancerre, Les Chais du Comte   14/20
Dry 👜👜 ▮
Fresh, grapefruity, négociant Sancerre, which struggles to get out of first gear. For all that, it's perfectly acceptable at the price.

1994 Petit Chablis, Louis Josse   13/20
Dry 👜 ▮
We can't think of any other appellations that are humble enough to inflict the description '*petit*' on themselves. But in the case of this light, characterless Chardonnay, the humility is justified.

50–80FF

FRANCE

1992 Tokay Pinot Gris Heimburger, Alsace Grand Cru, Sonnenglanz, Beblenheim   13/20
Medium dry ▮

Full, soft, overripe Alsace white whose flavours are leaden-footed and lacking in the necessary balancing acidity. Drink now, if at all.

1990 Gewürztraminer, Alsace Grand Cru, Sonnenglanz, Beblenheim   16/20
Medium dry 🍾🍾 ▮

From the same co-operative, this has more of the finesse and concentration we expect from a top *grand cru* site. With its toasty, lychee-like aromas and spicy freshness, this is much better value at just over 65 francs.

Over 80FF

FRANCE

1994 Chassagne-Montrachet, Louis Vinceur   15/20
Dry 🍾🍾 ▮

Louis Vinceur is one of a mind-boggling number of pseudonyms dreamt up by Nuits-Saint-Georges-based merchants, Labouré-Roi. This is a finely balanced, barrel-fermented white, showing some of the characteristic nuttiness and rich, full flavours of good Côte de Beaune Chardonnay. A good buy at just over 80 francs.

Red

Under 20FF

FRANCE

Comte de Feynes, Cuvée Prestige, Vin de Table de France, Raoul Johnston   14/20
Medium-bodied 👜👜 ❘
A mish-mash of southern French grape varieties made in a pseudo-claret style by Bordeaux merchant Jean-Marie Johnston. Chocolatey smooth, modern red with a note of oak character.

Merlot Vin de Pays d'Oc, Raoul Johnston   13/20
Full-bodied 👜 ❘
From the same stable, this stab at an ersatz-Saint Emilion is less successful, showing a pruney, baked character and a plonky aftertaste.

1995 Bordeaux, Château Ferrand   14/20
Medium-bodied 👜👜 ❘
From the best recent red wine vintage in Bordeaux, this soft, approachable, plumply fruity red represents the sort of value the Gironde needs to provide if it is to compete with the New World.

1993 Buzet, Les Vignerons de Buzet   15/20
Full-bodied 👜👜👜 ❘
The south-west French Buzet co-operative is a model operation, regularly turning out well-priced reds with plenty of flavour such as this. With its deep colour, prominent cherry fruit and smooth, oak-matured tannins, this is one to fill the boot with.

1995 Côtes du Rhône, Cuvée Prestige, Cellier des Dauphins
                    14/20
Medium-bodied 👜👜 ❘
Classic modern Grenache-based southern Rhône red with soft, raspberry fruitiness and a hint of pepper.

20–30FF

FRANCE

1994 Beaujolais, Paul Gibelet   12/20
Light-bodied 🍷
Prematurely browning, this uninspiring, basic Beaujolais badly needs a vintage update. Drink with giblets.

1993 Fitou Grande Réserve, Rocflamboyant, Mont Tauch   15/20
Full-bodied 👛👛👛 ⌇
Behind the garish, first-year design-school label, this oak-aged southern French blend of Carignan, Grenache and (crucially) 30 per cent Syrah, is a deliciously aromatic, garrigue-scented, broadly spicy red with cleverly-judged oak and masses of flavour.

1994 Saint Emilion, Prince Gonzalve du Puy, Yvon Mau   15/20
Medium-bodied 👛👛👛 ⌇
Saint Emilion is one of the biggest appellations in France, which means that style and quality can vary enormously. This affordable red from Yvon Mau, with its soft, grassy Merlot and Cabernet Franc-based fruit, is one of the good guys.

30–50FF

FRANCE

1994 Saint-Amour, Albert Dorival   14/20
Medium-bodied 👛👛 ⌇
Saint-Amour is usually the lightest of the ten Beaujolais *cru* villages. This floral, cherryish Gamay is true to type with elegant, maturing fruitiness. Halfway to red Burgundy.

1992 Savigny-lès-Beaune, Philippe de Malby   15/20
Medium-bodied 👛👛 ⌇
Philippe de Malby, as you may have guessed, is another of the many Labouré-Roi stage names. For a négociant Burgundy from a so-so vintage, this is a well-priced, commendably attractive Pinot Noir with some oak influence and wild strawberry fruitiness.

1992 La Tour de L'Impernal, Cahors, Côtes d'Olt   14/20
Full-bodied 🍾🍾 ▮
Robust, mint and sage aromas make this Malbec-based red from Cahors' largest
producer a good buy at just over 30 francs. Structured, oaky Cahors with dry,
rustic tannins.

Over 80FF

FRANCE

1991 Vosne-Romanée, Louis Josse   15/20
Medium-bodied 🍾🍾 ▬
A youthful, substantially splintered red Burgundy from one of the Côte de
Nuits' most famous villages. It's an attempt at a powerful, modern style, which
just about succeeds at this relatively modest price – for Vosne.

Sparkling

50–80FF

FRANCE

Champagne Rocheret, Special Selection Brut   14/20
Dry 🍾🍾 ▮
A yeasty, youthful fizz from the bargain basement, showing fresh, tangy fruitiness
and lemony acidity.

Victoria Wine ☆☆☆☆

Address: Unit 179, Cité de l'Europe, 62231 Coquelle

Telephone: 00 33 321 82 07 32

Opening hours: 10.00am to 8.00pm Monday to Thursday and Sunday;
10.00am to 9.00pm Friday; 9.30am to 8.00pm Saturday

Manager: Franck Trouiller

Payment methods: Access, Visa; Eurocheques, travellers' cheques; sterling;
French francs

Discounts: None

In-store tastings: Three to five wines available every day for tastings in-store

English spoken: Yes

A year ago, we commented on the slightly forlorn look of Victoria Wine's Cité de l'Europe store. There was nothing wrong with the range inside, which ranked – and still ranks – with the best on the other side of the Channel, but customers were scarcer than bylines in *The Economist*. Researching the 1997 edition of *Grapevine*, we noticed a considerable change for the better. There were customers aplenty, busy promotions and a real buzz of interest about the place.

The wines are a treat, too. The range is taken from Victoria Wine Cellars, the upmarket arm of the Woking-based off-licence chain, but the savings are often considerable. As the blackboard put it outside the shop: 'Wines you'll know at prices you won't.'

If Victoria Wine is struggling a little in the high streets of Britain, it's doing rather well in France, thank you. As managing director, Mike Hammond, puts it: 'Calais started as a little experiment, but it really took off after three months.' Hammond is pleased that his mainly French staff have started to sell wine to the locals as well as day-tripping Brits. 'We need a niche in France, and with New World wines, I think we've found it.' Jacob's Creek on French dinner tables? Now there's a thought.

Victoria Wine's Calais store stocks the full Victoria Wine Cellars range available in the UK (see pages 397–418 for details). Savings vary, but prices are at least £1 a bottle cheaper.

The Wine Society ☆☆☆

Address: Rue Fressin, 62140 Hesdin; UK address: Gunnels Wood Road, Stevenage, Herts SG1 2BG

Telephone: 00 33 321 86 52 07; Stevenage telephone and membership enquiries: 01438 741177; Stevenage order office: 01438 740222

Opening hours: 8.00am to 6.00pm Monday to Saturday (closed for lunch 12.30–1.45pm, Sundays and French public holidays)

Manager: Nathalie Delattre

Payment methods: Access, Visa; French cheques or banker's draft; French francs

Discounts: None

English spoken: Yes

In-store tastings: Yes

With over 100 wines and spirits to choose from, the Wine Society's range at its shop on the corner of Hesdin's cobbled town square offers its peripatetic members a fair selection from the main list of classic French wines, regional *vins de pays* and wines from the New World.

The advantage of a visit to Hesdin, apart from the charm of the little town itself, lies in the average saving of between £12 and £15 per case on excise duty and VAT. With the extra duty saving on fizz, there is the added incentive of bringing Champagne or sparkling wines back for parties and weddings.

If you time your visit to coincide with one of the Society's Soirées d'Hesdin, you can enjoy a themed tasting or supper, which this year included a Provençal dinner and a Bastille Day supper. Revolutionary stuff indeed.

You have to be a member to buy from the Wine Society at Hesdin, and the Society, which is run on co-operative lines, is keen for new recruits. All that's required is that you ask for details of how to join and pay £20 for a one-off lifetime share. The Society provides a list of hotels in and around Hesdin, with information, we're told, on the best bidet in town.

White

20–30FF

CHILE

1995 Casablanca Chardonnay, Casablanca Valley   16/20
Dry 🍾🍾🍾 ▪

Made by wunderkind oenologist Ignacio Recabarren at the Santa Carolina winery, this is an ultra-refreshing grapefruit and melon-style Chardonnay with a brushstroke of oak and butterscotch complexity. A wine that seems to get better with every vintage.

ENGLAND

1995 Midsummer Hill, Three Choirs   14/20
Dry 🍾🍾 ▪

A blend of Schönburger, Madeleine Angevine and Seyval Blanc, this is a pleasant, nettley English white with bracing elderflower crispness.

FRANCE

The Society's French Dry White, Vin de Pays de l'Hérault, P. Bésinet   12/20
Off-dry ▪

Basic, unbalanced, rather pricey southern French plonk with few redeeming features.

1995 Le Petit Bosc, Blanc de Blancs, Vin de Pays de l'Hérault, P. Bésinet   13/20
Dry 🍾 ▪

From the same producer, and for the same price, this is a fresher, fruitier, more modern style with pleasant cool fermentation characters of grapefruit and boiled sweets.

1995 Sauvignon de l'Arjolle, Vin de Pays des Côtes de Thongue   14/20
Dry 🍾 ▪

Soft, unoaked, southern French Sauvignon Blanc with fresh lemony acidity. A little short of depth and varietal character.

1994 The Society's Chardonnay, Vin de Pays de l'Hérault,
P. Bésinet   14/20
Dry 👜 🍾
Decent, no-frills Languedoc Chardonnay with pear-droppy, unoaked fruit and an optimistic price tag.

ITALY

1994 Bianco d'Alcamo, Duca di Castelmonte   15/20
Dry 👜👜👜 🍾
An intriguing blend of the Sicilian Catarratto, Damaschino and Grecanico grapes, made in a super-fresh, green-olive and lemon-zest style rounded off with a nutty, bitter twist. An excellent seafood white.

30–50FF

AUSTRALIA

1995 The Society's Australian Dry Riesling   14/20
Off-dry 👜👜 🍾
Clean, tangy, summer white with ripe, lime and melon fruit flavours made at the Mitchelton winery in Victoria.

FRANCE

1994 The Society's Sauvignon de Touraine, Oisly et Thésée,
Domaine Baron Ricard   15/20
Bone dry 👜👜 🍾
A subtle, elegant Loire Valley Sauvignon Blanc from one of the region's best co-operatives. Refreshingly crisp and grassy.

1995 Château Bel Air, Bordeaux   15/20
Dry 👜👜 🍾
Soft, quaffable, fruit-laden white Bordeaux blend in an attractive package, showing the progress that white Bordeaux has made over the last few vintages.

1994 The Society's White Burgundy, Mâcon-Villages, Jacques Dépagneux

13/20

Dry ▯

Gluey, grubby, old-fashioned white Burgundy with a hot, bitter aftertaste. Not the kind of society we'd like to keep.

1994 The Society's Vin d'Alsace, Hugel

14/20

Dry 👜 ▯

A reliable, lightly spicy blend of Gewürztraminer and Muscat made in a fruity aperitif style by the eccentric Hugel family.

NEW ZEALAND

1995 The Society's New Zealand Sauvignon Blanc, Marlborough, Selaks

15/20

Dry 👜👜 ▯

Typically assertive Marlborough style with tart, green-bean aromas and flavours, and an austere nip of acidity from Auckland winery, Selaks.

50–80FF

FRANCE

1994 Sancerre La Reine Blanche, Vacheron

16/20

Bone dry 👜👜👜 ▯

Subtle, complex Loire Sauvignon Blanc with notes of honey and nettle and a crisp, minerally aftertaste. The Vacheron family rarely lets you down.

1994 Pouilly-Fumé, Michel Bailly

14/20

Bone dry 👜 ▯

We found the aromas rather subdued and the fruit suffering from a lean, green streak on this eastern Loire Sauvignon Blanc. It may fatten up with another year in bottle, but don't call us.

1993 Riesling Cuvée Tradition, Kuentz-Bas

16/20

Bone dry 👜👜👜 ▭—

This is just starting to develop secondary characters from maturing in the bottle. And very nice they are too. Fresh, minerally, aromatic Riesling with fine concentrated lime fruitiness and subtle flavours.

1991 The Society's Gewürztraminer, Hugel   16/20
Dry 🍾🍾🍾 ▯
An evolved dry Alsace Gewürz with lanolin and rose-petal aromas, soft, honeyed fruit and considerable weight. Drink over the next year.

NEW ZEALAND

1995 Te Mata Castle Hill Sauvignon Blanc, Hawkes Bay   17/20
Dry 🍾🍾🍾 ▯
Made in a style that couldn't be more different from the bungee-jump-into-a-gooseberry-bush flavours of Marlborough Sauvignon Blanc, this is a restrained, almost European-like North Island white with subtle mineral and elderflower characters and excellent richness.

Red

20–30FF

CHILE

1995 Cono Sur Pinot Noir   14/20
Medium-bodied 🍾🍾 ▯
Still a good buy at around £5, but this juicy, green-tinged Pinot Noir from rangy California winemaker Ed Flaherty is a little leaner than in previous vintages. Perhaps too much of the best fruit has gone into the excellent Reserve.

1993 The Society's Chilean Cabernet Sauvignon, Rapel Valley, Carmen   14/20
Medium-bodied 🍾🍾 ▯
Intensely blackcurranty, spearmint-scented Chilean Cabernet Sauvignon made by the impressive Alvaro Espinoza. We suspect he sells his best wines under his own label.

FRANCE

The Society's French Red, Corbières
14/20
Medium-bodied 👛👛 🍷

A warm, peppery, unoaked southern French quaffer from the giant Val d'Orbieu operation. A better bet than The Society's white.

The Society's French Full Red, P. Lapascal, Vin de Table
14/20
Medium-bodied 👛👛 🍷

Benefiting from a change of supplier (we'd like to take some of the credit here), this is a supple, juicy, carbonic maceration-style red with smooth, raspberry fruitiness.

The Society's Claret, P. Sichel
14/20
Medium-bodied 👛 🍷

What Carlton Club and some Wine Society members might refer to as a good luncheon claret, this grassy Merlot-based red from Peter Sichel of Château d'Angludet is softly juicy and approachable.

1994 Château Jacquet de la Grave, Louis Vialard
14/20
Medium-bodied 👛 🍷

Soft Merlot-based claret from Louis Vialard of Château Cissac, with approachable tannins, but a raw bite on the finish.

1994 Domaine de Limbardie, Vin de Pays des Coteaux de Murviel
15/20
Medium-bodied 👛👛 🍷

Made by *pied noir* Henri Boukandoura in a modern, carbonic maceration style, this is a fresh, sweetly fruity, blackberryish Languedoc red with luscious tannins.

1995 Château de Péna, Côtes du Roussillon Villages
13/20
Full-bodied 👛 🍷

From grower Pierre Lapascal, this is a baked, raisiny, chewily tannic Roussillon red, which ought to be £1 cheaper.

1994 Cuvée de l'Arjolle, Vin de Pays des Côtes de Thongue, Teisserenc
14/20
Full-bodied 👛👛 🍷

Peppery, dry, firmly tannic Languedoc red with sweet, tobacco-ish oak and a rather dry, astringent finish.

1994 Cépage Syrah, Domaine de la Condamine l'Evêque, Vin de Pays des Côtes de Thongue
15/20

Medium-bodied 💰💰 🍷

From consultant oenologist Guy Bascou's own domaine near the Bassin de Thau, this is a stylish, southern French Syrah with plenty of ripe blackberry fruitiness, some oak, and a chewy bite of tannin.

ITALY

1994 Montepulciano d'Abruzzo, Roxan
15/20

Full-bodied 💰💰💰 🍷

Combining flavours of plain chocolate, date and raisin, this mouth-filling, warm-climate Italian red is packed with fruit and is good value at under £4.

1992 Cent'are Rosso, Duca di Castelmonte
14/20

Full-bodied 💰 🍷

Mature, heavily oaked Sicilian red with lots of alcohol, raisin and coffee-bean flavours and a drying, tannic finish.

SPAIN

1993 The Society's Rioja, Cosecheros Alavesas
13/20

Medium-bodied 💰 🍷

Coarse, splintery Rioja, which is beginning to dry out. At nearly £5, you can do a lot better than this from northern Spain.

UNITED STATES

Canyon Ranch Cellars Cabernet Sauvignon
12/20

Medium-bodied 🍷

Sweetened-up, confected California plonk with added acidity in a vain attempt to breathe a bit of zip into the wine.

30–50FF

AUSTRALIA

1992 Penfolds Bin 28 Kalimna Shiraz   16/20
Full-bodied 🍷🍷🍷 ▬-
A benchmark Penfolds red with masses of colour, sweet American oak and come-hither fruit flavours enhanced by an attractive minty, herby quality and smooth tannins.

FRANCE

1995 Château de Lacarelle, Beaujolais Villages, Jacques Dépagneux   14/20
Light-bodied 🍷 ▮
Pleasant, faintly bubblegummy Beaujolais Villages, which falls a bit flat on the palate. We expect more concentration at nearly £6.

The Society's Red Burgundy, Jean Germain   12/20
Medium-bodied ▮
Light, old-style négociant red Burgundy in which the Pinot Noir grape is struggling to assert itself.

The Society's Saint Emilion, Jean Pierre Moueix   14/20
Medium-bodied 🍷 ▮
A blend of 1992 and 1993 vintage Bordeaux, this is a mature Merlot-fruity claret with some chocolatey sweetness. Rather light.

1990 Château de la Grave, Côtes de Bourg   15/20
Medium-bodied 🍷🍷 ▮
A good, honest red Bordeaux from the excellent 1990 vintage with decent richness and a rustic edge.

1993 Côtes du Rhône, Claude et Nicole Jaume   15/20
Medium-bodied 🍷🍷 ▮
Juicy, easy-drinking, Grenache-based southern Rhône quaffer with pleasant cherry and strawberry fruit flavours and a hefty alcoholic punch.

SPAIN

1991 Viña Salceda Crianza Rioja   15/20
Medium-bodied 🍷🍷 ▮
Considerably more impressive than the Wine Society's own-label Rioja, with evidence of well-integrated oak and sweet, wild strawberry-like fruit flavours, pleasantly softened by barrel ageing.

50–80FF

FRANCE

1990 Château Beaumont, Haut Médoc, Cru Bourgeois   15/20
Medium-bodied 🍷🍷 ▮
Mature, sweetly supple, Merlot-like Left Bank claret, which would be ideal for Christmas drinking.

1989 The Society's Celebration Pauillac, Domaines Rothschild
16/20
Medium-bodied 🍷🍷 ▮
From the owners of Château Lafite, no less, this is a rich, complex, sumptuously textured red Bordeaux, showing the ripeness and concentration of the bicentenary vintage.

1993 The Society's Châteauneuf-du-Pape, Domaine du Vieux Lazaret, Quiot   16/20
Full-bodied 🍷🍷 ▮
A well-made, headily aromatic southern Rhône red with plenty of sweet, alcoholic fruit flavours and rich, leafy tannins. A good introduction to Châteauneuf-du-Pape at under £10.

Over 80FF

FRANCE

1990 The Society's Celebration Pomerol, Jean-Pierre Moueix
15/20

Medium-bodied 🛢 ▐

Pleasantly aged, Right Bank claret from the house of Moueix, with some sweet Merlot fruit and a surprisingly tannic bite for a 1990 claret.

Rosé

30–50FF

FRANCE

1995 Château Bel Air Cabernet Sauvignon, Bordeaux Clairet
15/20

Dry 🛢🛢 ▐

A pale pink, grassy rosé with the marked flavours of the Cabernet Sauvignon but none of the tannins. Attractively fruity and fresh.

Sparkling

30–50FF

FRANCE

Heritage Brut, Blanc de Blancs   13/20
Off-dry 💰 🍾
Basic Chenin Blanc fizz with coarse bubbles, a touch of appley sweetness and little or no sign of bottle development.

SPAIN

1991 Sumarocca Extra Brut, Cava   14/20
Dry 💰 🍾
Creamy, youthful, tangy Cava, which sounds more like an Italian car than a wine. Rather expensive at nearly £6.50.

50–80FF

FRANCE

1992 The Society's Celebration Crémant de Loire, Gratien & Meyer   15/20
Dry 💰💰 🍾
Attractive Loire Valley sparkler from the Saumur house of Gratien & Meyer, with honeyed maturity and a refreshing bite.

Over 80FF

FRANCE

Fleury Brut Champagne   15/20
Dry 💰💰 🍾
Appealingly youthful, Pinot Noir-based fizz at an affordable price, with pleasant sweetness from added reserve material.